THE OFFICIAL

America Online®

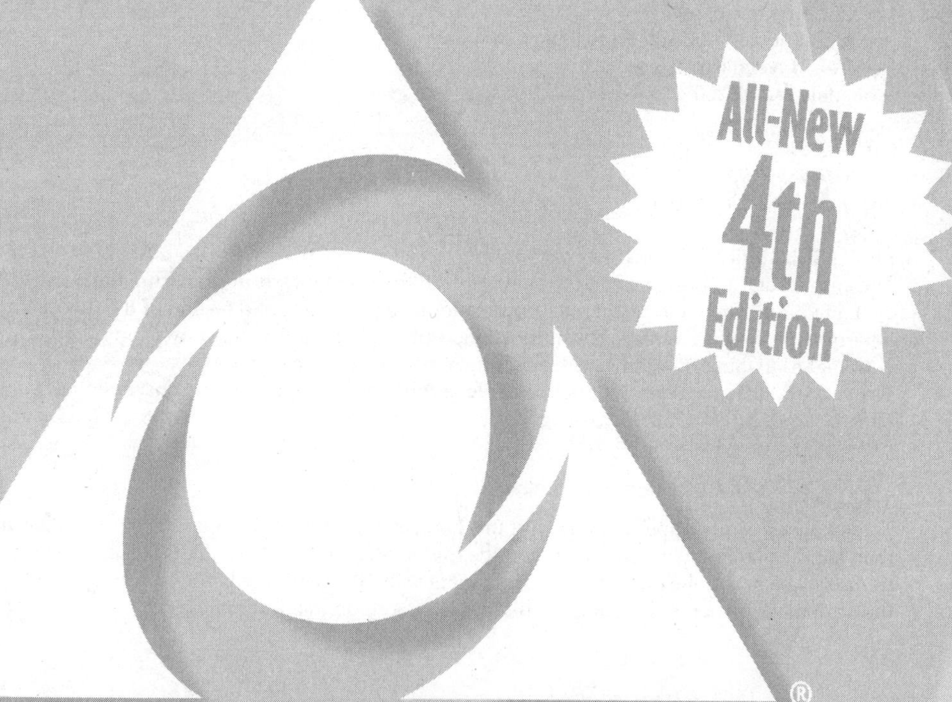

TOUR GUIDE

TOM LICHTY and JENNIFER WATSON

The Official America Online Tour Guide, Fourth Edition

Library of Congress Catalog Card Number: 97-81235

Fourth Edition 10 9 8 7 6 5 4 3 2 1

Printed in the United States of America

The Coriolis Group, Inc.
An International Thomson Publishing Company
14455 N. Hayden Road, Suite 220
Scottsdale, AZ 85260

(602)483-0192
Fax (602)483-0193
http://www.coriolis.com

Limits of Liability & Disclaimer of Warranty

The authors and publisher of this book have used their best efforts in preparing the book and the programs contained in it. These efforts include the development, research, and testing of the theories and programs to determine their effectiveness. The authors and publisher make no warranty of any kind, expressed or implied, with regard to these programs or the documentation contained in this book.

The authors and publisher shall not be liable in the event of incidental or consequential damages in connection with, or arising out of, the furnishing, performance or use of the programs, associated instructions and/or claims of productivity gains.

Trademarks

Trademarked names appear throughout this book and on the accompanying compact disk, if applicable. Rather than list the names and entities that own the trademarks or insert a trademark symbol with each mention of the trademarked name, the publisher states that it is using the names only for editorial purposes and to the benefit of the trademark owner with no intention of infringing upon that trademark.

Albany, NY • Belmont, CA • Bonn • Boston • Cincinnati • Detroit • Johannesburg • London
Madrid • Melbourne • Mexico City • New York • Paris • Singapore • Tokyo • Toronto • Washington

President
Michael E. Moran

Associate Publisher
Robert Kern

Editorial Operations Manager
Kerry L. B. Foster

Marketing Managers
Scott Johnson
Polly Wirtz

America Online Editorial Director
Brad Schepp

America Online Technical Editor
David O'Donnell

Acquisitions Editor
Neweleen Trebnik

Project Editors
Jennifer H. Mario
Paula Kmetz

Production Coordinator
Wendy Littley

Copy Editor
Judy Flynn

Technical Reviewer
Russ Mullen

Desktop Publisher
Jaimie Livingston

About the Authors

Tom Lichty is a freelance writer living near the base of Mount Hood in western Oregon. There he provides emotional support for his wife Victoria, who is completing her final year of medical school, manages a small farm, and skippers the tugboat *Auklet*, which journeys northwest waters whenever possible.

Jennifer Watson is first and foremost an America Online member, with a history dating back to the pre-9600 bps days and a collection of sign-up kits to rival a computer superstore. Her never-ending quest to get the most out of America Online has led her to volunteer as a "community leader," helping other members also get more. These days she is the founder and coordinator of AOL's online training center for other community leaders and content providers. She is also the author of two other books about America Online, *AOL Keywords* and *AOL Companion*, both by MIS Press, Inc.

Acknowledgments

If you're like us and you cringe whenever the stars take the stage to accept their Emmys with a large sheet of paper in their hand, relax. We're not going to assault you with the litany of people who participated in this book. There are scores of them.

There are nine, however, who deserve special mention: Joe and Elizabeth Woodman, Scott Johnson, Neweleen Trebnik, Jennifer Mario, Brad Schepp, David O'Donnell, Matt Wagner, and George Louie. Many of these people represent the Camelot we once called Ventana. Its loss is like that of an old friend.

Contents

Foreword

I first got interested in online services in the early 1980s. I didn't know much about them then, but I knew enough to realize that they had a lot of potential. So when I bought my first personal computer in 1982, I decided to buy a modem and get online. This proved to be a very frustrating experience. It took me several months before I had all the equipment properly configured and was able to connect for the first time. Once I got connected, I found the services themselves hard to use and expensive. Nevertheless, despite all the hassles and shortcomings, I thought it was amazing that such a wealth of information and services were out there waiting to be tapped into.

That was more than a decade ago. When we founded America Online, Inc., our objective was simple: to make online services more accessible, more affordable, more useful, and more fun for people like you and me. America Online now serves more than *11 million customers* and is the *world's leading Internet* online service.

Our success has been driven by a constant focus on making the power of online services accessible to everyone. In designing America Online, we worked hard to make it very easy to use. We didn't want people to have to read a book in order to get connected, so we made the software easy to install and easy to use. As a result, people are usually up and running with America Online in just a few minutes.

Although we've done a good job of making the process of connecting to America Online hassle-free, we still have a problem: Once you're connected, what do you do? America Online has grown so quickly, and now contains so many different services, that finding the services that best meet your specific needs can be a bit of a challenge.

That's where *The Official America Online Tour Guide* comes in. Think of it as your personal tour guide, helping you get the most out of America Online. It highlights a wide range of useful and fun services, so you can begin enjoying America Online immediately. After you're comfortable with the basics, it will take you to the next step by explaining some of the more advanced capabilities that are built into the service.

When Ventana Communications first contacted us about publishing an America Online book, we thought it was a great idea. Our members had been asking for a book for some time, so we knew there was interest. And we felt that by working with an independent publisher, we'd end up with a better book than if we tried to write it ourselves.

The choice of Tom Lichty as the author was inspired. Tom had written a number of popular computer books, so he knew how to communicate information in an interesting and humorous manner. (A lot of computer books are deathly dull; Tom's are funny and engaging.) And since Tom was a novice user of online services, we felt his insightful observations as a novice would help others get the most out of America Online.

When the first edition of *The Official America Online Tour Guide* was published in 1992, it got raves from readers; this new, fourth edition is certain to be even more popular.

As you'll soon discover, America Online is more than easy-to-use software and a collection of useful and fun services. It's a living, breathing, electronic community that comes alive because thousands of people all across the country don't just passively read the information that scrolls by on their screens, they get involved and participate, exchanging ideas on hundreds of topics. We provide the basic framework; beyond that, America Online is shaped by the collective imagination of its participants.

A new interactive communications medium is emerging, and it will change the way we inform, educate, work, and play. America Online is at the forefront of this exciting revolution. Come join us as we work together to shape this new medium.

Steve Case, Chairman & CEO, America Online, Inc.
AOL E-mail Address: SteveCase

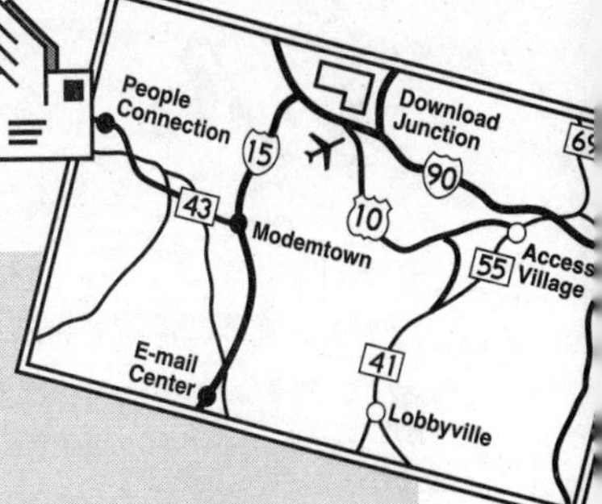

CHAPTER 1

Welcome Aboard

- What Is America Online?
- How to Use This Book

It's Friday night in America. In Dubuque, Iowa, a mother composes mail to her son, a lieutenant stationed in the Middle East. In Cheyenne, Wyoming, a teenager chats with her peers. In New York City, a business owner, working late, researches the availability of SBA loans. An 11-year-old in Washington state has just won his 11th straight round of cribbage. A father in Irvine, California, shops for a birthday present for his youngest daughter. A hundred miles to the west, somewhere in the Pacific, a tugboat skipper is watching radar images of an approaching storm.

Ten years ago, you'd be hard-pressed to find anything that these people have in common. Today, without thinking, few of us would fail to discover the common denominator: they're all online.

Like television and radio before it, the online industry has become ubiquitous—only it's done so much more quickly. Like television and radio, it emerged as a curiosity, was nurtured in controversy, and has matured as a viable and influential mass medium.

But unlike television and radio, this is a medium of the people. Any patron of the medium is a participant in its message. It's as multilateral as it is objective. There are no races, boundaries, castes, or even age groups here. The potential for such a forum is staggering.

But power has its price. In order to get online, you have to know how to use the tool, and the tool can be as vexing as Parisian traffic.

We can't help you with Parisian traffic (it's beyond hope), but we certainly *can* help you get online and find your way around. America Online is the easiest-to-use online service available, and some say its software is even fun. But America Online isn't without some complexity, and some of us prefer a little hand-holding when it comes to learning complex systems.

May we help? We're *The Official America Online Tour Guide*, and we're here to bring order to your chaos, confidence to your fears, and, hopefully, a little levity to the tedium of learning. This is an exciting place and these are exciting times, but we understand that it can also be awfully intimidating, and we're here to help. Pull up your computer, grab your mouse, and let's discover the future.

Instant Gratification

Empowerment. That's what this book is all about. Our mandate is to make you feel empowered by reading the *Tour Guide*. Thus, the following snippet of transcendental reward:

Sign on and stop at the Welcome screen. Move your cursor around on that screen and notice how the cursor changes. Passing over a button, for example, it becomes a pointing hand, ready to issue a command should you choose to click the mouse button.

Sometimes the cursor changes even when it is *not* over a button. This is not unique to the Welcome screen. When it changes unexpectedly like this, you should always experiment. This is no place for timidity.

Yes, there's a secret place within the Welcome window. It's intentional, and it changes every day.

Only you know about the arcanum of the Welcome window; it's our little secret. Be empowered by this knowledge. But don't tell anyone.

What Is America Online?

A term like *America Online* doesn't give many clues as to its composition. We can safely deduce its country of origin (it's in America, all right: northern Virginia, to be exact—just outside Washington, DC). But what's this "online" business? You won't even find the word in your dictionary if it's an older edition.

A definition is in order, and we are going to pursue that definition, not only in terms of features and functions, but also in relation to the "community" we join when we become AOL members. Over the next few pages, we'll allow America Online's technological capabilities to dazzle us, but by the end of this chapter, you'll see that the true rewards are found in the *people* who await us on AOL.

It's One Big Thunder-Lizard Computer

One way of defining AOL is by describing its hardware. Coordinating thousands of simultaneous phone calls and storing tens of thousands of files requires one thunder lizard of a computer complex. No little stegosaurus will do. We're talking brontosaurus here, a beastie who relocates continents whenever he feels the urge to sneeze. Forget prefixes like *kilo* and *mega*. Think *giga* and *tera*. When they turn on the power to this thing, lights dim along the entire eastern seaboard.

Open Architecture

We hate to disappoint you, but America Online isn't a single brontosaurus-sized mainframe; it is, in fact, a number of refrigerator-sized computers, each having more in common with the adaptable velociraptor than a leviathan as benign as the brontosaurus.

Figure 1-1: A few of the many systems that are the heartbeat of America Online. Products from a number of manufacturers are represented here—Silicon Graphics, Cisco Systems, Hewlett-Packard—each selected on the basis of suitability to a specific task. The homogenization factor is open architecture, which allows all of these diverse systems to work in concert.

Look carefully at the cabinets pictured in Figure 1-1: the equipment mounted in them carries a variety of brand names. This isn't a place where a single manufacturer's equipment monotonously dominates the scene. You might expect everything to say IBM or DEC on it, with matching colors and shapes like a model kitchen. Instead, what's inside of those cabinets is a mélange of electronic diversity more akin to a customized home entertainment system. AOL's cabinets hold equipment from a variety of manufacturers. IBM is there all right, but so are Hewlett-Packard, Cisco, Tandem, Silicon Graphics, Stratus, and a few others.

Using equipment from a single manufacturer and connecting it with proprietary cables and communications protocols—so-called *closed systems*—used to be commonplace in mainframe computer installations. Today, however, closed systems are no more tolerated there than they are in home music systems. In your living room, you might have a Pioneer receiver, a TEAC tape deck, and a Sony CD player. Each has the features you wanted when you bought it, and the price was right. You were able to plug them all together using standardized cables, with never a worry that they might not work together properly.

In the computer business, this is called *open architecture*, and it's almost a mantra at AOL. Because of the common standard (TCP/IP—or *Transmission Control Protocol/Internet Protocol*, for those of you who care about those things), AOL can now buy computer components much as we buy components for our stereo systems: the best one for each job, each at the best price.

All of which is to say that from a mechanical perspective, AOL is a diversity of computer systems interconnected with TCP/IP open architecture. Most of this hardware resides in that cavernous auditorium in Reston, Virginia, very close to Dulles airport, near Washington, DC.

Hosts & Clients

Let's define a couple of terms up front. You'll encounter them often in this book, and without clarification, they'll seem like that much more technobabble—and we all know how irritating that can be.

AOL's computer complex in Virginia is often referred to as the *host*. There are millions of us and only one AOL; we all "visit" AOL when we sign on; AOL's machines attend to our needs. These are the kinds of hostlike things that provoke the term.

Our computers—and the AOL software running on them—are the *clients*. Clients are served by the host, clients are numerable, and in this case, clients are patrons.

Client/host terminology is common in the networking industry, and when you think about it, AOL *is* a network. The meanings behind the terms aren't complex. Don't let the technobabble intimidate you.

Common Carriers

There's more to the technology of AOL than computers, however. There's also the nagging little problem of delivering the signal from your location to Reston and back. Again, an analogy is in order.

If you wanted to get a package to a friend who lives across the country, you could probably hop in your car and drive it there yourself. But compared to the alternatives, driving across the country would be impractical, to say the least.

More likely, you'd hire a *common carrier*—a service such as United Parcel Service or FedEx—to deliver the package for you. For a fraction of what it would cost you to do the job yourself, common carriers can do it more reliably, less expensively, and much more conveniently.

AOLnet

In the early 1990s, when AOL was first experiencing almost meteoric growth, even the largest common carriers couldn't keep up. It was as if everyone we know called FedEx for a pickup every 15 minutes.

Taking matters into its own hands, AOL established its own private network, *AOLnet.* AOLnet is your best choice of all the carriers because AOLnet has high-speed access numbers and AOLnet's backbones—the transcontinental lines that run from city to city—are state of the art. For more information about AOLnet, sign on, press Ctrl+K or Command+K (for keyword, AOL's navigational shortcut system), enter the keyword: **AOLnet**, and read the information you find there.

For much the same reason, AOL hires common carriers to deliver goods to its members. And, typical of AOL, it hires multiple common carriers to ensure reliability. There's SprintNet, a service of US Sprint, and there's Datapac, a subsidiary of Bell Canada, for Canadian members. There are others. These common carriers offer *nodes*—local telephone numbers—in most cities in North America. They charge AOL for phone calls (placed or received) just as FedEx would charge you to deliver a package.

AOL has installed AOLnet nodes in hundreds of cities, but for those few cities that AOLnet doesn't serve, SprintNet, Tymnet, or Datapac are used. No matter which carrier you use, the important thing to understand is that the carrier is as much a part of the AOL network as are the machines in Reston.

Welcome Back!

It's especially rewarding to welcome back readers from previous editions of the *Tour Guide*. You write to us with each new book, telling us what you like and don't like, and we appreciate the feedback.

The Fourth Edition describes Version 4.0 of the AOL software, including the following features:

- With one click the new spelling checker will find spelling and grammatical mistakes in your e-mail and AOL text documents.
- You can now sign on with one of your other screen names without losing your connection.
- The new Address Book now alphabetizes your address list. It also includes a place to add notes for each person listed, and a place to add a picture for each entry.
- The new toolbar is color-coded and customizable. You can right-click or Option-click to remove icons that you don't use and drag icons of your favorites onto the toolbar.
- If you don't want any icons on your toolbar, or you prefer your toolbar at the bottom of your screen, you can now make it happen.
- You can stylize your chat comments with the same options you use in e-mail. Add bold, italics, and colors to your words, and share links to your favorite areas—all in chat.
- You can put images right into e-mail; there's no need to attach a file.
- The new channel guide appears to the left of every main channel window. This streamlined navigation makes it easy to know where you are and faster to explore new channels.

We're sure you'll like these features as much as we've enjoyed exploring them on your behalf.

It's a Telecommunications Service

Now *there's* a polysyllabic mouthful: *telecommunications*. As the term is used here, it refers to two-way communications via telephone lines. A phone call, in other words, is a form of telecommunicating. Computers are another. If you have a computer and we have computers and we all have modems, we can use our existing telephone lines to connect our computers to one another. Once connected this way, our computers can exchange data: text, graphics, sounds, animation—even programs.

Of course, you have to be at your computer and we have to be at ours—at the same time—and we have to know how to make our computers talk to one another. Also, we have to check for errors encountered in the transmission, and we're just us and you're just you, and there's only so much computer data three people can exchange among themselves before the whole thing gets to be pretty dull.

What we need is a *service* that will store our data so that we don't have to be at our computers at the same time. Instead of calling your computer, we'll have our computers call the service and store our data and messages there. When you're ready for that data, you can instruct your computer to call the service and retrieve the data at your convenience.

And who's to say that we should have the service all to ourselves? We can let everyone else with a computer in on it as well, regardless of the type of computer they own. Carried to its extreme, this scenario might result in hundreds of thousands—millions, actually—of people using the service, exchanging and storing thousands of computer files. Most of this data can be public rather than private, so the exchange becomes multilateral.

Which is precisely what telecommunications services—and AOL—are: a vast network of "members," all using a computer, a modem, and a telephone line to connect with a common destination—to "go online." Members can exchange public and private files, they can send and receive e-mail, and members who are online at the same time can "chat" in realtime. They can even play online games with one another.

And what does this service cost? The economies of scale allow expenses to be distributed among the members. Moreover, even though AOL is near Washington, DC, very few members pay for long-distance calls. America Online has local telephone numbers in nearly every city in the contiguous United States. Even if you live in "the sticks," chances are you'll find a local number you can call—or one that's a "short" long-distance call away. If that's too expensive, there's always AOL's 800 number. (To find out more about access to AOL via the toll-free 800 number, sign on and use the keyword: **Access**.)

Allow Us to Introduce Ourselves

Jennifer Watson is an online pioneer who writes books about the online community. She is also founder and coordinator of the online training academy for AOL's community leaders and partners. She has had the good fortune to lead an amazing team and help thousands learn new skills, all from her home in Ypsilanti, Michigan. Her screen name is **Jennifer**.

Tom Lichty (say *lick'-tee*) is a full-time writer who lives on a small farm in rural Oregon where the air is clear and the politics are liberal. He often plies the waters of the Pacific Northwest aboard *Auklet,* his cruising tugboat. If you ever happen to be in Desolation Sound on a peaceful July evening and notice a small tug at anchor with a fellow bent over the keyboard of his laptop computer, it's probably Tom. His screen name is **MajorTom**.

We'd be flattered if you'd check out our home pages on the World Wide Web (the Web is discussed in Chapter 4, "Using the Internet"). Jennifer's home page is at **http://members.aol.com/jennifer/** and Tom's is at **http://members.aol.com/majortom/**.

Read our book. Visit our home pages. Then send us some mail. We'd love to hear from you.

It's Software Installed in Your Computer

Conceptualizing AOL as nodes and mainframe computers isn't very comforting. For many of us, America Online is much more parochial than that: AOL is software in our computers—software on a disk bundled with the computer, or ordered from a magazine ad.

Figure 1-2: America Online's logo appears whenever you run the software installed on your computer.

That's more like it. The software you use on your computer to sign on to AOL more accurately represents the personality of the service than anything we've discussed so far. It makes friendly noises (if your computer is equipped with sound), it's resplendent with windows and icons, and it automates tasks and procedures that only a few years ago used to exclude most seminormal people from using telecommunications systems.

We're getting closer to the mark. The phrase *user-friendly* is properly used to describe this service. America Online's new software is familiar, predictable, and comfortable for the Windows or Macintosh user. The File menu says Open, Save, Close, and Exit. Its windows have title bars and minimize buttons.

Another unique aspect of the AOL software is its interface and communication strategy. The software is highly graphical. However, most of AOL's graphical components are transferred to your machine only once; then they're stored on your hard disk. After that, text is the primary information that flows between you and AOL.

We Do Windows, Too!

AOL's client software is available for a number of different kinds of computers and their operating systems: Windows 95, Windows 3.1, and Macintosh.

Nearly everything described in this book applies equally to all of these operating systems, except for the illustrations. All of the screen shots in this book were captured on machines running Windows 95, which was the only software available to us at the time we wrote this book. If you're a Windows 3.1 or Macintosh user, don't feel left out. This book is about America Online, not Windows 95. Except for a few inconsequential cosmetics, operation of the AOL client software is the same for the Macintosh or Windows 3.1 as it is for Windows 95.

With that said, we acknowledge a few differences between the Windows and the Macintosh versions of the software. Though the differences are subtle and few, if you're a Mac user, be sure to look for the sidebar that precedes the "Moving On" section at the end of each chapter.

It's a Resource

News, sports, weather—sure you can get them on radio and television, but not necessarily when you need or want them. You can get them in a newspaper, too, but it's going to cost the environment a tree or two, the pictures are fuzzy, and about all you can do with a newspaper you've read is throw it away (consult the Environmental Forum at keyword: **Environment** for recycling information). America Online offers the news, sports, and weather as well—available at your convenience and without sacrificing any trees. It's in electronic form, so you can file it, search it, and include it in documents of your own.

On an average day, we begin by reading the latest news and weather (discussed in Chapter 5, "Finding Stuff"); then we check up on the investments in our modest portfolios and read our mail (discussed in Chapter 3, "Electronic Mail & the Personal Filing Cabinet"). Not long ago, Tom researched the purchase of a new modem for his computer (see Chapter 5), and we often make travel plans using AOL's airline reservation system. We constantly search the online video reviews before we rent a tape. Past issues of *Windows Magazine, WIRED, National Geographic,* and *Smithsonian* are online for our review, as is *Compton's Encyclopedia, The Merriam-Webster Dictionary,* and "the Gray Lady" (the *New York Times*). As professional members of the desktop publishing community, we constantly collect graphics, fonts, and utilities (AOL has tens of thousands of such files online—learn how to search for them in Chapter 5).

In other words, we could describe AOL as a resource of almost infinite potential. You don't have to drive anywhere to use it, it's continuously maintained and updated, and it's all electronic—available for any use you can imagine. Many members find the resource potential alone ample justification for signing on to AOL, but to limit your participation this way would be a disservice to AOL and to yourself. Above all, AOL is people: friends, associates, consultants—even lovers. It's a resource, all right, but it's also a community. And therein lies its greatest value.

It's a Community

We've taken the easy way out. Yes, AOL is a telecommunications service. Yes, it's the host computer. Yes, it's client software in your computer. And yes, it's a resource. But that's like saying that the fourth of July is just another day of the year. There's much more to it than that. July fourth is celebration and good things, but for many of us, it means people: family, friends, and community. AOL, too, is best defined by its people. America Online is a *community*. Our dictionary defines community as "a social group sharing common characteristics or interests," and that is the best definition we can imagine for AOL.

As members, we have common interests, we all have computers, and we love to share. *That's* what AOL is all about. After a few weeks, the novelty of interconnection and graphical images wears off. After a few weeks, we stop wondering about the host computer and data bits. After a few weeks, we all discover the true soul of AOL, and that soul is its people.

When we agreed to write the first edition of this book back in 1992, community was the last thing on our minds. We had been telecommunicators for years. We thought we'd seen it all. Now, however, we spend as much of our online time corresponding with friends—new friends in every part of the country—as we do conducting research. In Chapter 3, we admit to becoming despondent if we don't hear the familiar "You've got mail!" when the Welcome screen comes up. Throughout this book, we'll offer little tips on how to make friends online. Follow these tips and you'll become as much a part of this community as we are.

Futuring

This is certainly a medium for futuring—for envisaging, musing, and aspiring. We future with nearly everyone we meet at AOL: they're the people who are shaping the future of telecommunications, and they're always a couple of years ahead of the rest of us. Fascinating discourse.

Steve Case is the chairman and CEO of America Online. He is paid to envision the future, and he loves his job. Not long ago, on a spectacular fall afternoon, Steve chatted with us from his Virginia office about what lies ahead for telecommunications.

Fewer than 20 percent of American homes are online today. Steve compares this to television in the late 1940s: "No one remembers television then. It was in less than 20 percent of American homes. It was an emerging technology, a curiosity, and the things television did in the '40s are all but forgotten."

He goes on to cite television's emergent moment, which he feels was the 1960 presidential election. We couldn't help but take notice of television after that: the debates, after all, could very well have swayed the election.

Steve Case futures about the online medium in 10 years, when it has reached the same point along its developmental curve. Will the candidates appear in an online rotunda of some sort, debating issues and answering questions from members? Will they offer an e-mail address and respond to all queries? Steve suspects that the online industry might very well influence the viability of a third political party in this country. What medium is better prepared to develop a party of the people? The online medium is the embodiment of the elusive flat playing field, where everyone is equally empowered and there is little cause for class, race, gender, or age discrimination. In an era where political candidates are perceived as media stars—inaccessible, almost chimerical—we're primed for a candidate who seems to be one of us, and the online medium is where such a creature might best be nurtured.

We never asked Steve Case if he thought he might ever be president of the United States. We doubt that he would take the job. He's having too much fun being Steve Case.

How To Use This Book

It's true: this book is a "user's manual"—for America Online. You no doubt already know that documentation can be dull. Few people take a software manual to the hammock for a lazy afternoon of reading. As you might guess from the title, this is not your typical prosaic how-to instruction manual; you will find no inscrutable "technobabble." We hope you'll find it more of an odyssey—a pleasant journey of discovery—to the interesting places and people in America Online's virtual universe. Nonetheless, as your guides to all the diverse experiences AOL has to offer, we've included organizational and reference tools that will help you find your way around.

Finding Answers

We want you to be able to turn to *The Official America Online Tour Guide* whenever you have a question about AOL. We want you to be able to find the answer to your question with a minimum of effort, no matter how many different places the subject may appear in the book. Pursuant to that, a number of tools are at your disposal:

- The *table of contents* lists titles, section heads, and subheads for every chapter. When you need information on a specific subject, turn first to the table of contents. Nine times out of ten, it will be all you need.
- A thorough *index* appears at the end of the book, with references to subjects, procedures, and departments. If the subject you're after doesn't appear in the table of contents, turn to the index.
- A *listing of keywords* appears in Appendix B. Keywords are the interstate highway system at AOL. If you want to get somewhere in a hurry, use a keyword. As you discover places that appeal to you, add them to your list of favorite places in your Personal Filing Cabinet (described in Chapter 3, "Electronic Mail & the Personal Filing Cabinet").
- A *glossary* of terms used in the book follows the appendices. The glossary is especially thorough in its inclusion of telecommunications terminology that is unique to AOL. People often talk in shorthand when they're online—typing is so *slow*—and the glossary offers the necessary translations.

Activity Listings

With the exception of the first chapter, we've organized this book according to the way people use AOL. Chapters 2 through 10 each describe a typical online activity and how that activity is best pursued.

- Chapter 2, "The Abecedarium," comes up next. AOL is a big place. Lots of things are going on here, and when you first sign on, it's like your first day on a new job: everyone seems to know what to do except you.

Chapter 2 is like a neighborly coworker—showing you an *orderly, effective* approach for getting to know AOL and spending your time there productively. This chapter also defines the word *abecedarium.*

- Chapter 3, "Electronic Mail & the Personal Filing Cabinet," describes AOL's most popular feature: e-mail. You can communicate with people all over the world—not just fellow AOL members, but anyone with e-mail access to the Internet—using AOL's mail filing system, which is second to none.
- Chapter 4, "Using the Internet," introduces the Internet and AOL's tools for using it. You'll find newsgroups here, and e-mail, and, of course, the World Wide Web.
- Chapter 5, "Finding Stuff," helps you find your way around America Online and the Internet.
- Chapter 6, "Transferring Files," focuses on tricks and techniques for receiving (downloading) and sending (uploading) files from and to AOL.
- Chapter 7, "Chat," introduces you to chat rooms, where conversations occur in realtime and strangers rarely remain unacquainted for long, and Instant Messages, where long-distance conversations occur without extra charge, and no one remains a stranger. This chapter also discusses the groups who make up that community: kids, seniors, and everyone in between.
- Chapter 8, "Working Offline," shows you how to read and write your mail offline when you're not paying AOL for the time. You can also instruct your computer to perform your downloads automatically and unattended, in the middle of the night if you want, when the load on the system is minimal.
- Chapter 9, "Preferences," explores AOL's elaborate Preferences command. The AOL client is highly configurable, and the wealth of options requires explanation. Here it is.
- Chapter 10, "Destinations," makes an effort to acquaint you with the spectrum of interesting things you can do online. Though it's by no means comprehensive, this chapter includes online games; book, film, and television reviews; ABC, MTV, and Entertainment Weekly; the comics; and travel. You'll also visit AOL's massive computing resources, its reference area, and its extensive Personal Finance area.

Mac Lovers

Jennifer has a confession: Her true love is Mac.

No, not the guy in Apartment 2B—the Apple Macintosh computers that introduced her and much of the rest of world to personal computing. Sure, she does Windows too, but Macs always get first preference in her office. Their independent spirit rivals her own, and she strives to match the elegance and creativity that an Apple Macintosh displays so well.

So it should come as no surprise to you that she sticks to the Mac when using America Online as well. In truth, there are few differences in the America Online software developed for the Mac and for Windows—the latter being admittedly the software towards which this book is geared. Even so, if there *is* a difference, she has likely discovered it, tested it, and documented it.

If you're a fellow Mac Lover, Jennifer invites you to join her at the end of each chapter to get the skinny on the differences in the America Online software for the Macintosh. She'll also reveal the special features that only the Mac software boasts, plus shortcuts and tricks to mimic some of Windows' options.

Don't worry, though; the Apple doesn't fall far from the AOL tree.

Moving On

We remember renting a car in Paris last June. We left the airport at rush hour and immediately found ourselves in stifling Parisian traffic. Citroëns, Peugeots, and Renaults accompanied us, their drivers smoking French cigarettes. Motor scooters with loaves of French bread in their baskets whizzed by between lanes. Sonorous voices emanated from the radio, which was playing Parisian accordion music. The scene had more charm than menace, and we were eager for our journey to begin.

We hope you're feeling eager as well, because this journey too is about to begin. This will be a voyage of discovery and reward, challenge and triumph. You'll probably make some long-term friends here and return to visit every day. It's an honor to be able to introduce you to such a place.

The Abecedarium

CHAPTER 2

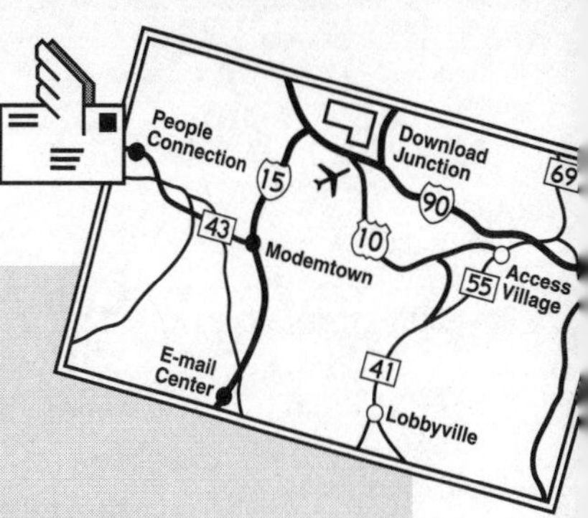

- Quick Start
- Road Trips
- Getting Help
- Guides
- My AOL
- Parental Controls
- Terms of Service (TOS)

Isn't that a *great* word? *Abecedarium*. Pronounce the first three syllables as you would pronounce the first three letters of the alphabet: "A-B-C," then add "darium" (it rhymes with "aquarium"). Indeed, the letters *A B C* are the root of the word, for in the original Medieval Latin, *abecedarium* meant "alphabet." Later the term was used to describe books for people who were learning the alphabet, and later still—as it is today— *abecedarium* was used to describe a primer on any subject. That's what we're doing with this chapter: presenting a primer for those of you who are new to this abecedary we call online telecommunications.

The Newbies, the Ditzels, & the Dummies

A long-term discussion broke out on the staff message boards at America Online a couple of years ago: what term do we use to describe people who are new to online telecommunicating? *Dummy* is popular, but it's not a very flattering term. Its success as a book title, we suspect, relates more to a person's self-perception than the person's status among others. *Ditzel* is perhaps too colloquial a term, and even less flattering than *dummy*.

The consensus among the staff was that *newbie* would have to do, though it wasn't a unanimous sentiment. The term is often used derisively in spite of its original intent.

We like *abecedarian*. No word with that many syllables can be derisive. No word that appears to be so confoundedly unpronounceable can possibly be colloquial. And its meaning is understood by so few that it will never be used unflatteringly—it's hardly used at all. Perfect. We'll call ourselves abecedarians and perplex them all with our pedantic pedagogy. They're all a bunch of dweebs anyway. ;-)

Quick Start

Somewhere, the Godiva people must have a chocolate warehouse. It must be huge. Imagine standing just inside of the door, confronted by shelves of chocolates stacked to the ceiling in a warehouse that's measured in acres. Your host just told you to "eat whatever you want." *Holy confections!* Where to begin?

Once the stupefaction wears off, most AOL abecedarians wander around aimlessly for their first few weeks, biting their nails and cultivating futility. This is no more productive a method of exploring America Online than it would be in exploring Godiva's warehouse. We need some direction here: something or someone to show us where the best stuff is so we can get down to the business of prodigal consumption.

We don't know about Godiva, but America Online offers such a place. To get there, use the keywords: **Quick Start**. Here you'll find the virtual equivalent of a signpost, expertly leading you in one of four directions depending upon your experience and needs (see Figure 2-1). The first path is recommended for beginners; it offers easy-to-follow instructions on adding new screen names, sending and receiving e-mail, and navigating the service. The second path offers a guided tour of the best of AOL and how to use buddy lists, send Instant Messages, and mark a favorite place. The third path matches your interests to the various areas online, allowing you to find the right stuff without needless wandering. Finally, the fourth path leads you to a collection of tips and tricks you won't want to be without. Don't be surprised if you discover Godiva Chocolatiers along your journey.

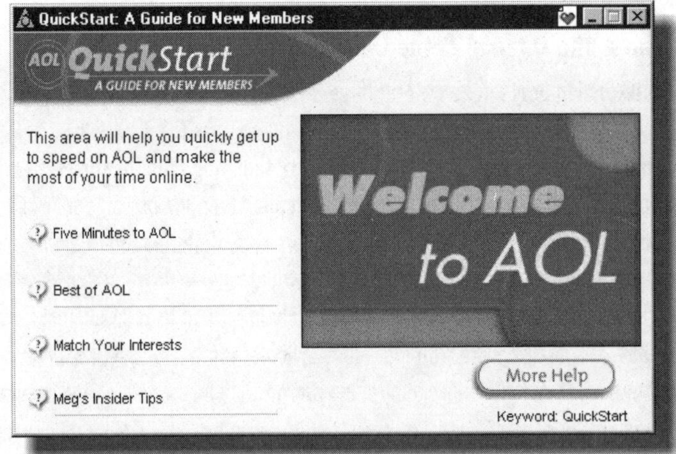

Figure 2-1: Quick Start is the best way to get the most out of AOL in the least amount of time.

Keywords

We mentioned *keywords* in the previous chapter and we just mentioned them again, but more emphasis is appropriate. Keywords are shortcuts to specific destinations within America Online. Without keywords, accessing Family PC Online, for example, via menus and windows requires that we click the Computing button in the Channels window, click the Magazine Rack button, and finally click the Family PC selection in the list. *Whew!* That's a lot of button-pushing, and we had to know which buttons to push. There's gotta be a better way.

There is: keywords. The keywords for Family PC Online are **Family PC**. Once we know the keyword(s), all we have to do is use it: type **Family PC** into the entry box on the toolbar (the toolbar is that bar of icons just under the menu bar) and press Go. Alternatively, you can press Ctrl+K or Command+K or choose Go To Keyword from the Favorites icon on the toolbar and type into the area provided. Once you've clicked Go, America Online takes you directly to Family PC Online, bypassing all the steps in between.

A list of keywords is available in Appendix B of this book and online at keyword: **Keywords**. Keywords are also available within Find Central (discussed later), which you can search right in the Keyword window. Just enter your criteria where the keyword would normally go and click the Search button.

A final note: keywords are not case sensitive. **FAMILY PC** works just the same as **family pc**. Spaces don't affect things either: **Family PC** works no better than **FamilyPC**.

Discover America Online

The lyrics from one of our favorite songs by Simon and Garfunkel express it best: "They've all come to look for America... Online." Well, perhaps the lyrics aren't *quite* like that, but it fits. You want to explore America Online beyond the brief introduction AOL Quick Start offers, and you can.

Thankfully, you don't need to rely on buses or hitchhiking to explore America Online. Just use the keyword: **Help**. This will take you to the AOL Member Services area, where all of America Online's ongoing member help is consolidated—and there's a wealth of it (see Figure 2-2).

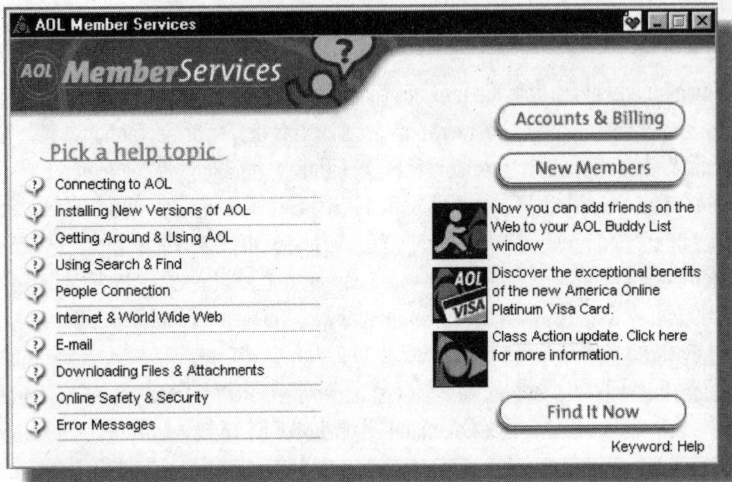

Figure 2-2: The AOL Member Services area is a clearinghouse of ongoing member help.

Learn AOL

Then again, maybe you're not ready for ongoing help. Perhaps you're a linear learner and you prefer your lessons in the "Step 1, Step 2, Step 3" format. AOL offers an area for that as well, and it's at keywords: **Learn AOL** (see Figure 2-3).

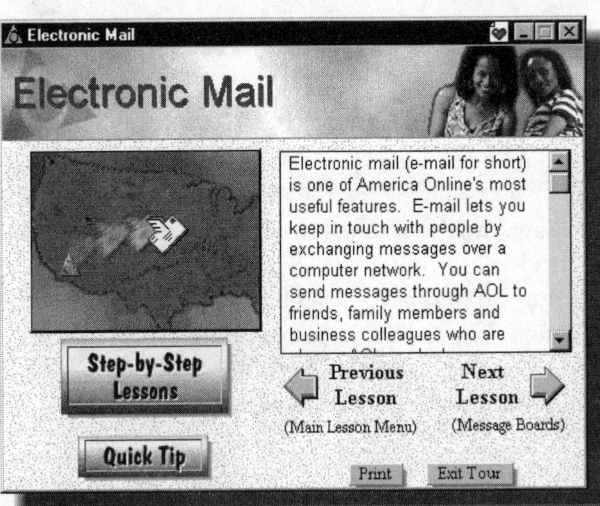

Figure 2-3: The Electronic Mail tutorial is just one of many "lessons" designed to make using America Online easy and fun.

As much as we like to think of this book as the perfect mechanism for learning about America Online, it does have its flaws. It's a single medium. It's not in 24-bit color. Its pictures don't move. It's difficult to change.

On the other hand, America Online offers a fluid, dynamic, and compelling multimedia environment—a medium that's perfect for learning. America Online is aware of this advantage, of course, and employs it well in the Learn AOL area that's under that placard.

There's a programmed learning area here: a dozen or so step-by-step lessons, each with colorful graphics, that you can browse to gain insight into the America Online experience. If you're new to the service, this is the place to begin.

Find Central

America Online is a vast and glorious place. It's easy to lose sight of the forest while you're looking at the trees. There are hundreds—perhaps thousands—of places you might miss if you don't know how to find them. You're probably not even aware that they exist.

So how do you learn how to discover places like this? How would we find all of the places that have to do with chocolate, for example, when the only place we know of for chocolates is the refrigerator? It's easy. Use Find Central.

Find Central is available on the toolbar so it's nearby regardless of where you are on the service. Find Central will show you how to find people, events, places, and things (see Figure 2-4).

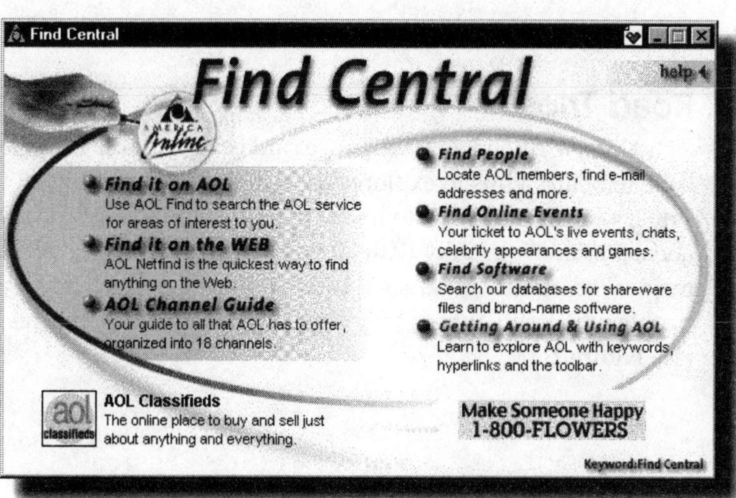

Figure 2-4: Here's the best way to learn how to explore America Online's universe: Find Central. Its button is always available on the toolbar.

Using Find Central today, we found almost 4,000 places that had to do with chocolate, including Godiva Chocolatier (at keyword: **Godiva**) and even a chocolate pizza Web site. Are you surprised?

AOL Insider

AOL Insider is one area you won't want to miss. Keywords: **AOL Insider**, this is a place you will want to visit every week, if not every day. It changes daily, and the information and tips are invaluable. If you want to get the very most out of America Online, visit AOL Insider regularly (see Figure 2-5).

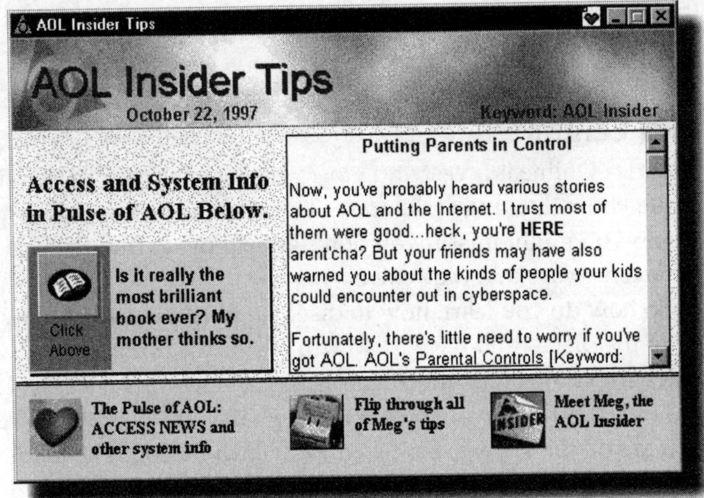

Figure 2-5: Use the keywords: **AOL Insider** for latest access information and member tips.

Road Trips

Actually, we fibbed a bit when we said earlier in this chapter that you don't have to board a bus to explore America Online. You'll want to for AOL Road Trips, which are guided tours of the service. Virtually speaking, you climb aboard a "bus" (usually with 20 or so other members) and take off on a magical adventure conducted by tour guides, better known as Roadies—people who know where they're going and identify features along the way (see Figure 2-6).

Figure 2-6: Road Trips are one of the best ways to get to know America Online. Take the hand of an expert and participate in a methodical, revealing tour of America Online—and have fun as you go. Road Trips are available at the keywords: **Road Trip**.

Are You Current?

Do you have the latest version of AOL's client software? Here's how to find out:

1. Sign on and use the keyword: **Upgrade.**
2. Find the latest copy of the AOL software available for download in the upgrade area; then read its description to discover its version number.
3. Choose About America Online from the Help menu and note the number of the version you're now using.
4. If the versions don't match, you need to download the upgrade. Begin by printing the file's description that appears on your screen. *Don't neglect this step.*
5. Download the upgrade and then sign off.
6. Exit from the AOL software; then follow the helpful directions in the description you have printed.

Road Trips aren't passive. At each stop, your Roadie will let you "off the bus" to explore the area for a while on your own. You can wander around in the Florida Wildflower Web page, for example (see Figure 2-7), and your Roadie will be at your side, ready to answer questions and point out features.

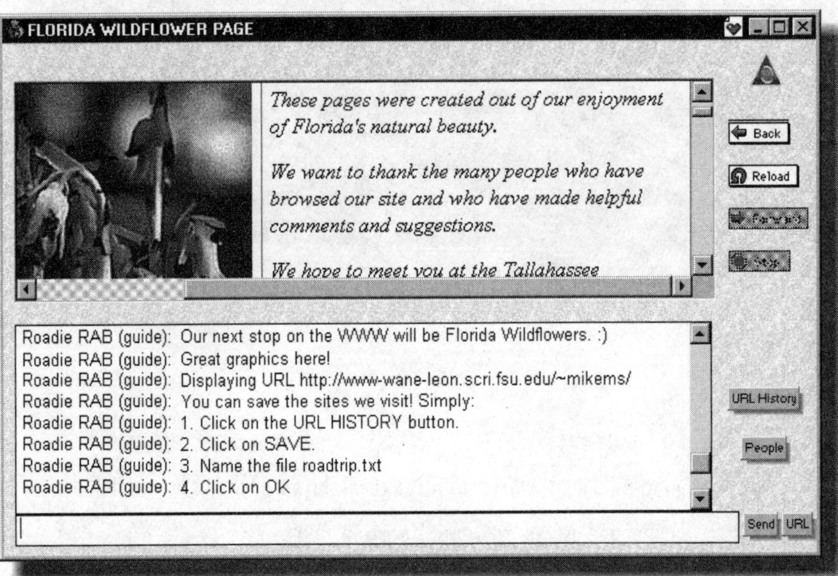

Figure 2-7: The Florida Wildflower Web page invites our exploration in the top half of the Road Trip window. In the lower half, our Guide is identifying features of the site. The very bottom of the window offers a text box where we can submit our questions and comments. The Guide or anyone else on the bus can reply.

Road Trips aren't the exclusive purview of AOL's Roadies, by the way. Anyone can be a "tour guide"—even you. It's a great way to introduce friends to America Online, even if they're in another part of the country (or world). It's really quite easy to prepare your own personal tour; press the Help button at keywords: **Road Trip** for more information.

Getting Help

Speaking of help, our first online experience is one neither of us can forget. It was many years ago for both of us—long before America Online. Like America Online, the services we subscribed to were commercial services, but the clock was running whenever we dialed their numbers. Anxiety had no finer ally.

In other words, we empathize with those of you whose fingers turn to cucumbers whenever you sign on—and so does America Online. Things have changed. Today there is help—plenty of help. Not only does America Online offer an abundance of help, it's most often free even to those who are not on an unlimited usage plan. We'd be five years younger today if the online industry had been that considerate in the early days.

Altruistically, America Online offers both online and offline help. One set of help files resides on your hard disk and is available at any time regardless of whether you're online or not. We call this version AOL's *Offline* help. The other version—*online* help—is always available online, without charge. We'll discuss both in this chapter.

Offline Help

Let's talk about offline help first. America Online's offline help is especially configured to answer the kind of questions you'll encounter when you're disconnected from the service. "How do I connect when I'm away from my usual location?" "How do I change my password?" "What's the technical support telephone number?"

A Familiar Face

Nowadays, in both the Macintosh and Windows environments, help is a separate program that's called by other programs whenever you choose Offline Help from the Help menu. When you choose Offline Help, America Online starts the Help application. When you ask for help from Microsoft Word, the same thing happens. The help files themselves are different; the Help application is the same.

This means there's no need to learn how to use the help feature over again for each application. Help is the same for all applications.

America Online utilizes the Help application to its fullest. The America Online help file is very large, and there are plenty of links to cross-reference help topics with one another. Any help topic can be searched and printed, bookmarks can be placed to lead you back to topics of particular interest, and an extensive list of tips and tricks is available.

As is always the case with items that aren't grayed out on the menus, Help can be chosen at any time, whether you're online or off. These help topics are stored in a file on your hard disk. Therefore, you don't need to go online to access them; you just need to launch the AOL software and choose Offline Help from the Help menu.

Getting Help: A Methodical Approach

If you have a question about America Online and require help, *don't write to us!* We're just two people, with two people's knowledge of the system. America Online offers an army of experts; each of them is thoroughly acquainted with the system, and each is trained in member assistance. To make effective use of them, we suggest you use the methods described below, in the order in which they appear. Most of the topics mentioned are explained in detail later in this chapter. To get help from America Online:

1. Look up the topic in the index of this book to see if your question is answered here. We'd like to think that most of your questions can be answered this way.
2. Run the AOL software (you don't need to sign on) and either choose Offline Help from the Help menu or click the Help button on the Sign On window. Offline Help is always available when you're offline (it's available online as well). It offers an extensive searchable list of topics and will often answer your question, especially if it has to do with the most commonly asked questions.
3. Sign on and choose Member Services Online Help from the Help menu. Click the Yes button in response if you get a message that begins with "Are you sure..." (but don't worry if you don't see this). This will take you to AOL Member Services, a particularly comprehensive (and free to all) resource. This is an amazingly comprehensive collection of answers to almost any question relating to America Online or the Internet you might have. You can even search this database and other help resources. There's a Member Services button on each channel's screen as well.
4. Sign on and use the keyword: **MHM**. This will take you to the Members Helping Members area. The highlight here is an active message board where you can post your questions. Within a day or so you will have a response to your question from another member. Peer help is often the best help you can get.
5. Sign on and use the keywords: **Tech Live**. This will take you to AOL Member Services again. Click any of the help topics, choose any of the subjects, and then read any of the articles to access the Troubleshooting button. Here you'll see several ways to obtain more help, including the option to speak to an AOL Technical Representative online. This feature is free for all and available from roughly 7:00 A.M. to 2:45 A.M. Eastern time, seven days a week except when the AOL system is down for maintenance.
6. Call Customer Relations at 1-800-827-3338 or 1-703-265-1184 (outside the United States and Canada). They're open from 8:00 A.M. to 2:00 A.M. Eastern time, seven days a week. It's a toll-free call in the continental United States, and there's never any charge for support from America Online.

Downloading the Help File

America Online's offline help file is an encyclopedic piece of work. It's so large, in fact, that it might not have been included with your installation of the AOL software. For these installations, America Online downloads the help file to you at the conclusion of (or during) your first online session. You'll see a message to that effect—probably just before you sign off—and the option to accept the download or ignore it. Unless you're calling America Online via a toll line (that is, unless you've had to dial a 1 before AOL's number), there won't be a charge.

In other words, when you're offered the download, take it. If you don't, you'll miss one of America Online's better help mechanisms.

How to Use Help

One of the topics on the Help menu is Offline Help. If you've never used the Help feature before, this is the place to start. Get to know Offline Help inside and out; become comfortable with it. Once you've gained that kind of confidence, you won't hesitate to use Offline Help the next time it's needed (see Figure 2-8).

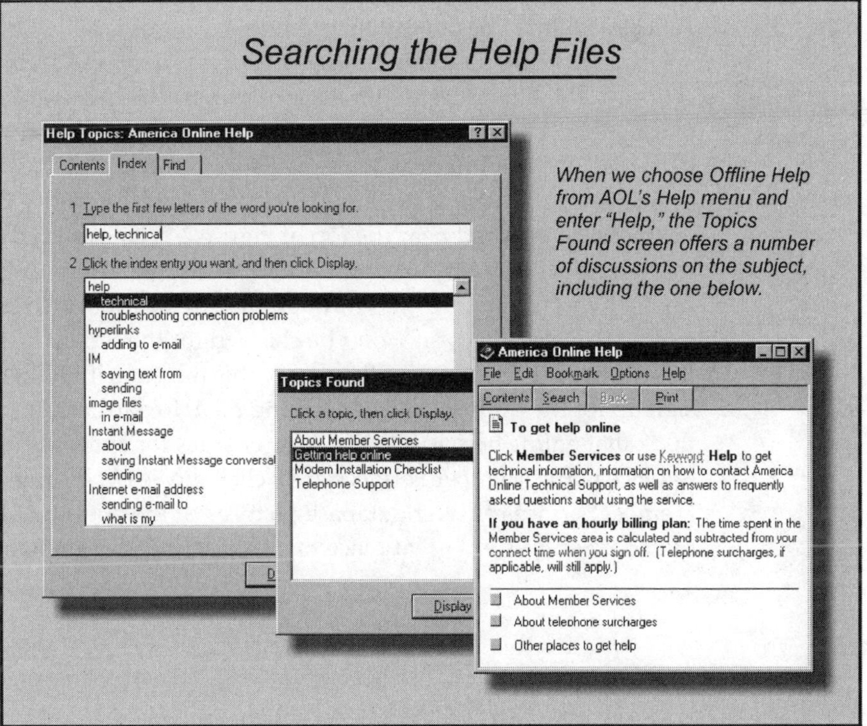

Figure 2-8: Searching America Online's Offline Help files for *Help*, you'll discover plenty of resources. This information is available whether you're online or off.

Victoria, Tom's wife, is a medical student. She learned a long time ago that it's impossible to memorize all of the things she has to know to become a successful practitioner. The sheer magnitude of the task was dragging her down until she realized that all she really had to know was where to look for information. She has a well-organized library and knows which books discuss which topics. When she needs assistance, she goes to her library and gets help.

You should do the same. Don't worry about memorizing all the petty details—for any computer program. Instead, learn how to use Offline Help. It will take 20 minutes, and it will be the most productive 20 minutes you'll ever spend with your computer.

Online Help

America Online's online help is especially comprehensive. Moreover, because the online help files are stored on the host computer (and not on your hard disk), they can be updated quickly, whenever an update is required. In addition to the help you get using the online files, AOL staff and members stand ready to help you as well. This is world-class help, and its breadth is unique to America Online.

Member Services

America Online doesn't call their online help area Online Help. In the true spirit of altruism, they call it *Member Services*. To access Member Services, choose Member Services Online Help from the Help menu or use the keyword: **Help**. You must be signed on for this; online help isn't stored on your hard disk. It's on America Online's host computer.

Just before you enter the Member Services area, America Online may flash the message pictured near the top of Figure 2-9. Unexpected dialog boxes like this often spell trouble, we know, but not this one. America Online is trying to say that you're about to pass through the "free curtain" (to use the online vernacular) and that you won't be charged for the time you're about to spend in Member Services. You will only see this message if you've elected not to sign up for the unlimited usage pricing plan. Regardless, it's comforting to think that online help is free of online charges for everyone.

Once in the Member Services area, click the Search button to scan the entire Member Services answer database pictured at the bottom of Figure 2-9. Member Services is a great place to poke around and get to know the service.

Random Acts of Help

The next time you sign on to America Online, go to keyword: **Help** and click any of the help topics. Once you're there, relax (the clock's not running) and explore this area casually. Poke around as you would at a flea market. Don't try to memorize anything. Get the feel of the place. Get to know what's there and where it's found. Consider this an exploratory mission without any particular agenda. After 20 minutes or so, move on to something else.

You will be amazed at what this kind of unstructured behavior can do for you. You will acquire a familiarity with the layout of the place, and you will gain confidence in the use of online help. Most important, the next time you need help, you won't hesitate to use the keyword. And that, in the long run, is perhaps the most productive attitude you can adopt toward the use of America Online.

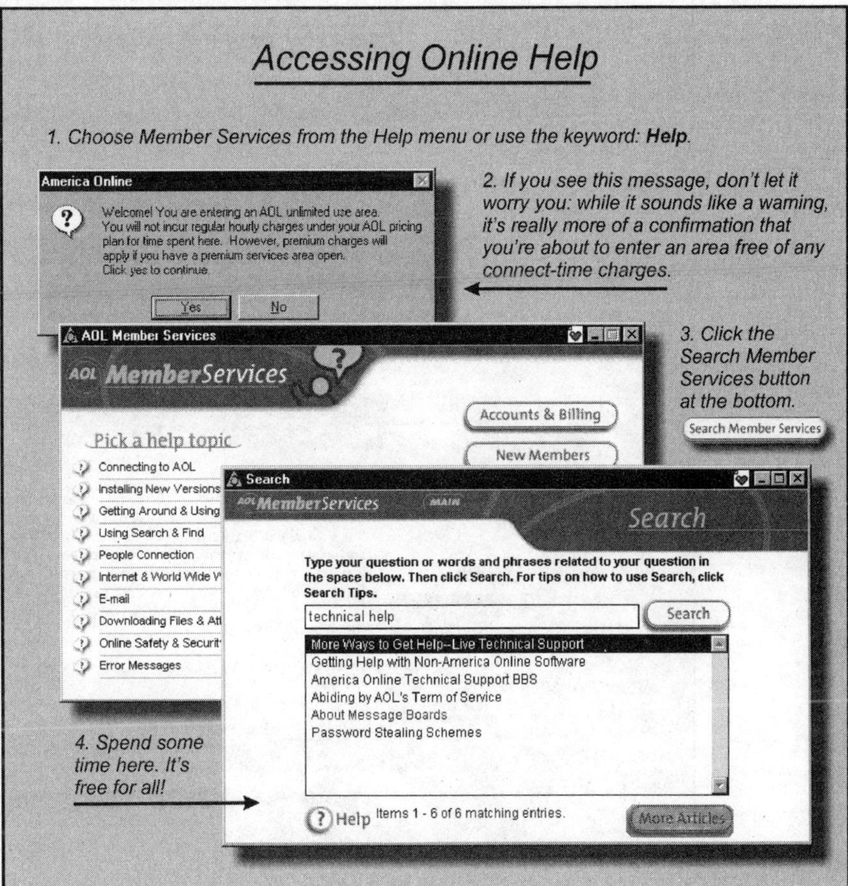

Figure 2-9: Online help is available whenever you're online by selecting Member Services Online Help from the Help menu. The best part: it's absolutely free.

The help topics pictured in the Member Services window offer immediate answers for nearly anything you encounter while online. Each of the topics can be saved, printed, or both. The list of topics is extensive, and the detail offered within each topic is bountiful (see Figure 2-10).

To save an online help article that's on your screen, simply choose Save (or Save As—they're the same command in this context) from the File menu. America Online asks you what you want to name the file and where you want to save it. Provide the information it needs, and that help article will be stored on your disk, ready for any purpose you might have in mind. You can open the file containing the information you saved with any word processor or your AOL software; just choose Open from the File menu.

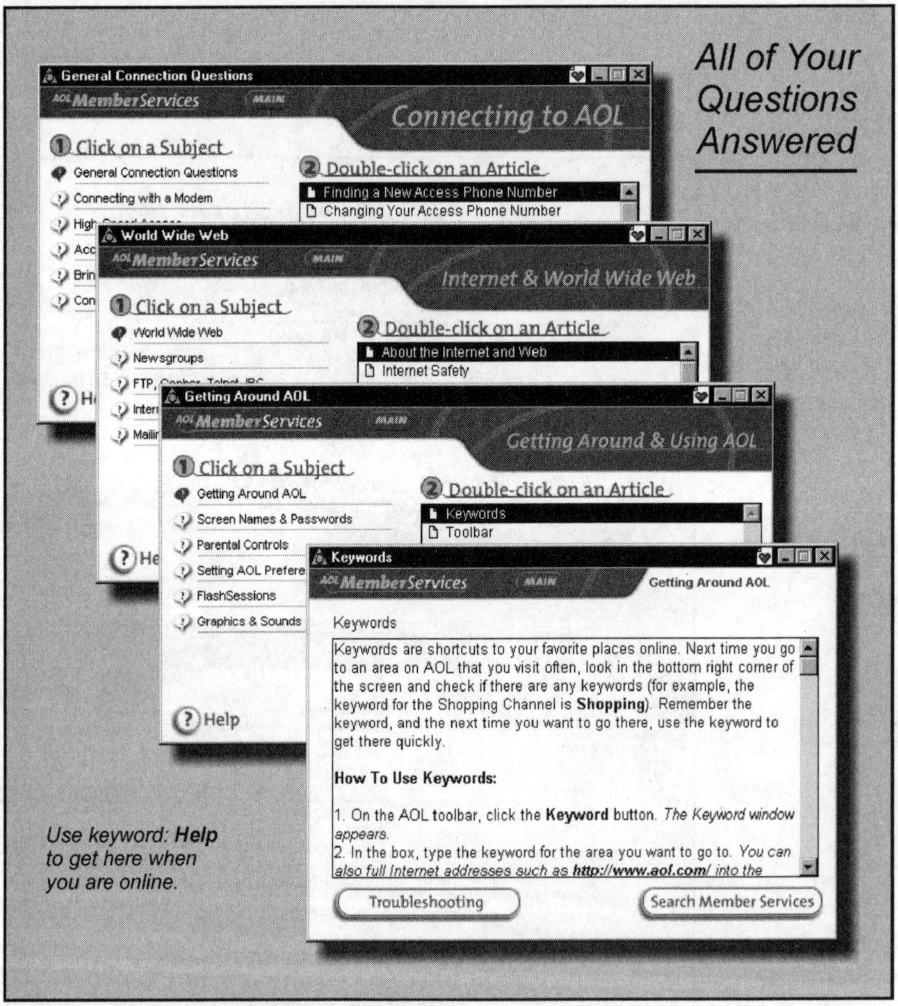

Figure 2-10: A few of the help topics available in the Member Services database.

Printing Help

More likely, you'll want to print a help article for ready reference. As you might expect, all you have to do is choose Print from the File menu or click the Print icon in the toolbar. Printing from America Online works about like printing from any other Windows application. You'll receive the Print dialog box associated with the printer you've selected via the Print Setup command under the File menu. Configure this dialog as you please and print. By the way, you can print just about any text file you read online, not just the online help articles. If you run across a file description or news article you want to print, just choose Print from the File menu or click the Print icon in the toolbar—America Online will print whatever text is in the frontmost (active) window.

Member Help Interactive

Let's talk about rooms for a moment. At America Online, a *room* (you might hear it referred to as a *chat room*) is a place where a number of people gather to talk about a subject of common interest. There are classrooms, for instance, where you'll find a teacher and students. There's People Connection (the waving-people button on the toolbar), where people go to mingle and meet other people. In fact, America Online offers scores of rooms, and we will explore a number of them in Chapter 7, "Chat."

Look again at Figure 2-10. There you'll see a button labeled Troubleshooting in the bottom window. If you click that button, which is accessible in any of the online help articles, you'll discover a wide range of ways to get additional help from America Online. If you accessed Troubleshooting from a help topic of a general nature (such as Getting Around & Using AOL), you can get general help in the Tech Live Auditorium. Here you will find yourself in a room with at least one online volunteer—you can recognize them by the letters MHMS in their screen name—and probably a number of other members, all with questions about the service. Conversations in the room are real-time; you don't have to wait for replies. This isn't mail, and it's not a message board. It's a room, and as in real rooms in real buildings, people there can hold real conversations.

Member Help Interactive is available from 9:00 A.M. to 2:45 A.M. Eastern time, 7 days a week, 24 hours a day. If you need an immediate response, this is the place to find it (see Figure 2-11).

Should your needs tend to be more technical, America Online also provides technical help. Rather than bring you to a room with others as with general help, technical help puts you directly in touch with an America Online representative for one-on-one help. When you first enter the technical help area (available under topics like Connecting to AOL), you are presented with a window explaining how technical help works and a countdown to let you know when the next available representative can help you (see top of Figure 2-12). This is much better than waiting on hold on the phone; you can explore the Member Services answer database while waiting and perhaps even find the answer on your own. The countdown will update automatically for you, so you'll always know how long you have to wait. When a representative is available, a small window will appear on your screen much like a private consultation room. The representative will ask how they can help you and you'll be on your way. We wish all customer service support was this easy.

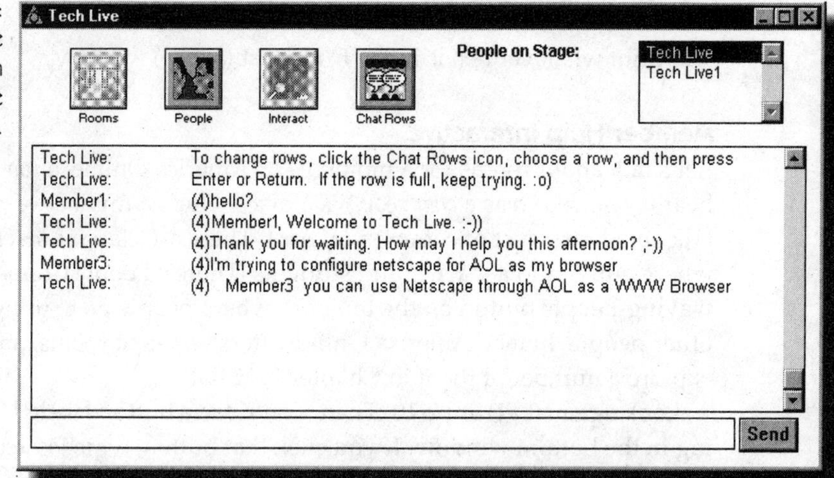

Figure 2-11: A glimpse of general help in the Tech Live Auditorium.

Take the Time

The Tech Live Auditorium, as you can imagine, is a popular place. At any one time, hundreds of members might be there, each asking questions to which they want answers *right now!*

Rather than toss everyone in the same "room" where they're forced to clamor for attention like reporters at a press conference, America Online arranges the general help room in a series of "rows," each with its own volunteer, and each with a limited number of members. Of necessity, it's an elaborate structure with strict protocols—a structure that takes a bit of understanding in order to use.

As you pass into the general help room, America Online offers a number of windows explaining the protocol and offering other methods of help you may wish to explore. When you make your first visit, take the time to read this information or search for a reply to a specific question. Once you get into the room and receive a prompt reply to an urgent question, you'll be glad you did.

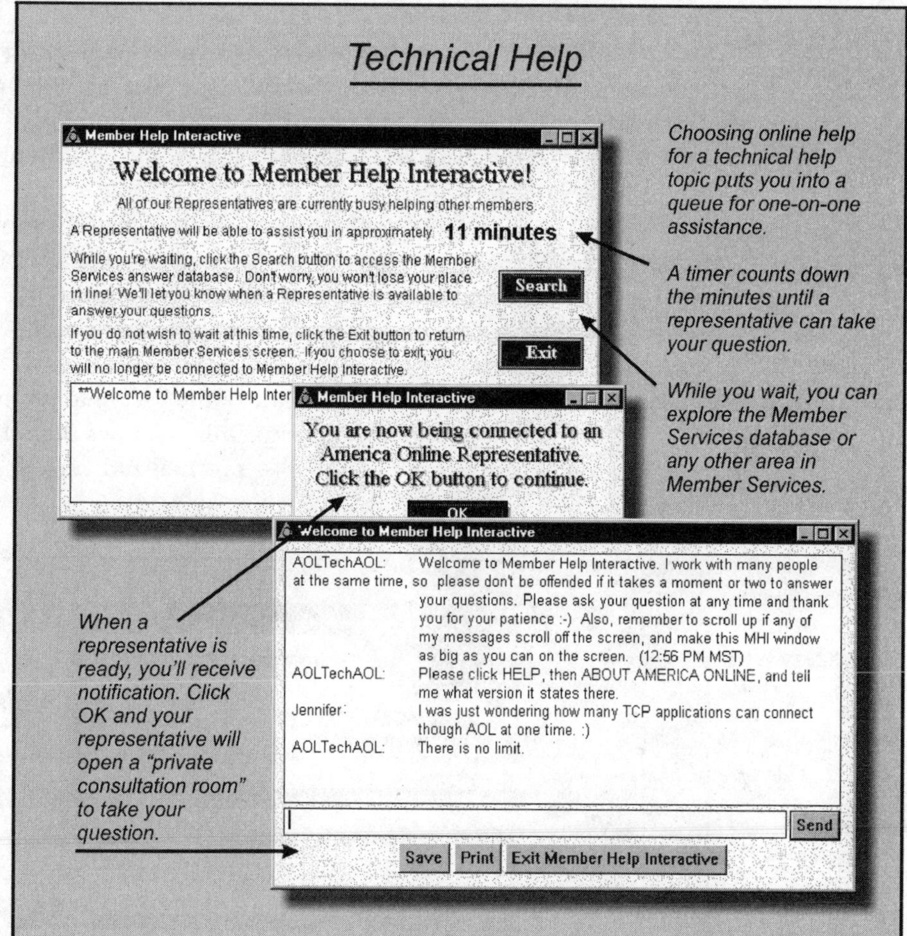

Figure 2-12: Technical help offers one-on-one help with a representative online.

The Help Rooms

Member Help Interactive is always free, and that often leads to a crowd. An alternative is the Help Room (more properly, the Help *Rooms*—there are usually more than one). The Help Rooms are chat rooms in the People Connection, and though they're not free, they're staffed by Guides and Rangers and open every day from 3:00 P.M. until 3 A.M. Eastern time. Read Chapter 7 to learn about People Connection and chat rooms.

Members Helping Members

On Tom's IRS 1040 form, right there next to the word *Occupation*, it says "educator." Though he's retired from the classroom, he still writes books and does some consulting. As an educator, he attends a number of conferences. Most of these conferences are academic, each featuring a number of speakers and seminar leaders.

Reflecting back on those conferences, he admits that the greatest benefit he received from them is not from the speakers or the seminars but from the other people attending the conference. He gets his education in the hallways and at lounge tables. People talking to people—peer to peer—that's where he finds the Good Stuff.

America Online is no different. Some of the best help online is that received from other members. America Online knows that; that's why it provides Members Helping Members—a formalized version of peer support (Figure 2-13).

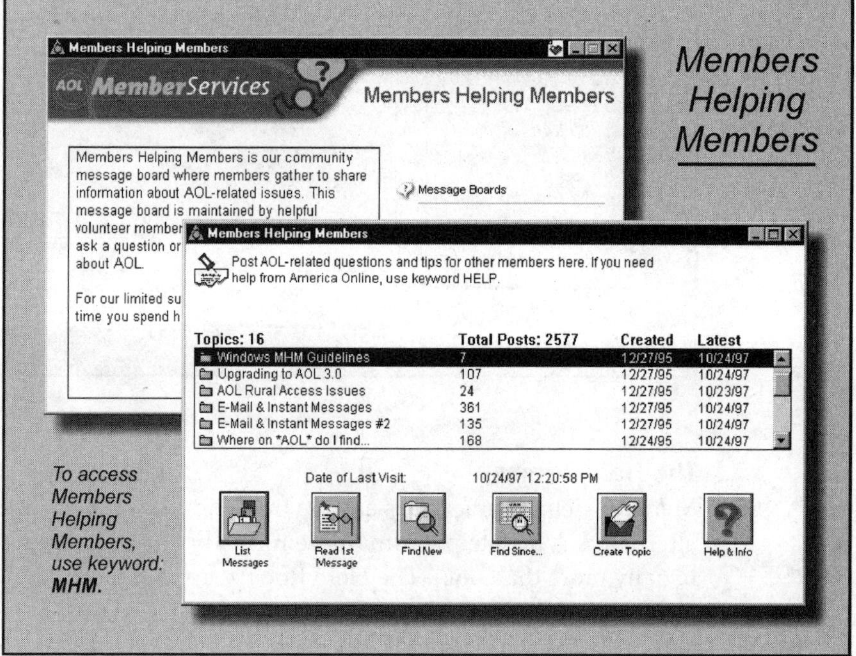

Figure 2-13: To access Members Helping Members, use the keyword: **MHM**.

Message Boards

Members Helping Members is a *message board*. Though we'll discuss message boards in Chapter 7, "Chat," the subject is worth a brief mention here as well.

A message board is analogous to the bulletin boards you see hanging in the halls of offices and academic institutions. People post things there for other people to see: postcards, lost mittens, announcements, and messages. America Online's message boards are exactly the same (though you might not see lost mittens on America Online's boards).

Look again at Figure 2-13. Note how America Online's boards are organized by using folders. The bulletin board analogy weakens a bit here, but AOL's boards get a lot of messages—the Members Helping Members board pictured in Figure 2-13 has 2,577. Unless they're organized in some fashion, 2,577 messages posted on a single board would be chaotic and overwhelming. The solution is folders.

You can read all the messages in a folder, browse through them (viewing only their subjects rather than the messages themselves), or specify only those messages that have been posted since a specific date. This very convenient message-reading system is described in detail in Chapter 7.

For the time being, let's select a folder and read its messages. We picked the General AOL Questions folder and found the series of messages pictured in Figure 2-14.

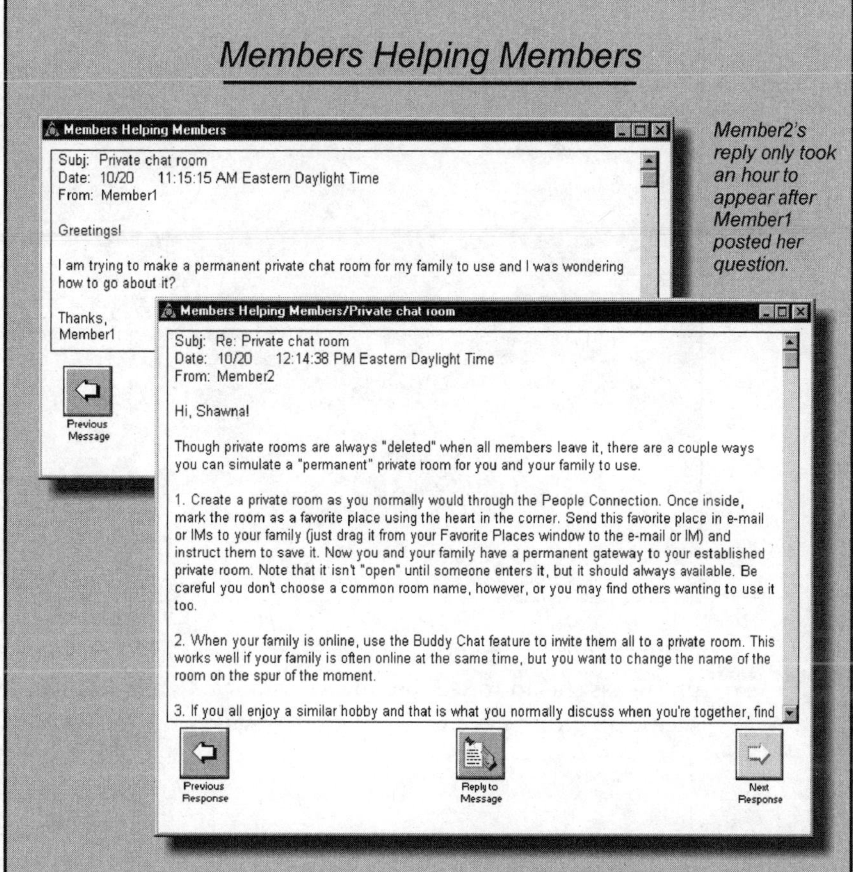

Figure 2-14: Member1 needed help on creating a private room for her family. Member2 was there to help.

The Value of Member Help

Look at the last message pictured in Figure 2-14. Not only does Member2 suggest three ideas for Member1, but she also explains why and when each idea would work best. This is superb help, and it came from another member. The full text of the message from Member2 appears in Figure 2-15.

Figure 2-15: Member2 offers not one but three solutions to a question.

Member2's Message

Hi, Shawna!

Though private rooms are always "deleted" when all members leave it, there are a couple ways you can simulate a "permanent" private room for you and your family to use.

1. Create a private room as you normally would through the People Connection. Once inside, mark the room as a favorite place using the heart in the corner. Send this favorite place in e-mail or IMs to your family (just drag it from your Favorite Places window to the e-mail or IM) and instruct them to save it. Now you and your family have a permanent gateway to your established private room. Note that it isn't "open" until someone enters it, but it should always available. Be careful you don't choose a common room name, however, or you may find others wanting to use it too.

2. When your family is online, use the Buddy Chat feature to invite them all to a private room. This works well if your family is often online at the same time, but you want to change the name of the room on the spur of the moment.

3. If you all enjoy a similar hobby and that is what you normally discuss when you're together, find a conference room in one of the forums that interests you and favorite place that. Keep in mind that this is a public room, however, and there probably will be structured chats or conferences in there from time to time.

I hope these ideas are helpful!

Member2

Note another small detail: Member2 must have looked up Member1's profile, as she addresses her message to "Shawna." That's a nice touch. Member2 didn't have to do that, but it makes her message all the more personable. (How, you may wonder, do we know that Member2 is a she? *We* looked up *her* profile! Profiles are discussed later in this chapter.)

We're reminded of community again. Visiting a big city a few months ago, Tom was struck by the isolation that seemed to surround everyone he passed on the street. Perhaps it's a defense mechanism for dealing with high population density, but it seemed that everyone was in a cocoon, oblivious to everyone else. No one smiled. No one ever looked anywhere but straight ahead. Thousands of people jostled together, yet no one was talking. An incredibly lonely place.

On the other hand, in Damascus—the little Oregon town closest to Tom's home—there are no strangers. People stop on the street and say hello, swap some gossip, and perhaps offer advice.

America Online is more like Damascus. We spent years on other services and never felt like we belonged. We never got mail, we never contributed to a message board, and we never knew where to find help. It was like a big city to us, and we were always anxious to leave. At America Online we're walking the street in a small town on a sunny day, and everyone is smiling. The first day we arrived at America Online, we got a letter from Steve Case. And people like Member2 go out of their way to offer assistance. This is our kind of place. We're at home here.

Guides

Among the many art galleries we've visited, one in Amsterdam stands out. There were a number of Rembrandts there, hanging on the wall just like any other picture. No glass cases or protective Lexan—just those radiant Rembrandts, emancipated and free. A gentleman in uniform stood nearby. He wasn't a guard; the uniform wasn't that severe. He was a guide. He was a volunteer. He got to spend his days in a room full of the Rembrandts he loved and at the same time share his interest with other people. He explained the Rembrandts to us in a fatherly way, exhibiting a proprietorial regard for his fellow countryman's legacy.

Which is precisely what America Online's *Guides* are. They're members just like the rest of us—experienced members with particularly helpful online personalities—but members all the same. They remain politely in the background, leaving us to our own explorations, silent unless spoken to. If we need help, however, Guides are always nearby, ready with friendly advice and information. If you have a question—any question at all—about America Online, its services, or its policies, ask a Guide.

Like the guide in Amsterdam, you can identify Guides by their appearance: their screen names have the word *Guide* in them. If Figure 2-15's Member2 was to be a Guide (she should be), she would probably be Guide2, or something like that.

Figure 2-16: A stop by the AOL Help chat room for some assistance.

A Help Chat Room

```
Zzz: how do i find the roots of a cubic equation when the
          leading coefficient is negative?
Guide ONE: TigerK9105, that's the ticket :)
TigerK9105: I see..
Guide ONE: Zzz, try keyword: AAC for Academic Assistance.
Guide TWO: MrLexum, thanks for waiting how may I help
          you? :)
MrLexum: Tried to download the new recommended browser
          for AOL.  I have 16 Mb memory.  Screen says
MrLexum: I dont have enuf memory
MrLexum: when I finished my screen looked different,
Guide TWO: MrLexum, did you try rebooting your computer
          to clear the memory?
MrLexum: Yes that is what i had to do...
MrLexum: OK Lexus, have you cleared your cache? :)
MrLexum: I closed all the windows that were open...
had to reinstall aol..
MrLexum: Haven't cleared my cache.  will try that..
Guide TWO: Sent you email on how to do that Lexum :)
MrLexum: Is 16 mb ram enuf to run the new explorer?
Guide TWO: For live detailed help, goto Keyword: HELP,
          choose
Guide TWO: a topic, then double-click on an article and
          hit the
Guide TWO: troubleshooting button.  There is a hyperlink
          called
Guide TWO: ONLINE that will take you to a technician. :)
Guide ONE: Queue (turn): MajorTom, KiddCyb
Guide TWO: MajorTom, how can I help you?
```

This is an ongoing conversation we walked in on.

Big smile. Turn your head counter-clockwise 90 degrees to see it.

The line of people (based on the order of arrival) waiting their turn to ask questions. Tom is next!

Figure 2-16 is a little hard to follow if you're not used to America Online's so-called chat rooms. Though chat rooms are discussed in Chapter 7, a little explanation seems in order here as well. Twenty-one people were in the room when we visited. Some were just watching (*lurkers*), but most were there to ask a question. The entire illustration is a *chat log* (look under My Files on the toolbar for the Log Manager).

The Guidepager

Sometimes you'll need a Guide in a hurry. Someone could be harassing you, or hassling people in a room. This kind of behavior, lamentable as it is, is a fact of life in online communities, many of which are larger than most cities in the country today.

Though I'll discuss this subject in Chapter 7, it's worth noting here that you don't have to wander the lobbies looking for a Guide when you need one in a hurry. Just use the keywords: **I Need Help** and select one of the categories there (see Figure 2-17).

Don't abuse the Guidepager feature. It's not there to help you learn how to cut and paste or download a file. Guidepager is America Online's life ring, and it should be used only as such.

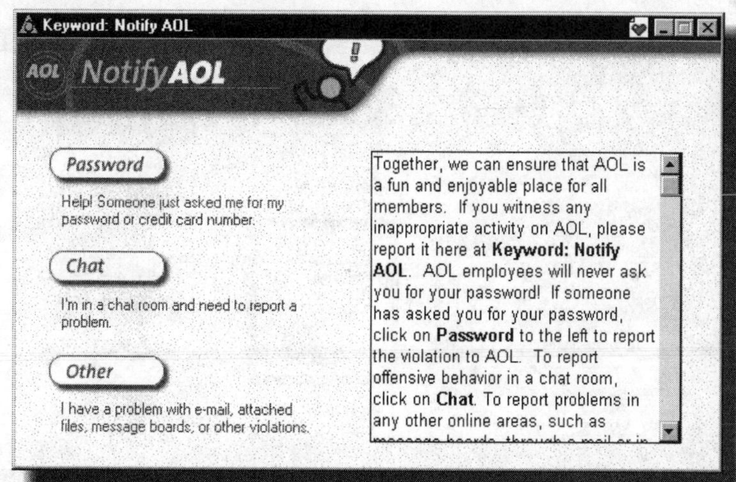

Figure 2-17: The keywords: **I Need Help** get you help fast!

Chat rooms can be intimidating to the first-time visitor. Don't be shy. Jump right in with a Hello, look for the Guide's name, and ask your question. More important, note that MrLexum received one immediate answer to his question and received instructions in e-mail from Guide Two. Most likely he got just what he needed and it only took 10 minutes.

Guides are on duty 24 hours a day, 7 days a week, 365 days a year. To find a Guide, click on the two-heads button on the toolbar or select the People Connection option from the Channels screen. Once in a Lobby, click the List Chats button and look for the AOL Help room—there's usually a guide there. You'll find them roaming throughout the other rooms too. They're easy to spot: they all have the word *Guide* in their screen names.

My AOL

We all have some degree of nesting instinct, some more than others. Faced with a new living space, many of us immediately turn to wallpaper samples and paint chips. A new office might sprout posters, bulletin boards, and a favorite lamp—all within minutes of taking possession. Or how about the people who put wobbly-head critters on the parcel shelf of a newly acquired automobile before they drive it off the lot? Regular robins in the spring, we are.

If you're a nester, you'll love the degree of personalization America Online offers. You can not only control America Online's environment, you can even control the way you're presented within that environment. America Online is a nester's Shangri-la.

All of these nesting controls are found at one location, appropriately called *My AOL*. To get there, select it under the My AOL icon on the toolbar.

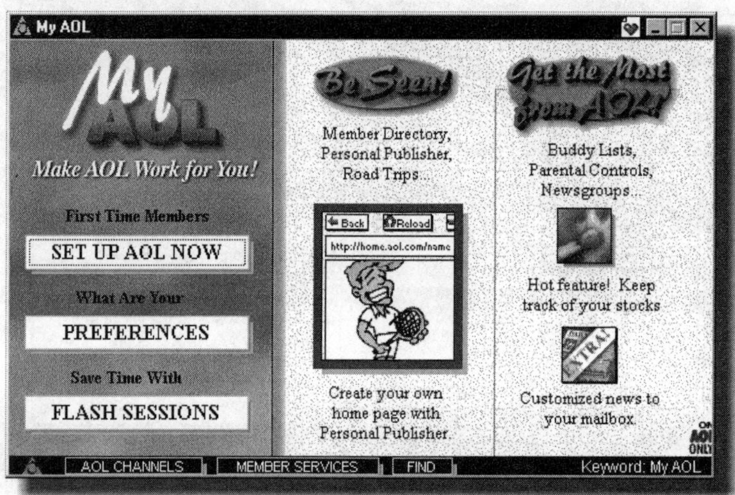

Figure 2-18: The My AOL button on the toolbar allows you to configure your online environment exactly as you wish.

A number of the My AOL controls are so extensive that we've dedicated whole sections of the book to them. Others are best presented in contexts other than this one. Though we'll discuss many of the My AOL controls here, others are addressed elsewhere in the book:

- *Preferences* deserve an entire chapter; look for them in Chapter 9.
- *FlashSessions* are discussed in Chapter 8, "Working Offline."

- The *Personal Filing Cabinet* is discussed in Chapter 3, "Electronic Mail & the Personal Filing Cabinet."
- *Favorite Places* are discussed in Chapter 5, "Finding Stuff."
- *Buddy Lists* are discussed in Chapter 7, "Chat."

There are a number of other features in the My AOL area, however, and we'll discuss them next.

Changing Your Password

While you are in the My AOL area, you'll be reminded that the AOL staff will never ask for your password and that you should change your password often.

That's good advice, but how, exactly, *do* you change your password? None of the admonishments explain the process.

It's easy; just use the keyword: **Password** and then follow the directions.

Member Profiles

America Online offers you the opportunity to post a voluntary *member profile*. Profiles are the way AOL members describe themselves: hobbies, home towns, age, gender—that kind of stuff. It's all very enticing, but the operative term here is *voluntary*. America Online values the individual's privacy, and if you wish to remain secluded in the online community, you may do so.

On the other hand, your profile is your opportunity to be anyone you want to be: if you've always wanted to be Jell-O Man, be Jell-O Man; if you have a fascination with wobbly-head critters, mention it in your profile and you'll probably meet some other wobbly heads online.

As we mentioned a moment ago, member profiles are voluntary. If you elect not to complete a profile, however, you will cut yourself out of a number of opportunities to become involved in the online community. If you elect to post a profile (or if you've already posted a profile and want to edit it), use the keyword: **Profile**. When you do, the Edit Your Online Profile window pictured in Figure 2-19 will be displayed.

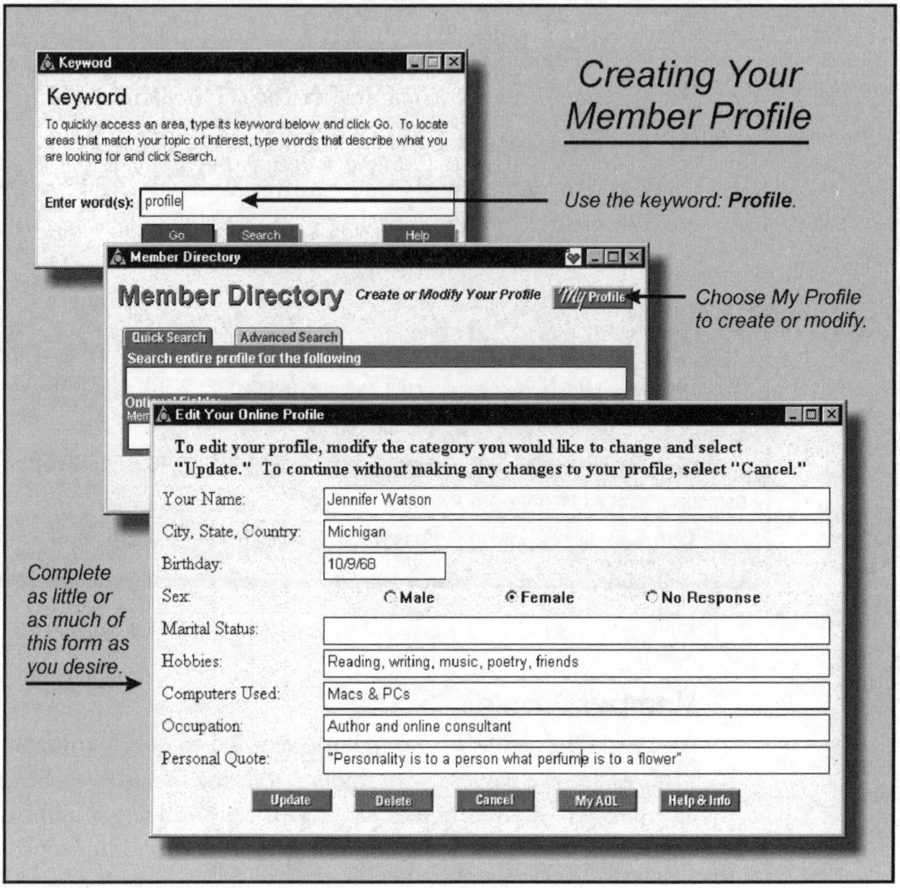

Figure 2-19: Be who you want to be; fill in as much or as little of this form as you wish.

The Masquerade

The text mentions your profile, but be aware that you are by no means limited to a single one. Your America Online account provides for up to five account names, and each of those account names can have its own profile. Businesses might use these account names for individual employees, and families might use them for individual family members, but most people use them as *noms de plume*. At America Online, you never know whether you're talking to a real person or someone behind a mask. It's a regular masquerade here, for better or worse.

And that's our point: if you want to avoid the potential of meeting a misdirected personality concealed behind a mask, withhold any confidentialities or personal information until you're on reliably firm ground. Anonymity breeds impudence in some people, as does any mask; and like a mask, one's visage is not necessarily one's self. Contrary to admonishments from Mother, feel free to talk to strangers here. Just don't get in the car with them until you know who's driving and where the journey might go.

This masquerade is all part of the America Online community, which is discussed in Chapter 7.

Figure 2-19 reveals a secret that many of America Online's members don't know: you can complete as much or as little of the profile window as you wish. If you don't want people to know your name, put your screen name there, or your first name only. Many people include only their birth day and month, preferring to keep the year of their birth to themselves (Jennifer has no such shame).

In fact, here are a few profile secrets:

- If you include your birth day and month, people can send you birthday wishes via e-mail.
- If you include your first name, last name, *and* your city and state, people can use directory assistance to reach you by phone (unless your number is unlisted). Is that what you want them to do?
- You must be online to make any changes in your profile.
- Definitely do fill out a profile. You can't really participate in America Online's online community until you do.
- The Hobbies, Computers Used, and Occupation fields are often used by people looking for others with similar interests. If you enjoy quilting and you include quilting among your hobbies, there's a good chance you'll meet up with other quilters online.
- You're not committed to the information you include in your profile. You can add, modify, or delete it whenever you want—just use the keyword: **Profile**.

There are two primary reasons for filling out a profile. Most often, someone will see your screen name online—in a chat room (chat rooms are discussed in Chapter 7) or in some e-mail—and they will want to know more about you. They'll choose Get AOL Member Profile from the People icon in the toolbar, enter your screen name, and your profile will be displayed.

The other use for profiles is the *Member Directory.* The Directory is AOL's database of everyone's profiles, and it's searchable. You can search for a member by real name, screen name, or by anything in their profile. You might wonder if a friend or relative is signed up with America Online; search the directory and you'll know in seconds. The Directory is discussed in more detail in Chapter 5, "Finding Stuff."

Parental Controls

In Chapter 1, we described America Online as a community. On a political level, communities range from socialism to anarchism. But in this country we think of something in between. There *is* a government, after all, but it's not authoritarian; people do pretty much as they please, within certain bounds.

Our politics are reflected in our families; we seek a balance between despotic authority and profligate anarchy. Parents struggle with this balance; equanimity is elusive. Nowhere is this more evident than in matters of censorship.

Every parent adopts a personal level of control; that's as it should be. Recently, however, the media have offered their assistance: all motion pictures are rated, many television cable companies offer selective channel blocking, a rating system is emerging for video games, and America Online offers a feature called *Parental Controls* (see Figure 2-20).

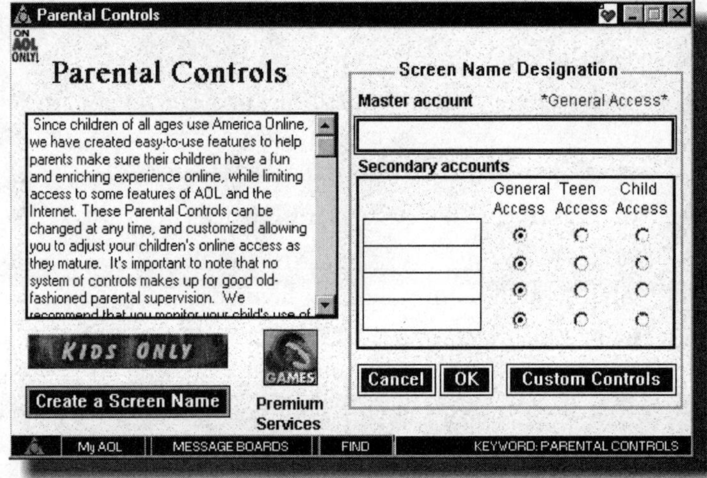

Figure 2-20: Parental Controls allow the master account holder to determine how much or how little of the AOL service is available to the screen names associated with the account.

Only the holder of the master account can use Parental Controls. The master account is the permanent screen name that was created during your first sign-on to America Online. Parental Controls enable the master account holder to restrict—for other names on that account, as well as itself—access to certain areas and features available online. It can be set for one or all screen names on the account, and once it is set for a particular screen name, it is active each time that screen name signs on. Changes can be made only at the master account level, and therefore only by the person who knows the master account's password. These restrictions are set at keywords: **Parental Controls**.

As shown in Figure 2-20, there are three account designation types used to control access to America Online: general, teen, or child. General access has no restrictions and is the default. Teen access restricts the screen name to World Wide Web sites selected for content appropriate to teens 13-16. Teen access is also blocked from newsgroups that allow file attachments and they cannot use premium (extra-charge) services. Child access only allows access to the Kids Only channel and World Wide Web sites appropriate to those under 12. Child access also restricts Instant Messages, Member Rooms, file attachments on e-mail, and premium services. These controls are particularly convenient if you are unfamiliar with all that America Online has to offer. If you prefer to tailor access, click the Custom Controls button for more specific options (see Figure 2-21).

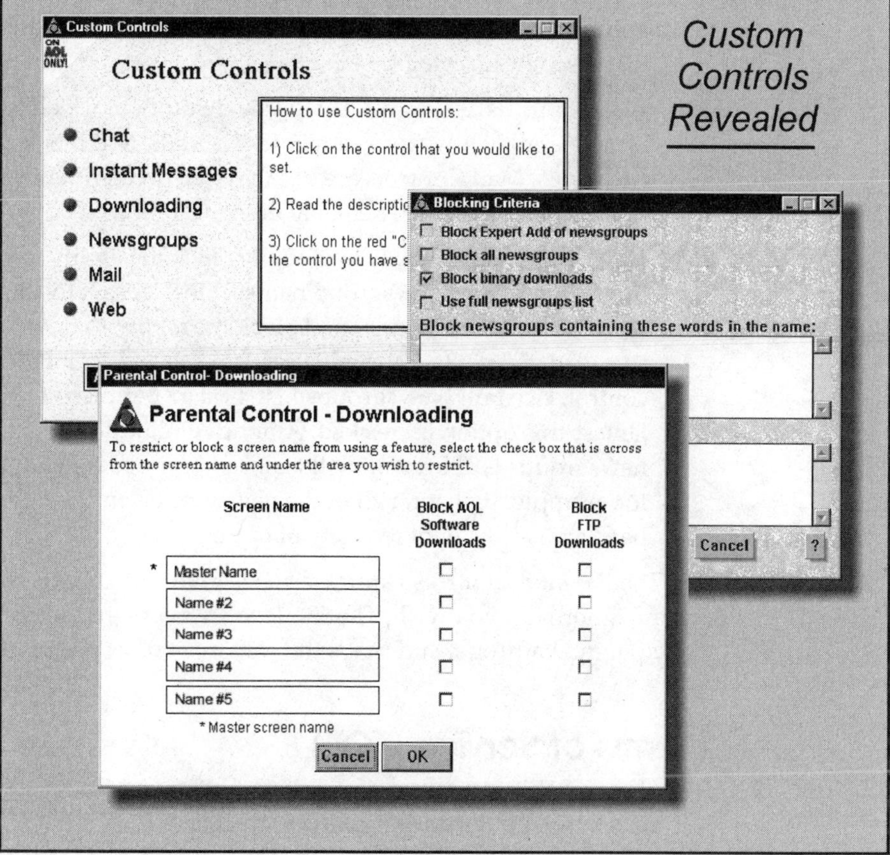

Figure 2-21: Using the master screen name, you are able to custom-control access to certain areas within the service for all your other screen names.

The master account holder can set any or all of the following four Parental Control features (refer to Figure 2-21):

- **Chat Controls.** Allow you to block all instant messages, block access to all rooms in the People Connection, block access to member rooms only, or block access to conference rooms found throughout America Online, such as the MTV Yack room in MTV Online.
- **Downloading Controls.** Allow you to block downloading of any data that's available on America Online, including programs, graphics, and multimedia (downloading is discussed in Chapter 6, "Transferring Files") as well as block FTP downloads, which are discussed in Chapter 4, "Using the Internet."
- **Web Controls.** Allow you to block all Web sites, allow only Web sites appropriate for children up to 12 years in age, allow only Web sites appropriate for teens, and allow all Web sites. The World Wide Web is discussed in Chapter 4.
- **Mail Controls.** Allow all e-mail (the default), block all e-mail, allow you to receive e-mail only from certain individuals, and block e-mail from certain addresses. Mail Controls are discussed in greater depth in Chapter 3, "Electronic Mail & the Personal Filing Cabinet."
- **Newsgroup Controls.** Allow you to block the ability to add newsgroups by typing in their newsgroup names, block access to all newsgroups regardless of their nature, and block the ability to download the Internet's so-called *binaries* (such as pictures, videos, and sounds). An additional control, Use Full Newsgroups List, is *more* permissive when it's checked. Unless this option is checked, America Online's available list of newsgroups is abbreviated: the alt.sex.* groups don't appear on the list, for example. By listing all of the newsgroups on the Internet, members have access to a wider variety of options.

The Parental Controls feature is an elective, not an imperative. Use it if you want; ignore it if you wish. That's a level of intervention that accommodates any parental attitude, and that's the way most of us prefer to have it.

Terms of Service (TOS)

You're probably not aware of it, but you have a contract with America Online, and even though it's not a signed contract, you waived the need for your signature when you first signed on. The contract defines exactly what you can and cannot do online, and it defines exactly what America Online can do if it determines that you have violated the terms of the contract.

The contract is called *Terms of Service*, or *TOS* for short. It's always available for review or downloading at keyword: **TOS** (see Figure 2-22). Time spent there is free of America Online's normal connect-time charges.

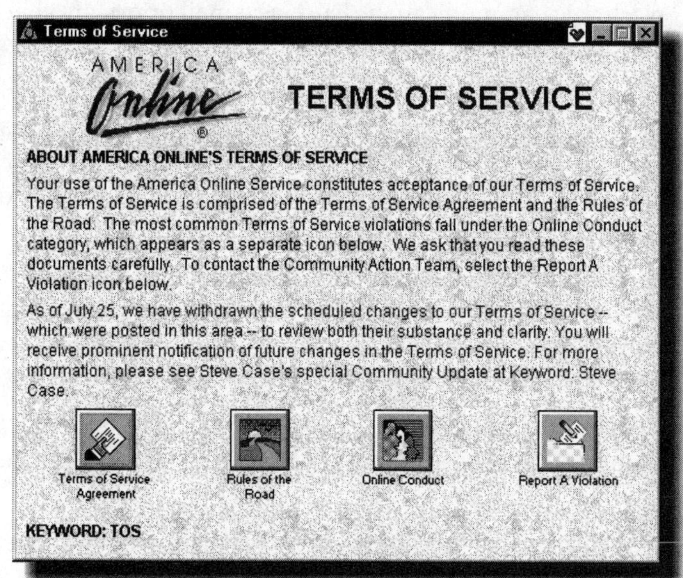

Figure 2-22: The contract that exists between all members and AOL is available at keyword: **TOS**.

Unless you have joined AOL with the specific intention of disrupting the service (snerts, phishers, and trolls are discussed in Chapter 7, "Chat"), TOS exists to protect you. Specifically, TOS describes violations such as offensive e-mail, impersonation of America Online staff, and online harassment. It also describes what you can do if you witness these violations. Look again at Figure 2-22: the Report a Violation button provides a number of ways for you to enforce your rights. Among other things, America Online's TOS team is the online "police," and they can take quick and conclusive action when provoked. We've seen it happen; it's not an experience soon forgotten.

TOS, like your local 911 service, exists to make the community a better and safer place to live. And like a 911 service, TOS can be abused—even by those with good intentions—because of ignorance. If you think you might ever require TOS enforcement, read this information.

Here are some interesting TOS conditions:

- You agree that you are an individual, not a corporation.
- You agree that you are at least 18 years of age.
- You agree to notify America Online within 30 days if your billing information changes (e.g., your credit card is stolen).

- You are liable for all expenses incurred on your account—even if someone steals your password—until you notify America Online by telephone.
- America Online does not intentionally monitor or disclose any private electronic communications (such as e-mail or private chat rooms) unless required to do so by law.
- America Online *does* monitor public communication (public chat rooms, message board postings), though America Online ". . . has neither the practical capability, nor does it intend, to act in the role of 'Big Brother' by screening public communication in advance." (Quoted from "Rules of the Road.")
- Unless you tell America Online otherwise (see Chapter 9, "Preferences"), America Online has the right to distribute your name and address to third parties (for example, mailing lists). This right does not extend to your billing information, however.
- Both the Terms of Service agreement *and* the Rules of the Road (review Figure 2-22) constitute your contract with America Online. You should read them both.

We mention all of this not to infuse you with an Orwellian fear of America Online but rather to offer a wake-up call. TOS has some very specific and significant conditions in it, conditions to which you have legally agreed. You should know your rights and know how to recognize others' wrongs. Read this agreement.

America Online's Voice

The male voice you hear when you sign on is that of Elwood Edwards, a professional announcer who, last we heard, works for Channel 50 in Washington, DC.

El's story is one of online romance made good. He was a member like the rest of us when, in the late 1980s, he met a female member online and began to chat with her. It turned out that the lady worked for America Online and was involved in the process of selecting a voice to add to AOL's software. When she discovered El's profession, she asked him if he would like to record the voice tracks.

El and his newfound acquaintance met face-to-face for the recording session, discovered lots of things they had in common, and were married soon thereafter.

MacHelp

Jennifer finds she has less need to consult AOL's help resources when using the Mac, even with new software and features. Whether this is due to the Mac's design or her own experience with it is hard to say. Regardless, knowing the resources are there when needed is a big help in itself, and help is available in abundant supply on both the Mac and Windows. The only real differences on the Mac are in the means of accessing it. So here's the scoop...

To find out what version of the AOL software you are currently running, choose About America Online... from under the Apple menu located on the far left of the menu bar.

Offline Help on the Mac also has a familiar face: It is based on Apple Guide and is called, appropriately enough, AOL Guide. You'll find it under the Help menu or, if you're using System 7, under the question-mark icon, which is always found at the far right of the menu bar. Links to the AOL Guide are also liberally scattered through the AOL software itself.

The Mac Help Desk is available at keywords: **Mac Help**.

Moving On

All of this talk about TOS notwithstanding, we hope this chapter has made you feel more comfortable and welcome here. America Online offers more help—and more kinds of help—than any software we know of. It's online, it's offline, it's Member Services, it's Members Helping Members, and it's Guides and other community leaders. Everyone at America Online—members included—helps someone else sooner or later. That's comforting. Not only is America Online a community, it's a *considerate* community, where no one remains a stranger for long.

Without a doubt, the mechanism that members most often use to communicate among themselves is electronic mail, or e-mail for short. America Online places notable emphasis on its e-mail features, and it shows. To see what we mean, turn the page.

CHAPTER 3

Electronic Mail & the Personal Filing Cabinet

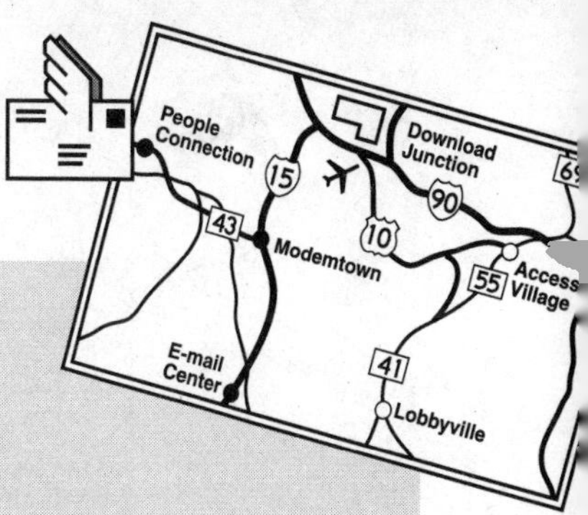

- What Exactly Is Electronic Mail?
- The Mail Center Icon
- Internet Mail
- The Address Book
- The Personal Filing Cabinet
- Express Delivery
- Reading Mail Offline

"I signed up so that I could exchange e-mail with my daughter in Connecticut."

It's not always a daughter, and it's not always Connecticut, but it *is* the most frequent rationale we hear from new AOL members when we ask them what prompted them to first go online. Indeed, we usually don't even have to ask. Electronic mail (*e-mail* for short) is the single most influential factor responsible for the meteoric growth of the online industry.

AOL, being the largest e-mail provider on the planet, certainly can vouch for e-mail's popularity. AOL handles over 200 pieces of mail *per second* and stores our e-mail on over 3,000 hard disks totaling more than 5 terabytes of storage.

The consequence of all this e-mail intrigue isn't entirely technological. There's an eloquent, affirmative social effect as well: people are writing to each other again, just as they did a hundred years ago during Emily Dickinson's age of eloquence. There's a renaissance of correspondence, a revival of colloquy. Personal communication is no longer a phone call that interrupts dinner; it's a thoughtful process. And again the writer awaits a reply, expectant and hopeful as a bride.

What Exactly Is Electronic Mail?

Electronic mail (*e-mail* for short) is simply mail prepared on a computer and sent to another computer. There are lots of private e-mail networks—computers wired together and configured to send and receive mail. America Online is one of them. Many of these networks (including AOL) are connected to the Internet (the Internet is discussed in Chapter 4; Internet mail is discussed later in this chapter), and you can send mail to (and receive mail from) any of the people who are connected across these networks (Figure 3-1).

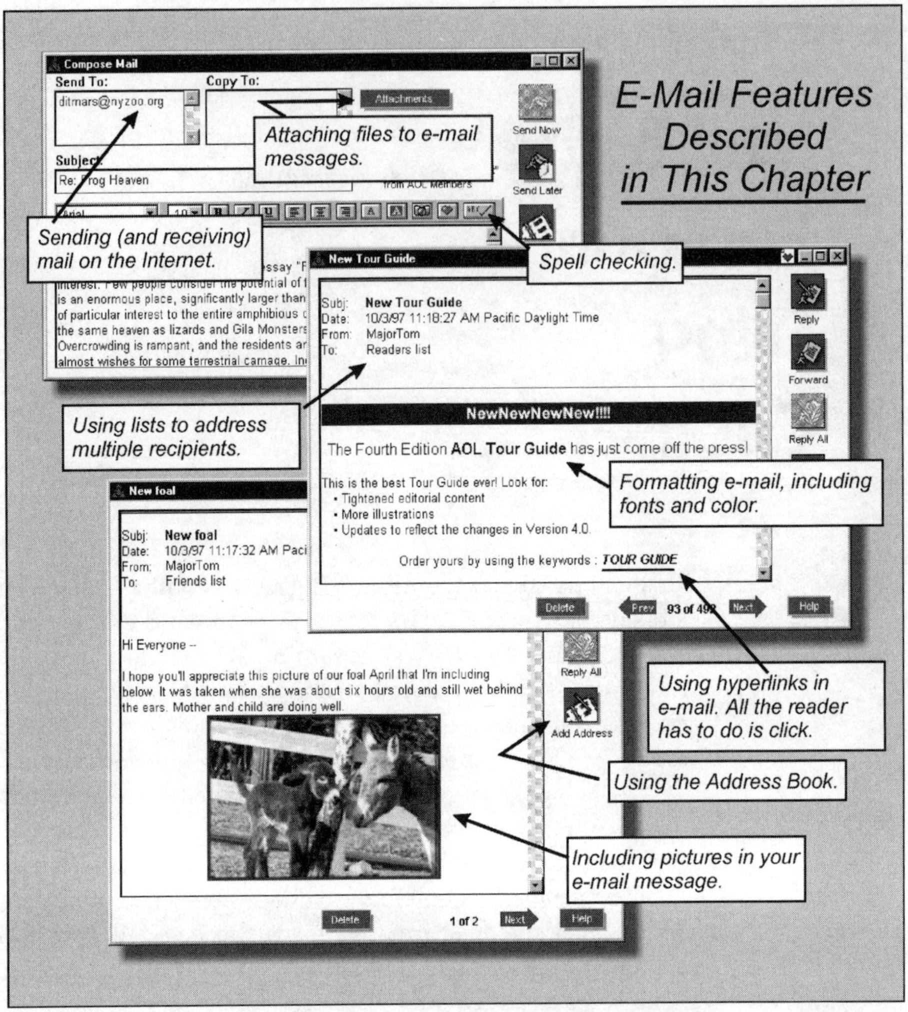

Figure 3-1: You can send mail over the Internet, "fancy up" your mail with changes in font and alignment, and even include pictures. Everything is described in this chapter.

AOL never charges extra for e-mail sent or received, e-mail when sent between AOL members is almost instantaneous, and e-mail can be sent anywhere in the world. There are no stamps to buy, no envelopes to lick, and no natural resources wasted. AOL offers an elaborate system for filing e-mail, and if you must, you can print your mail for filing the old-fashioned way or for circulating among those who aren't e-mail enlightened.

Instant Gratification

If you're like most of us, e-mail will eventually become a daily activity; you'll have plenty to answer and plenty to send. It will probably become a mixture of work and pleasure; it will certainly become a focus in your social and professional life.

In the meantime, however, you might be looking for things to do with e-mail that provide instant gratification. Not vacuous stuff like sending messages to yourself, but activities with a material reward. Here are some ideas:

- Use the keyword: **Reminder** to learn about AOL's e-mail reminder service. It will send mail to you upon your request, reminding you of important dates and activities. There's no charge.
- Use the keywords: **Interest Profiles** to tell AOL about yourself. AOL will respond—via e-mail—with an extensive message identifying places online that you might want to visit. This is a *great* way to become involved—immediately and productively—with the online universe. Again, no charge.
- Use the keyword: **Newsletter** to request receipt of an e-mailed online newsletter. Subjects range from online tips to conducting personal finance online; newsletters are sent monthly, weekly, and occasionally more often. Free of charge, of course.
- Of course, you can always send mail to us. We love to hear from readers, and we *always* reply**.** As we mentioned in Chapter 1, Jennifer's screen name is Jennifer and Tom's is MajorTom.

The Mail Center Icon

All of the essential e-mail commands are available via the Mail Center, which is the third icon from the left on the toolbar. Just click the Mail Center's downward-pointing arrow to access the pop-up menu (Figure 3-2). Most of the Mail Center's options are available only when you're signed on. Figure 3-2 illustrates these options in the signed-on condition.

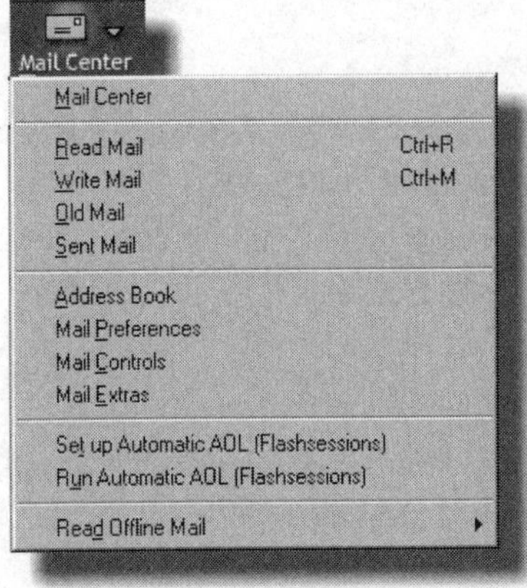

Figure 3-2: The Mail Center pop-up menu.

The Mail Center Window

In "AOLspeak," the phrase *the Mail Center* actually stands for two entities: the pop-up menu available on the toolbar (pictured in Figure 3-2), and the place where AOL gathers all of its support facilities for e-mail events (pictured in Figure 3-3). AOL's e-mail is like cheese: it seems simple at first, but a really good cheese (and a really good e-mail facility) is resplendent with complexity and reward. AOL's e-mail tools are like this, and occasionally you're going to want the advice of an expert to fully appreciate what AOL has to offer. Whenever you need help with e-mail, choose The Mail Center (Figure 3-4) from the Mail Center drop-down menu.

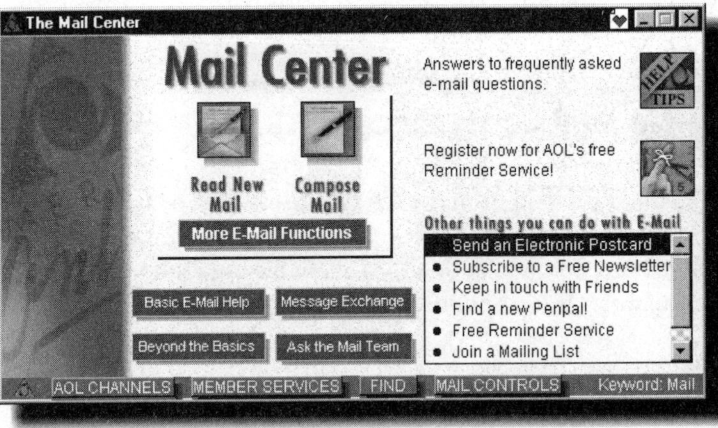

Figure 3-3: The Mail Center is a fountain of e-mail expertise.

Note that not only does the Mail Center offer basic e-mail help, it also offers advanced assistance (Beyond the Basics) and personalized replies to your specific e-mail questions (Ask the E-Mail Team). There's a reminder service, a message exchange (for assistance from other members), and access to all of AOL's e-mail controls. (Did you know that you can configure your AOL software to omit most "junk mail"? The feature is available by clicking the E-Mail Controls tab in the Mail Center window.)

Junk E-Mail

You always hear it said that no one likes junk mail, but surely *someone* does—somebody, after all, is sending us all of that stuff. They must have a reason, and it's not because they hate junk mail.

Nonetheless, most of us growl when junk mail appears in our mailbox, and the growls become louder when junk mail appears in our *electronic* mailboxes. Electronic mailboxes are favorite targets for junk-mail distributors; there's hardly any cost, after all, and often the originator cannot be traced.

Those very attributes make junk e-mail a thriving medium, and therein lies the problem. To the recipient, it's an annoyance, but to the Internet as a whole, it's a grave menace. Junk mail clogs the information superhighway like a jackknifed semi.

Perhaps, by the time you read this, the problem has been solved—AOL, among others, is investing an arsenal of legal resources in pursuit of junk e-mail's eradication. If, however, junk mail is hounding you, use the keywords: **Junk Mail** to learn what you can do about it.

The Read Mail Command

The Read Mail command is represented by the leftmost icon on the toolbar, and it's next on the Mail Center pop-up menu. Like the Mail Center command, this command is only available when you're online: when you choose either one of these commands, you're accessing information stored on AOL's computers. The Read Mail command allows you to read any new (unread) mail that's waiting for you, perhaps the thing you'll do the most while you're online.

The Read Mail command produces a list of all the new messages that have been sent to you. Any number of pieces of new mail may appear here, Internet mail as well as mail from other AOL members. If more than one shows up, they'll appear in the order in which they were received at America Online. The oldest mail will be at the top, the most recent at the bottom. In other words, to read your mail in chronological order from oldest to most recent, read your messages from top to bottom.

A number of potentially confusing buttons appear across the bottom of the New Mail window pictured in Figure 3-4. Let's discuss them.

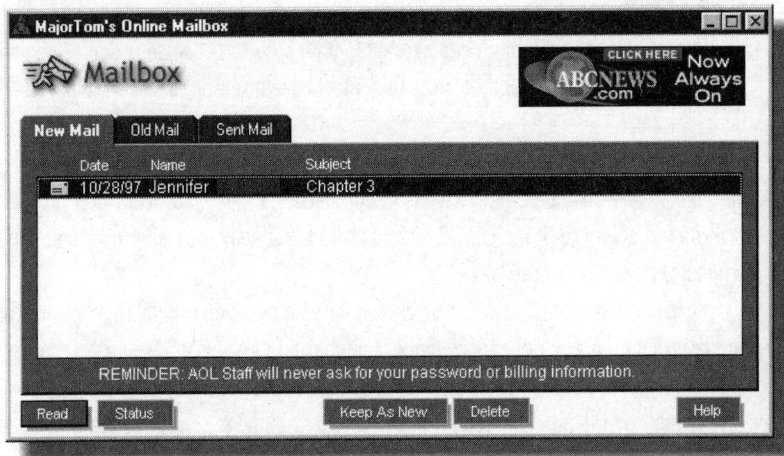

Figure 3-4: The three-tabbed dialog box for reading mail; the New Mail tab is frontmost. The Read Mail command is only available when you're online.

Night Mail

We love to read mail. E-mail is like Christmas morning to us. Our mail passion is shared by plenty of others. In *Night Mail*, the poet W. H. Auden once wrote:

> And none will hear the postman's knock
> Without a quickening of the heart.
> For who can bear to feel himself forgotten?

Perhaps that's e-mail's greatest virtue: it makes us feel appreciated. That little mailbox full of envelopes in the Welcome window says, "Somebody's thinking of you," and there are few of us whose hearts don't quicken a bit when we see it.

The Read Button

This button displays the selected piece of mail on the screen for reading. It's the default button; double-clicking an entry on the list does the same thing.

How Deep Is the Ocean?

People ask, "How long does AOL retain my mail if I don't read it?" On the average, it's 27 days. This number is subject to change, so if you're going on a long vacation and you don't want to miss any of your mail, it's best to take a computer along with you and check your mail on the road.

The Status Button

The Status button tells you when the message was sent and when the recipients read it (including you). It also tells you if any recipient *didn't* read it and instead deleted it. There's more about that coming up.

A Debatable Proposition

Though we'll talk about Internet mail later in this chapter, note that the times displayed when you click the Status button will be accurate for mail sent to other AOL members only—it doesn't apply to Internet mail, sent or received. AOL forwards Internet mail to the Internet within a few moments after you press the Send button, but when is it actually "sent"? When it's posted? When it's routed to the recipient's country, or mailbox? There are no answers to these questions. Thus, when you select a piece of Internet mail and click the Show Status button, AOL will display the message "Not Applicable."

The Keep as New Button

Clicking this button will return the selected piece of mail to your New Mail list, marking it as unread even though you have already read it. The mail is, however, still considered read as far as other AOL members' status checks are concerned. In other words, if someone checks the status of a piece of mail that you read and then kept as new, they will see indication that you've read the mail regardless of whether you kept it as new or not.

The Delete Button

This feature allows you to remove a piece of mail permanently from your new mail mailbox. Unlike ignored mail, deleted mail will not appear on your Old Mail list (we'll discuss the Old Mail command later), which means that once you've deleted some mail, you'll never be able to get it back. Status checks performed by other AOL members on deleted mail say "Deleted."

When clicked, the Delete button renders the selected piece of mail indelibly inaccessible—there's no bringing deleted mail back. It's great for junk mail that you unequivocally do not want to ever see again.

The Help Button

This button takes you to the e-mail section of the AOL help files that are stored on your hard disk. You can access these files at any time by choosing the Help option from the menu bar.

The Write Mail Command

The Write Mail command is next on the Mail Center menu. It's also the second (from the left) icon on the toolbar. You can write mail whether you're online or off; it's best to write mail offline and send it later—a feature we'll discuss in Chapter 8, "Working Offline."

When you choose the Write Mail command, America Online responds with a blank piece of mail titled Write Mail (Figure 3-5). Note the position of the insertion point in Figure 3-5. It's located within the Send To field of the window. America Online, in other words, is waiting for you to provide the recipient's e-mail address. Type it in. (If you don't remember the recipient's e-mail address, you can use your Address Book, which we'll describe later in this chapter.)

You can type multiple addresses in the Send To field if you wish, separating them with a comma and a space. If you want to send mail to Jennifer Watson and Tom Lichty, type **Jennifer, MajorTom** in this box. Note that the field is actually a scroll box. You can type as many addresses as you want, up to 14,000 characters.

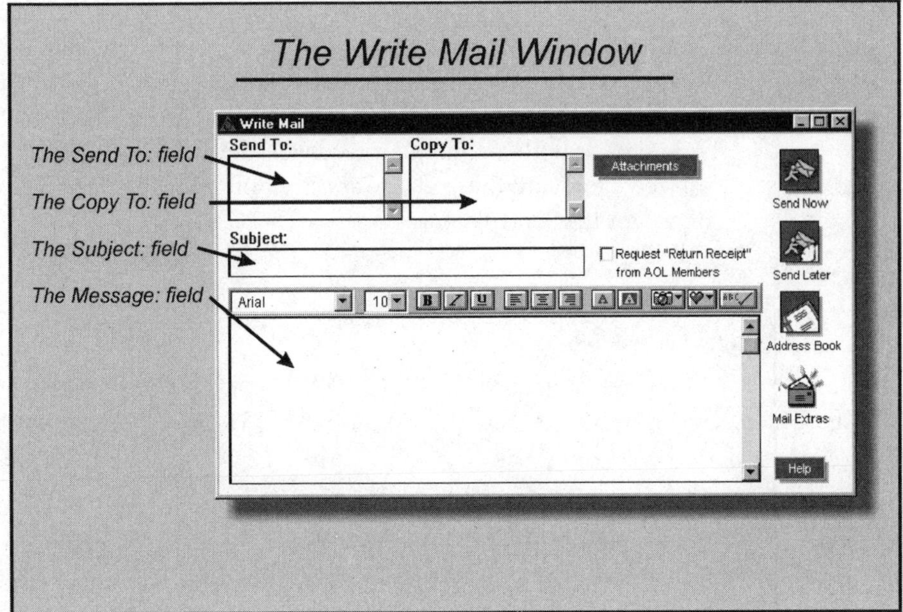

Figure 3-5: The empty Write Mail window.

The Mini Toolbar

The mini toolbar immediately above the Message field in Figure 3-5 is where you can change the font, the font size, style, and color, and the alignment of selected text in the mail window. You can even check your spelling.

Note that if you leave the cursor atop one of the buttons for a moment, a tool tip pops up, explaining the button's purpose.

Note also that the codes that describe formatting such as font, alignment, and color are removed before AOL mail is sent to the Internet. Internet recipients will still see your message, but they won't see the formatting. The same can be said for AOL members who are using AOL software that predates version 3.0.

Press the Tab key and the cursor jumps to the Copy To (carbon copy) field. Here you can place the addresses of those people who are to receive "carbon copies" of your mail. Carbon copies (actually, they're called "courtesy copies" now—carbon paper being almost an artifact) are really no different than originals. Whether a member receives an original or a copy is more a matter of protocol than anything else. Capacity limitations for this field are the same as those for the Send To field.

Blind Carbon Copies

As is the case with the traditional Copy To (or CC) at the bottom of a business letter, the addressee is made aware of any others who will receive an electronic carbon copy of the letter—a traditional courtesy.

On the other hand, you might want to send a copy of a message to someone without letting the other addressee(s) know you have done so. This is known as a *blind* carbon copy, and at AOL it works whether you're mailing to another AOL member, an Internet address (we'll discuss Internet mail later in this chapter), or a combination of both. To address a blind carbon copy, place the address (or addresses) of the blind carbon copy recipient(s), enclosed in parentheses, in the Send To or the Copy To field. The parentheses are the trick. No one but the recipient of the blind carbon copy will know what you've done. The ethics of this feature are yours to ponder.

Press the Tab key to move the insertion point to the Subject field. This field is mandatory—AOL won't take the message without it.

You can type your message within the Message field. There's a length limit of around 30K (about 15 typewritten pages).

Preparing Mail Offline

Always try to prepare your mail when you're offline. You can linger over it that way, perfecting every word. When you complete a message, click the Send Later button. Why not prepare mail while you're online? Because time spent online is like hot water: though you're really not paying for it (assuming you've chosen the unlimited access plan available at keyword: **Access**), if you squander it, there's that much less for everyone else.

For more information on preparing and reading mail offline, see Chapter 8.

Old Mail

Occasionally you may want to review mail you've already read. Even if you don't file mail you've read on your own machine, AOL retains (for a few days) everything you read and stores it on the host's hard disks. The Old Mail command accesses that mail. It's available under the Mail Center's pop-up menu (review Figure 3-2) or by clicking the Old Mail tab pictured in Figure 3-6.

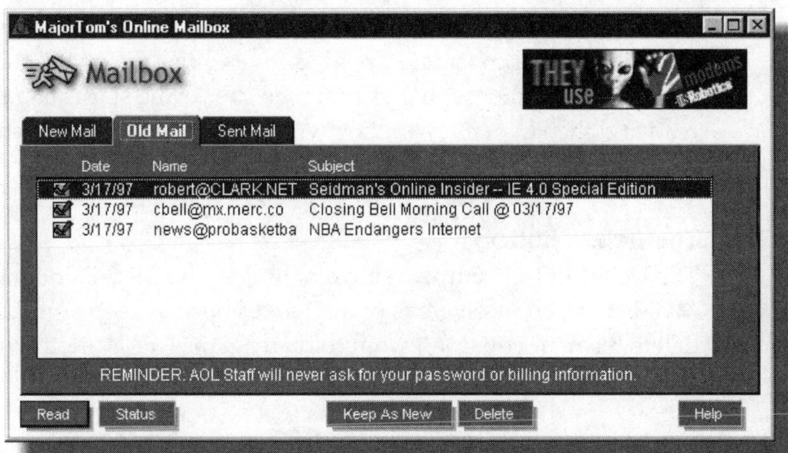

Figure 3-6: The Old Mail list in the Online dialog box.

Again, a variety of buttons appear across the bottom of the window. Refer to Figure 3-6 as we discuss them.

The Read Button

Select a piece of mail from the Old Mail list and then click the Read button to read a selected piece of old mail. Double-clicking a particular piece of mail in the window does the same thing.

How Deep Is the Ocean? (Part Two)

People ask, "How long does AOL retain my mail on the Old Mail list?" There's no specific answer. It has to do with the volume of mail AOL is handling, AOL's current e-mail policy, and whether or not all recipients have read any particular piece you've sent. In other words, don't expect AOL to do your filing for you. There's a much better way—the Personal Filing Cabinet—and we'll discuss it later in this chapter.

The Status Button

In this context, the Show Status button tells you when the mail was read by each of AOL members to whom it was sent. It does not apply to Internet mail recipients.

The Keep as New Button

The Keep as New button will return the selected piece of mail to your New Mail list, marking it as unread even though you have already read it. The mail is, however, still considered read as far as other members' status checks are concerned. In other words, if someone checks the status of a piece of mail you read and then kept as new, they will see the time you first read the mail regardless of whether you kept it as new or not.

The Delete Button

The Delete button simply removes the selected piece of mail from your Old Mail list. If you receive lots of mail and prefer to keep your Old Mail list brief, delete the mail you don't want to read again. This is another indelible command: once old mail is deleted, it's no longer available on the Old Mail list.

Sent Mail

Occasionally you may want to review mail you've sent to others: "What exactly did I say to Billy Joe that caused him to visit the Tallahatchie Bridge last night?"

Like the Old Mail list, the Sent Mail list isn't all-inclusive; it only goes back so far (see the "How Deep Is the Ocean" sidebars). It's a handy way to see what you said. Refer to Figure 3-7 as we discuss this tab.

Figure 3-7: The Sent Mail tab lists the mail you have sent recently.

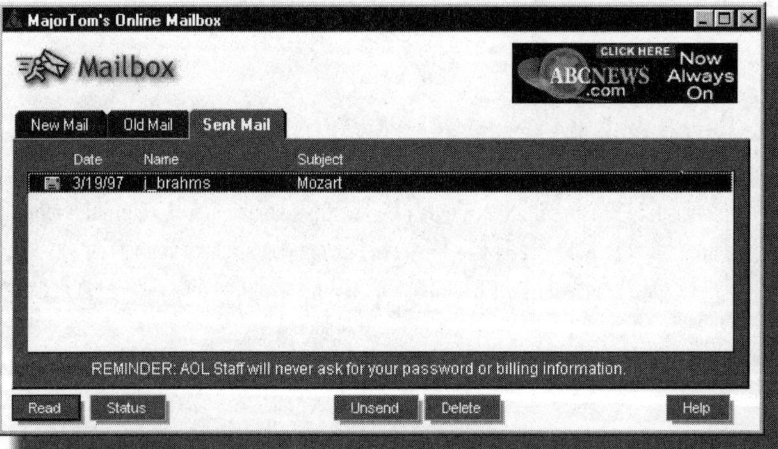

The Read, Status, Delete, and Help buttons are all the same as they are for the Old Mail list, though they pertain to mail you've sent rather than mail you've received from others. Note that sent mail that's deleted is only deleted *from the list*; it's not deleted from the recipients' mailboxes. If you want to do that, read on.

The Unsend Button

The Unsend button allows you to retrieve from the mailboxes of all recipients (as well as from your Old Mail list) mail you have sent. To unsend a piece of mail, highlight the mail you wish to unsend and click the Unsend button. This feature, however, will be disabled in the following circumstances:

- Any addressee was an Internet mail address.
- Any recipient has read that piece of mail (including you, if you were on the addressee list).

If you unsend a piece of mail, it will be permanently deleted from the AOL archives. It won't show up on your Old Mail list when you check it again. AOL will remind you of this when you click the Unsend button. If you want to modify or save an unsent message, open it while it still appears in the Old Mail list, and then either modify it (and resend it if you wish) or copy and paste it into some other document. Then you can unsend it without fear of losing the original.

Internet Mail

As much as Steve Case would prefer it to be otherwise, not everyone is a member of AOL. Some receive their mail via the Internet (which we'll discuss in Chapter 4); others prefer AOL's competitors (which, as you might suppose, this book doesn't discuss).

We haven't yet made it to Chapter 4, so discussing Internet mail is somewhat premature. But this is the e-mail chapter, after all, and e-mail is a big part of the Internet, so an Internet e-mail discussion follows.

For the time being, understand that the Internet is a worldwide interconnected network of networks, each of which is similar to AOL. Something like 75 million people use Internet mail, and you can send mail to (or receive mail from) any one of them via AOL, a privilege for which you pay nothing extra.

AOL NetMail

One of the troubles with any e-mail service is that you have to sign on via your Internet service provider (*your* ISP is America Online) before you can read or write your e-mail. Up until now, AOL was no exception, and though you can always sign on to AOL (as a guest) via a friend's computer, what if your friend doesn't have the AOL client installed?

The problem is solved. AOL's latest e-mail gadget is called *NetMail*, and what a boon it is. This free service lets you send and receive your AOL e-mail directly via the Internet—just as if you're logged on to your AOL account—even though the computer you're using doesn't have the AOL client installed. You can read (and write) AOL e-mail anywhere there's a computer that can access the World Wide Web. Use the keyword: **http://www.aol.com/netmail/home.html** to find out more.

Internet Addresses

The following is an example of the format that is used for Internet e-mail addresses: paul_williams@oregon.uoregon.edu.

Everything to the left of the at sign (@) in an Internet address is the user's name (paul_williams, in the example). Everything to the right of the @ sign is the addressee's *domain*—the name of the network the addressee is using (oregon.uoregon.edu, in the example—a computer network at the University of Oregon). Our domain is AOL, which is known as aol.com on the Internet. Tom's Internet address, then, is the combination of his screen name, an @ sign, and AOL's domain name: majortom@aol.com.

A Case for Exactitude

America Online is, perhaps, excessively lenient when it comes to e-mail addresses. At AOL, screen names are not case sensitive. MajorTom works no better than majortom. Even spaces are ignored; mail addressed to Major Tom is always delivered to MajorTom.

On the Internet, however, the e-mail address occasionally *is* case sensitive, and spaces simply aren't tolerated.

Even if you don't know what the Internet is (you will if you read this chapter and the next), and even if you think you'll never exchange mail on the Internet, it's wise to develop the habit of entering e-mail addresses exactly as you encounter them. If your friend tells you that she's JulAnnF, send mail to JulAnnF. If she tells you that she's julannf@umich.edu (an Internet address—you can tell by the @ sign), send mail to julannf@umich.edu. She might also be known as jul_ann@umich.edu (note the underscore—a common artifact in Internet usernames), thus you should address her mail accordingly. Like traffic lights, many matters in life require adherence to rules. This is one of them.

Sending Internet Mail

Internet e-mail is composed and sent conventionally. To address an e-mail message to an Internet user, simply place the recipient's Internet address in the Send To field of the Compose Mail form (see Figure 3-8).

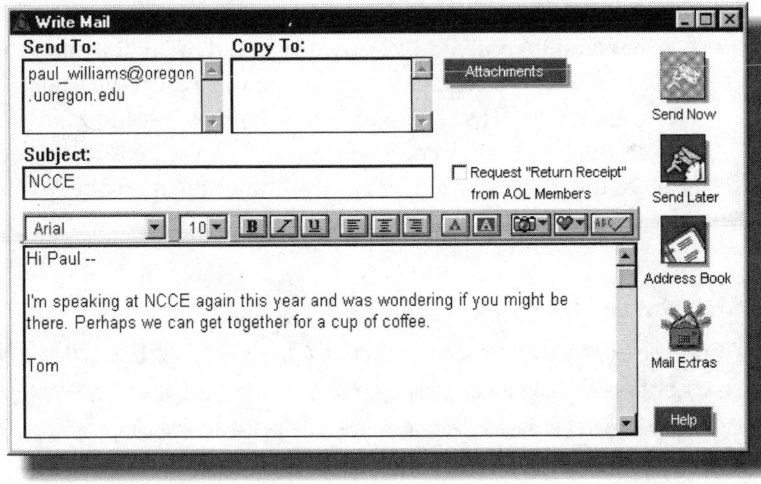

Figure 3-8: Sending mail via the Internet requires entries in the Send To, Subject, and Message fields. You can't leave any of them blank. Aside from the added complexity of the recipient's address, Internet mail is prepared exactly the same as mail to other AOL members.

The Directory of Internet Users

Users come and go on the Internet like nighttime talk-show hosts. There are probably around 75 million of us, after all, and thousands log in and out every day. Keeping a directory of them would be nearly impossible.

"So what?" you say. "There are well over 75 million telephone users in this country, and they're all listed in directories." Your point is well taken, but the telephone system is composed of a number of coordinated authorities, each charged with the responsibility, among others, of maintaining a directory of its users. Not so with the Internet. No one's charged with the responsibility of maintaining Internet member directories.

Nonetheless, you'll find a number of "Internet White Pages" if you poke around the Internet, including the one that appears under the Find button on the toolbar. Read Chapter 5 for more information.

Receiving Internet Mail

Internet mail is received like any other AOL mail: it's announced when you sign on, and you can read it by clicking the You Have Mail button on the Welcome screen. The only way you'll know it's Internet mail is by looking at the sender's address, which will contain an @ sign and a domain name. You'll also see the Internet "header" at the end of the message.

Internet Mail Conundrum

A perplexing mail question frequently received at AOL has to do with blind carbon copies and Internet mail. It's possible that you might receive a piece of Internet mail, yet your name will not appear in the header as a recipient. "Was the mail misdirected?" you'll ask.

Probably not. More than likely you were sent a blind carbon copy (a BCC). When you are a recipient of BCC Internet mail, your name will not appear among the recipients in the header, yet you will receive the mail. If you think about it, it makes sense: if your name appeared in the header—or anywhere else for that matter—the BCC effort would be thwarted. It's confusing, but it's comforting to know that your anonymity is assured.

America Online offers plenty of help with Internet e-mail, including a message board and an avenue for communication with the AOL Internet staff. Use the keyword: **Mail** to explore this feature.

Internet Mail Trivia

Actually, this isn't trivia at all. We're trying to attract your attention with a sidebar. If you're an Internet mail user, this is Really Important Stuff.

- Remember AOL's 30K limit on the length of an e-mail message. If you must send a message longer than that via the Internet, cut your mail into smaller pieces and mail the pieces independently. Identify your strategy in the Subject field: Letter to Mom 1/2, and Letter to Mom 2/2. This is common shorthand for split mail on the Internet.
- Little of AOL's fancy formatting—fonts, font sizes, styles, colors—is understood by other Internet e-mail programs. Most of them understand none of AOL's formatting at all. This is also true of embedded graphics and hyperlinks. These features are primarily intended for AOL member-to-member mail only.
- Don't use any special characters (such as copyright symbols or the "smart quotes" offered by some word processors) in Internet mail—including em dashes (—). The ASCII standard to which all Internet mail adheres doesn't recognize them, therefore it's unlikely they'll make it to the destination.
- America Online doesn't charge you anything extra for Internet mail, sent or received. Some services do. If you're counting your blessings, add that to the list.

The Address Book

America Online provides an address book just like the address book next to your telephone. It's available under the Mail Center pop-up menu. In effect, AOL's Address Book is a cross-reference, listing people's real names and their corresponding e-mail addresses. Our recommendation is that you use the Address Book, even if you only have a name or two to put there now. Typing e-mail addresses is too much work, and it's too easy to make mistakes.

Adding a Person to Your Address Book

No one memorizes e-mail addresses—especially Internet e-mail addresses. Internet addresses are eccentric composites of alphabet, punctuation, and symbol characters—for example, speterman@lemming.uvm.edu. Addresses like this are eminently forgettable. AOL's addresses are less complex, but like most addresses, they too are forgettable. That's why America Online provides the Address Book (Figure 3-9).

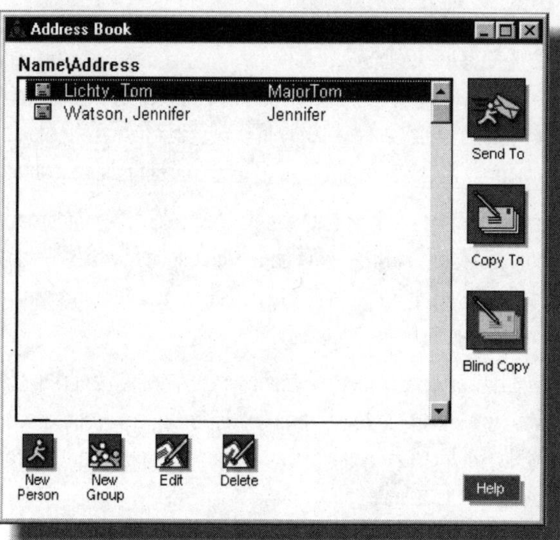

Figure 3-9: The Address Book window allows you to keep track of your favorite e-mail correspondents.

Of course, before you can use the Address Book you have to put some addresses there. There are two categories of entries available in the address book: individuals and groups. Let's discuss the individuals first.

To add a person to your Address Book, choose Address Group from the Mail Center pop-up menu and click the New Person button. AOL provides the editing form pictured in Figure 3-10.

Figure 3-10: Adding a person to your Address Book.

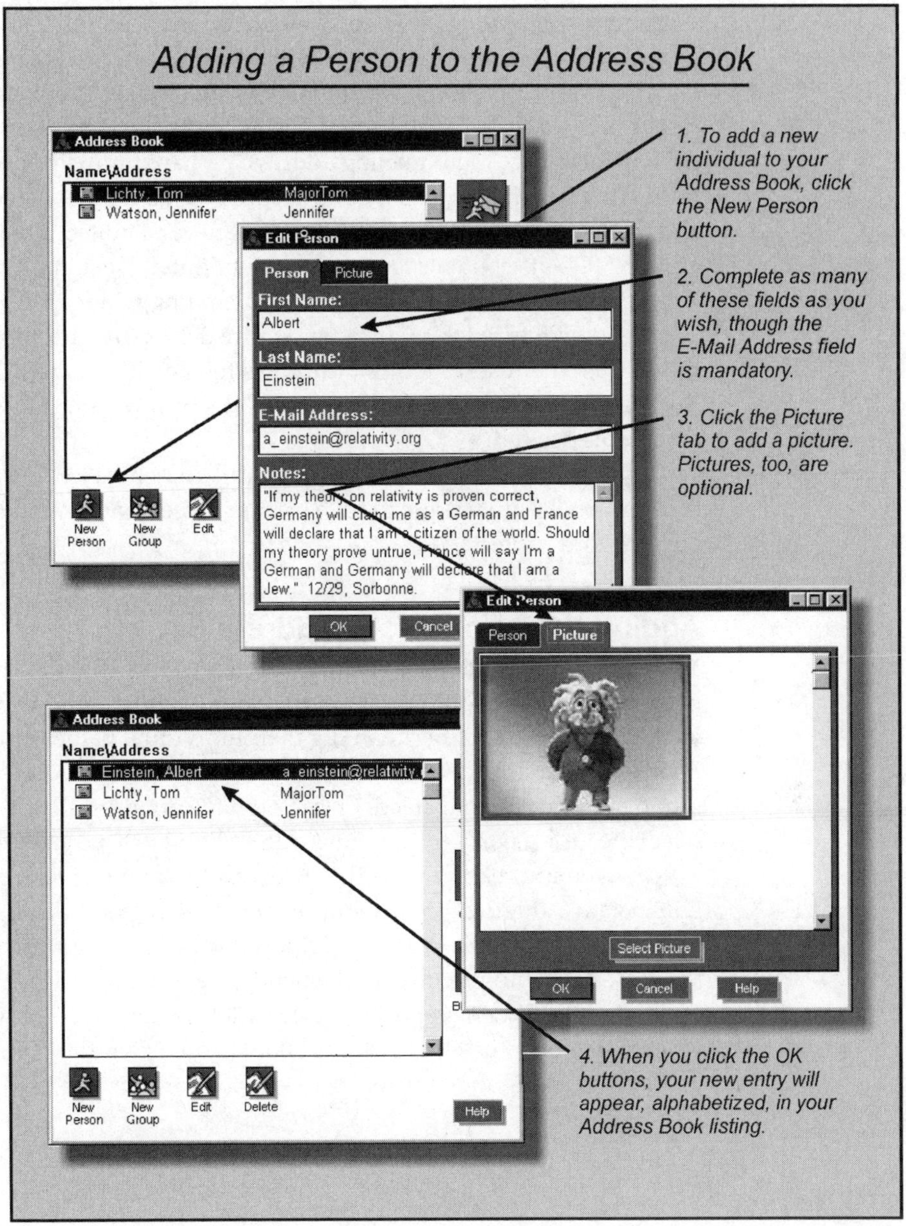

Adding a Person to the Address Book

Address Book

Name\Address

Lichty, Tom MajorTom

Watson, Jennifer Jennifer

New Person | New Group | Edit

Edit Person

Person | Picture

First Name: Albert

Last Name: Einstein

E-Mail Address: a_einstein@relativity.org

Notes: "If my theory on relativity is proven correct, Germany will claim me as a German and France will declare that I am a citizen of the world. Should my theory prove untrue, France will say I'm a German and Germany will declare that I am a Jew." 12/29, Sorbonne.

OK | Cancel

1. To add a new individual to your Address Book, click the New Person button.

2. Complete as many of these fields as you wish, though the E-Mail Address field is mandatory.

3. Click the Picture tab to add a picture. Pictures, too, are optional.

Edit Person

Person | Picture

Select Picture

OK | Cancel | Help

Address Book

Name\Address

Einstein, Albert a_einstein@relativity.

Lichty, Tom MajorTom

Watson, Jennifer Jennifer

New Person | New Group | Edit | Delete | Help

4. When you click the OK buttons, your new entry will appear, alphabetized, in your Address Book listing.

You must provide the person's e-mail address; all the rest of the fields are optional. It's best, however, to provide the first and last names along with the e-mail address so that the Address Book can alphabetize the entry properly.

The Notes field is for any comments you want to jot down regarding the person; their (U.S. Mail) mailing address, perhaps, or their phone number (birthday? favorite candy bar? dog's name?). This is a scrollable text-only field, and though it has a size limitation—we've never counted, but it's probably around 30K—its contents are otherwise unlimited. Text in the Notes field can be copied and pasted into other windows, including windows in other programs.

Note the Picture tab pictured in Figure 3-10. Any graphic can be inserted there (click the Insert Picture button) as long as it's in the JPEG, GIF, BMP (for PCs), or PICT (for Mac) format. AOL's proprietary ART format is acceptable as well.

The Address Book is saved automatically whenever you exit the program. Address Books are unique to each of your screen names, though they cannot be password protected.

Adding a Group to Your Address Book

You can also add groups of people to your Address Book. Perhaps you've engaged in a dialog on the subject of relativity with a number of other esteemed physicists. Rather than dig their individual names out of your Address Book every time you want to send e-mail to the group, you could create a group entry for them instead. Once you have done so, all you have to do is select the group entry from your Address Book to send mail to all of them.

Now you are ready to use the Address Book whenever you prepare mail. Look again at Figure 3-5. Do you see the Address Book icon in the Write Mail window? If your Address Book is current, you can use it to look up addresses and plug them into the Send To and Copy To fields of the Write Mail window. Whenever a Write Mail form is displayed on your screen, all you have to do is use that Address Book icon. From then on, it's only a matter of clicking the mouse.

Figure 3-11: Use group entries for groups of people to whom you regularly send e-mail.

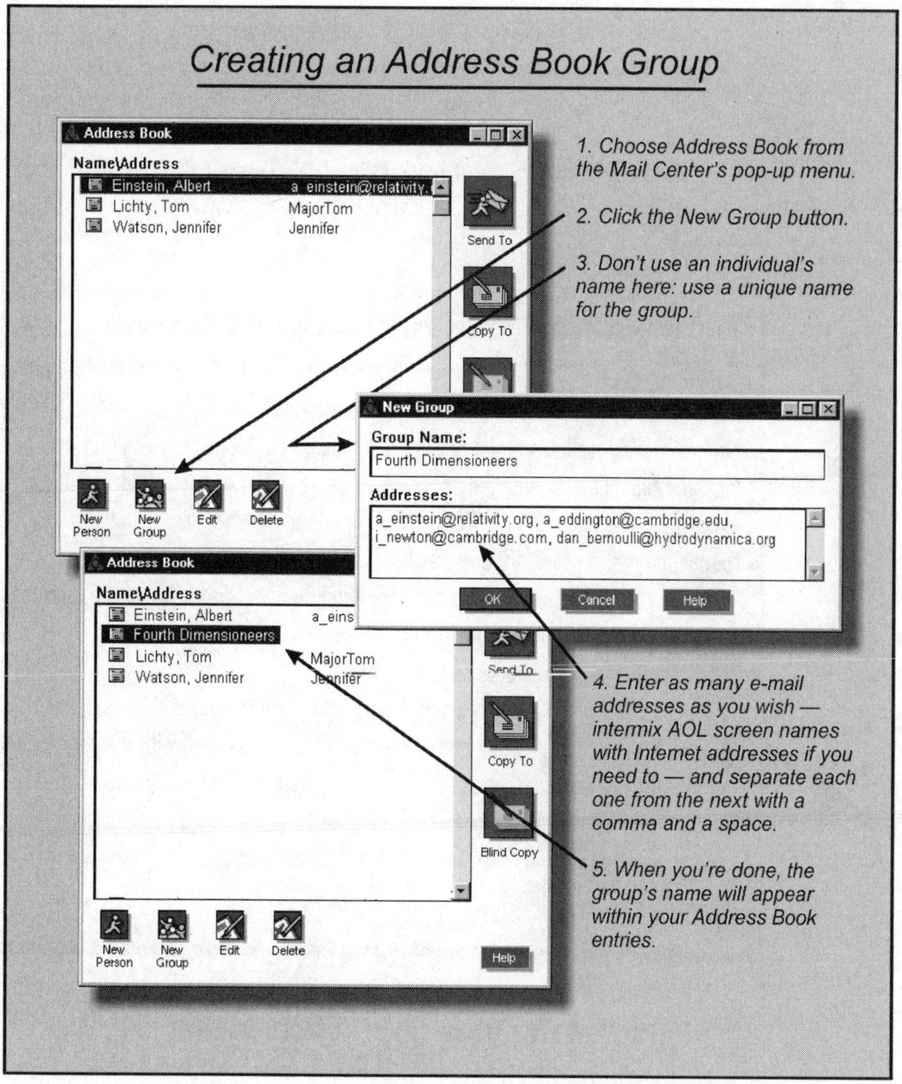
Creating an Address Book Group
Address Book
Name\Address
Einstein, Albert a_einstein@relativity.
Lichty, Tom MajorTom
Watson, Jennifer Jennifer
Send To
Copy To
New Person
New Group
Edit
Delete
1. Choose Address Book from the Mail Center's pop-up menu.
2. Click the New Group button.
3. Don't use an individual's name here: use a unique name for the group.
New Group
Group Name:
Fourth Dimensioneers
Addresses:
a_einstein@relativity.org, a_eddington@cambridge.edu, i_newton@cambridge.com, dan_bernoulli@hydrodynamica.org
OK
Cancel
Help
Fourth Dimensioneers
Blind Copy
4. Enter as many e-mail addresses as you wish — intermix AOL screen names with Internet addresses if you need to — and separate each one from the next with a comma and a space.
5. When you're done, the group's name will appear within your Address Book entries.

That's Relativity

Asked to explain relativity, Albert Einstein once said, "When you are courting a nice girl, an hour seems like a second. When you sit on a red-hot cinder, a second seems like an hour. That's relativity." (Quoted in *News Chronicle*, 14 March 1949.)

The Personal Filing Cabinet

When e-mail becomes something other than a casual dalliance, a system for filing it becomes strategic. Fortunately, such a system is included in your AOL software, and it's called the Personal Filing Cabinet. It's available under the My Files icon on the toolbar, and it's one of the most productive features offered by your AOL software.

The Personal Filing Cabinet vs. the Offline Mail Command

Though we discuss it later in the text, it's important to note the relationship between the Personal Filing Cabinet and the Offline Mail command (which, like the Personal Filing Cabinet, is also available under the My Files icon on the toolbar). If you look carefully at the Personal Filing Cabinet, you'll note a folder named Mail. Open that folder and you'll find the hierarchy that's found via the Offline Mail command. Indeed, that's all the Offline Mail command does: it opens a subset of your Personal Filing Cabinet.

The Personal Filing Cabinet route to this data, however, offers all of the commands—saving, new folder creation, compacting, searching—that are discussed on the upcoming pages. The Offline Mail command does not.

On the other hand, many of us find the Offline Mail command to be more convenient than the Personal Filing Cabinet simply because it's not cluttered with the very commands we refer to. You'll use both methods of accessing your offline mail, depending on your needs at the time. The Personal Filing Cabinet is the place where you'll perform your maintenance tasks; the Offline Mail command is best suited for daily mail activities—reading, writing, and filing.

Personal Filing Cabinet Preferences

Though preferences are discussed in Chapter 9, two mail preferences deserve mention here. Note the Retain All Mail preferences pictured in Figure 3-12. When they're selected, these two preferences cause your AOL software to save all your mail on your hard disk, where you can get to it whenever you please.

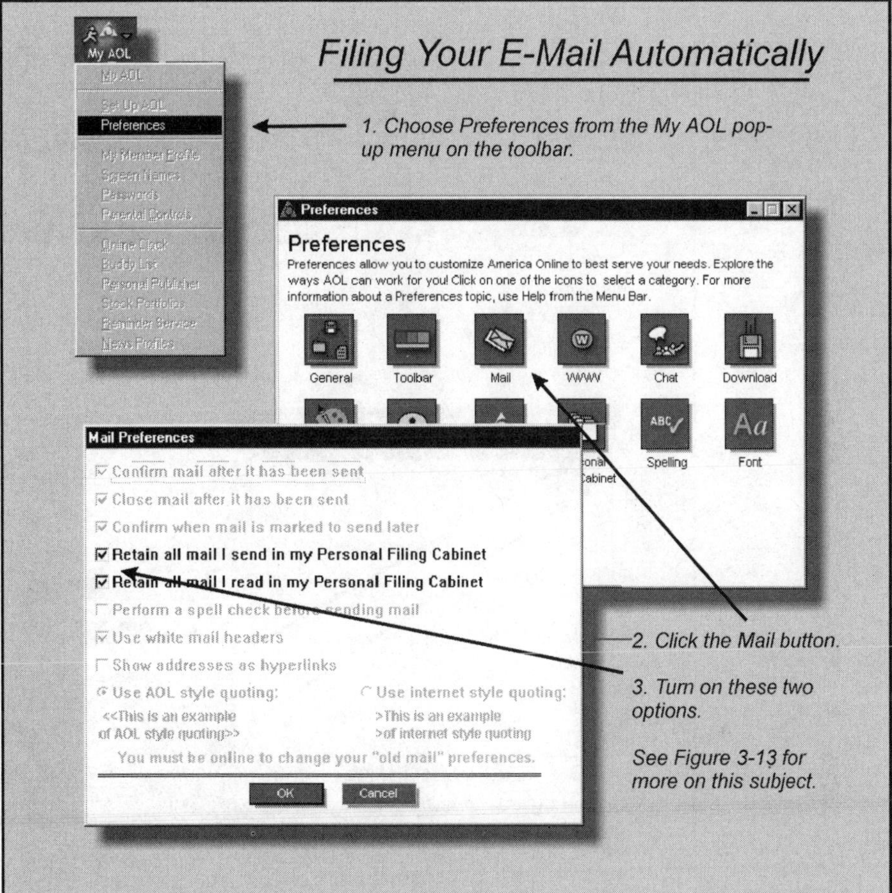

Figure 3-12: When they're turned on, the two Retain All Mail preferences, shown here in the "on" condition ("off" is the default), cause all of your mail to be saved automatically in the Personal Filing Cabinet on your hard disk.

When they're turned on, the Retain All Mail preferences make copies of all your mail—sent and received—and place those copies in the folders pictured in Figure 3-13. Once the preferences are on, copies of all of your mail are retained locally—on your hard disk—for your review, whether you're online or offline (thus the term *offline mail*). You can leisurely sort through your mail, reading, replying, filing, and deleting. You can store as much of it as you please, for as long as you please. If you use mail as much as we do, this is one of the best features AOL has to offer.

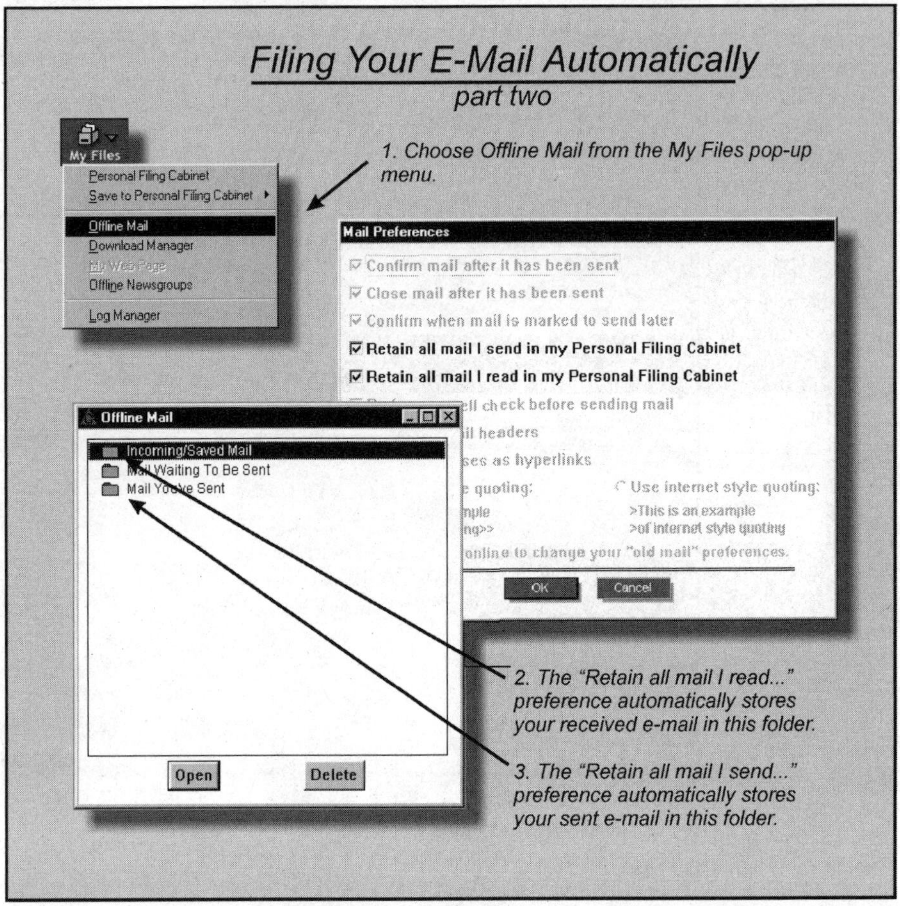

Figure 3-13: When they're turned on, the Retain All Mail preferences cause copies of all your mail to be stored in these two folders within your Personal Filing Cabinet.

"What does this all have to do with the Personal Filing Cabinet?" you ask. Try this: online or off, choose Personal Filing Cabinet from the File menu. This will open the Personal Filing Cabinet window, which will resemble Figure 3-14. Note that the hierarchy under the Mail folder matches the hierarchy of the Offline Mail window pictured in Figure 3-13. Indeed, they're the same thing, accessed in different ways (see the "The Personal Filing Cabinet vs. the Offline Mail Command" sidebar earlier in this chapter).

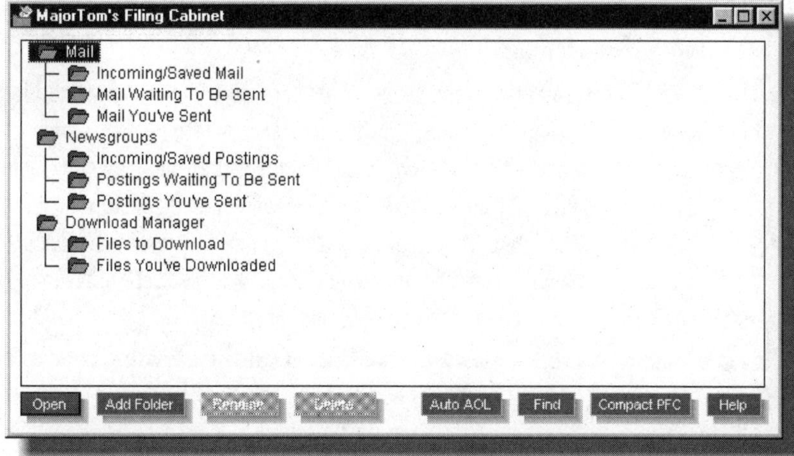

Figure 3-14: Your "offline mailbox" is actually a subset of your Personal Filing Cabinet.

Though the everyday method of accessing offline mail is via the Mail Center, the Mail Center's Offline Mail window lacks many of the controls offered by the Personal Filing Cabinet. Because we'll need the buttons displayed at the bottom of the window pictured in Figure 3-14—buttons that aren't available in the Offline Mail window—we'll use the Personal Filing Cabinet window for the remainder of our offline mail discussion.

Bypassing Go

We're becoming mired in specifics. When it comes to the Personal Filing Cabinet, that's probably just as well, but there's one generality we've omitted: there's more than one method of stashing mail in your Personal Filing Cabinet.

Whenever a piece of mail appears in the frontmost window, you can store it in your Personal Filing Cabinet by choosing Save to Personal Filing Cabinet from either the File menu or from the My Files icon on the toolbar.

The technique argues eloquently in favor of a tight filing hierarchy, for when you choose the Save to Personal Filing Cabinet command from either menu, a cascading menu appears, listing the complete hierarchy of your Personal Filing Cabinet. If you've succumbed to rampant folderism—if your Personal Filing Cabinet sports more folders than Bill Gates has bedrooms—then this technique is cumbersome, at best. But if you've kept your top-level hierarchy to, say, 10 or fewer folders, saving mail this way is a viable alternative to the Save All Mail preferences described in the text.

Keyword: Suggestions

The Retain All Mail preferences described in the text are not only some of the best features AOL has to offer for avid e-mail users; they also represent an idea that came from a member. That member used the keyword: **Suggestions** and then proposed the feature. Not long after that, the Retain All Mail preferences appeared in the AOL client.

In other words, AOL listens. If you have a great idea that AOL could use, tell them about it. Like any community, this one functions better when people give back to the community whenever they can, and AOL's suggestion box makes it easy.

Managing Your Mail

Leaving mail in your Incoming/Saved Mail folder and the Mail You've Sent folder is not a good idea. Though the mail will accumulate there in chronological order, there will be no other organization whatsoever. Once a few dozen entries pile up, you will realize that you need some kind of filing system. The mail exchange pictured in Figure 3-15 is an example of a mail system in need of organization.

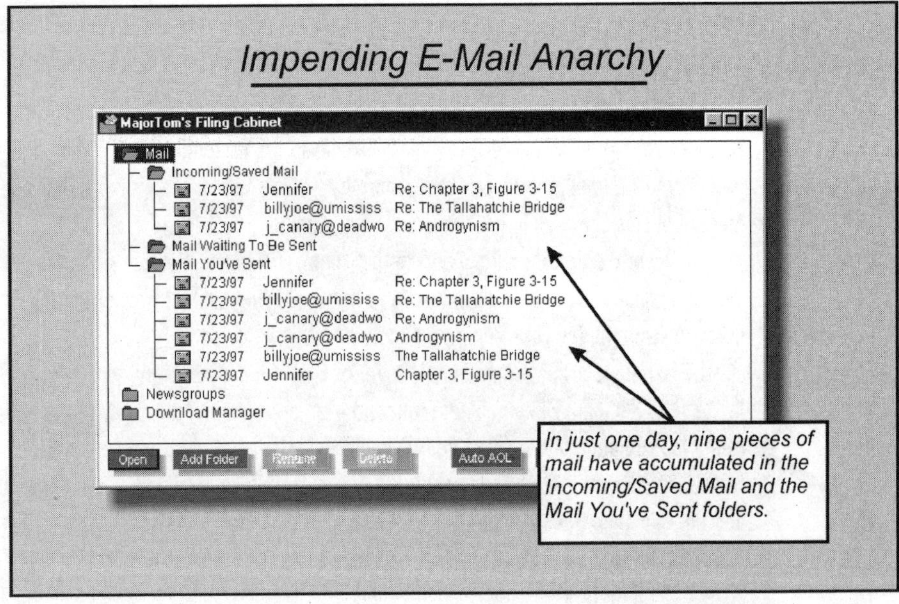

Figure 3-15: In only a couple of days, the Incoming/Saved Mail folder and the Mail You've Sent folder are overcrowded. It's time for some organization.

Do It Offline

You can conduct all of the Personal Filing Cabinet activities described in this chapter without having to sign on. The Personal Filing Cabinet resides on your hard disk, not at AOL, thus it's yours to do with as you please, whenever you please, whether you're online or off.

Filing Schemes

Filing schemes are very personal things. As you observe the illustrations in this section of the book, you'll note that Tom files his mail using folders with people's names on them. You may prefer to file by date, by project, or by geographical location. There are no limits. Filing schemes can be multilayered: you might have two primary folders—Friends and Business, for example, in which items are filed by date. Our friend Leonard gets so much mail that he has alphabetical sections—A-F, G-P, and Q-Z—and folders with people's names on them within each of those sections. Some people argue the merits of their particular system the way the boys down at the pub argue Fords and Chevys. It really doesn't make much difference how you set up your system; just pick one and do it. You can always reorganize later if you have to.

Making New Folders

No matter what kind of filing scheme you elect to use, it will be done with folders. Think of a real filing cabinet. To organize your stuff, you visit the stationery store and buy a box of tabbed folders. You label them according to your filing scheme, put them in the filing cabinet, and store papers inside them. You might even store folders inside of folders. That's the metaphor used in your Personal Filing Cabinet.

No More Prying Eyes

You might want to consider protecting your Personal Filing Cabinet with a password. Once your password is established, no one can access your files without it.

To establish a password, go online, click the My AOL icon on the toolbar, choose Preferences, and click the Passwords button. Put a little check mark in the Personal Filing Cabinet column for each screen name for which you want a password, then enter the password(s). The next time you try to open your Personal Filing Cabinet, AOL will ask for your password. Without it, your files might just as well be in a vault.

To make a new folder, select the folder you want the new folder to appear in and then click the New Folder button at the bottom of the Personal Filing Cabinet window (see Figure 3-16). You can name a folder anything you choose. Folder names can include spaces and punctuation, and the limit of 69 characters is more than you'll ever need.

Figure 3-16: Select the intended parent folder before you click the New Folder button.

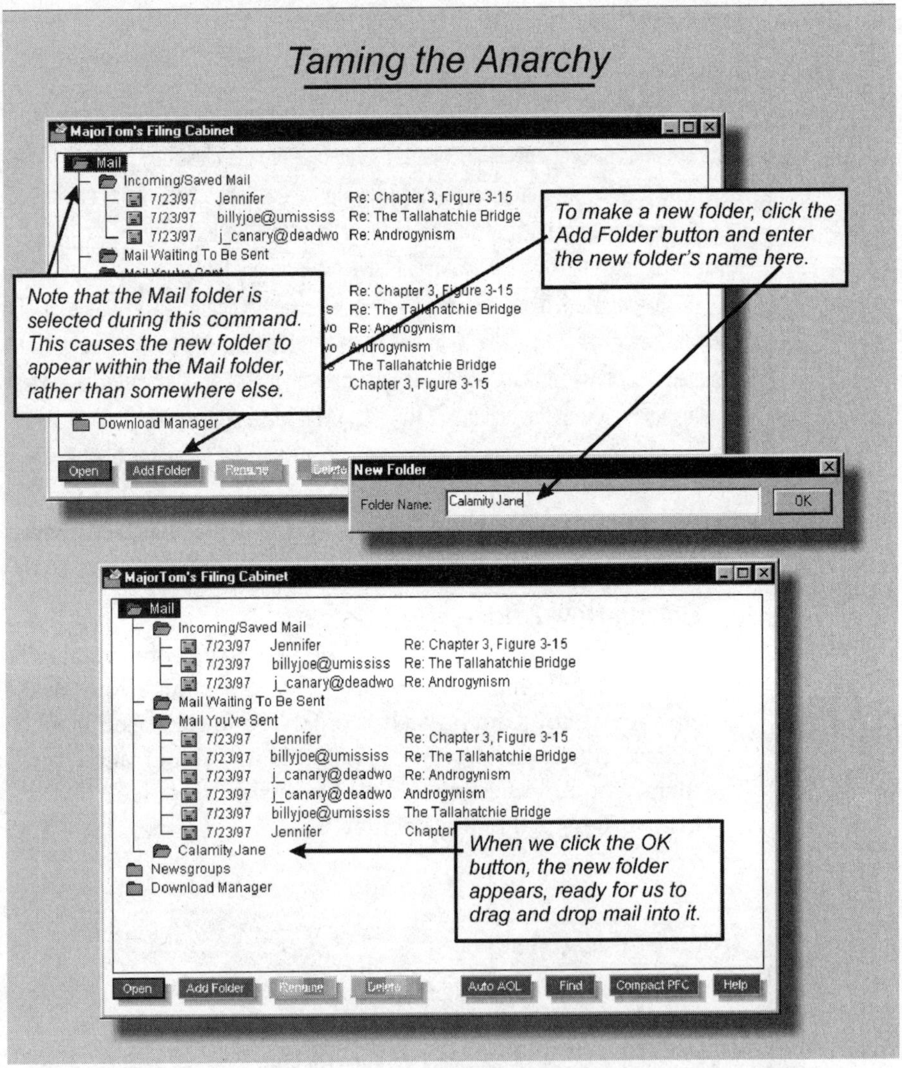

Your new folder will appear at the bottom of the list within the parent folder—the folder you selected when you issued the command. You can then drag and drop mail into the new folder as you please (Figure 3-17).

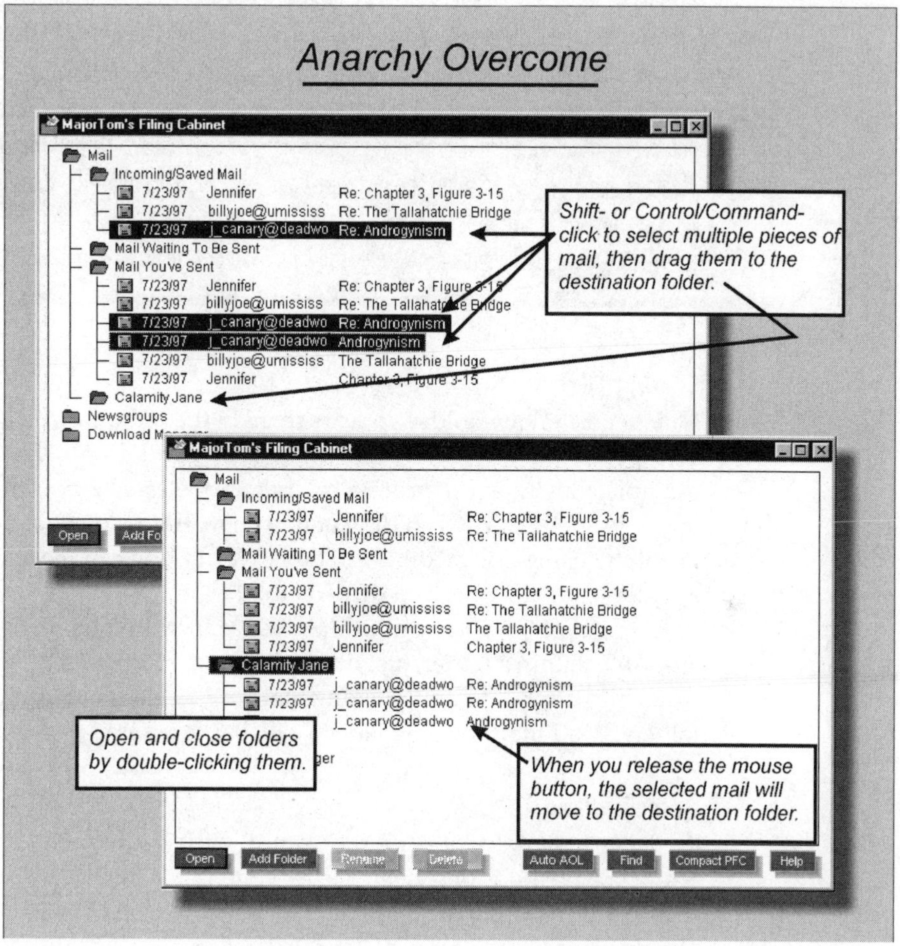

Figure 3-17: You can drop mail into the newly created folder as you please, organizing your mail just as you would organize the contents of any filing cabinet.

Multiple Selections

You can select multiple messages or folders—or a combination of both—in the Personal Filing Cabinet by using the modifier keys used by many Windows and Macintosh applications today. The discontinuous files pictured in Figure 3-17 were selected by clicking on the top message and then holding down the Control key (PC) or Command key (Mac) while clicking on the remaining two messages. This selected each of the messages as they were clicked.

If you prefer to select a list of contiguous messages, you could select the first message and hold down the Shift key to select the last message. This will select all of the messages in between. The Shift and Control/Command keys also work for folder selection.

Once selected, multiple folders or messages can be moved or deleted as if they were one.

Sorting Files

Mail deposited in a folder appears there in the order in which it was placed. To organize mail within folders, simply drag and drop it. Figure 3-17, for example, illustrates the process of dragging selected pieces of mail from one folder to another. You can drag and drop mail up, down, or across your hierarchy using this method—in other words, you can reorganize mail within a folder using the drag and drop method.

For example, if you want to alphabetize three entries named Baker, Charlie, and Able within a folder, just drag Able up to Baker and release the mouse. Note: This applies to reorganizing mail only; it does not apply to reorganizing folders. Read the "Sorting Folders" sidebar for more.

Deleting Mail

To delete mail, select it—use the Control-click (Command-click for Mac) or Shift-click methods described earlier—then click the Delete button pictured in Figure 3-17. You can delete folders the same way. AOL will ask for your confirmation before it completes the deletion. You can also delete mail by opening it and pressing the Delete button in the bottom of the mail window. The Delete key on your keyboard will do the same thing.

Sorting Folders

While rearranging mail within a folder is a simple matter of drag and drop, rearranging folders is not. If you try to move a folder within its parent—trying to alphabetize folders is a good example—you'll drop the folder you're dragging into another folder more often than not. Folders appear in chronological order, with the newest at the bottom (note how the Calamity Jane folder in Figure 3-16 appears at the bottom of the folders within the Mail folder). If you want to rearrange their order, you'll have to employ a little chicanery.

The method Tom uses is to shuffle them via their parent folder. To move the Calamity Jane folder to the top of the folders within his Mail folder, for example, Tom does the following:

1. He creates the Calamity Jane folder as described, and as described, it appears at the bottom of the list.
2. He drags all of the folders that are to appear *after* the Calamity Jane folder to the parent (Mail) folder and drops them there. This causes the folders he has dragged to be "added to" the list, thus they appear after the Calamity Jane folder.

This is much more difficult to describe than it is to accomplish. AOL is no doubt working on a more elegant solution, but until it's offered, this is the best way to do it.

Saving & Backing Up Your Mail

No matter how well it's organized, your Personal Filing Cabinet can become unwieldy if you don't clean it out now and then. Tom backs up his Mail folder—usually to a floppy disk—on the first day of each month; then he goes through it methodically and deletes all mail that's more than a month old. On May 1, for example, he backs up his Mail folder to a floppy and then deletes all the mail from March. This keeps the volume of mail in his Filing Cabinet at manageable levels. It also provides a comprehensive monthly backup, and if he has to refer to outdated mail, he can always open the mail file from the appropriate floppy.

You can save any folder in your Personal Filing Cabinet—or any folder within a folder—by simply right-clicking on it. In Figure 3-18, for example, we're saving the Mail folder to a floppy disk.

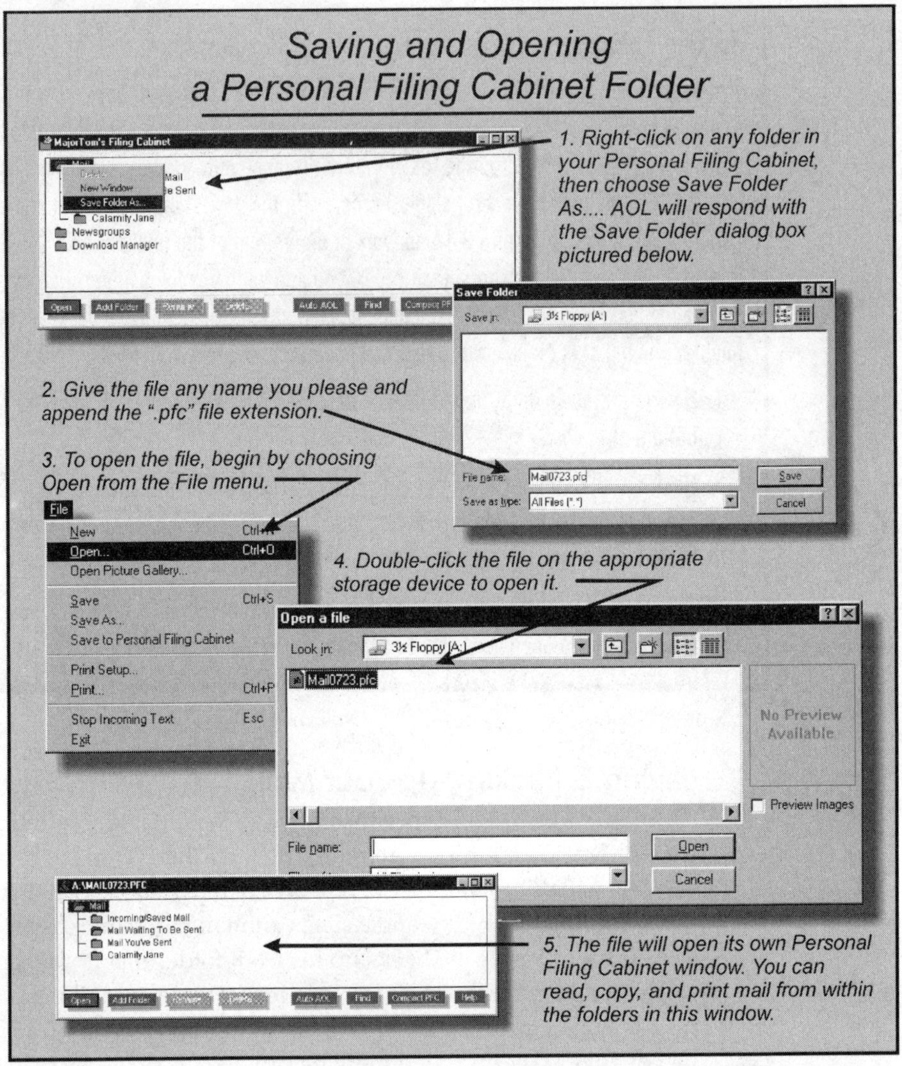

Figure 3-18: Right-click on any folder within your Personal Filing Cabinet to save that folder as a file with a .pfc extension (which stands for Personal Filing Cabinet). Note: The saving routine for Macintosh will be similar to that described here for Windows. Try Option-clicking on a folder to save it.

Saving and Opening a Personal Filing Cabinet Folder

1. Right-click on any folder in your Personal Filing Cabinet, then choose Save Folder As.... AOL will respond with the Save Folder dialog box pictured below.

2. Give the file any name you please and append the ".pfc" file extension.

3. To open the file, begin by choosing Open from the File menu.

4. Double-click the file on the appropriate storage device to open it.

5. The file will open its own Personal Filing Cabinet window. You can read, copy, and print mail from within the folders in this window.

You don't need to save your mail on a floppy disk. You can just as well save it on your hard disk. Saving mail to floppies, however, gets it off your hard disk where space is precious. We all seem to have an abundance of floppy disks lying around, doing little more than gathering dust.

Compacting the Personal Filing Cabinet

Deleting pieces of mail from your Personal Filing Cabinet doesn't really delete them from your hard disk; they just disappear from the Cabinet's display. They're still on your hard disk, and they still take up some room.

There's a reason for this: the physical process of deleting mail could take a lot of time. It's much faster for your software to simply mark a piece of mail as deleted—leaving it otherwise undisturbed—than it is to actually remove it.

Think of one of those sliding-tile games you might have played years ago. To fill a vacated space, many tiles have to be shuffled, a process that takes time. Physically deleting mail from your Personal Filing Cabinet would leave little "holes" on your hard disk, and utilizing that space vacated by deleted mail would require a process not unlike sliding game tiles.

Rather than shuffling hundreds of pieces of mail around on your hard disk every time you delete mail from your Personal Filing Cabinet, your AOL software offers a specific, automated routine for that process. That routine is available whenever the Personal Filing Cabinet window is open: just click the button marked Compact PFC (review the top window in Figure 3-18). Do this when you're offline and only when you have some time; the process can be lengthy.

There are a number of preferences to control the behavior of the Compactor feature. Refer to Appendix A for details.

Multiple Windows

It won't take long: shuffling files like a Vegas gambler, you suddenly discover that no matter how you manipulate your Personal Filing Cabinet display, you can't fit both the window containing the source file and its intended destination on the screen at the same time.

What you really need is another window—one showing the destination, for example—that can share the screen with the source.

And you can have it. All you have to do is point to the folder (the destination folder, in this example) and click on the alternate mouse button (try Option-clicking with the Mac). The menu pictured in Figure 3-19 will appear, allowing you to create a new window for the selected folder. With the second window on the screen, arrange your windows so that both the source and the destination are displayed and then drag and drop the message. This is much more difficult to describe than it is to do. Give it a try.

Figure 3-19: This pop-up menu appears when you click on a Personal Filing Cabinet folder with the alternate mouse button.

Searching the Personal Filing Cabinet

With all of the functionality described so far, the Personal Filing Cabinet offers even more, in the form of two elegant searching commands. Here's an example: working online with group of esteemed herpetologists, Tom has been arguing the existence of frog heaven—a profound topic that has provoked controversy worldwide. Tom remembers mention of Gila monsters in the dialog, but who wants to reread a score of e-mail messages to find a single mention of Gila monster?

The solution is the Personal Filing Cabinet's Find button, pictured in Figure 3-20. That button invokes the Search dialog box that's also pictured in Figure 3-20. All Tom needs to do is fill it in and tell it to find what he's after.

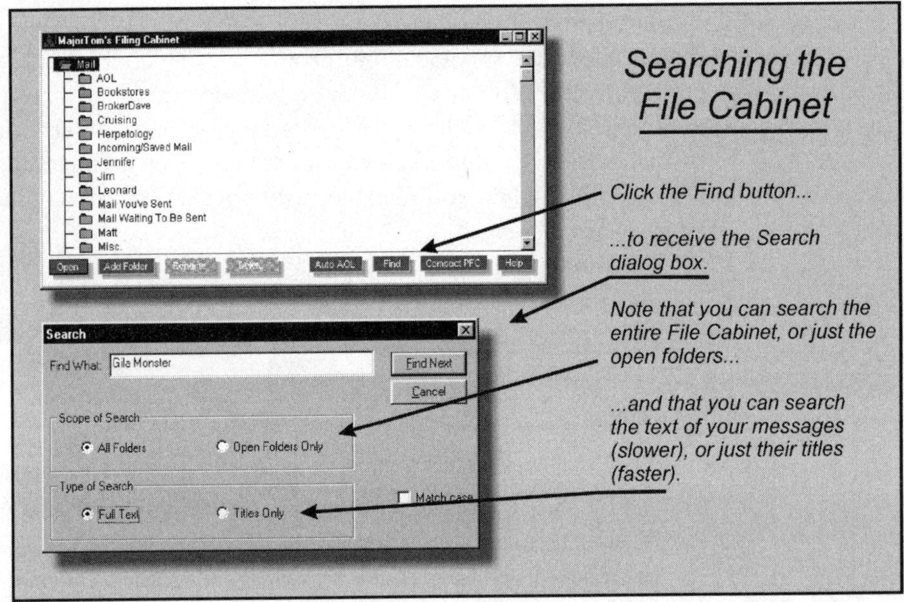

Figure 3-20: The Find button allows you to search your entire Personal Filing Cabinet, or any folder within it, for either a specific message title or a string of characters in the message body.

Searching through your messages in this way is remarkably fast—even a full-text search—and when AOL finds a match, it highlights the message containing the found text (see the top window in Figure 3-21). The Find Next button (Figure 3-20) will direct the software to find the next message containing the search text, if there is one. And so on.

Finding the message containing the text is only half the task, however. The other half is finding the text itself. This is accomplished with the Find in Top Window command that's pictured in Figure 3-21. Once the Personal Filing

Cabinet's Find command has found a message, open the message and choose Find in Top Window from the Edit menu. You'll see the Search window pictured in Figure 3-21, and once it's filled in, the matching text will be found in no time.

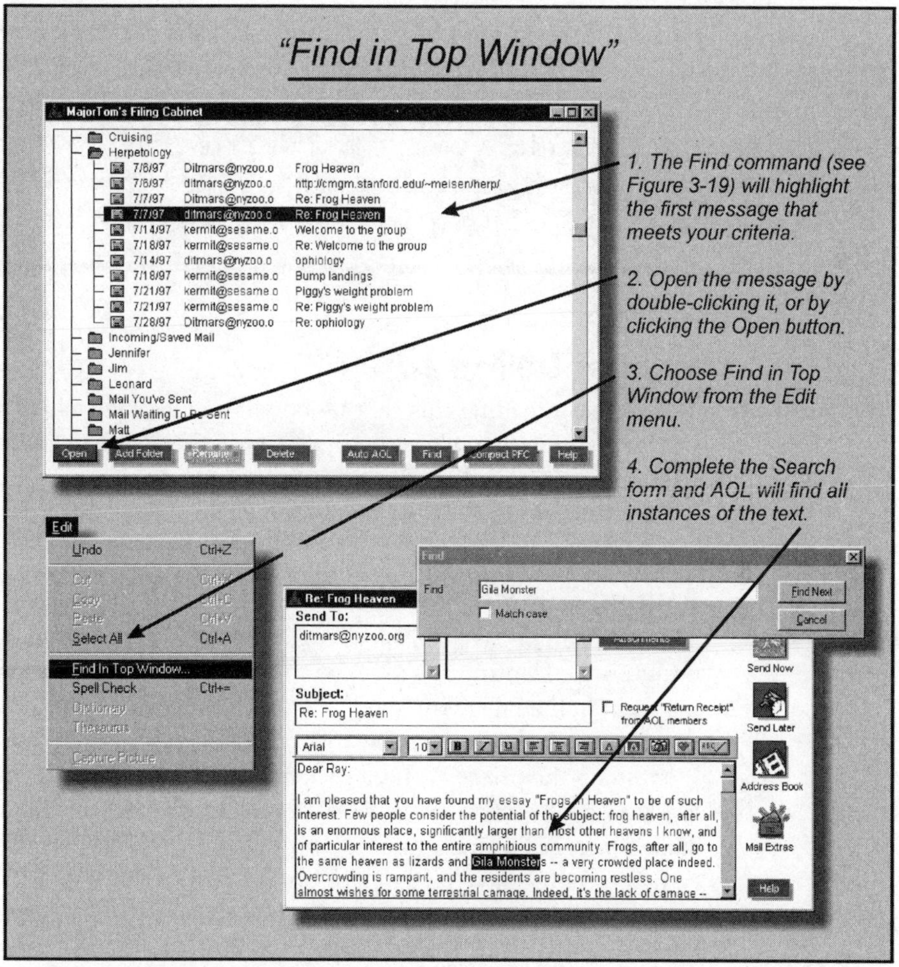

Figure 3-21: The Find in Top Window command finishes the job of searching for specific information in your Personal Filing Cabinet.

"Find in Top Window"

1. The Find command (see Figure 3-19) will highlight the first message that meets your criteria.

2. Open the message by double-clicking it, or by clicking the Open button.

3. Choose Find in Top Window from the Edit menu.

4. Complete the Search form and AOL will find all instances of the text.

The Find in Top Window command applies to any window, by the way, not just those windows containing mail in your Personal Filing Cabinet. You can use it to find text in articles, newsgroup postings—any text file you can open with AOL's Open command.

There Are No Frogs in Heaven

An illustration similar to Figure 3-21 has appeared in all previous editions of this book. Lots of people have read it and responded, asking us to send them a copy of "the 'Frogs in Heaven' essay."

Perhaps there are frogs in heaven, but to the best of our knowledge there is no essay about them. Frogs in heaven? We've never heard a celestial croak—only choirs, harps, and the wispy fluttering of angels' wings. Surely frogs don't grow wings. (In reviewing this manuscript, our technical editor commented that if frogs *did* have wings, "they wouldn't bump their butts when they hop." Good point and typically well put.) It's improbable enough that they ungrow their tails. Frogs in heaven: it's as implausible as metamorphosis.

Express Delivery

You can stop reading this chapter now if you like. It's a long chapter, and if all you're doing with e-mail is everyday stuff, there's no need to become involved with the particulars that are coming up. You can always return to this chapter later when you're ready for your e-mail black belt.

Printing & Saving Mail

You can print or save any piece of mail—any document, actually—that occupies the frontmost (active) window by choosing the appropriate command from the File menu or clicking the appropriate icon on the toolbar. If you choose Print from the File menu, AOL displays the standard dialog box identifying the printer you've specified via the Windows Control Panel or the Macintosh Chooser. Click the OK button to print, or change to another installed printer through the Setup button.

If you choose Save As, AOL responds with the traditional Save As dialog box. Give your mail a name (use the .txt extension for maximum compatibility with other programs if you're using a Windows system) and put it wherever you please. It will be saved as a standard text file and you will be able to open it not only with AOL's software, but with any word processor or text editor.

Alternatively, you can select and copy most text—mail included—that appears on your screen. Once it's copied, you can open any text file on your disk (or start a new one via the New command under the File menu) and paste your mail into that file. You can also paste copied AOL text into other applications' files if you wish.

Replying to Mail

You'll probably reply to mail more often than you print or save it. Actually, all the Reply button does is call up the Compose Mail window with the To and Subject fields already filled in with the appropriate information (see Figure 3-22). Aside from these two features, a reply is no different than any other message. You can modify the To and CC fields if you wish and discuss any subject that interests you in the message text. You can even change the Subject field or remove the original recipient's screen name from the To field, though this somewhat defeats the purpose.

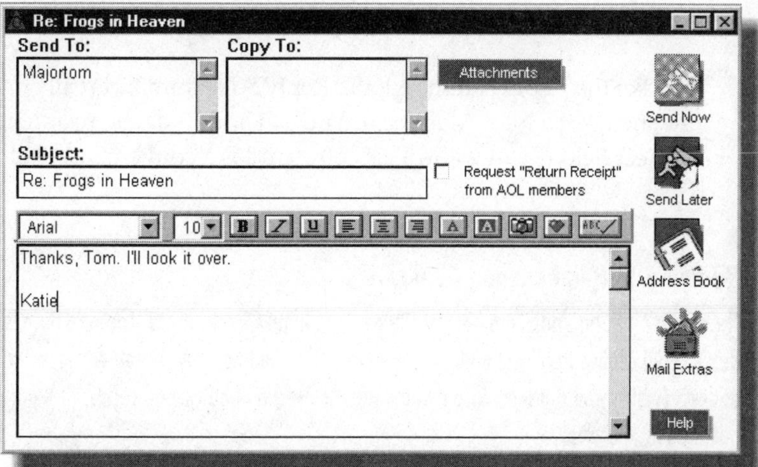

Figure 3-22: The Reply window. The Subject and To fields are already completed for you.

Replying to All

Look at Figure 3-23. Note that there are two reply buttons, including one marked Reply All. Reply All allows you to reply to everyone who was sent a message, including any CC addressees. In other words, you have your choice of replying only to the original sender (the Reply button) or to everyone who receives a message (the Reply All button).

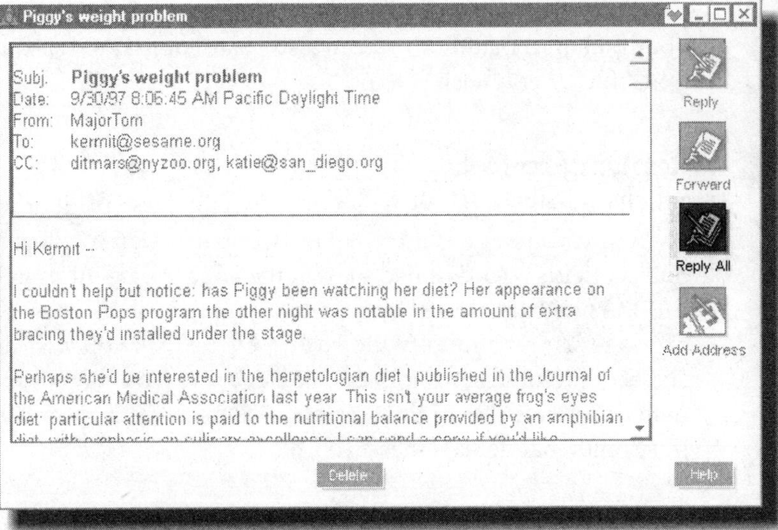

Figure 3-23: The Reply All button allows you to direct your reply to everyone who received the original message.

Like the Reply command, the Reply All command really only completes a few fields of a New Mail form. You can add or delete recipients and change the Subject field if you want. This command is a convenience, not an imperative.

> **Replying to Blind Carbon Copies**
>
> The Reply All button does not necessarily reply to blind CC addresses. The rule here is this: Reply to All replies to all the addresses visible in the Mail window. If you don't see an address (which would be the case if someone received a blind carbon copy), that person will not receive your reply.

Quoting

Some people get mountains of mail and don't remember everything they've said. You might be responding to something someone e-mailed to you a week ago, and even though their message is right in front of you at the moment, it might be hundreds of messages in the sender's past. If you respond with something like, "Yes. Next Thursday at 2:00 would be good," they might have to search laboriously through their mail filing system (assuming they have one) to discover what provoked your response.

To avoid such a situation, it's a common courtesy to quote the significant part(s) of the message to which you're replying. A typical quote might look like this: "In a message dated 5-12, you said <<Would you like to have lunch soon and discuss the contract?>>" Following that, your message, "Yes. Next Thursday at 2:00 would be good," makes a great deal more sense.

Those "chevron" brackets in the preceding paragraph (<< >>) indicate that you are quoting. Quoting can be tedious, but AOL's software makes it easy. Just select the portion of the sender's message that you want to quote before you click the Reply button. There's no need to copy the selection. When you click the Reply button, AOL will automatically quote the selection in either the AOL style (which we're using here as an example) or the Internet style (there's a preference command for this—see Chapter 9). It works with forwarded mail, too (see Figure 3-24).

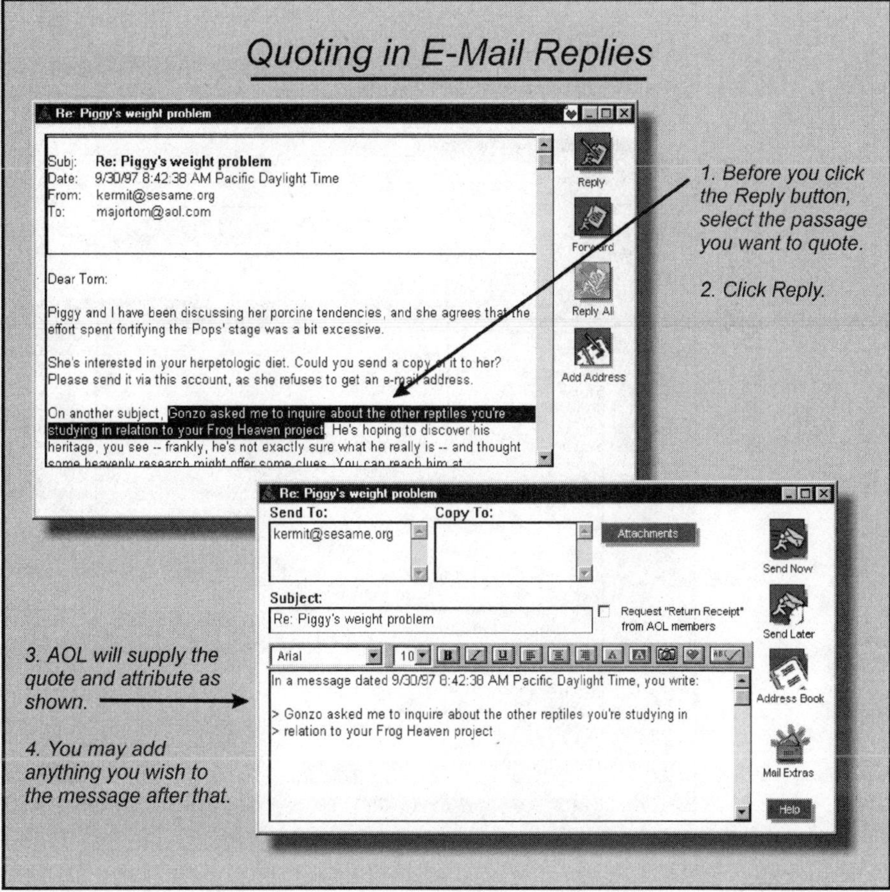

Figure 3-24: Quoting is easy: first select the text to be quoted; then click the Reply (or Forward) button.

Forwarding Mail

To forward a piece of mail to a third party, click the Forward button. America Online will respond with the slightly modified Compose Mail window that appears at the center of Figure 3-25.

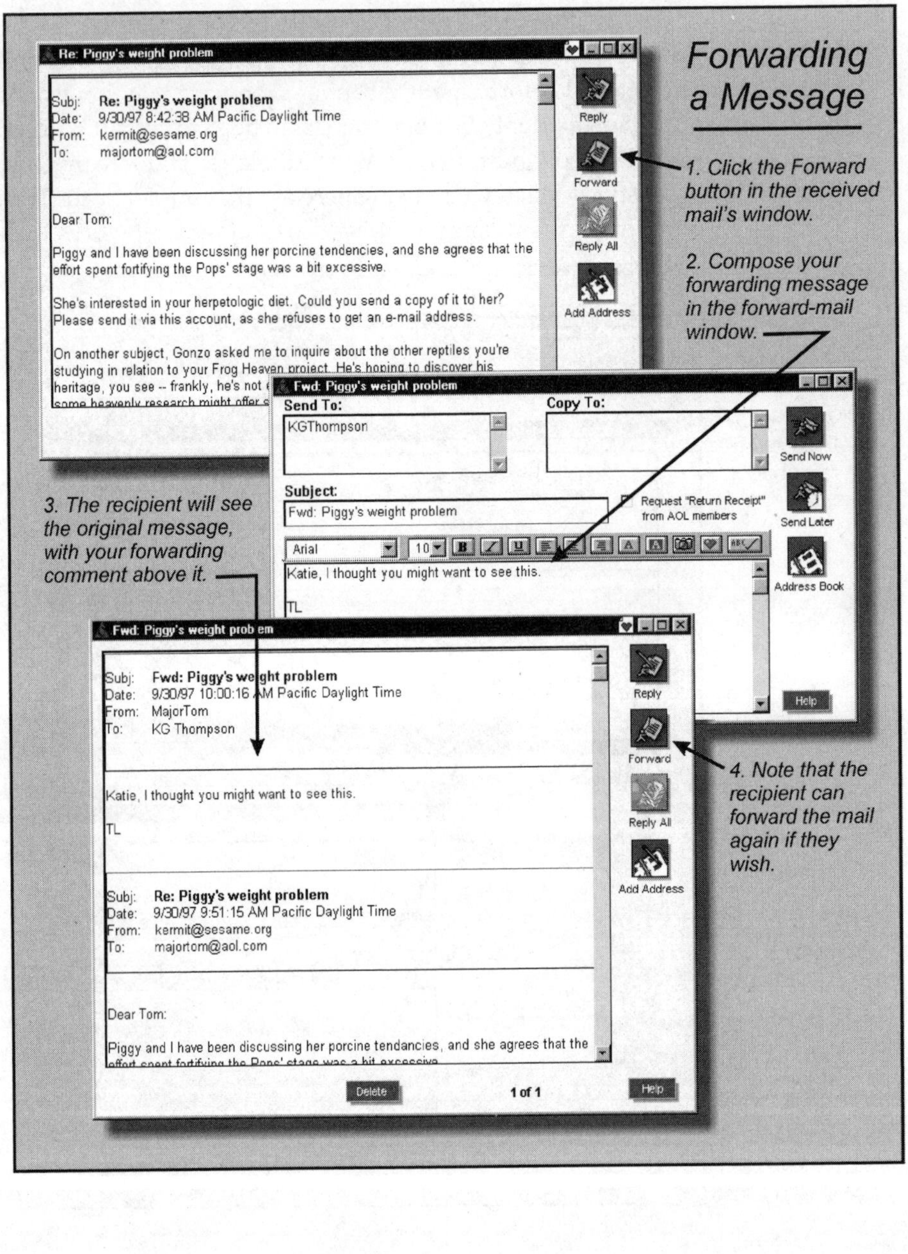

Figure 3-25: Forwarding mail is as easy as clicking a button, identifying the recipient, and typing your comments.

Forwarding a Message

1. Click the Forward button in the received mail's window.

2. Compose your forwarding message in the forward-mail window.

3. The recipient will see the original message, with your forwarding comment above it.

4. Note that the recipient can forward the mail again if they wish.

Re: Piggy's weight problem

Subj: **Re: Piggy's weight problem**
Date: 9/30/97 8:42:38 AM Pacific Daylight Time
From: kermit@sesame.org
To: majortom@aol.com

Dear Tom:

Piggy and I have been discussing her porcine tendencies, and she agrees that the effort spent fortifying the Pops' stage was a bit excessive.

She's interested in your herpetologic diet. Could you send a copy of it to her? Please send it via this account, as she refuses to get an e-mail address.

On another subject, Gonzo asked me to inquire about the other reptiles you're studying in relation to your Frog Heaven project. He's hoping to discover his heritage, you see -- frankly, he's not

Reply
Forward
Reply All
Add Address

Fwd: Piggy's weight problem

Send To: KGThompson
Copy To:
Subject: Fwd: Piggy's weight problem
Request "Return Receipt" from AOL members
Arial 10

Katie, I thought you might want to see this.

TL

Send Now
Send Later
Address Book
Help

Fwd: Piggy's weight problem

Subj: **Fwd: Piggy's weight problem**
Date: 9/30/97 10:00:16 AM Pacific Daylight Time
From: MajorTom
To: KG Thompson

Katie, I thought you might want to see this.

TL

Subj: **Re: Piggy's weight problem**
Date: 9/30/97 9:51:15 AM Pacific Daylight Time
From: kermit@sesame.org
To: majortom@aol.com

Dear Tom:

Piggy and I have been discussing her porcine tendancies, and she agrees that the

Reply
Forward
Reply All
Add Address
Delete
1 of 1
Help

The center window pictured in Figure 3-25 is where you enter your forwarding comment and the address of the person who is to receive the forwarded mail. The new recipient then receives the mail with your comment preceding the forwarded message. America Online clearly labels the mail as forwarded and identifies the person who forwarded it (note the details under Forwarded Message in the bottom window).

Checking Your Spelling

With version 4.0's spell checker, AOL finally took pity on those of us who qualify as illiterati. The spell checker is available whenever you compose mail, send an Instant Message (more about Instant Messages in Chapter 7, "Chat"), or compose any textual document. Look again at Figure 3-5; at the far right of the mini toolbar in the mail window you'll see the Spell Check button, the one with the checkmark on it. Simply click it and AOL will check the spelling of the mail in the frontmost window.

The spell checker is something of a grammar checker as well. It checks for proper capitalization, spacing, punctuation, formatting—even doubled words. This is no lightweight afterthought. It's fully integrated and exhaustively featured (see Figure 3-26).

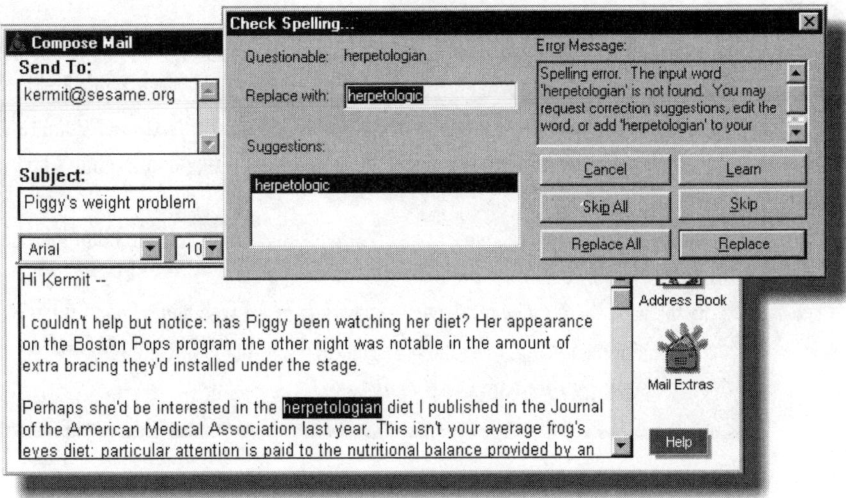

Figure 3-26: AOL's new spell checker rivals those in expensive word processing programs.

Of course, the spell checker is valuable only if you use it. Be sure to click that checkmark button before you send mail.

Hyperlinks in E-Mail

Speaking of buttons on the mail window's mini toolbar, have you noticed the hyperlink button there? It's the one with the heart-and-folder icon. Here's how it works.

Cruising the Net, you come across the Travelsickness Bag as Art Web page. Thinking of your friend Harry, who—how shall we say it?—can't keep it to himself when it comes to air travel, you compose some mail to tell him about it.

Telling him about it, however, could be a chore. You will have to tell him how to use the Web, and then identify the specific Web address for the page—a lengthy thing, filled with nonsense words and exacting punctuation.

There's an alternative. If you've already added the page to your Favorite Places list (Favorite Places and the World Wide Web are discussed in Chapter 4, "Using the Internet"), all you have to do is click the heart icon on the toolbar (to open the Favorite Places window) and then drag the Travelsickness entry from the Favorite Places window to the message field of the Compose Mail form. When you do, the Travelsickness entry will appear in the Compose Mail form, underlined and in a different color than the rest of the message (if you have a color monitor).

When Harry receives the mail, all he has to do is click the underlined text. AOL will launch the Web browser and connect with the page, all automatically. It's a great way to exchange the names of interesting places with friends.

Any entry on your Favorite Places list will work. It doesn't have to be a Web address. In fact, the entry doesn't even have to be on your Favorite Places list: just highlight some text in the message field of a Compose Mail form and right-click (PC) or Option-click (Mac) on it. AOL will produce a dialog box where you can supply a location's address—a hyperlink—manually.

The fine print: Harry will have to be an AOL member using version 3.0 or later of the AOL client. So will you.

By the way, there really is a Travelsickness Bag as Art Web page. Pages of this ilk are fleeting and it might be gone by the time you read this, but it's worth a try; we found it at **http://www.pvv.unit.no/~bct/spypose/**.

Requesting a Return Receipt

If you're sending mail to another AOL member, the Return Receipts Requested From AOL Members check box (pictured in Figure 3-5) makes sense. If you check it, the AOL host will send you an e-mail message the moment the recipient reads your mail. The host's message will tell you when your e-mail was sent and when it was read. You can discover this information using the Read Mail command (discussed earlier in this chapter), but many people prefer the convenience of the Return Receipt command.

Remember, however, that this feature only applies to mail sent to other AOL members. There's no way to tell when (or if) mail sent to addressees outside of the AOL system (Internet addressees) was read.

Attaching Files to Messages

Try as we might, language often fails us. When Tom's jenny Molly foaled on April Fools' Day, he sent announcements to his e-mail friends, describing the newborn with all of the creativity he could muster. His friends were indifferent. Who cares about a baby donkey?

Later, he sent them pictures of baby April, six hours old. That's all it took. They all wanted him to package her up and send her overnight, FedEx. She's that cute (see Figure 3-27).

Understand that we're not talking in the abstract here; files are files. Files can include text, graphics, data, sound, video, databases, spreadsheets—even programs. Any of these files can be attached to a piece of e-mail using AOL's software, and any attached file can be downloaded in its native format (the format used by the creator of the file), ready for viewing, hearing, or (in the case of program files) running.

Remember also that you can *insert* graphics into the body of an e-mail message that's destined for another AOL member, a process we will soon discuss. Inserted graphics, however, are limited to graphics (no sound, no video, no spreadsheets), and only AOL members—indeed, only AOL members using the latest version of AOL's client software—can receive them successfully.

File transmission requires elaborate protocols and error checking. Not a single bit, nibble, or byte can be displaced. Forget all of that. You need not become involved. America Online handles it all invisibly, efficiently, and reliably. If you want to send a file, all you have to do is click the Attach button (see Figure 3-28) and AOL takes care of it from there.

Figure 3-27: Sending a baby donkey across the country is as easy as clicking a mouse.

Sending a File Via E-Mail

It's a girl!!

Send To: (A long list of e-mail friends appeared here)

Copy To:

Attachments

April.jpg

Send Now

Subject: It's a girl!!

Request "Return Receipt" from AOL members

Send Later

Arial 10

Hi everyone --

I've taken the liberty of attaching a picture of April, our new foal born April Fool's Day (appropriate, as she was entirely unexpected). The picture was taken when April was about six hours old.

Mother and daughter are doing fine.

Tom

Address Book

Mail Extras

Help

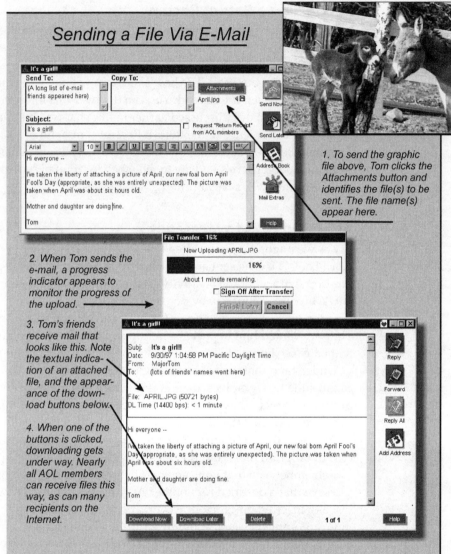

1. To send the graphic file above, Tom clicks the Attachments button and identifies the file(s) to be sent. The file name(s) appear here.

File Transfer - 16%

Now Uploading APRIL.JPG

16%

About 1 minute remaining.

Sign Off After Transfer

Finish Later Cancel

2. When Tom sends the e-mail, a progress indicator appears to monitor the progress of the upload.

3. Tom's friends receive mail that looks like this. Note the textual indication of an attached file, and the appearance of the download buttons below.

It's a girl!!

Subj: It's a girl!!
Date: 9/30/97 1:04:58 PM Pacific Daylight Time
From: MajorTom
To: (lots of friends' names went here)

File: APRIL.JPG (50721 bytes)
DL Time (14400 bps): < 1 minute

Hi everyone --

I've taken the liberty of attaching a picture of April, our new foal born April Fool's Day (appropriate, as she was entirely unexpected). The picture was taken when April was about six hours old.

Mother and daughter are doing fine.

Tom

Reply

Forward

Reply All

Add Address

Download Now Download Later Delete 1 of 1 Help

4. When one of the buttons is clicked, downloading gets under way. Nearly all AOL members can receive files this way, as can many recipients on the Internet.

Cheap Insurance

If your work involves travel and you take your laptop with you on the road, you can send e-mail to yourself, attaching important files you've constructed while away from the office. America Online will hold them for you—at least during AOL's 27-day limit on held mail. If something untoward should happen to your data while you're on the road, you can always download your files when you return. It's cheap insurance.

Attaching a Single File

You can attach a file to any e-mail message by clicking the Attach button in the message's window. America Online will respond with the sequence of windows pictured in Figure 3-28.

Figure 3-28: Attaching a file amounts to little more than clicking a button and locating the file on your disk.

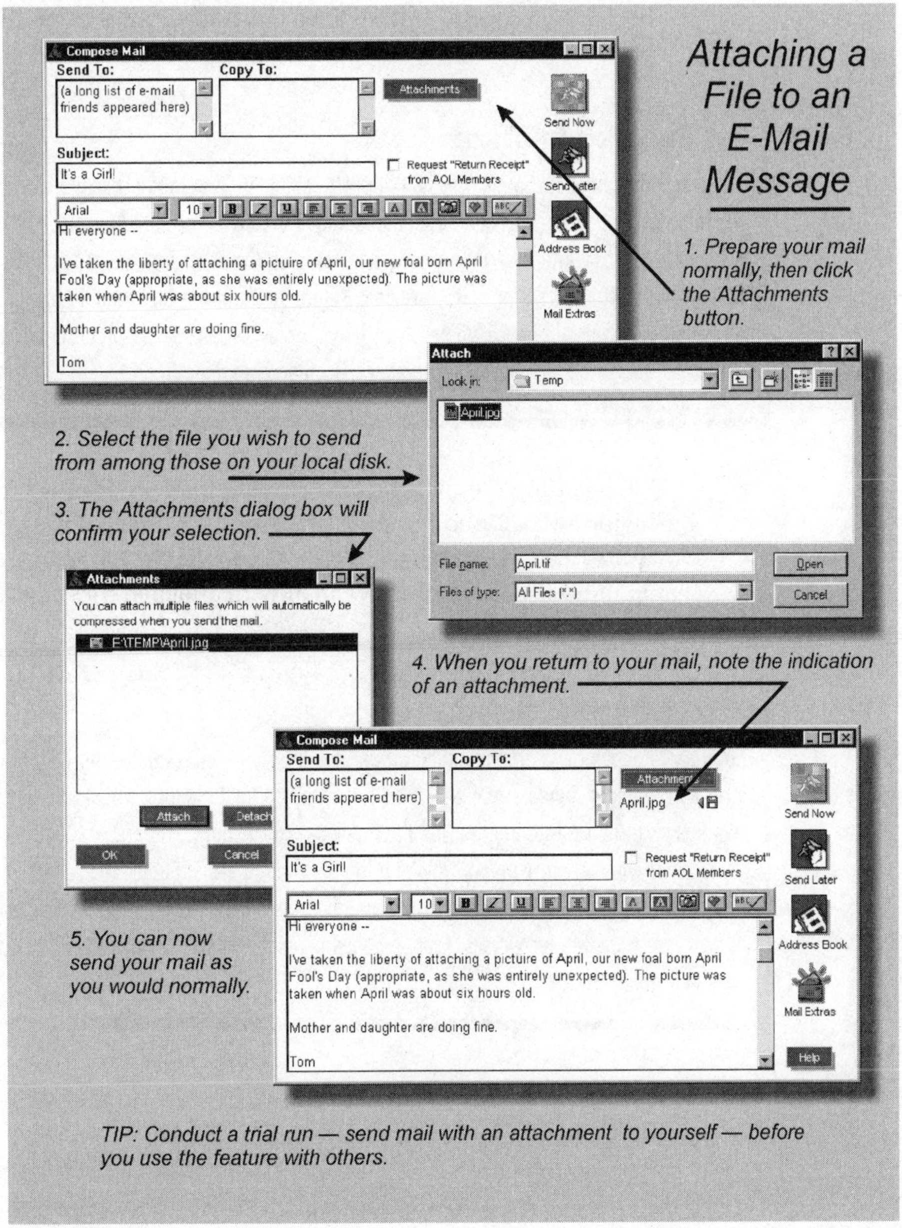

Attaching a File to an E-Mail Message

1. Prepare your mail normally, then click the Attachments button.

2. Select the file you wish to send from among those on your local disk.

3. The Attachments dialog box will confirm your selection.

4. When you return to your mail, note the indication of an attachment.

5. You can now send your mail as you would normally.

TIP: Conduct a trial run — send mail with an attachment to yourself — before you use the feature with others.

When you click the Send Now button pictured in the bottom window of Figure 3-28, you trigger the sequence of events pictured in Figure 3-27. America Online will hold the mail and the file (or files—more about that in a moment) until the addressee is ready to read the mail and download the file. If you address the mail to multiple recipients—even if they're receiving carbon copies or blind carbon copies—each will be given the chance to download the file.

Not Everyone's Enlightened

While AOL members exchange attached files with abandon, don't expect similar success on the Internet. Not all Internet software understands the conventions used to attach files, and even when the convention *is* understood, the person on the other end might not know what to do with an attached file once it's received. Before you attach a file to mail destined for any addressee with whom you've never exchanged files, send them a regular e-mail and ask if they are familiar with file attachments. It's the polite thing to do.

Downloading files attached to received mail is optional. Though the It's a Girl! window pictured in step 4 of Figure 3-27 offers both Download File and Download Later buttons, the recipients might elect to ignore them both. (Keep that in mind if you ever receive mail with attached files you don't want.)

Your Mail Is Safe, Unless...

Contrary to popular rumors circulating around the Internet, you cannot acquire a computer virus by reading a simple e-mail message. However, if that message contains an attached file, there's a chance that the file (not the message) could contain a virus.

In other words, before you download a file attached to e-mail, know the sender. If you're convinced of the sender's integrity, go ahead and download the file; but before you open it, check the file for viruses. Even good people inadvertently send virus-infested files once in a while.

Attaching Multiple Files

You can attach more than a single file to an e-mail message if you wish, in the form of a *zip archive*. Though zip archives are beyond the scope of this book (sign on and explore the Mail Center—it's on the Mail menu—if you want to know more), you should know that a zip archive is often a collection of several files rolled into one. Typically, a zip archive is compressed as it's compiled, streamlining the file-transfer process even further.

But that's enough tech talk. When you select more than one file for use in an attachment, the AOL client automatically combines them into a zip archive and attaches it to your mail. It's a complex process, but you needn't worry; the client does it all. All you have to do is issue the appropriate commands (see Figure 3-29).

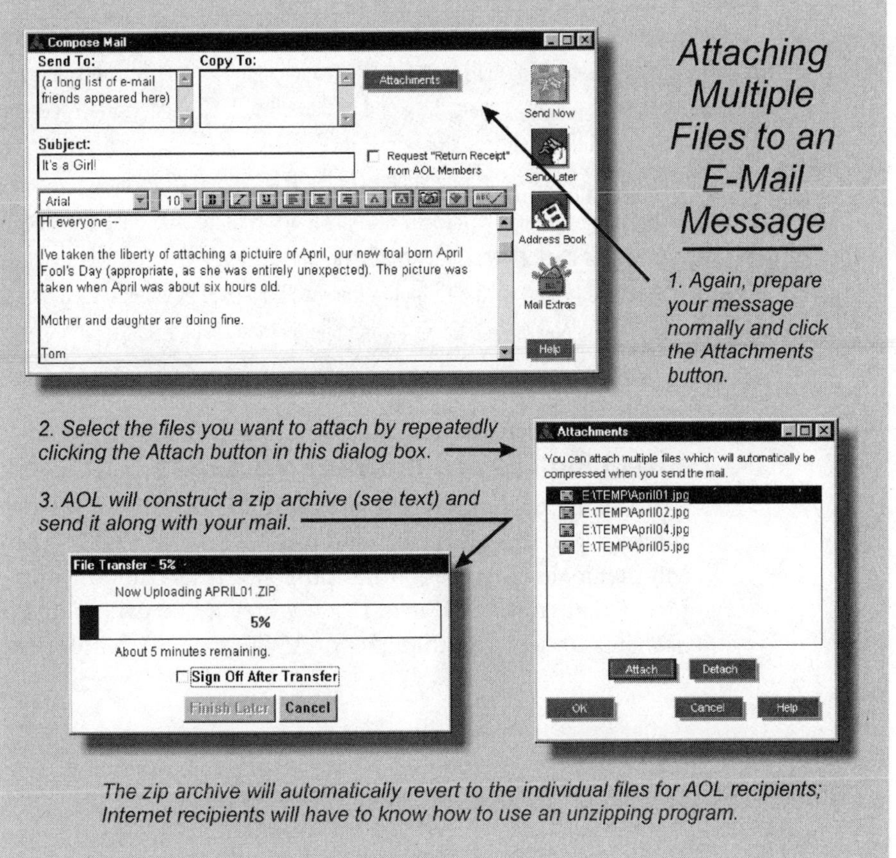

Figure 3-29: Attaching multiple files amounts to nothing more than repeating the process you used to attach a single file.

Our comment about file attachments and Internet recipients (see the "Not Everyone's Enlightened" sidebar) goes double for multiple file attachments on the Internet. Internet recipients will have to employ a decompression program (something that's built in to your AOL software, so you don't have to worry about it) *and* viewing (or hearing, or playback) programs (which are also built in to your AOL software) before they can make sense out of your attachments. Before you send multiple file attachments to an Internet address, discuss the matter with the addressee first. It's usually best to send the attachments singly under these circumstances.

Which Format to Use?

Commonly used graphics formats include the GIF (Graphics Interchange Format), JPEG (Joint Photographic Experts Group), BMP (bitmap, unique to Windows), PICT (unique to Macs), or ART (AOL's proprietary format) formats. Of them all, only GIF and JPEG are universally understood among today's computers, and of those two, JPEG usually offers the smallest file size. Moreover, GIF only offers 256 colors; JPEG offers millions.

In other words, send your graphics files in the JPEG format if you have a choice. You can convert almost any graphic to JPEG by opening it first with the AOL client (version 4.0 of the client opens all of the formats discussed above) and then saving it as a JPEG file (just choose Save As from the File menu and configure the saved file as JPEG). You'll save connect time—both yours and the recipients'—and telecommunication resources.

Attaching Files to Internet Messages

Because there's no universal standard for attaching files to e-mail on the Internet, you can't directly send files (or receive them) via Internet mail. Internet mail, like all e-mail, is pure ASCII text, and most files take the form of binary data, not ASCII text. Don't worry if you can't define the term *binary data;* just understand that it's not ASCII text and therefore not native to e-mail.

With that said, it will seem contradictory when we tell you that you can attach a file to Internet mail, but it's true. A few comments follow:

- If you attach a file to Internet mail, AOL will convert it to text before it's sent. This may seem anachronistic; how can you send a picture of a frog (or the sound of a frog), for example, as text? Simple: use a program that converts binary data into ASCII text. AOL does this for you via a technique called MIME (Multipurpose Internet Mail Extensions) base64 encoding.
- The recipient's e-mail program must understand MIME base64 encoding and be able to decode it. If that's not possible, the recipient will have to decode it manually. There are a number of programs that can do this, most notably a little shareware application called MIME64. It's available in AOL's software libraries. Downloading files from AOL's libraries is discussed in Chapter 6, "Transferring Files."

There are other binary-to-text-and-back techniques for transferring files on the Internet—one called *uuencoding* comes to mind, and Macintosh users are fond of *BinHex*—and if someone sends an attached file to you, it might be encoded using one of these other techniques. If that happens, your AOL software will not be able to automatically decode the message and offer to download the file to your machine. You'll have to do this manually. A description of that process—a process that can take many forms depending on the encoding method used—is beyond the scope of this book, but again, you can find answers (and ask questions) by visiting the keyword: **Mail**.

It should be apparent that file attachments to Internet mail are not universally supported, just barely standardized, and fraught with the potential for error. Both you and the intended recipient should be prepared for a period of experimentation and adjustment. The system doesn't always work the first time it's tried.

With all of the disclaimers out of the way, and though the convert-to-text-and-back process sounds a little bit like a sow's ear, it is in fact a technique that's been used for years on the Net. It works flawlessly when it works, and thousands of people do it every day. Don't hesitate to try.

Receiving an Attached File

When you receive mail with an attached file, whether it's from another AOL member or someone on the Internet, two buttons marked Download Now and Download Later will appear at the bottom of the message (see Figure 3-30).

Figure 3-30: Pay particular attention to the Download Manager dialog box in the center window. You'll need to know where you saved the file and what you called it when you want to use it later.

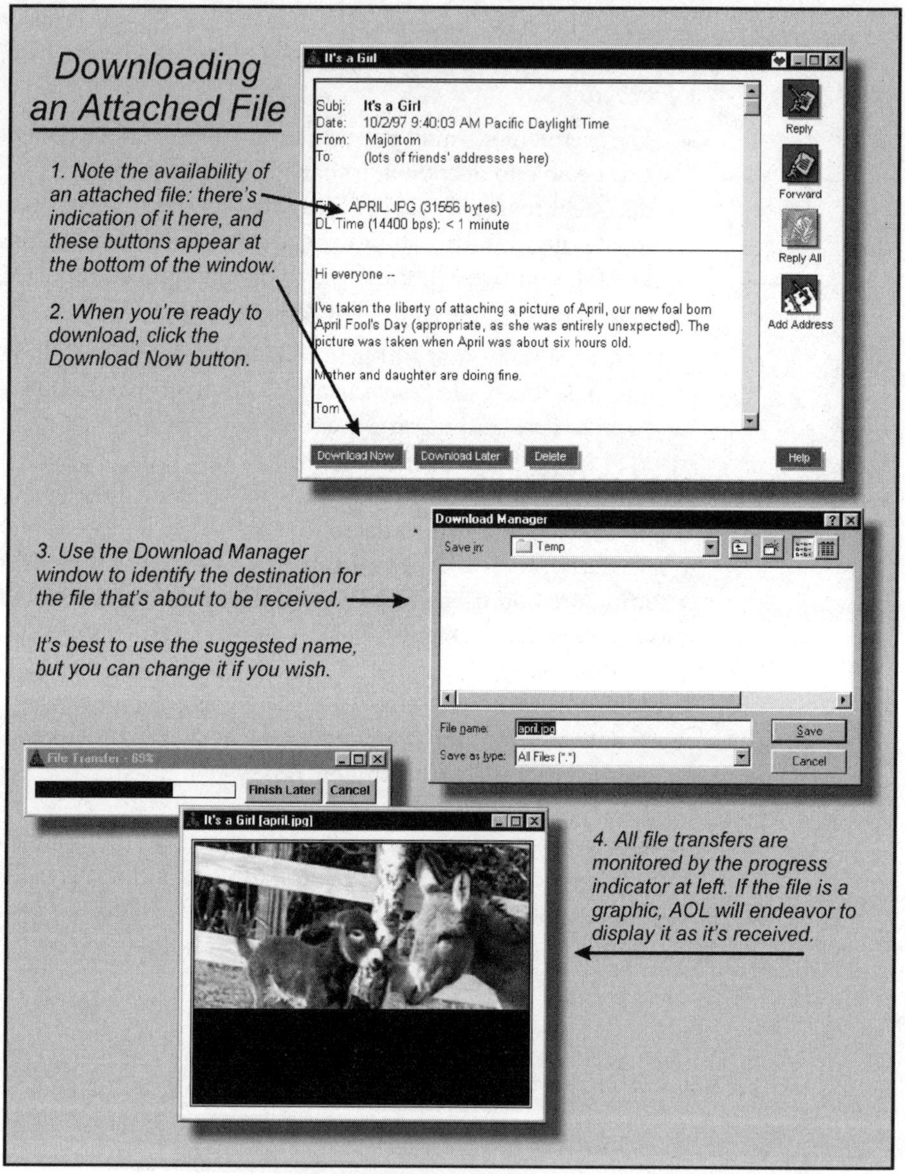

Downloading an Attached File

1. Note the availability of an attached file: there's indication of it here, and these buttons appear at the bottom of the window.

2. When you're ready to download, click the Download Now button.

3. Use the Download Manager window to identify the destination for the file that's about to be received.

It's best to use the suggested name, but you can change it if you wish.

4. All file transfers are monitored by the progress indicator at left. If the file is a graphic, AOL will endeavor to display it as it's received.

It's a Girl

Subj: It's a Girl
Date: 10/2/97 9:40:03 AM Pacific Daylight Time
From: Majortom
To: (lots of friends' addresses here)

File: APRIL.JPG (31556 bytes)
DL Time (14400 bps): < 1 minute

Hi everyone --

I've taken the liberty of attaching a picture of April, our new foal born April Fool's Day (appropriate, as she was entirely unexpected). The picture was taken when April was about six hours old.

Mother and daughter are doing fine.

Tom

Download Now | Download Later | Delete | Help
Reply | Forward | Reply All | Add Address

Download Manager
Save in: Temp
File name: april.jpg
Save as type: All Files (*.*)
Save | Cancel

File Transfer - 69%
Finish Later | Cancel

It's a Girl [april.jpg]

The Download Later button is actually a function of the Download Manager, which is discussed in Chapter 8, "Working Offline."

The Download Now button will produce the standard file-saving dialog box, allowing you to give the file a name and declare its destination. Pay attention to this dialog box. It determines where the file will be after you've signed off and are trying to remember where you put it. The file-saving dialog box also allows you to declare the file's extension, which, if you're using a Windows system, can determine the software that will be able to open it.

When you click the file-saving dialog box's OK button, AOL will download the file and save it where instructed. A progress indicator will keep you abreast of the process.

Inserting a Picture

As you can see, this attachment business can become complex, but it can be simplified. If the recipient is another AOL member and all you want to do is include a picture with your mail, simply insert it. This feature only applies to pictures, and it only works if the recipient is an AOL member using version 4.0 (or later) of the software, but it's the best choice under those circumstances.

To insert a picture, simply position the cursor within your e-mail message area where you want the picture to appear and then click the "camera" button on the Write Mail window's mini toolbar. An Open dialog box will appear. Select the file and click the Open button. That's all there is to it. You can insert as many pictures as you want, no limits (see Figure 3-31).

Practice on Yourself

If you've never done it before, send e-mail with attachments (or pictures) to yourself before you explore the feature with others. See how long it takes, and how the mail appears when it comes up on your screen. Get a feel for the process.

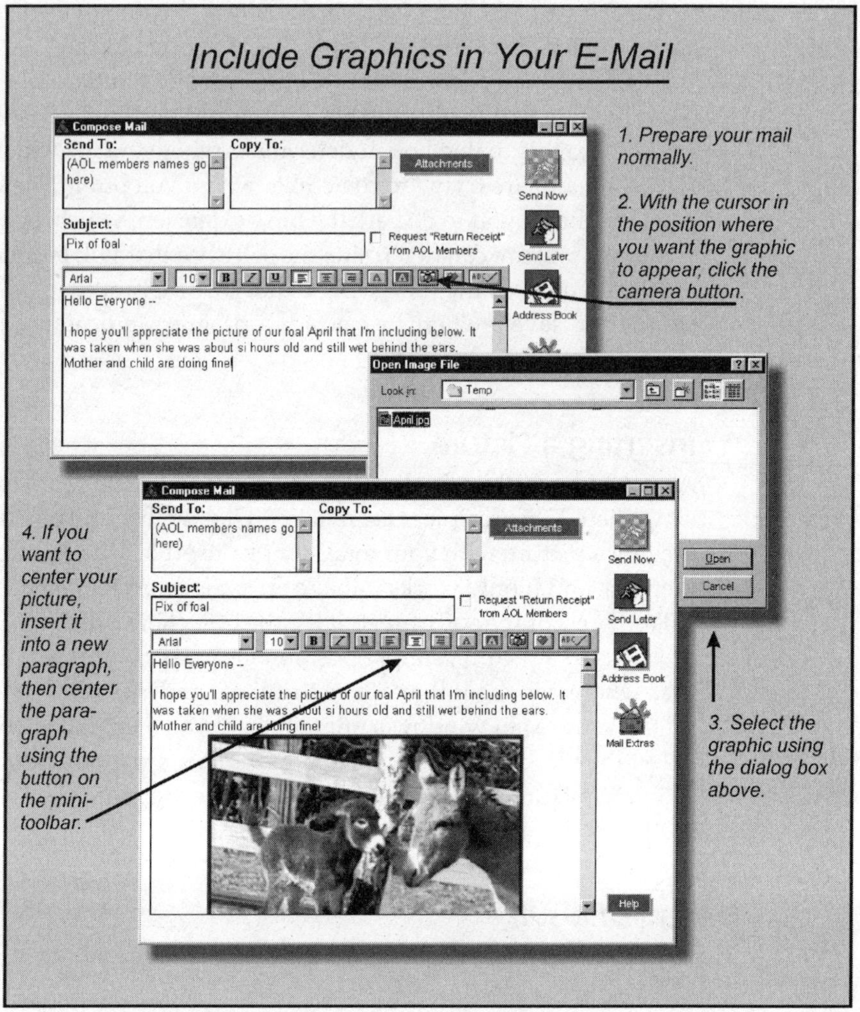

Figure 3-31: Inserted pictures can add considerable interest to e-mail.

Include Graphics in Your E-Mail

1. Prepare your mail normally.

2. With the cursor in the position where you want the graphic to appear, click the camera button.

3. Select the graphic using the dialog box above.

4. If you want to center your picture, insert it into a new paragraph, then center the paragraph using the button on the mini-toolbar.

Pictures in the GIF, JPEG, BMP (Windows), PICT (Mac), or ART (AOL's proprietary format) formats are acceptable, but again, this feature only works if the recipient is an AOL member using version 4.0 (or later) of the client software.

Undeliverable Internet Mail

Because Internet addresses are complex, you might occasionally misaddress a piece of Internet mail. Fortunately, your fallibility has been anticipated in the form of Internet daemons. In spite of their onerous-sounding name, daemons are simply computer programs that (usually) run without much human intervention. Our dictionary defines *daemon* as "an attendant spirit," which is exactly what Internet daemons are. In Figure 3-32, for example, the University of Oregon's e-mail system tried to find the user name pd_williams and couldn't, so a daemon sent mail back to me telling me so.

Should you try to send e-mail to a nonexistent domain name or a nonexistent username, a daemon somewhere will intercede and send mail back to you. The daemon will generally send back the body of the message as well (note the bottom of the lower window in Figure 3-32). All you have to do is select and copy the message text, paste it into a new mail window, enter the proper address, and resend the mail. Your mail won't end up in some kind of Internet dead letter box; the Internet always delivers.

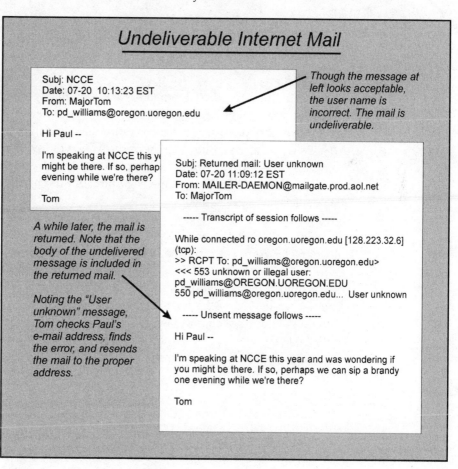

Figure 3-32: At top, a misaddressed Internet mail message looks as good as any other, but a few minutes later we receive the "User unknown" message pictured in the center window.

Undeliverable Internet Mail

Subj: NCCE
Date: 07-20 10:13:23 EST
From: MajorTom
To: pd_williams@oregon.uoregon.edu

Hi Paul --

I'm speaking at NCCE this y
might be there. If so, perhap
evening while we're there?

Tom

Though the message at left looks acceptable, the user name is incorrect. The mail is undeliverable.

Subj: Returned mail: User unknown
Date: 07-20 11:09:12 EST
From: MAILER-DAEMON@mailgate.prod.aol.net
To: MajorTom

----- Transcript of session follows -----

While connected ro oregon.uoregon.edu [128.223.32.6] (tcp):
>> RCPT To: pd_williams@oregon.uoregon.edu>
<<< 553 unknown or illegal user:
pd_williams@OREGON.UOREGON.EDU
550 pd_williams@oregon.uoregon.edu... User unknown

----- Unsent message follows -----

Hi Paul --

I'm speaking at NCCE this year and was wondering if you might be there. If so, perhaps we can sip a brandy one evening while we're there?

Tom

A while later, the mail is returned. Note that the body of the undelivered message is included in the returned mail.

Noting the "User unknown" message, Tom checks Paul's e-mail address, finds the error, and resends the mail to the proper address.

E-Mail Anonymity

Occasionally, you might want to send e-mail anonymously. There are legitimate reasons for wanting to do this, and when you encounter the need, you'll appreciate the services of an *anonymous remailer.* Anonymous remailers are free services that strip off all of the return-address information from your e-mail and send the mail in such a way that its source can not be traced.

Want to know more? Use the keyword: *http://www.cs.berkeley.edu/~raph/remailer-list.html.*

By the way, remailers are *not* services intended to disguise the originators of junk e-mail. It would be anathema for a remail service to broadcast junk mail. If you're thinking about it, don't even try.

Mail Extras

No one could have predicted e-mail's rise in popularity or significance over the past 10 years. No one can predict what will become of it in the next 10. And no one is more aware of e-mail's unpredictable plight than AOL.

That's why there's a button in the Write Mail window marked *Mail Extras.* It's AOL's expansion module: it's conspicuous, it's convenient, and—if you'll remember the numbers cited at the beginning of this chapter—it's in front of 200 people's faces every second.

Currently, under Mail Extras there's *Card-O-Matic*. It's a simple concept: you provide a short e-mail message and the people at Card-O-Matic create a full-color electronic postcard that they e-mail to the recipient (see Figure 3-33). It's probably more effective than a snail-mail postcard because of its uniqueness; it's much faster (a godsend if you've forgotten an occasion), and it's about the same price.

There's all kinds of clip-art here too, including photographs and cartoons. You'll find stationery, color, hyperlinks, and smileys—and Help files for every one. There's no excuse for old-fashioned, lackluster e-mail any longer: just click the Mail Extras button.

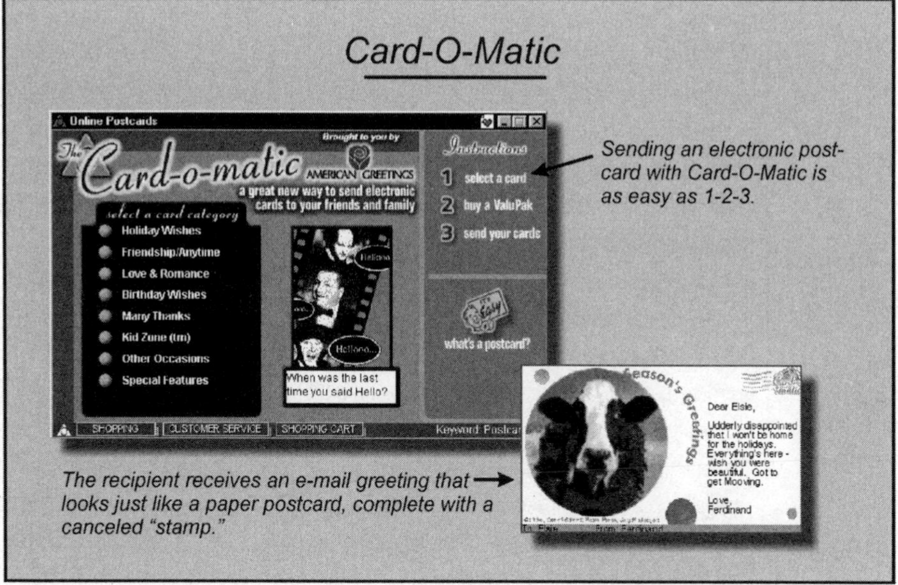

Figure 3-33: When you care enough to send the latest, Card-O-Matic makes it easy.

Reading Mail Offline

It's October 31st as we write this chapter, and mysterious things are bumping in the night. Among them are our computers, signing on at 4:00 A.M., getting our mail, and signing off again—all automatically, while we sleep. Or try to sleep. Things really *are* going bump out there.

You can instruct your software to sign on, unattended, at any time of the day, get any mail that's waiting for you, send any mail that's waiting to be sent, and sign back off. This is a great feature if, like us, you like to have your e-mail waiting for you first thing in the morning without having to sign on. Once the workday begins, our computers also sign on every hour to check for mail, again unattended, even if we're doing something else with our computers at the time.

Have we piqued your curiosity? This feature is so consequential that we've devoted an entire chapter to it. See Chapter 8, "Working Offline," for more on the subject.

MacMail

Jennifer knows mail. She gets over 500 pieces a day on her various names and has come to know the mail features well—maybe too well—on both the Mac and Windows. If you've followed along in this chapter on your Mac, you'll have noticed what seem like big differences. Most are just variations in form, not function. And those features that truly differ on the Mac tend to be in its favor.

Mail windows on the Mac look a bit different, but all the features we've detailed in this chapter are present. If something appears to be missing, look for it in another place in the window. You may notice some extra things, too, like the small arrow in the upper left-hand corner when you're reading mail. This arrow is a useful, Mac-only feature that lets you toggle between two different window formats (one fancy, one simple). You can also bring your mailbox to the front by clicking the box between the forward and back arrows—the one that reads "456 of 462" on Jennifer's screen right now (your numbers will be different, or so we hope for your sake). Macs can even change the amount of space allotted to the Send To and message fields with the double arrow at the bottom of the Send To field. Give it a try.

Composing mail on the Mac is similar to doing so on a PC, with one distinct difference. Rather than a separate Copy To field for sending carbon copies like that shown in Windows, you type all recipient screen names into the Send To field and then select CC (for carbon copy) or BCC (for blind carbon copy) from the drop-down menu to the left of each name. You can even save time and mouse clicks by first typing an open bracket—[—or an open parens—(—immediately before you type the recipient's screen name. This automatically designates the recipient as a carbon copy or blind carbon copy, respectively. Typing either a close bracket—]—or a close parens—)—at the end of a screen name sets the next address you type as a regular To (as opposed to a CC or BCC).

Members on Mac also have the additional formatting feature of text background color available in the Compose Mail window. To use it, select the text you'd like to change by dragging your mouse over it; then click on the arrow to the right of the outlined "A" icon and choose your color. Only the background color of the text you highlighted changes.

There's another added feature in the Mac's Address Book: You can view its contents alphabetically by name (the default) or by address (screen names or Internet addresses). Just click the appropriate column label at the top of the window to toggle between the two formats—the column you select will change to a darker gray.

The Mac Preferences window looks a bit different from the Windows version, but most functions remain the same. Read your preferences carefully, however: Not all preferences are in the same location or use the same phrasing. For more detail on preference differences, see the end of Chapter 9.

Last but not least, the Personal Filing Cabinet on the Mac has a couple of added benefits. Like the Address Book, you can view the contents alphabetically by name (default), by address/location, or by date—just click the appropriate label at the top of the window. You can even switch the order of the contents between first to last and last to first by clicking the down arrow in the upper right-hand corner of the window. New folders are easy to create on the Mac, too—simply click the New Folder icon, and when a new folder appears in your Personal Filing Cabinet, type in its name. You'll notice the resemblance to creating new folders in your Finder. And also like the Finder, you can select a group of continuous items by dragging your mouse over the rows; you can also select multiple, discontinuous files by using the Shift key while selecting each one. One feature we're missing is the ability to save the contents of individual folders in the Personal Filing Cabinet. You can easily compensate for this by making a new folder on your desktop (in the Finder), selecting all the mail you'd like to save (if it is all the mail in a folder, use Command+A) and, with your new folder visible in the background, drag the selected mail over the top of the folder. It will all be saved to the folder, using the subject lines as the titles.

Moving On

As you can see, AOL's e-mail facility is effective and easy to use. It holds your mail for you, even after you've read it, and even if you don't file it yourself. It allows you to reply to and forward mail at the click of a button. It offers a filing system that's the best in the business. Perhaps best of all, it rarely costs you any more than your monthly AOL membership fee.

Very impressive indeed.

E-mail, however, is not a local thing. Just like U.S. Mail, you aren't limited to sending and receiving mail within your community (AOL) itself when you use AOL's mail feature. You can send e-mail to anyone who can receive it and vice versa, regardless of the community—or even country—they live in. The tool for that is the Internet. We've mentioned the Net a number of times in this chapter; now's the time to get to know it better. Read on.

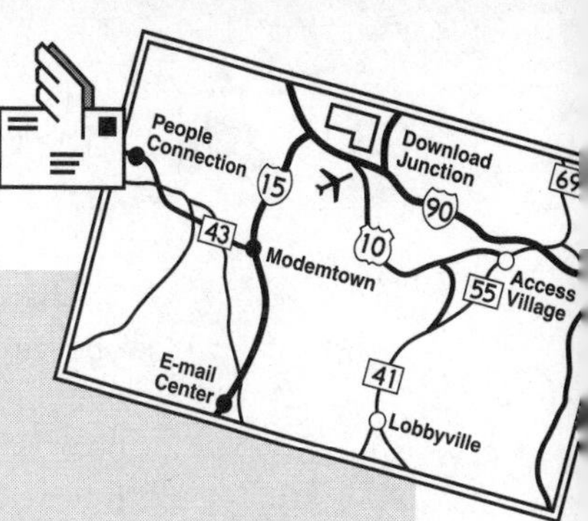

CHAPTER 4

Using the Internet

- Internet Addresses
- The World Wide Web
- Favorite Places
- Mailing Lists
- Newsgroups
- Gopher
- FTP
- Telnet
- net.help

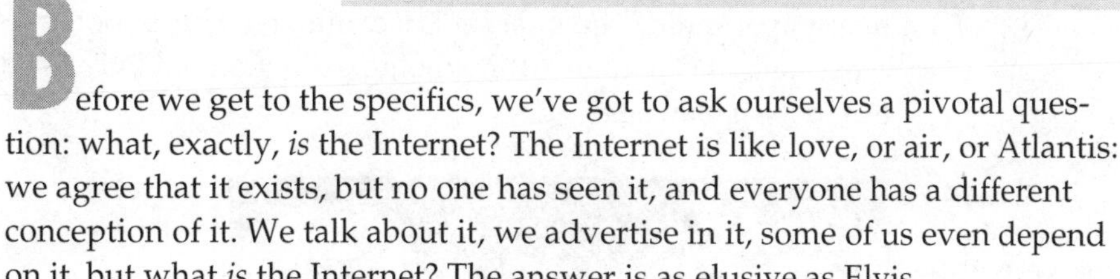

Before we get to the specifics, we've got to ask ourselves a pivotal question: what, exactly, *is* the Internet? The Internet is like love, or air, or Atlantis: we agree that it exists, but no one has seen it, and everyone has a different conception of it. We talk about it, we advertise in it, some of us even depend on it, but what *is* the Internet? The answer is as elusive as Elvis.

The convenient answer to the question is to identify the Internet as a system of wires and computers. Physically speaking, it's a system of *inter*-connected computer *net*works—the Internet. AOL is one of those networks—the largest—but there are thousands of others. They're all connected via a web of fiber-optic cables that encircles the world like a chrysalis encircles a moth.

Figure 4-1: *NET01*, by Jeff Stewart, is the artist's conception of how the Internet might appear in virtual reality. Jeff has a number of images posted online. Look for them at keywords: **PC Graphics**.

There's more to the Internet than a chrysalis of fiber-optic cables, however. The Internet is also a political phenomenon, and therein lies its most enigmatic—and frustrating—virtue: it's an anarchy. There's no chairman of the board, no central data bank, and no country of origin. No one owns the Internet: the networks attached to it fund it. No megalithic corporation controls the Internet: a committee administers it, and the committee is composed of volunteers. No one polices the Internet: anything goes—and everything does. The Internet is the epitome of anarchy, with all of the circumspection anarchy implies.

The Internet is an economic anarchy too. Despite the hopes and efforts of its founders, the Internet has become a commercial medium. Unlike other commercial media, there's no Federal Communications Commission or newspaper guild. The Internet is a commercial hippopotamus trampling the ecosystem of economics, threatening extinction not only to its environment, but to itself as well.

Figure 4-2: Artist Mike Keefe's editorial cartoons are always entertaining and often provocative. Use the keywords: **In Toon** to download a new one every day.

So why does it survive (and thrive)? Perhaps best of all, the Internet represents the potential for the consummate community. It has no borders and it has no eyes. It reaches tens of millions of people but knows nothing of their ethnicity, gender, or age. Its only criteria for membership are a telephone line, a computer equipped with a modem, and a willingness to interact with others. There are no uniforms, no authorities, no boundaries, and no castes. This unparalleled equanimity offers the potential for an ideally democratic community: one where the common denominators are a desire to speak and a willingness to listen, and where superficial values are simply impracticable. Thomas Jefferson would have loved this place.

Nouns & Adjectives

If you're going to live in the neighborhood, you're going to have to speak the language. Used as a noun, the Internet is referred to as "*the* Internet." One would never say, "Send me a message on Internet"; it would be, "Send me a message on the Internet."

When *Internet* is used as an adjective, the article is dropped. It's "Internet mail," not "the Internet mail."

We used to call it "the Net," but then Sandra Bullock made a movie and popularized the term, and everyone knows how much us dweebs loathe common language, so we're back to "the Internet." It's our neighborhood, after all. We give it our respect.

Internet Addresses

We touched on the subject of Internet addresses briefly in Chapter 3, but they deserve more than that. They're really not much different from the addresses the U.S. Postal Service uses, though rather than being sent to you at your home, Internet mail is sent to your *domain*. Domain or domicile, they're the same thing: they're the places where you "live" on the Net—where you keep your mailbox and, perhaps, your Web page.

International Top-Level Domains

When our friend Kyoko writes to us from Japan, the address she places on the envelope goes from the specific to the general: she starts with our name and ends with U.S.A., in the name/address/city/state/country format.

International Internet addresses are exactly the same. At the far right you'll find the name of the country. This is called the *top-level domain*. Well, almost always. The Net's an anarchy, after all. Figure 4-3 identifies the abbreviations for some common international top-level domains.

Abbreviation	Country
au	Australia
at	Austria
ca	Canada
dk	Denmark
fi	Finland
fr	France
de	Germany
it	Italy
jp	Japan
no	Norway
uk	United Kingdom
us	United States

Figure 4-3: Country abbreviations are the top-level domain of international Internet addresses.

A well-known example of an international top-level domain is **username@well.sf.ca.us** indicating a user on the Whole Earth 'Lectronic Link (the WELL) in San Francisco (sf), California (ca), U.S.A. (us).

Note that the segments of Internet addresses are separated by periods. It's always that way. (Well, here again, almost always. You occasionally will see other address formats. They're rare, however, and assuredly the exception to the rule.)

U.S. Top-Level Domains

At the risk of sounding politicocentric again, most domains are within the United States, and the **us** top-level domain is typically omitted from American domain names, just as it is on paper mail that's to stay within our borders. Instead, top domains for U.S. users typically identify the type of system they're using. Figure 4-4 identifies the common U.S. top-level domains.

Abbreviation	Affiliation
com	business and commercial
edu	educational institutions
gov	government institutions
mil	military installations
net	network resources
org	other (typically nonprofit)

Figure 4-4: U.S. top-level domains identify the nature of the user's affiliation.

Tom's Internet address, as mentioned in Chapter 3, is majortom@aol.com. Jennifer's is jennifer@aol.com. Anyone looking at our top-level domain can determine that we're affiliated with a commercial organization—in this case, America Online.

Domain Names & Computer Names

Immediately to the left of the top-level domain is the location of the network that's actually connected to the Internet. Thus, a domain name such as uoregon.edu implies that there's a network named uoregon somewhere, and it has a direct line to the Internet. AOL has a direct line to the Internet also (several of them, actually), thus it's known as aol.com.

Many institutions—especially business and educational ones—have more than one local area network (LAN), and though these LANs are connected to the Internet, they're only connected indirectly, through some kind of central host. Most of Tom's academic associates work at the University of Oregon, but the U of O has at least seven satellite networks connected to the university's central mainframe, which in turn is connected to the Internet. One of those networks is located within a building called Oregon Hall, and the users on that network add *oregon* to the string, identifying their LAN within the University's hierarchy. Thus, their domain becomes oregon.uoregon.edu, which identifies the Oregon Hall (oregon) LAN, which is connected to the University of Oregon domain (uoregon), which is an educational institution (edu).

Usernames

Most Internet activity takes the form of e-mail, and e-mail is sent to individuals. To identify an individual, the format username@oregon.uoregon.edu is used. Everything to the left of the at sign (@) in an Internet address is the user's name.

Many people on the Internet use their first initial and last name as their Internet name (fmorgan@mit.edu). This format is unique (at least to the domain), and it's not gender specific (an issue that many Net users prefer to avoid). Spaces aren't allowed (so you'll often see underscores in their place: fred_morgan@mit.edu), and Internet addresses are usually not case sensitive. None of this should make a whit of difference to you: your screen name (minus any spaces) automatically becomes your Internet username. Your domain (sounds regal, doesn't it?) is aol.com.

WIRED Magazine

WIRED is the "magazine of the digital generation" covering interactive media, the networking community, and the toys of technology. Started in early 1993, *WIRED* has quickly advanced to the vanguard of the literary aristocracy. Its design is precocious, its content acerbic, its language always provocative (and often offensive to some). The information age has few perspectives that can match *WIRED*'s insight, candor, or irreverence, and none can match them all.

Best of all, *WIRED* is available online at AOL. Only past issues of *WIRED* are available—you'll have to visit your newsstand for the latest edition—but its focus isn't so myopic that its content becomes obsolete in a month or two. If this chapter interests you and you're not yet a *WIRED* devotee, read this magazine. Use the keyword: **WIRED**.

PS: If you don't care for *WIRED* once you've checked it out, use the keyword: **http://www.covesoft.com/underwired/Contents.html**. Leave it to the Web to provide an alternative medium to the alternative media.

The World Wide Web

True to its anarchical roots, the Internet matured—if one can use the term to describe a technology that's just turning 30—in fits and starts. As computers became more powerful, so did the Internet, and as the Internet became more powerful, it expanded.

Expansion, however, introduced more users—people who weren't computer professionals. Though the Internet started as a military contrivance in the late 1960s, by the early 1980s, educational institutions had joined the fray. By then, the military's technologists were outnumbered by academics with .edu at the end of their addresses—students from fine art departments, theologians, history professors—proponents of the humanities, far removed from high technology. These people were uncomfortable with Internet commands like *grep* and *ping*. They were more interested in parsing Chaucer than in conjugating UNIX. Like most of us who have followed, they were searching for a method of bringing unity and simplicity to the Internet. It was time for the Internet to descend from the stratosphere and come down to earth.

By the late 1980s, the scientists at CERN—the European Particle Physics Laboratory in Geneva, Switzerland—decided to do something about it. The result was the *World Wide Web*: a gathering of FTP sites, Gopher holes, WAIS gateways, e-mail, and newsgroups—all the fragments that were diffracting the Internet—in familiar and convenient surroundings. The Web was released in 1990 and suddenly the Internet became as familiar as our living rooms. Indeed, today's Web is so obliging, it's the *only* means of using the Internet for many people, and if industry pundits are to be believed, it might just become our only means of using our *computers*.

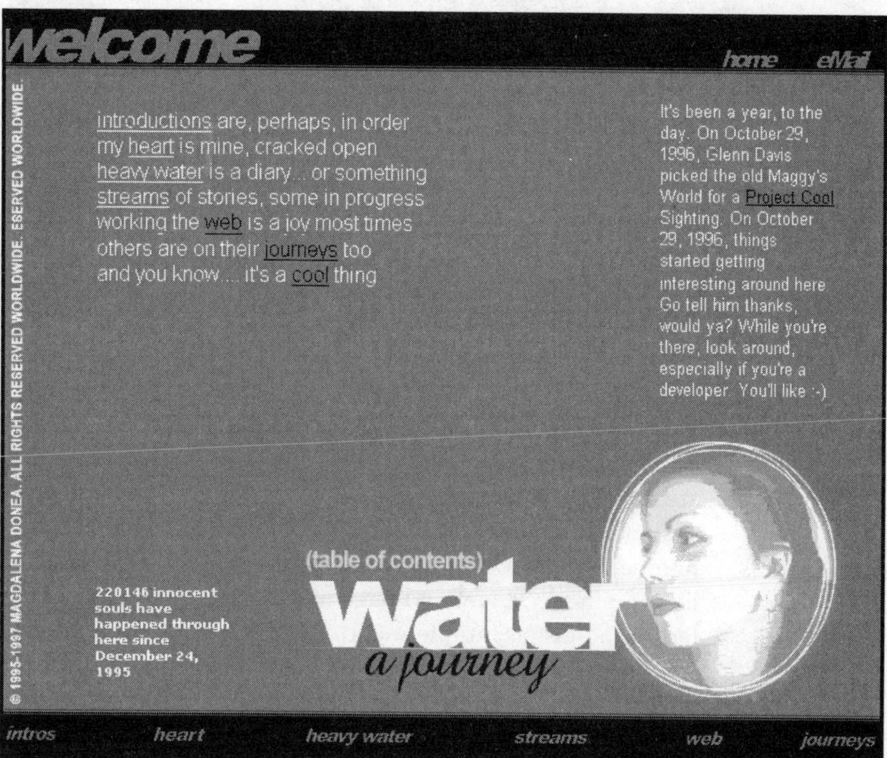

Figure 4-5: Water, the personal Web page designed by Magdalena Donea at **http://www.kia.net/maggy/**. Awards and citations include the *Wall Street Journal*, *Mediafile*, and *USA Today*. This site was voted Cool Personal Web Site of the Year in 1997. You can have a personal Web site as well. We'll tell you how in this chapter.

The important thing for you to understand is that the World Wide Web is simply another method of accessing information on the Internet. You can travel to St. Louis, for example, by plane, train, or boat; the only difference is the method of transportation. St. Louis is St. Louis no matter how you get there. The same goes for, say, an updated printer driver from Microsoft: you can get it on the Web, or through e-mail, or via FTP (we'll discuss FTP later in this chapter). Regardless of how it's accessed, the driver is the driver, no matter how you got it. As far as the Web is concerned, it's all a matter of getting there.

A Sterling History of the Internet

Our history of the World Wide Web is necessarily brief; this isn't a history book, after all. But the genesis of the Web really *is* fascinating, even if you don't care for history. To learn more, follow the path illustrated in Figure 4-6. Bruce Sterling's excellent *History of the Internet* is only one of the resources available by following the links in that illustration. Be sure to investigate them all.

Hypermedia

The Web's universe consists of *hypermedia*. To our experience, the use of polysyllabic buzzwords like this usually indicates that the words' true meanings are obtuse and opaque. The word *hypermedia* is no exception, but it's the heart of the Web, and you must understand one to understand the other. Perhaps Figure 4-6 will help.

Each Web page consists of text and graphics (and more—such as sound and animation—if it's a really ambitious page), usually marked with links (*hyperlinks*, actually), or areas on the page that when clicked lead to something else. Links can lead you to more Web pages, graphics, sounds, or videos; there are no limits other than the capability of your hardware and the link designer's imagination. The path shown in Figure 4-6 is only one of an infinite number of paths we could have explored. A click on the Arts or Computing links on the AOL NetFind page would send you down other paths, just as fertile and just as infinite as the one in the illustration. Indeed, the Web is a vast cosmos of resources that are linked to related resources all over the world. These resources are constantly being changed—npr.org, for example, changes at least every hour—thus the term *hyper*links, meaning "active links."

Figure 4-6: Hypermedia provides a nonlinear pathway to the infinite potential of the World Wide Web.

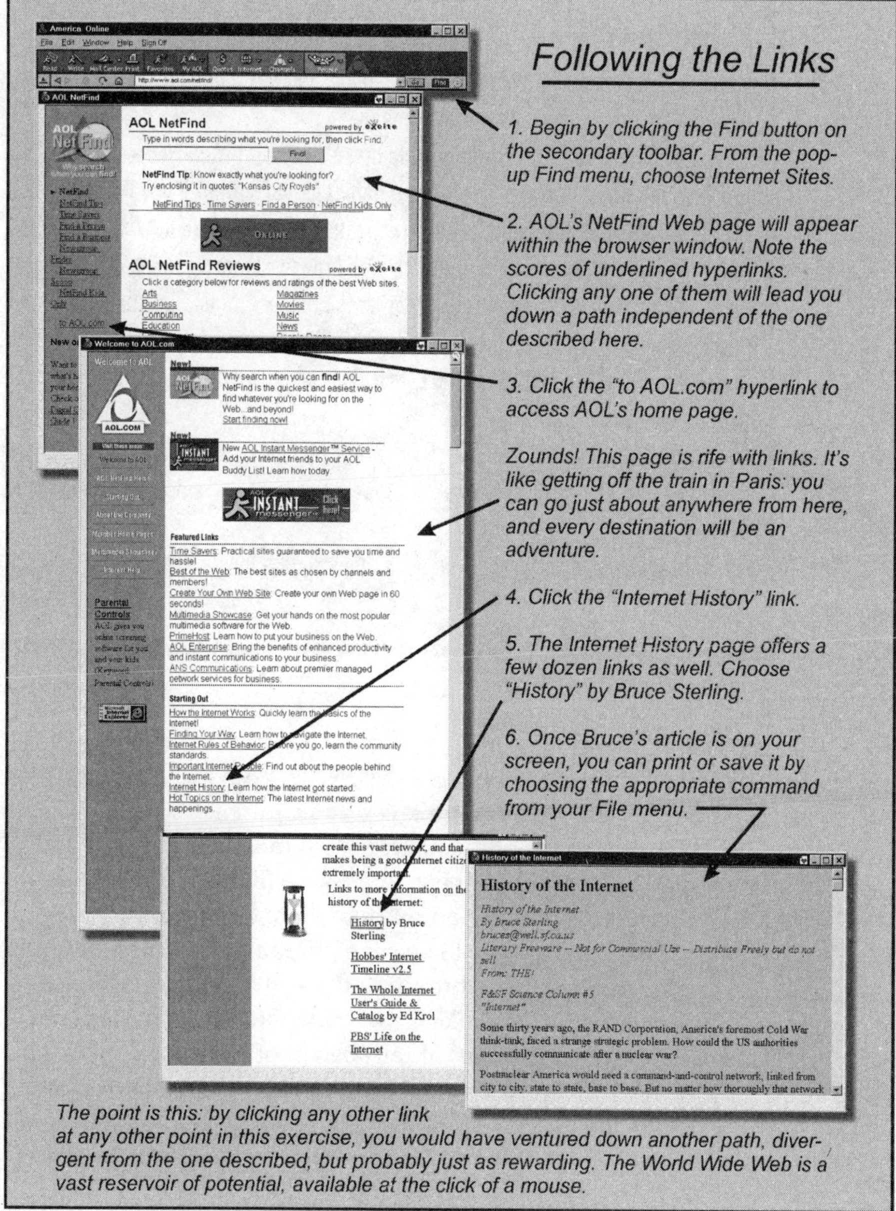
Following the Links
1. Begin by clicking the Find button on the secondary toolbar. From the pop-up Find menu, choose Internet Sites.
2. AOL's NetFind Web page will appear within the browser window. Note the scores of underlined hyperlinks. Clicking any one of them will lead you down a path independent of the one described here.
3. Click the "to AOL.com" hyperlink to access AOL's home page.
Zounds! This page is rife with links. It's like getting off the train in Paris: you can go just about anywhere from here, and every destination will be an adventure.
4. Click the "Internet History" link.
5. The Internet History page offers a few dozen links as well. Choose "History" by Bruce Sterling.
6. Once Bruce's article is on your screen, you can print or save it by choosing the appropriate command from your File menu.
The point is this: by clicking any other link at any other point in this exercise, you would have ventured down another path, divergent from the one described, but probably just as rewarding. The World Wide Web is a vast reservoir of potential, available at the click of a mouse.
AOL NetFind
AOL NetFind Reviews
Welcome to AOL.com
History of the Internet

Nomenclature

So far, we've defined the *World Wide Web*, *page*, and *link*, but there are a few other terms that require interpretation before we continue.

A *Web browser* is software designed to access the World Wide Web—the Internet's graphical interface. Web access requires a hefty piece of software; you'll see Web browsers for sale at software stores and in mail-order catalogs, and they're not cheap. You needn't fret: your AOL software contains a superb Web browser; there's nothing else to buy.

A *URL* is the *Uniform Resource Locator*, or the address for each article of text, and each graphic, sound, or video, on the Web. A typical URL is **http://www.att.com**—for AT&T, in this case. There are millions of URLs, thus their addresses are lengthy and specific. URL is pronounced "you-are-el," not "earl."

HTTP stands for *HyperText Transfer Protocol.* Appearing at the left end of a keyword, HTTP tells your AOL client to invoke the browser and treat the remaining text in the keyword as a URL.

HTML is *HyperText Markup Language*, the scripting language that's used to create Web pages.

Browsing

The World Wide Web is a vast place. With the acceptance of Web page advertising, every commercial enterprise has established a presence on the Web, and many of them have spent millions of dollars making their pages sparkle. We're the benefactors, as we flit from one bouquet of pages to another, butterflies in a bountiful field of opportunity.

This is not a place to become mired in procedural details. As the AOL software presents it, browsing the Web really requires no instructions. It's a place for discovery, like an art gallery (try the WebMuseum at **http://sunsite.unc.edu/wm/**) or the shelves of books in a public library (try the World Wide Web Virtual Library at **http://vlib.stanford.edu/Overview.html**). This is the Internet at its best; it will bring you back time after time.

Using the Web Browser

The browser in your AOL software is one of the best: Microsoft's *Internet Explorer.* You can use other browsers as well—more about that later—but Internet Explorer is integral to your AOL client, and, therefore, the most convenient browser at your disposal.

Invoking the Browser

AOL's built-in browser is invoked automatically whenever you issue a command that refers to the World Wide Web. The keyword: **Web** will invoke it. The little house icon on the toolbar will invoke it too. So will the Go to the Web and AOL NetFind options on the pop-up menu that appears when you click the Internet icon on the toolbar. You'll invoke the browser if you choose a Favorite Place that contains a legitimate URL (we'll discuss Favorite Places later in this chapter). You can type a URL into the text box in the toolbar or click a Web hyperlink in e-mail—all of these things invoke the built-in browser.

Among the myriad ways of invoking the browser, our preference is the use of keywords; any URL can be entered as a keyword. Press Ctrl+K or Command+K (or click the Keyword button on the secondary toolbar), and then type a legitimate URL into the Keyword dialog box— **http://www.aol.com/best.html** is a good example. Use it as a keyword and you'll soon be at AOL's Best of the Web page, an ideal place to begin exploring the World Wide Web.

> **Be Specific**
>
> Don't be fooled by media shorthand. AT&T, for example, includes the AT&T Web address in their TV ads, but in the interest of brevity, they often leave significant portions out. While the complete address is **http://www.att.com**, you might see it advertised as **att.com**, which won't work if you plug only that into your browser. The advertisement assumes you know the rest—and now you do.

You can copy and paste URLs into the Keyword dialog box as well. Let's say a friend sends you e-mail inviting you to visit his favorite Web site. In the midst of your friend's e-mail, he includes the URL **http://www.henson.com/muppets/Kermit.htm**. You decide to visit the site to see what's up.

Rather than painstakingly reenter a lengthy URL, all you have to do is the following:

1. Select the URL in your friend's e-mail.
2. Press Ctrl+C or Command+C to copy it.
3. Press Ctrl+K or Command+K to call up the Keyword dialog box.
4. Press Ctrl+V or Command+V to paste the URL into the dialog box.
5. Press the Enter key and you're on your way (see Figure 4-7).

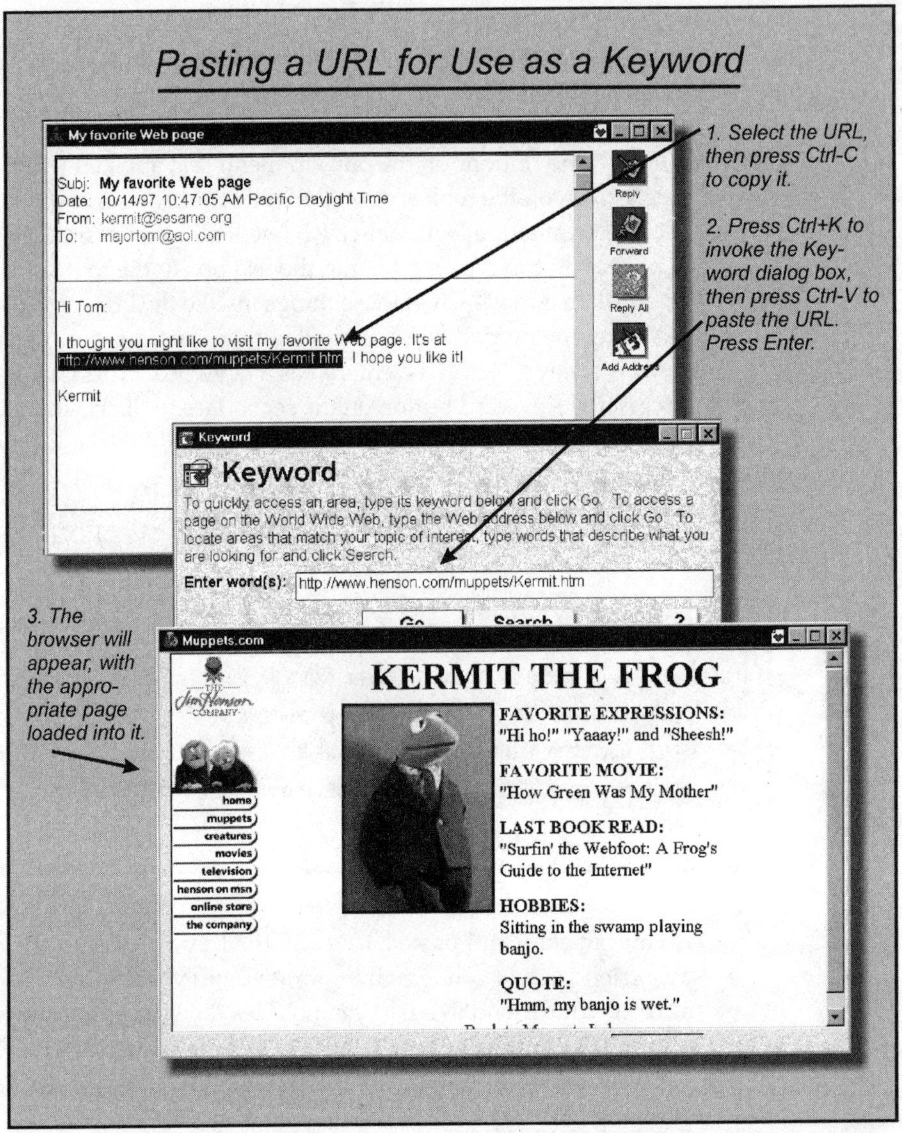

Figure 4-7: Our favorite method of accessing the Web: using URLs as keywords.

Pasting a URL for Use as a Keyword

1. Select the URL, then press Ctrl-C to copy it.

2. Press Ctrl+K to invoke the Keyword dialog box, then press Ctrl-V to paste the URL. Press Enter.

3. The browser will appear, with the appropriate page loaded into it.

Home Pages

A *home page*, according to QUE's Computer and Internet Dictionary (keywords: **Que's Dictionary**), is "...a document intended to serve as an initial point of entry to a web of related documents. Also called a welcome page, a home page contains general introductory information, as well as hyperlinks to related resources. A well-designed home page contains internal navigation buttons, which help users find their way among the various documents that the home page makes available."

In other words, a home page is the first page you see when you visit a site. Most sites have a number of linked pages—the "web of related documents" the dictionary refers to. The home page usually offers some mechanism to access the remaining pages: a menu, a map, or a toolbar. Domestic diva Martha Stewart's home page (**http://www.marthastewart.com**), for example, offers little more than a greeting message and a picture of a front door (Figure 4-8). To explore the remainder of her site, you click the door.

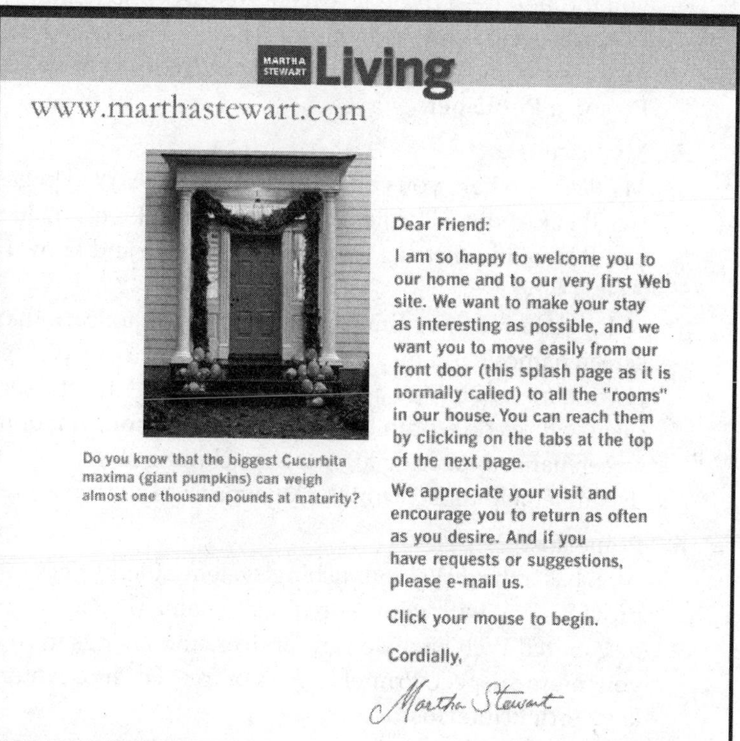

MARTHA STEWART Living
www.marthastewart.com
Do you know that the biggest Cucurbita maxima (giant pumpkins) can weigh almost one thousand pounds at maturity?
Dear Friend:
I am so happy to welcome you to our home and to our very first Web site. We want to make your stay as interesting as possible, and we want you to move easily from our front door (this splash page as it is normally called) to all the "rooms" in our house. You can reach them by clicking on the tabs at the top of the next page.
We appreciate your visit and encourage you to return as often as you desire. And if you have requests or suggestions, please e-mail us.
Click your mouse to begin.
Cordially,
Martha Stewart

Figure 4-8: Perhaps the very definition of a "home" page, Martha Stewart's home page is little more than a hello and a door. The door—which changes with the season—opens to admit visitors to the site.

Three Men in a Tub

It all depends on how much of a dweeb you want to be. Most of the people you meet on the street would pronounce WWW as "double-you, double-you, double-you," which is a mouthful, especially when you're trying to say it quickly. Dweebs (or people trying to be 'hipper than thou'), however, say "dub dub dub." Dweebness is a delicate thing. Pocket protectors and horn-rim glasses might be taking it a bit too far, but saying "dub dub dub" is probably okay, even among non-dweebs.

Your Personal Home Page As a member of America Online, you can have your own Web site, with your own home page. AOL even offers a number of tools to help you construct and maintain it.

- Personal Publisher
  Personal Publisher is an area within AOL where you can create your own World Wide Web home page and post it online for others to see. Construction of a Web page can be a daunting task, but Personal Publisher walks you through it—a tutorial-driven experience something like Microsoft's Wizards—and soon enough you'll have a Web page you can call your own. There's no charge for this service. To learn more, use the keywords: **Personal Publisher.**

- My Place
  My Place is where you can post more complex Web pages and FTP files (we'll talk about FTP later in this chapter). There's no hand-holding here; you'll have to construct your own Web page and know how to upload to AOL's server.

  If you know these things, you'll be happy to learn that each of your screen names has 2 megabytes of storage for your Web pages and supporting materials, and again there's no charge for the service. Your Web page will reside within the **http://members.aol.com/** domain, with your screen name appearing after the concluding slash. Look for My Place (and its ample help files) using the keywords: **My Place**.

- PrimeHost
  AOL has a third Web publishing system called *PrimeHost*. PrimeHost provides you with your own domain name (i.e., www.yourbusiness.com), discounted Web page design services, and listings in 20 search engines. As you might suspect, PrimeHost is not free. For more information, see keyword: **PrimeHost**.

- AOL Press
  AOL also offers Web page development software called *AOL Press.* The software accommodates tables, scripts, and a number of multimedia features. Incredibly, AOL Press is also free. Find it at keywords: **AOL Press**.

Everyone's a Star

Using My Place and AOL Press, both Jennifer and Tom have constructed personal Web pages. Jennifer has a Web page at **http://members.aol.com/jennifer** and Tom's is at **http://members.aol.com/majortom**. Jennifer's page offers a tour of her bathroom (*ahem!*); Tom's page takes you aboard his boat. Both pages offer information about our dogs, a synchronicity we never arranged.

Your Default Home Page Your *default home page* (see Figure 4-9) is the page your browser automatically displays when it's first invoked. Unless you tell it otherwise, the built-in browser defaults to AOL's NetFind page on the Web—the one pictured in Figure 4-6.

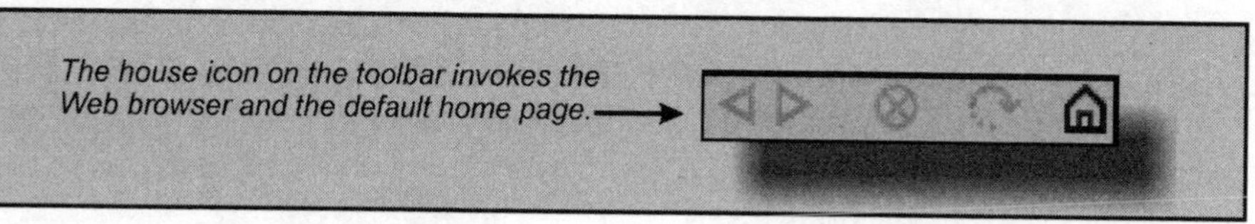

The house icon on the toolbar invokes the Web browser and the default home page.

Figure 4-9: Click the house icon on the toolbar to display your default home page. The keyword: **Web** will do the same thing.

You can change the built-in browser's default home page. Though AOL's NetFind page is a great jumping-off point, it's a complex page, and complex pages take time to load. It's also on the Web, and anything accessed on the Web is slow compared to, say, things stored on your hard disk, especially during periods of peak Web usage.

To change your default home page, click the My AOL icon on the toolbar and then choose Preferences. You can do this offline. Click the WWW button and then click the Navigation tab (see Figure 4-10).

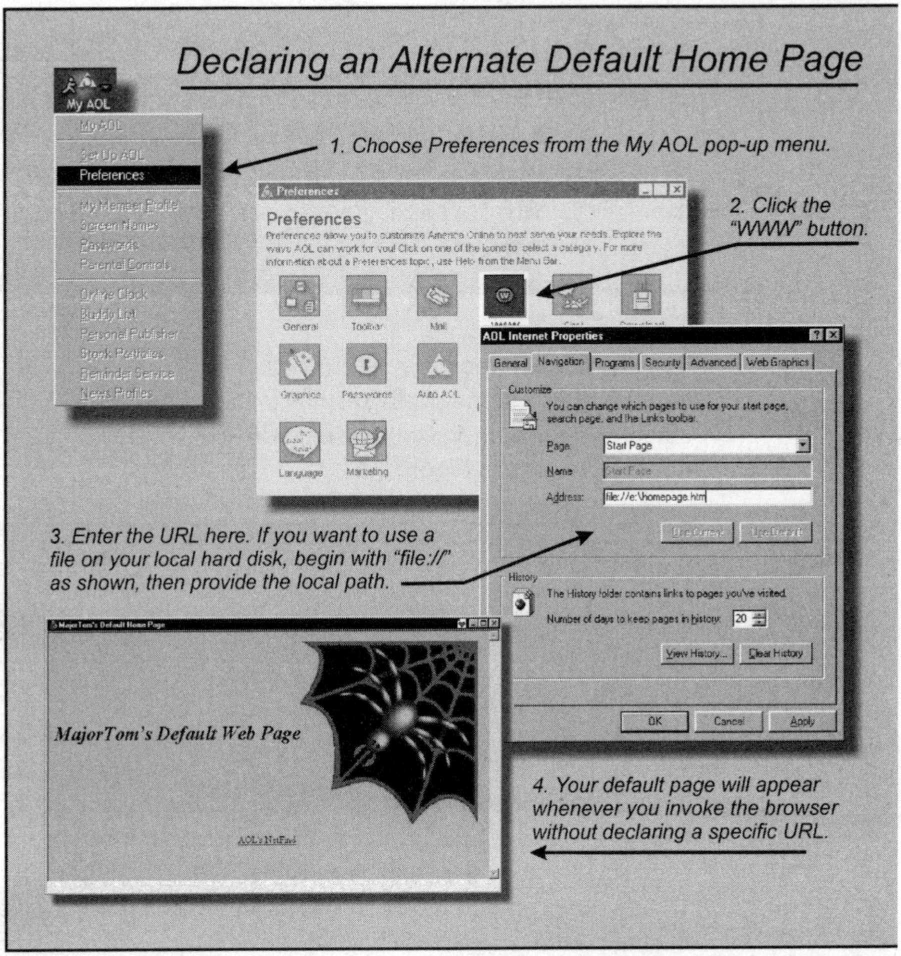
Declaring an Alternate Default Home Page
1. Choose Preferences from the My AOL pop-up menu.
2. Click the "WWW" button.
3. Enter the URL here. If you want to use a file on your local hard disk, begin with "file://" as shown, then provide the local path.
4. Your default page will appear whenever you invoke the browser without declaring a specific URL.
MajorTom's Default Web Page

Figure 4-10: You can change your default home page to any Web page you like—including one stored on your hard disk.

If you would like to reference a Web page you've stored on your hard disk, look carefully at the address in the AOL Internet Properties window pictured in Figure 4-10. The file:// prefix there tells the browser to access a file on your hard disk rather than one on the Web. Fill in a path pointing to a local file (see the example in Figure 4-10) after the double slashes.

Forward & Back

Browsing the Web is often an exploratory venture, and like any exploration, you will encounter a number of dead ends on your journey on the Web. When you start down a path you'd rather back out of, just click the Back arrow on the toolbar (see Figure 4-11). The Back arrow backs you out of the page on your screen and displays the page you viewed previously.

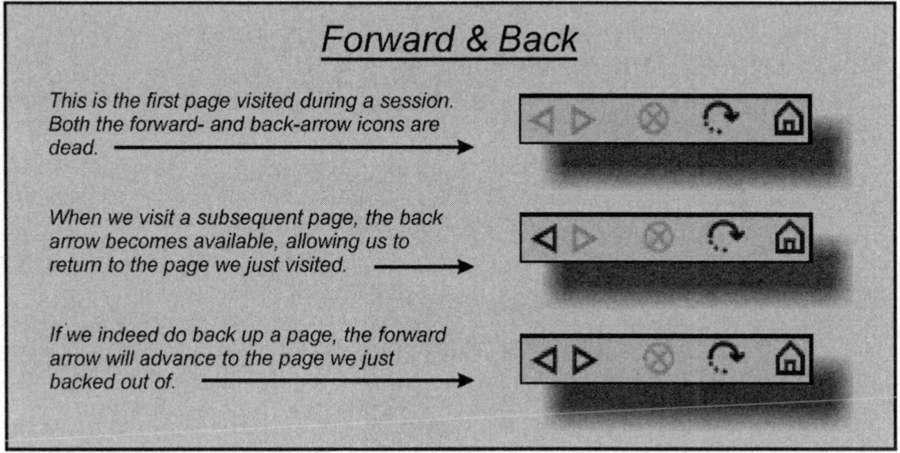

Figure 4-11: Navigate forward and back along the path you're following with the Forward and Back arrows on the secondary toolbar.

You can back up as much as you want with the Back arrow—until you reach the first page you viewed during the session. Once you've backed up, you can go forward again using the forward arrow, revisiting the pages you just backed out of. The Forward arrow is only available if you've backed up, of course.

The History Trail

The Forward and Back arrows are always linear: using them, you will retrace your steps, one step at a time, in the order (or reverse order) in which you originally took them.

But what if you want to revisit a place you visited 10 or 12 steps back? Perhaps you checked the news, then 2 or 3 weather pages, and now you want to go back to the news page again. How do you do that?

It's easy: just pull down the *history trail* available on the toolbar (see Figure 4-12).

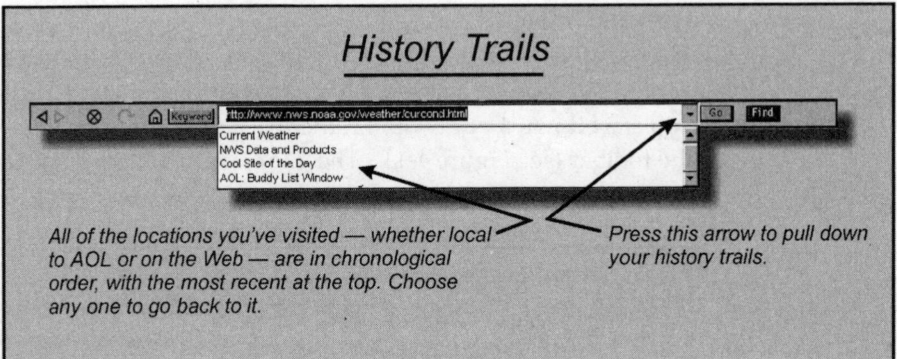

History Trails
Http://www.nws.noaa.gov/weather/curcond.html
Current Weather
NWS Data and Products
Cool Site of the Day
AOL: Buddy List Window
All of the locations you've visited — whether local to AOL or on the Web — are in chronological order, with the most recent at the top. Choose any one to go back to it.
Press this arrow to pull down your history trails.

Figure 4-12: You can revisit any location you've visited during a session—whether it's on the Web or local to AOL—by choosing the site from the pull-down history trail on the secondary toolbar.

A few notes about the history trail:

- The trail is only available when you're online.
- The trail lists not only Web sites you've visited, but AOL sites you've visited as well.
- While only 16 sites appear on the trail at a time, it *is* a scroll box. If you need to visit an ancient site (sounds like archaeology…), scroll down. It'll be there.
- History trails are unique to screen names, but they're remembered. If you change screen names you'll have access to the trail most recently visited by the changed-to screen name. When you return to the screen name you were previously using, you'll again see the sites visited by *that* name.
- The history trail doesn't clear until you exit the software, so the sites you visited during an earlier session are available even if you sign off and sign back on again, just as long as the client remains loaded in memory.
- Use history trails to retry Web sites that are sluggish: stop the sluggish site (we'll discussing stopping in a moment), visit some other places, and then use the history trail to try the sluggish Web site again.

Nothing Magical

There's nothing magical about a Web site: it's just a collection of files on a computer (called a *server*) connected to the Web, configured to respond to requests for information. While some sites are powered by stellar arrays of mainframe computers, many others are little PCs not unlike the one you're using. Although large sites can handle thousands of connections (*hits*) at a time (AOL's Web site handles 350 million hits a day), some smaller sites become bogged down when the number of connections goes to double digits.

Traffic at Web sites comes and goes, sometimes dramatically changing the sites' ability to respond—especially the smaller ones. A site that wasn't responding half an hour ago might perk up if you try it again now.

The time of day makes a difference too. In the evening—especially after 6:00 P.M. Eastern Time—millions of anxious people are connected to the Net, impatient as a kindergarten class at an art museum. Like visiting any popular attraction, you might find yourself "standing in line" to access a popular Web site. To avoid this, do your surfing during another time of the day.

Stopping a Page

If you read the "Nothing Magical" sidebar, you know that some Web sites can be frustratingly slow at certain times of the day. At times like this, after watching the AOL logo at the right end of the toolbar glitter for a few minutes, it's tempting to think unflattering thoughts about America Online. Your frustration, however, is probably rooted in the site (or the Internet), not AOL.

Frustration is what the Stop icon on the toolbar is for (see Figure 4-13). If a page seems unreasonably slow, don't be lenient. If activity isn't forthcoming within 15 seconds or so after you've declared the URL, the site is slow—stop loading the page (by clicking the Stop icon) and do something else online. (We use unread mail for little time fillers like this.) Later—even if it's only 10 minutes later—use your history trail to try the site again.

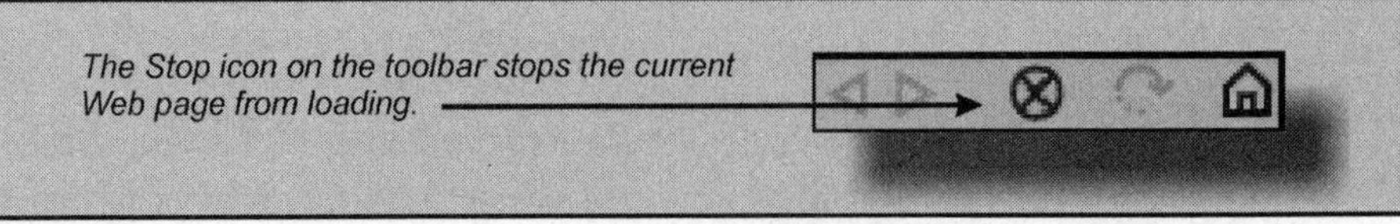

The Stop icon on the toolbar stops the current Web page from loading.

Figure 4-13: Don't tolerate slow Web sites. Stop them, do something else for a while, and then try again.

Reloading a Page

In spite of its youth—it's less than 10 years old, after all—the Web frequently exhibits Alzheimer's-like symptoms. In the middle of a page, as if it forgot the subject of conversation, the Web will suddenly halt, staring off into space, waiting for Minnie and Mickey to stop by for tea. Nobody knows why the Web does this. For such a technical thing, the Web's uncannily organic sometimes. Things, it seems, occasionally slip its mind.

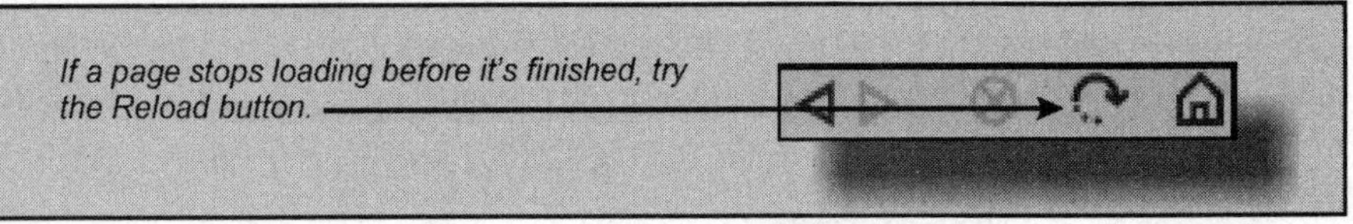

If a page stops loading before it's finished, try the Reload button.

Figure 4-14: The Reload button "tickles" stubborn Web pages, often succeeding in obtaining elements the first load could not.

If a page stops loading—if the AOL logo on the toolbar stops glittering and there is still stuff to come—try reloading the page. The Reload button (see Figure 4-14) is something of a poke in the Web's ribs: the browser will go out on the Web and fetch the page again, as if it had never arrived in the first place. Sometimes, a reload is all it takes to complete a page.

Printing a Page

Generally, Web pages print exactly as they're presented on the screen. If the designer had printing in mind, even page breaks will be properly placed.

To print a Web page, be sure the page occupies the active window; then choose Print from the File menu. Printing a Web page is no different than printing a page from your word processor or graphics program. You cannot print a Web page until it has loaded completely, and background elements generally don't print—a good thing—though everything else usually does.

Saving a Page

Many, though not all, Web pages can be saved to a local disk (see Figure 4-15). You have two choices: a page saved as text is suitable for loading into a word processor; a page saved as HTML is suitable for viewing in an HTML editor, such as AOL Press. This is a great way to get to learn Web page scripting.

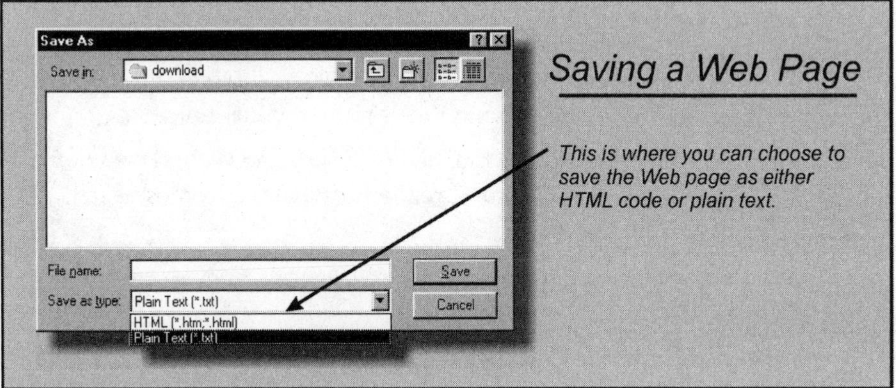

Figure 4-15: Choose Save As from the File menu to save a Web page.

One important note about saving: you cannot save graphics. The Save As dialog box allows you to save a page as text or HTML—which is itself text—but not graphics. There is a significant exception: if a page is nothing *but* a graphic—no text, no additional graphics—the Save As dialog box might allow you to save the graphic in the ART, GIF, or JPEG format. If these formats are offered, remember that the ART format is unique to AOL and is not available to other graphics programs. The other two are pretty much universal. Review Chapter 3 if you've forgotten the advantages and disadvantages of these formats.

How do you get a Web page that's nothing but a graphic? Try clicking on a graphic within a more complex page. Sometimes, graphics are links, and the links lead to the graphics themselves rather than pages that contain the graphic. If you see a graphic you love that you'd like to save (and you don't have any commercial intentions for it—anything published on the Web is copyrighted), try clicking on it to see if you can get the original. You just might.

Remember too, you can always use your Print Screen key to capture the whole screen and then paste it into some kind of graphics program. What you get will be what you see.

Using a Third-Party Browser

You've probably heard about the competition between (Netscape) Navigator and (Microsoft) Internet Explorer. Which browser is better?

We choose not to jump into the fray, and neither does AOL. If you don't like the version of Microsoft Internet Explorer that's built into the AOL client, use another one. Here's how:

1. Start the AOL client and sign on.
2. Start the browser of your choice.
3. Maximize the browser's window if you wish, but even if you don't, the AOL client will recede into the background. Your browser will load its default Web page, and you're ready to motor on down the information superhighway in the vehicle of your choice.
4. When you're finished browsing the Web, close your browser and the AOL client will return, ready for whatever comes next.

Favorite Places

As you explore the Web, you'll discover pages you'll want to return to on a regular basis. And when you return, you won't want to type their arcane URLs again and again from the keyboard. That's what the Favorite Places feature is for. Favorite Places is where you store references to the destinations you like to visit repeatedly: places that have become your favorites; places with addresses you don't like to type.

Like the Personal Filing Cabinet discussed in Chapter 3, Favorite Places is a hierarchical "filing cabinet," composed of folders and places (see Figure 4-16). You make the folders, you decide what to call them and where they go, and you determine the favorite places that go inside of them.

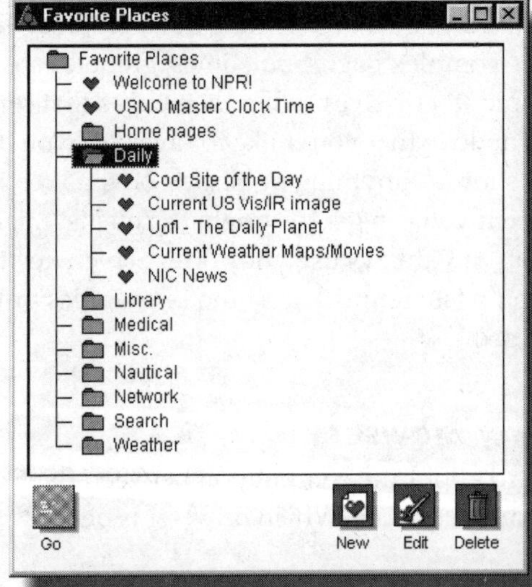

Figure 4-16: Tom's Favorite Places window. The Daily folder is open to reveal the places he likes to visit every day.

Adding Favorite Places

Of course, before you can have a Favorite Places list, you have to put some places on the list. This is where the hearts come in (see Figure 4-17).

Note that the Travelers Advantage Sweepstakes window pictured in Figure 4-17 is *not* a Web page. Although this is the Internet chapter, and though Travelers Advantage is an AOL-only feature, we want you to know that your favorite places are not limited to Web pages. Any window with a heart on it can become a favorite place, including those available only on AOL.

Figure 4-17: Any window that offers a little heart icon on its title bar is fair game for your Favorite Places list.

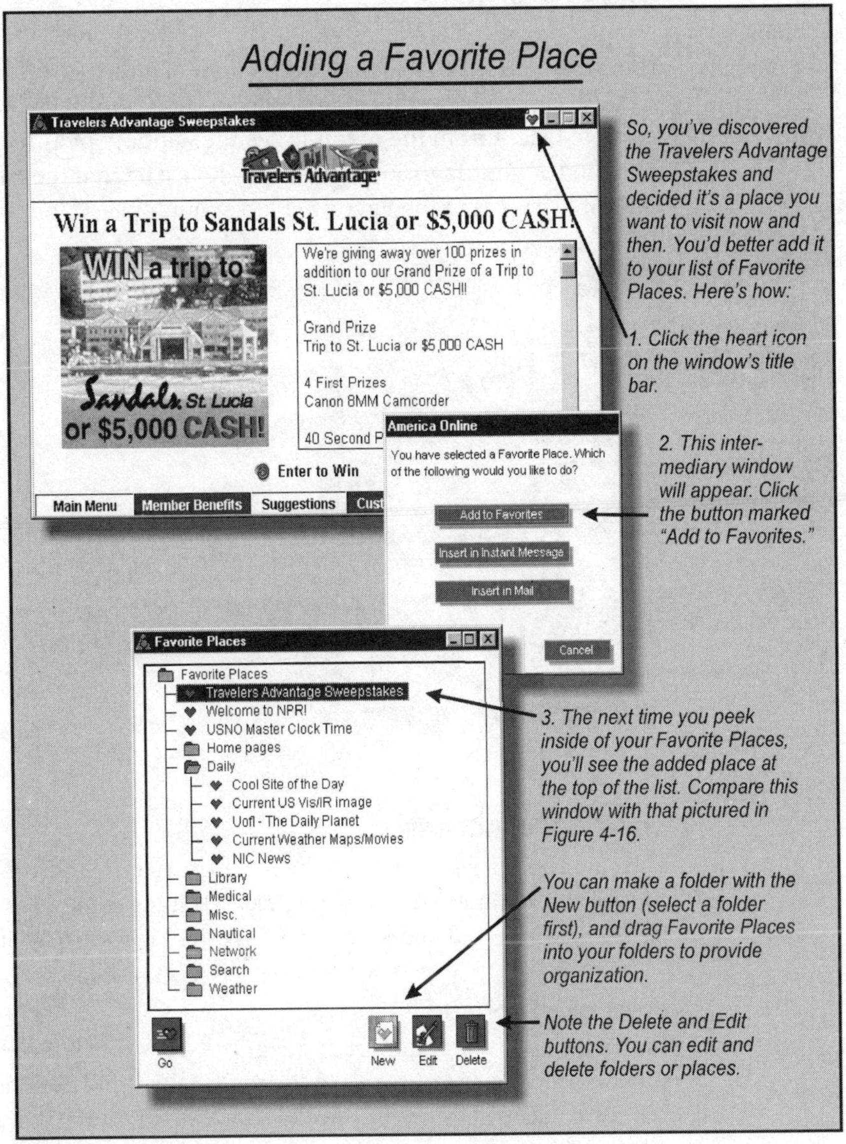

Adding a Favorite Place

So, you've discovered the Travelers Advantage Sweepstakes and decided it's a place you want to visit now and then. You'd better add it to your list of Favorite Places. Here's how:

1. Click the heart icon on the window's title bar.

2. This intermediary window will appear. Click the button marked "Add to Favorites."

3. The next time you peek inside of your Favorite Places, you'll see the added place at the top of the list. Compare this window with that pictured in Figure 4-16.

You can make a folder with the New button (select a folder first), and drag Favorite Places into your folders to provide organization.

Note the Delete and Edit buttons. You can edit and delete folders or places.

Heartless?

You say you can't find hearts on your Web page's title bars? They *all* have them, so if you can't find them, you've probably maximized the browser's window. Just click its Restore button (the square-within-a-square above the AOL logo) and you'll see the heart.

Using Favorite Places

To open the Favorite Places window, click the Favorites button on the toolbar. You can do this at any time, whether you're online or off. Your Favorite Places will appear in a hierarchical menu format (see Figure 4-18), or you can choose Favorite Places from the menu to see the window pictured in Figure 4-16. To go to one of your favorite places, just choose it from the Favorite Places menu or double-click it in the Favorite Places window.

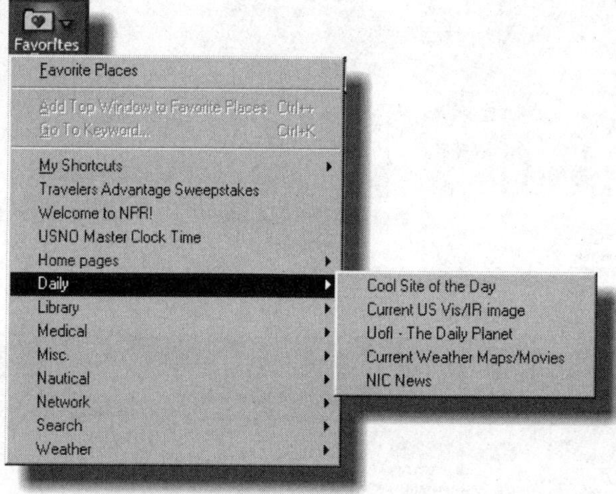

Figure 4-18: Your favorite places are also available in menu format by clicking on the Favorites button on the toolbar. If you want the maintenance commands pictured in Figure 4-16—New, Edit, Delete—you'll need to choose Favorite Places from this menu.

Immediate Access

The Favorite Places window—the one pictured in Figure 4-16—provides controls for maintenance of your places, but it's somewhat inconvenient in terms of access, and access is what Favorite Places are all about.

Keystroke Shortcuts

The pull-down menu pictured in Figure 4-18 is much more accessible, but you still have to mouse your way to the toolbar and pull a menu down to get there. What we really need are keystroke shortcuts to our favorite places—and we can have them. To assign these keystroke shortcuts, pull down the menu under the Favorites button on the toolbar and then choose My Shortcuts | Edit Shortcuts. There you'll find the places assigned to each of the 10 editable keyboard shortcuts, Ctrl+1 through Ctrl+0 (see Figure 4-19). (For the Mac, these would be Command+1 through Command+0.)

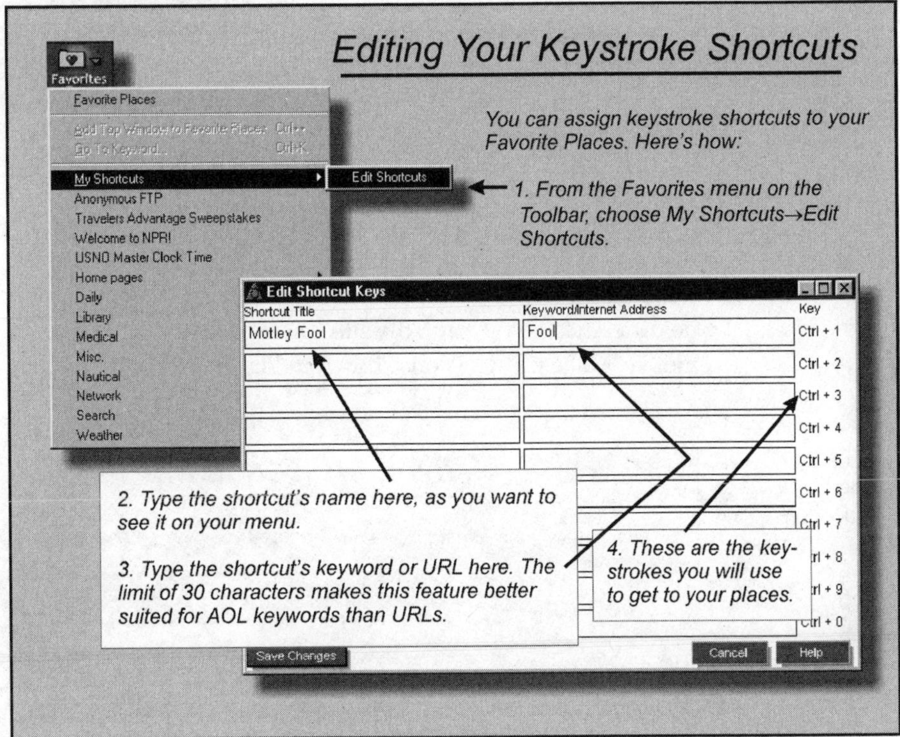

Figure 4-19: Assign keystroke shortcuts to those places you need to get to in a hurry.

Don't feel obliged to keep the default keyboard shortcuts AOL provides, by the way. You can delete theirs and substitute yours whenever you like.

Changing Toolbar Icons

The ultimate in immediate access is toolbar icons, and like keystroke shortcuts, you have control over a limited number of them.

It all depends on the resolution and size of your screen. A standard VGA screen—640 by 480 pixels—has no room for any extra icons on the toolbar, but a Super VGA screen—600 by 800 pixels—has room for three, and an EGA screen—1024 by 768 pixels—has room for seven.

To add icons to your toolbar, you might first have to remove some of those that are already there. Only those appearing against the dark background—those to the immediate left of the AOL logo—can be removed. Remove them by *right*-clicking (or Option-clicking) on them. A one-element menu will appear (see Figure 4-20); use it to remove any icon you don't want.

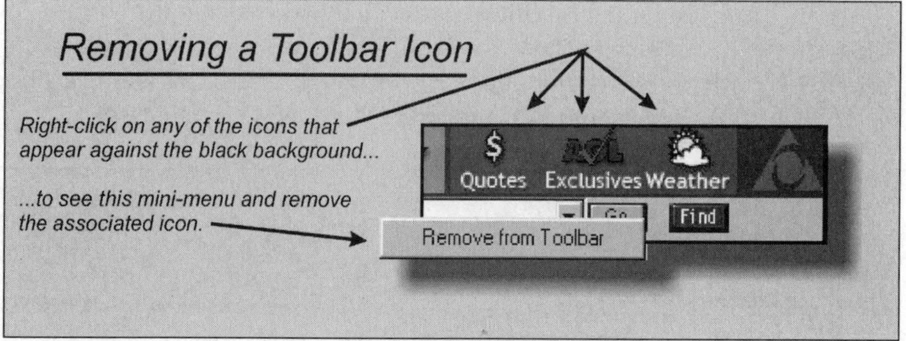

Figure 4-20: Right-click on toolbar icons to remove them.

Once an icon has been removed, you can fill its "hole" by going online and navigating your way to the site you want to add to the toolbar. (The site, by the way, can be any site with a heart on its toolbar—Web site or AOL site, it makes no difference.) Now drag the site's heart icon to the toolbar and release the mouse. Make the decisions shown in Figure 4-21 and *voilà*, you have a new icon.

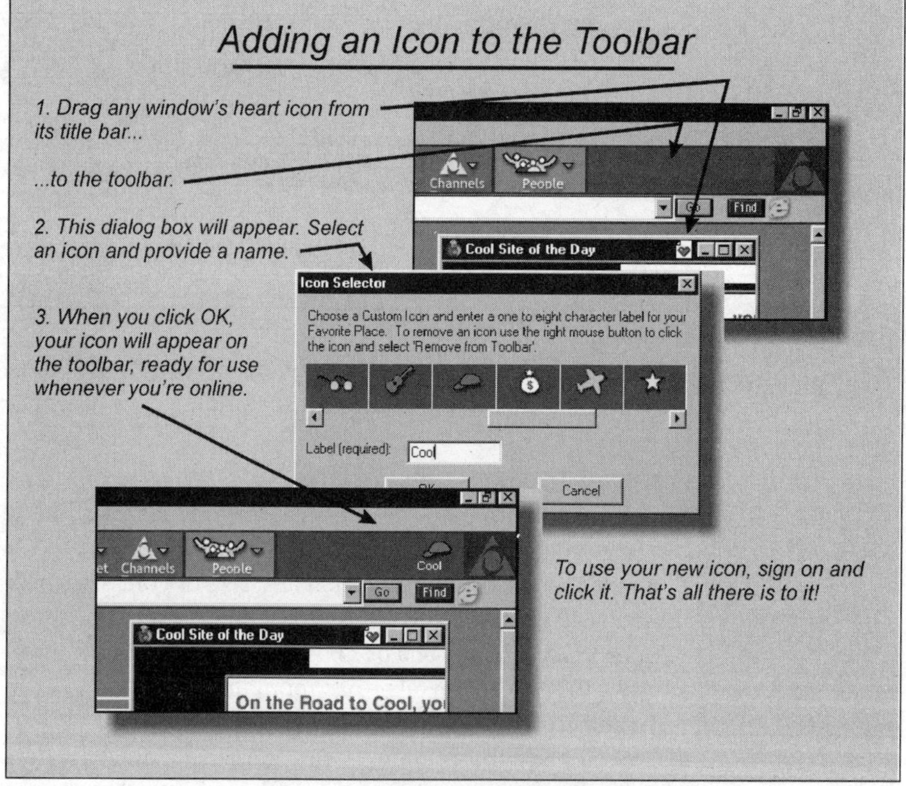

Figure 4-21: Drag and drop title-bar hearts to add icons to the toolbar.

Backing Up Favorite Places

You might recall our discussion of the Personal Filing Cabinet in Chapter 3. The Personal Filing Cabinet has its own facility for backing up data, so we didn't discuss technicalities, like where it's located on your local disk.

In fact, all of your personal data—your Personal Filing Cabinet, your Address Book, and your Favorite Places—is contained in the Organize subdirectory of the America Online 4.0 directory (your AOL directory may have another name; look around) on your hard disk. You will find a number of files within the Organize subdirectory, each composed of one of your screen names. These are the files you should back up if you want to back up your Address Book or your Favorite Places.

To back up Tom's MajorTom file, for example, Tom simply copies the MajorTom file in his Organize subdirectory to a floppy disk. If he should lose the data on his hard disk, he simply copies the MajorTom file from the floppy back to the Organize subdirectory. The next time he runs the AOL client, everything is intact up to the date he last backed up.

Mailing Lists

Internet *mailing lists* are something of a cross between Ed McMahon and Rush Limbaugh (a vivid, if not particularly adept, analogy if there ever was one).

Mailing lists are like Ed McMahon in that they arrive in your mailbox frequently and seemingly unbidden. They're like Rush Limbaugh in that they accept material from listeners (subscribers in this case) and broadcast those contributions to everyone else on the list. Mailing lists are where people discuss issues of common interest. There are thousands of lists, and the issues range from ablation to zymurgy.

What Is a Mailing List?

An Internet mailing list is, quite simply, a vehicle by which e-mail messages sent to the list are broadcast (via e-mail) to all members of the list, complete with the sender's identity. Indeed, many lists are run by machines that simply route everything sent to them to the entire list membership in the form of e-mail. Some lists are riveting; some lists are wearisome; some lists are mesmerizing one day and humdrum the other.

America Online offers a direct line to its Internet mailing list feature; just use the keywords: **Mailing Lists** (see Figure 4-22).

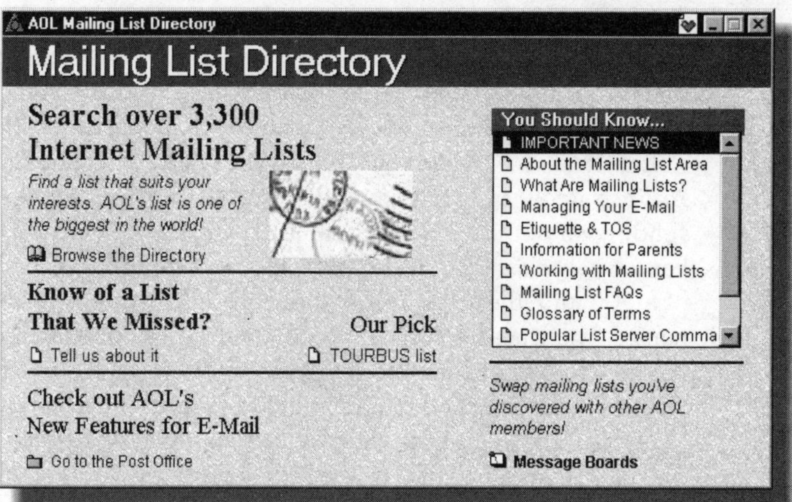

Figure 4-22: The keywords: **Mailing Lists** provide access to Internet mailing list information, including a searchable database of lists currently available.

Sorry, Ed

Internet mailing lists are not like the mailing lists used by Ed McMahon and his colleagues for marketing purposes. In fact, most Internet mailing lists discourage commercial posts. Although there are Internet mailing lists that may discuss such topics as advertising, business, and the Internet, they *discuss* these topics—they're not advertising vehicles per se.

Finding a Mailing List

AOL offers a searchable directory of lists (see Figure 4-23) called, officially, the America Online Mailing List Directory. Colloquially, it's known as AOL's "list of lists." To get there, click the Browse the Directory icon shown in Figure 4-23 (then, if you want, add the resulting Web page to your Favorite Places). Spend some time exploring the directory: if you search the list descriptions by content, you'll discover all kinds of interesting things. A search using the criterion *flying*, for example, produces all the lists with the word *flying* in their descriptions, including "high-flying" and "flying by the seat of your pants." While searches like this can drift off the subject quickly, you never know what gems you'll unearth.

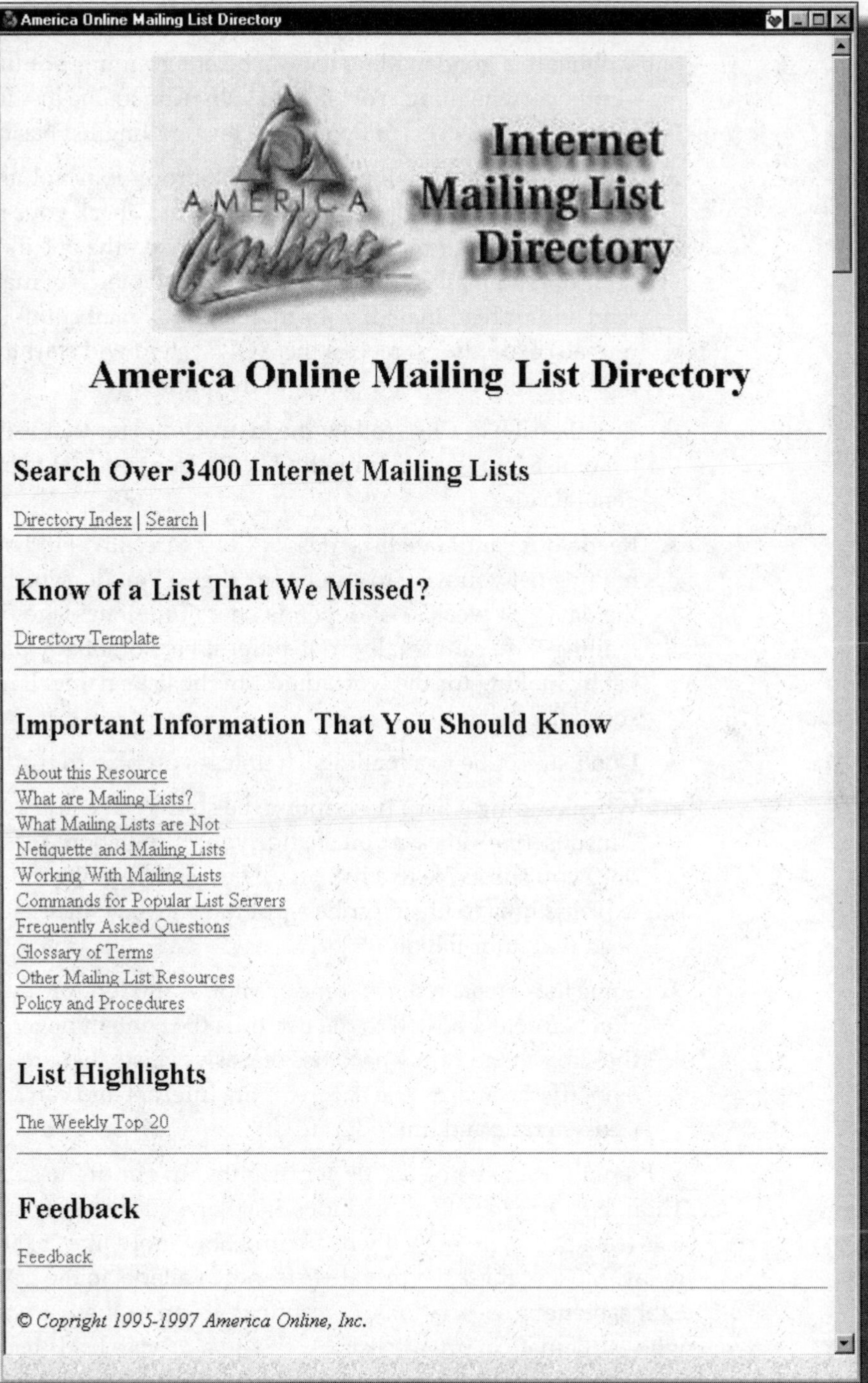

Figure 4-23: To search AOL's "list of lists," click the Search link on the Mailing List Web page.

Subscribing to a Mailing List

Subscribing to a good mailing list can be entertaining, stimulating, enlightening—and overwhelming. You should subscribe to one just for the experience. Before you do, however, understand a few mailing list basics:

- It's not unusual for a list to generate a prodigious volume of mail. For this reason, it is important that you sign on and check your mailbox often to avoid losing your mail. Your AOL mailbox—the one in Virginia, where your unread mail is held—is limited to 550 pieces of mail, including both read and unread mail. If your total mailbox mail count (both read and unread) exceeds 550 pieces, the AOL system will start to delete excess mail, starting with read mail and then unread mail.
- To subscribe to a list, follow the instructions for that list included in the list of lists. Subscription methods vary from one list to another. There's no general rule.
- Read your candidate lists' descriptions carefully. Find out whether any mailing list you wish to join has a "digest" mode, which compiles all of the day's (or week's—it depends on volume) messages into a single mailing. You can usually spot a digest version of any particular mailing list by looking for the word digest in the list's name. If a digest is offered, subscribe to it.
- Don't subscribe to a mailing list unless you plan to read it.
- When reading a list's description, be sure to take note of how to "unsubscribe" in case you change your mind about receiving it. (Often, once you subscribe to a list, you'll be a sent a confirming message that also explains how to unsubscribe—put this message in a safe place in case you need that information.)
- Some lists are *moderated*; some are not. A moderator reviews each submission before it's posted to the list, thus the content never strays too far off the subject and rarely becomes offensive. Lists that are not moderated embody the anarchistic nature of the Internet and can become quite idiosyncratic and immoderate.

Frankly, we're being a little shortsighted in our discussion of lists so far. Though AOL's list of lists includes 3,000 or 4,000 publicly accessible mailing lists (review Figure 4-22), there are probably more like 25,000 lists on the Net today. Most of these are private lists, not available to the general public. Clubs, owners' associations, investment groups—these are the kinds of people who participate in private lists. Access to a private list is usually by invitation.

If you're just starting out and you're a little hungry for e-mail, subscribing to a mailing list—especially a dynamic, dialogue-oriented list—is a quick way to populate your mailbox. You'll meet people there too, people with whom you share an interest. Mailing lists are a great way to feel as if you belong on the Net.

There's a funny thing about mailing lists. Most of us go through an Internet cycle: we begin by jumping into everything online with both feet. We join lists, recruit pen pals, and browse the Web incessantly. Eventually, however, we discover that our non-virtual lives—family, friends, jobs—are decaying; we reevaluate ourselves and pull back from the Internet, sticking with only the two or three most valuable contacts we've made there. Invariably, a few of the artifacts are mailing lists. Mailing lists are often the most provocative and inestimable contacts we make on the Internet, second only to e-mail. In an era of technoglitter, they're frequently overlooked by newcomers to the Net, but like old friends, they're often the only thing that matters when the blush is off the rose.

Newsgroups

Newsgroups (see Figure 4-24) are similar to mailing lists in that they provide forums for the free exchange of ideas, opinions, and comments, usually confined to a specific field of interest. You visit a newsgroup, read the messages you find there, reply to those that inspire a response, post new messages when you have a new topic to propose, and come back another day to see what responses you've provoked.

Unlike mailing lists, no mail is involved with newsgroups, and you needn't subscribe—you can drop into and out of newsgroups with little more than a few clicks of your mouse. Most activity occurs while you're online, including reading and responding to postings. Thus, some will say that newsgroups are more immediate, more interactive, and more conversational than mailing lists. Newsgroups or mailing lists? For most it's a matter of preference. You probably will want to dabble in both for a while.

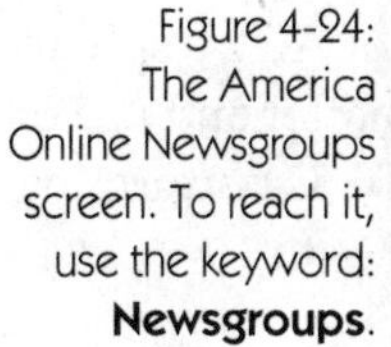

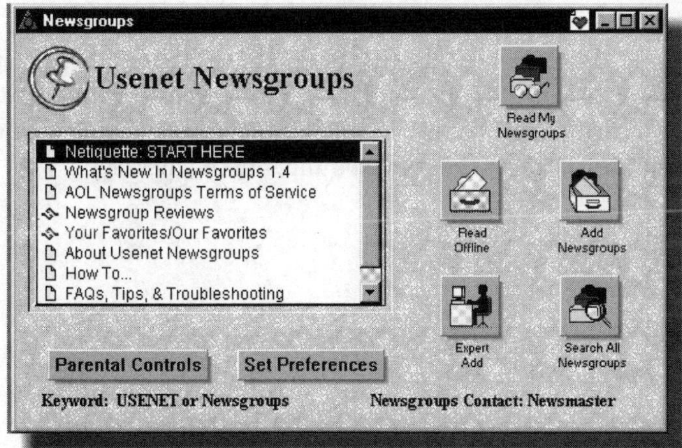

Figure 4-24: The America Online Newsgroups screen. To reach it, use the keyword: **Newsgroups**.

There are tens of thousands of newsgroups on the Internet. The number has been doubling or tripling every year and if it keeps it up, we'll have more than half a million of them by the turn of the century.

One thing's for sure: few newsgroups have anything to do with the news. Newsgroups aren't groups assembled to discuss *Washington Week in Review.* This is an anarchy: there are no restrictions whatsoever on newsgroup topics. That's why there are thousands of them.

What's Usenet?

You'll often hear newsgroups referred to as Usenet. There's a good reason for that. Newsgroups began as a number of sites (not a network per se) that agreed to the protocols described by Usenet. It's not that the original Usenauts had anything against the Internet; they were experimenting, and they preferred to experiment independently, where privacy was assured and failure didn't threaten the academic or military communities.

The experiment was successful, as we all know, and eventually most (though not all) newsgroups migrated to the Internet. The Usenet name remains, however, a vestige of the past, like the "trunk" of a car.

Here's a sidebar within a sidebar: In fact, not all newsgroups participate in Usenet. Many are accessed through gnUSENET, a peculiar circular acronym, meaning "GnUSENET is Not USENET." Anarchy prevails, even when faced with order.

The Internet doesn't have a monopoly on newsgroups. America Online has hundreds of them, though AOL prefers to call them message boards (which we discuss in Chapter 7, "Chat"). They're all the same, and they all exist to satisfy our passion for discourse. Accordingly, newsgroups are arguably the most popular resource on the Internet.

And they *are* an Internet resource, meaning they're outside of AOL's sphere of influence. No one polices the Internet. Newsgroup subject matter and use of language are appropriate to the Internet anarchy. In a way, AOL is performing a service similar to that of the telephone company when it comes to newsgroups: AOL is just the medium, not the message.

Because newsgroups are an Internet resource, AOL's own internal Terms of Service (TOS) don't apply. There are guidelines, however, and AOL's Usenet Newsgroups TOS is a codification of these guidelines. The Usenet TOS is always available in the list box at the keyword: **Newsgroups**, where it's called AOL Newsgroups Terms of Service. Be sure to read it—it might save you considerable newsgroup face. Another good place to turn is keyword: **Netiquette**, which discusses the whole issue of Internet etiquette in greater detail.

The Learning Curve of Sisyphus

Don't let the magnitude of the Internet overwhelm you. Tens of thousands of newsgroups aren't stifling, they're liberating. Electronic Frontier cofounder John Barlow once wrote, "On the most rudimentary level there is simply terror of feeling like an immigrant in a place where your children are natives—where you're always going to be behind the eight-ball because they can develop the technology faster than you can learn it. It's what I call the leaning curve of Sisyphus. And the only people who are going to be comfortable with that are people who don't mind confusion and ambiguity.... We've got a culture that's based on the ability of people to control everything. Once you start to embrace confusion as a way of life, concomitant with that is the assumption that you really don't control anything. At best it's a matter of surfing the whitewater."

Getting Help with Newsgroups

Help is never far away when you're using AOL's Internet features. A number of methods are available for accessing help—from AOL, from other members, or from the Internet community at large.

Online Help

Newsgroups take a bit of learning. We'll do our best to help you with that during the next few pages. AOL offers a mountain of help online, however—content that can be changed whenever the Internet staff wants to change it. These help files (see Figure 4-25), in other words, continually respond to suggestions from users as well as changes in the Net itself.

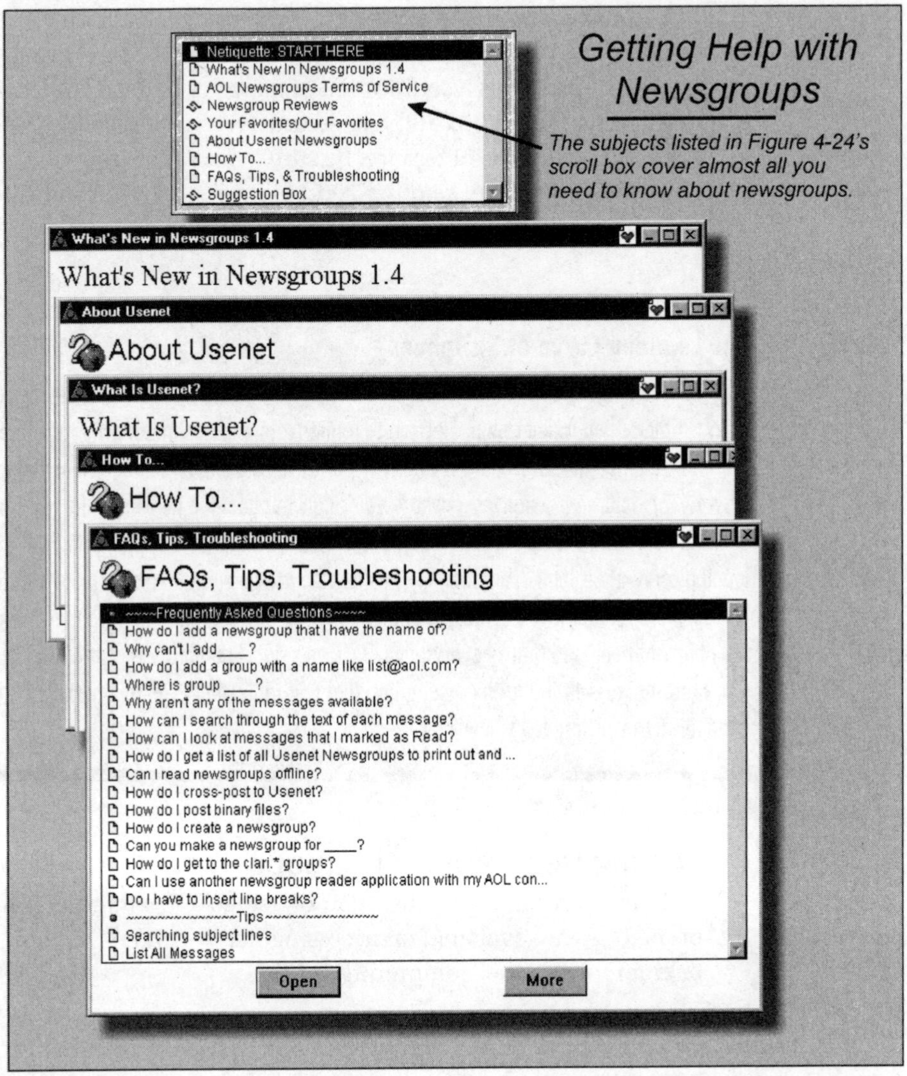

Figure 4-25: AOL's online help topics are always timely and relevant.

aol.newsgroups.help

Perhaps the most availing source of newsgroup help is a newsgroup itself. The aol.newsgroups.help newsgroup (it is part of the default newsgroup subscription list—you're probably already subscribed) is a great place to begin. This is the most active location for newsgroup assistance, and it's not broadcast throughout the Internet—your questions are only seen by fellow AOL members, and your responses will come from fellow AOL members. Peer assistance is often the most valuable source of help around.

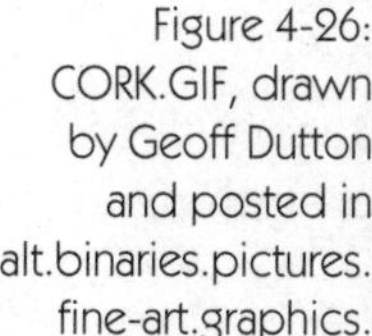

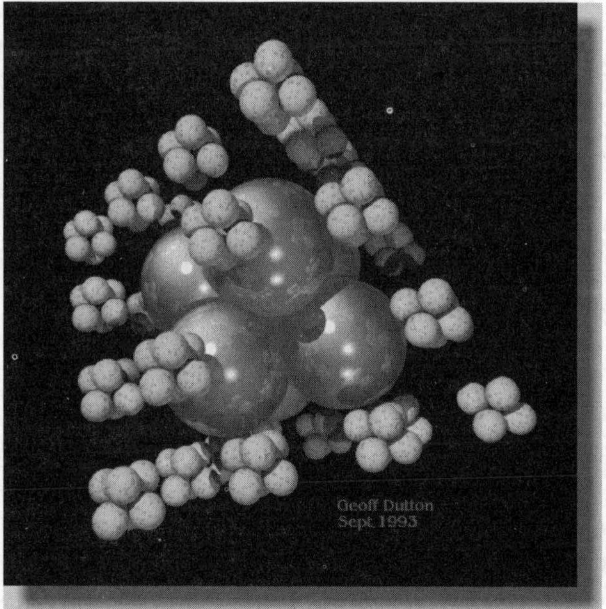

Figure 4-26: CORK.GIF, drawn by Geoff Dutton and posted in alt.binaries.pictures. fine-art.graphics.

Newsgroup Names

That striking image in Figure 4-26 was posted to **alt.binaries.pictures.fine-art.graphics**, a newsgroup where exceptional computer graphics are posted for the rest of us to enjoy.

The graphic, however, isn't the subject of our discussion. The newsgroup is. Specifically, the newsgroup's *name* is. Let's take a moment to dissect it.

Unlike e-mail addresses, newsgroup names go from the general to the specific as you read from left to right. Thus, in the name **alt.binaries.pictures.fine-art.graphics**, the term *alt* is the most general; the term *graphics* is the most specific.

Properly speaking, seven "official" categories of newsgroups exist on the Internet, along with a number of "alternative" ones. One of these categories always appears at the very beginning of a newsgroup name:

- **comp.** Newsgroups that discuss computer science and computers in general, including hardware and software.
- **news.** Groups concerned with newsgroups themselves. These include **news.newusers.questions** and **news.announce.newsgroups**. You are automatically subscribed to these groups. Please read them; it's the best way to become familiar with newsgroups.
- **rec.** Recreation, including hobbies and the arts.

- **sci.** Discussions of scientific research other than computer science.
- **soc.** Social issues. That's a *very* broad term, and so is this category. Topics range from **soc.women** to **soc.men**. (As you might expect, everything in between is available too.)
- **talk.** Debate and controversy ranging from the ridiculous (**talk.bizarre**) to the sublime (**talk.environment**).
- **misc.** Anything that doesn't fit into the categories above.

In addition to the seven conventional categories just listed, there are at least half a dozen *alternative* categories, but their inclusion among accessible newsgroups differs from site to site: some Internet sites carry them; some don't. They include the following:

- **alt.** Bizarre things are posted here, but you'll also find groups that simply have elected to bypass the bureaucratic process of formal inclusion in one of the preceding seven categories. Most alt groups, however, *are* alternative (and typically antic) in nature. Try **alt.barney.dinosaur.die.die.die** or **alt.swedish.chef.bork.bork.bork** for examples.
- **bit.** Redistributions of the more popular mailing lists, in newsgroup format. The *bit* refers to Bitnet, one of the academic networks that originally carried mailing lists.
- **biz.** Business-related groups.
- **clari.** The ClariNet system consists of commercial news systems such as UPI and the Associated Press. The stock exchanges are here as well. As you can imagine, this is a commercial resource that subscribers pay for. If you'd like a sample, try **biz.clarinet.sample**.

Back at our discussion of the newsgroup name **alt.binaries.pictures.fine-art.graphics**, the second part—**.binaries**—identifies this group as one where binary, rather than textual, information is posted. Binary information is usually composed of computer programs (you'll find a lot of binaries in the **comp**. newsgroups), but computer graphics are a close second. We'll discuss binary postings later in this chapter.

The third part of our **alt.binaries.pictures.fine-art.graphics** newsgroup name—**.pictures**—distinguishes this newsgroup name from other binary newsgroups, especially the programming newsgroups in **comp**.

The fourth part—**.fine-art**—identifies the nature of the pictures. There are cartoons on the Net, and ASCII pictures (remember the Christmas-tree graphics composed entirely of Xs?), and a number of others that simply don't qualify as fine arts. (The jury is still out on **alt.art.bodyart** and **alt.binaries.pictures.furry**. Try them and decide for yourself.)

Uuencoding

The newsgroup is a textual medium. Nontextual data—programs, spreadsheets, graphics, sounds—won't transfer from one machine to another via newsgroups without some uncommon maneuvering.

Impetus for the transfer of nontextual (binary) data was encountered early in the history of the Usenet. In its early days, many (perhaps most) of the machines on the Net ran the UNIX operating system, and UNIX programmers wanted to exchange programs with one another. For many of them, newsgroups were their only common link.

Enter *uuencoding*, the conversion of binary information to textual data and back again. The term stands for UNIX-to-UNIX encoding, but it's used by all systems now. Uuencoding is how binary information—graphics in particular—is shared via most newsgroups.

The bad news is that if you want to participate in a binary newsgroup—one where binary information is shared—you need a conversion program. The good news is that such a program is built in to the AOL system.

When AOL detects a binary newsgroup posting, it offers the options shown in Figure 4-27. You don't have to do anything; the dialog box pictured in Figure 4-27 appears automatically. You can choose to cancel the operation (unless you want the binary, canceling is a viable option; binaries are *long*); you can choose to download the article (which doesn't decode the posting); or you can choose to download the file (which decodes the file and saves it on your local disk).

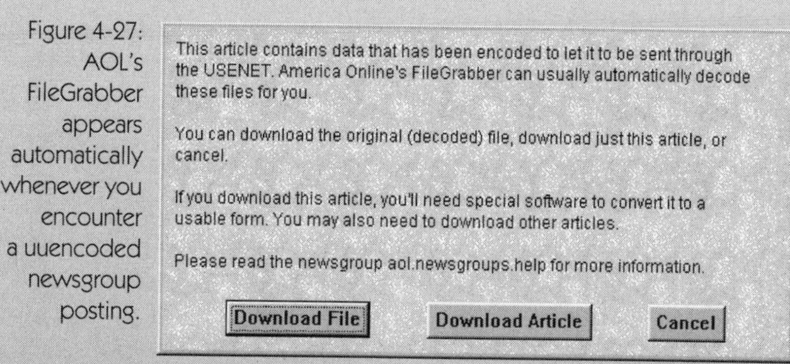

This article contains data that has been encoded to let it to be sent through the USENET. America Online's FileGrabber can usually automatically decode these files for you.

You can download the original (decoded) file, download just this article, or cancel.

If you download this article, you'll need special software to convert it to a usable form. You may also need to download other articles.

Please read the newsgroup aol.newsgroups.help for more information.

Download File | Download Article | Cancel

Figure 4-27: AOL's FileGrabber appears automatically whenever you encounter a uuencoded newsgroup posting.

Indeed, the *FileGrabber* (as it's called) will even display the binary—if it's a graphic—on your screen as it's being downloaded, providing you with the opportunity of canceling the download should you not like the picture you're receiving. Compared to the old days when we used to have to decode and view uuencoded graphics with a repertoire of programs, this is a piece of cake.

The final part—**.graphics**—distinguishes this newsgroup from **alt.binaries.pictures.fine-art.d**, where discussions of the postings (rather than the postings themselves) occur.

Most newsgroup names are self-explanatory once you've learned the conventions. The best way to learn the conventions is to browse through the list of active newsgroups. We'll discuss the list later in this chapter.

Finding Newsgroups

You probably don't want to subscribe to tens of thousands of newsgroups just to find one you like. That's a bit like standing under an avalanche to get ice for your tea. Subscribing to more than half a dozen exceeds the limits of human tolerance. The task of finding an appropriate few, then, is a high priority for us all.

Searching AOL's List

Naturally, there's a list of currently available newsgroups, and naturally, it's posted in a newsgroup (more about that later), but with tens of thousands of newsgroups, reading the list is a bit like inviting the population of China to dinner. What we really need is some form of database mechanism—preferably one that's convenient and free—by which we can search the list.

Take a look at Figure 4-28. Note specifically the Add Newsgroups and Search All Newsgroups buttons. These are your entry points to the list of newsgroups.

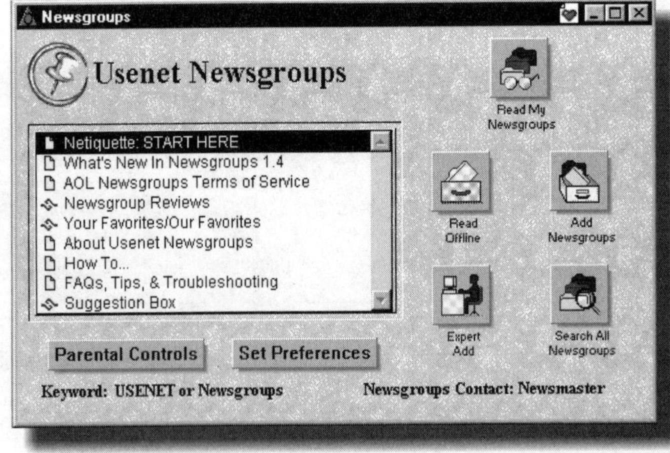

Figure 4-28: The Add Newsgroups and Search All Newsgroups buttons allow you to perform online searches of the tens of thousands of newsgroups available.

Add Newsgroups The Add Newsgroups button doesn't perform a search per se; it's more like navigating through a hierarchy of menus (see Figure 4-29). Its most useful feature is its ability to display actual messages from within a newsgroup without your having to subscribe to the newsgroup itself.

Not that subscribing to a newsgroup isn't revocable; it's just inconvenient when you're on a newsgroup scouting expedition to add a newsgroup to your list, read a message or two, and then remove the group from your list when you decide it's not to your liking. The Add Newsgroups feature eliminates the need to have to go through those hassles for each sampling.

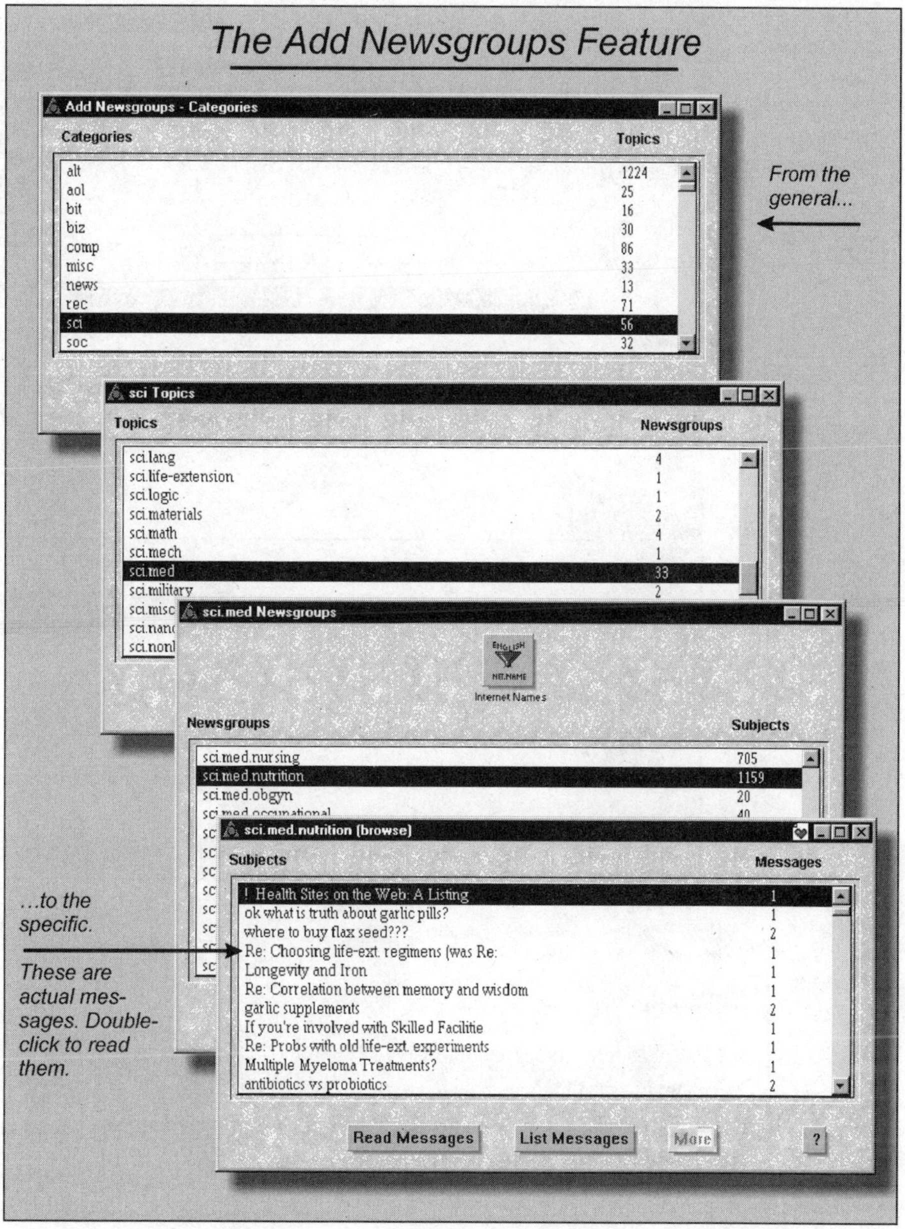

Figure 4-29: The Add Newsgroups feature allows you to peek at a group's messages without having to add the group to your list.

The Add Newsgroups Feature

Add Newsgroups - Categories

Categories	Topics
alt	1224
aol	25
bit	16
biz	30
comp	86
misc	33
news	13
rec	71
sci	56
soc	32

From the general...

sci Topics

Topics	Newsgroups
sci.lang	4
sci.life-extension	1
sci.logic	1
sci.materials	2
sci.math	4
sci.mech	1
sci.med	33
sci.military	2
sci.misc	
sci.nan	
sci.nonl	

sci.med Newsgroups

Internet Names

Newsgroups	Subjects
sci.med.nursing	705
sci.med.nutrition	1159
sci.med.obgyn	20
sci.med.occupational	40

sci.med.nutrition (browse)

Subjects	Messages
! Health Sites on the Web: A Listing	1
ok what is truth about garlic pills?	1
where to buy flax seed???	2
Re: Choosing life-ext. regimens (was Re:	1
Longevity and Iron	1
Re: Correlation between memory and wisdom	1
garlic supplements	2
If you're involved with Skilled Facilitie	1
Re: Probs with old life-ext. experiments	1
Multiple Myeloma Treatments?	1
antibiotics vs probiotics	2

Read Messages | List Messages | More | ?

...to the specific.

These are actual messages. Double-click to read them.

Search All Newsgroups Alternatively, you can search the list using the Search All Newsgroups button pictured in Figure 4-28. This button leads to a searchable online database of newsgroups that's not only complete, but also remarkably fast (see Figure 4-30).

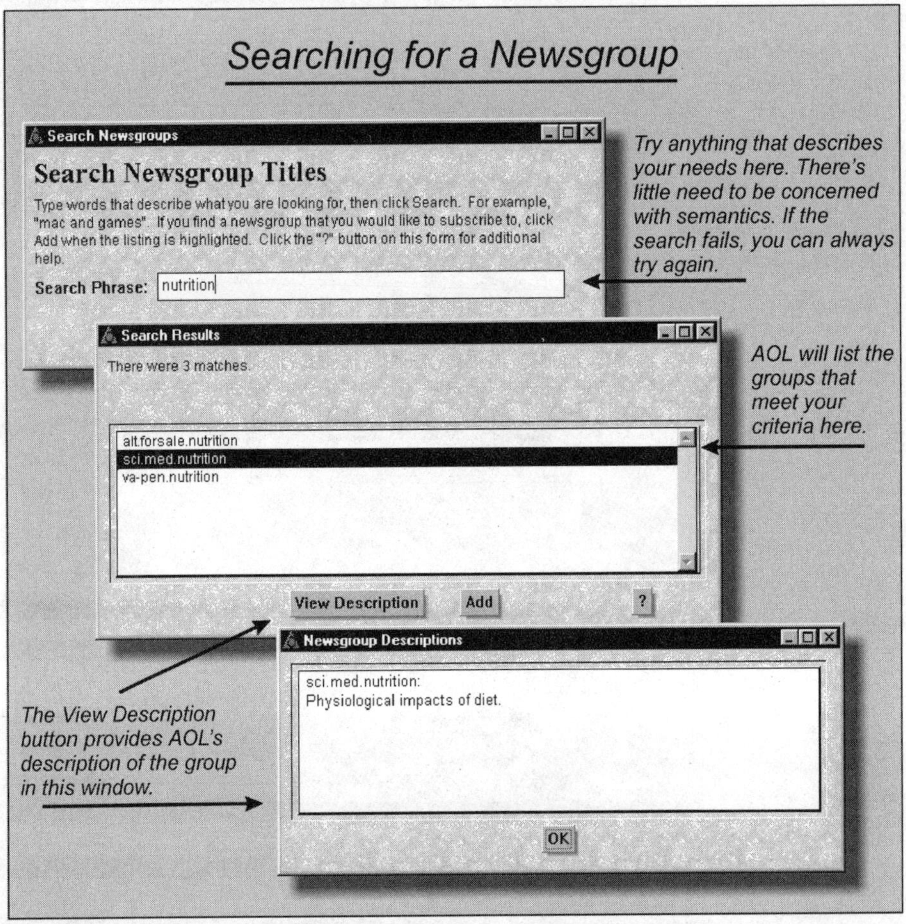

Figure 4-30: The Search All Newsgroups button allows you to conduct an online search for newsgroups that interest you.

Follow the Scent

The Search All Newsgroups feature stops short of offering individual messages for browsing. You might try using the Search All Newsgroups button to find the name of a specific newsgroup or two and then use the Add Newsgroups button to sniff through individual messages before actually adding the group to your list.

Using the Web to Find a Newsgroup

Frankly, AOL's newsgroup-searching mechanism is the best for searching through the tens of thousands of newsgroups available simply because it's fast. Nonetheless, you might find a newsgroup via the World Wide Web that AOL's search didn't turn up, or perhaps you simply prefer using the Web whenever possible. Regardless, if the Web's your preference, by all means use it to search the list. Use the keyword: **http://www.aol.com/netfind/newsgroups.html**, and then conduct your search from there (see Figure 4-31).

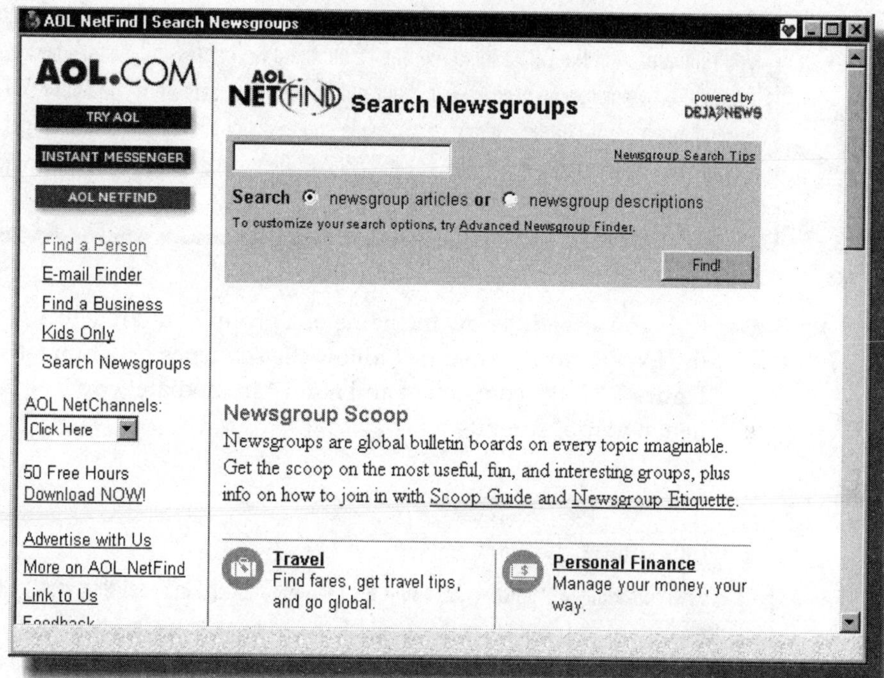

Figure 4-31: The Search All Newsgroups Web page offers a number of options—mostly links—that aren't available in the Newsgroups window, including e-mail and business searches.

Finally, there's the list itself, available for downloading at **http://www.netmeg.net/faq/internet/usenet/newsgroups/big-eight-newsgroup-list/**. This is a *huge* file—one that's growing every day—but it's comprehensive and you can use your favorite list-searching software to search it whenever you please, online or offline. Remember that you can use URLs such as the one above as keywords; just press Ctrl+K or Command+K and then type in the URL. Typos will not be tolerated.

Expert Add

Now that you've found a newsgroup, it's time to add it to your list. You can do this by using the Add Newsgroups button that we've already discussed or by using the Expert Add button, which we'll discuss next. Both buttons are pictured in Figure 4-28.

Pick Your Philosophy

Before we continue, a word about enthusiasm. Newsgroups are like a quart of ice cream: you're gonna want the whole thing, but the whole thing isn't necessarily what's best for you. A single, active newsgroup can take an hour out of your day, every day, and bury you with unread messages if you miss a day or two while you're away pursuing your nonvirtual life. As they say, "Moderation is a virtue." Then again, as Oscar Wilde once said, "Moderation is a fatal thing.... Nothing succeeds like excess."

If you already know the name of a group you'd like to add to your list, use the Expert Add button. Just follow the sequence of commands pictured in Figure 4-32. It's convenient and almost immediate; you'll be reading the group in a matter of seconds.

Internet Names

If you look carefully at Figure 4-32, you'll see a button marked Internet Names. Use this button whenever you want to see the actual Internet name of any particular newsgroup. Occasionally, AOL abbreviates them or even renames them within this window. If you want to see the real thing—and the whole thing—click this button.

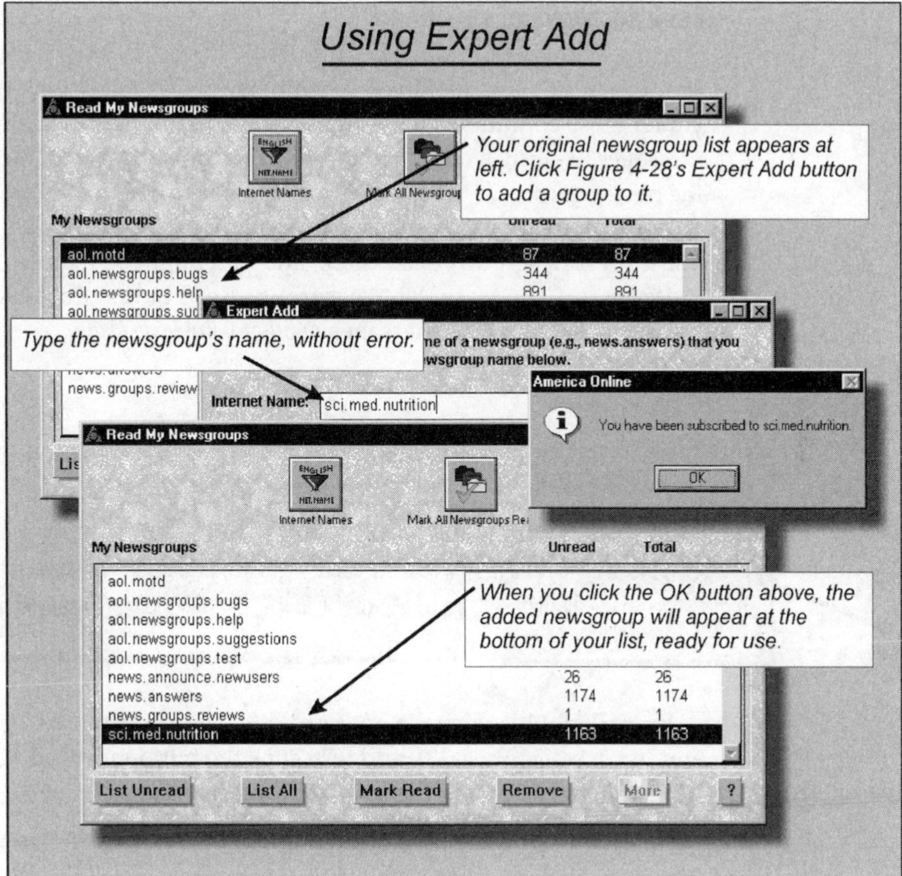

Figure 4-32: If you already know the name of the groups you want to add, use the Expert Add button.

Reading Posts

Once you've added a newsgroup to the list, you'll probably want to read the posts that are there. Though you might be tempted to double-click the newsgroup's name within the Read My Newsgroup's window, that might not be your best strategy.

The **sci.med.nutrition** group pictured in Figure 4-32, for example, contains 1,163 messages, of which 1,163 are unread (which makes sense, we just added the group, after all). If we double-click the group's name, all 1,163 messages are going to appear, some of which might be a couple of months old. Reading them could take hours.

Mark All Newsgroups Read

Starting a newsgroup journey with 1,163 unread messages is like starting with abalone recipes in a cookbook when what you're really looking for is zucchini. Under these conditions, you might consider eliminating all those unread messages, waiting a day or so for new ones to appear, and *then* start reading the newsgroup.

Look again at the lower window in Figure 4-32. There's a button labeled Mark All Newsgroups Read there, and you might be tempted to click it.

Watch out! The Mark All Newsgroups Read button does exactly what it says: it marks all of the messages *in all of your newsgroups* as read. This is rarely your intention.

The Vacation Button

We call the Mark All Newsgroups Read button our *vacation button.* When we're away from newsgroups for a period of time, the quantity of messages that accumulates is overwhelming. That's when we use this button. It's a bit like cutting in line, but who's to reprimand you for it?

Instead, double-click the newsgroup's name to produce that group's window (see Figure 4-33), and *then* click the button marked Mark All Read. AOL will then, *for that newsgroup only*, update all of the messages as read, which is usually your intention.

List All

Updating a group's messages as read doesn't eliminate them forever. You can always read old newsgroup messages—whether you've read them or not—by clicking the List All button pictured at the bottom of Figure 4-33.

Clicking this button will produce a listing of every message that AOL is holding for that group, regardless of whether you've read it or not.

Figure 4-33: One way of easing into newsgroups is to mark all postings in a newsgroup as read before you start.

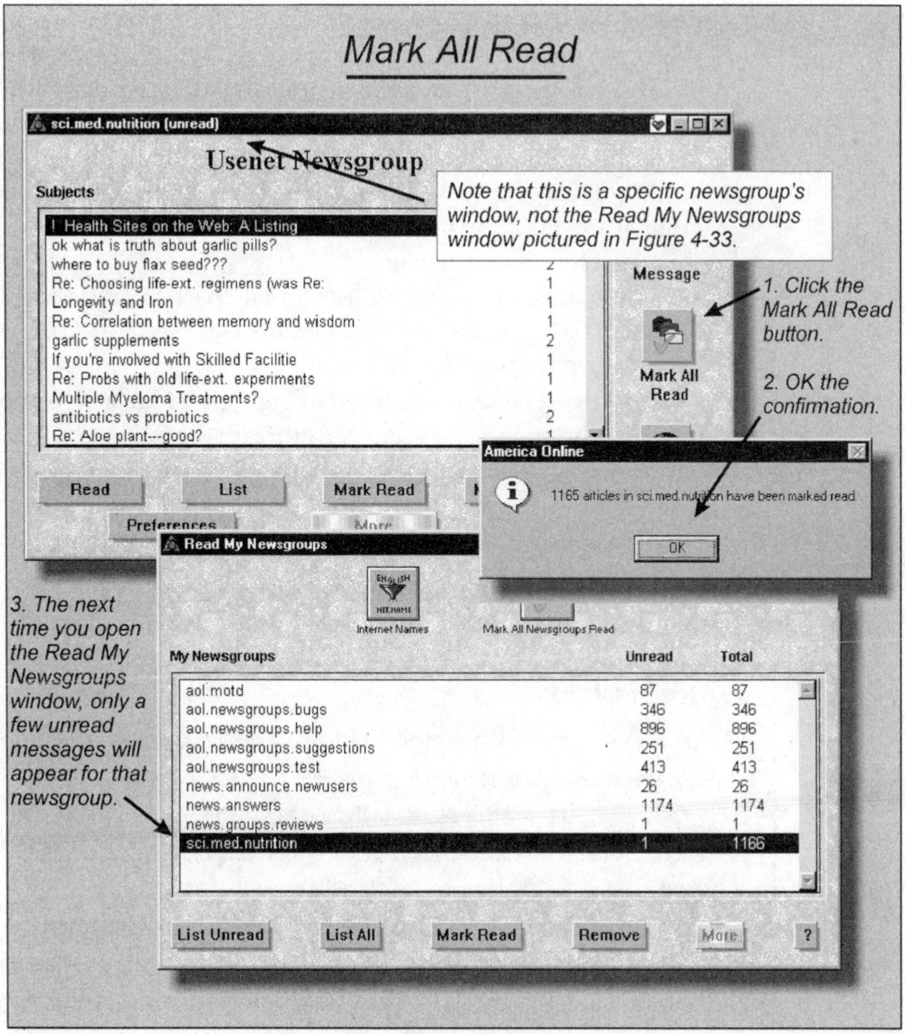

All of this talk about updating unread messages might give you the wrong impression. You should always get to know a newsgroup—get to know it well—before posting a message of your own there. If that means reading 1,163 messages, then read them. But if you're in no hurry to post, take your time, get a fresh start, and become acquainted with your newsgroup at a leisurely pace. Haste rarely enhances any journey.

Reading a Thread

Whenever anyone responds to a message, the message and its response form a *thread.* Some threads can become quite lengthy, composed of scores of messages. By threading messages, AOL's newsgroup software eliminates the need to sift through hundreds of messages, looking for a response to a particular posting. Threading not only tells you if any responses exist, it also gathers the original and all the responses together regardless of how much they might be separated by time or distance.

It's easy to tell if a thread exists for any particular message: just look at the Number column in the group's window (see Figure 4-34). If the number exceeds 1, you're seeing a thread.

The Message buttons pictured in Figure 4-34 are active only when the message you're reading is part of a thread; the Subject buttons take you from one subject on the list of subjects to the next. Though they become inactive when they're inappropriate, it's easy to click the Subject ->> button, for example, when you mean to click the Message -> button, thereby skipping who knows how many responses in a thread.

Delayed Responses

With tens of thousands of newsgroups on the Internet, gigabytes of messages are generated each day. These messages aren't stored in some central repository. Each site has to hold all of the messages that might be of interest to its members. In the interest of storage space, each site establishes a time limit on the retention of Usenet messages. Because of its size, AOL's limit is one of the most generous in the industry.

Occasionally, someone will respond to a message for which the original has been deleted. When this happens, the message will appear as an original message (there will be a 1 in its Number column) with Re: in front of it. There are three or four of these pictured in Figure 4-34's upper window. Typically, the message that you're reading will quote the original (more about quoting later in this chapter), so catching up with the thread won't be much of a problem.

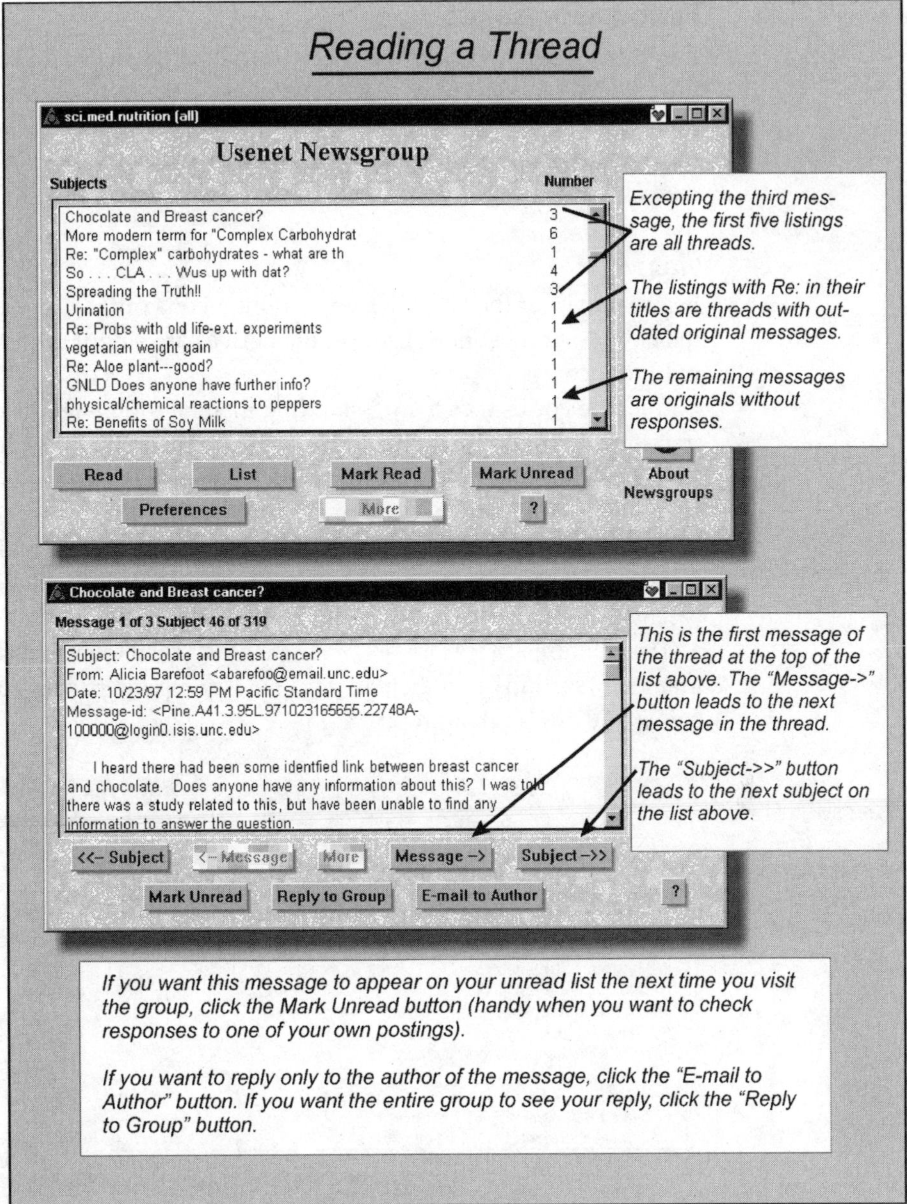

Figure 4-34: Watch the Number column when you're reading newsgroup postings.

Posting Messages

For the most part, people are attracted to the Internet because of its dialog. The Internet isn't the morning newspaper, *General Hospital*, or the news on the hour. The Internet not only encourages dialog; when it comes to newsgroups, the Internet *is* dialog. It stands to reason, then, that you can post your own messages to newsgroups as well as read those posted by others.

FAQs

Before you litter the USENET with spontaneous piffle, you should get to know the natives. In most newsgroups, the natives are singularly intolerant of redundancy.

Imagine yourself as a long-standing member of the tennis newsgroup (**rec.sport.tennis**), engrossed in an ongoing discussion of ballistic stretching. There are differing opinions about the value of this form of exercise, and the arguments are often eloquent and enlightening.

Each day, two or three messages interrupt your thread with the question, "What's ballistic stretching?" Over time, your limits of patience might be reached.

The solution is a FAQ: a list of Frequently Asked Questions (see Figure 4-35). Many newsgroups post them; if your newsgroup offers one, you should read it before you post to that group.

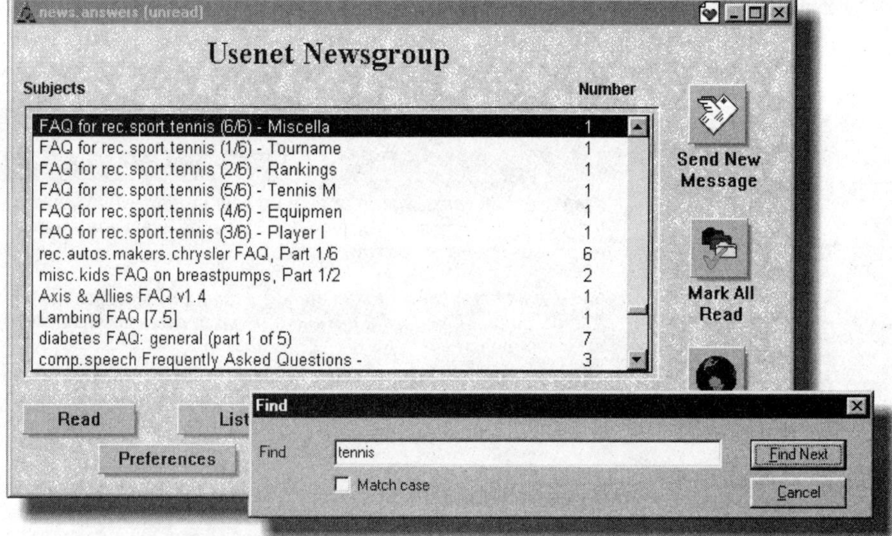

Figure 4-35: A number of FAQs appear regularly in the **news.answers** newsgroup. Use the Edit menu's Find in Top Window command to search for your newsgroup.

FAQs are usually reposted every couple of months or so—more frequently for large, active groups. Though each newsgroup posts its own FAQ within the group periodically, the mother lode of FAQs is the **news.answers** newsgroup pictured in Figure 4-35. Join this group (if you haven't already) and find (and read!) the FAQs for the groups in which you're participating. Loss of newsgroup face is a terrible thing to have to endure.

Starting a Thread

Assuming you've discovered and read the FAQ, the time will come when you will want to start a thread of discussion within a group. That's what the Send New Message button is for (it's pictured in Figure 4-35). This button provokes the Post New Message window pictured in Figure 4-36. Note that the name of the newsgroup is already filled in and that the cursor is positioned within the Subject field, waiting for you to declare one.

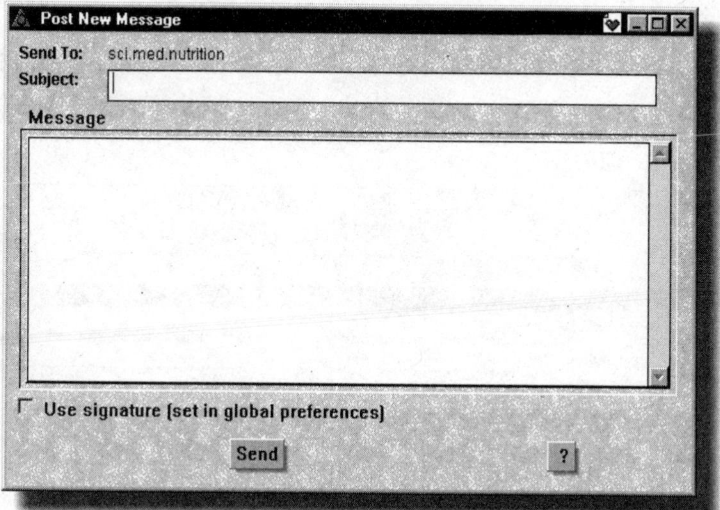

Figure 4-36: The Post New Message window. Posting here will begin a new thread.

Consider the subject carefully. Look again at the Subject column in Figure 4-34's upper window: most subjects there are provocative and compelling. They invite inquiry. Try to emulate them, and avoid subjects like Question or Comment—subjects that provoke about as much curiosity as Bob Dole.

Now you're ready to compose your message. Thousands of people in scores of countries are liable to read it. Give thought to what you're about to say. Say it succinctly, and oblige netiquette (discussed later in this chapter). Your newsgroup experience will be more rewarding if you do.

Your Signature

You'll see a lot of *signatures* at the ends of newsgroup postings. Most newsgroup software—including AOL's—automates the process of including one. Signatures are short (no more than four lines, ideally) disclaimers at the ends of messages identifying the sender, the sender's affiliation (all of the early participants in Usenet were associated with a military or educational institution, you'll remember), and the sender's e-mail address.

You don't have to use a signature, but if you want to, spend some time looking at the signatures of others before you construct your own. When you're ready, sign on, use the keyword: **newsgroups**, click the Set Preferences button, and then type your signature in the space that's provided. From then on, it's a simple matter of checking the appropriate boxes (displayed in Figures 4-36 and 4-37) whenever you post.

Responding

Compare Figure 4-37's Post Response window with the Post New Message window pictured in Figure 4-36. They're both intended to get your message onto Usenet, yet they share practically nothing in common.

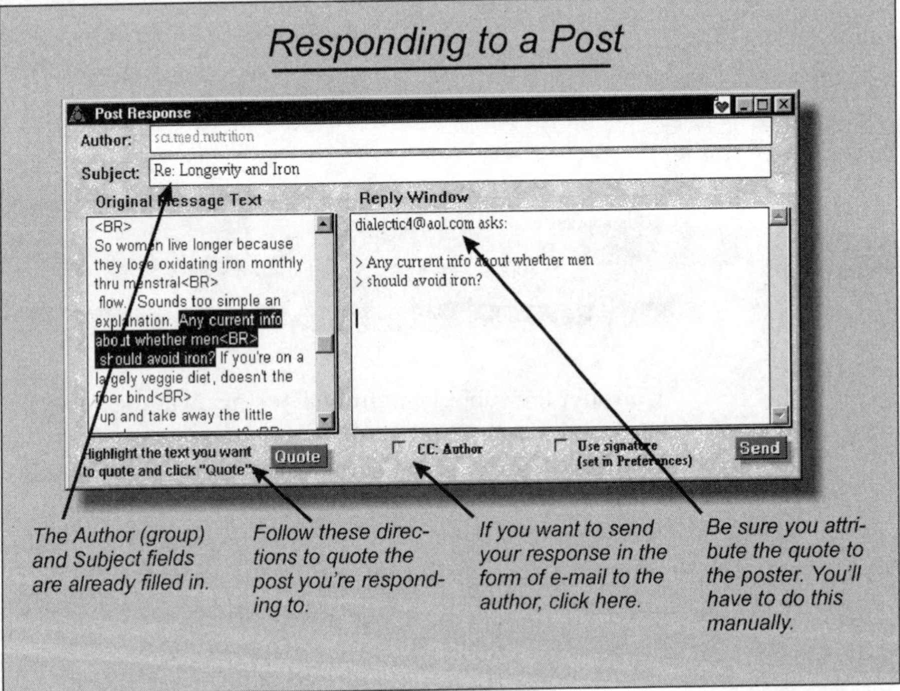

Figure 4-37: The Post Response form makes it easy to quote and reply via e-mail to the author of the original post.

As well they shouldn't. A response is a dialog, and newsgroup dialogs infer all kinds of things: quoting, e-mail to the sender, cross-posting, and more.

Sweaty Palms?

Newsgroups are subject to worldwide participation. Posting to one implies not only a vast readership, but an *international* one. Whenever you post to a newsgroup, you're emissary as well as discussant.

Kinda gives you sweaty palms, doesn't it?

Perhaps you should consider the benefit of conducting your newsgroup activity offline. You can program the AOL client to sign on—whenever you want, as often as you want—retrieve all of the newsgroup postings you haven't read, post all of the newsgroup postings you haven't sent, and sign back off again, all automatically. When such a session concludes, your unread newsgroup postings remain on your hard disk where you can read and reply to them in the quietude of the offline milieu. Emissaries are nurtured by quietude.

Paranoia aside, reading newsgroup postings offline also allows you to file them, both incoming and outgoing, just like e-mail.

Want to know more? Read Chapter 8, "Working Offline."

Quoting It's customary to quote the text that provoked your response. It's especially beneficial when the original post has been dropped from the thread (provoking one of those Re: subject lines you see in Figure 4-33).

If you've read Chapter 3, you already know what quoting is. Figure 4-38 illustrates an appropriate quote pulled from the **sci.med.nutrition** newsgroup; Figure 4-37 illustrates a quote in construction. In either case, the quotes are properly attributed to the original poster (something you'll have to do manually using AOL's software) and relatively short.

Attribute your quote and quote only the salient portion(s) of the originator's message—not the whole thing. Otherwise, follow the brief instructions appearing at the bottom of the Post Response form (review Figure 4-38), and remember to quote whenever it's appropriate, ignoring admonitions from people like humorist Gelett Burgess:

> Ah, yes, I wrote the *Purple Cow*—
> I'm sorry, now, I wrote it!
> But I can tell you, anyhow,
> I'll kill you if you quote it.

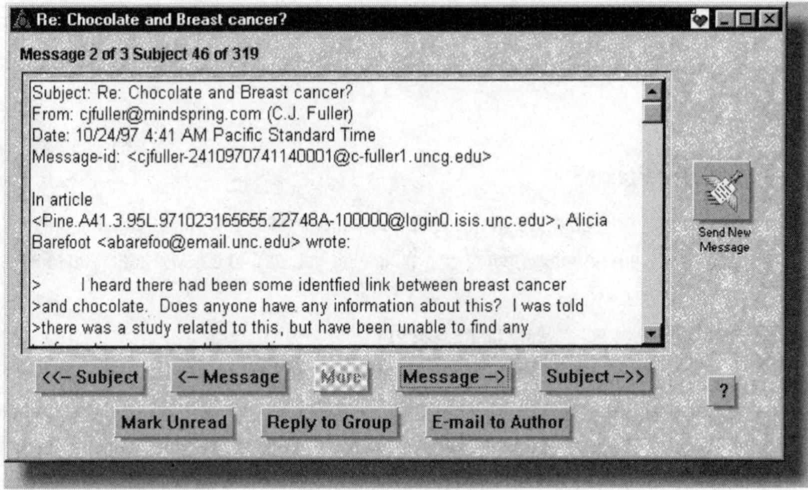

Figure 4-38: The beginning of a message in **sci.med.nutrition**, including a quote. Note the proper attribution.

E-Mailing the Originator It's considered polite to send a copy of your reply to the individual to whom you're responding. That person might not read the newsgroup regularly or might have removed the newsgroup from his or her list, but it's a sure bet they'll want to read your post. All you have to do is click the CC: Author check box that's pictured in Figure 4-37. We've made a number of long-term online friends by doing so.

When E-Mail Makes More Sense

Whenever you're about to respond to a newsgroup posting, ask yourself, "Would e-mail be better?" Many replies are better suited to e-mail—not that they contain sensitive information or personal information (though they may); the argument for e-mailed replies is usually more mundane than that. Many replies are simply not newsgroup material. They're questions or requests; often they're replies or suggestions; sometimes they're simple hellos.

Think of talk radio: would you rather your comment be broadcast to a vast audience, or would a personal phone call serve the purpose more effectively?

To send e-mail to the originator of a posting, just click the E-mail to Author button pictured in Figure 4-38.

Removing a Newsgroup From Your List

There's a practical limit to the number of newsgroups you'll want to participate in. Time is an important factor; surely you've got a life outside of the Internet....

You'll also want to try a "trial subscription" once in a while, and sometimes the trial will prove to be unfruitful.

No matter what the reason, removing a newsgroup is easy. Simply select the newsgroup to be removed (in the Read My Newsgroups window) and click the Remove button (see Figure 4-39).

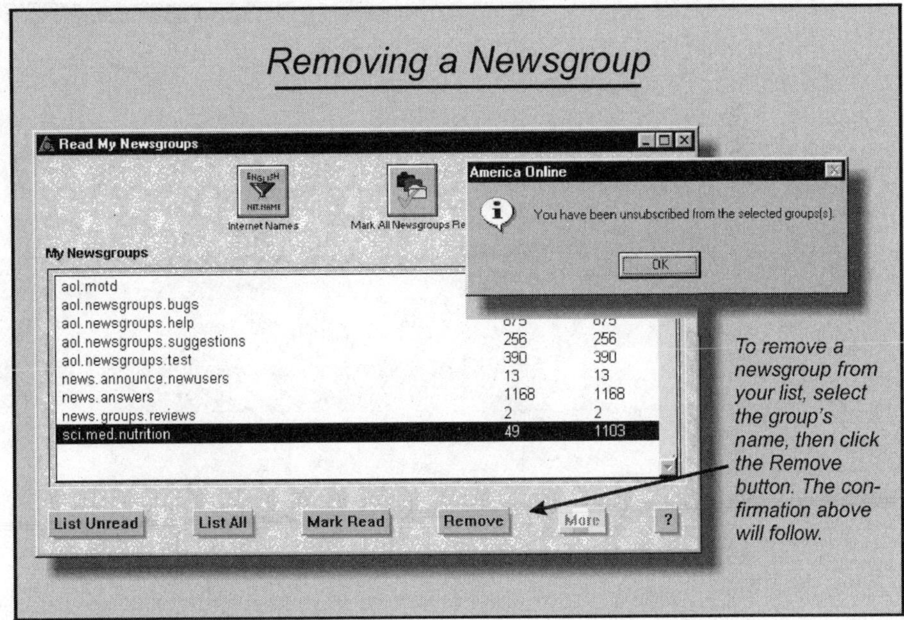

Figure 4-39: Remove newsgroups from your list with the Remove button.

Testing

Newsgroup posting is a little like entering cold water: some jump right in; others prefer to adjust gradually. When it comes to newsgroups, if you're among the latter group, there's help.

Most newsgroups, you'll remember, are broadcast throughout Usenet. This is not the place to experiment. If you're not sure of your ability to post to newsgroups, experiment using the **alt.test** or **aol.newsgroups.test** newsgroups (see Figure 4-40). Don't *ever* post a test message to a working group.

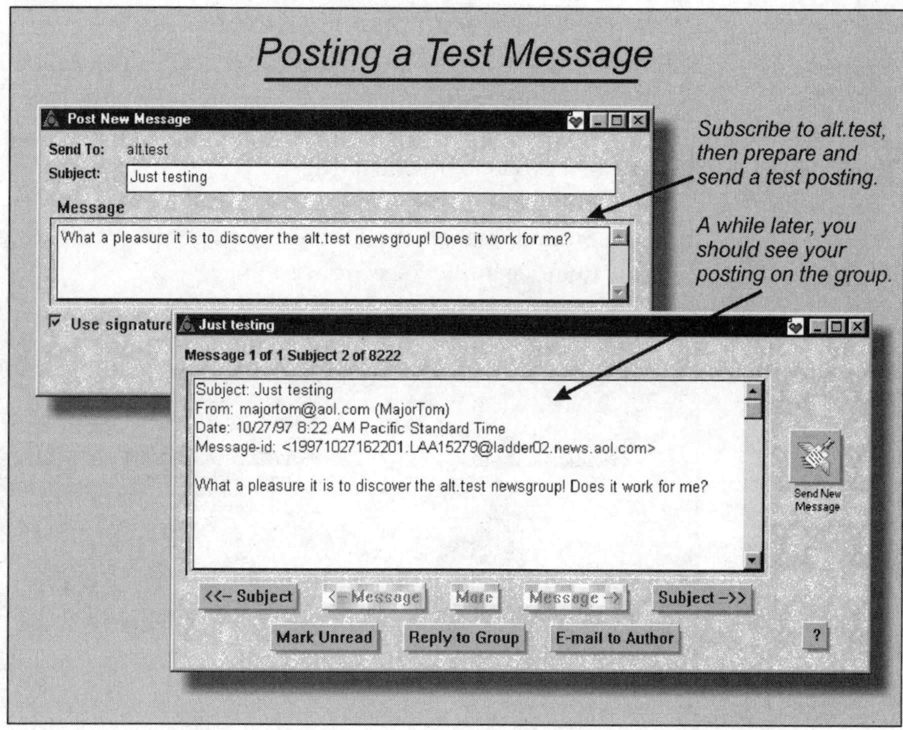

Figure 4-40: Posting a test message to **alt.test**.

Autoresponders

A number of machines constantly monitor the **alt.test** newsgroup for activity and automatically respond to any postings in that group in the form of e-mail.

Consequently, don't be surprised if you receive some unexpected e-mail messages after you post a test. And look carefully at the addresses from the senders; some come from all over the world!

Netiquette

Nowhere is the etiquette of online conduct more critical (or more abused) than in newsgroups. Most *faux pas* are committed by people who are new to the Internet, but that makes little difference; the *faux pas* are an annoyance to the people who've been here for a while, and they're an acute source of chagrin to well-meaning innocents who commit them. The Internet is a community, after all, one with a particularly stalwart camaraderie and an intense adherence to a set of unwritten guidelines for interactions with others. Most specialized social organizations are that way, and to become a member of one without first becoming familiar with its catechism invites disgrace. A minicourse in Netiquette, then, might help.

Having stung ourselves a number of times, we've taken to writing our missives and waiting for at least a couple hours before posting them. We save them and recall them the next time we sign on. For some reason, this obliges us to read them again before we click the Post button. It has often saved us considerable newsgroup face.

- There are real people on the other end of the line, people with emotions and feelings. Honor them.
- Honor yourself as well. You are known on the Internet by what you write. Project the image you want others to see.
- Brevity is admirable; verbosity is disfavored (among other things, because it wastes time, disk space, and network bandwidth). Say what you have to say succinctly; your words will carry greater authority and impact.
- Read before writing. Add something to the conversation; don't simply repeat what's already been said. Subscribe to the **news.answers** newsgroup and read the FAQ for your newsgroup before posting. By reading before you write, you'll have a better sense of the tenor and conventions of the newsgroup to which you are posting.
- Quote the messages to which you're responding. Edit the quoted material for brevity (and indicate when you've done so), use the quoting fashion you see in other messages, and always acknowledge the person you're quoting. (Quoting is also discussed in Chapter 3, "Electronic Mail & the Personal Filing Cabinet.")
- Contribute something. Some people speak simply to be heard; these same people post mainly to see their material online. Don't contribute to the tedium: look for a new perspective, ask a probing question, make an insightful comment. If none come to mind, wait for another opportunity. There are plenty of opportunities on the Internet; we all have something worthwhile to contribute eventually.
- Use Help. If the help files described in this chapter don't answer your question, post a message in **aol.newsgroups.help**. Lots of people are willing to help you if you ask.

Gopher

Growth on the Internet is a stupendous thing. Most everyone agrees that it exceeds 100 percent a year; some contend that it's as high as 20 percent *per month.* Regardless of the figure, navigating the Net has become about as convenient as navigating the Atlantic Ocean: relatively easy if you have the right tools, but impractical—some might say perilous—if you don't.

One such tool is *Gopher*. Originating in 1991 at the University of Minnesota (where the school mascot is the Golden Gopher), Gopher is a system of sites containing amazing numbers of files (mostly text), all listed in hierarchical menus. All you have to do is keep choosing menu items until you find what you're after; then Gopher "goes for" (it's kind of a double pun: mascot and "gofer") your material on the Net.

People new to the Internet tend to think of e-mail, Usenet, and the Web as the only resources available. Those who do are doing themselves a lamentable disservice. The Gopher system has been around for ten years now—nearly a third of the Internet's lifetime—and the amount of data that's stored there is extensive and for many Internet users, undiscovered (see Figure 4-41).

Figure 4-41: The keyword: **Gopher** takes you to AOL's Gopher service where vast—and often overlooked—Internet resources await your exploration.

The Gopher system is actually composed of a number of Gopher servers located around the world. Each server is like a good librarian: it organizes content for your convenience. (Librarians organize libraries with card files; Gophers organize the Internet's content with menus.) When you find what you're looking for, the Gopher retrieves the information for you. Better yet, Gophers reference other Gophers: AOL's Gopher, for example, offers access to hundreds of other Gophers. It's as if you were given access to a librarians' convention, and the librarians, every one, brought their card files with them.

Though there are a number of Gopher servers, you're rarely aware of them individually: AOL simply groups them all into one massive menu tree that you're free to peruse as you wish. In a way, that's too bad, because you're usually unaware of the vast distances you're traveling when you access the various Gopher servers on AOL's menus. You might be in Switzerland one moment and Germany the next. That's the nature of the Net; distance has no meaning in cyberspace.

That's about all there is to lament, however. AOL wraps up Gopher in a fine cloak of colors, offering its Gopher menus in the Web browser window where everything is familiar and comfortable. If you're used to browsing the Web, you won't have any trouble using Gopher. In fact, some folks are beginning to rediscover Gopher thanks to some enterprising individuals who are making Gopher content available via the Web.

FTP

Gopher, newsgroups, and the Web are nifty tools, but what if you want more direct access? What if you want to log on to another machine on the Net, see a directory of its files, and download a few of them? We're talking now about the "engine room" of the Internet, where you access other machines' files as if they were on your own hard drive. FTP, or *File Transfer Protocol*, provides that kind of access; it's how you download files (including programs, sound, sound video, and graphics) from other machines.

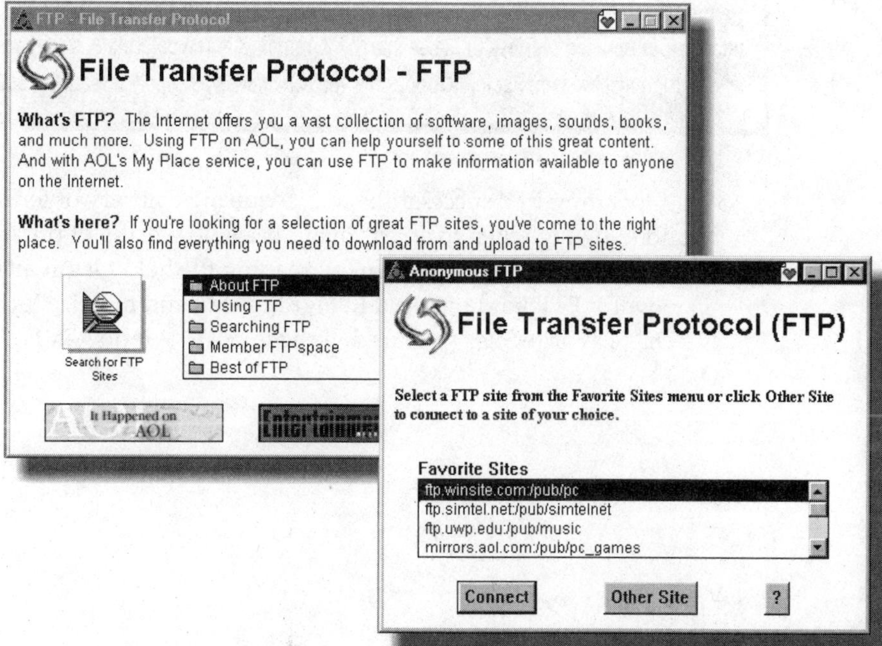

Figure 4-42: Use the keyword: **FTP** to download software from other sites.

FTP is two things, actually. First, it's a protocol, allowing machines on the Internet to exchange data (files) without concern for the type of machine that originated the file, the file's original format, or even the operating systems of the machines involved. FTP is also a program that enables FTP. Just as the word *telephone* denotes both a device you hold in your hand and a system for international communications, FTP is both the message and the medium.

The term is also used as both noun ("It's available via FTP") and verb ("FTP to **ftp.aol.com** and look in the pub directory"). It's hard to misuse the term, in other words. Just don't try to make a word out of FTP when you say it aloud—always use the initials.

Anonymous FTP

Originally, most FTP sessions occurred between a site and a person at a remote location who had an account at that site. The person would log on by supplying an account name and a password and then conduct the appropriate file activities.

The need soon became apparent, however, for less restrictive access. What if a site wanted to post a file for anyone to download? A number of publicly funded agencies required such an arrangement. NASA's space images, for example, are funded by public money; therefore, it was decided that the public should have access to them.

The solution is *anonymous* FTP. During an anonymous FTP session, the user logs on to the remote site using the account name anonymous (AOL does this for you unless you supply a specific username). The password for anonymous login, typically, is the user's Internet address—a common courtesy so the people at the remote site can determine, if they wish, who is using their system. Again, AOL does this for you unless you supply a specific password.

Operating FTP successfully and acquiring a library of fertile FTP locations (and knowing when to access them) is a skill worthy of pursuing, but it does require time to develop. Begin by reading the help files available at the keyword: **FTP** (and pictured in Figure 4-42), and practice for a while using AOL's Favorite Sites (pictured in the forward window in Figure 4-42).

Telnet

Yet one more tool remains for us to discover: Telnet. A number of Internet users require operating-system access to machines on the Net, not for the purpose of transferring files (which is FTP's job), but to run programs on those remote machines. Often these programs are games, but chat applications are common as well; so are databases.

People who require Telnet access to the Internet have specific needs, and most of these people have favorite programs—Telnet clients—that they prefer to use for the task. This isn't a situation where AOL can provide a client for you; Telnet is too idiosyncratic for that.

Instead, AOL provides a "socket" into which you plug your Telnet client. The AOL client recedes to the background under these circumstances, and the Telnet client assumes command. At AOL's end, signals from your computer are routed directly to the remote computer you're accessing. AOL's host computers remain transparent until your Telnet session concludes.

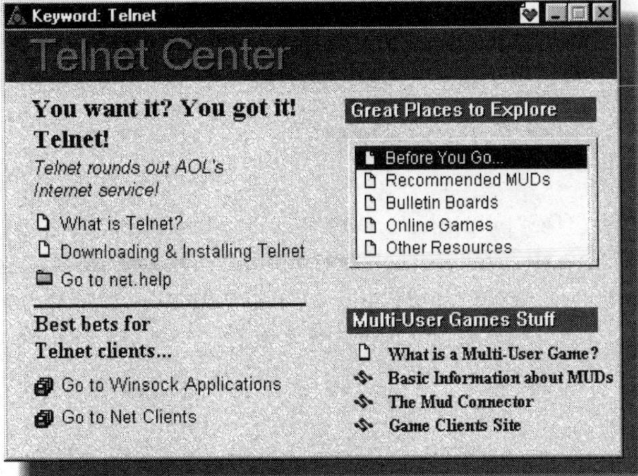

Figure 4-43: Telnet allows you to connect the client of your choosing directly to the Internet.

If you require Telnet access to the Net, use the keyword: **Telnet**. You'll find a number of clients available there, as well as the sockets we've mentioned. Take the time to review the informational resources pictured in Figure 4-43 if you're not already familiar with this technology.

net.help

We're about to wrap this up, the longest chapter in the book, but before we do we want to leave you with a continuing resource. To get help about the Internet—at any time of day, on any subject—use the keywords: **Net Help**, and investigate the net.help area pictured in Figure 4-44.

Figure 4-44: Find answers to your Internet questions at keywords: **Net Help**.

Net.help offers help files on every subject we've talked about in this chapter and then some. It offers searchable databases of information on the Net, access to live classes, and the Surf Shack message boards. It's constantly updated and always current. If you remember nothing else from this chapter, remember the keywords: **Net Help**. You'll find the answers you need there.

MacInternet

The Internet is Mac-friendly. Jennifer encounters few differences on her Mac when she's actually "out there" on the Internet. Web pages, mailing lists, newsgroups, and FTP files look for a warm computer, not the color of your operating system. The differences she finds are "back home" in the AOL software; they tend to be minor.

Changing your default home page requires fewer steps on the Mac. Just choose Preferences from the My AOL icon on the toolbar, click the WWW button, and type the new URL into the Home Page field.

While browsing the Web, you can get a menu of available options by pressing your mouse button down (and keeping it down) inside the browser window. If your mouse is over a graphic, your options will include saving a copy of the graphic; if over a link, you have the option of opening the link in a new window.

To assign keystroke shortcuts to your favorite places, choose Edit Shortcuts from the My AOL button on the toolbar or from the Window menu.

You can add your own icons to the toolbar by dragging them from your list of favorite places. If you want to share a favorite place you've added to your toolbar, you can copy it right from the toolbar by holding down the option key while dragging the icon to your mail, Instant Message, or post. You can restore your original toolbar buttons in your Toolbar Preferences, or by simply holding down the Command key when you click on the toolbar and selecting Restore Original Buttons from the drop-down menu. If you prefer to remove the custom toolbar items individually, make sure your trash can (on your Desktop) is visible in the background and then drag the icon to the trash while holding down the Option key.

Macs can back up the Personal Filing Cabinet too! Just copy it from the Data folder inside the America Online preference folder (located in the Preferences folder in the System Folder) to a floppy or another location on your hard disk.

Moving On

Each Internet resource described on these pages is an existing AOL feature. Others will no doubt come along. That's part of the fun of telecommunications; this is just the beginning, and there's always more to come. Becoming a member of AOL (and exploring the Internet) is a little like planting a fruit tree: there are many rewards (blossoms, bees, fruit, firewood), and each year there's a more bountiful harvest than there was the year before.

It's positively organic. ;-)

In this chapter, we might have temporarily lost our focus. This is a book about America Online, not the Internet, and AOL offers a mother lode of resources for the intrepid electronic explorer. There are places to go, people to visit, files to download—a universe of potential that's the fastest-growing entity on earth. But how do you *find* all of this stuff? To find out, see the next chapter.

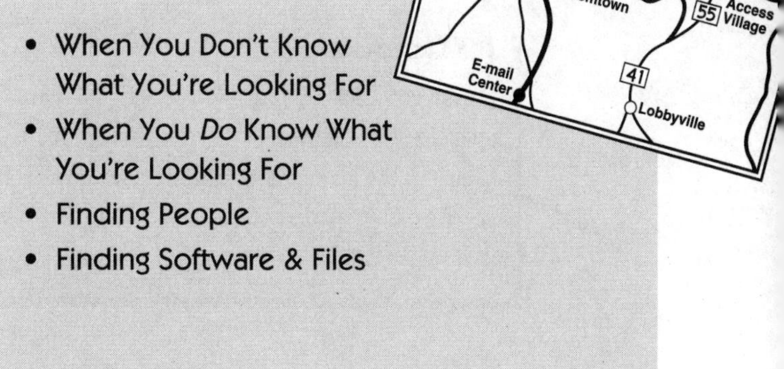

CHAPTER 5

Finding Stuff

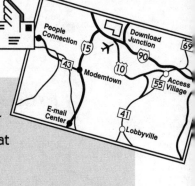

- When You Don't Know What You're Looking For
- When You *Do* Know What You're Looking For
- Finding People
- Finding Software & Files

Tom visited Bordeaux, France, last spring along with his friend Doyle. Both Doyle and Tom are fond of wine, and Doyle is in the wine business. Bordeaux is the mecca of the trade.

Bordeaux is also home to VinExpo, an exclusive, international winesellers' exposition: five covered acres of wine booths—well over a thousand of them—all pouring free samples. It was staggering to walk into that room. It's a place we've always wanted to be, but few people spoke our language, everyone there was an expert, and it was our first visit.

Walking into AOL for the first time is a similar experience. It's a little intimidating at first, but you're here because you want to be, and you know the rewards will far exceed any unease you're feeling. You're psyched, El Edwards's voice just said, "Welcome," and AOL proffers a virtual glass, waiting for you to take your first sip. If only you knew where to begin.

When You Don't Know What You're Looking For

Although this chapter is titled "Finding Stuff," your first couple of visits will probably be exploratory. That's the best way to get to know a place, after all, whether it be VinExpo, a new hometown, or AOL: spend some time "walking the aisles" before you decide on a location for your first lengthy stay.

We've talked about Discover America Online, Learn AOL, Find Central, and the AOL Insider in Chapter 2. In other words, you probably know a bit of the language by now. You can say *merci beaucoup* and *bonjour*. You've gained a smidgen of confidence and now you're ready for adventure. You're standing inside the main gate saying, "Give me your best shot!"

The Classifieds

Though this chapter is titled "Finding Stuff," it doesn't discuss finding *stuff,* like stereos and used cars. That kind of stuff is available online, however, and there are plenty of bargains to be had. Use the keyword: **Classifieds** to discover more about AOL's Classifieds. They're just like the classified section of your Sunday newspaper, so you'll have no trouble finding your way around.

Getting Around & Using AOL

But wait! What if you don't know your mouse from a hockey puck? What if you've never heard of the term *scroll bar,* and menus are something you expect at a restaurant? If this is your level of computer expertise, don't feel intimidated. The Getting Around & Using AOL area was created by AOL's online help experts (who certainly know what AOL's members require) with new members in mind. It'll take no more than half an hour of your time and you'll be clicking and dragging with the best of them.

To get to this area, use the keywords: **Find Central** (or click the Find button on the toolbar) and then choose Getting Around & Using AOL (see Figure 5-1).

Be sure to take half an hour to explore the Autotutor, pictured at the bottom of Figure 5-1 (use the 1-2-3 icon). If your learning is better served by a linear path than a random one, this is the place for you.

The Channels

Linear, however, is not the appropriate strategy when you've gone online to wander around—to browse. The word *browse* certainly has changed. Ten years ago it was a literary term, something we did at the library or bookstore. Five years ago it was something we did with the TV remote. Today, it's an online term, and nowhere is it more appropriate than among AOL's *channels.*

The Channels window could be right behind your Welcome window when you sign on. (If the Channels window doesn't appear when you sign on, click the My AOL icon on the toolbar, choose Preferences, and then click the General button. Turn on the Channels option—it's the first one.) Alternatively, click the Channels icon on the toolbar, or click the Channels button in the Welcome window. No matter how you do it, all of AOL's channels will appear on your screen with a profusion of potential for the online browser (see Figure 5-2).

Figure 5-1: The Getting Around & Using AOL area is the place to begin. Although this chapter discusses the tools for discovering online content, first you have to know how to unlock the toolbox. This area shows the key.

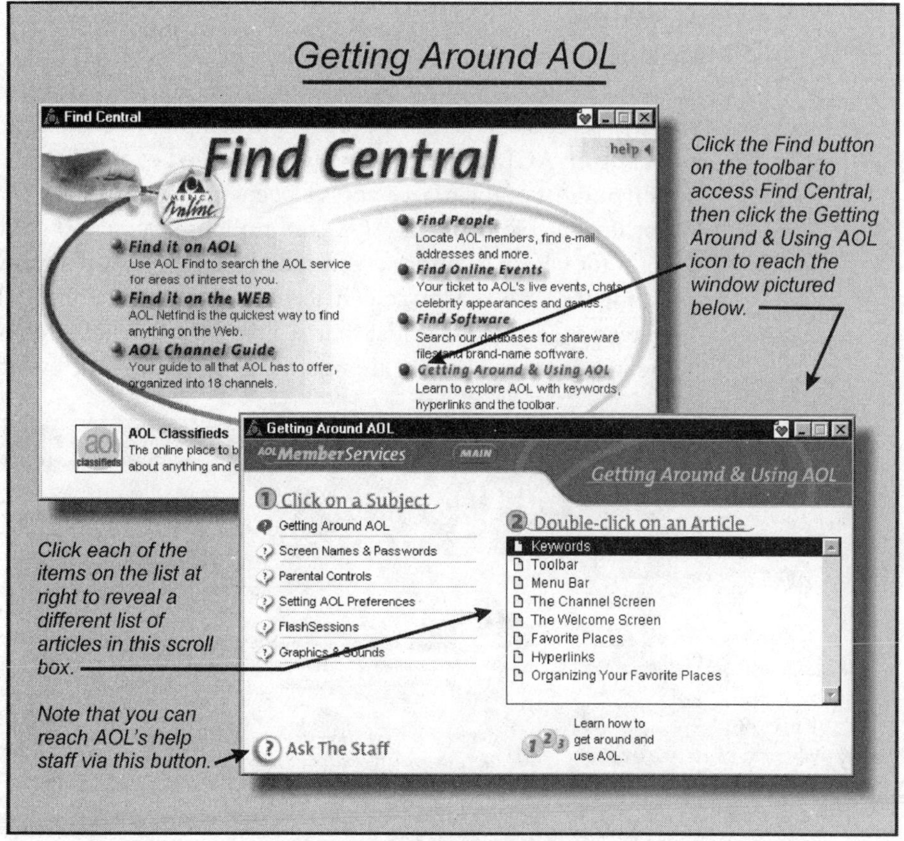

Figure 5-2: The remote is in your hands: The Channels window is a great way to browse around AOL.

AOL Today

The trouble with channel surfing is that to really do a thorough job, you have to spend a couple of minutes watching every channel your cable company provides. It could take two hours just to sample them all. The same is true of browsing on AOL: by the time you've sampled everything, you will have forgotten most of the places you've been.

Fortunately, someone at AOL is sampling for you and gathering the best of the best for you in a single screen called AOL Today. It's a never-ending job, updating the AOL Today screen, as it's constantly changing. The snapshot displayed in Figure 5-3 is just that, a snapshot. In a half an hour, the contents of the window are likely to change, accommodating the events of the day.

Figure 5-3: The workplace, travel, personal finance, world news—even the *New York Times* crossword. They were the richest places to visit at noon, November 4. You'll find AOL Today at the top of the list of channels every day.

Hyperlinks

Look again at the text in Figure 5-3. See how the words *balance work and family, stocks, bargain*, and others are underlined? They're all *hyperlinks*. Although we've discussed links before, they bear mention again: not only will a click on the icons—the baby, the dollar sign—lead you to the featured site, clicks on the *links* will lead you to sites that are supplementary to the events of the day, sites not unlike this sidebar is in its relation to the main text. How else would you have discovered the $199 round-trip fare between Orlando and Duesseldorf that was being offered November 4?

The Workplace Channel

We detoured by the Workplace Channel the other day simply because it might be the last place you'd think to browse (Figure 5-4). Browsing is usually something you do with your leisure time, and leisure is pretty rare at the workplace.

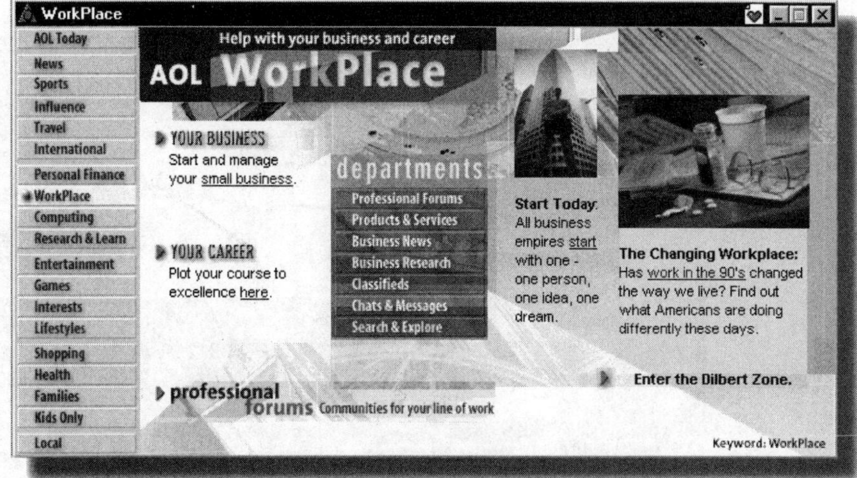

Figure 5-4: The Workplace Channel offers sympathetic support for the working individual and plenty of suggestions for improving your working conditions and the quality of work you perform there.

Indeed, one of the articles we encountered claimed that many baby boomers and gen-Xers have a difficult time justifying long-term employment with the same employer in today's labor market. In a feature on employee loyalty, we listened to an interview with a factory worker in Dallas who proudly predicted that he planned to stay at his job for "maybe another year" and a traveling saleswoman who was searching for a way to get off the road and back into her home. People don't stay with jobs forever nowadays. It made us thankful for our six-year affiliation with the *AOL Tour Guide*.

Here's the point: we spent half an hour browsing the Workplace Channel, engrossed in the plights of people and their jobs. We listened to their voices and even took in a few Dilbert comics. It was an enriching and wholly unexpected diversion. The Channels window took us there.

Weather on the News Channel

The News Channel is, perhaps, AOL's most ambitious undertaking. If you're one who watches the evening news every night, you'll not only feel right at home (the News Channel is freckled with video and sound), you'll delight in having the news when you want it. There's no waiting for the news at AOL.

Nor is there for the weather. Indeed, television's evening news rarely presents the weather when you want it: you want the weather when you're about to go out into it, and though we all go out into the weather at all times of the day, early evening usually isn't one of them. Enter the Weather department on AOL's News Channel. Figure 5-5 shows you how to get there and what you'll find once you do.

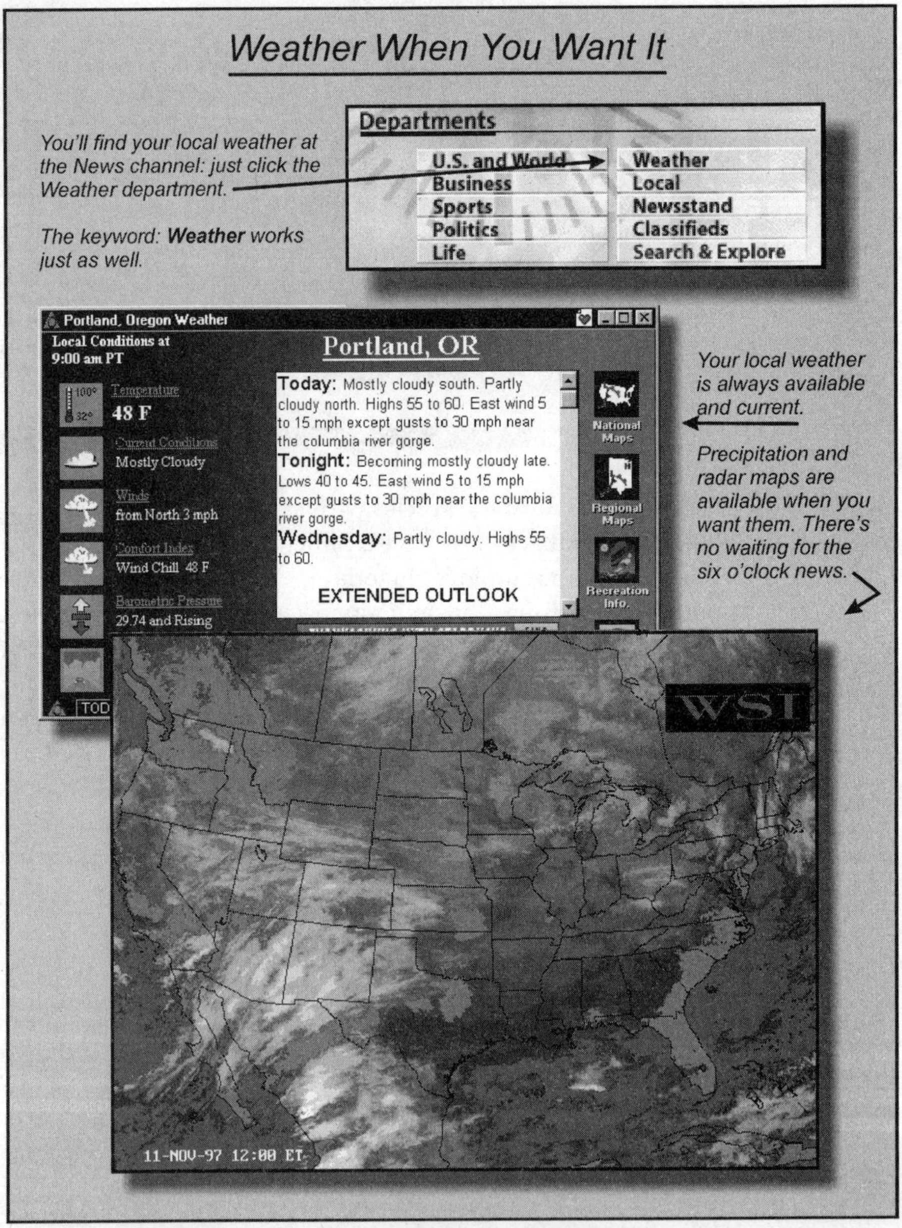

Figure 5-5: The Weather department at the News Channel is available 24 hours a day and is always current.

Weather When You Want It

You'll find your local weather at the News channel: just click the Weather department.

*The keyword: **Weather** works just as well.*

Departments
U.S. and World
Business
Sports
Politics
Life
Weather
Local
Newsstand
Classifieds
Search & Explore

Portland, Oregon Weather
Local Conditions at 9:00 am PT
Portland, OR
Temperature 48 F
Current Conditions Mostly Cloudy
Winds from North 3 mph
Comfort Index Wind Chill 48 F
Barometric Pressure 29.74 and Rising
Today: Mostly cloudy south. Partly cloudy north. Highs 55 to 60. East wind 5 to 15 mph except gusts to 30 mph near the columbia river gorge.
Tonight: Becoming mostly cloudy late. Lows 40 to 45. East wind 5 to 15 mph except gusts to 30 mph near the columbia river gorge.
Wednesday: Partly cloudy. Highs 55 to 60.
EXTENDED OUTLOOK
National Maps
Regional Maps
Recreation Info.

Your local weather is always available and current.

Precipitation and radar maps are available when you want them. There's no waiting for the six o'clock news.

WSI
11-NOV-97 12:00 ET

The Research & Learn Channel

Before we explore other browsing methods, we'll visit one more channel: Research & Learn. There we discovered UCAOL, the University of California Extension, where online classes are accredited by the University of California, Berkeley. We found courses ranging from "The Art of Film" to "The Environmental Behavior of Pollutants"—over a hundred in all, and all offering college credit (see Figure 5-6).

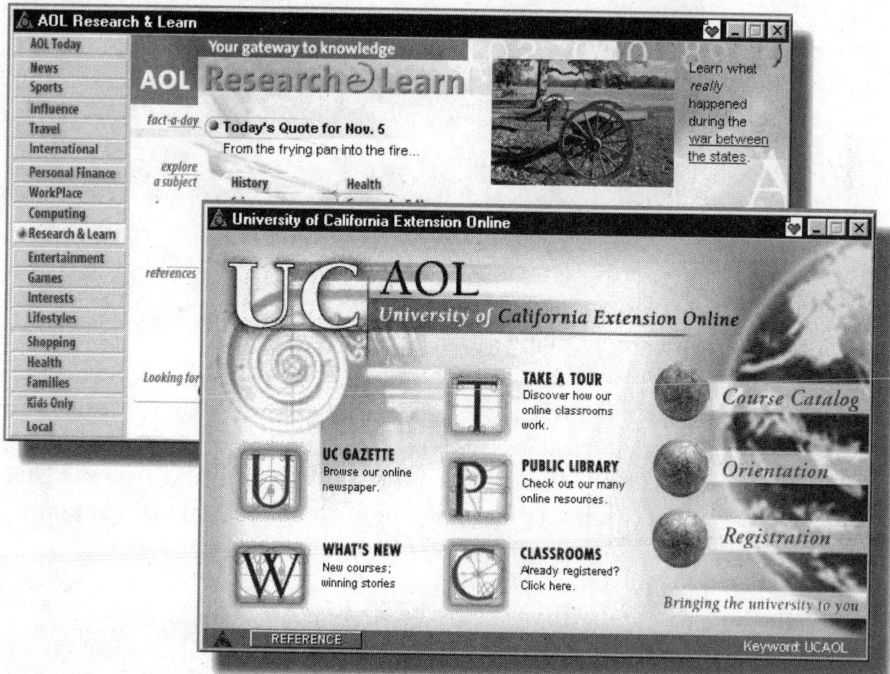

Figure 5-6: UCAOL and the Research & Learn Channel. Earn academic credit while you're online!

Members' Choice

The Channels window is for the *very* casual browser. It reminds us of the traffic circles in Bordeaux. Often, half a dozen roads spun off of them: Tom and Doyle would occasionally circle two or three times and then take one of the roads at random to see where it would lead. That's what the Channels window is like.

Perhaps you're looking for something a little more focused. You want to browse, but you'd like to see some direction offered in the process. May we suggest Members' Choice? This is where you'll find AOL's top 50 sites—the 50 most popular AOL offerings, based on member visitations. The places listed there might surprise you, but they're all great sojourns for the casual browser (see Figure 5-7).

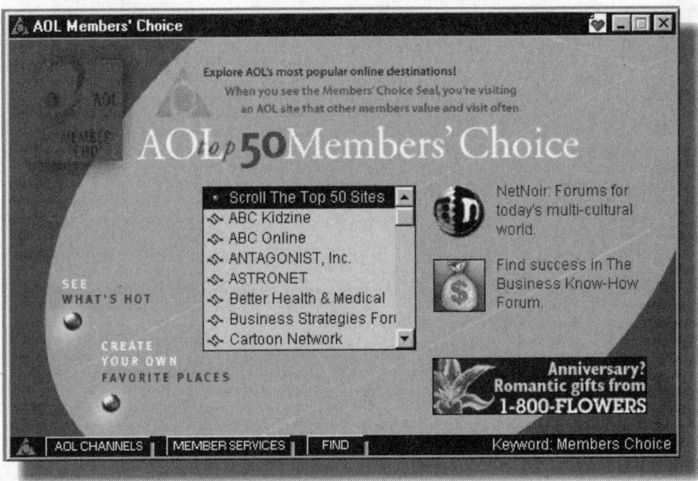

Figure 5-7: Members' Choice offers AOL's 50 most popular sites. Use the keywords: **Members Choice**.

Hecklers Online

One place that's always among the top 50 is Hecklers Online. With ten million members, AOL is bound to have a few outrageous wags, and most of them gather at Hecklers Online. Wag or not, everyone enjoys a giggle or two, so Hecklers Online is a popular spot. You want to browse? This place is a great distraction—a place you might never think to visit, but once you do, it becomes a destination (see Figure 5-8).

Figure 5-8: Hecklers Online is a great place to stop by for a morning chuckle. Use the keyword: **HO**.

The Three-Line Novel

Among the Hecklers Online diversions, you'll discover the *Three-Line Novel.* Members are asked to submit novels consisting of three lines (sentences) and prizes are awarded to the top four entrants. Here's one by a member named Pamela, a veterinary student and satirist:

"Following a bitter divorce, she returned to school where she studied more diligently than any student her professors had known during their careers. She graduated with honors and immediately went to work for a genetics laboratory, often buried in her research long after her co-workers were asleep in their beds. One late evening her shrieks of triumph could be heard echoing through the vacant halls as she gazed lovingly at the product of her labors; a tall, muscle-bound male, the obvious lack of intelligence showing in his glazed eyes, breathing deeply through his ears, and sitting silently due to his lack of vocal cords."

ABC Online

Okay, so you've had your yuks. Now you're in the mood for something with a little more meat on the bone. Many people aren't aware of it, but the online medium is perhaps the best medium for the delivery of the daily news: stories are updated continually, the news is available when you want it. AOL is capable of not only words and pictures, but *moving* pictures, and *spoken* words. Of course, glitz and glitter are nothing more than that if there's no integrity behind the news organization, but at AOL, ABC News is the primary news provider, and their integrity is undeniable (see Figure 5-9).

Be sure to try ABC's slide shows, RealAudio, and streaming video. Soon, everything online will look (and sound) like this.

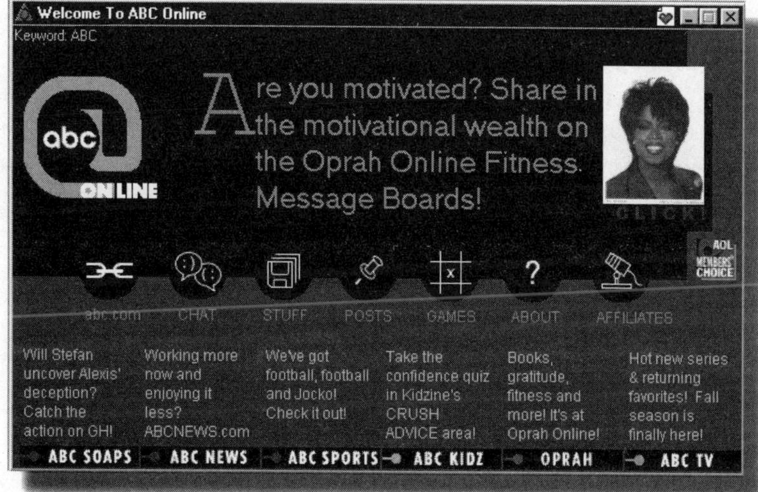

Figure 5-9: ABC Online offers not only the news, but sports and entertainment as well. Use the keyword: **ABC**.

Market News Center

When Wall Street suffered a 500-point "adjustment" in November 1997, no one jumped from a tall building. Indeed, few people panicked whatsoever. The reason? Today's stock market is largely composed of private investors, and private investors are usually in the market for the long haul. They don't panic in response to daily fluctuations.

Those private investors, of course, are people like us. And while we don't panic in response to daily fluctuations in the market, we *do* follow the developments on Wall Street. And here's where the online medium shines through: the market news here is immediate, including continually updated graphics of the stock market's condition (see Figure 5-10).

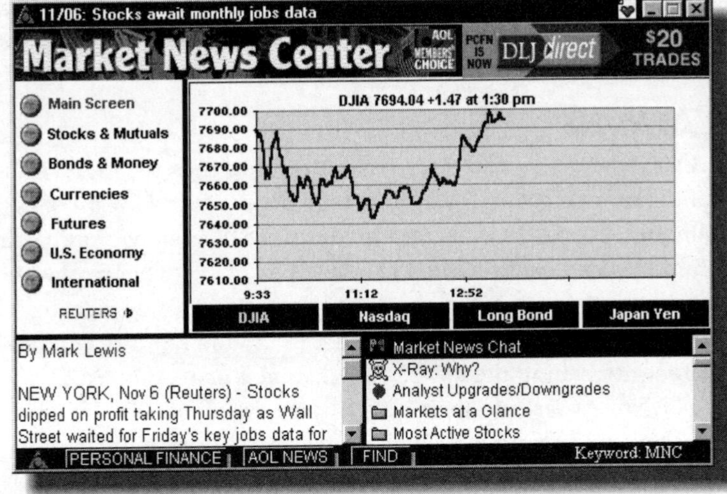

Figure 5-10: The Dow is up! The Market News Center is your launch pad to all of AOL's features for the private investor. Use the keyword: **MNC**.

The Sporting News

Our last visit among AOL's Top 50 sites is The Sporting News. Using the newspaper metaphor, The Sporting News is the *Wall Street Journal* of sports. In addition to the baseball, football, basketball, and hockey features—all immediate and up-to-the-minute—The Sporting News offers comment (including readers' comments) and a photo gallery (see Figure 5-11).

The Hot 5

The only trouble with the Top 50 is its number: 50 places to visit when you only have a half an hour to browse is like touring the Louvre on a motorcycle. If you want even more focus, try AOL's Hot 5 (Figure 5-12).

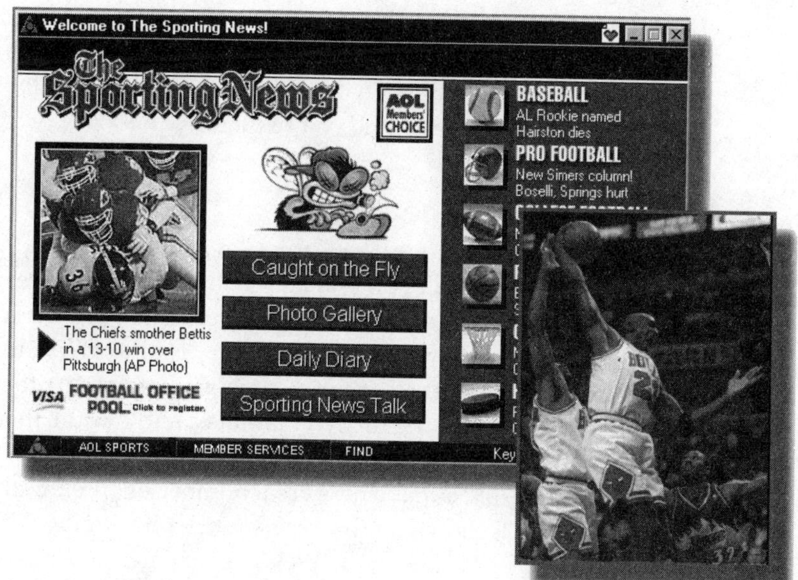

Figure 5-11: The Sporting News offers up-to-the-minute sports, when you need them, at keywords: **The Sporting News**. That's Michael Jordan, airborne again, from The Sporting News Photo Gallery.

Figure 5-12: Today's stop at the Hot 5 netted visits to three notables in the news: Dennis Rodman, Richard Gere, and MajorTom's namesake, David Bowie. Use the keyword: **New** to get here.

AOL's Hot 5 is actually a subset of What's New, AOL's springboard for new features online. The Hot 5 twirl in the center of the What's New window, and they change every day. That means you can visit the Hot 5 every day and find something new every time you're there.

Yahoo!'s Picks of the Week

So far, we've discussed only the features available at AOL proper. The World Wide Web is just as rich in potential, with available resources not only from AOL, but from everyone and everyplace else on the Web as well.

It would be a daunting proposition to try to find great stuff on the Web efficiently and effectively. We need someone to bird-dog the world's millions of Web sites, find the really great ones, and bundle them for us, all in one tidy package.

It's been done, of course. There are a number of "preferred selections" services, and we'll show you two of them here, beginning with Yahoo!'s Picks of the Week. Yahoo! is one of the Web's search mechanisms—we'll discuss those later in this chapter—and each week Yahoo! offers half a dozen or so sites the staff has selected as particularly interesting and rewarding (see Figure 5-13). Typical of the Web, Yahoo!'s picks are complete with hyperlinks. All you have to do is click your mouse.

Figure 5-13: (From upper right) Yahoo!'s Picks of the Week reveals Steve Hart's A Bronx Family Album, Stephen Hawking's Universe, a John Deere Model H tractor (from the Antique Tractor Society), and "Dark Coaches," from The Internet Hearse Society. Use the keyword: **http://www.yahoo.com/picks**.

Yahoo!'s Picks of the Week is available as a mailing list, by the way. You can receive it automatically—as e-mail—every week, free. Visit the site for details.

Cool Site of the Day

Yahoo's Picks of the Week is, of course, weekly. Perhaps you'd rather browse more often. The Cool Site of the Day offers a new pick every day, along with scores of previous picks. The Cool Site of the Day is to Web sites what the Pulitzer is to literature. It's quite a badge of honor to be selected as a Cool Site of the Day (see Figure 5-14).

Figure 5-14: The Forgotten (**http://www.forgotten.com/**) is a spectacularly videoactive site from Ransom International, a publisher of cutting-edge computer games. The Myst-like interface is continued throughout the site. We found this site via the Cool Site of the Day, at **http://cool.infi.net/index.html**.

Cool Site of the Day is from InfiNet, who also publishes Live Online (**http://www.live-online.com**), a Web page of spectacular audio and video clips, including streaming audio from a number of "Left of the Dial" radio stations around the country. Their Modem Moshpit is a Cool Site of the Day for streaming audio. Do you have speakers and a 28.8 (or better) modem? Give the Moshpit a try.

When You *Do* Know What You're Looking For

Browsing is an intemperate kind of thing. It consumes time with a chain-saw appetite. And while we all like to indulge ourselves occasionally, browsing is at best a digression.

More often than not, your online pursuits will be guided by a purpose: you'll sign on with a goal, a destination, a specific need. Five years ago, the online universe was primarily social—e-mail, chat, newsgroups—but lately it has returned to its roots; it's becoming a resource, a repository of the world's knowledge, encyclopedic and abundant.

Back in its military and scholastic era, the Internet was a place people accessed to search for information. Their tools were primitive and the scope was narrow, but the searching process—something humans have never been good at—was done at the speed of light.

The tools are no longer primitive, nor is the scope of information narrow. The problem today is knowing where to find what you're looking for and how to phrase your query, challenges we'll discuss for the remainder of this chapter.

Finding Stuff on AOL

Much to our benefit, AOL offers one granddaddy of a search mechanism, capable of finding nearly everything the service has to offer. You don't need exacting terminology or technical expertise; just type in a few words and let AOL locate it for you. (Note that we're talking about AOL here, not the Internet. Searching the Internet is an entirely different matter—one that we'll discuss in a few pages.)

To access AOL Find, use the keywords: **AOL Find**, click the Find button on the toolbar (then choose AOL Find), or—handiest of all—use Ctrl+K or Command+K, as if you're about to enter a keyword (see Figure 5-15), enter your search criteria, and click the Search button.

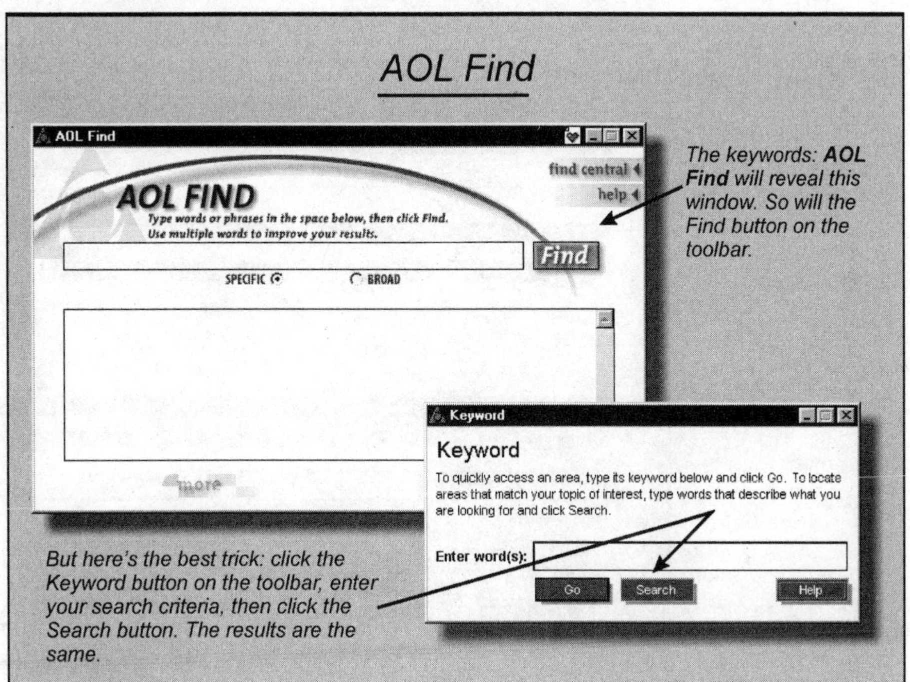

Figure 5-15: AOL Find is your one-stop shop for searching AOL's local content.

A Simple Search

Let's conduct a little search of our own. Our old 1200 baud modem, we admit, is past its prime. It's time to purchase a new one, but we'd like to conduct some research before we buy. Perhaps AOL can help. We call up the Keyword dialog box, enter "modem" and click the Search (*not* the Go) button. AOL finds 18 matches and one of them—*Business Week* magazine's Maven—offers exactly what we were looking for: scores of modems tested, complete with ratings and prices (Figure 5-16).

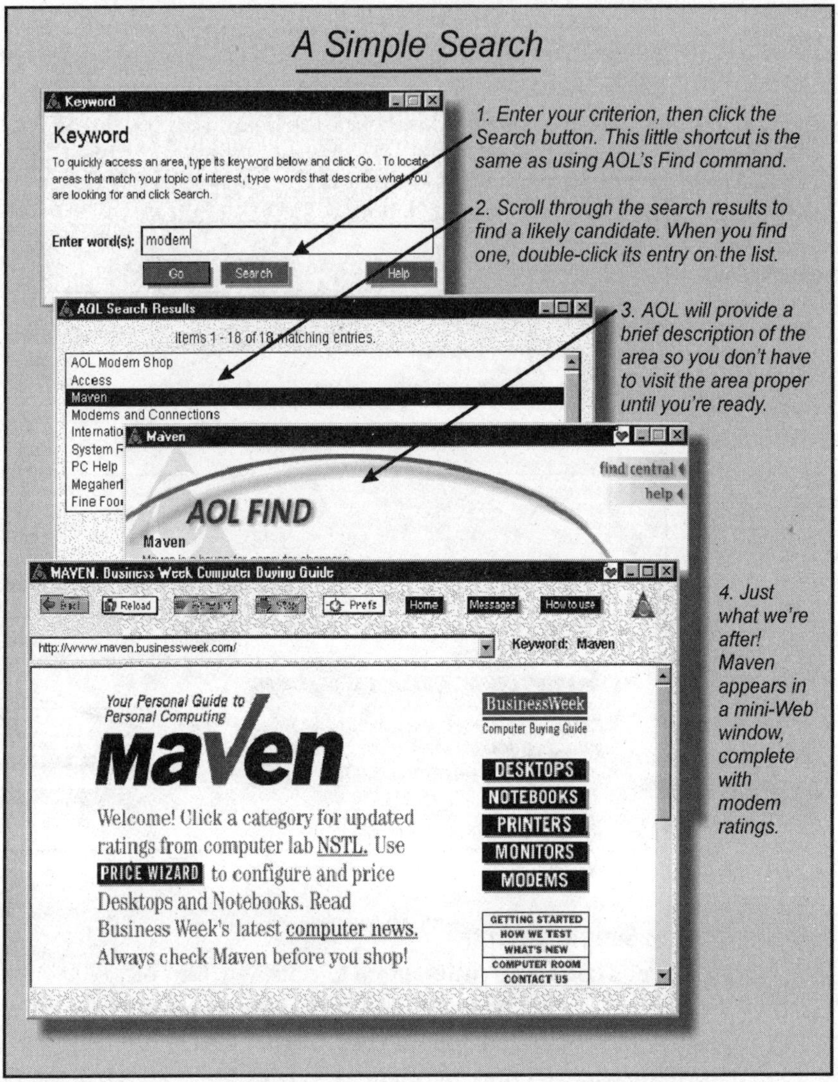

Figure 5-16: A search on the word *modem* produces a manageable number of hits, one of which was exactly what we wanted.

A Simple Search

1. Enter your criterion, then click the Search button. This little shortcut is the same as using AOL's Find command.

2. Scroll through the search results to find a likely candidate. When you find one, double-click its entry on the list.

3. AOL will provide a brief description of the area so you don't have to visit the area proper until you're ready.

4. Just what we're after! Maven appears in a mini-Web window, complete with modem ratings.

By the way, Maven's listings of the National Software Testing Lab's ratings identified the Sportster from U.S. Robotics as a likely choice. We read a little bit more about high-speed modems on the PC Hardware Forum, we found U.S. Robotics online at AOL and discovered the specifications for the modem we were considering, and we found the modem itself on sale at the AOL Modem Shop. All of these online locations were revealed in Figure 5-16's second window, and they're all pictured in Figure 5-17.

Figure 5-17: Not only an effective search, but a purchase as well: we researched high-speed modems at the PC Hardware Forum, found the vendor online, and purchased the product at the AOL Modem Shop.

Change Is Everything

That's the mantra of the online universe: "change is everything." In the 14 years that we've been online, we've seen the online universe undergo the virtual equivalent of a big bang: it's the same stuff, but nothing is as it was; everything has changed. If transportation had undergone the same changes the online industry has, we'd all be teleporting now. Scotty would be a very busy fellow.

We mention change because this section of the book contains many specific examples, presented in a workbook-like fashion. We invite—encourage—you to follow along, duplicating our exercises at your computer. But don't expect the same results. Comprehend the concepts; don't chide the change.

A Complex Search

Most of your searches will be as effortless as the one pictured in Figure 5-16. You needn't become involved with Boolean functions and other search modifiers until the situation warrants them, and when you're searching for something on AOL, the situation rarely does.

Rarely. But occasions do arise when a couple of words as search criteria simply aren't enough. Let's say we sold a couple of thousand cases of wine and made a few dollars on the deal. Now it's investment time, and—lately—the stock market has been an excellent (if not harrowing) investment. We sign on, press Ctrl+K or Command+K, identify our interest in the stock market, and click the Search button (Figure 5-18).

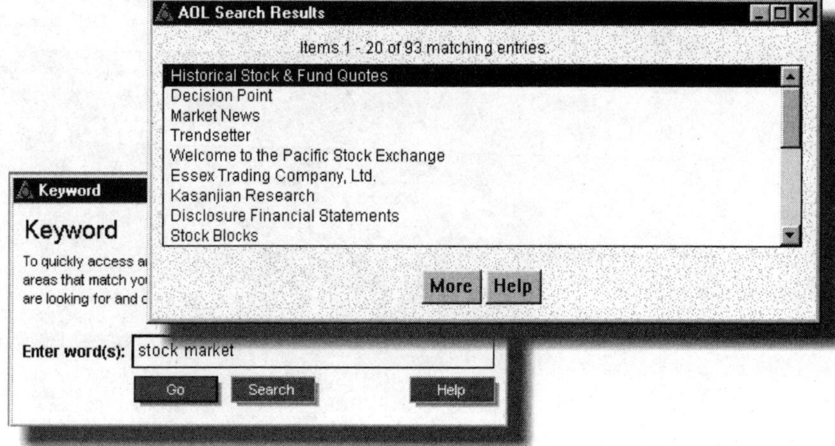

Figure 5-18: A simple search using the criterion "stock market" proves to be too broad.

Although it doesn't happen often, the search pictured in Figure 5-18 is too broad. Ninety-three articles are too many to plow through looking for a home for our investments.

This calls for some heavy artillery. We'll have to dispense with the convenience of the Keyword dialog box and make use of the AOL Find dialog box (keywords: **AOL Find**). The Find dialog box allows us to specify a *specific* search rather than the broad one that's provided by the Find dialog box (Figure 5-19).

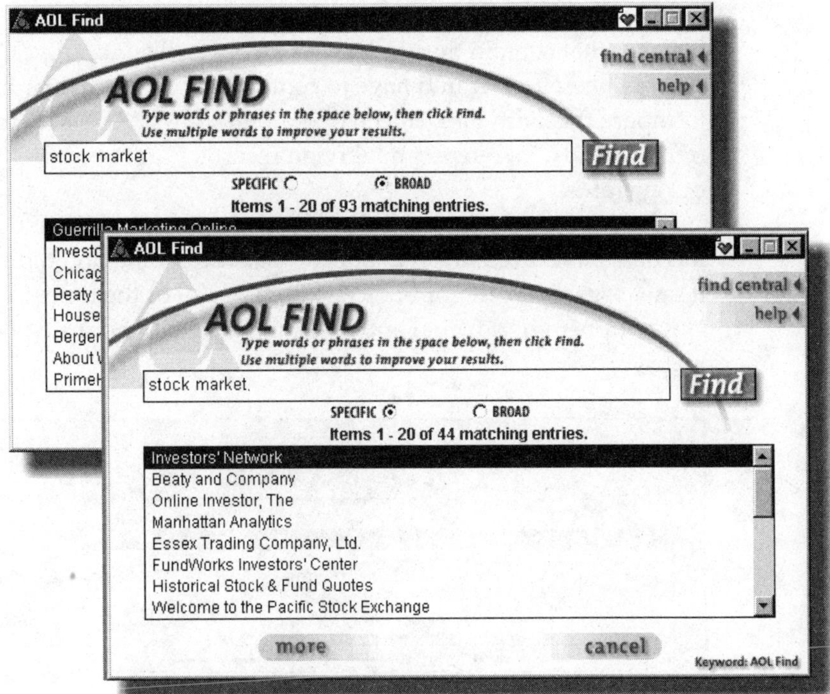

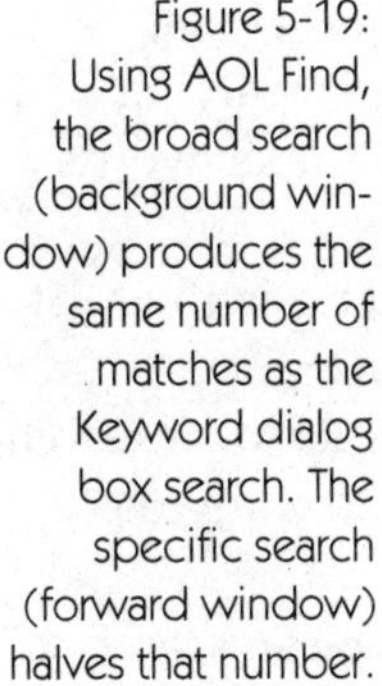
Figure 5-19: Using AOL Find, the broad search (background window) produces the same number of matches as the Keyword dialog box search. The specific search (forward window) halves that number.

The descriptions associated with each of the areas in AOL's database contain both verbal descriptions and keywords (there's an abbreviated view of the Maven area's description in step 3 of Figure 5-16). AOL's broad search searches both the description and the keywords. The specific search searches only the keywords. The broad search searches the verbal descriptions as well as the keywords and is usually more useful—you might find some interesting places by association—but not always. In other words, if you get too many matches, try AOL's Specific button first.

Good as it may be, the specific search has left us with 44 matches, which is still too many to investigate online. Since we've decided that we'd like to make our investment in mutual funds, perhaps we can narrow the search even more. *Boolean operators* are the solution, and in this context, they're the words *and*, *or*, and *not*. Think of them the way you would think of any other mathematical operator (+, -, *, ÷) and they're self-explanatory. If we say "stock market *AND* mutual funds," for example, we mean, "provide a list of all matches that contain the words *stock market* and *mutual funds*." Qualifying records, therefore, would have to contain *both* terms in their list of keywords. Compare this with the Boolean operator *or*. If we say "stock market *OR* mutual funds," we expect qualifying records to contain *either* term in their list of keywords.

Boolean operators, by the way, usually appear in UPPERCASE. Most search mechanisms require them to appear that way; some don't. If you want to play it safe, use uppercase for Boolean operators all of the time.

The upper window in Figure 5-20 is the result of our first Boolean search: 25 matches.

Figure 5-20: Boolean operators narrow the search even more.

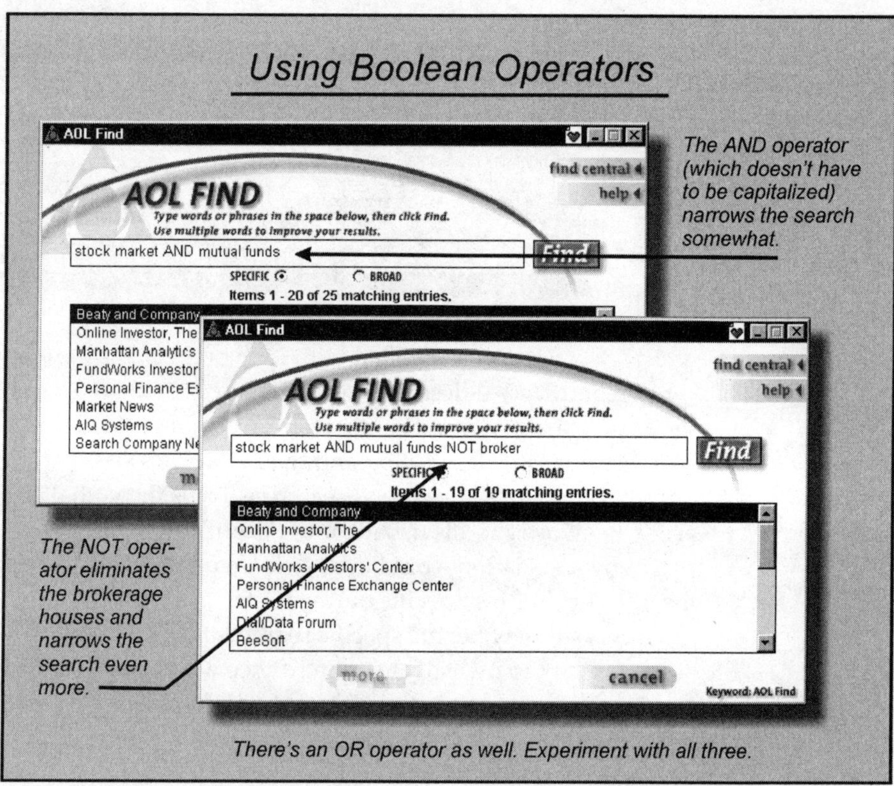

The list in Figure 5-20's upper window really isn't unmanageably long, but we can't help but note that it contains a number of brokers. As we're still in the research phase of our investment, we add the second Boolean operator pictured in Figure 5-20 and narrow the search even further.

By the way, we ended up with more than ample information and even discovered a place to invest in our mutual funds online. See Figure 5-21.

Figure 5-21: First Call offers a number of timely reports for the investor at keywords: **First Call**. Stock Talk is a forum where beginners and experts alike swap stock tips, debate the market, and discover the resources America Online offers to online investors (keywords: **Stock Talk**). Morningstar is one of the industry's most respected ratings services for mutual fund performance (keyword: **Morningstar**). And the Brokerage Center offers access to a number of brokers for online trading (keyword: **Broker**).

Leave It to George

Einstein failed mathematics; George Boole—the British mathematician for whom the Boolean operators are named—was self-taught. Indeed, he was a full professor of mathematics, yet never attended a university. In 1854, in *An Investigation of the Laws of Thought* (no demure title, that), Boole described the binary algebraic system that is the essence of all computer logic today.

The Motley Fool

It takes a charmer to be perceived as both a prankster *and* a prophet, but that's what the Motley Fool does (Figure 5-22). Brothers David and Tom Gardner hold court at keyword: **Fool**, where they couch the complexity of high finance in everyday, almost jocular language. They take beginners by their funny bones and walk them through the halls of finance, injecting providential wisdom almost without the reader's awareness.

Figure 5-22: The Motley Fool serves as court jester and financial advisor with uncanny skill every day at keyword: **Fool**.

The result is an unexpectedly savvy and thriving following. People are attracted by the presentation; they stick around for the reward. The Motley Fool is one of AOL's greatest success stories—for both the brothers and their followers. If you're an investor—especially if you're thinking about becoming one—check out the Motley Fool.

If you're not familiar with Boolean operators, AOL's Find window is a great place to learn about them. Since it's not subject to the occasional overcrowding of the World Wide Web, the AOL Find window searches quickly—a perfect platform for practice searches.

Let's try one more searching exercise. Again use the keywords: **AOL Find**, or click the Find button on the toolbar and choose Find it on AOL. Click the Specific option and enter the criterion "news." AOL will respond with scores of "hits," including some significant surprises (see Figure 5-23).

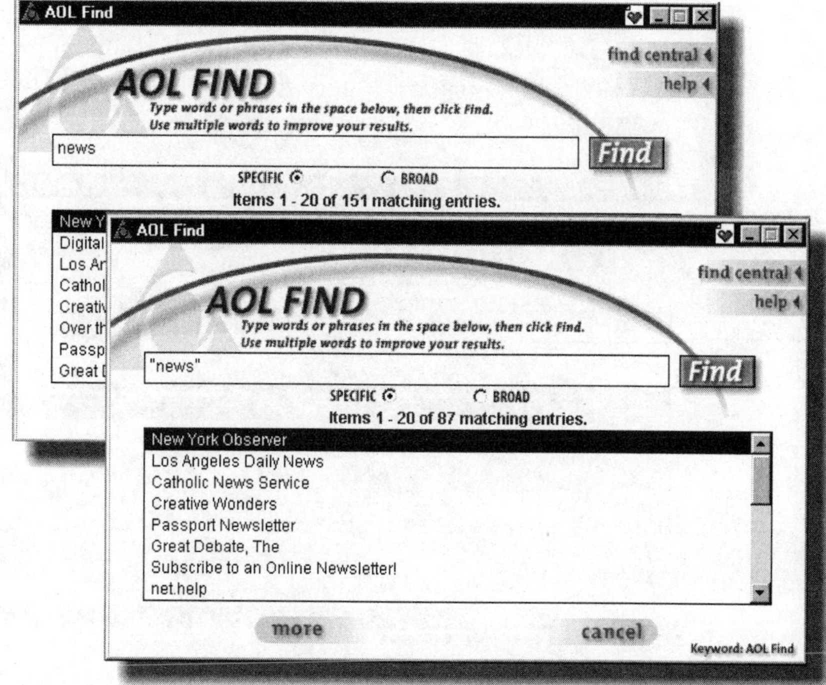

Figure 5-23: A search on the word *news* produces a few surprises. Using a whole-word search eliminates most of them.

AOL has responded with a whopping 151 hits, including "classical music," "AOL 3.0," and "Spiritual Mosaic." What does classical music have to do with the news? Or AOL's latest (at the time) software? Or Spiritual Mosaic, which is a site for pagans, Wiccans, and astrologers?

They all offer newsletters, that's what, and the word *news* occurs within the word *newsletter*. In other words, AOL is finding our keyword *within* other keywords—matches that relate to our intentions only remotely.

The solution is to place quotes around the criterion: "news." This is a common way of telling a database that we want it to search on the whole word only and not to consider our criterion as a word within a word. The whole-word search pictured in the lower window in Figure 5-23 cuts the number of hits in half.

Another useful exercise is to practice using the OR Boolean operator. The upper window in Figure 5-24 shows the AND operator, which we've seen before. The 27 matches that AOL lists are those sites that offer *both* news and sports.

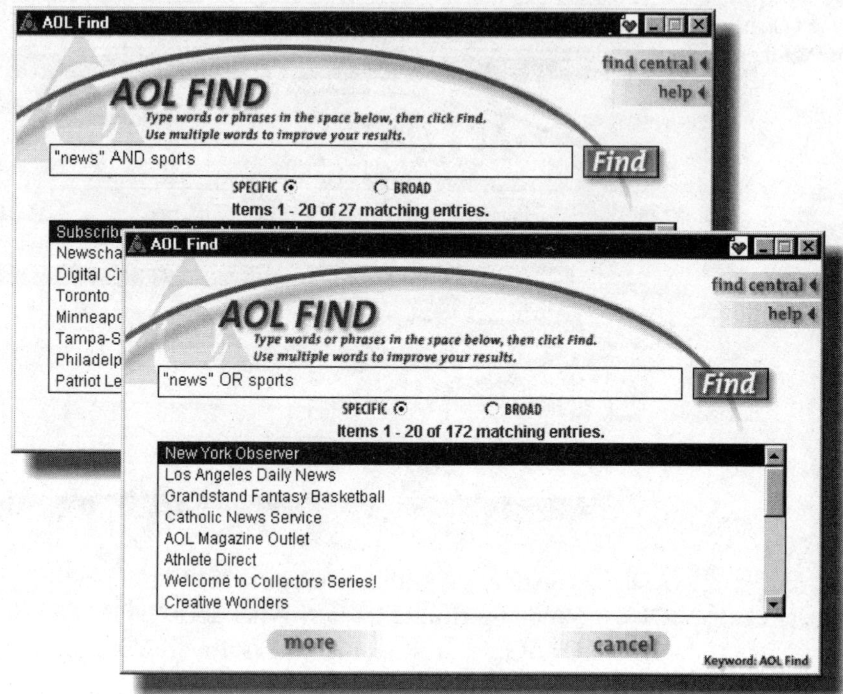

Figure 5-24: The OR Boolean operator expands the potential for hits; the AND operator decreases it.

The lower window in Figure 5-24 illustrates what happens when the OR operator is substituted. More than three times as many sites offer *either* news or sports, a significant difference.

Our search was gratifying, by the way. Figure 5-25 identifies some of the interesting destinations we visited as a result of our pursuit of news and sports.

Figure 5-25: AOL's Grandstand (keyword: **Grandstand**) is a forum for sports dialog; the Real Fans Sports Network (keyword: **Fans**) provides real-time sports reporting (be sure to use the ticker); Digital Cities (keywords: **Digital City**) offers local news, sports, and weather for scores of localities around the nation; AOL's News Search (keywords: **News Search**) allows you to search all of the news articles currently online; The Newsstand (keyword: **Newsstand**) centralizes all of AOL's magazines and newspapers for easy access; and the venerable New York Times Online (keyword: **Times**) offers "all of the news that's fit to digitize."

Finding Stuff on the Web

Searching AOL is like searching your bedroom for a missing sweatshirt. Searching the Web is like searching 100 million bedrooms for a missing sock. Consequently, a number of search *engines*, as they're called, have appeared—sites that have the ability to search the entire Web using your criteria and return the results within a few seconds. This requires an arsenal of hardware and telephones lines that we can only imagine, but the expense is repaid: search engines are hosts to the choicest advertising opportunities on the Web. Millions of people visit these sites every day; ads there reach every one of them, and many of their owners/operators have consequently become multimillionaires virtually overnight. In the next few pages, we'll visit five of them to see what they have to offer.

No Place for Arachnophobia

Spiders—so named because they crawl around on the World Wide Web—are elaborate computer programs that periodically go out on the Web and examine pages. Most spiders read every word on every site they find and then index those words, building indices similar to the one at the back of this book. The search engines themselves search the indexes (not the sites), which is why most search engines are so fast.

No one knows how many Web sites are out there—some say the number doubles every couple of months—but fifty to a hundred million is a good guess. Can you imagine browsing fifty to a hundred million Web sites? Every day?

AOL NetFind

AOL's NetFind (keyword: **NetFind**, or click the Internet icon on the toolbar) is the most accessible search engine for AOL members (Figure 5-26).

NetFind, like a lot of other search engines, defaults to the OR operator, which, as you'll recall, is less selective than the AND operator. A search using the criterion "search engine" netted over three million hits. Searching with the criterion "search AND engine" netted a little over one hundred thousand. (NetFind, by the way, requires Boolean operators in uppercase.)

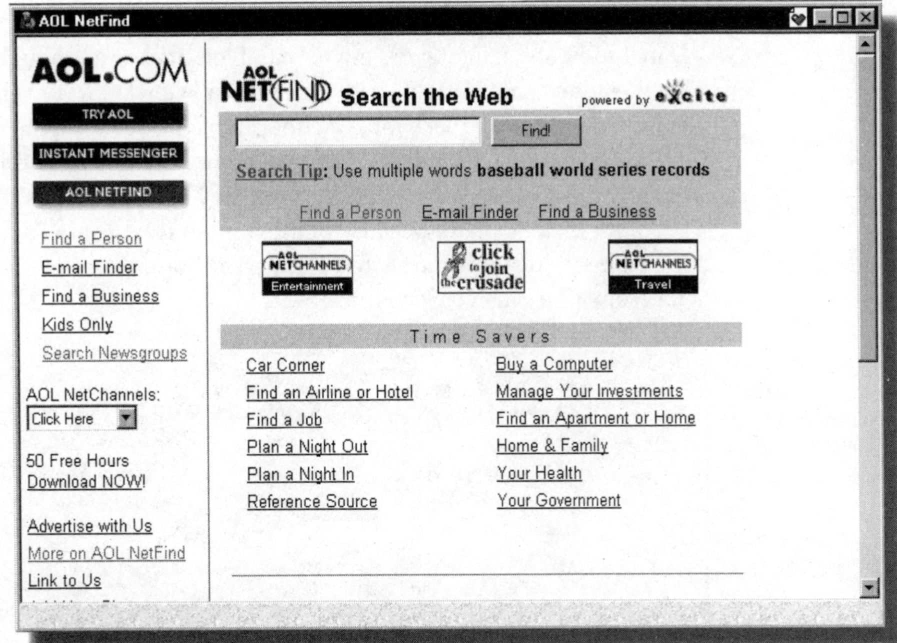

Figure 5-26: AOL's NetFind is a relatively simple search engine. Super-complex searches—the kind we don't even try to discuss in this book—aren't supported, but NetFind *does* support all of the Boolean operators we've mentioned.

NetFind offers a couple of tasty features you might like: (1) Hits are ranked by quality (100%, 99%, etc.), and (2) *query by example* is supported. The term *quality* refers to how well the site matches your search criteria. Query by example is a way of refining your search by telling the engine what kind of hit worked well for you. When you find a hit that's especially appropriate to what you were looking for, return to the results page and click the link labeled More Like This. Do this a few times and you'll hone your query to a razor-sharp edge *without* acquiring a PhD in computer science along the way.

You'll hear about another search engine called *Excite!* (keyword: **http://www.excite.com/**). We won't discuss it here because NetFind really *is* Excite—the AOL-branded version, in fact. NetFind has a different look and feel to it, but it's Excite underneath.

Yahoo!

We include Yahoo! in our review of search engines even though it really isn't a search engine at all. Yahoo! is what's called a Web *directory*. Yahoo! doesn't use a spider (see the "No Place for Arachnophobia" sidebar). Instead it relies on humans. Members of Yahoo!'s staff visit some 500,000 sites periodically and update Yahoo!'s directory to reflect what they find. Sites must be submitted to Yahoo! for inclusion, but because of the human role, Yahoo!'s directories often provide better results than search engines, although Yahoo!'s 500,000-site listing is far from all-inclusive. See Figure 5-27.

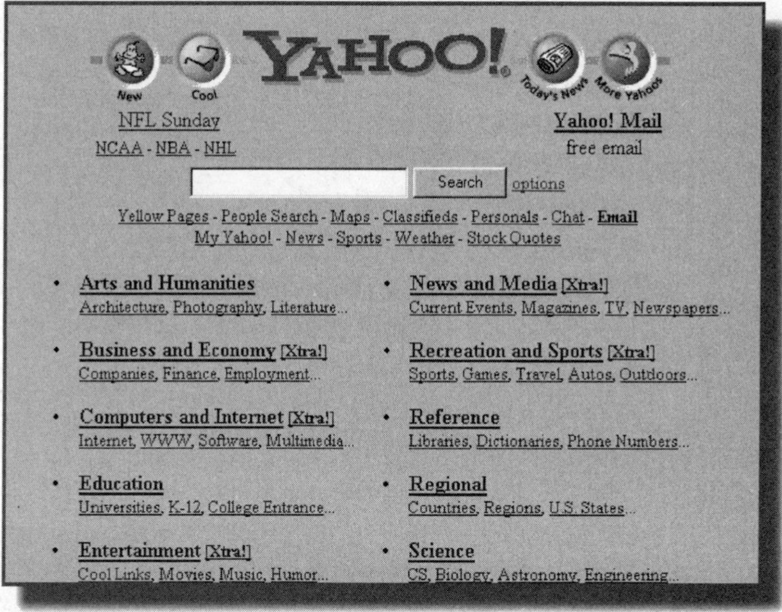

Figure 5-27: Yahoo! (keyword: **http://www.yahoo.com**) is actually a directory of Web pages built by humans rather than spiders.

The people at Yahoo! recognize their directory's imperfections and offer quick links to selected search engines (AltaVista is the preferred one). With a click of the mouse, queries sent to Yahoo!'s directory are "piped" to any of the major search engines. Look for the AltaVista link on any Yahoo! results page.

This Is the Place for Arachnophobia

Unusual words are more likely to return valid search results than common words. This goes especially for single-word searches. *Arachnophobia*, for example, will produce a more focused search than *spiders*.

AltaVista

Digital Equipment Corporation owns AltaVista, which began as a technology demonstration for Digital's Alpha AXP servers. Quickly, however, AltaVista has become one of the most popular search engines on the Web (see Figure 5-28). And search engine it is: using spiders (some of which crawl the Web daily), AltaVista indexes almost every word of every site it visits—perhaps as many as 50 million sites.

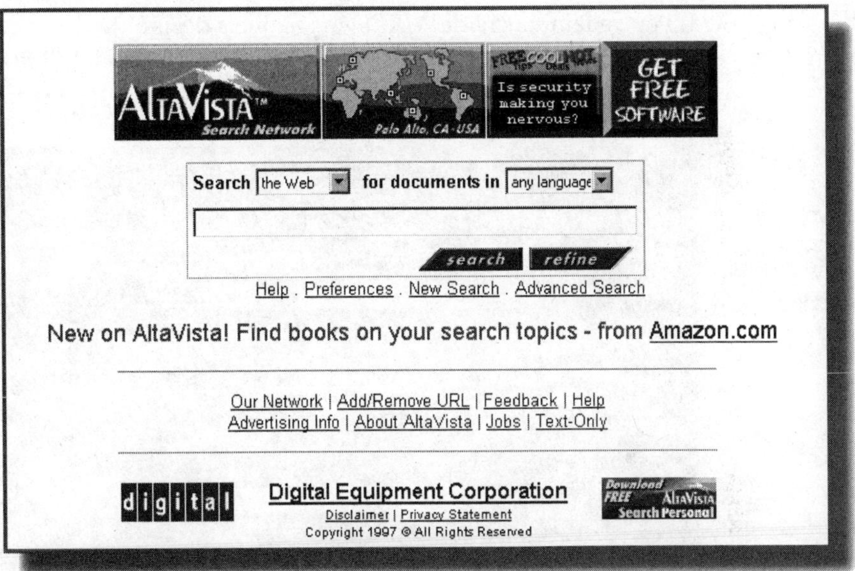

Figure 5-28: AltaVista is the Mac truck of search engines, at keyword: **http://www.altavista.digital.com**.

Because of its ponderous index of sites, AltaVista frequently returns matches numbering in the millions, with the best ones buried somewhere in the middle of the list. Knowing how to phrase a query really counts here, though it won't take long to learn. *Do* take the time to learn it, however, or stick to something less complex like NetFind.

Stopwords

Stopwords are terms so common on Web sites that search engine developers routinely exclude them. Search AltaVista for the word *computer*, for instance, and you'll get "No documents match the query" in return. Many engines won't search for a phrase beginning with a number, and others won't search for phrases that include one-letter words. Don't search for "Vitamin C," use "ascorbic acid" instead. Words like *sex*, *free*, *shareware*, *Web*, and *Windows*—so-called *Spamdex* words—return so many hits as to be useless.

HotBot

HotBot is from *WIRED* magazine, and as you might expect, it's the most graphical search engine of them all (Figure 5-29). It offers drop-down menus to let you compose a search, and you can configure it to find only certain types of files (applications, images, VRML, and so forth) and save customized settings. It's the only one that allows you to confine a search to a specific geographical location, and it attempts to resolve the common problem of duplicate matches by checking documents for sites mirrored on other servers. If you're familiar with *WIRED* magazine's design (take a look at keyword: **WIRED**), you're familiar with HotBot's look and feel. It'll find phosphors on your screen you never knew you had.

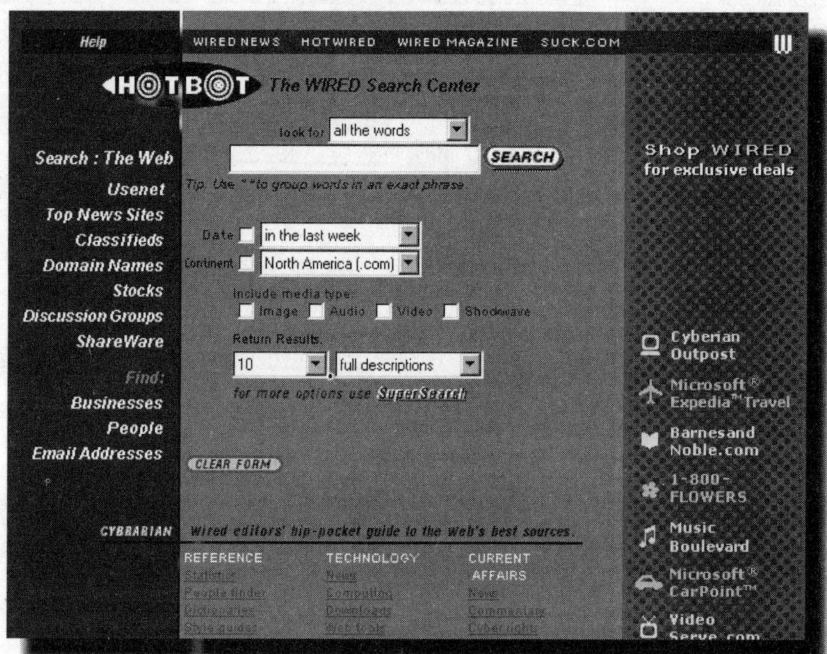

Figure 5-29: HotBot (keyword: **http://www.hotbot.com**) is *WIRED* magazine's search engine entry.

Search Engine Watch

If the topic of search engines intrigues you, or if you just want to do a better job of searching the Web, visit Search Engine Watch at keyword: **http://searchenginewatch.com/**. Here you'll find sections on how search engines find and rank Web pages, tips on how to use search engines better, periodic reports on how search engines are performing, search engine links, and even a game to test your search engine knowledge.

Finding People

Enough of this Web page stuff. Though we all browse the Web at one time or another, many of us find our long-term contentment in the people we meet online. We stumble to the computer every morning not to browse the Web, but to read our mail. The Web is sexy and enticing, but it's the people of the online community that make it a community. It's these people who bring us back every day.

Of course, before you form online relationships with people, you first have to find them. How do you find people online? That's our topic for the next few pages.

Finding AOL Members

Let's be candid: AOL is a beehive of social activity. If you haven't read it yet, Chapter 7 ("Chat") will make that abundantly clear. You should expect, then, for AOL to offer a number of people-finding mechanisms, and you won't be disappointed.

The Member Directory

You might recall our discussion of member profiles in Chapter 2. Profiles are descriptions of yourself that you provide; they identify your name, interests, locality, and so on. There are two primary reasons for filling out a profile. Most often, someone will see your screen name online—in a chat room (chat rooms are discussed in Chapter 7) or in some e-mail—and they will want to know more about you. They'll choose Get AOL Member Profile from the People icon on the toolbar, enter your screen name, and your profile will be displayed.

The other use for profiles is the Member Directory. The Member Directory is AOL's database of everyone's profiles, and it's searchable. You can search for a member by real name, screen name, or by anything in their profile. You might wonder if a friend or relative is signed up with AOL: search the directory and you'll know in seconds.

Profilers Only

Although AOL has more than 10 million members, only those who have posted their profiles are available when you search the Member Directory. Some people are here strictly for business, others are single-purpose accounts with no social intentions, and a few others are simply shy. Whatever their reasons, these people would rather be left alone, and they guarantee that by omitting their profile.

One of the more interesting things you can do with the directory is search for people with interests similar to yours. Once you've found them, you can send them mail and, perhaps, strike up a friendship. It's all part of the electronic community.

Tom, for instance, enjoys cruising the waters of the Pacific Northwest aboard his tugboat. Thinking he might find someone to share his mania, he searches the Member Directory for members with similar interests by specifying "cruising AND boat*" as his criteria (Figure 5-30).

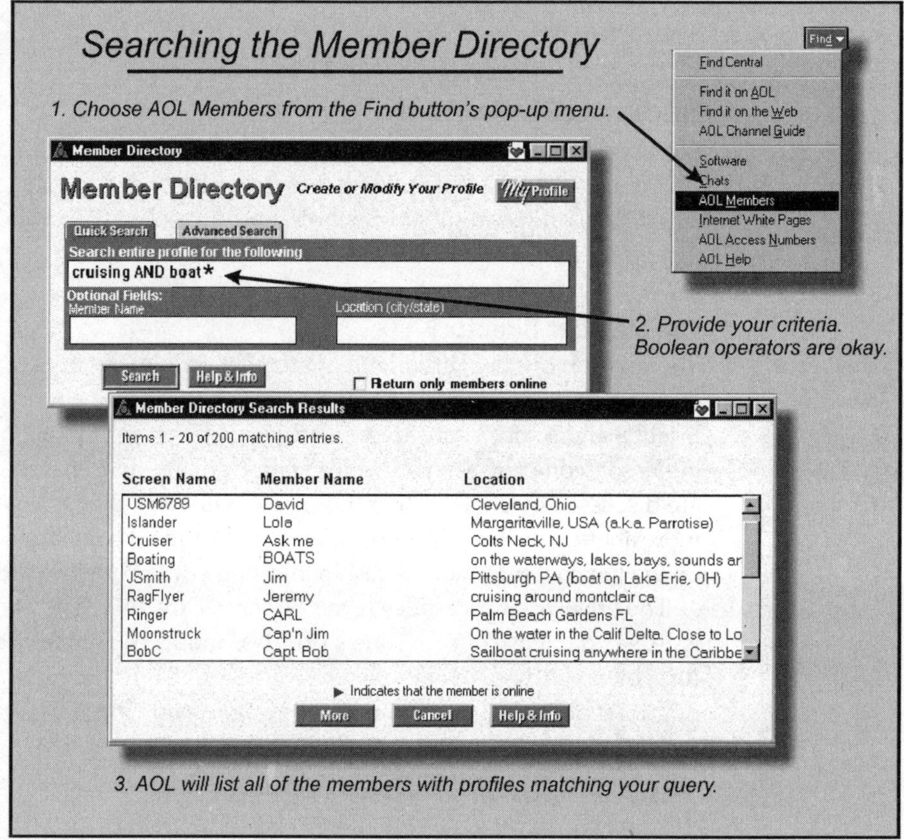

Figure 5-30: Much to Tom's delight, there are lots of other aquatic cruisers on America Online. (The screen names in this illustration have been changed to protect members' privacy.)

Note that one of Tom's criteria was "boat*" and that he used the Boolean operator AND. The asterisk is a wildcard, and most Boolean operators are supported. (There's help available with wildcards and Boolean operators; just click the Help & Info button pictured in the upper window of Figure 5-30.)

The Personals

We mentioned the AOL Classifieds briefly at the beginning of this chapter. Like any good community communications vehicle, AOL offers an extensive "classified section," but unlike newspaper classifieds, these classifieds are searchable. Sure, you'll find sections containing vehicles, real estate, computers, and employment, but you'll also find a section dedicated to personals as well (see Figure 5-31).

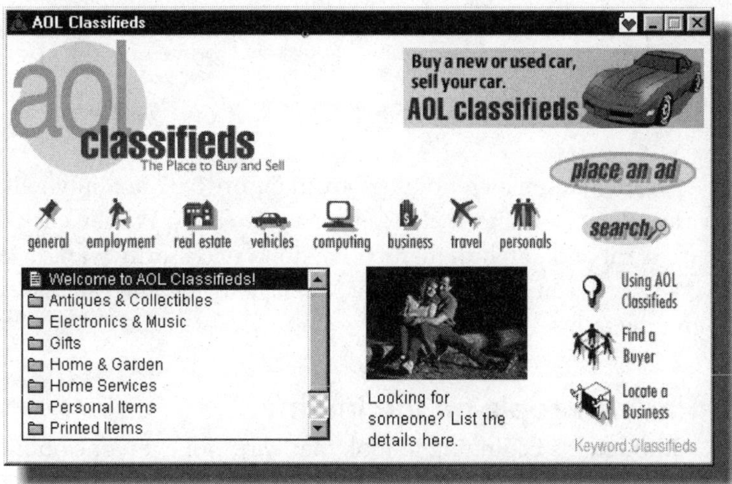

Figure 5-31: The AOL Classifieds are a great way to find not only computers and cars, but people as well.

Expect to find the "SWF" kind of stuff here—all moderated by AOL staff and on the up-and-up, by the way—but you'll also find people looking for pen pals, weight-loss partners, softball players, relatives, and roommates and reunions looking for members of the class of 1977. There's no charge for the service.

Finding People Online

There's one other way of finding someone online, but only if they're online at AOL and only if you know their screen name. The feature is called Locate a Member Online.

If you suspect that a friend of yours is online (and your Buddy List window isn't showing—see Chapter 7 for a description of Buddy Lists), just press Ctrl+L or Command+L to locate a member online (see Figure 5-32).

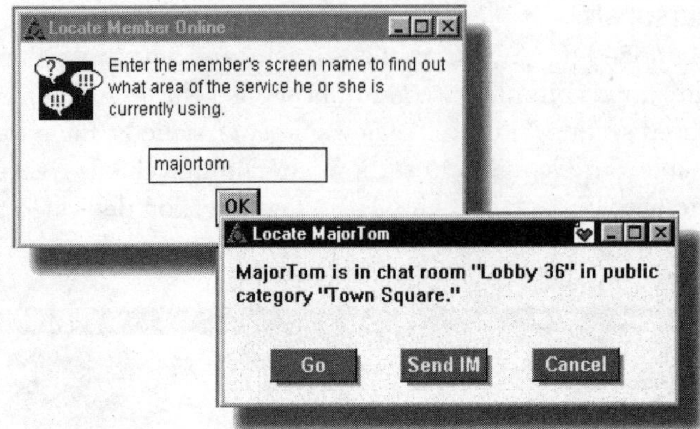

Figure 5-32: Want to know if a friend is online? Press Ctrl+L. You'll not only discover if they're online, but if they're in a chat room, which chat room they're in as well.

Note that the lower dialog box in Figure 5-32 not only tells us that MajorTom is online, it also tells us where he is. We can click the Go button if we want and join him there. If we don't necessarily want to join him in Lobby 36, we can send him an Instant Message instead. It's all just a matter of clicking the mouse.

Finding People on the Internet

Although it's beginning to look that way, not everyone online is an AOL member. Indeed, there are 50 to 100 million people using the Internet, and nearly every one has an e-mail address. How do you find them? You use any of the many online services that specialize in finding people online.

Internet Instant Messages

You can maintain a Buddy List and send Instant Messages (Buddy Lists and Instant Messages are discussed in Chapter 7) to anyone who is currently signed on the Internet and is using AOL's Instant Messenger service. This is a great way to stay in touch with online friends who aren't AOL members, and it sure beats the price of a phone call. For more information, read Chapter 7, and use the keyword: **http://www.aol.com/aim/home.html**.

AOL Switchboard

No doubt the most convenient tool for finding Internet users is the AOL Switchboard. Not only does Switchboard list Internet users, it lists businesses as well and even offers an Ad Studio for the construction of elaborate "Yellow Pages" business listings.

But business isn't what we're discussing. If you want to track down an old friend or distant relative, or you wonder what happened to your former roommate, or you're assembling a class reunion, the people you're looking for are probably available via the AOL Switchboard (Figure 5-33). To get there, click the Find button on the toolbar and choose Internet White Pages.

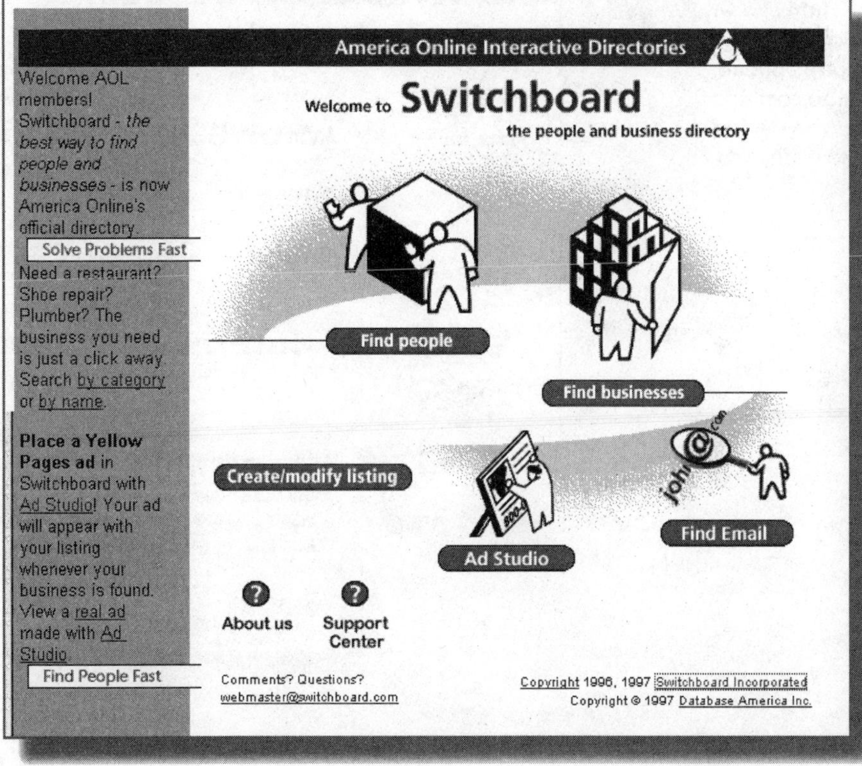

Figure 5-33: AOL's Switchboard lists tens of millions of Internet users. You can search for them here and add your own listing as well. Use the keyword: **http://aol.switchboard.com/**.

Other Internet White Pages Services

There are a number of Internet White Pages services available. Most of them are listed at keyword: **http://www.internic.net/tools/wp.html**, where you'll find mini-search forms and links to each one as well. We've pictured a few of these in Figure 5-34.

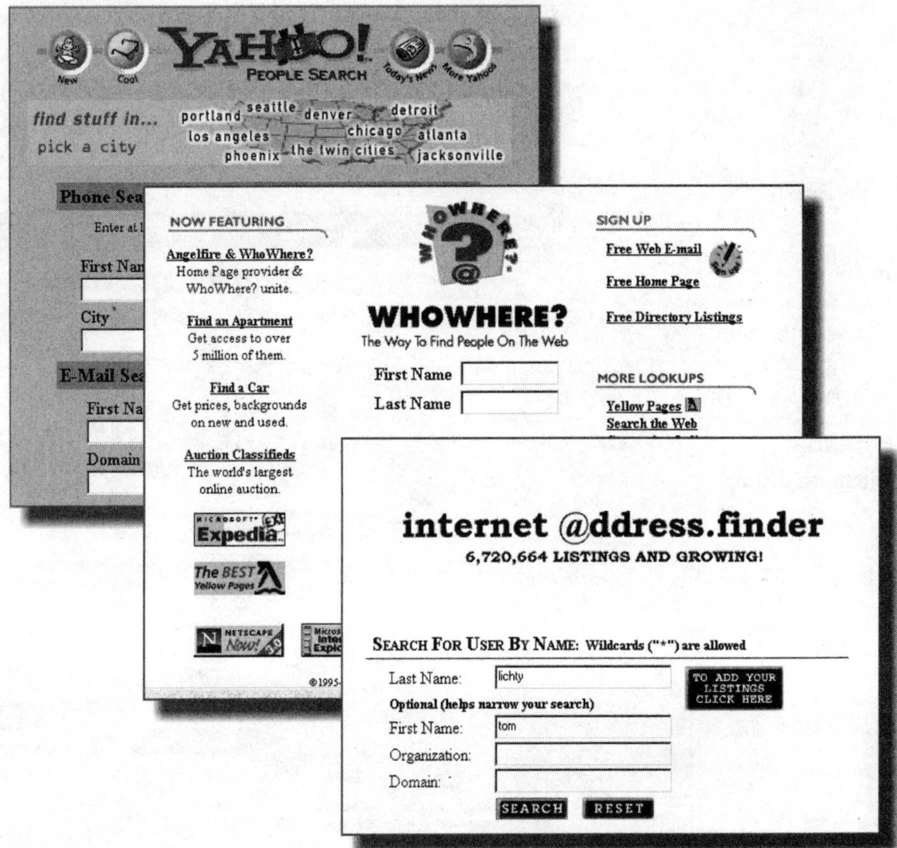

Figure 5-34: Three of the White Pages services offered on the Internet. Use the keywords: **http://www.whowhere.com**, **http://phone.yahoo.com**, and **http://www.iaf.net** to reach them.

Finding Software & Files

Be sure to read Chapter 6, "Transferring Files," for a discussion of AOL's File Search mechanism. It searches AOL's massive library of files—both programs and data—and returns results in a matter of seconds.

There are millions of files available on the Internet as well. Most hardware and software companies post updates and drivers on the Internet; all you have to do is find a company's site (you shouldn't have trouble finding stuff now!) and navigate to its download area.

Here's an example. We've had our Zip drives for over a year now, and we've heard that there are new drivers—maybe even a new program—available for our hardware. We use AltaVista to search the Internet for Zip drivers from Iomega Corporation and come up with just what we were looking for (Figure 5-35). In other words, you already know how to find files on the Internet: just use the search tools you've read about in this chapter.

Figure 5-35: Using AltaVista to find updated drivers for our Iomega Zip drives.

MacStuff

You may have trouble finding stuff on your desk, but you won't on America Online. And you won't find any variations between the Mac and Windows when it comes to finding things on AOL either.

Moving On

Frankly, the Iomega search shown in Figure 5-35 is a bad example. You don't have to look very carefully to see that Iomega directs us to "use the keyword: **IOMEGA**" at America Online. Indeed, AOL offers all of the Iomega files that Iomega does, and AOL servers are usually faster than those on heavily used sites such as Iomega's.

So how do you find *those* files? And how do you download them once you've found them? It's all in Chapter 6, "Transferring Files." Read on.

Transferring Files

CHAPTER 6

- What Is Downloading?
- Uploading Files

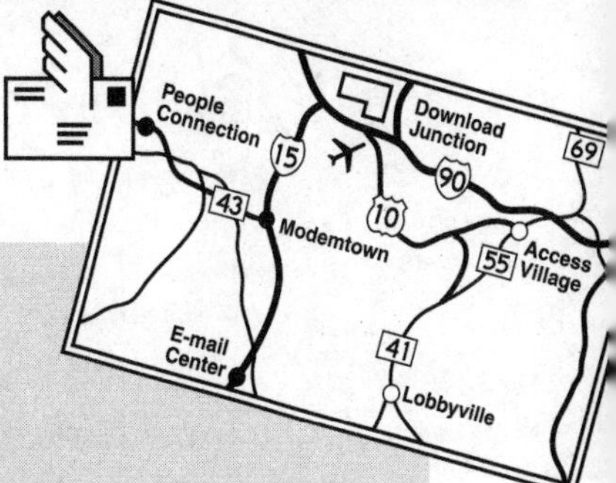

An AOL community leader once wrote, "If I had a nickel for every time I was asked how to download or what a download is, I would be a rich woman."

Exaggeration, perhaps—it takes 20,000,000 nickels to make a millionaire—but her message is clear: people want to know what this "downloading" business is all about. And well they should; downloading is one of the top five activities people do online, and more than 100,000 files, spread across the service like flowers in a meadow, are available for downloading on America Online. Members graze this meadow, smiling, downloading bouquets of files. People must be on to something here, and those who aren't want to be. A chapter on the subject (as well as on uploading—transferring a file from your computer to America Online's computer) seems warranted. Here it is.

What Is Downloading?

Simply put, *downloading* is the process of transferring files—for example, transferring a file from America Online's computers to your computer. Files can be programs, utilities, drivers, fonts, graphics (many of the graphics in this book have been downloaded), sound, animation, and, of course, text.

On America Online, there are three kinds of downloads: the first two are e-mail downloads (which we discussed in Chapter 3) and File Transfer Protocol (FTP) downloads (which are done via the Internet and discussed in Chapter 4). The third type of download is via a *file library* and can be either *freeware* or *shareware* (both of which cost nothing to download beyond your normal connection charges) or retail software (which you must purchase before you download). The majority of files on America Online are freely distributed, and all retail software is clearly marked (and kept in special libraries).

Retailware

Don't let this chapter's emphasis on shareware fool you. There's plenty of retail software available online as well—hundreds of titles of boxed software identical to that found in software and computer stores everywhere. The difference is convenience: You can buy retail software online without having to leave your keyboard, and it arrives in your mailbox a few days later. Use the keywords: **AtOnce Software** to peruse 3,500 products you can download. Also, visit the AOL Software Shop (kewords: **Software Shop**).

You may have heard horror stories about downloading, but they probably had something to do with complex downloading protocols. Fortunately, those are things of the past. The AOL software handles the protocols automatically.

A Downloading Session

Note: This section of the chapter describes a typical downloading session for Windows users only. Macintosh readers should skip to the section entitled "Finding Files for Downloading."

Perhaps the best way to explain downloading is to download a file for you and explain the process as it's happening. If your computer is nearby, you might want to sign on and follow along.

Finding the File

Before you can download a file, you have to find it. There are lots of ways to find files, but for the purposes of this exercise, we'll go directly to a known location. Later, we'll discuss methods of finding a file when its location is *not* known or when the name of the file isn't at hand.

Begin by signing on and using the keyword: **Win**. Most forums offer libraries, as does this one. Simply stated, a library is an online reservoir of files. Some of these files are placed online by the forum's staff; others are uploaded by America Online members (we'll discuss uploading later in this chapter). There's usually a forum staff member who maintains the library, ensuring files are virus-free, clarifying file descriptions, and removing out-dated entries.

By now you should see the Software Library button in the PC Windows Forum window. Click it (see Figure 6-1). The Windows Forum Software window will appear, offering a variety of file categories.

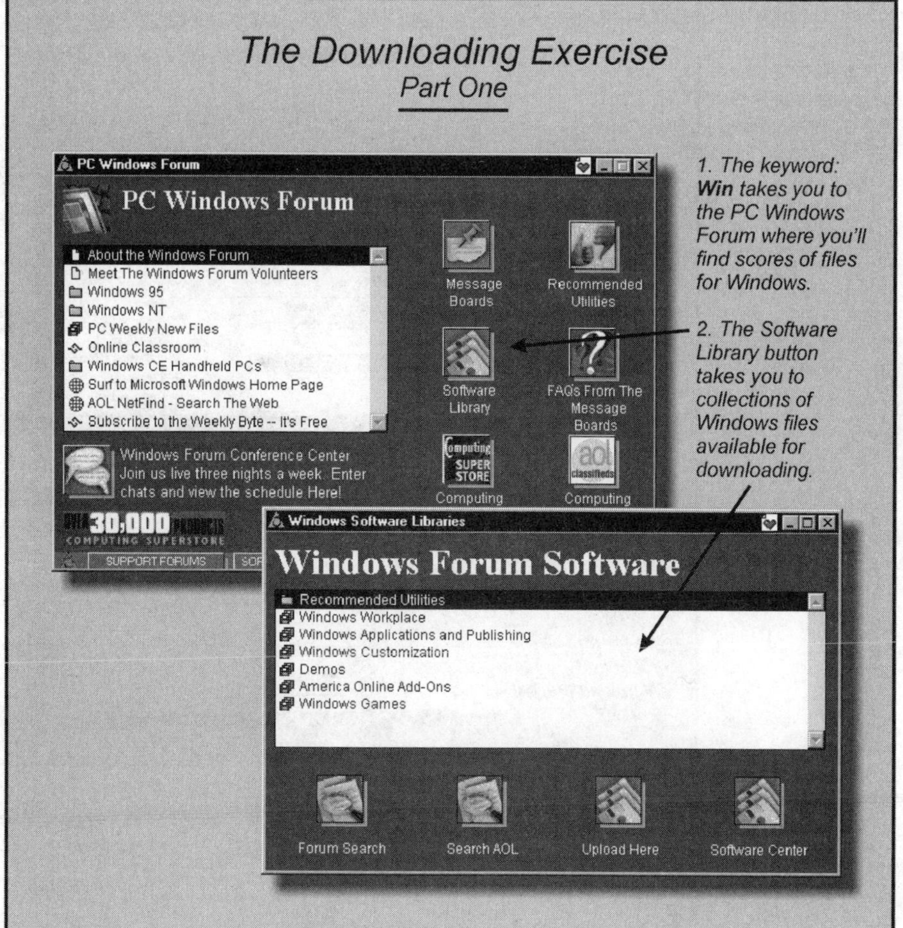

Figure 6-1: The PC Windows Forum is an especially rewarding place to find Windows files for downloading.

Writing on Water

This exercise is a litany of specifics, and when it comes to the telecommunications industry, describing specifics is like writing on water. By the time you read this, the appearance of the PC Windows Forum may have changed, the forum's libraries might have been restructured, and existing files could be superseded by new versions.

Assuming this *fait accompli*, we suggest adaptability. A forum of some kind for Windows will always exist, and so will its file libraries. Tolerate change; if you do, your online life—not to mention your experience with this book—will become a lot easier.

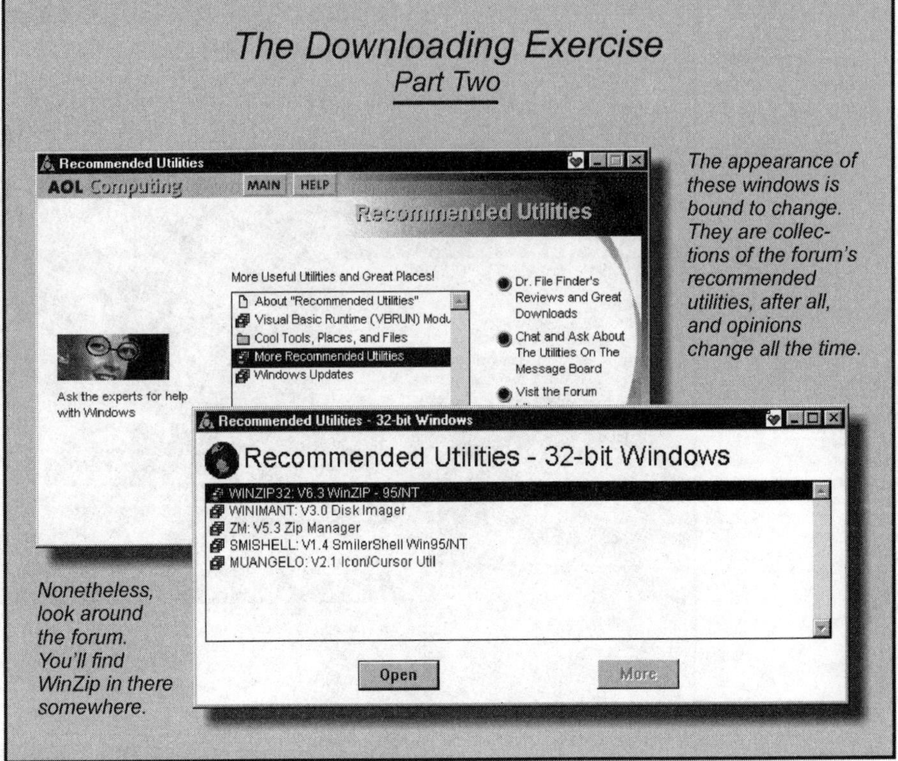

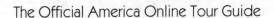

Figure 6-2: WinZip is one of the forum's most popular shareware utilities.

WinZip

You can't survive long in the downloading environment without some form of compression/decompression software. Compression and decompression are as common to downloading files as stink is to skunks. Though we'll discuss file compression later in this chapter, you're going to need file compression software eventually, and now's a good time to get some. WinZip is an excellent choice, and since this exercise requires that you download something, we might as well make it something useful.

Downloading the File

The Windows 95/NT version of WinZip (there's also a version for Windows 3.1) is selected in Figure 6-2 and is appropriate to our needs. We found it first by selecting the Recommended Utilities folder shown in Figure 6-1 and then opening the 32-bit Windows library within the More Recommended Utilities folder. To download it, simply:

1. Double-click it and then click the Download Now button in the file description window that results. The standard Windows file-saving window appears next.
2. Choose a place for WinZip on your hard disk and click the OK button.

The progress indicator shown in Figure 6-3 appears, estimating the amount of time required to download the file and providing visual indication of the file's progress. When the transfer is finished, the announcement you see at the bottom of Figure 6-3 appears and the process concludes. It's as easy as that.

Figure 6-3: Determine where you want the file to go on your hard disk and then click OK. The remainder of the transfer is automatic.

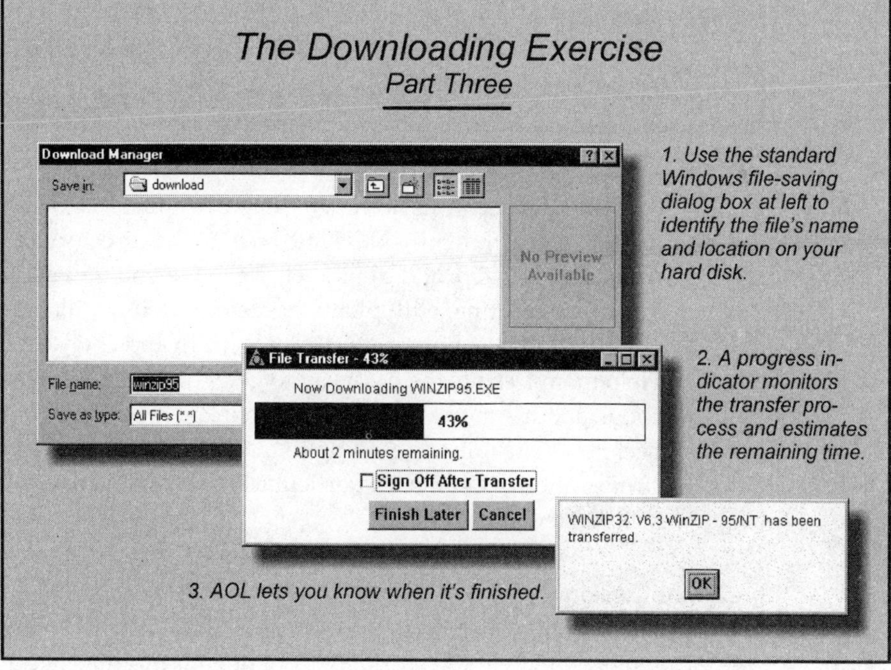

Filenames & Destinations

Look again at Figure 6-3 and note the proposed filename. If you want to use a filename other than the one proposed, all you have to do is select the name (if it isn't selected already) and start typing. We don't recommend changing the filename unless the proposed filename conflicts with one already on your disk. The file's documentation, for example, might refer to the file by the original name; if you change the name, the reference might be unclear. Also, forum discussions might refer to the file's original name. If you search for an update to the file, you'll need to use its original name. So stick to the original name unless you have a good reason not to.

The \AOL40\DOWNLOAD directory pictured in Figure 6-3 is the default destination for downloaded files. Some would say that this directory isn't the best one to use; there will no doubt be an update to version 5.0 some day, and when it comes along you will probably have a new directory for it—something like C:\AOL50. When the installation of the update is complete, you might be tempted to delete the old \AOL40 directory, forgetting that you have a number of valuable downloads in there. By the time you remember, it might be too late. The file-saving dialog box in Figure 6-3 allows you to declare any directory on any disk as a destination. Don't hesitate to change the destination.

Sign off now if you've nothing else to do online (the Sign Off command is under the Sign Off menu). Navigate back to the directory to which you downloaded WinZip, and double-click the file you downloaded. WinZip's installation is routine, with plenty of Help buttons available along the way. When installation is finished, execute WinZip and choose Brief Tutorial from its Help menu. That's the best way to get to know the program, and since this is a book about America Online—not WinZip—we'll move on to a different subject now. The important thing to mention is that you have downloaded a file from America Online—a particularly useful file—and all you had to do was click a few buttons.

Multitasking

America Online offers three ways to download files: (1) you can simply click the Download Now button and sit in front of your machine like a fossil; (2) you can queue files for downloading and wait until the end of your online session (or for another part of the day) and download then (this is a function of the Download

Manager, which we'll discuss in Chapter 8, "Working Offline"); or (3) you can do something else with your computer while the download concludes in the background, like write that letter you owe your mother or pay the bills.

Doing more than one thing at a time with your computer is known as *multitasking*, and it might come as a surprise to you to discover that your AOL software offers true multitasking capabilities (even many veteran America Online members are ignorant of this feature): start a download, then do something else with your computer.

Here's how it's done:

1. Sign on, locate the file you want to download, and start the downloading process.
2. Once the progress indicator appears (pictured in Figure 6-3), you can do whatever you please with the programs on your computer, even within AOL itself. If you want to read mail or visit a forum, do it. If you want to run another program on your computer, minimize America Online and run the program. The file will continue downloading in the background in either case. Note that you cannot simultaneously upload and download a file using AOL.
3. When the download concludes, America Online will announce that it has completed the task. If you are working in another application, the AOL software will become the active program and make its announcement.

With all that said, a few caveats are in order:

- You will notice some slowing of your system. It's doing double duty after all, and each task gets its little slice of your computer's power.
- Some software doesn't tolerate multitasking very well, especially software that relies heavily on disk activity or your computer's central processing unit. Games are notoriously unsuited to the multitasking environment.
- If you've got an external modem, watch the lights. If the Receive Data (RD) light goes out or flickers badly while you're multitasking, you're asking too much of your system. Let America Online have your system to itself while you stretch a bit or go for a walk. If that won't do, find another task to perform with your computer that isn't quite so demanding.

Multitasking seems a bit magical. But it works. In four years neither of us have had a download go bad or a file become corrupted because of a multitasking problem. In fact, Jennifer is writing this sentence as a download is underway. It's a great way to magnify your potential.

Finding Files for Downloading

Now that you've seen how easy it is to download a file, you probably have come to realize that it isn't downloading that requires your understanding, it's *finding the files* for downloading. America Online offers over 100,000 of them, after all, and like prospecting for gold, the search is 99 percent of the expedition.

Searching through 100,000 files would be a horrendous task were it not for AOL's searchable database of online files. This database contains information on all of the files stored in the computing forums, and it's constantly maintained. Every file in the computing forums' libraries appears in this database within a few hours after it's posted. As you might expect, access to the database requires only a click of your mouse.

Finding Files While You're Online

There are two ways you can find files while you're online: you can search for them or you can browse among them. Searching implies that you know what you're looking for; browsing is a more leisurely activity. Each requires its own strategy.

File Search You can search at any time, from any place online—you don't have to be in a specific forum to do so. All you have to do is type the keywords: **File Search** in the toolbar, and click the Downloading Software button to reach the database of freely distributed files (see Figure 6-4).

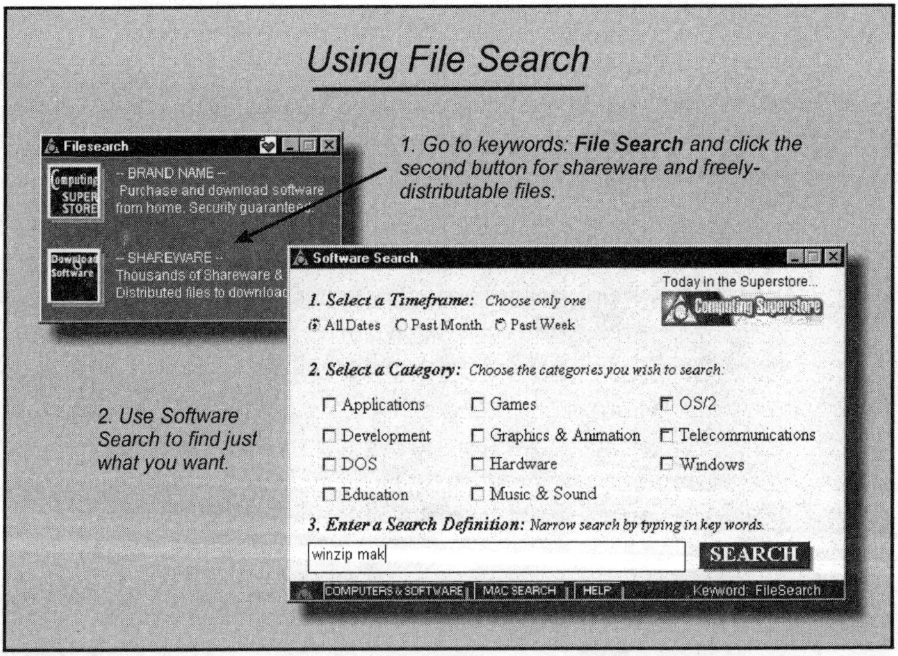

Figure 6-4: At keywords: **File Search**, you can enter specific criteria to help you find exactly the file you want.

Look again at the Software Search dialog box pictured in Figure 6-4. Two sets of check boxes are provided: you can specify only those files that have been uploaded recently (the Past Week option is great for finding only new files) or only those files that fit certain criteria.

More important, there's also a text box at the bottom of the Software Search window. Here you can specify your own criteria. Words entered here are matched against all file descriptions in the database.

There are three special words you can use in a match phrase: *AND*, *OR*, and *NOT*. These are called Boolean modifiers, and we discussed them in detail in the last chapter. You might receive dozens of matches to the search phrase "Versailles," most of which would be references to the suburb of Paris or the palace, not to our objective—the Versailles font. The search phrase "Versailles AND font," on the other hand, narrows the search. (The AND modifier is the default, by the way. Whenever more than one word appears in a search phrase, America Online assumes there's an *AND* between them. Thus the phrase "Versailles AND font" is the same as the phrase "Versailles font.") Perhaps you want the Utopia font as well as the Versailles font. Here is where the OR modifier comes in. The phrase "Versailles OR Utopia" finds either one.

The NOT modifier narrows the search by excluding material matching the criterion that follows it. The phrase "Versailles NOT France" would provide a listing of all references to Versailles that aren't associated with France.

Combining modifiers can be unclear. The phrase "Versailles OR Utopia AND font" is ambiguous. Do we mean "Versailles, or Utopia and font," or do we mean "Versailles or Utopia, and font"? To clarify, use parentheses. The phrase "(Versailles OR Utopia) AND font" says "Look for Versailles or Utopia, excluding everything but fonts from either category." It pays to be specific.

File Descriptions In our haste to download earlier, we neglected to fully explain an important item: the file description. Every file offers one—it's the window with the Download Now and Download Later buttons in it—and you should display this window before you download the file. Be sure to read these descriptions. Figure 6-5 pictures WinZip's file description—the example file we downloaded earlier.

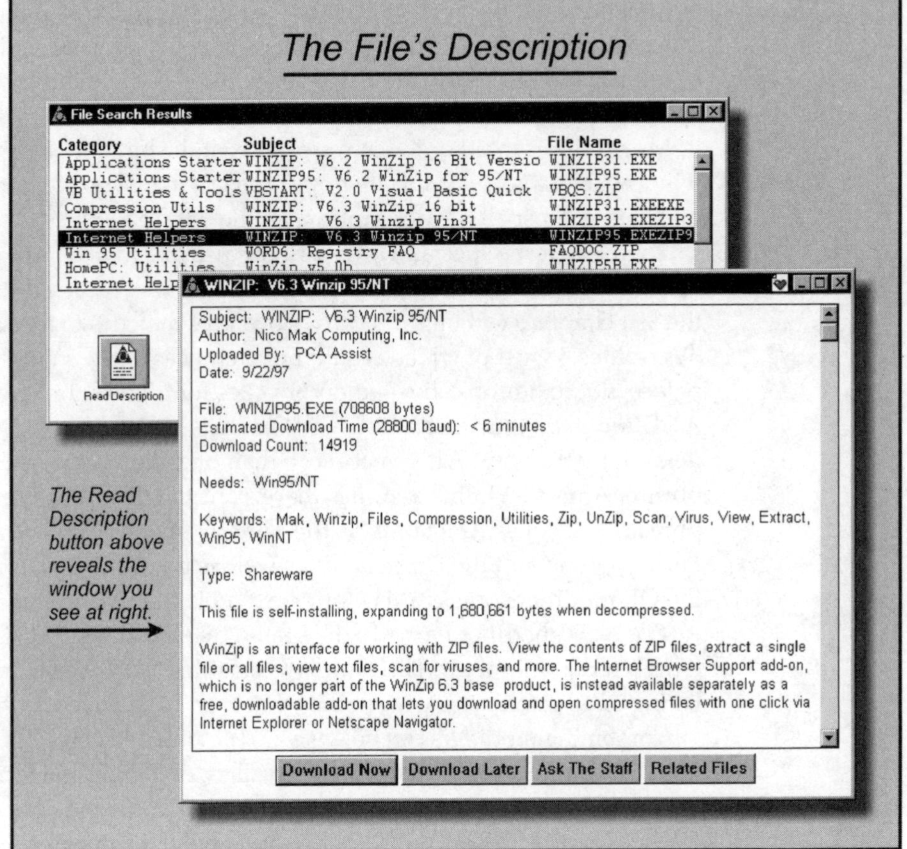

Figure 6-5: Read file descriptions before you download.

When we click the Read Description button, America Online provides a complete description of the file. This intermediate step is critical. There are lots of things we need to know about this file before we can decide whether to download it. Let's look at WinZip's file description in its entirety (see Figure 6-6).

All information in the file description is searchable, though you'll get the best results in matching the *Subject*, *Author*, *Uploaded By*, *Date*, and *File* lines. Don't confuse the Uploaded By line with the Author line. The Uploaded By line contains the name of the person who uploaded the file. That person is often a Forum Assistant or another member, not the author.

Figure 6-6:
A wealth of information is found in file descriptions.

WinZip's File Description

```
Subject:  WINZIP:  V6.3 Winzip 95/NT
Author:  Nico Mak Computing, Inc.
Uploaded By:  PCA Assist
Date:  9/22/97

File:  WINZIP95.EXE (708608 bytes)
Estimated Download Time (28800 baud):  < 6 minutes
Download Count:  14919

Needs:  Win95/NT

Keywords:  Mak, Winzip, Files, Compression, Utilities, Zip, UnZip, Scan,
Virus, View, Extract, Win95, WinNT

Type:  Shareware

WinZip is an interface for working with ZIP files. View the contents of
ZIP files, extract a single file or all files, view text files, scan for
viruses, and more. The Internet Browser Support add-on, which is no longer
part of the WinZip 6.3 base  product, is instead available separately as a
free, downloadable add-on that lets you download and open compressed files
with one click via Internet Explorer or Netscape Navigator.
Several changes have been made between the 6.3 beta 5 version and the 6.3
version.  Previously, all the WinZip shell extension menu entries were not
shown when WinZip was used with the latest IE 4.0 and Memphis betas.
Adjustments ensure that all menu entries now appear on all systems.

The Configuration dialog box layout for the Internet Browser Support add-
on has been revised, and support has been added for scan32.exe, part of
McAfee NetShield 3.0. Miscellaneous bug fixes and adjustments have been
made as well.

Author's Email Address:  support@winzip.com
Author's Web Address:   http://www.winzip.com

To run, enter:  WINZIP95
This file is self-installing, expanding to 1,680,661 bytes when
decompressed.

Documentation:  Online Help, Readme.txt, License.txt, Vendor.txt,
WinZip.txt, Whatsnew.txt, Order.txt

Downloads of previous version:  71,004
```

The *Date* is used when you specify All Dates, Past Month, or Past Week in the File Search dialog box.

File indicates the actual name of the file as it will download to your machine. This is what you'll see on your computer after you've downloaded the file. Note that the File line tells you both the file's name and its size.

What Is Shareware?

You might note that WinZip is *shareware*. There are two major channels for the distribution of computer programs and data. The traditional commercial channel involves the publisher, the distributor, and the retailer—each of whom, in order to make a living, must add a bit to the cost of the product. There's a considerable distance between the creator of the software and the people who purchase and use it.

A software product distributed by the alternative method is called *shareware*. With shareware, there's usually a direct connection between the user and the creator. Shareware programs and data are posted on online services like America Online where they can be downloaded whenever we, the users, please. Individuals or user groups also can distribute shareware among themselves without fear of recrimination. As a rule, shareware authors welcome this kind of distribution.

If you download a shareware program, you normally get the complete program—not a limited version. It usually comes with documentation as well. You can try it out for a few weeks before you decide to buy. If you decide to keep it, in most cases the author expects you to send money. Since the money goes directly to the author—no publishers, distributors, or retailers are involved—shareware usually costs less than commercially distributed software. The author's share is all you pay for shareware.

With shareware, there's also a direct channel for communication between user and author. If you have a question, complaint, or a suggestion for improvement, send e-mail to the author. Chances are you'll get a reply. This is a significant feature: to whom do you send mail if you think your car or your refrigerator can be improved? And do you really think anyone will ever reply?

While most shareware authors request financial remuneration, a few simply give their material away (freeware). Others request a postcard from your city or town (postcardware), or a donation to a favored charity.

The shareware system only works if users pay, and payment is voluntary. Sadly, only about 10 percent of the people who use shareware programs actually pay for them. This is undoubtedly the biggest fault in the shareware concept. Shareware can be a boon to us users, but only if we obey the honor code that's implicit in the system. In other words, if you use shareware on an ongoing basis, pay for it—and encourage others to do the same.

The *Estimated Download Time* is America Online's best guess as to how long it will take to download the file. The time is estimated based on the baud rate at which you're connected. If you're connected at 28.8 kbps, the estimate is based on that baud rate. This number is only an estimate. If you signed on during a peak-use period (for example, around 9 P.M. Eastern time), this number might be slightly optimistic. If you're signed on at 4 A.M., this number will be pessimistic. Jennifer downloaded WinZip—which America Online estimated to be a six-minute download—in less than five minutes during a mid-morning session at 28.8 kbps.

The *Download Count* is a rough indication of the file's popularity. If you're looking for a graphic of a cat, for example, and 40 files match your search criteria, you might let the number of downloads direct you. Often, however, the number of downloads says more about how catchy a file's name or description is than it does about its content. Sometimes you have to balance the download count and date to gauge the quality of a file. If something has been online for a year and only has 20 downloads, you can normally assume that it's of limited usefulness. WinZip 6.3, on the other hand, was only uploaded in September 1997 and by October of the same year had already racked up over 14,000 downloads (in addition to the tens of thousands of downloads accumulated by previous versions). It's a pretty safe bet that this is a good program. You'll get a feel for this sort of thing as you peruse and sample the various files available.

The *Equipment* line, if present, indicates any hardware and/or software beyond a basic PC you'll need to run the file. Sometimes, though, this line is used to indicate what hardware or software the author used to create the file.

The *Needs* line is critical: if your PC isn't up to the task, or if you need special software, it's nice to know before you download the file. For example, you'll need Windows 95 or NT to take advantage of all the features in this version of WinZip.

Keywords are those that provide matches when you enter your own search criteria. Read these. They offer valuable insight into how to word your search phrases. That's how we knew to specify "WinZip Mak" when we originally declared our search phrase.

Note: In this context, a keyword is a word assigned to a shareware file and used to help categorize and describe it for easy search and retrieval. These keywords are separate from and can't be used by America Online's navigational keyword function (accessed by typing Ctrl+K or Command+K, or by typing the keyword in the toolbar).

The *Description* itself is provided by the person who uploaded the file. WinZip's description, for example, indicates that a help file is available with the program—an important consideration for a program like this.

File descriptions can be saved for later reference. Choose Save from the File menu before you close the description window. America Online will ask where you want to store the description, which it saves in a simple text format. It can be read offline (after you've saved it to a separate file) with any word processor or the AOL software (just choose Open from AOL's File menu).

Browsing for Files File Search is not the only way to locate files while you're online. What if you're simply looking for a nice picture? You don't necessarily know *which* picture you're looking for, just a picture.

Here's a real-life situation: the other day Tom needed a provocative graphic for use as Figure 4-1 in the Internet chapter. He had no idea which graphic that would be, so File Search was out—"provocative" isn't a very precise search criterion.

An abyssal reservoir of graphics resides in the PC and Mac Graphic Arts Forums. Whenever he's in the mood for something pretty to brighten up his screen, or something intriguing to pique his visual curiosity, this is where he goes to browse.

He used the keyword: **Graphics**, clicked the Software Libraries button, and began to browse (see Figure 6-7).

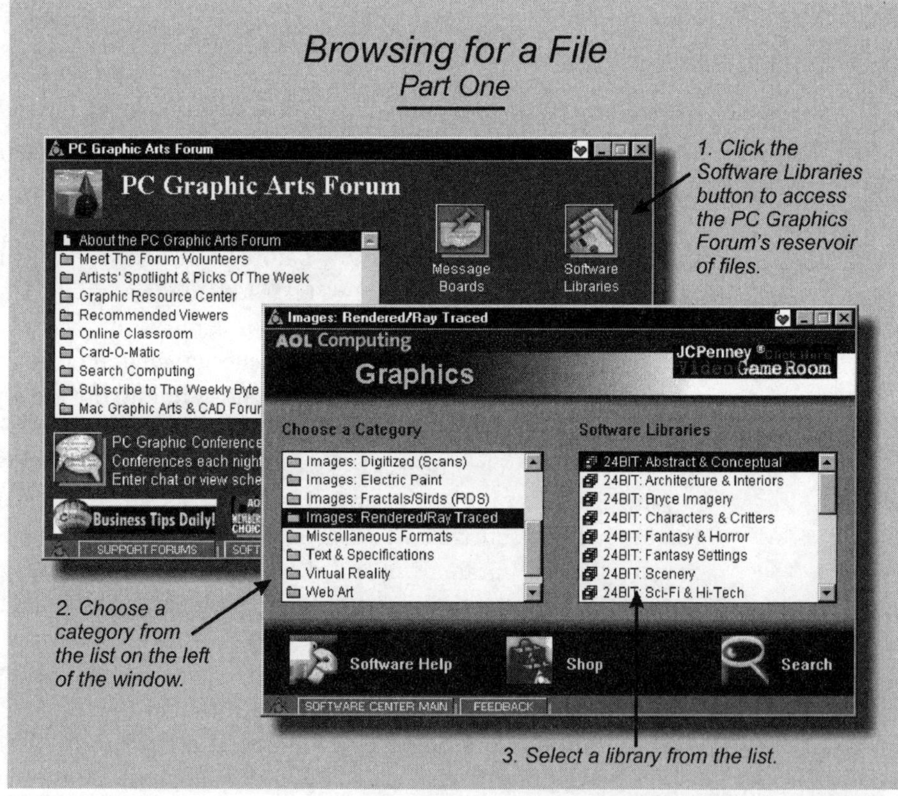

Figure 6-7: The PC Graphic Arts Forum at keyword: **Graphics** is a great place to browse for images. A similar forum is available for Mac users at keywords: **Mac Graphics**.

Tom knows from experience that the graphic libraries contain thousands of particularly sublime images—the kind that make our books look better. He's always raved about the ray-traced images, so it was no surprise when he chose the Images: Rendered/Ray Traced folder pictured in Figure 6-8. Among the various libraries within that folder, he selected the Abstract & Conceptual library. These decisions are illustrated in Figure 6-8 along with the library listing for "The Internet 1," Jeff Stewart's evocative image of the Internet, which we eventually chose to use as Figure 4-1.

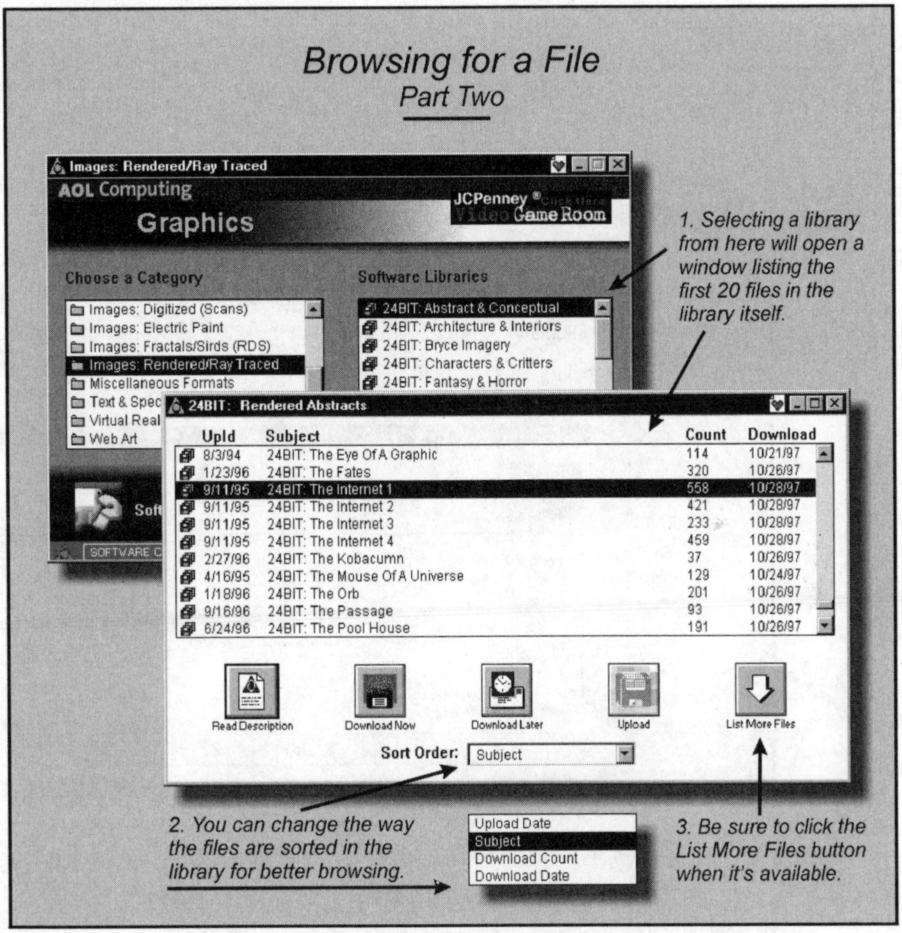

Figure 6-8: Among the most captivating images available online are 24-bit rendered ray tracings.

Note that he could have chosen any other library or folder along the way. He could have browsed the graphics forums for hours, peeking at thumbnails (see the "Thumbnails" sidebar) and downloading images that caught his eye. Each library offers the opportunity to change the order of the files with the drop-down menu at the bottom of the window. The default sort order is Upload Date, with Subject, Download Count, and Download Date. Looking for the most popular files? Try sorting by download count—you'll get a list of files in order from most downloaded to least. Taking that one step further, you can sort by download date to list the files starting with those that were most recently downloaded. In Figure 6-8, you'll notice Tom sorted the files by subject, which eventually led him to the graphic he chose.

Browsing for files is a leisurely pursuit—most browsing is—with plenty of opportunity for detours and new discoveries. Finding files on America Online is like shopping: if you know what you're after, you can go directly to your destination and nab the merchandise, or you can meander, grazing in meadows of opportunity. The choice is yours.

Thumbnails

A useful feature of the AOL software allows you to view *thumbnails* of graphics files before they're downloaded. This is a boon to members; thumbnails allow us to see a graphic before we spend time downloading it. Thumbnails appear in the upper left corner of a graphics file's description window (see Figure 6-9). You can't miss them.

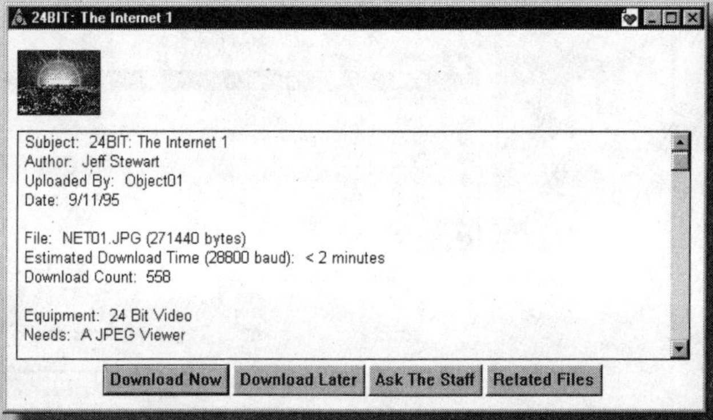

Figure 6-9: Most graphics offer thumbnail views so you can preview the graphic before you make the decision to download it.

24BIT: The Internet 1

Subject: 24BIT: The Internet 1
Author: Jeff Stewart
Uploaded By: Object01
Date: 9/11/95

File: NET01.JPG (271440 bytes)
Estimated Download Time (28800 baud): < 2 minutes
Download Count: 558

Equipment: 24 Bit Video
Needs: A JPEG Viewer

Download Now | Download Later | Ask The Staff | Related Files

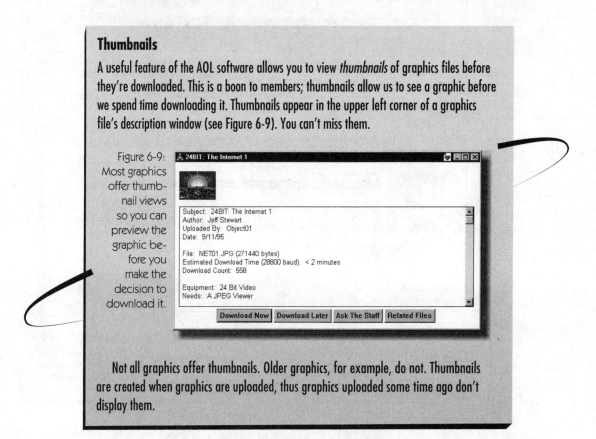

Not all graphics offer thumbnails. Older graphics, for example, do not. Thumbnails are created when graphics are uploaded, thus graphics uploaded some time ago don't display them.

The Graphics Viewer Your AOL software offers a graphics viewer that allows you to see graphics as they're downloaded. The viewer is especially valuable when there's no thumbnail (see the "Thumbnails" sidebar) available and you're downloading in the dark, so to speak.

Assuming the graphic you're downloading is in the PCX, BMP (for PCs), PICT (for Macs), JPG, or GIF format (more about formats later in this chapter), America Online will display the graphic on your screen as soon as enough of it is received for you to see. (There's a preference available to turn the viewer off, though its default setting is On. Preferences are discussed in Chapter 9.)

You don't need to do anything to invoke the viewer; it just appears when it's supposed to. Figure 6-10 shows the viewer in action as Jeff Stewart's graphic is being received.

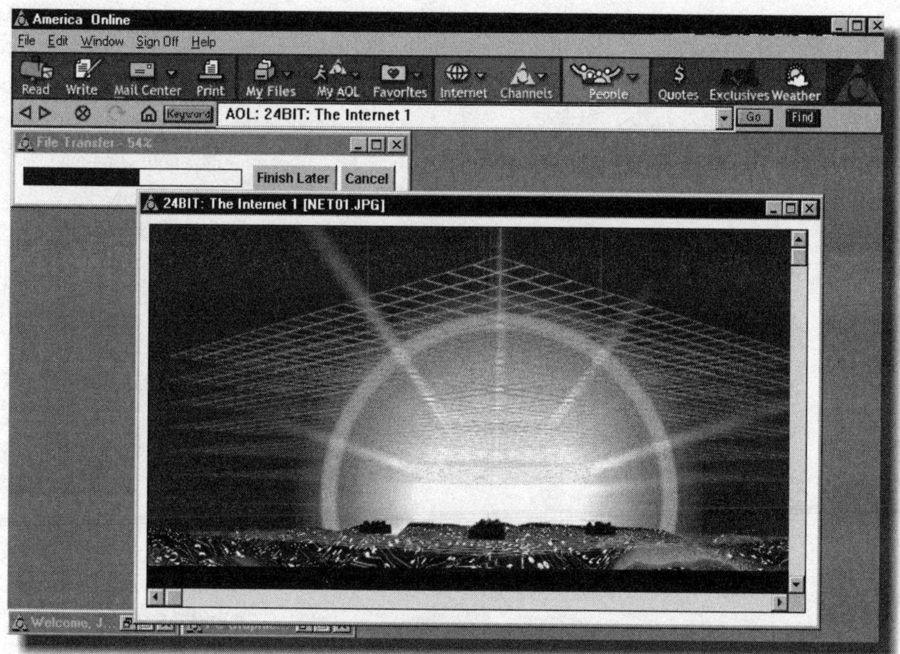

Figure 6-10: The graphics viewer allows you to see graphics as they're received.

Let's face it, not all graphics are of archival quality. You'll occasionally encounter one that, in spite of an acceptable thumbnail, isn't worth the time it takes to download. File descriptions and thumbnails go a long way toward avoiding that potential, but sometimes you just have to see an image full size to pass judgment. That's what the graphics viewer is for. By the time a third of a graphic is received, you'll probably know whether you want it or not. Just keep your eyes on the screen and be ready to click that Cancel button (look for it in Figure 6-10) if you don't like what you see.

Graphics Viewer Trivia

Many regular users aren't aware of it, but America Online's graphics viewer can be used to open existing graphics stored on your hard disk—whether you're online or off. You can also edit them there and then store them in either the BMP (for PCs), PICT (for Macs), GIF, or JPG format. In other words, not only can you use your AOL software to download graphics, but you can also use it to open and edit them whenever you want—online or off—and change their formats if you need to.

Eleven image modification tools (see Figure 6-11) are available whenever you open an existing graphic from your hard drive. You can rotate, flip, or mirror the image, crop it to the size you want, adjust the brightness and contrast, invert the colors, or convert it to grayscale. And if you make a mistake, you can always revert back to the original saved image. You can even insert graphics in e-mail—see Chapter 3 for details on using images in e-mail.

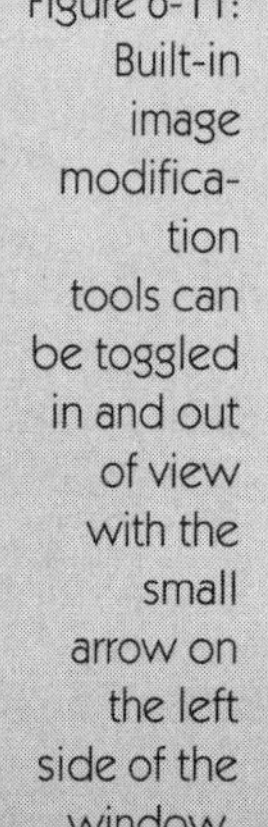

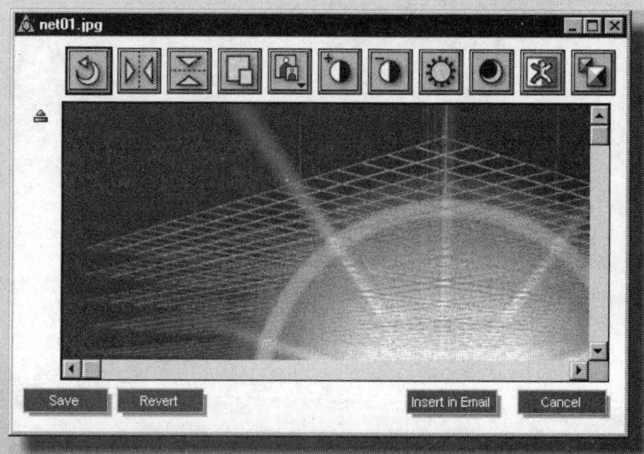

Figure 6-11: Built-in image modification tools can be toggled in and out of view with the small arrow on the left side of the window.

To change a graphics format, choose Save As from the File menu whenever a graphics window is open, then select the format you desire from the Save as Type menu in the file saving window. America Online will change the format automatically.

Aimless Roving The graphics example we've been using assumes your browsing is focused. Tom was looking for a graphic when he found that picture—a graphic that was to serve a specific purpose.

Often, browsing is less deliberate. Sometimes you go to a bookstore for a novel; sometimes you go to a bookstore for a book. There's a big difference. Browsing for files is much the same.

If you're browsing for browsing's sake, investigate America Online's Download Software Center at keyword: **Software** (see Figure 6-12). The Download Software Center is a bookstore of files. As you would expect, it supports browsing of the specific variety, but it also offers a splendid opportunity to browse aimlessly.

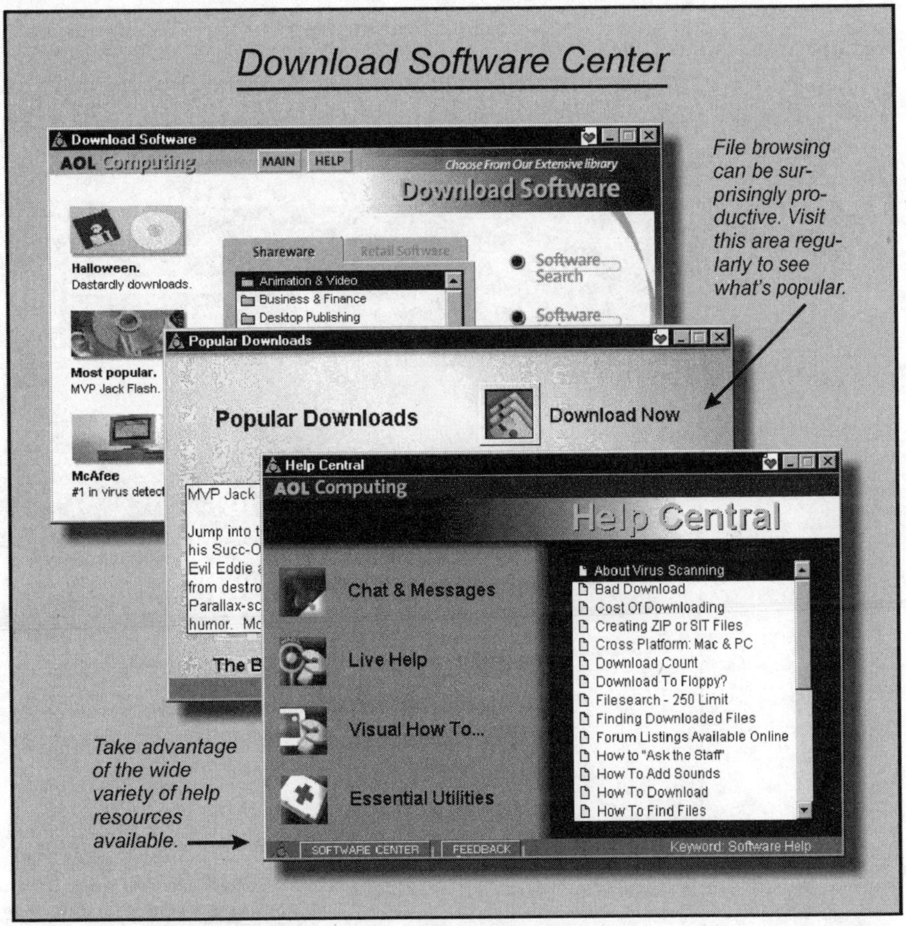

Figure 6-12: The Download Software Center is the place to find AOL's best downloading fare.

Look at those help categories in Figure 6-12: Chat & Messages, Live Help, Visual How To—the list goes on, as you can see.

The libraries in the Download Software Center are updated every week; make it one of the places you visit on a regular basis.

Finding New Files

If you're a downloading zealot, you should know about the Software Center's weekly listing of new files. Just click on Today's Highlights and open the Weekly New Files area. You'll find up-to-date lists of all the files that have been added to the forum libraries within the past week. You can browse them online—using the blue, underlined hyperlinks to go directly to the new files—or save them for reading offline (see Figure 6-13). It sure beats poking around.

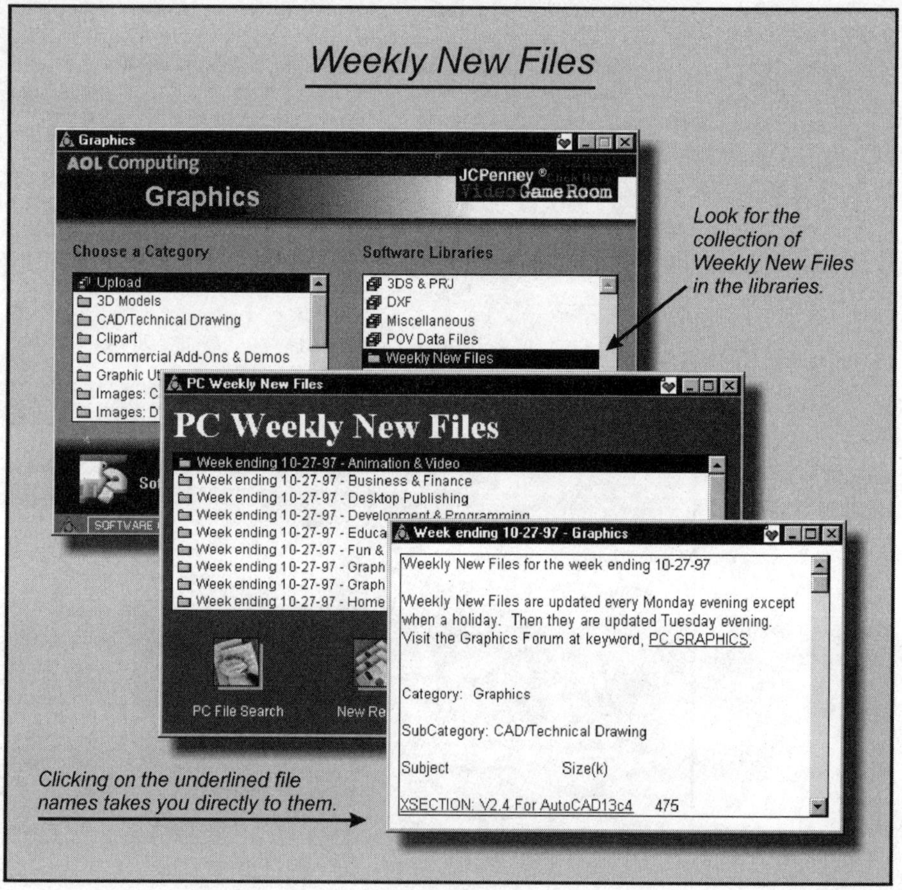

Figure 6-13: The Weekly New Files listings are updated with the latest files every week.

Weekly New Files

Look for the collection of Weekly New Files in the libraries.

Clicking on the underlined file names takes you directly to them.

Filenames & File Compression

The number of potential file formats for downloaded files is staggering. Fortunately, some standards and conventions help to organize the confusion.

Filenames for Windows Users

Nearly all downloadable files for Windows allow a maximum of eight characters followed by a period and ending in a three-character filename extension; WINZIP95.EXE, for example. The three-character extension is particularly useful. All you have to do is look at an extension to see what kind of file it is. Filenames ending in .xls are Excel worksheets, for example. Those ending in .txt are text files and are readable by most word processors and text editors, including the AOL software itself. Those ending in .zip are files compressed using a file compression utility (more about these later in this chapter). And those ending in .jpg are graphics files.

The chart pictured in Figure 6-14 identifies some of the common filename extensions and their meanings. Your AOL software is compatible with a large number of these formats. Not only can it open sound and video files, but it can play them too—assuming you have the hardware for it.

Figure 6-14: Filename extensions for some of the most common file formats you'll find online. Those marked with an asterisk can be opened with your AOL software.

Filename Extensions

Text formats

*TXT Unformatted ASCII text
RTF Rich Text Format
DOC Microsoft Word

Graphic formats

*BMP Windows bitmaps
TIF Tagged-Image Format
*GIF Graphic Interchange Format
*JPG Joint Photographic Experts Group
*ART AOL's proprietary graphics format
WMF Windows MetaFile
EPS Encapsulated PostScript

Compressed formats

ZIP PKZip, WinZip (AOL unzips automatically)
EXE Executable self-extracting archive
SIT StuffIt (Macintosh)
ARC Archives (AOL decompresses automatically)

Other formats

*WAV Windows audio
*MID Musical Instrument Digital Interface
*AU Sun workstation audio
*AVI Video for Windows
MPG Motion Picture Experts Group

File Compression

Look again at Figure 6-14. Four *compressed* formats are identified there, and they require further explanation.

Why compress files? There are three good reasons: (1) compressed files are much smaller than files that haven't been compressed and thus take significantly less time to download; (2) compressed files require less storage space; and (3) compressed files are often stored in an archive (several files compressed into a single file). Archives are a convenient way of grouping multiple files for storage and downloading.

Amazingly, compressed files can be reduced to as little as 20 percent of their original size, yet when they're decompressed, absolutely no data are lost. We don't know how they do it. Smoke and mirrors, we suppose.

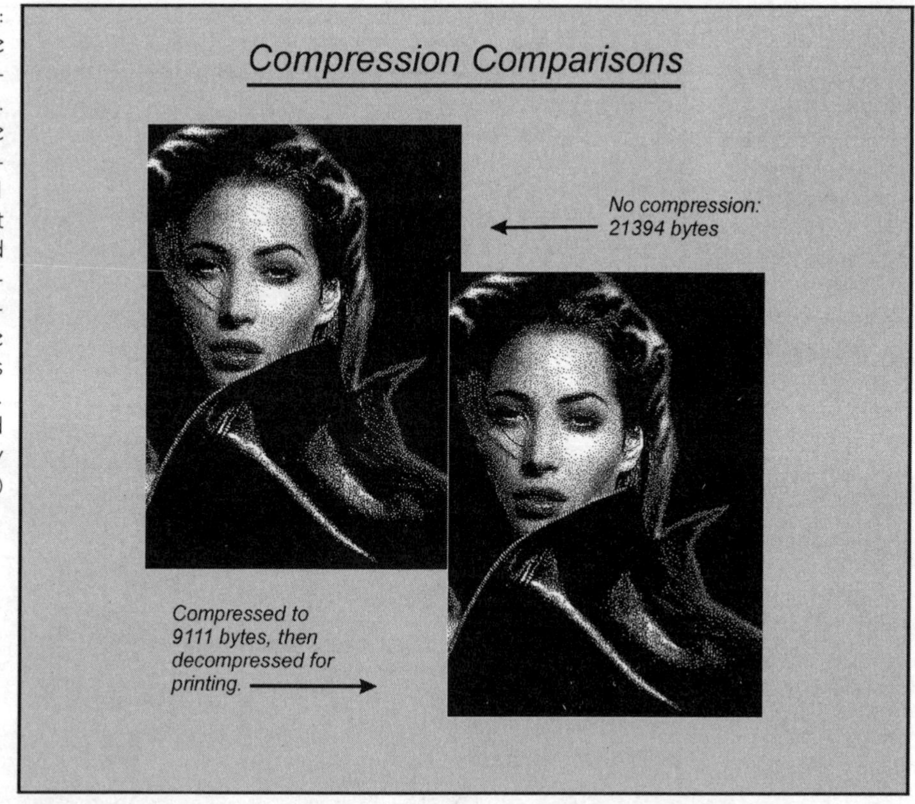

Figure 6-15: The original image on the left measures 21,394 bytes. The image on the right was compressed to 9,111 bytes (43 percent of the original) and then decompressed for printing. No data were lost; both pictures are identical. (Scanning and retouching by David Palermo.)

What's wrong with compressed files? They're useless until they're *de*compressed. The compressed image in Figure 6-15 couldn't be included in the illustration until it was decompressed. In other words, you must have decompression software before you can use compressed images. That's the bad news. The good news is that you already have decompression software; it's part of the AOL software package installed in your PC.

WinZip As we mentioned already, a shareware program called WinZip is responsible for a great deal of the file compression encountered in the Windows environment. WinZip can compress (or *zip*, as it's called) a single file or a multitude of files into a single file—an archive. WinZip archives are identified by the .zip filename extension.

Like all archives, WinZip archives must be decompressed (*unzipped*) before use, and incredibly, it happens automatically when you use AOL. If compression is done with smoke and mirrors, automatic decompression must be done with smoke and mirrors and an eye of newt. Whatever the technique, it works—and we're the beneficiaries.

When your AOL software downloads a file with .zip in its filename, it makes a note to itself to unzip the file immediately after you sign off. (You must have this option in effect. It's a preference, and preferences are discussed in Chapter 9 of this book.) An unzipped copy of the file appears on your disk after decompression, ready for use.

Available in versions for both Windows 95/NT and Windows 3.1, WinZip is fully contained and does its work effectively. It's fully compatible with the original compression software—PKZip—and easy to use. Even so, WinZip offers an extensive help file for those few occasions when you need it.

The download exercise at the beginning of this chapter describes how to locate and download WinZip.

To Zip or Not to Zip The automatic unzipping feature can be disabled if you want. Allowing AOL to decompress files automatically might create files in places you'd rather not have them, such as the \AOL40\DOWNLOAD\ directory, which is the default designation for downloads. To avoid that problem, you can override the feature and do it yourself later. There's a preference available to disable the automatic decompression feature, though its default setting is On. Preferences are discussed in Chapter 9.

There are also preferences available to allow you to configure the AOL software to automatically delete the original ZIP file after decompressing. Though you might want to activate this preference in deference to disk space, we recommend leaving it turned off. Once the download is complete (and once the AOL software has decompressed the file), copy the ZIP file somewhere, and *then* delete the ZIP file.

America Online doesn't only give you the unzipping part, it also lets you zip (compress) files or groups of files. If you want to zip your own files, follow the directions in Chapter 3 that describe attaching files to e-mail. You can do this while you're offline.

You're also welcome to acquire a copy of WinZip for yourself. It's available online as we mentioned earlier in the chapter. Use the keywords: **File Search** and then search for WinZip. You'll find a number of files meeting the criterion; be sure you get the latest. WinZip is shareware. If you like the program, pay the shareware fee and you can use it indefinitely with a clear conscience.

Self-Extracting Archives You now know all about compressed files, but there is another type of archive you'll find online: the *self-extracting archive.* Just as the name implies, these are archives that decompress themselves when you run them. Self-extracting archives usually end with the .exe filename extension. But so do many decompressed files, so check the download's description. (Refer again to Figure 6-3; WinZip is a self-extracting archive.)

For example, let's say you find a file online called dummit.exe, and you see this line in the file description:

```
This file is self-extracting, requiring 112,500 bytes.
```

That tells you dummit.exe is a self-extracting archive, and it gives you an idea of how much space it will take up on your disk when you extract it. You would download it just as you would any other file, but because it's self-extracting, America Online's decompression feature won't work here. That's not a worry. All you have to do is run the .exe file. The files contained within dummit.exe will decompress themselves, if there are more than one (it might be a single file), and you're ready to run the program according to the instructions contained in the online file description.

StuffIt While WinZip is the file compression standard for Windows, a program called *StuffIt* is the standard for the Macintosh platform. Instead of being zipped and unzipped, StuffIt files (followed by the .sit extension) are *stuffed* and *unstuffed*. A number of files suitable for use on either platform—graphics, mostly—were originally constructed on Macintoshes and are stuffed rather than zipped. (This is beginning to sound like a recipe for baked turkey: First stuff, then zip the carcass, then bake at 350 degrees for four hours.)

Stuffed files won't decompress automatically on a PC, nor are they self-extracting archives. To use them, you have to acquire unstuffing software. Our favorite is a program called UNSTUFF. We forgive its DOS command line interface because it's written by the people who wrote StuffIt, which means compatibility is ensured. UNSTUFF is available as freeware on AOL. Use the keywords: **File Search** and search for UNSTUFF.

Download 101

Even with America Online's automation and downloading conveniences, downloading can be confusing. And though we've tried to explain it thoroughly here, some people are better served by another voice. We're not offended if you're one of them.

If you have any downloading questions, try using the keywords: **Download 101**. Download 101 is AOL's center for downloading questions and answers, and it's rich in downloading tips and techniques (see Figure 6-16). There's also a downloading exercise there that walks you through the process, explaining each step along the way.

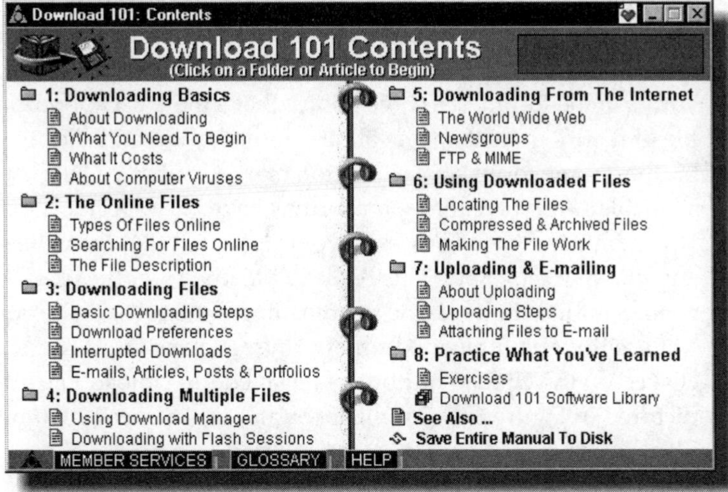

Figure 6-16: Download 101 is the place to get hands-on downloading experience, free of charge.

Best of all, Download 101 is free, regardless of your pricing plan. Spend as much time there as you need to become familiar and comfortable with the downloading process. All it costs is your time.

Uploading Files

With all this talk about downloading, it's easy to forget that before a file can be *down*loaded, it first must be *up*loaded. True to its community spirit, America Online depends on its members for most of its files—members like you and me. Uploading isn't the exclusive realm of AOL employees and forum staff, nor is it the realm of the weenies and the dweebs. Most of the files you can download from America Online—we'd guess more than 90 percent—have been uploaded by members using computers just like yours.

Earlier we defined downloading as the process of transferring a file from America Online's computers to your computer. Uploading is just the reverse: the process of transferring a file from your computer to America Online's computers. Once received, it's checked for viruses and the quality of its content, and then it's posted. The process rarely takes more than a day. Upload a file on Monday, and you'll probably see it available for downloading Tuesday morning.

The Uploading Process

Begin the uploading process by visiting the forum where your file seems to fit (finding forums is discussed in Chapter 5, "Finding Stuff"). If it's a graphic, post it in the Graphic Arts Forum. If it's poetry, post it in the Writers' Club. Once you're in the forum, select the library that's the most appropriate place for your file (if there's more than one library in the forum) and click the Upload File button. (Some forums have a button marked Submit a File; use this button if it's available.) Also note that some forums have very specific libraries marked Free Uploading and New Files; send your uploaded files there. Be sure, too, to read any files marked "Read This Before Uploading," or the like. They usually contain information specific to uploading material to that forum.

Recently Tom uploaded a magazine article to the Writers' Club. When he clicked on the Upload button, he received the Upload File information form pictured in Figure 6-17. You'll encounter this form every time you upload a file to AOL.

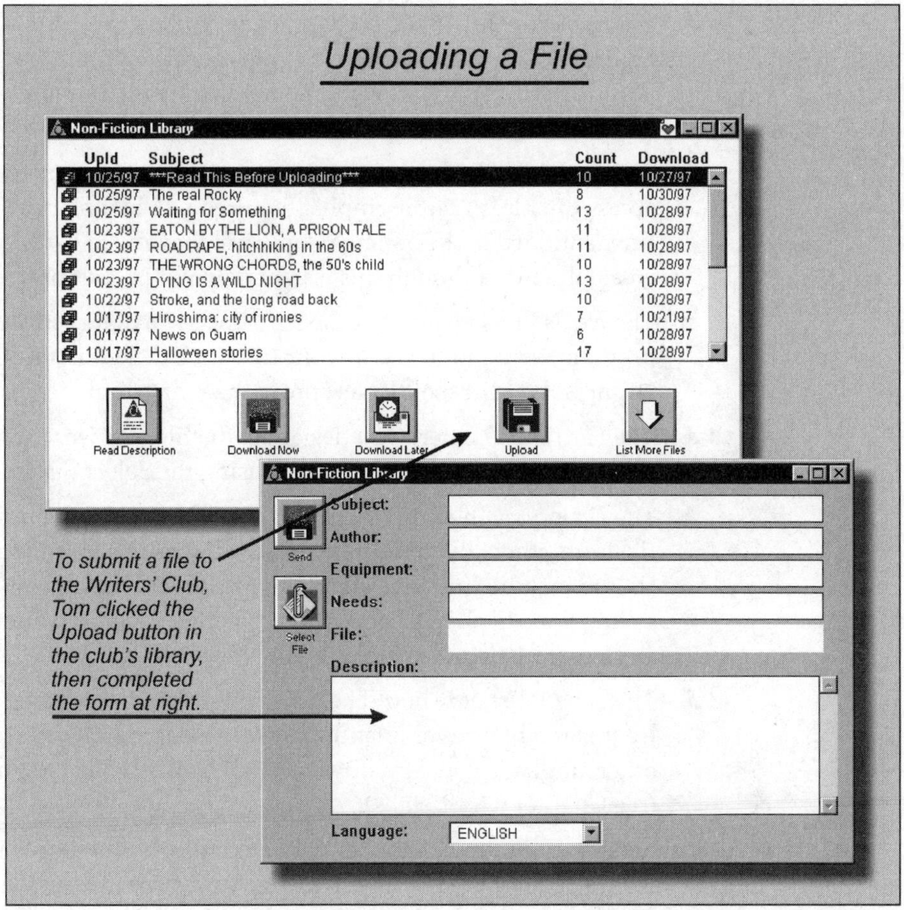

Figure 6-17: You'll be asked to fill out the Upload File information form for every file you upload to America Online.

Uploading a File

Non-Fiction Library

Upld	Subject	Count	Download
10/25/97	***Read This Before Uploading***	10	10/27/97
10/25/97	The real Rocky	8	10/30/97
10/25/97	Waiting for Something	13	10/28/97
10/23/97	EATON BY THE LION, A PRISON TALE	11	10/28/97
10/23/97	ROADRAPE, hitchhiking in the 60s	11	10/28/97
10/23/97	THE WRONG CHORDS, the 50's child	10	10/28/97
10/23/97	DYING IS A WILD NIGHT	13	10/28/97
10/22/97	Stroke, and the long road back	10	10/28/97
10/17/97	Hiroshima: city of ironies	7	10/21/97
10/17/97	News on Guam	6	10/28/97
10/17/97	Halloween stories	17	10/28/97

Read Description · Download Now · Download Later · Upload · List More Files

Non-Fiction Library

Send · Select File

Subject:
Author:
Equipment:
Needs:
File:
Description:
Language: ENGLISH

To submit a file to the Writers' Club, Tom clicked the Upload button in the club's library, then completed the form at right.

The Upload File Information Form

All too often, uploaders fail to complete the Upload File information form adequately. This form "sells" your file to other members, and what you have to say about it influences whether a member will take the time to download it. On the next page are listed some hints for creating accurate, useful, and compelling descriptions of files you upload.

- The *Subject* field should be descriptive and catchy, in that order. Look at Figure 6-17. Do you see how the subjects are listed there? The subject line is your headline. If you want members to read your story, hook 'em with a really great subject line.
- The *Equipment* line should identify any special equipment required to access the file. A 24-bit graphic requires a 24-bit color card; VGA won't do. As mentioned earlier, some people use this line to list what they used to create the file, although this is generally not proper protocol.
- The *Needs* line is where you specify the particular software application or program required to access your file. An Excel worksheet, for example, requires the Microsoft Excel spreadsheet program.
- The *File* field is where you designate the file you want sent from your hard disk to AOL's computer. Attach it using the Select File button.
- The *Description* field is where you get specific. Here you differentiate your file from others that might be similar. If you're submitting a program, you should include the version number. Be specific and persuasive; you're selling your file here. Think about what you would want to know if you were considering downloading the file.
- The *Language* field should be set to English for uploading to libraries frequented by predominantly English-speaking members. You will see other languages here if you've added them to your Language Preference (see Chapter 9 for details).

If you're submitting a number of related files, or if your file is larger than about 100K, compress it (or them) using WinZip, StuffIt, or something equivalent. This saves downloading time, and it's the polite way to offer your material.

Concluding the Uploading Process

America Online's by-now-familiar progress indicator will keep you entertained while the upload is under way; following it will be a dialog box announcing your success. The time spent uploading your file will be credited back to you if you are not on the unlimited pricing plan. Though you might not see the credit before you sign off, it will appear soon thereafter.

To check your billing information, use the keyword: **Billing**. A day or so after your upload is completed, you should see a note crediting your account with any time you have spent uploading files. The billing area is free, so you won't be charged for whatever time you spend online checking your account's billing information.

MacFiles

The Mac may speak a different language, but it makes a good attempt at being bilingual. And so does your Mac AOL software. Other than the obvious difference in the kinds of files you download, which you are automatically directed to when you use any of the commands or keywords in this chapter, the only real variations are in how you download them. Jennifer has "filed" away a few tips for you.

As we mentioned, StuffIt is the compression standard for the Mac. Just about everything you need to "stuff" and "unstuff" files compressed with StuffIt is already built-in to the Mac AOL software. You can also obtain a standalone shareware version of the software by going to keywords: **File Search**, clicking on the second button, and searching on the criterion StuffIt Lite. In addition to "stuffed" files, the Mac AOL software also automatically decompresses ZIP files, the Windows decompression standard.

The default destination for downloads is the Online Downloads folder within your America Online 4.0 folder. You can change the default folder with the Save To button in the Download Manager under the My Files icon in the toolbar.

The Mac software is able to display many types of graphics, but it does not have the editing capabilities described for Windows. If the need arises, Jennifer suggests you use a shareware graphics editor such as GraphicConverter, by Thorsten Lemke (available online in the file libraries). On the plus side, you can capture graphics with the Capture Picture command under the Edit menu.

Thanks to the flexibility of the Mac, file-naming conventions are considerably more varied than Windows' typical eight-character titles and three-character extensions. Don't be surprised if you download files in these name formats, however: Software from the Windows libraries, or those that are multiplatform, will often conform to the more limited filename standard to ensure everyone can use it.

Moving On

It's time for you to get your second wind. Though we've covered a parking lot full of technicalities, there's more. Computers are inherently technical, and almost everything discussed in this chapter has been technical as well.

But America Online is much more than technicalities. Many members use it for the community alone: chat, e-mail, kids, and seniors. In fact, community is at the heart of AOL. There are millions of wonderful people here. Turn the page. We want you to meet a few of them.

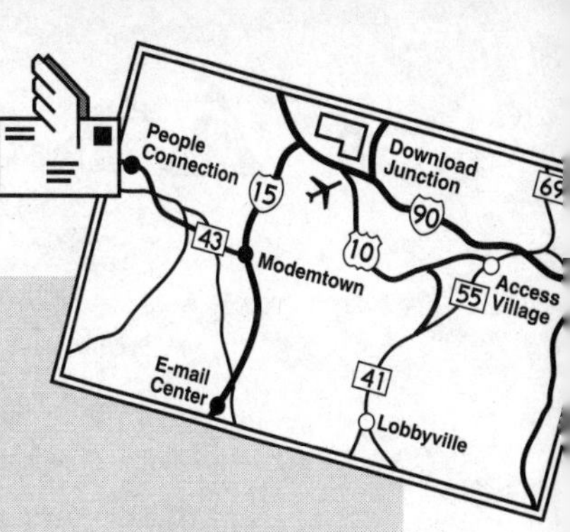

CHAPTER 7

Chat

- People Connection
- Auditoriums
- Instant Messages
- Buddy Lists
- Kids & Parents
- Women's Issues
- Message Boards
- Guttersnipe

For many America Online members, chatting in the online community is what it's all about—telecommunicating in real-time with real people all around the world. This is a two-way medium; it's a level playing field; it's egalitarian, attainable, and less expensive than cable TV. On the other hand, these very qualities are its greatest weaknesses: parity of access and freedom of expression don't necessarily promote honor and virtue. Thieves and scoundrels find this medium to be just as inviting as do scholars and prophets. Along with brotherhood and beneficence, there be dragons here. It's a community as diverse as America itself, and like America, America Online warrants scrutiny under strong light. Thus, this chapter examines chat, conferences, Instant Messages, Buddy Lists, and message boards—the real-time community of no-holds-barred dialog. This is what makes the online industry so invigorating—and so controversial. It's fascinating stuff, and we think you'll find this chapter to be fascinating reading.

Construction Ahead

By the time you read this chapter, chat rooms may look considerably different than they do in this book's illustrations. America Online is working on a new look and feel for the People Connection that will offer greater flexibility and accessibility. Development is still in early stages, however, and we would be doing you a disservice to preview it before its time. Take comfort in the fact that help will be available if you need it.

A Haven for Shy People

America Online is a haven for shy people. Shy people usually like other people and they're likable themselves; they just don't do well with strangers. Most shy people want to make friends—and all friends were once strangers—but they aren't very adept at doing it.

This is why shy people like America Online. Nobody can see them online, nobody seems to notice if they don't talk much, and if they're uncomfortable, they can always escape when they wish by signing off. Perhaps best of all, if you're a shy person, you can use a *nom de plume* and no one will even know who you are. We're back at the masquerade ball we mentioned in Chapter 2: you can wear the mask of a different screen name and be whatever or whomever you want to be. There's something comforting yet exciting about those possibilities.

Shy people can begin the America Online journey in a "safe" place like a forum, where no one's the wiser when they read a few forum messages or download a file or two. The next step would be to make an online friend and exchange some mail. Regardless of the path taken, it takes some time to work up the courage to venture into People Connection. It invariably means ending up in a room full of strangers, and this is not where shy people feel most comfortable.

The irony is that shy folks love People Connection once they become acquainted with it. It's the perfect outlet for years of pent-up longing for sociability. We are both shy. It took us each months to work up to People Connection. Yet now it's one of our greatest online rewards. We go there whenever we have time. You will too, once you get the hang of it.

People Connection

We discussed e-mail in Chapter 3 and newsgroups and mailing lists in Chapter 4. All of these tools foster dialog between people, but none of the dialogs occur in real-time. *People Connection* is the real-time, member-to-member communications headquarters of America Online. We were about to compare People Connection dialogs with telephone conversations, but at People Connection any number of people can be involved, there's rarely a long-distance toll to pay, and many of the people you talk to are strangers—but never for long.

People Connection is the heart of the America Online community and the ultimate chat experience. Here is where you make the enduring friendships that keep you coming back, day after day. Here, in a "diner," you can order a short stack and a cup of coffee and talk over the weekend ahead (or past). You can also sip a brew in a "pub" after a long day on the job. There are "events" here as well, where you can interview eminent guests and hobnob with luminaries.

Doesn't that sound like a community to you? This isn't couch potato entertainment; this is interactive telecommunication—where imagination and participation are contagious, and the concept of community reaches its most eloquent expression.

It sure beats reruns.

The Lobby

Unlike other areas within America Online, a visit to People Connection requires first passing through the "Lobby." The Lobby is one of AOL's so-called *chat rooms*, where real people communicate in real-time. No messages are left here. There are no files to download. America Online's Lobby is similar to the lobby of a hotel: it's an area people pass through, often on their way to some other destination. Every so often, people bump into an acquaintance. Or they just sit there a moment to rest.

If you've never visited People Connection, come along with us and we'll give it a whirl. Click the family-waving icon on the toolbar, choose People Connection from the Main Menu window, or use the keyword: **Lobby**. No matter which method you use, you will soon find yourself in the Lobby (see Figure 7-1).

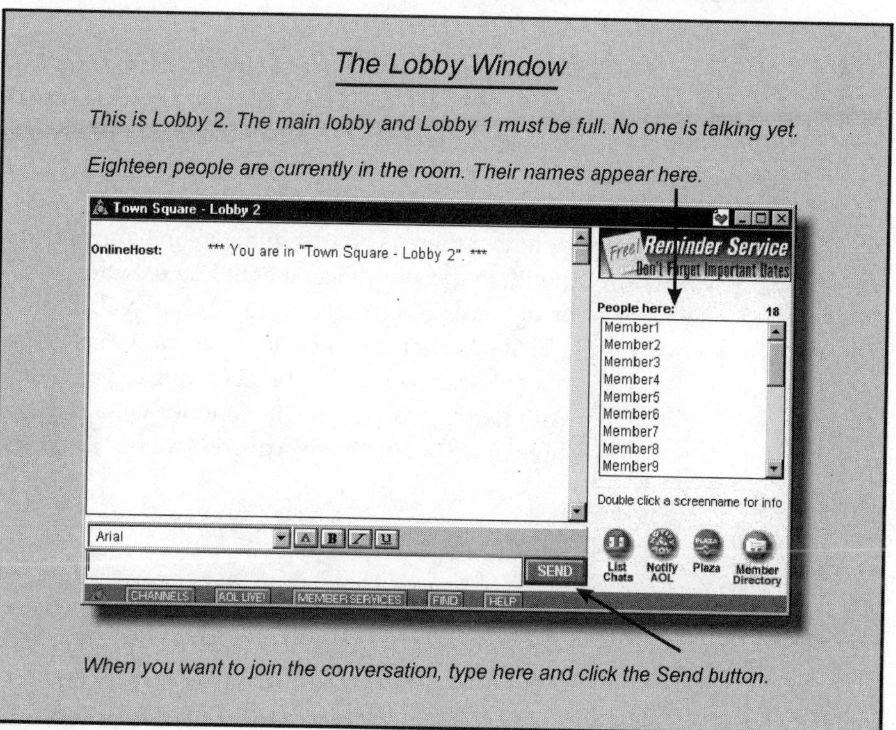

Figure 7-1: The Lobby screen seems empty just after we enter.

Note that the message in the chat room window pictured in Figure 7-1 says "You are in Lobby 2." When we entered the Lobby, America Online routed us to Lobby 2. This happens whenever traffic on the system is heavy. When the main lobby reaches capacity (rooms are considered filled when they contain 23 members), America Online places people in the secondary lobby—Lobby 1. It, too, must have filled by the time we arrived, so we were placed in Lobby 2. Note that it was also approaching capacity, so new arrivals were about to be routed into yet another lobby. This isn't uncommon. There are often hundreds of lobbies in operation at any one time.

Have Faith

If you really are following along with us, you've been in a lobby for a couple of minutes now. Your screen is full of chat, some of it indecipherable, some of it scurrilous, and some of it from people just as confounded as you are. If your first experience in a lobby doesn't pique your interest in America Online's chat rooms, don't give up. Finish this chapter: there are rooms where the conversation is enlightening, urbane, and predictably polite. Read on and we'll tell you how to find them.

Also note that of the 23 people in Lobby 2 at the time, a few of their names appear in the scroll box in the upper right corner of Figure 7-1's window. Our preferences are set to arrange these names alphabetically (preferences are discussed in Chapter 9). Your scroll box may list the members in the order they appear.

Finally, note that there is no text in the main (conversation) portion of the window other than the announcement telling us where we are. The only true conversation appearing here occurs after our arrival, and we have just walked in the door. That situation changes the moment we speak (see Figure 7-2).

Look again at Figure 7-2. This lobby is active today. People are rushing through it with hardly a pause. By the time we've said hello—a matter of seconds—three more people have arrived. America Online's lobbies are something like a hotel lobby just after a large meeting has let out: people are scurrying everywhere. (This is particularly true during periods of heavy usage. The session pictured occurred on a Sunday morning. America Online is almost always busy on the weekends.)

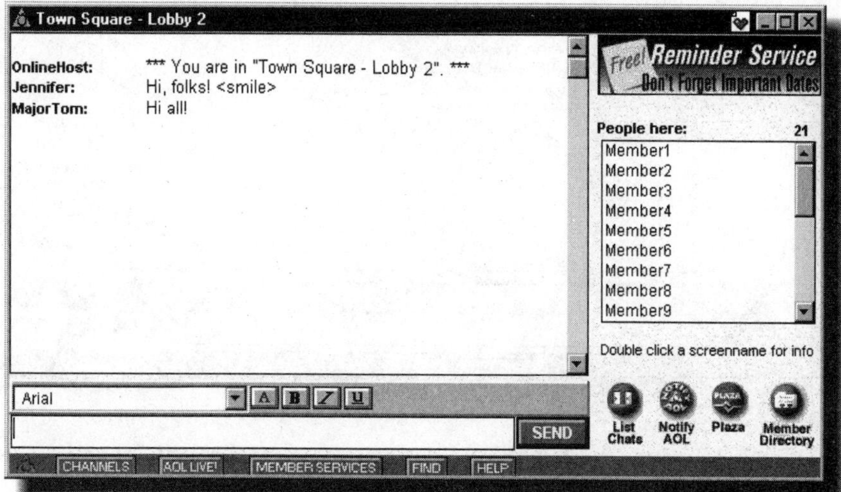

Figure 7-2: No matter how shy you're feeling, say hello when you enter a room.

Password Surfing

You've no doubt seen messages to this effect already, but if you're new to People Connection it's worth repeating here: *no one from America Online's staff will ever,* **ever** *ask you for your password.* We don't mean to imply that other people won't ask you for your password; password thieves are always a problem. We'll discuss the problem of password thieves later in this chapter, but just in case a message pops up on your screen asking for your password while you're "lobbying" with us, simply close its window and forget about it—at least for the time being. You probably won't hear from that person again.

Seconds later, a conversation has begun (see Figure 7-3).

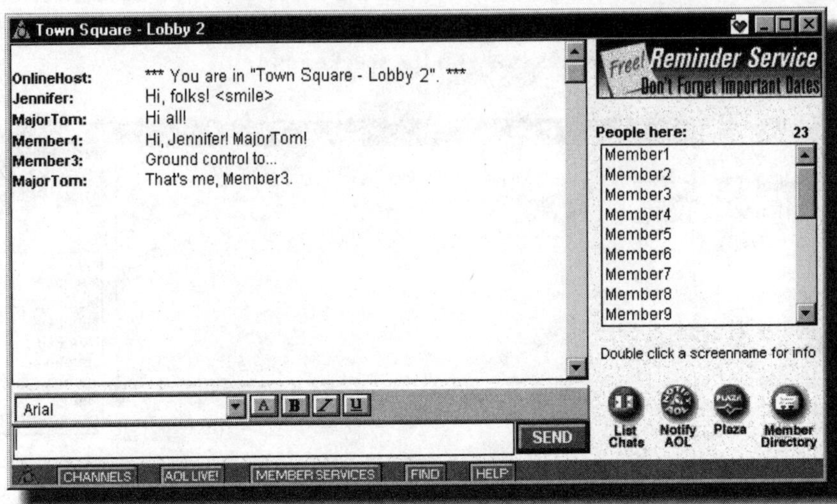

Figure 7-3: Catchy screen names come in handy when you first enter a room.

Though Tom immediately became involved in a conversation, don't feel obligated to do so yourself. It's perfectly all right to say hello and then just watch for a while. In fact, we recommend it. It gives you a chance to adapt to the pace of the conversation—to get to know who is in the room and what they're like. Lobbies are good for this. They're lobbies, after all. It's perfectly natural for people to sit in a lobby and watch other people.

Lurkers

It's not a very flattering term: *lurker*. It always makes us think of dark alleys and trench coats. In the online context, however, a lurker is one who visits a chat room and chooses not to participate in the conversation. There's nothing wrong with online lurking. We always lurk for a few minutes after we enter a room and say hello, to see who's in the room and to get a feel for the tenor of the conversation. You can lurk online for as long as you want to, but leave the trench coat in the closet.

As is the case with hotel lobbies, however, you won't want to stay in America Online's lobbies indefinitely. Awaiting you are lots of other rooms where conversations are more focused and residents less transitory. These rooms can be great fun; all you have to do is find the one that suits you best.

Kinds of Rooms

People who are new to America Online often have trouble understanding all of the kinds of rooms America Online has to offer. Each type of room serves a different purpose. Entering one without understanding what's inside is a bit like randomly opening meeting room doors in a large hotel: some might welcome you enthusiastically, others might make you feel unwelcome, and still others might be engaged in conversations that are of no interest to you whatsoever.

Public Rooms

If you're still in a lobby, you'll soon discover the List Chats button at the bottom right of the lobby's window (review Figure 7-2). This leads to the Public Rooms window pictured in Figure 7-4. Here, you can scan lists of all the public rooms available at the moment and choose the one that suits you best.

Figure 7-4: This Public Rooms list appears whenever you click the List Chats button in a room's window.

Help's on the Way!

People write to us all of the time telling us how overwhelmed they once were by all of the activity going on in People Connection. All of those rooms, all of those people, the shorthand—it can be downright intimidating.

Don't let it be. Find out all you can. Read this chapter, of course, but be sure to also click the question mark button in the lower right corner of any People Connection screen. That button leads to People Connection Help (Figure 7-5), where you can learn about chatting in the People Connection. The People Connection is a great place to meet people. Some would say it's the heart of the online experience. You owe it to yourself to learn all you can about People Connection and give it a good try.

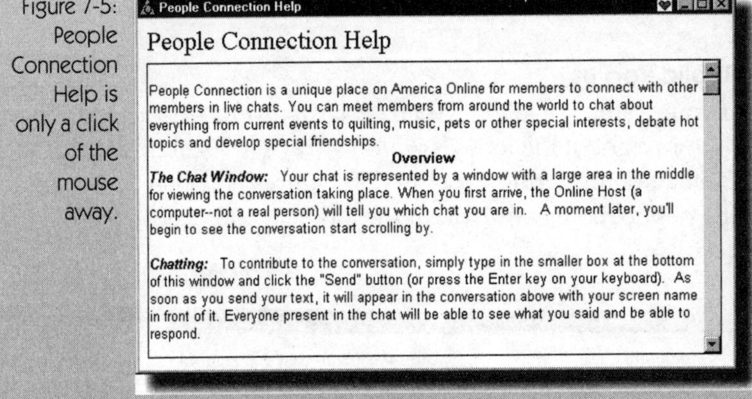

People Connection Help
People Connection Help
People Connection is a unique place on America Online for members to connect with other members in live chats. You can meet members from around the world to chat about everything from current events to quilting, music, pets or other special interests, debate hot topics and develop special friendships.
Overview
The Chat Window: Your chat is represented by a window with a large area in the middle for viewing the conversation taking place. When you first arrive, the Online Host (a computer--not a real person) will tell you which chat you are in. A moment later, you'll begin to see the conversation start scrolling by.
Chatting: To contribute to the conversation, simply type in the smaller box at the bottom of this window and click the "Send" button (or press the Enter key on your keyboard). As soon as you send your text, it will appear in the conversation above with your screen name in front of it. Everyone present in the chat will be able to see what you said and be able to respond.

Figure 7-5: People Connection Help is only a click of the mouse away.

The rooms appearing in the list box in Figure 7-4 all represent so-called *public* rooms at America Online. Public rooms share a number of common characteristics:

- As you might expect, they're open to the public. Anyone can enter (unless the room is full) and leave whenever they wish.
- Most public rooms are limited to 23 people (there are exceptions, but they're few). We don't know where that number came from, but it's appropriate. Conversations in rooms with more than 23 people would be hard to follow, especially if those people were all in a garrulous mood.

- Public rooms are named by America Online employees. Most of them are *self-replicating*: when Lobby 2 fills, for example, Lobby 3 is automatically created.
- Guides visit public rooms occasionally, either to offer assistance or to generally police the place. (Guides were discussed in Chapter 2, "The Abecedarium.") Aside from the occasional Guide or host (discussed later), however, most public rooms are occupied by members only; there are no staff members present.
- The names of all public rooms are "published" via the windows pictured in Figure 7-4.

The Best Seat in the House

The best way to find a "seat" in a self-replicating room is to attempt to enter one that's already full. If you want to enter the Sunrise Diner, for example, try selecting it—even if it's full. America Online will display a message telling you that room is full and asking you if you want to enter another one like it. Answer yes. Chances are, someone just walked out of one of the full rooms and you'll get that person's seat. America Online always tries to find you the best seat in the house if you use this technique.

To enter a public room, select the category, then scroll the list box shown in Figure 7-4 until you find the room you want, and then double-click its name. (Be sure to read the sidebar "The Best Seat in the House," to find a good seat.) As soon as you arrive (the chat window on your screen will tell you—review Figure 7-2), be sure to say hello.

To find out more about the people in the room, refer to the scroll box in the upper right corner of the room's window. The screen names of all of the people in the room are listed there. To see the profile of someone in a room, double-click his or her screen name and then click the Get Info button (see Figure 7-6). Not only will you be able to call up a profile of that person (profiles were discussed in Chapter 2), but you can send them an Instant Message as well (we'll discuss Instant Messages later in this chapter).

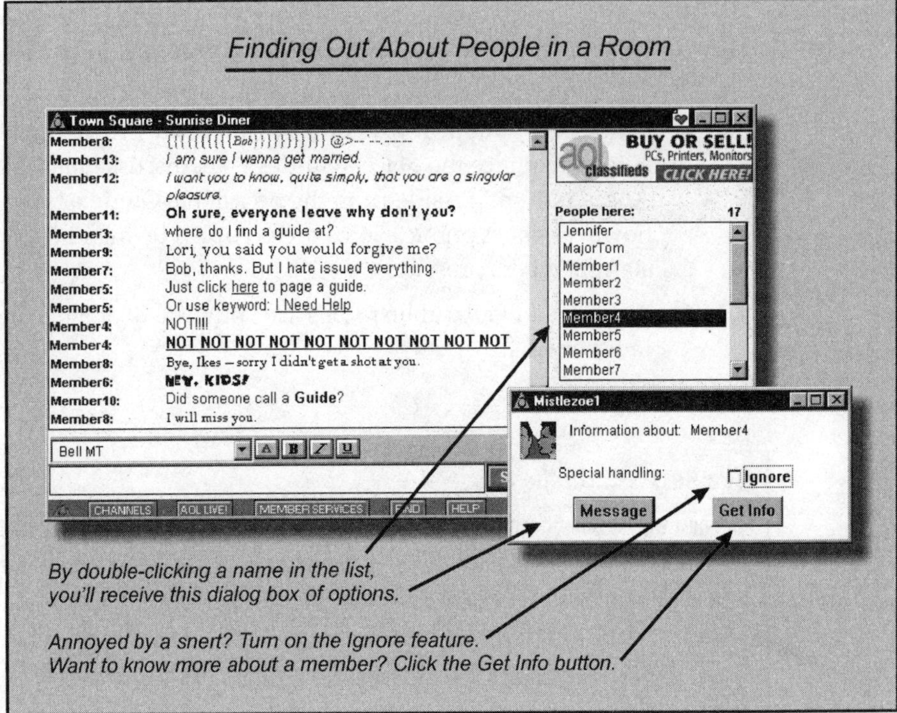

Figure 7-6: Double-click any name on a people list to find out more about that individual.

Special Handling

Member4 in Figure 7-6 was harassing the room, posting nonsense like the "NOT" pictured in the middle of the Sunrise Diner window. (We've changed his name and cleaned up his language—Member4 was a vile little muck.) Though there are a number of ways of dealing with his type, we simply double-clicked his name in the list box and then clicked the Ignore option illustrated in Figure 7-6. From that moment on, Member4 was out of our lives. It appears that the other room residents did the same thing, for everyone is ignoring him. Don't you wish real-life solutions could be this convenient?

Conference Rooms

While the Sunrise Diner illustrated in Figure 7-6 is a public room, the Writers Cafe is a *conference room*. Conference rooms are usually associated with forums and are typically accessed through those forums. You can't get to them via the Lobby, and they're not listed when you click the List Chats button shown in Figure 7-2. Other than that, conference rooms aren't much different than public rooms, but since they require a bit more savvy to find, they're less privy to the kind of harassment we alluded to in the sidebar "Special Handling."

Refer to Figure 7-7: the Writers Cafe is only available via the Writers Club. You can't get there with the People icon on the toolbar; you've got to venture through the Writers Club first—and encounter a friendly prequel about the room—before you get to the Writers Cafe.

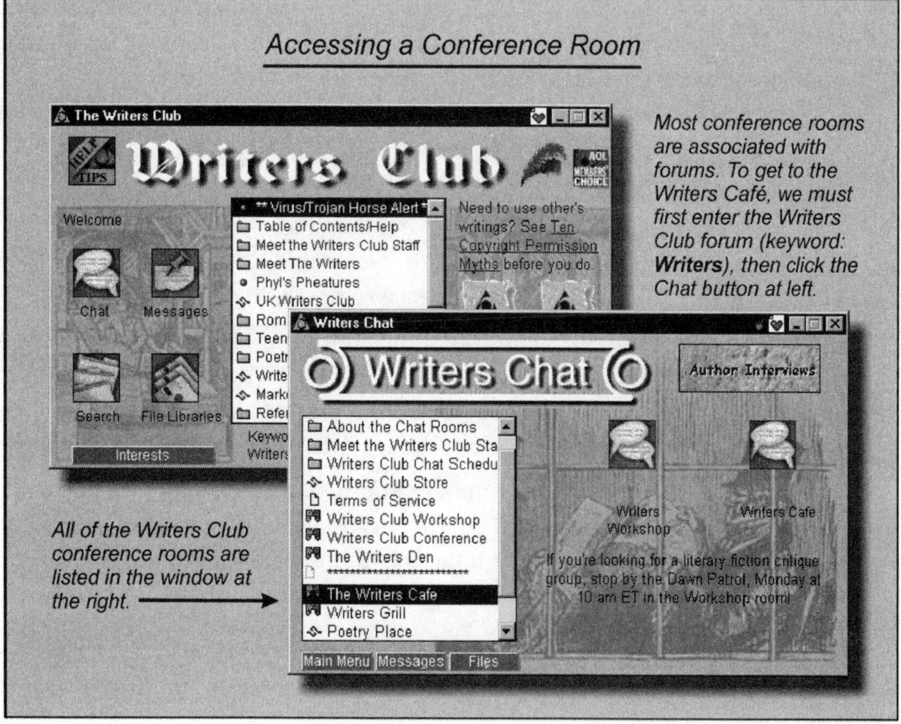

Figure 7-7: You have to travel through a forum to reach most conference rooms.

Because they're associated with forums (the Writers Club is a forum), and because they're slightly less accessible than public rooms, conference rooms exhibit some characteristics not common in public rooms:

- Most conference rooms can hold more than a public room's maximum of 23 people. It's not uncommon for thirty or forty people to be in a conference room. In spite of the crowd, conversations are rarely difficult to follow due to the use of *protocol* in most conference rooms. (See the sidebar "Protocol Rooms.")
- You're more likely to find staff members in conference rooms. They're forum staff—not Guides—and sometimes you can't determine they're staff without checking their profiles, but their presence usually makes a room more orderly and focused.
- Conference rooms are often scheduled: forums hold regularly scheduled meetings in their conference rooms during which a staff member is usually present and the subject matter is carefully regulated. Become familiar with a conference room's schedule before you enter it; you don't want to walk in on a scheduled conference unaware of what you're doing.
- Even during unscheduled times, conference room topics are more focused. We wouldn't expect to find people discussing model airplanes in the Writers Cafe (unless they were writing *books* about model airplanes), and hobbyists wouldn't expect to find us talking about agents and deadlines in their conference rooms either.
- The people in conference rooms are less transitory. People often graze among public rooms, looking for The Perfect Chat like a remote-wielding couch potato seeking The Perfect Channel. Such is not the case with conference rooms. People often stay in conference rooms for hours.

We're trying to make a subtle point here: if you're attracted by chat but underwhelmed by public rooms, seek out a forum that aligns with an interest of yours and see if it has a conference room. If it does, pop in. You might find yourself coming back again and again.

Protocol Rooms

At times, some conference rooms operate with *protocol*, usually when there is a guest speaker or a specific topic under discussion.

You can usually tell when you've entered a protocol room because you'll be greeted by a message informing you of the protocol. Protocol rooms invariably have a moderator as well, and the moderator's influence on the conversation will be readily apparent. One way or another, it doesn't take long to tell you're in a protocol room; just watch the conversation. Here are some of the conventions you'll see:

- Type a question mark **(?)** if you have a question and wait until the moderator calls on you.
- Type an exclamation point **(!)** if you have a comment and, again, wait.
- Type **GA** (for Go Ahead) or **/end** when you're done with your question or comment. It's also wise to have your material typed and ready to go before you're called on.

Game Rooms

A particular type of protocol room (see the sidebar "Protocol Rooms") that's dedicated to games is the *Game Parlor*, where mental challenges mingle with casual socializing (use the keyword: **Parlor**, and see Figure 7-8).

Figure 7-8: Parlor games are one of the best ways to get to know people online.

Each game has an official host and scorekeeper, and most have a greeter. The greeter will provide you with the host's and scorekeeper's names and some of the rules. The action is usually fast and erudite, but don't let that intimidate you; everyone has a first time and new visitors are always made to feel comfortable.

Parlor game schedules are always changing; you can see the latest at keyword: **Parlor**.

Member Rooms

Member rooms are named and created by members. A list of them is available by clicking the Member Rooms button pictured in Figure 7-4. The subject of a member room is entirely up to the member who creates the room and is usually identified by the room's name (see Figure 7-9).

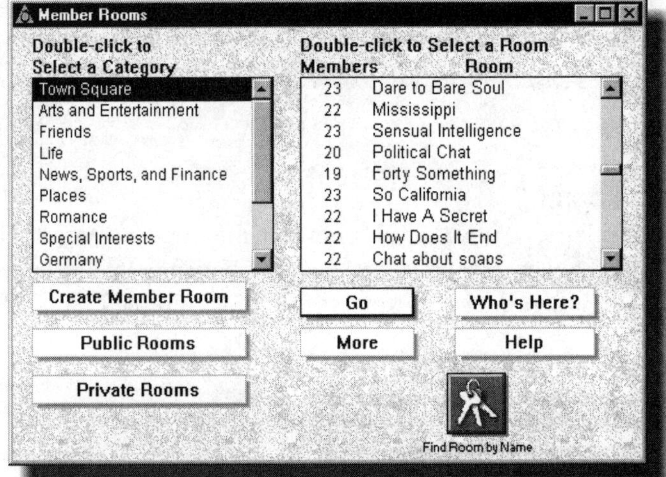

Figure 7-9: Member room topics vary from the innocuous to the scurrilous.

Note that member rooms are grouped by the same categories as public rooms. Since they're created by members—who aren't obliged to follow any kind of room category rules—member rooms often blur AOL's category distinctions. (Note that the Mississippi room pictured in Figure 7-9 really belongs in the Places category, though its popularity hasn't suffered from its misplacement.)

Member rooms share a number of common characteristics:

- Member rooms are open to the public unless they're full.
- Member rooms have a maximum capacity of 23 people and are not self-replicating.
- Member rooms are created and named by members (we'll tell you how in a moment). Member room names must abide by AOL's TOS (Terms of Service—TOS is discussed in Chapter 2); those with names found to be in violation of TOS are closed by People Connection staff.
- Member rooms are never hosted by staff members, though they *are* often hosted. The hosts in these circumstances are often host "wannabes." We're not using that term derogatorily: many conference room hosts get started by hosting a member room.
- Member rooms are rarely patrolled by Guides. Guides only enter member rooms when summoned via the Guidepager (see "The Guidepager" later in this chapter for more).

Figure 7-10 shows the same Member Rooms window that's pictured in Figure 7-9, though in Figure 7-10, the Places category has been selected. Note that the More button is dimmed in Figure 7-10 (all of the Places category rooms are available within the list box on the right); you would have to click Figure 7-9's More button—perhaps more than once—to see all of the rooms in the Town Square category.

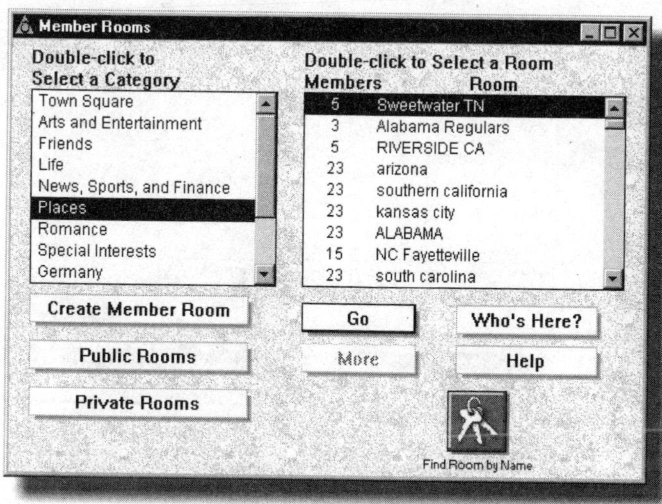

Figure 7-10: Member rooms in the Places category.

Anyone can create a member room. Just follow the sequence that's described in Figure 7-11.

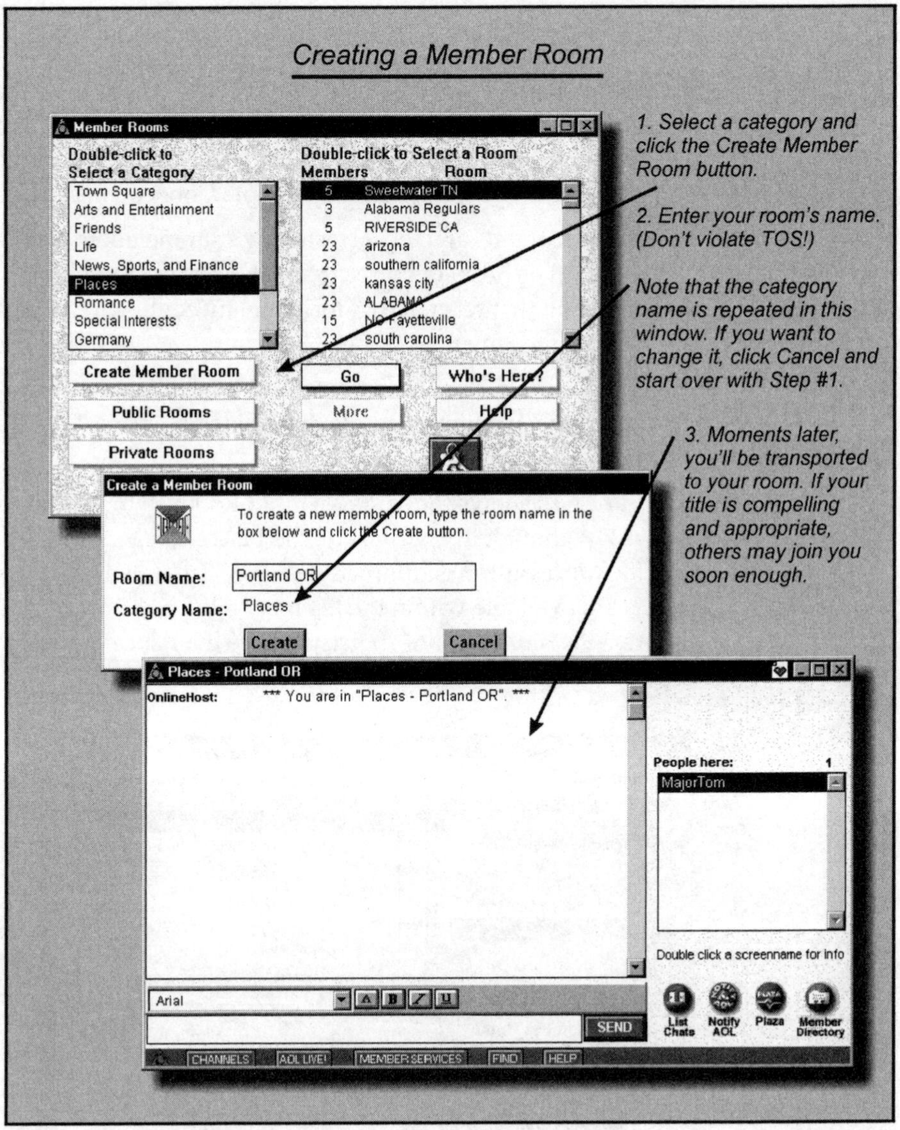

Figure 7-11: Creating a member room of your own amounts to little more than clicking a button.

Creating a Member Room

1. Select a category and click the Create Member Room button.

2. Enter your room's name. (Don't violate TOS!)

Note that the category name is repeated in this window. If you want to change it, click Cancel and start over with Step #1.

3. Moments later, you'll be transported to your room. If your title is compelling and appropriate, others may join you soon enough.

Member Rooms

Double-click to Select a Category

Town Square
Arts and Entertainment
Friends
Life
News, Sports, and Finance
Places
Romance
Special Interests
Germany

Double-click to Select a Room

Members	Room
5	Sweetwater TN
3	Alabama Regulars
5	RIVERSIDE CA
23	arizona
23	southern california
23	kansas city
23	ALABAMA
15	NC Fayetteville
23	south carolina

Create Member Room | Go | Who's Here?
Public Rooms | More | Help
Private Rooms

Create a Member Room

To create a new member room, type the room name in the box below and click the Create button.

Room Name: Portland OR
Category Name: Places

Create | Cancel

Places - Portland OR

OnlineHost: *** You are in "Places - Portland OR". ***

People here: 1
MajorTom

Double click a screenname for info

Arial | SEND

List Chats | Notify AOL | Plaza | Member Directory

CHANNELS | AOL LIVE! | MEMBER SERVICES | FIND | HELP

We hope the picture is coming into focus by now: the content, quality, and integrity of member rooms differ considerably from room to room. Some of the best rooms on the service are found here; so are the worst. Tom often visits the Portland OR (Oregon) room: one of his local TV meteorologists hangs out there, and weather is a subject about which Oregonians *always* have an opinion. However, there are other member rooms that are like the dark under the stairs: their names are all you have to go by.

Private Rooms

Like member rooms, private rooms are created by members and can hold 23 people. That, however, is where the similarity ends. Here are the specifics:

- Private rooms are not available to the public. There's no way to see a list of private rooms.
- Since you can't see a list of private rooms, you must know the exact name of a private room in order to enter it. You'll never know about a private room unless you create one of your own or someone invites you into theirs by providing you with its name.
- Private rooms are never patrolled—America Online's Terms of Service, in fact, specifically prohibits AOL staff from monitoring private room conversations (TOS is discussed in Chapter 2).
- You can leave a private room whenever you want to; just click its Close box.

Refer to Figure 7-12. The Private Rooms button pictured there allows you to create or visit a private room. When you click this button, America Online asks you for a room name. If you enter a name and the room already exists, America Online takes you into that room. If it doesn't exist, America Online creates it and takes you there. If you create a room, the only people who can enter it are those who know its name.

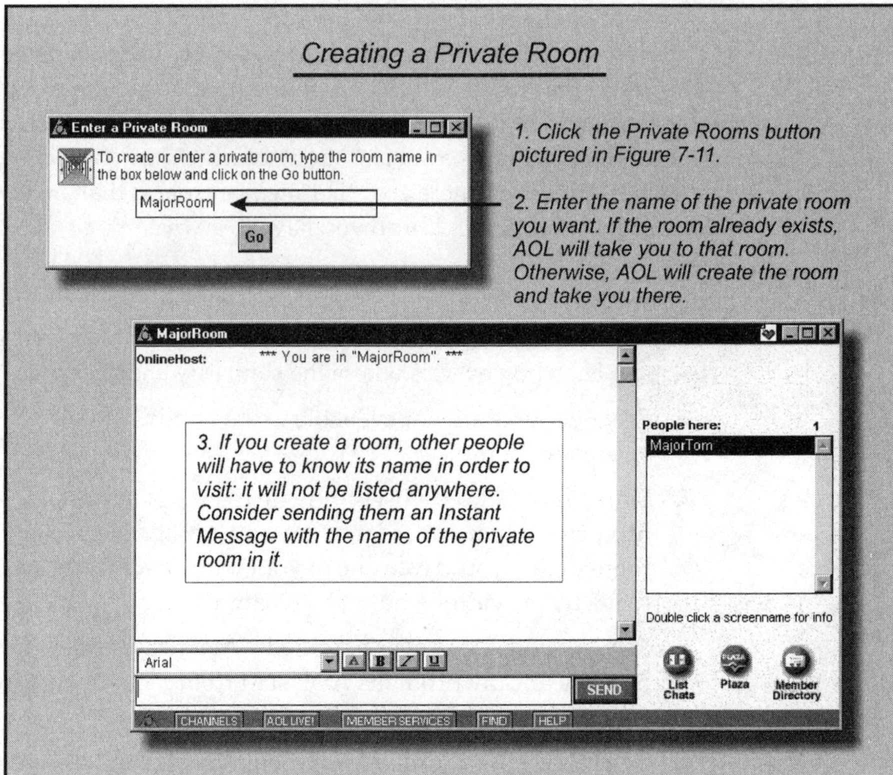
Creating a Private Room
Enter a Private Room
To create or enter a private room, type the room name in the box below and click on the Go button.
MajorRoom
Go
1. Click the Private Rooms button pictured in Figure 7-11.
2. Enter the name of the private room you want. If the room already exists, AOL will take you to that room. Otherwise, AOL will create the room and take you there.
MajorRoom
OnlineHost: *** You are in "MajorRoom". ***
3. If you create a room, other people will have to know its name in order to visit: it will not be listed anywhere. Consider sending them an Instant Message with the name of the private room in it.
People here: 1
MajorTom
Double click a screenname for info
Arial
SEND
List Chats
Plaza
Member Directory
CHANNELS
AOL LIVE!
MEMBER SERVICES
FIND
HELP

Figure 7-12: Private rooms are created in exactly the same fashion as member rooms.

Online Conference Calls

Consider the private room as an alternative to the conference call. We don't tend to think of them that way, but private rooms are essentially mechanisms whereby people from around the country can hold real-time conferences. America Online's private rooms are much less expensive than the phone company's conference calls, and participants can keep a log of the conversation for review once the conference has concluded. Conferences are often more productive when participants have to write what they say (makes 'em think before they speak) and vocal inflections don't cloud the issue.

To hold a private room conference call (or to simply meet some friends for a chat in a private room), tell the participants the name of the room and the time you want to meet beforehand; then arrive a few minutes early and create the room. Instruct the participants to enter the Lobby (the two-heads icon on the toolbar gets you there in a hurry) when they sign on, click the List Rooms button, click the Private Room button, and then type in the name of your room (keep the name simple). Try it: it's in many ways superior to a conference call—and cheaper to boot.

Using Favorite Places to Get to a Room

We discussed Favorite Places in Chapter 5, "Finding Stuff." Any window with a little heart icon in its upper right corner can be added to your Favorite Places list. Once a location is added to the list, you can return to it quickly and easily by choosing Favorite Places from the Go To menu or clicking the folder-and-heart button on the toolbar.

With that said, you might notice that most of the rooms we have discussed so far offer Favorite Places hearts on their title bars. The implication, then, is that you can add any room to your Favorite Places list and return to it later with a few clicks of the mouse. Are you fond of the Star Trek Club's The Bridge conference room? Add it to your Favorite Places list. The next time you want to go there, call up the list and double-click the entry for The Bridge. You'll bypass the Lobby and the List Rooms windows and be teleported directly to your destination. It's as if Scotty were handling the controls.

Remember too that your Favorite Places list is available even when you're offline. If you're offline and want to sign on and visit The Bridge, just call up your Favorite Places list and double-click the entry for The Bridge. America Online will sign on (and ask you for your password if you haven't stored one—see Chapter 8 for a discussion of stored passwords) and burrow directly to The Bridge. You'll hardly have time to dust off your communicator pin.

Chat Room Tips & Etiquette

Here are a few comments about chat room etiquette and technique:

- Review America Online's Terms of Service (discussed in Chapter 2 and available free at keyword: **TOS**) and get to know terms like *scrolling, impersonation, disruption, polling, chain letters,* and *pyramid schemes* as they pertain to the online environment.
- Don't give your password to anyone, no matter how convincing their argument to the contrary might be (see "Guttersnipe" later in this chapter).
- Say hello when you arrive in a room. Say good-bye before you leave.
- When you first enter a room (and after saying hello), watch the conversation for a few minutes to see which way the wind is blowing. Only then should you enter into the conversation.
- Speak when spoken to, even if you say nothing more than "I don't know."
- A catchy screen name works wonders. When Tom enters a room using his business screen name—which isn't catchy at all—he encounters far fewer rejoinders from its inhabitants than he does when he enters using his MajorTom screen name.

- Your screen name should contain a convenient "handle"—ideally your first name. Talking to TLic6865 is like talking to a license plate. "MajorTom" allows people to use "Major," or "Tom," or even "MT."
- Keep a log of your first few chat room visits. Review the log offline when the session has concluded. You'll learn a lot about chats this way.
- Get to know *smileys* and *emoticons*. These are the shorthand symbols you'll encounter online, such as ROTFL (rolling on the floor laughing), BTW (by the way), ;-) (a wink: turn your head 90 degrees counterclockwise), and hundreds of others. There are a number of files available for downloading that list them all. Use the keywords: **File Search** and search with the criterion "Emoticons." We're fond of the *Unofficial Emoticons Dictionary* by L.L. Drummond.
- You might want to see who's in a room before you enter it. A screen name often tells a lot about a person. You can see who's in a room by clicking *once* on any name in the Public Rooms window (review Figure 7-4) or the Member Rooms windows (review Figure 7-10) and then clicking the Who's Here? button.
- Learn what to do if you witness a TOS violation.

That last item points us directly toward the subject of the Guidepager: AOL's equivalent of an online 911. Read on.

The Guidepager

Freedom within the online community is threatened by a number of things—legislation, access, resources—but the most insidious and menacing threat to online freedom is abuse of the medium. And abuse, most frequently, appears in chat rooms.

Often the abusers are simply ignorant of the society. Sometimes they're brats on a lark, and a few are vandals, plain and simple. In all cases, the best way to deal with them is to report them, quickly and resolutely. This isn't tattling or hiding behind Mommy's apron; it's an imperative that we should all observe if we want to keep this community a healthy place. Those who would inflict online abuse represent a "social virus" to the online community; the scourge spreads like typhoid if left unchecked.

America Online's Guides are much more than the charitable souls they might seem to be. Think of them as you would think of the police: while they prefer to travel about benevolently assisting people in need, they are also vested with considerable authority. Guides can remove a member from a room, sever a member's access to People Connection for a period, or even terminate an account.

The *Guidepager* is a device used to summon a Guide for help, especially in the event of a TOS violation. The Guidepager is *not* a method of getting general help on AOL: read Chapter 2, "The Abecedarium," for information on that. The Guidepager may be accessed at any time, 24 hours a day, 7 days a week, by clicking the Notify AOL button in any chat room window (see Figure 7-13).

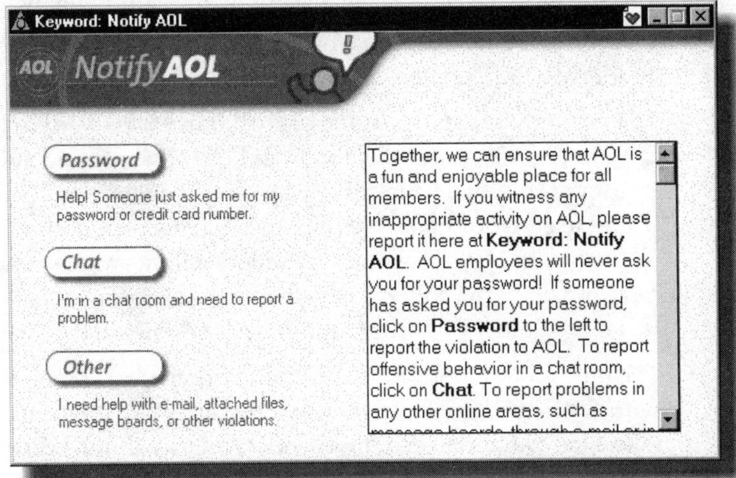

Figure 7-13: Use the Guidepager whenever you witness a violation of AOL's Terms of Service. The keywords are: **Notify AOL.**

Before you use the Guidepager, be sure to note the category and name of the room you are in, the screen name of the member causing the problem, and a brief description of the problem. Within five minutes, the Community Action Team Advisor or an on-duty Guide will come to your assistance. Don't abuse this service: sending false or frivolous pages can result in the termination of your account.

Chat Room Sounds

Interestingly, the online medium offers potential for much more than the textual exchange of dialog. In a few years (perhaps less), you will probably command an *avatar*—an online visual presence of yourself—just as you "wear" a screen name now. When your avatar enters a chat room, you will see other members' avatars in the room. Members in the room will likewise see your avatar when you enter, just as they see your screen name when you enter a room now.

It's all very radical, we suppose (and aptly described in the novel *Snow Crash*, by Neal Stephenson), but not inconceivable. In fact, part of this scenario is here now, in the form of *chat room sounds.*

You can broadcast chat room sounds to a room just as you send text; people in the room will hear the sound just as they would read the text. There are a few caveats, however:

- Your PC needs a sound card and speakers. If you don't hear "Welcome" when you sign on, you won't hear sounds in chat rooms. Almost any sound card and speaker combination will work, but buy the good stuff if you can afford it. This is fast becoming a multimedia medium.
- Likewise, the only people who will hear sounds you send are those with similarly equipped computers.
- The person playing the sound and all those who want to hear it must have the sound already installed on their hard disks. America Online doesn't transmit the actual sound file when you send a sound (sending the actual sound itself would take too long using a modem); rather, it sends an *instruction* to play the sound. Members will hear the sound only if they have obtained the sound (usually by downloading—read the "Finding & Installing Sounds" sidebar) and have it stored on their hard disk.
- The only sound files for the PC that work in chat rooms are those that end with the filename extension .wav. You already have a number of them: take a look at your \Windows and \America Online directories.
- To broadcast a sound in a chat room, type a line matching the format below and then click the chat window's Send button: **{S WELCOME.WAV}**

  Notice that the command is enclosed in braces {} and that it begins with a capital *S* (a lowercase *s* won't do). There's a space after the *S*, then the name of the sound. The .wav filename extension is optional in the command.

Finding & Installing Sounds

Hundreds of sounds are available online, where they're referred to as *waves* because of their .wav filename extension. For a listing of some of them, use the keywords: **PC Music** and browse the WAV Sounds & Utilities library. A similar library of sounds is available in the Macintosh Music and Sound Forum (keyword: **MMS**).

Sound files are great fun, especially in those chat rooms where they're used extensively. LaPub (keyword: **LaPub**) is a good example. More than a room, LaPub is a microcosmic community complete with its own library of sounds. With a sound card, speakers, and LaPub's library of sounds on your hard disk, a visit to the Pub is reminiscent of the TV series *Cheers*, replete with the clinking of glasses and the occasional splat of a pie hitting a face.

Earmuffs

Under some circumstances, chat room sounds can be disruptive. There are both technical and societal reasons for this, but the important thing is that chat room sounds can be turned off if you don't want to hear them. Read Chapter 9, "Preferences," for more information.

Keeping a Log

Your rendezvous is less than an hour away. You've cleaned your monitor screen, stocked up on soda, and you've got on your best pair of sweats. You want this chat to be everything you've hoped—and more. You go over and over what you want to say in your mind, even going so far as to jot down notes on your screen. Your palms begin to sweat and you worry you won't be able to remember what you said later on. How do you keep a permanent record of it?

The solution is found in America Online's Log Manager feature, whether you have the Chat of the Year or just a really good conversation. When a log is turned on, all chat appearing in your chat room is recorded on your disk. First, enter your chat room and get yourself situated. Now select Log Manager from the My Files icon in the toolbar. Once there, you'll see the name of the chat room you're currently in displayed (see Figure 7-14)—just click on the Open Log button below that, save the new file to your disk, and return to your chat. As the chat progresses, it will all be recorded in the log you opened—this includes anything you say as well. When you are done logging, just click the Close Log button. You can now open your log using America Online, or you can use an application like Microsoft Word if it is too large.

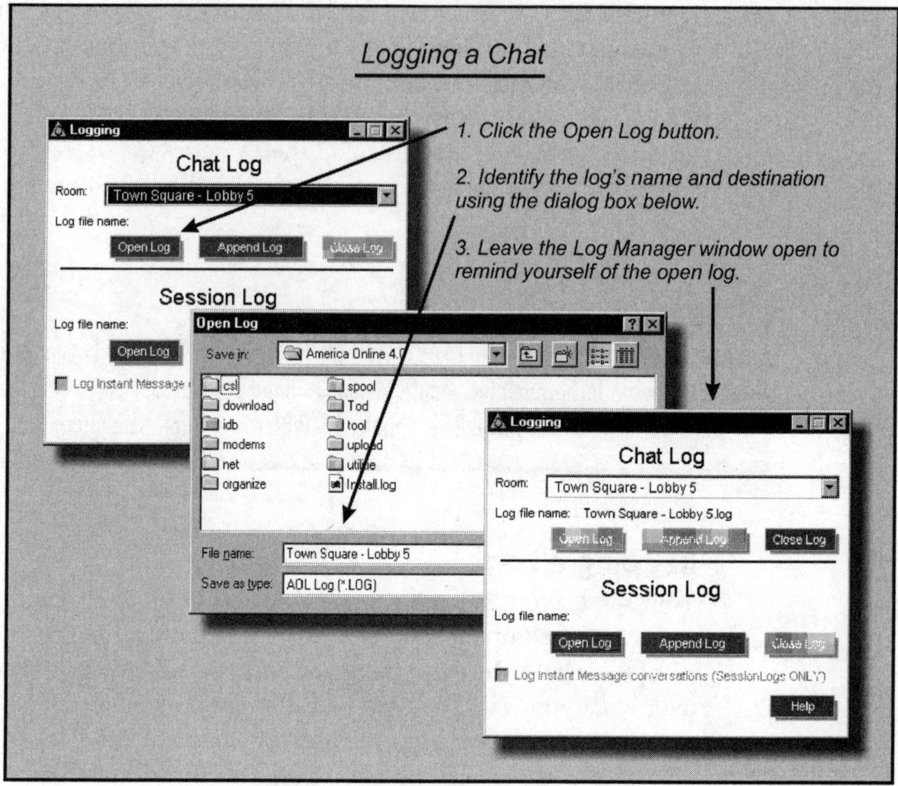

Figure 7-14: Log files capture and save chat for later review.

Here are a few notes about logs:

- You can always close the log or append an existing one by using the buttons in the Log Manager window (refer again to Figure 7-14). This is handy when you want to turn your log on and off: you can use the Close Log and Append Log buttons as you would the Pause button on a tape recorder, capturing the material you want and excluding what you don't want.
- Log files can be as large as you want them to be, but they grow quickly if you don't pay attention, especially in a chatty room. Monitor your activity online while a log file is open as you would monitor your fuel gauge while traveling through Death Valley. Remember too that if the log file is too large, you will not be able to use the AOL software to open it—you'll have to open it within another application.
- If you look carefully at the bottom window in Figure 7-14, you will note that there is another kind of log. The Session log is the one that captures articles like the one pictured in Figure 7-15. It will also capture Instant Messages (discussed later) when the option is checked.

Auditoriums

So far, all we've discussed are rooms with a relatively small capacity: 23 persons, for the most part. But what if President Clinton were to make an online appearance? (It has happened.) How about Billy Joel, Oprah Winfrey, Anthony Edwards, or David Bowie? (They all have appeared.)

A vehicle for such an appearance exists. In fact, a number of them do. Collectively they're known as *auditoriums*, and each one has a name: Cyberplex, Odeon, Globe, Bowl, Coliseum—there are 11 of them in total. Collectively, America Online's auditoriums can hold up to 55,000 people at a time (see the sidebar "Media Melding"). When you enter, you're assigned a "row" in the auditorium. Each row holds 8 or 16 people, and all of you can talk among yourselves all you want; no one else can hear your conversation.

Participating in an Auditorium Event

America Online's auditoriums are significantly different from other chat rooms. They have to be: thousands of people populate the auditoriums—many, many more than a normal chat room's maximum of 23. Here's how it works:

- When you're ready to interact with the people on stage, click the Interact button pictured in Figure 7-15. Your question or comment will be placed in a queue for the moderator's consideration. With audiences numbering in the thousands, not all questions are answered, but the dialog is always engaging whether you participate or not.

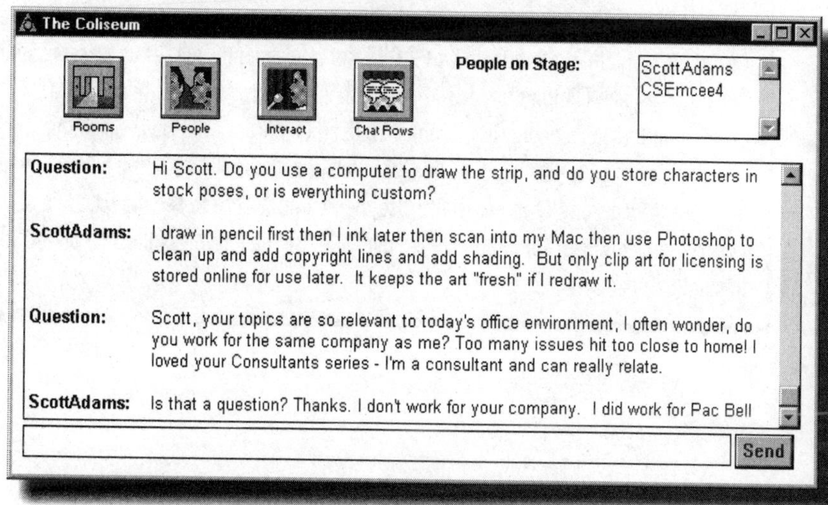

Figure 7-15: In the auditoriums with Scott Adams, creator of the "Dilbert" comic strip.

- If you simply type a comment into the lower text box pictured in Figure 7-15 and click the Send button, your comment will appear in the main text box, *but only on the screens of the people in your row.* Comments such as this are easy to recognize: they're preceded by your row number, which appears in parentheses.
- Figure 7-15's People button will display a listing of the other people in your row. You can send them Instant Messages or view their profiles as if you were in a normal chat room (review Figure 7-6).
- The Chat Rows button in Figure 7-15 will produce a listing of all of the rows in use within the auditorium and the number of people in each one. You can use this button to jump from one row to another or to find out about people in the auditorium who aren't in your row.

Media Melding

It was a media first: Michael Jackson appearing in a simulcast with America Online and MTV. It also set a record for auditorium attendance at AOL. In fact, over 16,000 people were "in" the auditorium with Michael Jackson that night, sitting in virtual seats, reading the conversation on their computer monitors while they watched The Man on their television screens. It wasn't the first, nor will it be the last multiple-medium online event: President Clinton's appearance was simulcast on the *Larry King Live* program on CNN, and the cast and crew of *Wings* appeared online while an episode was being taped!

Out of context, 16,000 is a meaningless number. Let's put it in perspective: the previous record for auditorium attendance was 2,035, set a few months earlier by actress Sandra Bullock. President Clinton drew 1,364 and Anthony Edwards (from NBC's *ER*) drew 1,846.

Michael Jackson's auditorium event was, in other words, a Big Deal. Since then, only one other event has beat his record: Rosie O'Donnell had almost 17,000. You owe it to yourself to witness at least one of these events. Use the keyword: **Live** to see the schedule of celebrity appearances. On the appointed evening, use the keyword indicated on the schedule to join the fun.

At the time we're writing this, America Online has 11 auditoriums: AOL Live, Bowl, Coliseum, CyberPlex, CyberRap, Digital City Plaza, Globe, International (1 & 2), News Room, and Odeon. Each can hold up to 5,000 people. There really isn't any difference among them besides their names—they all have the same capacity and they all work the same way. There are 11 of them so that America Online can accommodate simultaneous online events. America Online's auditoriums are similar to the auditoriums in a multiscreen theater: some want to watch *The Rocky Horror Picture Show*; some want to watch *On Golden Pond*. To each his own.

With all of these luminaries appearing online—sometimes over a dozen a day—how do you tell who's appearing, and when, and where? And how can you get there? Read on.

Auditorium Help

People, hosts, guests, etiquette, protocol—they can overwhelm the first-time visitor, we know. Any large gathering is that way.

Fortunately, there's help, and it's available right from the AOL Live! Main Screen. Use the keyword: **Live**; then click the Help button.

AOL Live!

Auditoriums and conference rooms—at any moment (especially in the evenings), scores of them are active. Keeping track of them all would be an unrealistic undertaking were it not for *AOL Live!*

Simply put, AOL Live! is your *TV Guide* for online events. Want to know what's playing? Use the keyword: **Live** and look over the schedule of Coming Attractions (see Figure 7-16). You can check the schedule according to time of day or search for a specific guest, room, or time.

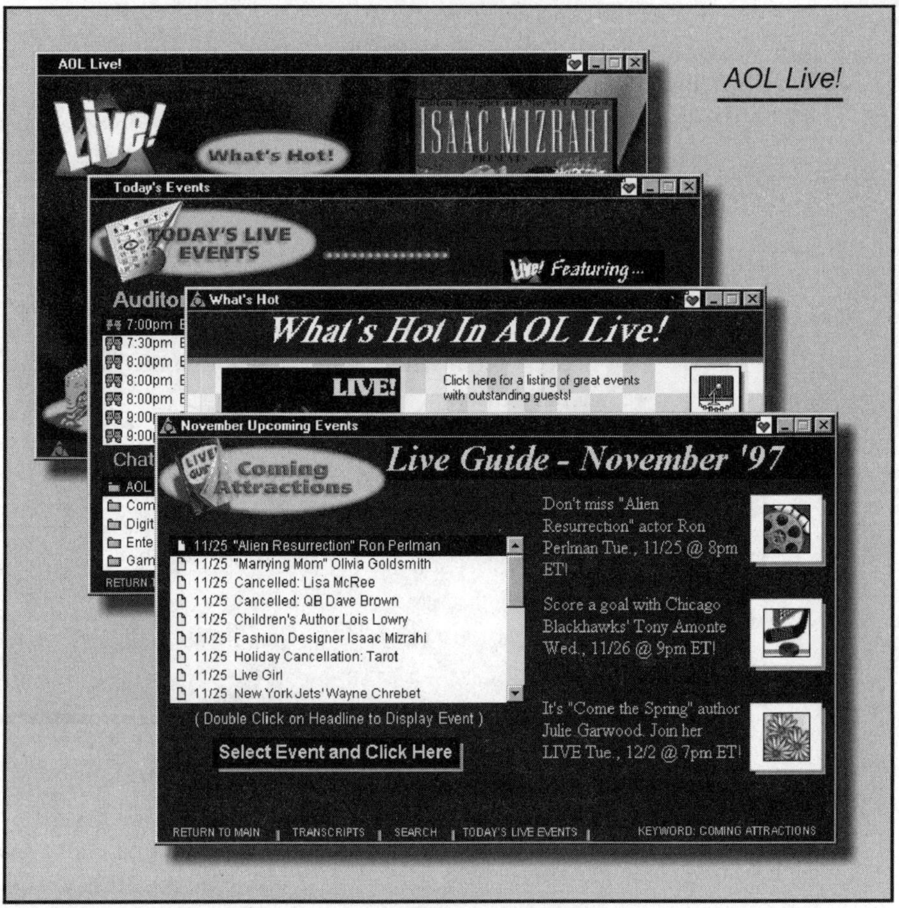

Figure 7-16: Use the keyword: **Live** to see what's happening in AOL's auditoriums and conference rooms.

So how do you get to all of these nifty auditorium events? Here's a tip: you can get to any auditorium, at any time, by using the keyword: **Intermission** and then clicking the Auditorium Entrances button. When auditorium events are advertised (especially on the Welcome screen), you're usually given a keyword that will take you to the forum or sponsor for the event. That's fine—especially if you want to know more about the sponsoring organization—but if you simply want to get there fast, use the **Intermission** keyword.

Express Delivery

Often, online promotions for auditorium events—you'll see them on the Welcome screen all the time—mention the name of the auditorium in which the event is occurring.

When you know an auditorium's name and want to get there as if Scotty beamed you up, use the auditorium's name as a keyword, *preceded by an @ sign.* If something is happening in the Odeon at 7:30, for example, wait till 7:30 and then use the keyword: **@Odeon**. You'll materialize in the Odeon just like Kirk and Spock on a distant planet, ready for action.

Instant Messages

An *Instant Message* is a message sent to someone else online. Don't confuse Instant Messages with e-mail or chat rooms. Unlike e-mail, Instant Messages work only if both the sender and the recipient are online at the same time. Like chat rooms, Instant Messages occur in real-time, but only two people can participate in an Instant Message: there's no "room" for others.

You'll probably encounter Instant Messages most often when you're in a room. It's then, after all, that the greatest number of people know you're online. Under those circumstances, an Instant Message is something like whispering in class, though you'll never get in trouble for it. Instant Messages aren't limited to chat rooms, however: they work whenever you're online, wherever you might be.

You'll also often receive Instant Messages from people who have your screen name on their Buddy List. Receiving an Instant Message from a buddy is always a welcome intermission.

Earlier in this chapter, we suggested a private room as an alternative to conference calls. You might also consider Instant Messages as alternatives to long-distance phone calls. Tom and Jennifer need to have a number of discussions nearly every week. Unfortunately, Jennifer, located in Michigan, is about as far away from Tom's home in Oregon as one can be without being in a different country. Instead of making long-distance telephone calls across the country and four different time zones, we go online, which allows us to "talk" without worrying about the cost. The cost amounts to nothing more than the normal connect-time charge. A conversation we had today appears in Figure 7-17.

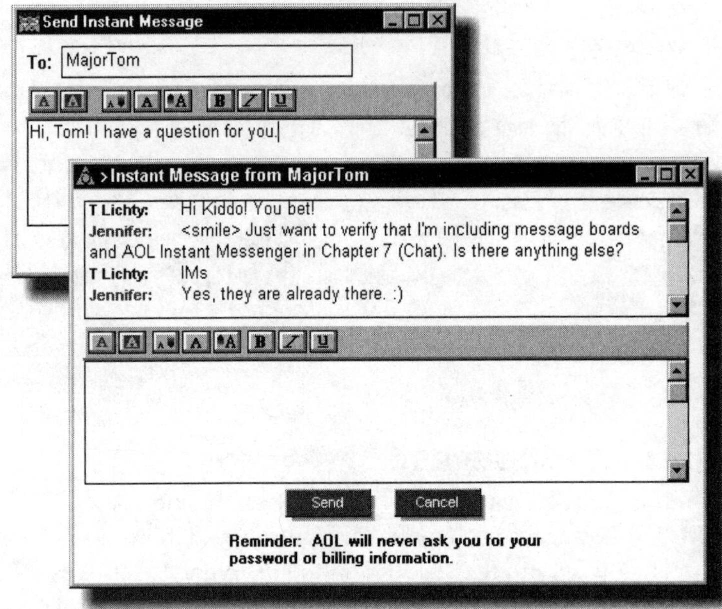

Figure 7-17: The Instant Message from MajorTom window contains a running log of our conversation in the upper text box along with a text box where Jennifer can compose her response below.

To send an Instant Message, choose Instant Message from the People icon in the toolbar. Enter the recipient's screen name and your message, as shown in the upper window of Figure 7-17, and click Send. After that, a running log of the conversation is maintained in the Instant Message window, as pictured in the lower window of Figure 7-17.

A few notes regarding Instant Messages:

- Before you send an Instant Message, use the Available? button in the Instant Message window or the Locate AOL Member Online command under the People icon. If the recipient isn't online when you send an Instant Message, America Online tells you, and you'll have to wait for another opportunity. (If a member is not available online, consider sending e-mail instead. Electronic mail is discussed in Chapter 3.)

- Figure 7-17's lower window has been enlarged from the default. Like all of America Online's windows, the Instant Message window can be resized. If you want to change the size of a window permanently, choose Remember Window Size Only from the Windows menu after you have sized the window to your satisfaction.
- You cannot send Instant Messages while in a "free" area (for those of you who did not elect the unlimited usage plan), though you can compose them while you're there. America Online closes any open Instant Message windows when you enter an unlimited usage area and exits it as soon as you attempt to send an Instant Message.
- Use the Available? button in the Send Instant Message window to determine where the intended recipient is before sending an Instant Message. This feature tells you if the recipient is online and, if so, whether he or she can receive Instant Messages. It also tells you if a member is in a chat room, in which case you might want to go to that room rather than send an Instant Message.
- Instant Messages are accompanied by a "Tinkerbell" sound (assuming your machine is equipped to play sounds), and the Instant Message window will appear on your screen. See the sidebar "Ongoing Instant Messages" for more.

Available or Locate?

The Available? button in the Send Instant Message window does the same thing as the Locate a Member Online command under the Members menu. We prefer the button. Most of the time, if a member is online, you're going to want to say hello, right? If you discover the member online via the Locate command and want to say hello, you have to call up the Send Instant Message dialog box anyway, but in the time it takes to produce that box, you might lose your opportunity.

Okay, it's a small matter, and locating members online isn't like locating pike: they aren't liable to disappear in a matter of seconds. Nonetheless, it's one less command to learn, and every time you don't use the Available? button, you'll wish you did.

Ongoing Instant Messages

Occasionally, you'll find yourself engaged in an ongoing Instant Message conversation. You might want to do something else online while it's underway—read the postings on a board, for example, or check the weather.

Doing something else online, however, pushes the IM window to the back, and if your PC can't play sounds, you'll need another method of determining when your correspondent has replied. How can you tell with the IM window in the background?

Easy: before you pursue another task, position the IM window on your screen (it's a window like any other and you can move it by dragging its title bar) so that its title bar will show, even if it's in the background and other windows have come to the front. While you're working on another task, keep your eye on the IM window's title bar. When your friend sends a reply, the > symbol will appear in the IM window's title bar, even if it's in the background. Then it's a simple matter of bringing the IM window to the front and composing your reply.

- You can log Instant Messages (handy for telephone-style Instant Messages such as those we exchanged) by choosing Log Manager from the My Files icon. Open a Session log: it records Instant Messages as well when you enable the option at the bottom.
- If you don't want to be disturbed by Instant Messages, you can turn them off at any time by sending an Instant Message to "$im_off" (without the quotation marks but with the dollar sign). Include a character or two as text for the message; otherwise America Online will respond with a "Cannot send empty Instant Message" error. A single character will do. To turn Instant Messages back on, send an Instant Message to "$im_on."

AOL Instant Messenger

Earlier we cautioned you not to confuse Instant Messages with e-mail. Yet there is one similarity: like e-mail, Instant Messages can be exchanged with those on the Internet as well as those on America Online. We owe this to AOL Instant Messenger, a program that allows those who install it to use Instant Messages and even Buddy Lists.

Sending and receiving Instant Messages is little different for those of us on America Online. AOL members do not need to install anything extra—we already have everything we need to exchange Instant Messages with folks using AOL Instant Messenger. We can place Internet friends who have AOL Instant Messenger right in our Buddy List (discussed later) like any other member and send them Instant Messages in the normal way. The only difference is in receiving Instant Messages—the first time you receive one from an AOL Instant Messenger user, you have the ability to accept or dismiss the message before you ever see it. From there on, it's familiar territory.

Best of all, AOL Instant Messenger is free to all your Internet friends. They can download it themselves at AOL's Home Page (http://www.aol.com/), or you can have the software sent to them using the keywords: **Instant Messenger** (see Figure 7-18). It is currently only available for Macintosh, Windows 95/NT, and Java users, but a Windows 3.1 version may be ready by the time you read this. Once the software is installed, your friends only need to register and choose screen names. There is no additional cost for this service. It is America Online's contribution to the Internet community and, ultimately, our own.

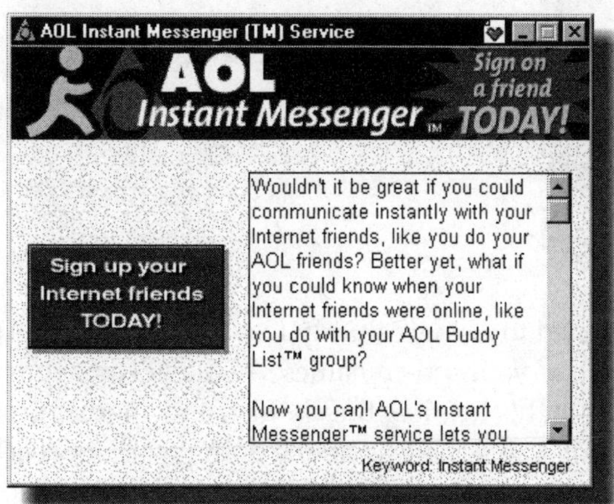

Figure 7-18: AOL Instant Messenger brings our Internet friends a little closer.

Buddy Lists

Supply and demand: classical economics expounds on the balance between equilibrium and chaos, citing theories and pointing to business graphics that look like the Grand Tetons and apple pies—all very arcane and inscrutable.

It's not that complex at America Online. At AOL, the supply-and-demand theory is simple: if we the members demand it, America Online will supply it. Such is the case with *Buddy Lists*. The demand from members for Buddy Lists warranted America Online's examination of the matter. Six months later, the feature was available.

What's a Buddy List? The wrinkle in the Instant Message scenario that we've been discussing is that you have to know if the recipient is online before you can send an Instant Message. The Locate a Member Online command under the Members menu serves the need after a fashion, but what if the person you're trying to locate signs on four seconds after you've tried to locate him or her? What if that person is online when you sign on? Wouldn't it be nice to know that as soon as the "Welcome" greeting is finished?

Buddy Lists are the solution. Once defined, your Buddy List patrols America Online's front gates like a faithful doorman, checking all members' screen names as they sign on. If there's a match—if a member signing on is on your Buddy List—you're immediately notified. And if a buddy of yours is already online when you sign on, you'll be notified similarly (see Figure 7-19).

Figure 7-19: Once a Buddy List is active, you'll receive automatic notification of a buddy's arrival whenever the buddy signs on.

You're not limited to a single Buddy List. You can have as many of them as you like—for each of your screen names. As MajorTom, Tom might have a group of buddies on his Readers Buddy List, and another group of buddies on his Business Buddy List. If he was online doing work, he'd activate his Business list. If he was there to be social, he'd use the Readers list.

You can create Buddy Lists, and you can add, edit, or delete buddies on those lists using the windows pictured in Figure 7-20 (at keyword: **Buddy**). You can also specify those members whose Buddy Lists you want your name to appear on (and those you don't) by using the Buddy List preferences discussed in Chapter 9.

Figure 7-20: Create, add, edit, and delete buddies and Buddy Lists using these routines.

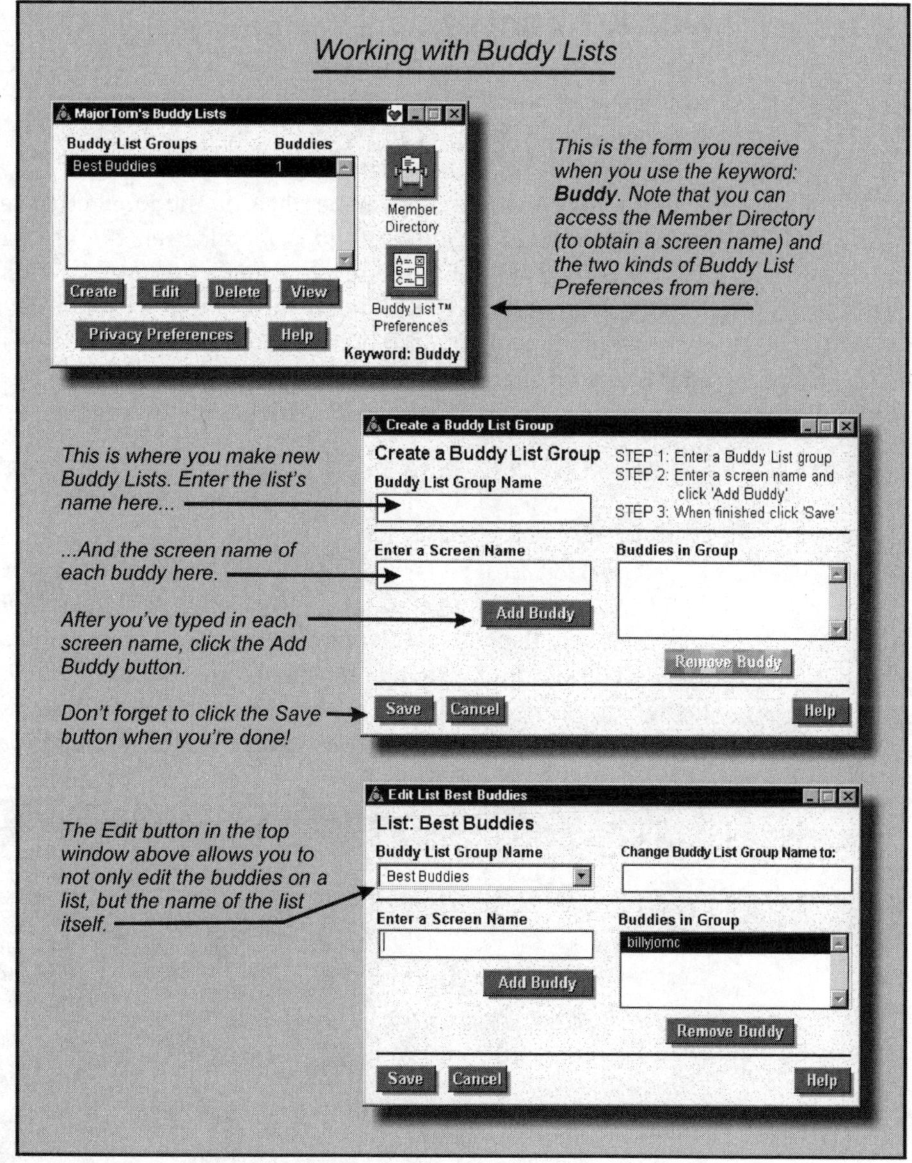

Kids & Parents

In its early years, the online industry was almost exclusively composed of adult males. The online services of the early 1980s concentrated almost exclusively on computer topics and issues. (America Online was no exception: it was called *PC Link* in those days and was devoted exclusively to users of the Commodore computer—remember the Commodore Pet?) The Internet was up and running then, but military and academic users dominated its use—hardly a forum for kids, or seniors, or even women.

Things have changed. Kids, women, and seniors are the fastest-growing segments of the online community. Probably no other segment of our society adapts as well to computers as our kids do, and kids have no qualms about striking up a new online friendship, uploading original art, or speaking their minds on a board topic.

Kids Only

Kids Only (keyword: **Kids**) is a full-fledged channel on America Online. It's AOL's place for kids to interact with each other and to find information appropriate to their age level. Not surprisingly, parents (and other adults) are asked to refrain from posting on the kids' boards or chatting in the rooms, though browsing the channel is a delight for people of all ages (just look at Figure 7-21 for an indication of the wealth of offerings in this area).

Figure 7-21: The visual abundance of Kids Only is apparent even in black and white.

Take Five for Online Safety

We're lifting these five rules directly from the Kids Only Channel. It's important for kids to realize that people online aren't always who they say they are. These five rules will help kids—of all ages—manage in our community to their greatest benefit:

- Don't give your AOL password to anyone, even your best friend.
- Never tell someone your home address, telephone number, or school name without asking a parent.
- Never say you'll meet someone in person without asking a parent.
- Always tell a parent about any threatening or bad language you see online.
- If someone says something that makes you feel unsafe or funny, don't just sit there—take charge! Call a Guide (keywords: **KO Help**). If you're in a chat room, leave the room. Or just sign off.

Kids Chat

If there's one thing kids like to do even more than exchange their creations, it's exchange their opinions. All kids have an opinion about something, and most of them have opinions about everything. And there's no medium better suited for that purpose than America Online.

There are chat rooms all over the Kids Only Channel. Nickelodeon has the Blabbatorium, Warner Brothers has the Chat Shack—there are lots of others. These rooms serve a distinct audience; they're not the same as conference rooms or the rooms in People Connection. Here are a few suggestions and specifics on features, restrictions, and unacceptable behavior:

- Some kids rooms (all of those in Kids Only, for example) are for kids of a specific age. Determine a room's age restrictions before you enter.
- The age restrictions are for participants, not observers. Parents should visit these rooms—to observe the conversations—before their children become participants.
- Most kids rooms are staffed at peak times; some are staffed round the clock. It's not uncommon to find three or four "nicks" (Nickelodeon staff) in the Blabbatorium, for example, on any weekday afternoon.
- Profanity is not allowed anywhere on America Online. Use of such language in chat rooms and message boards constitutes a TOS violation. Using symbols to disguise these words is also a violation.

- Rudeness to a guest, verbally or by behavior, will be considered a room disruption and is subject to TOS review.
- Harassing a staff member or another member in a chat room is not allowed. If someone harasses *you*, do not respond in the same manner. If the harassment appears in the form of an IM, use the Ignore feature (discussed earlier in this chapter) and report the violation to TOS. Don't let one person's rudeness make you behave in the same way.
- Talk of illegal activity is forbidden on America Online.
- *Scrolling* (when a user repeatedly presses the Return key so that previous chat room messages move too fast for the users to see) is forbidden. Scrolling is specifically defined as a TOS violation.
- *Polling* (asking a question and requiring all present to post a specific letter, number, or word in response, such as "Type '3' if you love David Bowie.") isn't specifically a TOS violation, but it's a little moronic and always disruptive.
- Before coming to a kids chat room, check the calendar. If there is a scheduled event, the room is reserved. You're welcome to join the event in progress, of course, but if you're looking for a social chat, wait until the scheduled event is finished.
- Do not post age/sex checks (requests for room occupants' age and gender) during scheduled events. This disrupts a discussion, is rude to a guest, and makes it difficult to play a game. Ask in Instant Messages if you really can't wait till the event is finished.

Parental Considerations

Though it occurs throughout the service, harassment and exploitation are particularly obstructive in any kids area. To be effective, America Online must be a place where kids are made to feel welcome. It's their online home, and a home—above all—must always be comfortable.

TOS & Kids

America Online's Terms of Service (TOS is discussed in Chapter 2) clearly define the rules of acceptable online behavior—for all members, including kids. Parents should understand these rules and make sure their children understand them before signing on. In the perspective of TOS and kids, it's important to remember that the person who is the master account holder is responsible for all of the users whose screen names are on the account.

An Extra Measure of Security

Here's a nifty little tip from remote forum leader Tom Quindry: use the Passwords preferences available in your Preferences (from the My AOL icon) to store your kids' passwords. The kids won't need a password to sign on—which might be convenient—but more important, they won't be able to see the passwords on the screen even if they look at the Passwords preference. (Note in Figure 7-22 that stored passwords are displayed as asterisks.)

If your kids don't need a password to sign on, if they can't see their stored password onscreen, and if you don't tell them what it is, they can't possibly reveal it to friends or password surfers, no matter how persuasive the come-on. An interesting proposition. Give it some thought.

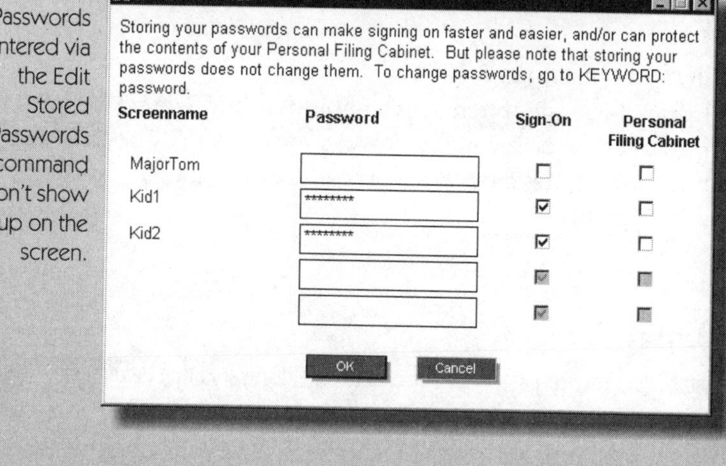

Figure 7-22: Passwords entered via the Edit Stored Passwords command don't show up on the screen.

KO Help

When your child witnesses a TOS violation, he or she should be encouraged to use the keywords: **KO Help** and ask a Guide to enter the room where the violation is occurring (see Figure 7-23). KO Help is sort of a Guidepager for kids. It's a bit more kid-friendly, but it carries the same degree of authority as any other Guide online. Not only will the offender be made to understand the significance of TOS enforcement (that's as politely as we can put it), but your child will see what happens when these rules are broken. A witness to a "TOS event" rarely forgets the experience.

Figure 7-23: Making America Online a better place for all kids: KO Help is only a keyword away.

Instant Messages & Kids

Instant Messages often arrive unbidden, and when kids are involved, these messages are occasionally unwelcome as well. Your child should know how to turn Instant Messages off, a procedure described in "Instant Messages" earlier in this chapter.

Online Time

A friend of ours once recounted her horror when she discovered that her daughter had fallen asleep for two hours while making a call to a 900 number. Those of you who didn't elect the unlimited usage plan already know that America Online's charges can add up quickly when a child—who can hardly be expected to understand the significance of a month of six-hour Saturdays in the KOOL Tree House—is left unattended online. The Kids Only staff suggests you teach your children how to use Automatic AOL sessions for collecting and posting mail (Automatic AOL is discussed in Chapter 8, "Working Offline"). Set limits on the amount of time they are allowed online, in much the same way you limit their television viewing. KOOL should be a fun electronic clubhouse but not a financial burden. America Online cannot be held responsible for charges you might deem excessive.

The Internet & Kids

As we mentioned in Chapter 4, the Internet is a vast superset of America Online extending around the world. It is, therefore, an environment over which America Online has no control. There is no Internet TOS, and even if there was one, there would be little authority for its enforcement: the Internet is still an anarchy in many ways.

On the other hand, an increasing number of schools are going online via the Internet, and the array of services available there is constantly growing. This is not an appropriate resource for parents to prohibit, though it *is* one to restrain and monitor (we'll discuss that later in this chapter, when we get to "Parental Controls").

By all means, encourage your children to explore the Internet, but do so only after you've explored this section of the book and visited the keywords: **Parental Controls**. Should you become aware of the transmission, use, or viewing of child pornography while on the Net, immediately report it to the National Center for Missing or Exploited Children by calling 1-800-843-5678. The Center has an excellent brochure on this subject titled *Child Safety on the Information Highway* (Figure 7-24).

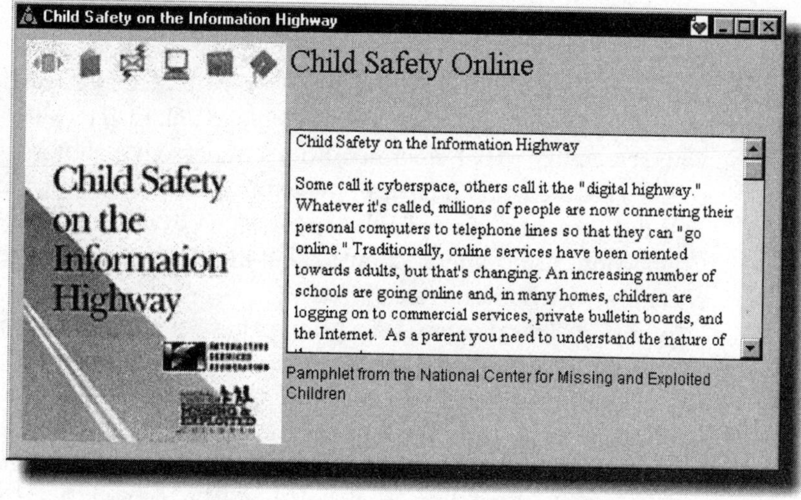

Figure 7-24: Parents who intend to allow their children to explore the Internet should order this brochure from the National Center for Missing or Exploited Children. Call 1-800-843-5678 to order.

Women's Issues

Sitting at your computer, probably in private, it's difficult to imagine the sheer magnitude of the America Online community. There are over 10 million people here: more people "live" in the America Online community than in the metro areas of San Francisco, Madrid, or Sydney. Every community this size has its share of societal rewards—and problems. America Online is no exception.

Perhaps no segment of America Online's society benefits more from these rewards—and suffers more of the problems—than women. A section on women's issues, then, is not only appropriate for this book, it's integral to the understanding of the community. This is a responsibility we don't take lightly.

Tom is not a woman, nor would he be so arrogant as to assume that he can speak on their behalf. Jennifer, on the other hand, has a wealth of experience as a woman online—from the early days of being a "girl geek" to our current climate of relative sophistication. Add to that the voices of four more women of online significance and vision—all active participants in the online community and all here long enough to have things in proper perspective—and you have the following dialogue. Short biographies appear as sidebars; we use the women's screen names to identify them.

Screen Names

Any woman who has ventured into People Connection with a gender-specific screen name probably has a shocking tale to tell. Instant Messages overlap on your screen like paper emerging from a hyperactive photocopier. Most of the senders are men, and most are shy and relatively innocent. Some are not.

What's a woman to do? Take a gender-neutral screen name? Avoid People Connection? Cancel her account? All of the women on our panel use gender-specific screen names. Here's why.

Jennifer: "I've always used a primary gender-specific screen name simply because, quite simply, *I'm* gender-specific. <grin> After I'd been on AOL for a few weeks, I considered the idea of having a gender-neutral name, but it seems like 'hiding' or sacrificing my identity in some way. So I didn't, and I'm glad I made that choice. I've met many women who refuse to use a gender-specific screen name because they feel that they will be harassed and/or discriminated against. I've only been harassed while in the People Connection chats (and that is no big deal to me), and rarely (if ever) discriminated against. So I use a gender-specific screen name because I like my name (most names have been a variation on Jennifer) and because I am female. It is just who I am."

EvaS: "I've always used my own name. The only time I didn't was in order to see how different my experience might be were I to sign on and go to a chat room using a man's name. It was interesting. I was ignored. :(. . . I'm a woman and like being one. I like my own name. I've learned how to deal with harassment. I ignore it completely. . . ."

SueBD: "In contrast to some of the rest of you, I do get sick of harassment in chat rooms. Most of the time I deal with it by either not going in there to begin with, or by going in under a gender-neutral name. I have noticed, however, as Eva has, that I get less attention that way. Entirely naively, I may have gotten myself into a worse situation than those who 'merely' have female screen names. SueBD was really just my initials when I joined AOL in 1993, but I have discovered since then (to my chagrin) that B & D also stands, in some circles, for bondage and discipline, and suggests all *kinds* of kinky things to some folks. Since doing kinky things is the *last* place I want to be online, I finally resorted to making a pretty blatant statement in my profile. As someone else suggested, it works most of the time. I've toyed with the idea of changing my screen name, but I'm on a billion mailing lists, and everyone online knows me by this name, and it just seems like a big undertaking at this point. Furthermore, SueBD is the top name on my account, and if I delete the whole account to get rid of it I lose my mailing list names, too."

SueBD

SueBD works as a medical professional and in her "spare time" owns and operates the Women's Web Construction Company, doing Web site design, graphics, and consultation regarding online community building (at http://wwcoco.com). She also moderates a medical professionals' mailing list (mailing lists are discussed in Chapter 4) with over 1,200 members around the world.

GwenSmith: "Both [my business screen name] and my 'civvie' one . . . are gender-specific. Why? Because I like to feel that I am showing 'me' online, that I am not hiding myself from others. When I started on AOL, I did have a more 'obscure' name, which allowed me to wander around without anyone knowing who I was—in fact (as it's my original log-on) I still have it and use it, now and again. However . . . people can see a gender-specific name and, well, hormones get the best of 'em, I guess. But I am not going to hide myself because they can't control themselves."

Sooze50: "I closed my account and restarted twice, out of paranoia, to get new screen names. If I were giving advice, I'd say, stow your main screen name, never use it, create one suitable changeable alter ego screen name, and use that for actual online activities. That way, you can dump the alternate screen name without going through the bother of canceling the account. My local police suggested I should never use my real name or give my real address. That proved impractical, since I wanted to exchange books and manuscripts with writers I met online. There is something of depth, an opportunity for mind-to-mind communication, a surprisingly high level of intimacy of thought, that is worth the risk. E-mail cuts across all the boundaries—age, gender, race, religion, location, time of day. It sounds corny, but, since the picture of the earth that was taken from the moon, I think that the biggest opportunity for world peace is going to be worldwide communication by e-mail and the Internet. In worrying about the problems, I say, let's not lose sight of the Big Picture."

Self-Defense

Using a gender-specific name, however, eventually provokes an unwanted advance or two. Here's how the members of our panel deal with them:

Jennifer: "I got a lot of these my first year here, and I almost never get them now. I think the biggest reasons are that I don't frequent the same places (People Connection chat rooms), I don't attract that kind of attention anymore, and I know what to do with those who do bother me. There are definitely places online that will bring more unwelcome advances than others, but that shouldn't be a reason to stay away if you want to visit them. Women just need to know that they don't have to respond to all the IMs they get (it *is* okay to close that IM window if you don't want to reply!), how to turn off IMs if necessary, and how to report problems. These days I just ignore the IMs, but if I'm in a particularly talkative mood, I may try to explain to them that asking a woman what she looks like isn't necessary when you are online and that they have the opportunity to get to know someone from the inside out here. . . .

"Another more 'controversial' way to avoid unwelcome advances is to not call attention to yourself. That means skipping the 'cute' screen names, sticking to basics in your profile, and not giggling and blushing a lot in a chat room. It is similar to walking with confidence down a street when you are worried about muggers. If you act in a strong, self-confident manner online, you will be overlooked more often in favor of those who don't. This doesn't mean you have to act tough at all. Just that you won't take any nonsense."

GwenSmith: "I find if I'm entering a room I haven't been in before, I tend to lurk and get the feel of the area. This often 'comes off' as 'avoiding being cute'—and saves me a lot of trouble! Another thing is to be wary about how much personal information you give out—like addresses and phone numbers, stuff like that. I never list my actual city in my profile (I'll use geographic locales instead), and will usually tell others who ask where I am that I'm 'Near (name a nearby city), CA'. . . ."

GwenSmith

GwenSmith has been an America Online member since spring of 1993 and has seen the system—and herself—grow and change during that time. Gwen works as an online community consultant and spends much of her time online with a very close circle of friends in the Gazebo chat room. She has a Web page at http://members.aol.com/gwensmith.

EvaS: "[The] first line of defense is to ignore unwelcome IMs. If they're salacious, lewd, report them to TOS. In other words, there I am—or, actually, was—hosting The Womens Room in People Connection. And an IM comes in: 'Wanna go private?' I don't answer. I just click the IM box off. . . . Same is true of unwanted e-mail.

"Before I was a host, though, I tried this technique. It would go something like this:

```
IM to EvaS:     Wanna go private?. . .
EvaS's reply:   Hey, I'm old enough to be your grandmother!
IM to Eva:      How old are you?
Reply:          52 (which is what I was five years ago;))
::long pause::
IM to Eva:      I like older women!
```

"So, with that kind of reply, I decided they weren't going to be put off by my age, that this approach was useless, that most of them are lonely guys of various ages . . . and that every woman who's willing to engage in cybersex looks the same. ;) From then on—and it did take me a couple of months to learn that my response was not working—I simply ignored them."

EvaS

EvaS was one of the founders and the Online Coordinator of the Women's Network on AOL. She is also the forum leader of Evenings With Eva, a women's issues conference series. In addition, in September 1991, she started The Womens Room, now Womens POV, in People Connection. "I'm really excited by the fact that more and more women are signing on to AOL," Eva says. "What I'd like to see is a true representation of women reflecting the population. Fifty percent women is my goal. And I do think we'll get there someday!"

Sooze50: "I was expecting to meet Stephen Hawking online and argue chaos theory. Virgin me, I knew nothing about 'hot chat.' I ventured innocently into the chat rooms with a feminine screen name . . . and, via IM, immediately met 'Lefty' of Florida who claimed to make 'XXXX videos.' There was also 70-year-old Frank from Maryland who was interested in writing 'personal erotica.' I teach testosterone, and consider myself a 'woman of the world,' and I am familiar with the male libido. But I was surprised to find the Electronic Bonejumpers online, so quickly!, so eager to peek up my Cyberskirts, and with so little foreplay! Initially I was frightened by the horny porny guys. I found, however, that simply saying I 'was not interested in that sort of thing' put an end to it. My advice on the handling of this problem is a combination of a sense of humor, caution, and faithful logging. You can always 'forward' to TOS."

Sooze50

Sooze50 has taught courses and written textbooks on biological clocks, the pineal gland, and endocrinology in Philadelphia. She is 53, writing and pursuing an active life with her retired husband in the Rocky Mountains.

GwenSmith: "Undesired IMs are promptly ignored. If the conversation isn't going to go past 'What are you wearing?,' then what's the point. Of course, if it's vulgar, off it goes to the TOS staff. A couple tips I have passed on to folks include:

"1. Don't bother to IM with a person who won't enter the chat room [you're in]. If they won't enter the room and talk, but want to carry on a conversation with you, then there is probably good reason to be suspicious of their intentions. Usually, I will 'invite' the person to come in and talk, just to see what their response is.

"2. Add something to your profile. Just putting a quick 'No Cybersex' or such in a profile can really help keep people away. A lot of the 'cruisers' check those profiles, and if they see 'No'—well, some of them will actually listen."

The Value of Online Friends

Most of us who have used this medium over time can attest to its greatest reward—finding and making friends online. Of Tom's very few "best friends," he's met two online. Over the years they've shared death, marriage, retirement, and of course, philosophy. Intellectual and emotional exchange with these people tends to be more intimate and intense than it is with his other good friends. The medium does that.

Tom has an unfair advantage, however. Scores of readers write to him every day, so he doesn't have to look very far for opportunities to make online friends. People tend to write to him using their primary account names rather than their alter egos. And Tom is a man: few who write to him have ulterior motives. These are advantages few other people have, and for women, soliciting friendships online is an exceptional vulnerability.

Sooze50: "In the beginning, I thought, what the heck can I do with this? As an author, I had talked only to editors and readers. Wouldn't it be fun to be friends with some authors? So, I thought, I'll try to find some. I found them, and some surprises, by searching the AOL Membership Directory. For example, searching Melville produced everybody interested in Herman Melville—and also everyone who lived in the town of Melville. I found Edward (name changed) while searching for the ghost of Moby Dick. He wrote 'please write anytime' and launched into a discourse on Skylab blowing up. Edward was as scary as Stephen King with the black humor of John Irving. Edward and I wrote over 600,000 (!) Strictly Platonic biting witty words to one another in the course of a year before he got [angry with me] the second, and Final time. . . . Therein lies the pleasure, and the danger. Because, when Edward disappeared, both the first and the second time, my feelings were hurt . . . we wrote for a long time, and I still miss him."

EvaS: "I have Chronic Fatigue and Immune Dysfunction Syndrome. Being online saved my life. I started a CFS support group, The Womens Room in PC, and so on. To put it yet another way, I found support through finding others with this rotten illness. And I found friends in the support group, people who didn't think I was a malingerer, who knew the illness was/is real. . . . One of the things I've learned about a lot of people online is that they find out new things about themselves. They can try out being more assertive, are less shy. They can speak up more. And all these experiments they try finally do leak over into their offline life. They actually try their wings here, unseen, unheard, and learn to speak out—not only here, but at work and at home."

GwenSmith: "All of my closest friends (other than my spouse and some long-time friends from high school) are from friendships gathered online . . . . Back in [the] halcyon days of '93, I met friends who are *still* here, friends that I have since met offline and who mean a lot to me. We all, I think, have had to make the first step in gaining friends, whether it was from opening up rooms, or from seeing someone else online who seemed like a nice person, and opening up a dialogue. I know that I usually get folks contacting me over hobbies, etc., in my profile, and think the [idea of an] 'extended profile' is a great idea!" (**Note:** No sooner said than done. Read "Personal Publisher" in Chapter 2, "The Abecedarium.")

Community awareness comes slowly. We tend to explore first, exchange some mail, and maybe visit a room or two. Later, we might develop a few friendships and find a few favorite haunts. Most of us, however, take a year or two before we become members of the America Online community as a whole. It's a revelation when we do: AOL is vibrant and diverse, and like any vital community, it requires teamwork to prosper and grow. Gwen, Sue, Eva, and Sooze all endeavor to put back into the community more than they take from it. We should all aspire to their benevolence.

Message Boards

There's another place where communities form and thrive: message boards. America Online's message boards are the electronic analogue of the familiar corkboard and pushpins. Message boards (call them "boards") are especially conducive to community. One of the unique advantages boards offer is convenience: you can drop in any time of the day or night, read the messages, and post your replies.

Most of us visit our favorite boards every time we sign on and eagerly read all the messages posted since the last time we visited. The feeling is remarkably immediate, and withdrawal symptoms set in after about three days' absence. In other words, boards—and the communities you find there—are addictive. But that's part of the fun.

Reading Messages

It seems appropriate in discussing community that we begin at the mecca of communities: the AOL Lifestyles Channel's Communities area at—what else?—keyword: **Communities**. This isn't one large community, but a collection of many, many special communities, with something for everyone. Broad topics include Ages & Stages, Beliefs, Ethnic, Gay & Lesbian, Self Improvement, and TalkWomen. Jennifer is particularly fond of the Generation X message boards in the Ages & Stages section (though she's quickly making her way up to the Thirties Board).

But we're getting ahead of ourselves. We've chosen this area because it's an excellent example of message boards. In fact, there are so many throughout the various communities that we lost count at 50. For this discussion, we'll examine message boards in the Ages & Stages section (see Figure 7-25).

Note the categories pictured in the center window of Figure 7-25. The three at the top are direct links to message boards. The Thirties Board is a particularly active message board—thirty-somethings have plenty to talk about, if prime-time television is any indication. A double-click on the Thirties category produces a list of folders representing topics (see the bottom window).

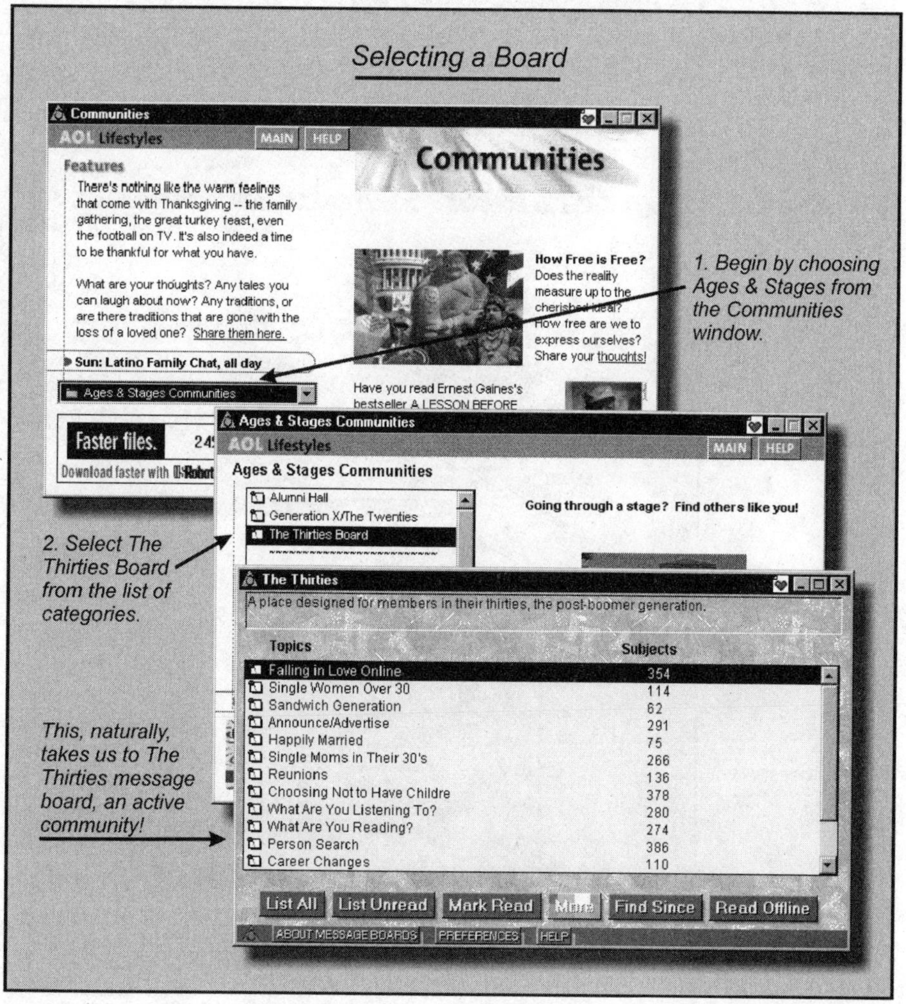

Figure 7-25: Type the keyword: **Communities** to open the AOL Lifestyles Channel's Communities main window; then choose Ages & Stages from the drop-down menu.

The bulletin board metaphor is distorted a bit here. Individual messages aren't normally posted on boards; topics are created on boards (the messages themselves are in the topics). Look at the top window of Figure 7-26: this board is currently holding over 3,500 posts. If all 3,500 were posted independently, the board would be a mess. You would never find a thing. The board's nested topics are merely organizational tools intended to help you locate topics of interest to you.

Figure 7-26: The 15 topics available within The Thirties board often contain hundreds of member messages.

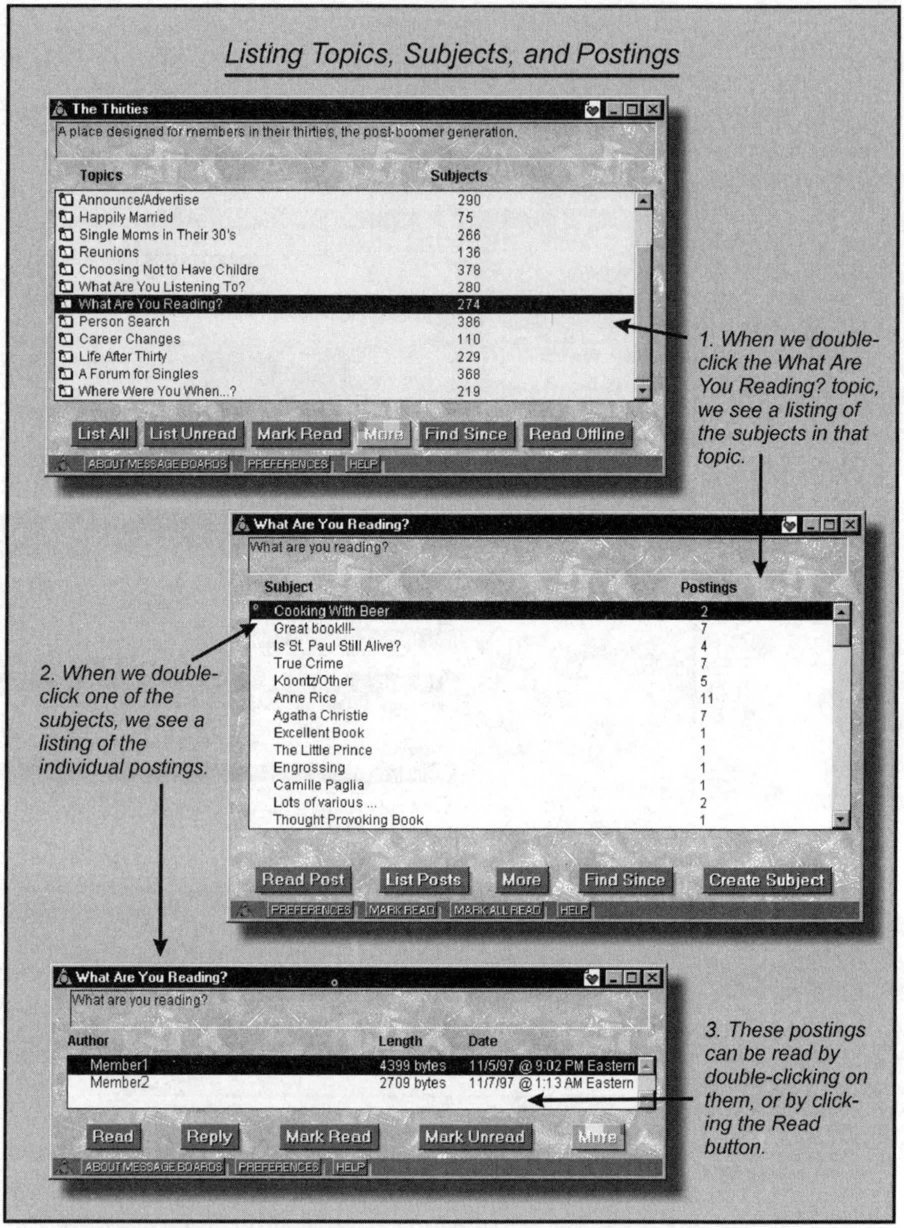

Listing Topics, Subjects, and Postings

The Thirties

A place designed for members in their thirties, the post-boomer generation.

Topics	Subjects
Announce/Advertise	290
Happily Married	75
Single Moms in Their 30's	266
Reunions	136
Choosing Not to Have Childre	378
What Are You Listening To?	280
What Are You Reading?	274
Person Search	386
Career Changes	110
Life After Thirty	229
A Forum for Singles	368
Where Were You When...?	219

List All | List Unread | Mark Read | More | Find Since | Read Offline

ABOUT MESSAGE BOARDS | PREFERENCES | HELP

1. When we double-click the What Are You Reading? topic, we see a listing of the subjects in that topic.

What Are You Reading?

What are you reading?

Subject	Postings
Cooking With Beer	2
Great book!!!-	7
Is St. Paul Still Alive?	4
True Crime	7
Koontz/Other	5
Anne Rice	11
Agatha Christie	7
Excellent Book	1
The Little Prince	1
Engrossing	1
Camille Paglia	1
Lots of various ...	2
Thought Provoking Book	1

Read Post | List Posts | More | Find Since | Create Subject

PREFERENCES | MARK READ | MARK ALL READ | HELP

2. When we double-click one of the subjects, we see a listing of the individual postings.

What Are You Reading?

What are you reading?

Author	Length	Date
Member1	4399 bytes	11/5/97 @ 9:02 PM Eastern
Member2	2709 bytes	11/7/97 @ 1:13 AM Eastern

Read | Reply | Mark Read | Mark Unread | More

ABOUT MESSAGE BOARDS | PREFERENCES | HELP

3. These postings can be read by double-clicking on them, or by clicking the Read button.

To read the messages placed in a topic, double-click the topic. By double-clicking the What Are You Reading? topic shown in Figure 7-26's top window, we reveal the subjects listed in the window at the center of that illustration.

Although only 13 subjects are listed in the window, you can scroll down to view the rest. Note the More button—when this is highlighted, it means there is more to display (which you can do by clicking it). The subjects are further subdivided into postings and replies (see the bottom window).

Double-clicking a subject will open the first message in a topic (which does the same thing as clicking Read Post). You can use the Next Post button to read the next post in sequential order or the Subject button to see the first post of the next subject (see Figure 7-27).

Figure 7-27: Once you have read the first message in a topic, click the Next Post or Subject button to read the remaining messages in the order they were posted.

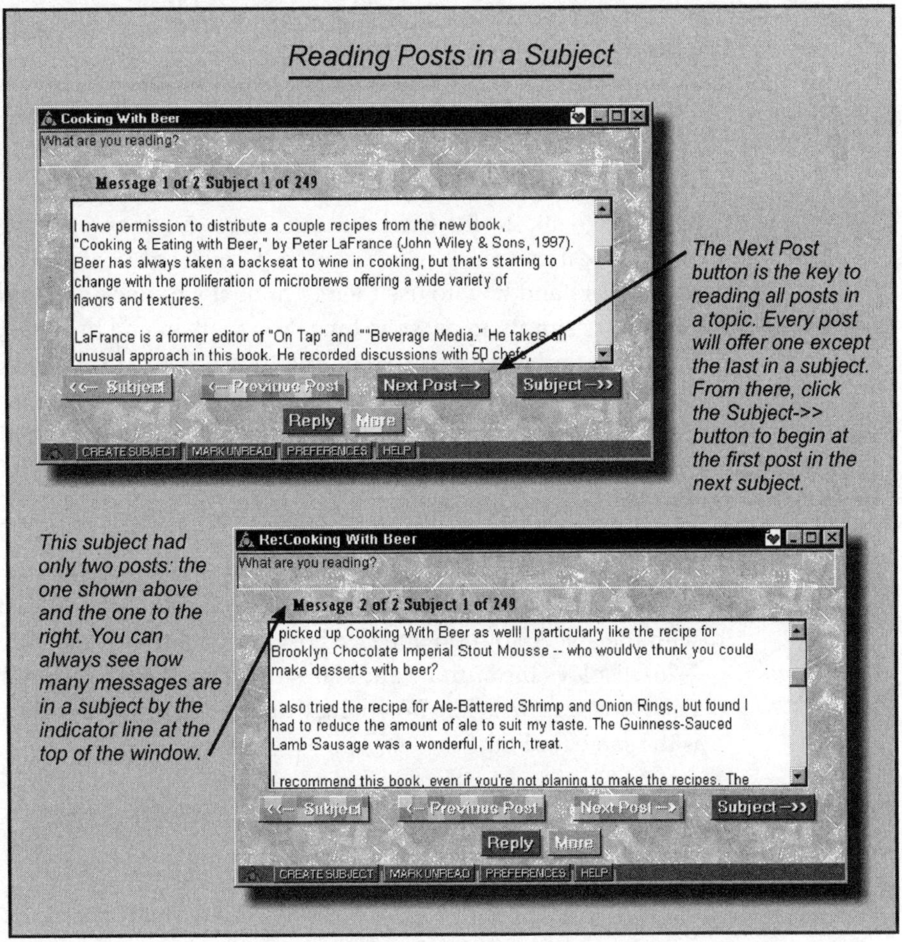

Reading Posts in a Subject

Cooking With Beer
What are you reading?
Message 1 of 2 Subject 1 of 249
I have permission to distribute a couple recipes from the new book, "Cooking & Eating with Beer," by Peter LaFrance (John Wiley & Sons, 1997). Beer has always taken a backseat to wine in cooking, but that's starting to change with the proliferation of microbrews offering a wide variety of flavors and textures.
LaFrance is a former editor of "On Tap" and ""Beverage Media." He takes an unusual approach in this book. He recorded discussions with 50 chefs,
<<— Subject | <— Previous Post | Next Post —> | Subject —>>
Reply | More
CREATE SUBJECT | MARK UNREAD | PREFERENCES | HELP

The Next Post button is the key to reading all posts in a topic. Every post will offer one except the last in a subject. From there, click the Subject->> button to begin at the first post in the next subject.

This subject had only two posts: the one shown above and the one to the right. You can always see how many messages are in a subject by the indicator line at the top of the window.

Re:Cooking With Beer
What are you reading?
Message 2 of 2 Subject 1 of 249
I picked up Cooking With Beer as well! I particularly like the recipe for Brooklyn Chocolate Imperial Stout Mousse -- who would've thunk you could make desserts with beer?
I also tried the recipe for Ale-Battered Shrimp and Onion Rings, but found I had to reduce the amount of ale to suit my taste. The Guinness-Sauced Lamb Sausage was a wonderful, if rich, treat.
I recommend this book, even if you're not planing to make the recipes. The
<<— Subject | <— Previous Post | Next Post —> | Subject —>>
Reply | More
CREATE SUBJECT | MARK UNREAD | PREFERENCES | HELP

If you would prefer to see all the postings in a subject first, click the List Posts button. From the resulting list, you can read or reply as you wish.

Record Those Messages

Reading messages is one of the most time-consuming activities America Online offers. Rather than read messages online, use the Automatic AOL feature to gather and read them offline—we'll discuss how later and also in Chapter 8. You can also save a log of them as they download to your computer. This is convenient when you only want to read certain messages and not an entire topic. Open a session log and let the messages scroll off your screen as fast as they can; don't try to read them while you're online. When you have finished the session, sign off, open the log (choose Open from AOL's File menu), and read it at your leisure.

Browsing & Finding Messages

We need to take a side trip here. The verbs *browse* and *find* have particular, unequivocal meanings when it comes to message boards. It's important that you understand how to use them. Think of a public library; you might go to the library simply to pass the time. You walk in and browse, picking up a book here and there as different titles strike your fancy. On another day, you might visit the library with a specific title already in mind, in which case you go straight to the card or electronic files and find that particular book.

America Online attaches the same meanings to these verbs. Look again at The Thirties window at the top of Figure 7-26, representing variations on the verbs we're discussing.

The List All button displays the topic's message subjects and number of postings, not the messages themselves. Once you have listed the messages with the List All button, the List Post button (see the middle window in Figure 7-26) displays the authors and dates of the messages. Using the List All and List Posts feature is like browsing through the books in a library; the concept is the same for both.

What Are You Seeing?

When you click List All and List Posts, do you actually want to see every single subject or message in a topic since the day it began? Or would you prefer to only get recent ones, say, in the last three months? Whatever your preference, you can set it—and other aspects—with your message board preferences (see Figure 7-28). Use the Preferences button at the very bottom of the window (see the bottom window in Figure 7-27) to bring up your options. Here you can set your signature (the text at the bottom of your post) and America Online will automatically "sign" your post with it each time you make one (unless you don't want it to). You can also change your sort order to see posts from oldest to newest (oldest first), newest to oldest (newest first, the default), or in alphabetical order. Of course, you can set the number of posts you want to see, from 1 to 9999 days (30 days is the default). Finally, you can designate the number of messages you want downloaded when you click the Read Offline button and run Automatic AOL (discussed later). Remember to save all your changes with the OK button. Note that preferences apply to all message boards, not just the one you're currently in.

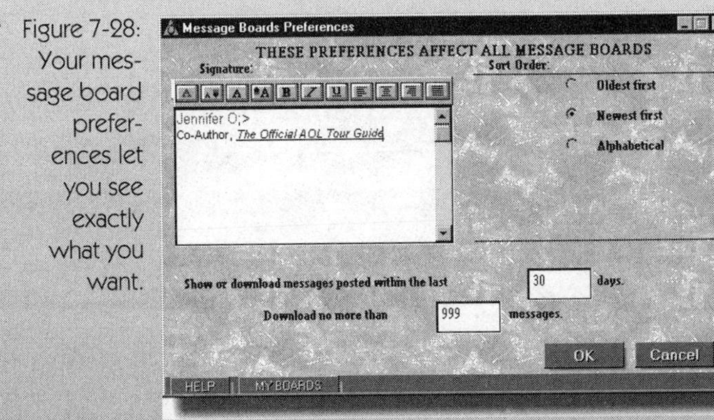

Figure 7-28: Your message board preferences let you see exactly what you want.

This might be a board you read often. If you do, you can go right to the List Unread button, which displays only those messages you haven't read yet (see Figure 7-29). Alternatively, if you've read all the messages you're interested in and don't want to be bothered with the others the next time you visit, select the board and click the Mark Read button. This will tell America Online that you've "read" the messages (even if you really haven't), enabling you to see only new messages the next time you click List Unread.

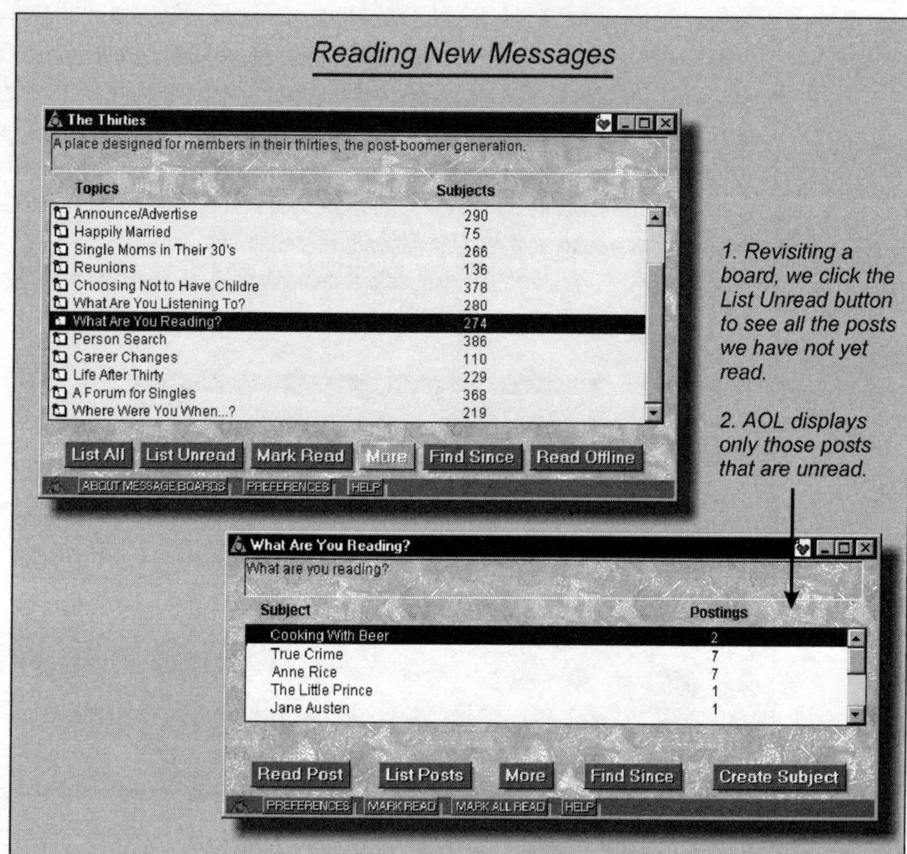

Figure 7-29: Only the messages you haven't read yet appear when you click the List Unread button.

Most boards contain hundreds if not thousands of messages. No matter how interested in the subject you may be, it's doubtful you'll want to read every message the first time you visit a board. Or maybe you've been away from the board for a few months and don't want to be deluged with all the messages posted since your last visit. These are two of the reasons why America Online provides the Find Since button (see Figure 7-30).

Figure 7-30: The Find Since button allows you to specify the extent of a message list.

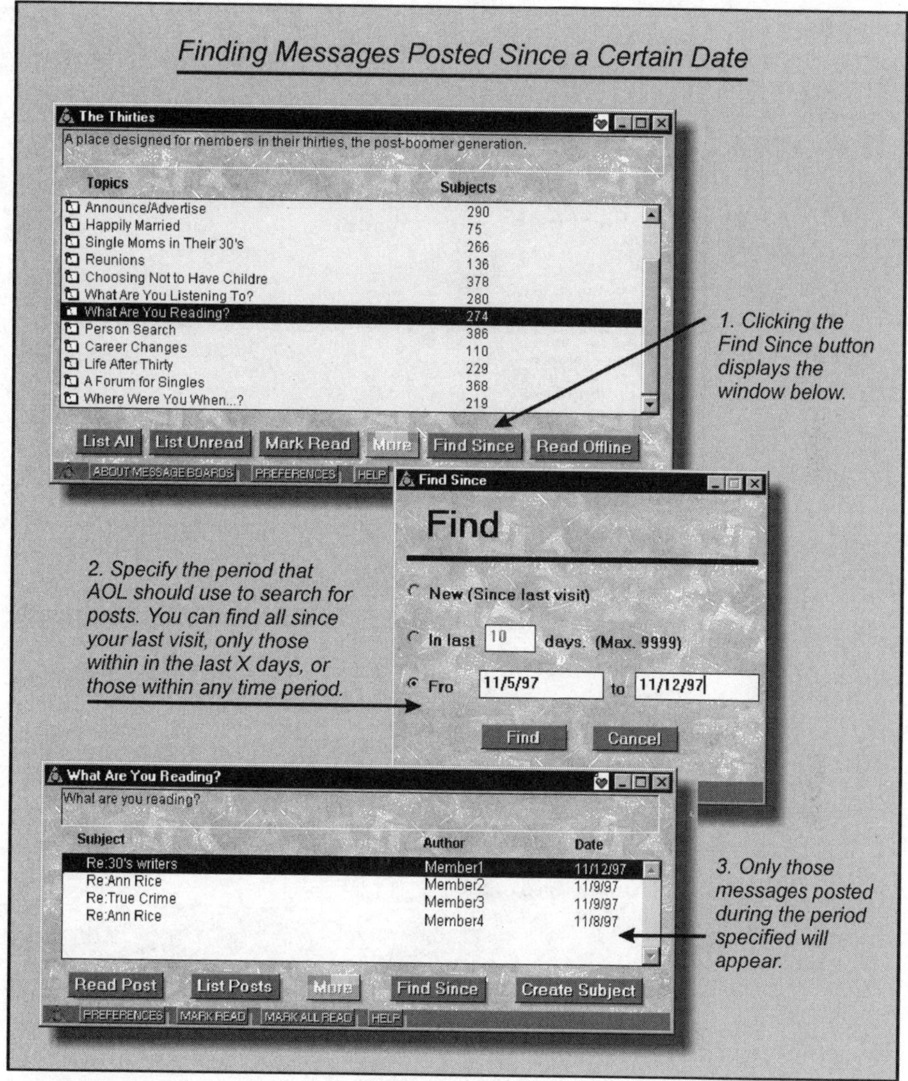

Those hundreds and thousands of posts are yet another reason for the last button in Figure 7-27: the Read Offline button. Click this button and all unread posts in a topic will be marked for later download when you run Automatic AOL (discussed in Chapter 8). You can view all your "offline" boards at the keywords: **My Boards**. If you decide you'd rather not download the topic to read offline, just click the Read Offline button again and it will be unmarked (see Figure 7-31).

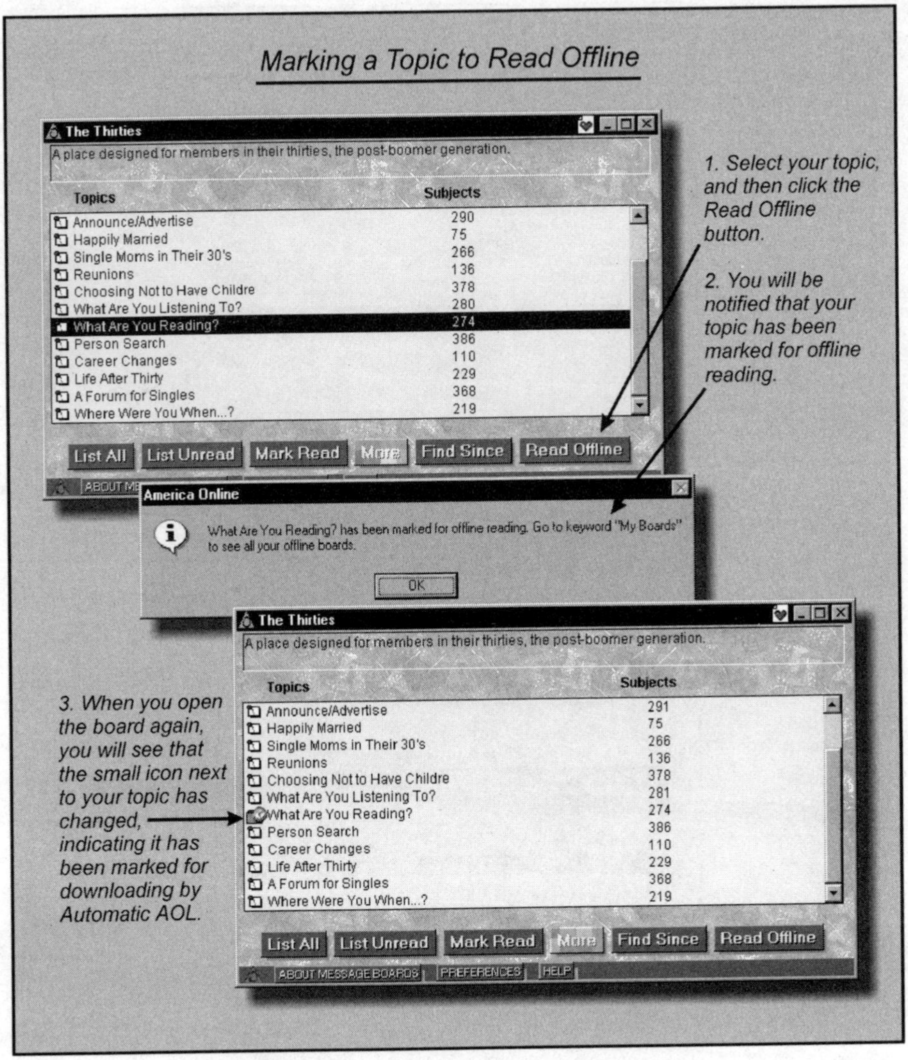

Figure 7-31: Topics can be marked for later downloading to read offline at your leisure.

Marking a Topic to Read Offline

The Thirties

A place designed for members in their thirties, the post-boomer generation.

Topics	Subjects
Announce/Advertise	290
Happily Married	75
Single Moms in Their 30's	266
Reunions	136
Choosing Not to Have Childre	378
What Are You Listening To?	280
What Are You Reading?	274
Person Search	386
Career Changes	110
Life After Thirty	229
A Forum for Singles	368
Where Were You When...?	219

List All | List Unread | Mark Read | More | Find Since | Read Offline

1. Select your topic, and then click the Read Offline button.

2. You will be notified that your topic has been marked for offline reading.

America Online

What Are You Reading? has been marked for offline reading. Go to keyword "My Boards" to see all your offline boards.

OK

The Thirties

A place designed for members in their thirties, the post-boomer generation.

Topics	Subjects
Announce/Advertise	291
Happily Married	75
Single Moms in Their 30's	266
Reunions	136
Choosing Not to Have Childre	378
What Are You Listening To?	281
What Are You Reading?	274
Person Search	386
Career Changes	110
Life After Thirty	229
A Forum for Singles	368
Where Were You When...?	219

List All | List Unread | Mark Read | More | Find Since | Read Offline

ABOUT MESSAGE BOARDS | PREFERENCES | HELP

3. When you open the board again, you will see that the small icon next to your topic has changed, indicating it has been marked for downloading by Automatic AOL.

Regardless of the procedural details, find a board that interests you and start reading its messages. Start with just one or two topics, read the last week's worth of messages, and become familiar with the subject and the people. When you feel confident, post your own messages. It is at that moment—when you have joined the fray—that message boards start to get really interesting. This is part of the fun; don't deny yourself the opportunity.

Posting Messages

Did you notice the Create Subject and Reply buttons in Figure 7-26? This is how you add messages—whether they be new subjects or replies to existing messages—to a topic. All you need to do is click the appropriate button, enter the subject (if needed) and text of your message, and select any of options at the bottom if you wish. Here are some brief descriptions of those options:

- **E-mail to Author.** Lets you send your message to the author of a post if you are making a reply and not a new subject. The default is Off.
- **Post to Board.** Submits your message to the board for everyone to see. By default, this option is checked, but you can deselect it if you wish a message to go only to the author.
- **Use Signature (Set in Preferences).** Places the signature you set in your preferences (discussed in the sidebar "What Are You Seeing?") at the end of your post automatically. If you have no signature set, this option is turned off by default. Otherwise the option is on by default.

When your message is ready, click Send to submit your effort. Your message will be added to the topic immediately. If you chose to create a new subject, you'll see it listed when you open the topic folder again. If you replied to an existing subject, you'll see your message when you list the posts for that subject. For the entire process, take a look at Figure 7-32.

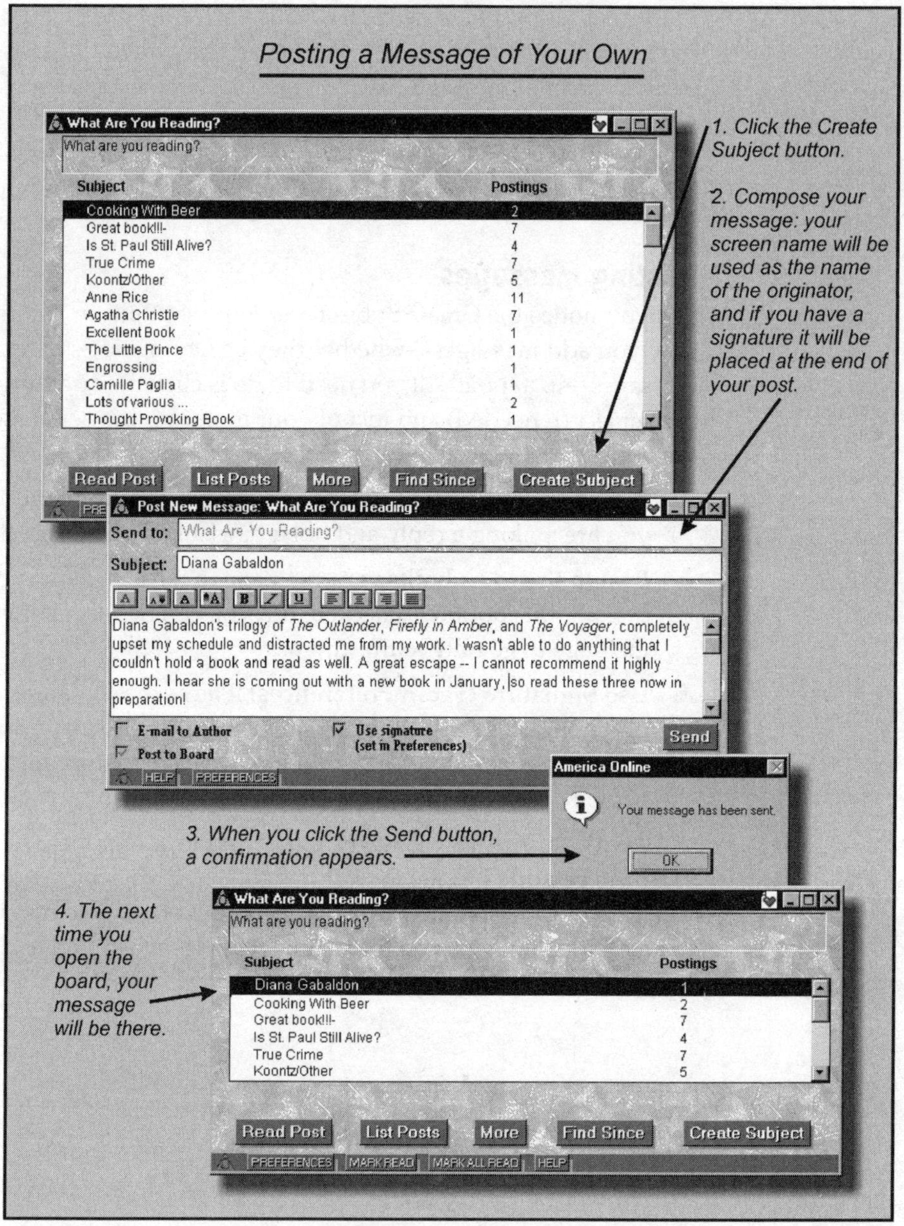

Figure 7-32: Posting your own message is as simple as clicking a button.

Posting a Message of Your Own

What Are You Reading?

What are you reading?

Subject	Postings
Cooking With Beer	2
Great book!!!-	7
Is St. Paul Still Alive?	4
True Crime	7
Koontz/Other	5
Anne Rice	11
Agatha Christie	7
Excellent Book	1
The Little Prince	1
Engrossing	1
Camille Paglia	1
Lots of various ...	2
Thought Provoking Book	1

Read Post | List Posts | More | Find Since | Create Subject

1. Click the Create Subject button.

2. Compose your message: your screen name will be used as the name of the originator, and if you have a signature it will be placed at the end of your post.

Post New Message: What Are You Reading?

Send to: What Are You Reading?

Subject: Diana Gabaldon

Diana Gabaldon's trilogy of *The Outlander*, *Firefly in Amber*, and *The Voyager*, completely upset my schedule and distracted me from my work. I wasn't able to do anything that I couldn't hold a book and read as well. A great escape -- I cannot recommend it highly enough. I hear she is coming out with a new book in January, so read these three now in preparation!

E-mail to Author | Use signature (set in Preferences) | Post to Board | Send

HELP | PREFERENCES

America Online

Your message has been sent.

OK

3. When you click the Send button, a confirmation appears.

4. The next time you open the board, your message will be there.

What Are You Reading?

What are you reading?

Subject	Postings
Diana Gabaldon	1
Cooking With Beer	2
Great book!!!-	7
Is St. Paul Still Alive?	4
True Crime	7
Koontz/Other	5

Read Post | List Posts | More | Find Since | Create Subject

PREFERENCES | MARK READ | MARK ALL READ | HELP

Message Board Etiquette

If you want to be heard, if you want replies to your messages, and if you want to be a responsible online citizen, you should comply with a few rules of telecommunications etiquette. Because Emily Post and Miss Manners haven't yet spoken on the subject, we'd best discuss it here:

- Post messages only when you have something to say, phrase the subject header effectively, and be succinct. The best messages have provocative headers and pithy prose. If your message fills more than a screen of text—if it requires a trip to the scroll bar to read—edit it.
- Stick to the subject. If the topic you're participating in is entitled "Weasels in Wyoming," don't discuss armadillos in Arizona.
- If your message wanders, summarize before responding. You might quote a previous posting (do so in brackets: "When you said <<I really prefer Macintosh>> were you talking about apples or Apples?"). This will help others stick to the topic.
- Don't post chain letters, advertisements, or business offers unless the board was created for it. And never send junk mail to unsuspecting recipients.
- HEY YOU! CAN YOU HEAR US??!! (Did we get your attention? Did you like the way we did it?) All-caps are distracting, hard to read, and worse, arrogant. Use all-caps only when you really want to shout (and those occasions should be rare). For emphasis, put your text in bold or italics: "I **told** you he was a *geek*." Do be careful not to overdo it on the styles and colors, though.
- Do not issue personal attacks, use profanity, or betray a confidence. If criticism is specifically invited, remember that there is no vocal inflection or body language to soften the impact and remove the potential for misinterpretation. E-mail is a better forum for criticism than boards are.
- For the same reason, subtleties, double entendres, and sarcasm are rarely effective.
- Avoid emotional responses. Think before you write. Once you've posted a message, you can't take it back.
- Remember your options. Some replies are better sent as mail than as messages. If you're feeling particularly vitriolic, send mail to the perpetrator. This saves face for both of you.

Posting effective messages is something of an art. Messages like "Me, too," or "I don't think so" don't really contribute to a board. Before you post a message, be sure you have something to say, take the time to phrase it effectively, and give it a proper subject header.

Proper Replies

Be sure you post replies to messages properly. The Create Subject button adds a message to the subject level of a board; the added message is posted independently and not identified as a response to any other message. A message posted via the Reply button will appear as a response in the list of postings within a subject, similar to those pictured in the lower window of Figure 7-32. It's not just a matter of semantics; it's an organizational imperative. Give consideration to your replies on boards: post them where they're most appropriate.

What we've described so far is a *threaded* board, with messages arranged in subjects and replies as we mentioned earlier. Not all boards are threaded, however—some simply display all postings in the same list regardless of whether they are replies or not. Some boards lend themselves to threading, some don't. Some of our favorites aren't threaded, and we're glad: threading discourages the kind of browsing that favored boards merit. Don't look upon an unthreaded board as anarchistic or simplistic. Welcome them and celebrate their diversity.

The Boardwalk

The message boards are gradually evolving to a new level of functionality. We've shown you the new era of message boards, but chances are some of the older-style message boards will still be around when you read this. These "classic" boards are still worth your attention; their features are just fewer in number. You cannot, for example, download all the messages from a classic board with Automatic AOL to read offline. Yet you can still browse, read, and reply. Enjoy them—they evoke a simpler time (if such a thing ever existed online).

Guttersnipe

In a community of 10 million, it should come as no surprise to learn that there are a number of interlopers online. And typical of an industry that embraces acronyms and sobriquets, America Online members fastidiously categorize these gremlins according to the severity of their pestilence.

Trolls

Least sinister are the *trolls.* Trolls dawdle along the information highway, impeding traffic and undermining good will. Trolls enter chat rooms with palaver like "Is anyone horny?" or "Press 3 if you like Spam." They're a bit more loquacious on message boards, but their posts usually disappear when the staff makes its first sweep of the day. Trolls send us e-mail all the time that says, "Did you know your name is in the Tour Guide?" Recondite discourse, that.

Trolls are easy to manage: just ignore them. They're seeking attention, after all, and if it's granted, they have their reward. Trolls are the first category of urchin to ignore in a chat room (the Ignore button was discussed earlier in this chapter). If a troll sends you e-mail or IMs you, copy his screen name and close his window. He probably won't be back. Use the copied screen name to block yourself from his Buddy List (blocking Buddy Lists is a preference and is discussed in Chapter 9) and forget about it. You just passed a ragamuffin on the street; don't break your stride and he won't break his.

Phishers

We're moving up the scavenger's food chain now. *Phishers* are trolls who have graduated from misdemeanors to larceny. Phishers snack on passwords, and they feast on credit card numbers.

The common phisher appears in the form of an unsolicited IM on your screen. The message therein identifies the phisher as a member of AOL's staff. There will be a comment about damaged files at America Online and a request for your password "so that we can reconstruct our database."

More sophisticated phishers will send you an IM or e-mail claiming to be a member of AOL's staff and offering an irresistible discount on an article of merchandise. Who can resist a 28.8 modem for $24.95? The hitch, of course, is that they're not staff, they have no modems, and the conversation will eventually get around to a request for your credit card number.

Other phishers, also masquerading as AOL staff, will ask you to send specific files on your hard disk to them. Though the files might seem benign and the request might seem sanctioned, this is phishing nonetheless. The requested file probably contains your encrypted password—for use by unattended Automatic AOL sessions, for example—and some phishers are sophisticated enough to decipher them.

If you ever receive a message—e-mail or IM—asking for your password, a file, or your credit card number, you can be sure it's a phisher. It is *not* a member of America Online's staff, no matter how eloquent or convincing the request.

FOOLED YOU!

Many phishers use the old "0 and L" trick. The word *GUIDE* will be rejected if it appears anywhere within a proposed screen name, but the word *GUlDE* will not (the third character is a lowercase *L*, not an *I*). Thus, you might receive a message from "GUlDE Tom" and think he's an official of some sort. Beware of zeros as well: "A0L Tom" is not a staff member. Though A-O-L is a blocked sequence for screen names, A-*zero*-L is not.

Phishers should always be reported. Don't close that IM window! Instead, click somewhere within the message, choose Select All from the Edit menu, and then choose Copy from the same menu. Write down the phisher's screen name, then use the keyword: **Guidepager**. You'll find your way from there.

The term phisher probably originated with the phone freaks of the 1970s and early 1980s—they called themselves "phreaks." They were the first (phirst?) of the breed, and unfortunately this breed is especially prolific. They can be very sophisticated: don't be phooled.

Snerts

Trolls troll for attention. Phishers phish for passwords. *Snerts,* however, are virtual voyeurs. Their primary goal is an indiscriminate assault on privacy. They live under tenement stairs where there is no light and an abundance of virulence. There they concoct schemes specifically designed to wreak havoc online, and harassment is their preferred bounty. When they discover a technique that seems especially repulsive, they broadcast it to other snerts (usually via the Internet) and come knocking on America Online's electronic doors.

A small army of America Online technicians vigilantly patrols for snerts, but the battle is often an impasse.

Unfortunately, snerts are as hard to catch as an arsonist and every bit as destructive. When you encounter one, use the keywords: **Notify AOL** immediately and report them.

Recidivistic Trolls

The word snert is an acronym: Sexually Nerdishly Expressive Recidivistic Trolls. Hard-core snerts, however, eschewed sex in the traditional sense of the word a long time ago—if they ever knew about it in the first place. They prefer the online medium for their carnal romps now; they don't have time for the triviality of substantive matters. Perhaps we should be thankful for that: their arrogance suppresses procreation. Snerts may be a vanishing species.

MacChat

Jennifer discovered America Online through its chat rooms. Her first six months were almost exclusively spent almost ensconced in the People Connection and surrounded by Instant Messages. In the process, she became intimately familiar with the sometimes subtle and often obvious variations between Mac and Windows chat. Thankfully, the differences these days are far fewer—intercomputer relationships are actually possible now.

Macs can play any sound installed (just place in your System file to install), but remember that other members in chat rooms will hear your sounds only if they also have the same sound file installed. You can convert a Mac sound file to a Windows WAV file (and vice versa) by using one of the sound converters available at keywords: **File Search**. Jennifer prefers Balthazar, by Craig Marciniak.

Members on Macs have the unique capability of talking chat rooms, thanks to Apple's Text-to-Speech feature. Use your Speech preferences to set it up, and make sure your sound is turned on and up. Speech works on more than chat rooms too; the Speak Text and Stop Speaking commands under the Edit menu are invaluable if you take advantage of this feature.

The Mac Log Manager offers three types of logs: System (the equivalent of Windows' Session Log), Chat, and Instant Message (unique to the Mac AOL software). Operation is the same for all three types.

In addition to other formatting options, Mac AOL offers a drop-down font menu in the Instant Message window. Like sounds, fancy fonts are visible to others only if they also have them installed in their System file. If they do not, they'll see the text in their default font (usually Geneva on the Mac and Arial on Windows).

Moving On

Chats, conferences, Instant Messages, Buddy Lists, message boards, e-mail—they all come together to form the framework of our online community. Into this we fill bytes and bytes of information, almost all exclusively generated by members. Trying to absorb even a minuscule percentage of it can easily overwhelm even a seasoned member. How do you participate in the community and still retain your sanity?

Let your software do the hard work! Your America Online software is capable of conducting all your postings at the same time, so your new messages are already retrieved and waiting for you first thing in the morning. It can also send postings you've composed offline as well as send and receive all your e-mail. It can even download multiple files in one session. And it can do all of this *unattended*—in the middle of the night, if that's when you choose (and you might: system activity is minimal in the middle of the night). These are the features of Automatic AOL and the Download Manager. We discuss them next.

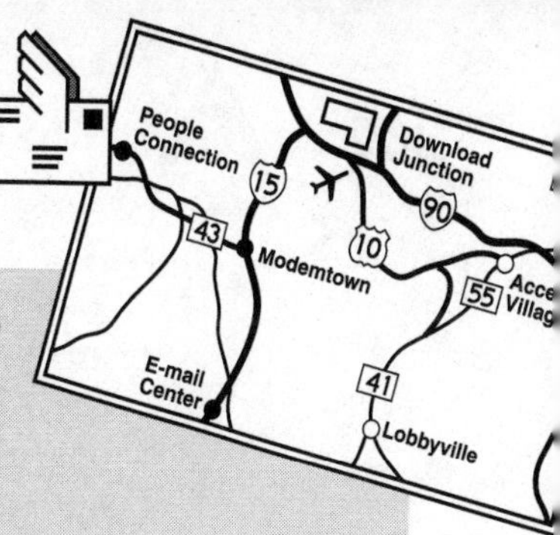

CHAPTER 8

Working Offline

- What Is Automatic AOL?
- Scheduling Automatic AOLSessions
- Attended Sessions
- Unattended Sessions
- Offline Mail
- Offline Postings
- The Download Manager

The greatest volume of mail we receive from our *AOL Tour Guide* readers comes in response to this chapter. These people are thrilled. They've discovered AOL's two automation features—Automatic AOL and the Download Manager—and they are dancing rapturously on the virtual sidewalks of the electronic community. If America Online has to deliver your mail with a forklift and you've been reading and responding to it online, you're going to love what this chapter has to say.

There's more: if you're a downloading zealot—if you collect shareware, utilities, fonts, and graphics the way Woody Allen collects troubles, you too will want to read this chapter. Your AOL software can sign on in the middle of the night—to take advantage of minimum online traffic and maximum transfer speeds—and retrieve a queue of files you've scheduled for downloading. It can even resurrect partially downloaded files—files that were interrupted in mid-download when you lost the connection or the cat chewed the phone line in half.

America Online offers solutions to all of these problems: Automatic AOL and the Download Manager.

What Is Automatic AOL?

Automatic AOL is a feature that lets you automate online sessions. At its highest level of automation, Automatic AOL signs on at a predetermined time, downloads all of your incoming e-mail, downloads all your unread message board and newsgroup posts from those you marked to read offline, downloads any files you identified earlier for transfer, and uploads any e-mail, message board posts, or newsgroup posts you've prepared but not sent. When all of that is completed, Automatic AOL signs off, telling you what happened and when and notifying you of any errors encountered.

Many people use Automatic AOL in a spontaneous fashion, invoking it manually as they work online (Jennifer just invoked a session a moment ago to check her mail while she writes this paragraph) or at the conclusion of an online session—sort of an "I'm ready to sign off now; clean everything up for me and sign off" command.

Others—people who conduct business via e-mail and need to check their mailboxes frequently during the day—schedule Automatic AOL to run like clockwork every hour or half-hour, maintaining an almost continuous connection with AOL and therefore with their e-mail community.

There are even a few people who schedule Automatic AOL to occur in the wee hours of the morning, preferring to conduct the majority of their online events when network traffic is light and connect times are minimal. These are people who delight in seeing their e-mail waiting for them when they awaken, sort of like breakfast in bed.

Futility Revisited

In Chapter 3, you sent yourself a letter. Yes, it was an exercise in futility, but you saw e-mail in action. We're about to repeat the exercise, but this time we'll have the computer do it for us. We'll experience not just futility; we'll experience *automated* futility. This is *not* what computing is supposed to be, but it might prove to be enlightening. To watch automated futility in action, follow the steps below:

1. Do not sign on. Rather, run your AOL software and click the Write icon on the toolbar. As you did in Chapter 3, prepare a short message to yourself. Your Write Mail window should look something like the one pictured in Figure 8-1. (Be sure to put *your* screen name, *not Jennifer's*, in the To box. You'd be amazed at the amount of mail she receives with "This is a test of Automatic AOL" in the message field.)
2. Note that the Send button is dimmed. Since you're not online, this command is not available. Instead, click the Send Later button. Unless you've changed your preferences from the default (preferences are discussed in Chapter 9), America Online will reply with the message pictured in Figure 8-2.

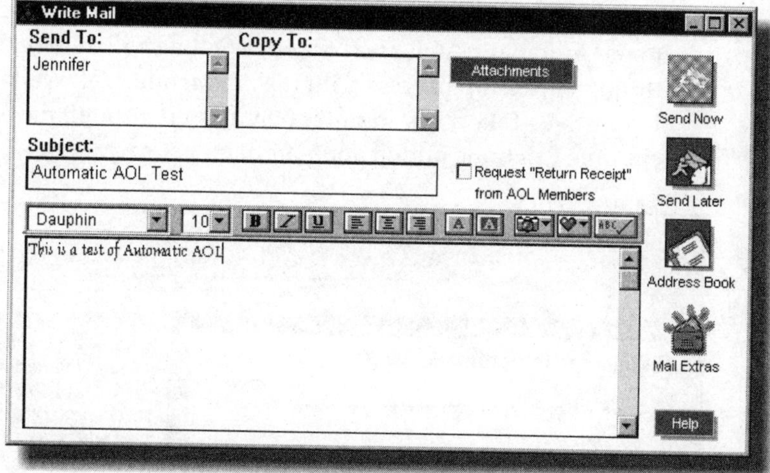

Figure 8-1: Compose a message to yourself, typing *your own* screen name in the To field.

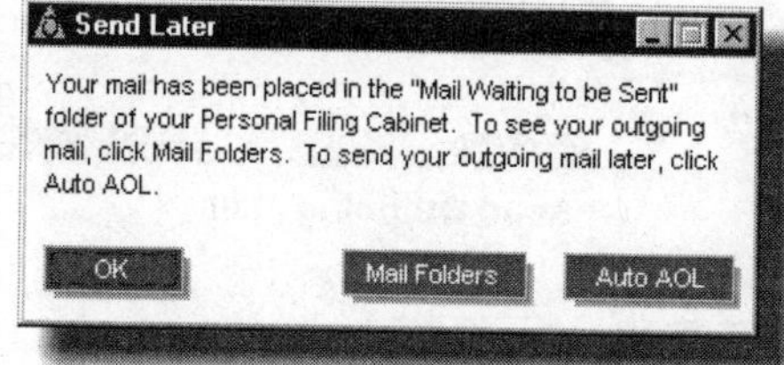

Figure 8-2: America Online confirms your request to send later.

3. Note that the dialog box shown in Figure 8-2 suggests that you "...click Auto AOL" to send your mail later. Do that now by clicking the Auto AOL button in the dialog box.

   The Automatic AOL window will appear (see Figure 8-3), including all the check boxes.

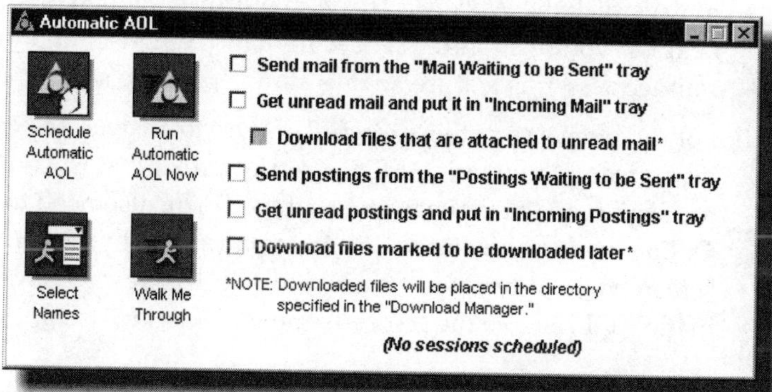

Figure 8-3: You can configure Automatic AOL from this window.

4. To begin, click the Run Automatic AOL Now icon. If this is your first visit to the Automatic AOL area, America Online will automatically escort you through the setup process with the Automatic AOL Walk-Through (see Figure 8-4). Take a few minutes here to step through the tutorial—just click the Continue button and you're on your way.

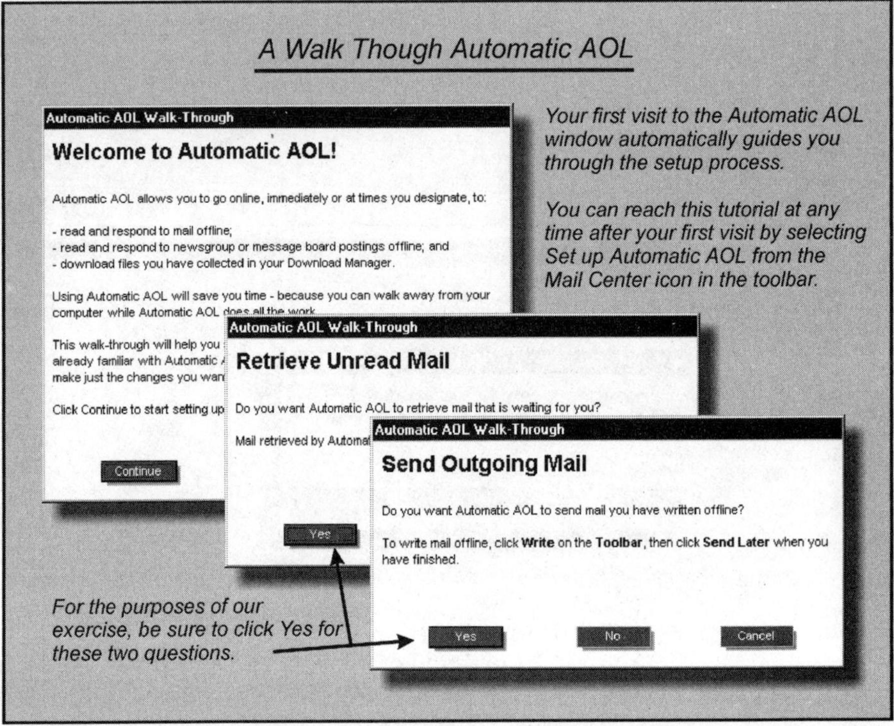

Figure 8-4: If you are new to Automatic AOL, take a walk through this tutorial first.

The Walk-Through only executes automatically once. After that, you can always click the Walk Me Through button shown in Figure 8-3 to invoke it again. If you're an infrequent Automatic AOL user and prone to absent-mindedness, this feature always stands ready to serve.

5. For the purposes of this exercise, be sure to answer Yes when you're asked if you want Automatic AOL to "retrieve mail that is waiting for you" and to "send mail you have written offline." You also need to let America Online know you want to use Automatic AOL by enabling it for your screen name. When you're asked to select your screen names for Automatic AOL, enable the screen name you want to use (for this text, select

the screen name you are sending your test mail to if you have more than one screen name) and enter the password you use (for that screen name) when you sign on to AOL (see Figure 8-5). Your screen name(s) will appear in place of Jennifer's, and the number of characters in your password may differ as well. (Notice that your password isn't displayed as you type; asterisks representing each letter in your password appear instead. That's as it should be. You never know who's looking over your shoulder.) When you have completed the Select Screen Names form, click the Continue button.

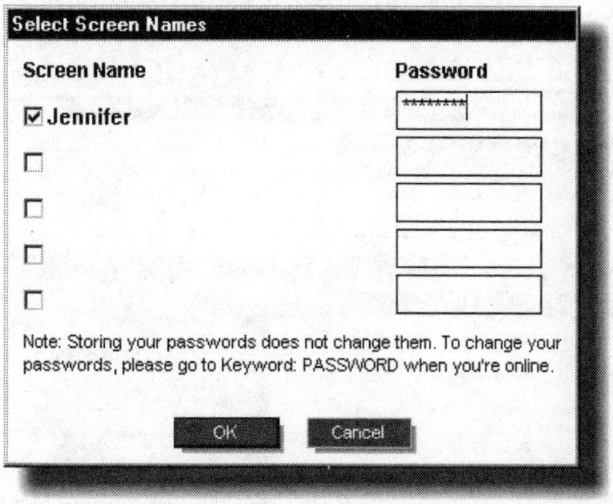

Select Screen Names

Screen Name | Password
☑ Jennifer | ********

Note: Storing your passwords does not change them. To change your passwords, please go to Keyword: PASSWORD when you're online.

OK Cancel

Figure 8-5: Complete the Select Screen Names form.

6. When you are asked to schedule Automatic AOL, click No this time—we'll come back to scheduling later. And that's it! Click OK. Now get it started by choosing Run Automatic AOL Now from the Mail Center icon's menu on the toolbar and then clicking the Run Automatic AOL Now icon (shown in Figure 8-3). America Online will respond with the form pictured in Figure 8-6.

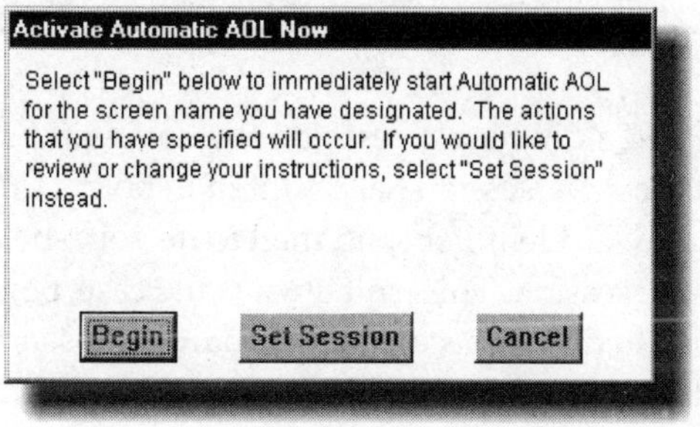

Activate Automatic AOL Now

Select "Begin" below to immediately start Automatic AOL for the screen name you have designated. The actions that you have specified will occur. If you would like to review or change your instructions, select "Set Session" instead.

Begin Set Session Cancel

Figure 8-6: If this is your first Automatic AOL session, read these instructions carefully.

7. Click the button marked Begin. America Online takes over (Figure 8-7).

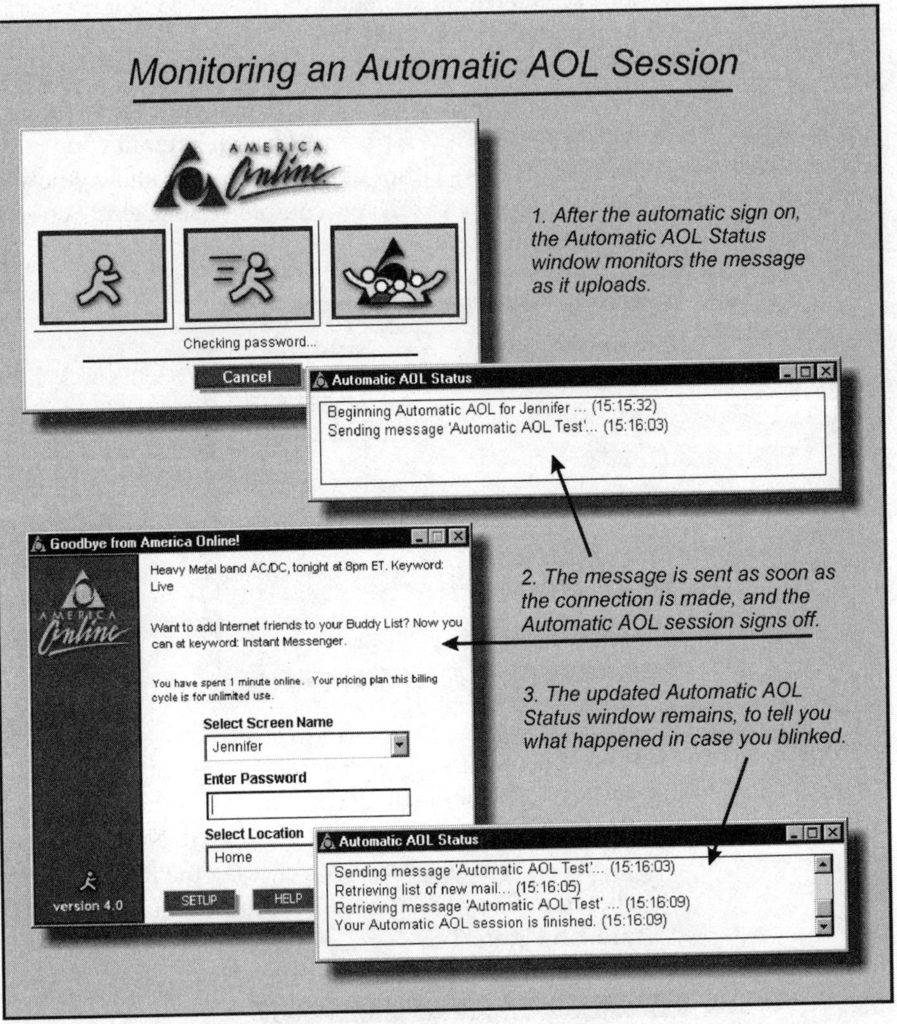

Figure 8-7: Automatic AOL signs on, "flashes" your mail to AOL headquarters in Virginia, and signs off—all in seconds.

8. AOL must have had a double espresso on the day that we produced Figure 8-7: This Automatic AOL session has resulted in both an upload and a download. Not only did Jennifer send mail to herself, she also received it—all during the same session. This isn't always the case. Sometimes the e-mail system is too busy to turn a piece of mail around and send it back before the session signs off. Don't be surprised if you have to run Automatic AOL a second time in order to receive the sent mail.

Regardless of whether you've had to run a second Automatic AOL or not, you've got mail, and you need to read it. But you're not online. How do you read mail when you're offline?

Click the Mail Center icon and pull down the menu. Choose the Read Offline Mail command, and then choose Incoming/Saved Mail from the resulting menu. Your Filing Cabinet will appear (see top of Figure 8-8). You'll find the mail you sent yourself in the folder marked Incoming/Saved Mail, which should already be "open" (if it isn't, just double-click the folder itself or select it and click Open). Now double-click (open) the entry representing your test.

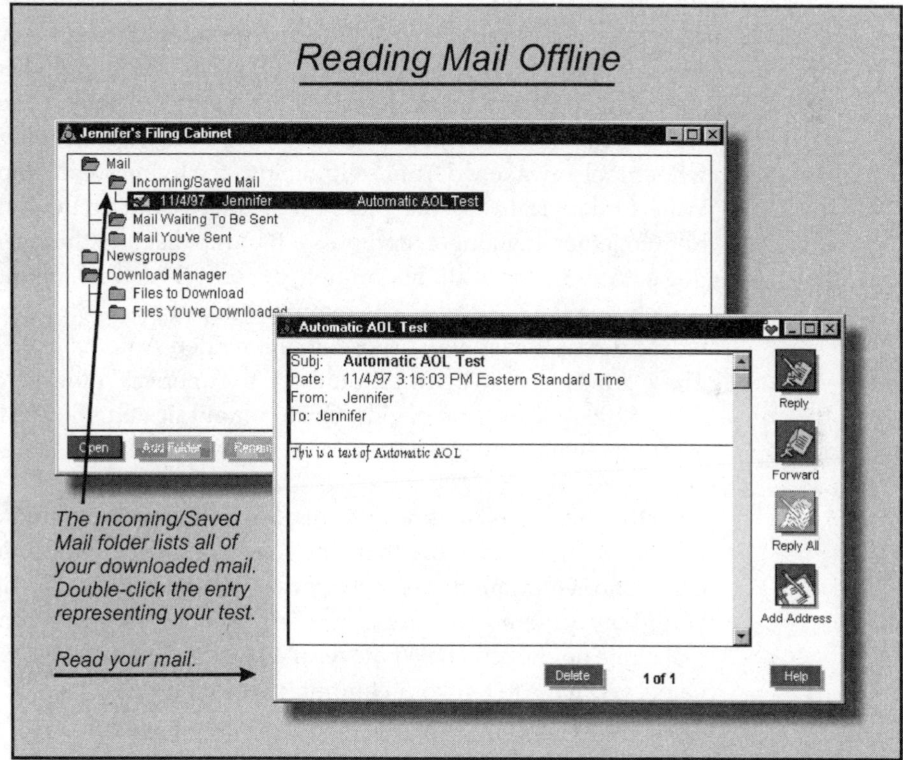

Figure 8-8: You can read mail offline when it's convenient for you and the clock's not running.

A second window will open (Figure 8-8, bottom) containing the text of your test. After you've read it, delete it by clicking the Delete button at the bottom of the window.

We're reminded of the big Mercedes sedan Tom's friend Doyle drives. In an irrational effort to remain the technological leader among automobiles, Mercedes equipped the car with *motorized headrests*. Now *that's* technology. Our exercise was a little like that. We threw technology at a task that was no doubt best left undone. At least we're in good company.

Scheduling Automatic AOL Sessions

You can invoke an Automatic AOL session at any time, whether you're online or off. Alternatively, you can schedule Automatic AOL sessions to occur at predetermined intervals: every day, every hour—whenever you please. Before any session can get under way, however, you have to tell AOL some things it needs to know.

Automatic AOL Session Setup

We can hear it now: it's 5:00 A.M. and El Edwards's voice calls from Jennifer's computer in the other room. "Jennifer," he says, "come in here and type in your password!" Bleary-eyed, Jennifer stumbles to her desk and types in her password. She crawls back into bed and starts to drift off when he calls again. "Jennifer," (is that a smirk in his voice?) "come out here and tell me which screen name to use!" Again, she stumbles to the desk, tripping over her dog, who, rudely awakened, runs yelping into the living room, knocking over the Waterford crystal vase. She picks up the pieces, hiding those that don't seem to fit together any longer, and puts a Band-Aid across the laceration on her dog's nose. She does all this smiling, of course. Always smiling.

Do we make our point? The manual entry of passwords and screen names would defeat the whole purpose of unattended Automatic AOL sessions. These things have to be communicated to America Online before the first Automatic AOL session begins. Once communicated, they're stored on your computer, eliminating the need to reenter them for each subsequent session.

Selecting Screen Names & Entering Stored Passwords Many America Online members use more than one screen name. Perhaps more than one member of your family uses the service. Maybe you have an alter ego. Perhaps you're shy, or famous, or reclusive, and you don't want anyone to see your real name on the screen. Whatever the reason, if you use more than one screen name, you have to tell your computer which names to use for Automatic AOL sessions, and if you want the sessions to run unattended, you'll have to enter a password for each screen name.

Selecting names and entering passwords is easy, and once it's done, you won't need to do it again unless you want to reconfigure Automatic AOL. We won't linger here, as we've already selected a name and entered a password during the exercise that led off this chapter. Figure 8-9 shows you how to do it.

Though Figure 8-9 illustrates the selection of a single screen name (and entry of a password for that screen name), the Select Screen Names window will include all of the screen names you are using for your account, up to the maximum of five. Activate only the check boxes for the screen names you want included in your Automatic AOL sessions, and include the password for each (only if you intend to have your sessions occur while you're away).

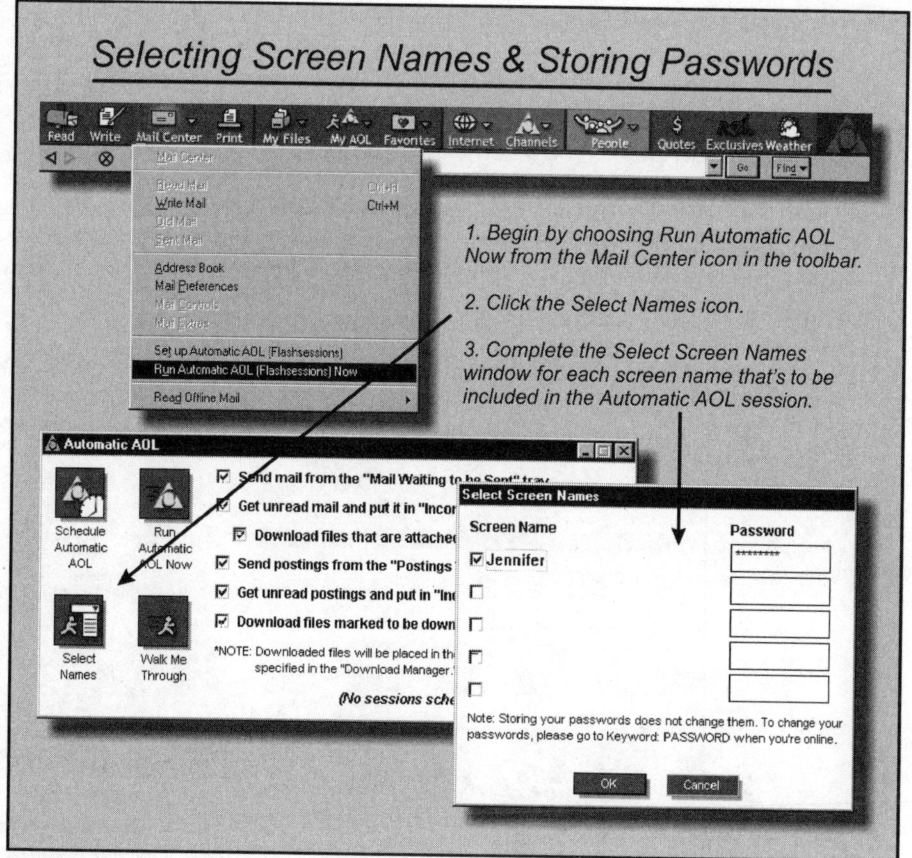

Figure 8-9: The Select Screen Names icon takes you to the entry form for selecting names and storing passwords.

Caution!

There's a minor potential for unauthorized use of your account whenever you store your passwords, even if you store them only for the use of Automatic AOL sessions. Normally, Automatic AOL signs on in response to the operator's command, does all of its activities, and then signs off. That last step, however, can be bypassed if the Escape key is used before Automatic AOL finishes. In effect, this allows anyone with a little computer savvy to run an Automatic AOL session on your account and then stay online to do as he or she pleases for as long as he or she wishes—all without needing to know your password. If there's a potential for this kind of abuse around your machine (and there always is with laptops, which are prime targets for theft), don't store passwords.

Declaring the Download Destination One more setup task remains before you can start an Automatic AOL session: you must declare a destination for downloaded files. Just choose Preferences from the My AOL icon on the toolbar, select the Download button, and change the path at the bottom—you can either type a new path directly in if you know it or use the Browse button to set it (see Figure 8-10).

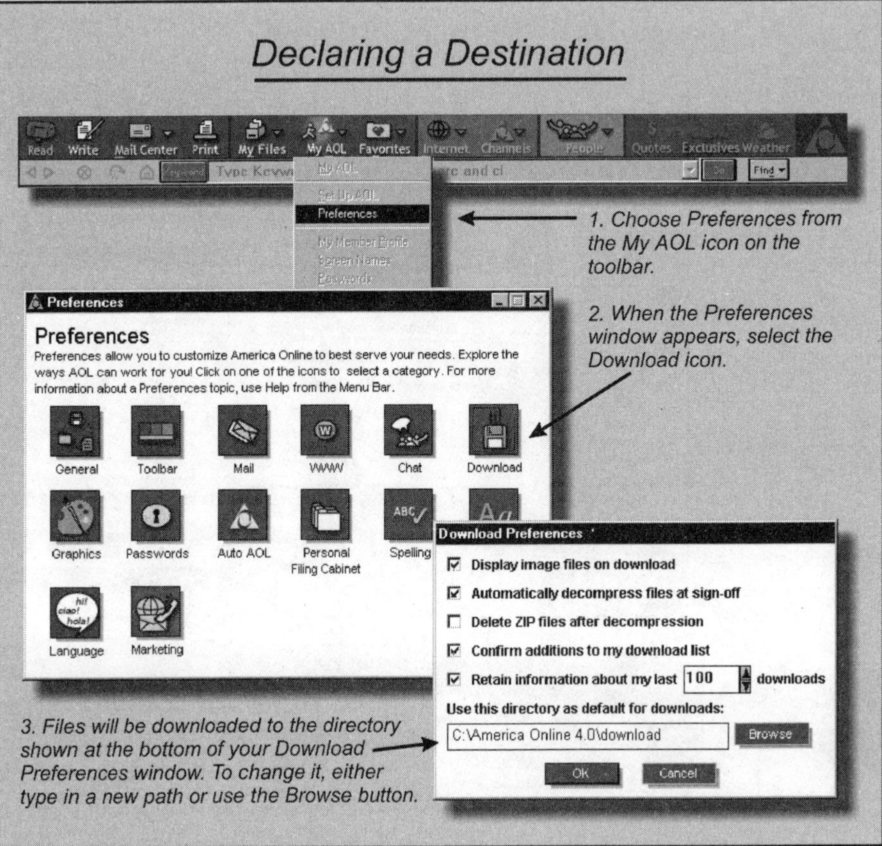

Figure 8-10: In the Download Preferences window, you can specify where you want to save downloaded files. The Download subdirectory in your America Online 4.0 directory is the default.

Attended Automatic AOL Sessions

Now that you've stored your screen names, passwords, and destinations, you're ready to run an Automatic AOL session. The exercise that began this chapter describes an *attended session*—one that occurs when you issue a command manually. Let's examine attended Automatic AOL sessions first.

Many Automatic AOL sessions occur when you're about to wrap up an online session. There's something organic about the flow of an online session: after a couple of months online, you'll glide from one task to another with all the fluidity of warm honey. About the last thing you'll want to do is interrupt your progress with a download or the transmission of a piece of mail. Instead, you can schedule an Automatic AOL session to take care of these things when you are done online. More about this in a moment, when you're finished with your online session.

Another kind of attended Automatic AOL session occurs when you're offline and want your computer to sign on; transfer mail, postings, and files; and sign off. As you saw during the earlier exercise, the advantage here is speed. Automatic AOL sessions "know" exactly what they're doing; they waste no time, they waste no money, and you don't have to stick around while they're under way.

Offline Attended Automatic AOL Sessions This is exactly what we did during the earlier exercise in this chapter. You begin an offline Automatic AOL session not by signing on but rather by choosing Run Automatic AOL Now from the Mail Center icon's menu (shown in Figure 8-3). When the Activate Automatic AOL Now window appears (see Figure 8-6), click the Begin button.

Normally, this is all you need to do to run an offline attended Automatic AOL session. When you click the Begin button, your computer signs on, does everything it's been told to do, then signs off. It repeats the process for each of the screen names you've indicated. When the dust settles, an Automatic AOL Status window remains on your screen to inform you of what happened (Figure 8-12). This is more a necessity than a convenience. Without the Automatic AOL Status window, you might have to perform some major sleuthing to find out what happened during a session, especially one that occurred in your absence.

Figure 8-11: Once your screen name and password are stored, a menu selection and a couple of mouse clicks are all it takes to run an offline attended Automatic AOL session.

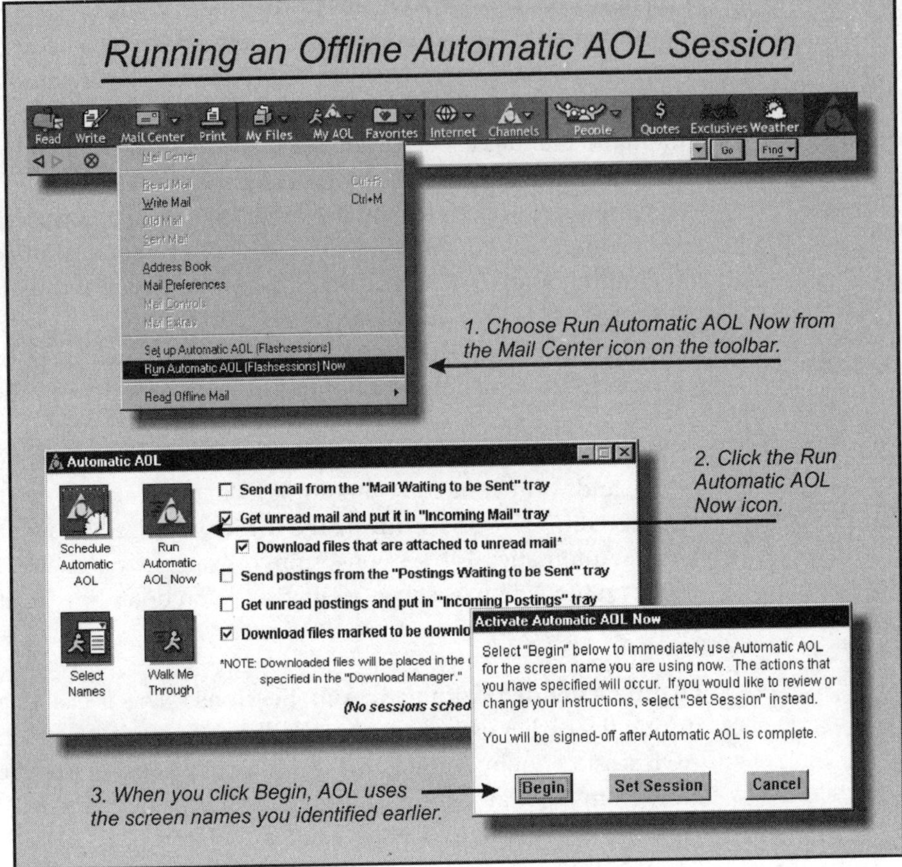

Do You Know Who You Are?

There's a bit of a trap waiting for you if you follow the three steps illustrated in Figure 8-11 and aren't paying attention. It's not apparent what screen names AOL will use during the upcoming Automatic AOL session. Review the Select Screen Names window shown at the bottom of Figure 8-9, if necessary. Note that AOL will run a session for each name that's selected in the Select Screen Names window, not just the screen name that's currently showing in the Welcome (sign-on) window. Be sure you know which names are selected in the Select Screen Names window before you allow your Automatic AOL sessions to run.

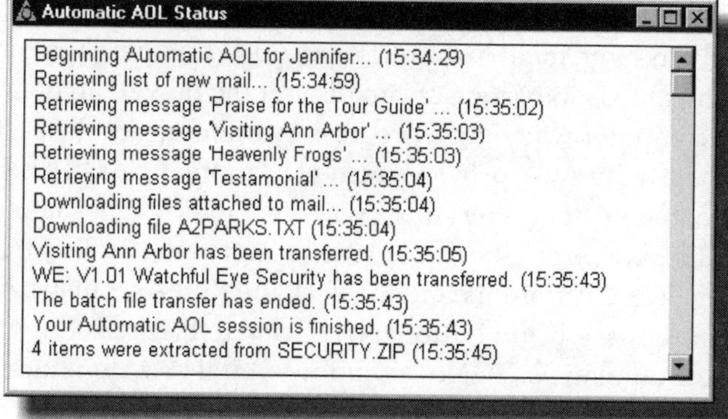

Figure 8-12: The Automatic AOL Status window lets you know what happened during an Automatic AOL session, just in case you weren't watching.

Look again at Figure 8-12. Jennifer received four pieces of new mail (one with an attached file) and downloaded a file she'd scheduled for download. The America Online software even extracted (decompressed) the downloaded file for her.

It isn't uncommon for only four or five entries to appear in the Automatic AOL Status window—two representing the start and finish of an Automatic AOL session, with two or three in between letting you know there was no new mail, no unread postings, and so on. This isn't as meaningless as it might seem. If there was no activity during a session Jennifer had scheduled for the middle of the night, she would be aware of that the next morning, and she wouldn't waste time looking for mail or files that weren't there. Of additional benefit is notification of errors. If Jennifer incorrectly addressed some mail or if the session was interrupted for some reason, she'd read about it here.

Online Attended Automatic AOL Sessions Another form of attended Automatic AOL session is the one that occurs at sign-on or sign-off. If you've queued mail or postings to be sent later, when you sign on, you'll be notified that you have items waiting and given the opportunity to send them now that you're online (see Figure 8-13). If you click the Send Now button, an Automatic AOL session will run for you. If you'd rather not get this reminder in the future, check the Do Not Ask Me Again check box.

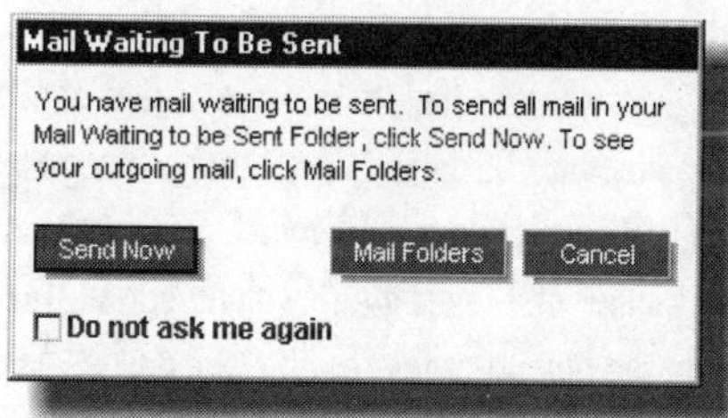

Figure 8-13: America Online reminds you upon sign-on when you have mail or postings waiting to be sent.

Once online, you might visit a forum or two, mark some files for downloading, reply to some mail, make a few postings, and perhaps compose some new mail. Downloads in particular can disrupt the flow of an online session. Sitting at your computer watching a progress indicator is not the best use of your time. That's why AOL provides sign-off Automatic AOL sessions.

When you've done everything you want to do online, choose Run Automatic AOL Now from the Mail Center's icon in the toolbar (rather than choosing Sign Off from the menu), click the Run Automatic AOL Now icon, and then click the Begin button (refer again to Figure 8-11). As noted in the Activate Automatic AOL Now window, you'll be automatically signed off after the Automatic AOL session is complete. This is one alternative to the Sign Off command; the other is the Download Manager, which we'll discuss later in this chapter. Either one will work if activity remains that doesn't require your involvement.

One more thing: if you accidentally sign off while mail, postings, or files are queued for later, America Online reminds you of your oversight (see Figure 8-14). One way or another, you always have an opportunity to run your Automatic AOL session.

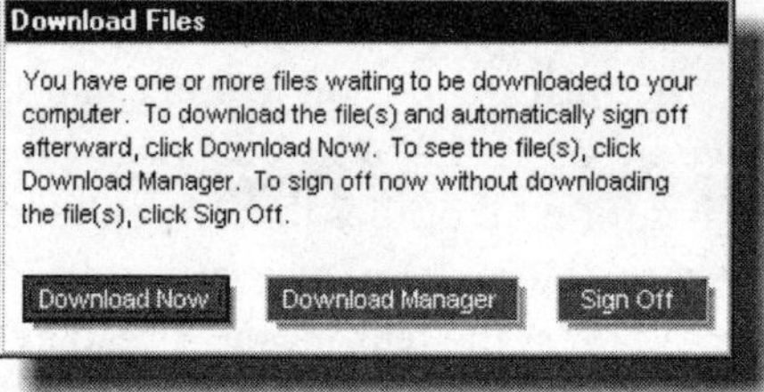

Figure 8-14: Before you sign off, you have the opportunity to run an Automatic AOL session if you have items already queued.

Where'd That File Go?

Automatic AOL sessions not only receive any mail that America Online is holding for you, they also download any files that are attached to that mail. Unfortunately, the destination of those downloads is often obscure and you're forced to scour your hard disk after the Automatic AOL session looking for the e-mail attachments it has downloaded.

Like all computer programs, AOL only does what it's told. In the case of files attached to e-mail, it defaults to the directory identified by your Download Preferences. Though we'll discuss them a bit later in this chapter, all you have to do to find your files is choose Preferences from the My AOL icon on the toolbar and select the Download button. The path to the downloading directory will appear at the bottom of the resulting window.

Unattended Automatic AOL Sessions

Our agent uses e-mail. Our publisher uses e-mail. Our editor uses e-mail. Indeed, most authors and many others in the book-publishing business work at home, and most manuscripts and related communications are exchanged electronically. There are days when communication sparks across the continent like migrating locusts. Contracts are negotiated, manuscripts are edited, illustrations tweaked—sometimes five or six times a day.

The literary profession isn't unique in its reliance on e-mail. For lawyers, salespeople, brokers, and others who need to send messages—across town, across the country, or around the world—*unattended sessions* are beyond mere conveniences, they're necessities.

On locust days like these, we instruct Automatic AOL to check for mail every half hour. This it does, in the background, as reliably as clockwork, regardless of what we're doing with our computers. There's no need to interrupt our train of thought: Automatic AOL simply signs on, sends queued mail, receives new mail, and signs off. We don't even have to be in the building. That's why they're called "unattended Automatic AOL sessions."

You're not limited to a half-hourly schedule either: you can run unattended Automatic AOL sessions as frequently or as infrequently as you desire. Some people even run them in the predawn hours to take advantage of off-peak hours when traffic is light.

Predawn Automatic AOL Session Tips

Lots of people run Automatic AOL sessions in the middle of the night. Many of these people are downloading zealots: their download sessions often last for hours. Under these conditions, downloading when system activity is minimal—around 5:00 A.M. Eastern time—makes significant economic sense.

If a 5:00 A.M. Automatic AOL session appeals to you, be sure to leave your computer on with the AOL software running. Don't forget to leave the modem on too (if it's the external variety), but turn off the monitor if you can: monitors (color, especially) consume a lot of power.

Scheduling Unattended Automatic AOL Sessions In addition to choosing screen names and entering stored passwords, one significant task remains: scheduling the time of day and the days of the week that you want AOL to conduct its Automatic AOL sessions. Figure 8-15 illustrates the procedure.

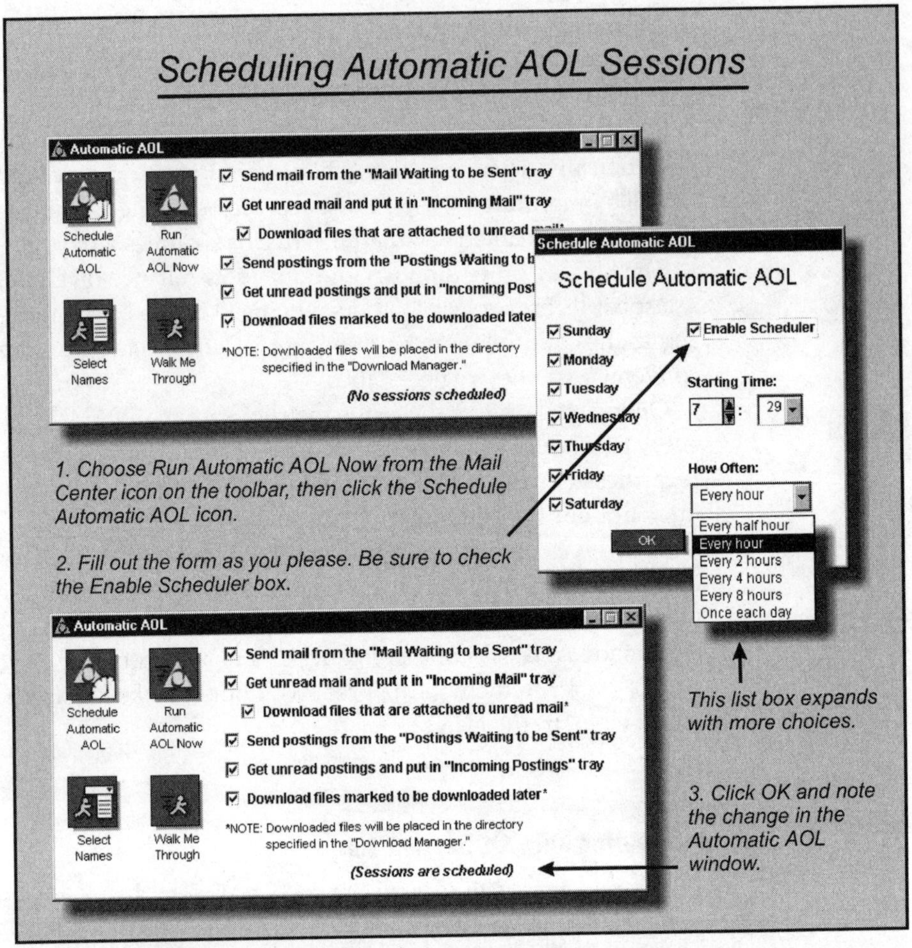

Figure 8-15: The Schedule Automatic AOL window lets you declare the days and times you want unattended Automatic AOL sessions to run. Be sure to check the Enable Scheduler box (it's easy to neglect) or the Automatic AOL session won't run.

Scheduling Automatic AOL Sessions

Automatic AOL

Schedule Automatic AOL | Run Automatic AOL Now | Select Names | Walk Me Through

☑ Send mail from the "Mail Waiting to be Sent" tray
☑ Get unread mail and put it in "Incoming Mail" tray
☑ Download files that are attached to unread mail*
☑ Send postings from the "Postings Waiting to be Sent" tray
☑ Get unread postings and put in "Incoming Postings" tray
☑ Download files marked to be downloaded later*

*NOTE: Downloaded files will be placed in the directory specified in the "Download Manager."

(No sessions scheduled)

Schedule Automatic AOL

☑ Sunday ☑ Monday ☑ Tuesday ☑ Wednesday ☑ Thursday ☑ Friday ☑ Saturday

☑ Enable Scheduler

Starting Time: 7 : 29

How Often: Every hour

Every half hour / Every hour / Every 2 hours / Every 4 hours / Every 8 hours / Once each day

OK

1. Choose Run Automatic AOL Now from the Mail Center icon on the toolbar, then click the Schedule Automatic AOL icon.

2. Fill out the form as you please. Be sure to check the Enable Scheduler box.

This list box expands with more choices.

3. Click OK and note the change in the Automatic AOL window.

(Sessions are scheduled)

We've assumed here that you've used the Automatic AOL sessions window (pictured at the top of Figure 8-15) to check all the activities you want AOL to carry out during an Automatic AOL session. Usually you'll want to select all the activities shown in the illustration.

We've also assumed that you have declared the appropriate screen names (and stored passwords) for which you want Automatic AOL to apply. Review Figure 8-9 if you're unsure.

Look again at Figure 8-15. Note that Jennifer's Automatic AOL sessions are scheduled for 29 minutes after the hour. In fact, she only has two choices: 29 or 59 minutes after the hour. America Online arbitrarily assigned these times when she joined. Yours will differ from hers, and so will those of everyone else. America Online staggers Automatic AOL session times to distribute the load on AOL's host machines. If given our druthers, most of us would probably choose to run our Automatic AOL sessions on the hour or the half hour—that's human nature. But AOL's machines would bog down answering thousands of simultaneous phone calls. Offering limited random times is AOL's way of avoiding Automatic AOL overload.

Excepting Incoming Files

Just last week, Tom attempted to send some e-mail to a friend. Attached to the message was a 270K file. Unfortunately, he misspelled his friend's screen name in the To box of the Write Mail form. Even more unfortunately, the misspelling meant the mail went to another legitimate AOL screen name—along with the 270K file. Though Tom resent the mail to the proper person later, the person who was on the receiving end of the misdirected mail was no doubt quite displeased with Tom if his Automatic AOL session downloaded the file. Tom's error might have cost him a couple minutes of connect time.

In other words, to protect yourself from encountering a mistake like the one Tom inadvertently inflicted on that unsuspecting AOL member, you might want to deactivate the Download Files That Are Attached to Unread Mail option in the Automatic AOL window (see the bottom window in Figure 8-15). We strongly suggest you disable this option. Not only can you end up downloading files you don't necessarily want, but you could inadvertently download a computer virus along with them. If you also have the Automatically Decompress Files at Sign-Off option enabled in your Download Preferences (see Chapter 9 for more details), you might accidentally activate the virus.

Remember, you can always sign back on to download files, but you can't undo the cost of a lengthy unwanted download once it's done.

Reading Offline Mail

It only makes sense that America Online lets you read incoming mail you've captured in an Automatic AOL session. What's interesting is that you can read *outgoing* mail you've marked to send later as well. This is especially comforting for those of us who suffer from occasional bouts of irresolution. Until it's actually sent, outgoing mail is ours to edit, append, or "wad up and throw away." (Now that we think about it, you can edit, append, or wad up and throw away mail even after it's sent—as long as it's not Internet mail and as long as no one has read it. Refer to Chapter 3, "Electronic Mail & the Personal Filing Cabinet," if you're not familiar with this feature.)

Reading Incoming Mail

Incoming mail is stored in the Incoming/Saved Mail folder in your Personal Filing Cabinet. (The Personal Filing Cabinet is discussed in Chapter 3.) To read incoming mail, use the Read Offline Mail command under the Mail Center icon in the toolbar (or choose Personal Filing Cabinet from the My Files icon in the toolbar), select Incoming/Saved Mail, then open the Incoming/Saved Mail folder if it isn't already open. Most folks use the Read Offline Mail command under the Mail Center icon. To read incoming mail using this command, follow the steps illustrated in Figure 8-16.

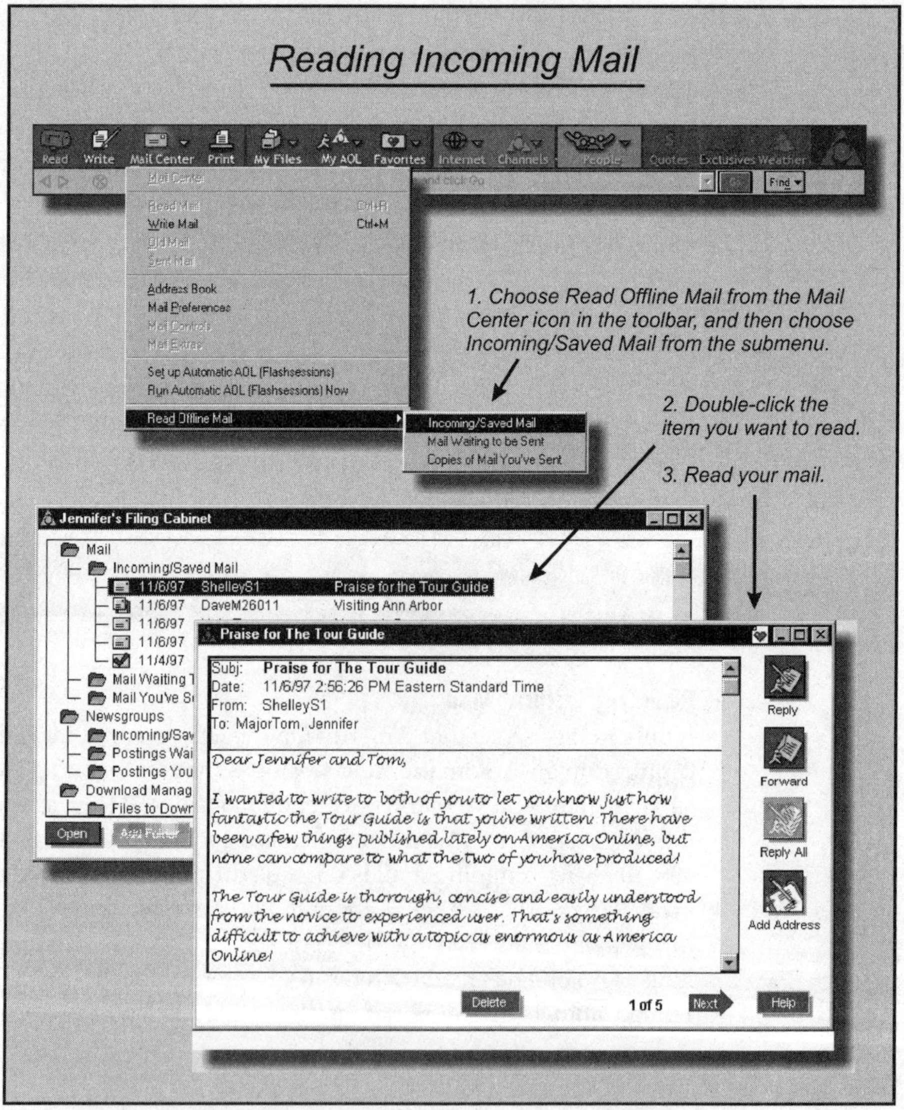

Figure 8-16: Reading incoming mail is easy. Because incoming mail is stored on your machine, not America Online's, you can read it when you're offline.

Reading Incoming Mail

1. Choose Read Offline Mail from the Mail Center icon in the toolbar, and then choose Incoming/Saved Mail from the submenu.

2. Double-click the item you want to read.

3. Read your mail.

Don't confuse the Read Offline Mail command with the Read Mail or Old Mail commands, which also appear under the Mail Center icon. These are both online commands that allow you to review new mail or mail you've already read. The Read Offline Mail command discussed here is usually issued offline, after an Automatic AOL session has concluded. (Again, review Chapter 3 for a thorough explanation of e-mail commands.)

Watch Those Screen Names!

It's important to note that the only mail appearing in the Personal Filing Cabinet window is mail addressed to the screen name currently appearing in the window that was onscreen when you issued the Read Offline Mail command. If you've used an Automatic AOL session to download mail for more than one screen name, you must change the screen name in the Welcome window (or the Goodbye window, if you've signed on and signed off earlier) to identify incoming mail for each of your screen names. Only then will you find all the mail that came in during the session.

Avoid Clutter

As we mentioned earlier, incoming offline mail is stored in the Incoming/Saved Mail folder in your Personal Filing Cabinet. All incoming offline mail messages are stored there until they're deleted or moved, even after they have been read. This is no place to file your mail. Mail left in this folder continues to appear in the Incoming/Saved Mail window, with the newest at the top. Discovering new offline mail under these circumstances can be awkward, and you might even miss a piece or two. Either file incoming offline mail in your personal mail folders, or delete it after you've read it.

The Personal Filing Cabinet is discussed in Chapter 3. Mail preferences are discussed in Chapter 9.

Reading Mail Waiting to Be Sent

The Read Mail Waiting to Be Sent command under Read Offline Mail in the Mail Center's menu allows you to read outgoing mail before you send it. This command can be invoked either online or off as long as you've prepared mail for sending but haven't sent it yet.

Again, don't confuse this command with the Sent Mail command. Sent Mail is an online command that lets you review mail you've sent during the past five days. The Read Mail Waiting to Be Sent command pertains only to mail you've scheduled for delivery but haven't sent yet (Figure 8-17).

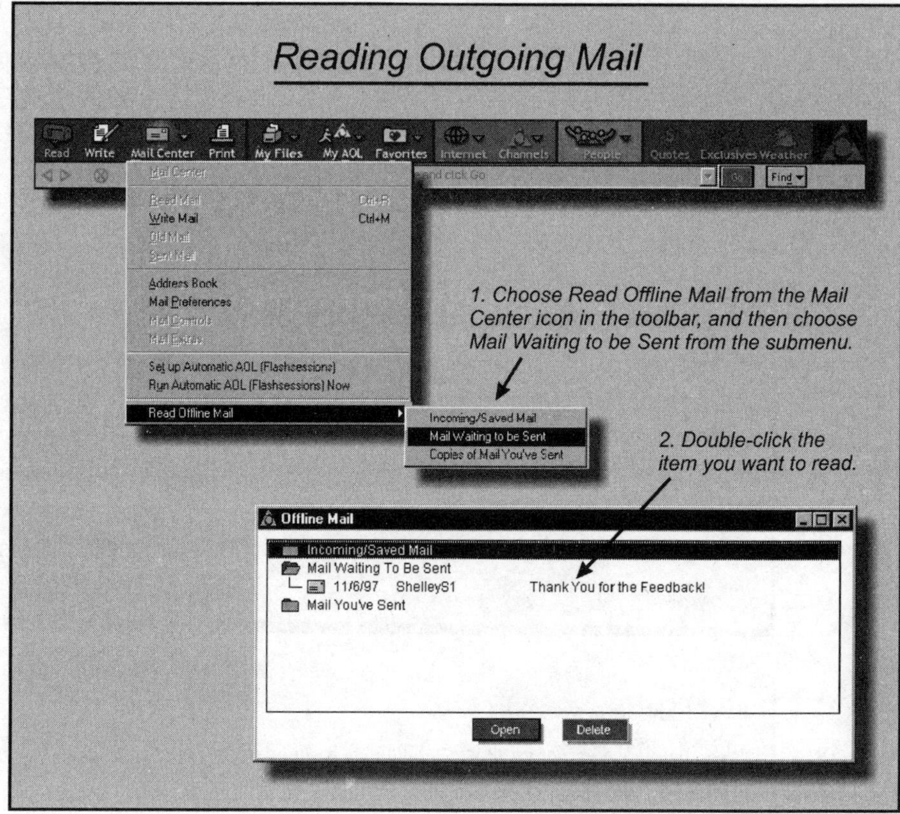

Figure 8-17: The Read Outgoing Mail command is available only when mail has been scheduled for delivery but hasn't been sent.

Offline Postings

Message boards and newsgroups—with their banter between members—also lend themselves well to offline reading. Like mail, America Online gives us the ability to "download" our posts in a batch from a message board or newsgroup to read offline at our leisure. This is more than simply convenience. Reading postings offline also saves time as we no longer need to wait online for each post to download to our screen—America Online will gather them in a batch and have them waiting for us. Better yet, it saves our sanity—when you're reading postings offline, the "flaming" posts just don't burn as bad.

Marking Postings to Be Read Offline

From your visit to newsgroups in Chapter 4, "Using the Internet," and your foray into message boards in Chapter 7, "Chat," we're guessing you've already found some favorites along the way. If they are anything like those we visit, keeping current with them while online can be tedious—offline reading is a real gift from the gods.

The first step to offline posting pleasure is to tell America Online which message boards and newsgroups you'd like to have retrieved by Automatic AOL. You wouldn't want all of them—it would probably take several lifetimes to read all the message board and newsgroup postings on AOL. Start with just one or two good ones. Just select the message boards and/or newsgroups you want to read offline (you may need to open them first) and click the Read Offline button in the lower right corner for each (see Figure 8-18).

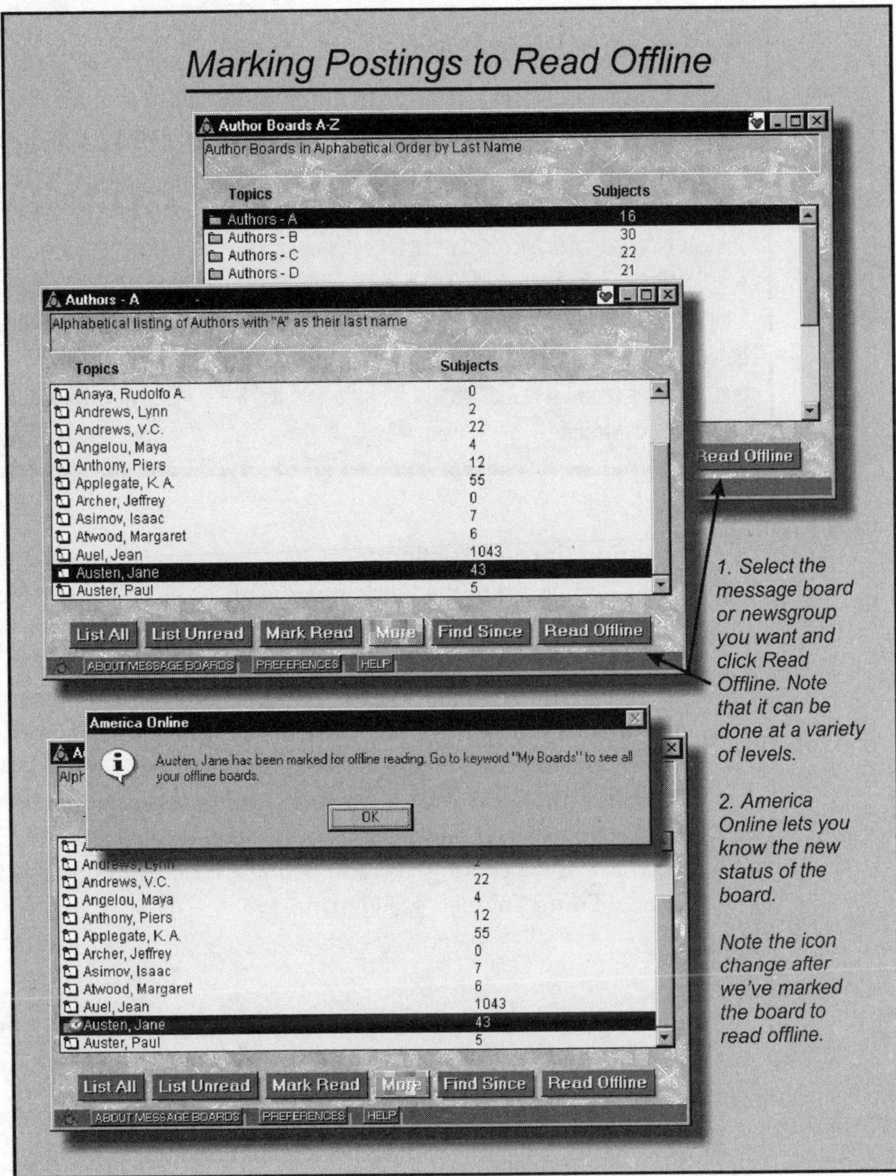

Figure 8-18: The Read Offline button marks unread postings in a message board or newsgroup for later retrieval.

A small icon of a clock on a file folder indicates that the unread postings inside are marked for later retrieval. You can toggle offline reading off again just by clicking the Read Offline button once more—you'll notice the icon return to the original pushpin and board. Once marked, a message board or newgroup stays marked indefinitely until you change it. To see all your marked boards and newsgroups, use the keywords: **My Boards** while online.

The Case of the Missing Button

There's a mystery afoot. Some of our favorite message boards don't have this Read Offline button anywhere within them. Are we missing it? Or, dare we say it, has a hacker run off with it?

Actually, neither; not all message boards can be read offline. As we discussed in Chapter 7, some older message boards exist on the system still, and they do not have the offline functionality built in. But not all hope is lost if you'd like to read their postings offline. Simply turn on your Session Log (within your Log Manager, discussed in Chapter 7 also) before you open your message board, and then click Read New for each message board and/or folder you wish to read offline. It isn't automatic, but it will capture the text for later perusal at your leisure.

Gathering Unread Postings

You've done most of the work already—now simply run Automatic AOL and reap your harvest. First, close any message boards you may be reading if you're currently online. Next, select Run Automatic AOL Now from the Mail Center icon in the toolbar. Verify that the "Get unread postings and put in the 'Incoming Postings' tray" box is checked. Then either start an Automatic AOL session now or schedule one for later, as we discussed earlier in this chapter. When the Automatic AOL session concludes, every unread posting from the message boards and newsgroups you marked earlier will be downloaded and placed in your Incoming/Saved Postings in the Newsgroups folder of your Personal Filing Cabinet (see Figure 8-19).

Figure 8-19: Automatic AOL captures all of your unread postings and organizes them in your Personal Filing Cabinet.

Gathering Postings with Automatic AOL

Automatic AOL

Schedule Automatic AOL

Run Automatic AOL Now

Select Names

Walk Me Through

☐ Send mail from the "Mail Waiting to be Sent" tray

☐ Get unread mail and put it in "Incoming Mail" tray

☐ Download files that are attached to unread mail*

☑ Send postings from the "Postings Waiting to be Sent" tray

☑ Get unread postings and put in "Incoming Postings" tray

☐ Download files marked to be downloaded later*

*NOTE: Downlo... specifie...

1. Verify that you've selected the postings options in your Automatic AOL preferences window.

Activate Automatic AOL Now

Select "Begin" below to immediately use Automatic AOL for the screen name you are using now. The actions that you have specified will occur. If you would like to review or change your instructions, select "Set Session" instead.

You will be signed-off after Automatic AOL is complete.

Begin | Set Session | Cancel

2. Run Automatic AOL to collect all your unread postings.

Automatic AOL Status

Retrieving unread postings... (10:49:52)
Retrieving message "Re: Mansfield Park and Fanny"... (10:49:53)
Retrieving message "Re: Mansfield Park and Fanny"... (10:49:54)
Your Automatic AOL Session is finished. (10:49:55)

3. The Automatic AOL Status window keeps you informed.

Jennifer's Filing Cabinet

- Mail
- Newsgroups
  - Incoming/Saved Postings
    - Non-Fiction
    - Austen, Jane
      - Create New Posting
      - Northanger Abbey
      - Mansfield Park and Fanny
        - Mansfield Park and Fanny
        - Re: Mansfield Park and Fanny
        - Re: Mansfield Park and Fanny
      - Lady Susan
        - Lady Susan
        - Re: Lady Susan

Open | Add Folder | Rename | Delete | Auto AOL | Find | Compact PFC | Help

4. Your new, unread postings are placed in your Personal Filing Cabinet.

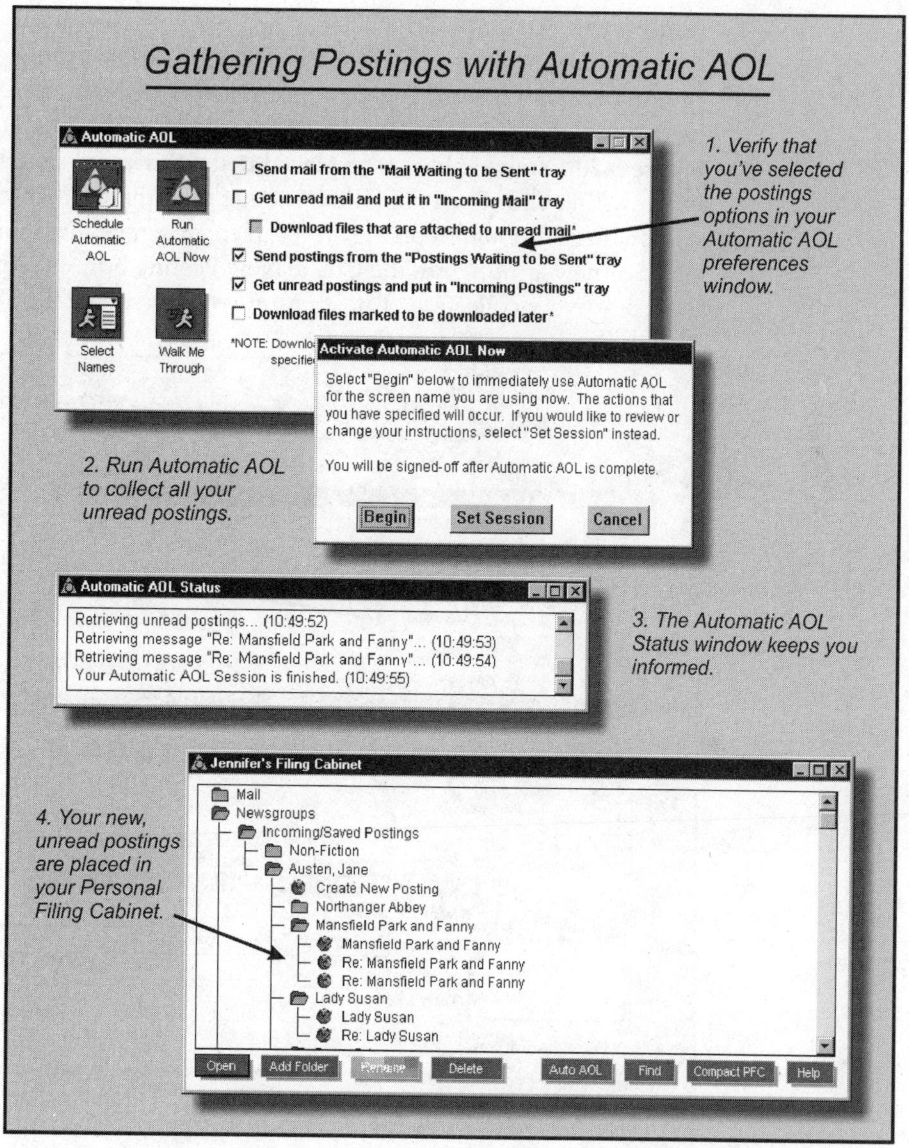

Replying to Postings Offline

Not only does America Online let you read postings offline, but you can respond to them offline as well. To compose a reply to a posting, simply read it while offline and click the Respond to Group button (as shown in Figure 8-20). Your reply will be placed in the Postings Waiting to Be Sent folder within your Personal Filing Cabinet until the next Automatic AOL session. In addition to replying, you can create a new thread in a message board or newsgroup with the Create New Posting button, which you'll find at the top of every collection of postings in your Personal Filing Cabinet.

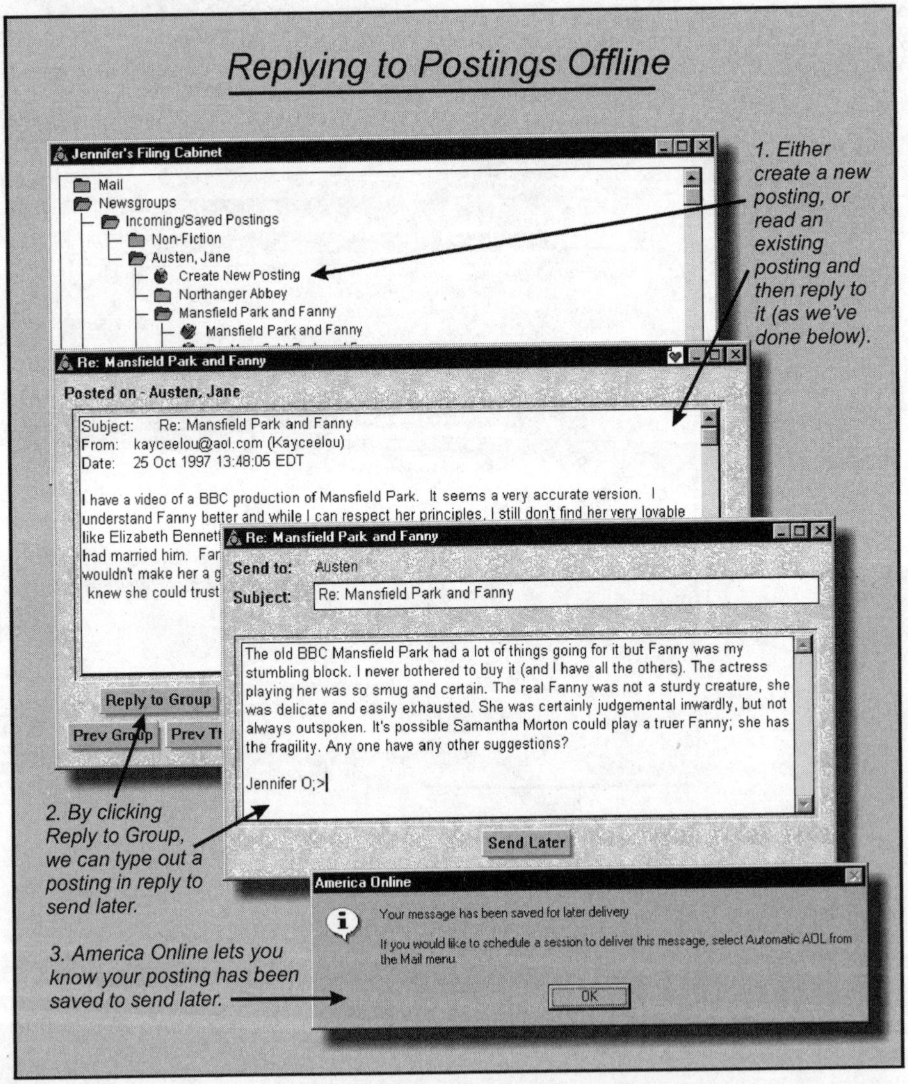

Figure 8-20: Reply to postings offline at your leisure.

Replying to Postings Offline

Jennifer's Filing Cabinet
Mail
Newsgroups
Incoming/Saved Postings
Non-Fiction
Austen, Jane
Create New Posting
Northanger Abbey
Mansfield Park and Fanny
Mansfield Park and Fanny

1. Either create a new posting, or read an existing posting and then reply to it (as we've done below).

Re: Mansfield Park and Fanny
Posted on - Austen, Jane
Subject: Re: Mansfield Park and Fanny
From: kayceelou@aol.com (Kayceelou)
Date: 25 Oct 1997 13:48:05 EDT

I have a video of a BBC production of Mansfield Park. It seems a very accurate version. I understand Fanny better and while I can respect her principles, I still don't find her very lovable

Reply to Group
Prev Group
Prev Tl

Re: Mansfield Park and Fanny
Send to: Austen
Subject: Re: Mansfield Park and Fanny

The old BBC Mansfield Park had a lot of things going for it but Fanny was my stumbling block. I never bothered to buy it (and I have all the others). The actress playing her was so smug and certain. The real Fanny was not a sturdy creature, she was delicate and easily exhausted. She was certainly judgemental inwardly, but not always outspoken. It's possible Samantha Morton could play a truer Fanny; she has the fragility. Any one have any other suggestions?

Jennifer O;>

Send Later

2. By clicking Reply to Group, we can type out a posting in reply to send later.

America Online
Your message has been saved for later delivery
If you would like to schedule a session to deliver this message, select Automatic AOL from the Mail menu.
OK

3. America Online lets you know your posting has been saved to send later.

If you have the "Send postings from the 'Postings Waiting to be Sent' tray" box checked, Automatic AOL will send each of your postings to the appropriate message board or newsgroup during your next session. If AOL is quick, you may even wind up downloading the postings you authored to read offline before the session ends.

The Download Manager

Downloads probably offer more potential than any other America Online feature. There are tens of thousands of files on AOL's hard disks, and every one of them can be downloaded to your computer. There are millions more on the Internet, and many of those are available to you as well. Using the Download Manager, you can establish a queue of files while you're online, where you can read descriptions and estimate time. When your session is almost over, you then instruct the Download Manager to download the files and sign off—or schedule an Automatic AOL session to download your files for you later when system activity is less intrusive. Either way, once the process has begun, you can walk away.

Let's watch a typical Download Manager session to see what the screens look like. We'll schedule two files for downloading; then we'll instruct the Download Manager to handle the downloading process and sign off automatically.

Selecting Files for Downloading

Figure 8-21 illustrates the process of selecting a graphic from The Grateful Dead Forum (at keyword: **Dead**). This is a particularly rewarding area if you're looking for something to download. It's full of graphics, sound, and even video.

Figure 8-21: The last step in selecting a Grateful Dead graphic for delayed downloading is to click the Download Later button, which calls up the dialog box at the bottom of the illustration.

Selecting a Photo for Download

1. Begin by using the keyword: **Dead.**
2. Click the downloads button.
3. Select the category from the Forum Software Library.
4. Select the graphic you want to download.
5. Click the Download Later button and conclude with the dialog box at right.

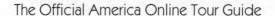

We might as well give the Download Manager more than one thing to do, so let's select another file to add to the download queue. A Mike Keefe political cartoon seems appropriate (see Figure 8-22).

Figure 8-22: Selecting a Mike Keefe cartoon for delayed downloading.

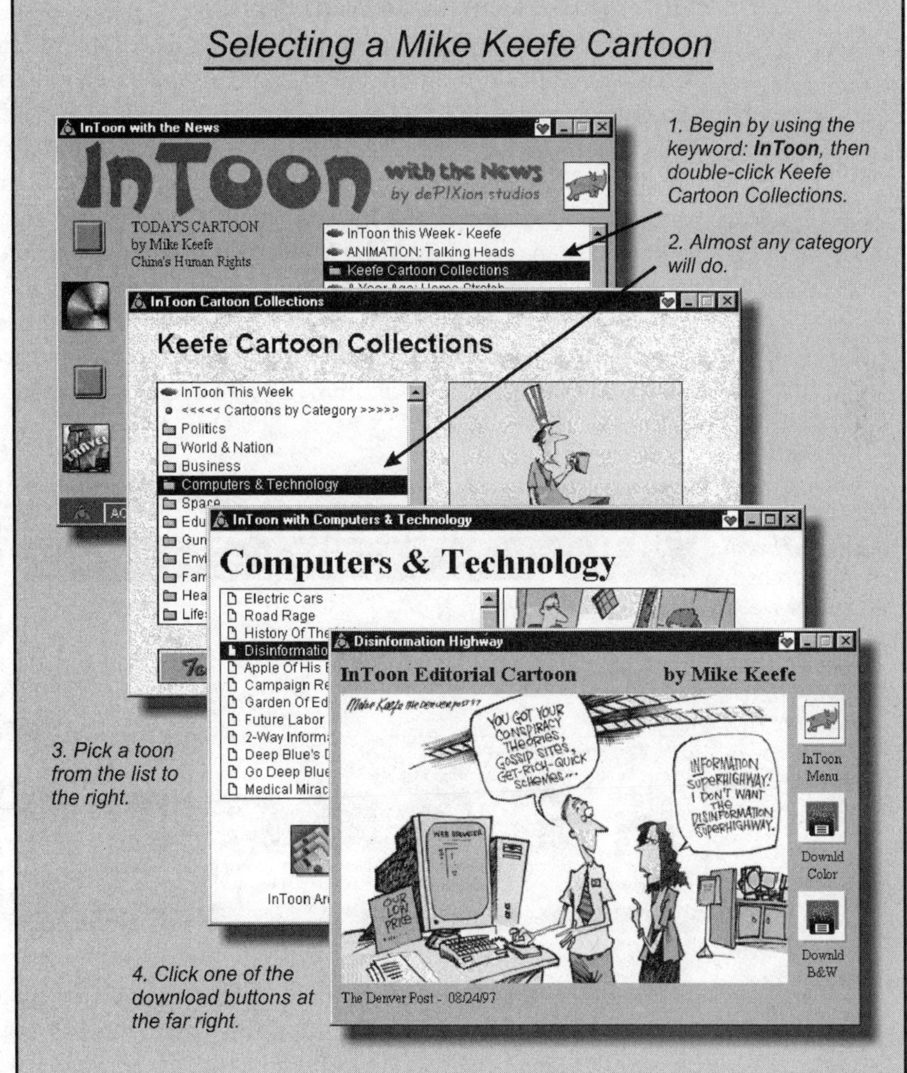

Running the Download Manager

Eventually, the time will come to reap the harvest. Rather than sign off, choose Download Manager from the File menu. This is a second alternative to the Sign Off command (the first being Activate Automatic AOL Now—under the Mail Center icon—described earlier in this chapter). The Activate Automatic AOL Now command accommodates both delayed mail and downloading activities, but it doesn't offer the control the Download Manager does. The Download Manager—under the My Files icon—doesn't send or receive queued mail or message postings, but it offers access to all the options pictured in Figure 8-23. If you have mail to send and files to download when you sign off, choose Activate Automatic AOL session Now (and configure the Download Manager ahead of time). If you have only files to download, choose the Download Manager.

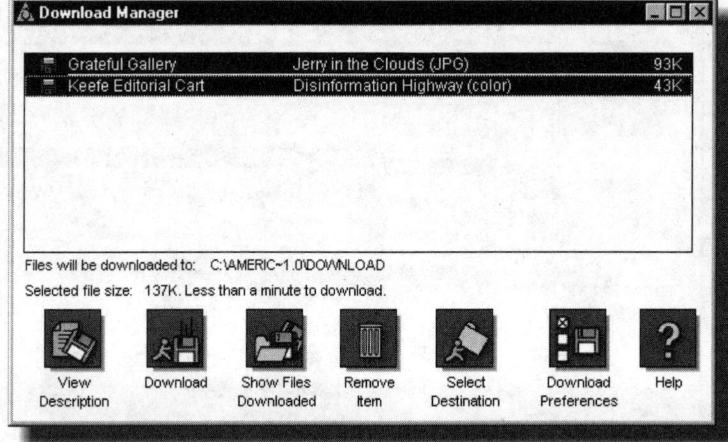

Figure 8-23: The Download Manager window lists all files scheduled for download and includes sizes, destinations, and the estimated amount of time required to download the entire queue.

Note the buttons across the bottom of Figure 8-23. This is an impressive array of commands. America Online wants you to have complete control over the downloading process, especially now that it's about to begin. Let's examine these buttons now:

- **View Description.** The same as the View Description button you encounter when you're browsing a file library. It's handy to have this command here. Though you probably read the file's description a half hour ago, chances are you remember nothing about it now that you've reached the Download Manager window. Lots of things could have happened in the interim. This button saves a long trip back to the file's original location to review its description.

- **Download.** Begins the downloading process. We'll use it in a moment.
- **Show Files Downloaded.** Lets you review your past downloads. The number of downloads available for review is set with the Download Preferences button (which we'll discuss in a moment). There's no value in downloading the same file twice. Though America Online will warn you if you try to download a file you've already downloaded, you can save yourself the trouble by checking this list first.
- **Remove Item.** Allows you to remove a file (or two, or three) from the list. Sometimes enthusiasm exceeds resources.
- **Select Destination.** Allows you to declare a destination folder other than the **aol40\download** folder, which is the default. **Note:** All the files in the queue must download to the same folder.
- **Download Preferences.** Allows you to determine whether images are displayed during an attended download. (See Chapter 6, "Transferring Files," for a discussion of the online graphics viewer.) A number of decompression options are presented here (again, see Chapter 6), as is the number of downloads available for review when you click the Show Files Downloaded button. Refer to Chapter 9 for a comprehensive discussion of all the America Online preference options.
- **Help.** Produces the Download Manager help topic. This is the offline help database—it references the help files that are stored locally on your hard disk—thus it is available whether you're online or off.

Pick Up Where You Left Off

Occasionally, the downloading process is interrupted. Lightning strikes. A power cord gets tripped over. The phone line develops a stutter. These kinds of things don't happen often, but when they do, they always seem to occur when you're 80 percent of the way through a 47-minute download. *Poof!* There goes 35 minutes of connect time.

Don't worry about it. If a file was interrupted during a download, your AOL software makes a note of it and will resume the download queue where you left off the next time you return to the Download Manager.

The downloading process commences when you click the Download button (see Figure 8-24).

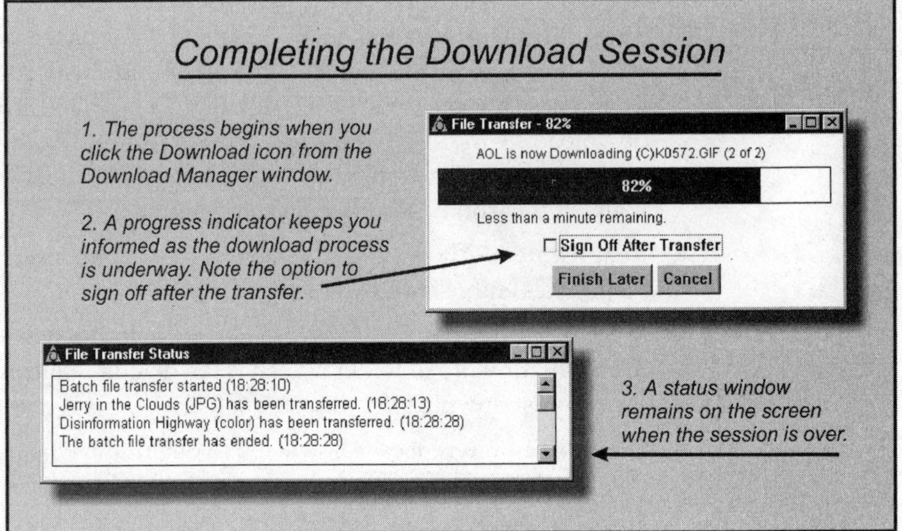

Figure 8-24: The Automatic AOL session ends with a display of the File Transfer Status window.

Look again at Figure 8-24. When the Sign Off After Transfer option is selected, you can walk away from the computer while all this is going on, secure in the knowledge that the Download Manager will sign off when everything has been downloaded satisfactorily (Figure 8-25).

Figure 8-25: Tack a couple of downloaded printouts to your wall each day; people will think you're clever, erudite, and urbane.

MacOffline

Jennifer admits she tends to forget what being offline is like. On those rare occasions when she finds her life again, Mac AOL's offline features are a blessing. They differ little from the Windows features we've described in this chapter. Here are the facts.

Automatic AOL offers the same features on Mac AOL as on the PC version; you just tend to find them in different places. Configuration and scheduling, for example, are done directly through your preferences: Auto AOL and Passwords to be exact. If you get lost, walkthroughs are available by clicking the small question mark icon on the bottom of your preferences window. If this is the first time you've used Automatic AOL, Jennifer suggests you select Set Up Automatic AOL from the Mail Center icon on the toolbar for step-by-step help.

The Mac Download Manager is integrated into your Personal Filing Cabinet, with similar features. Most differences are still intuitive—to view a file description, select it in the Download Manager and click Open, or just double-click it. You can change your download destination via Download Preferences.

Moving On

All this time spent talking about Automatic AOL sessions and the Download Manager might make you feel like a real yahoo if you don't use them. Don't worry about it: not all AOL members get enough mail or download enough files to make Automatic AOL sessions and the Download Manager worthwhile. In other words, you've got plenty of company: the yahoos are the majority.

There's a political statement there, we're sure, but to explore it would hardly be the way to conclude a chapter. Instead, reward yourself for reading this far by turning the page. The preferences chapter follows. Yahoos or not, we've all got preferences and America Online offers plenty of choices. Read on.

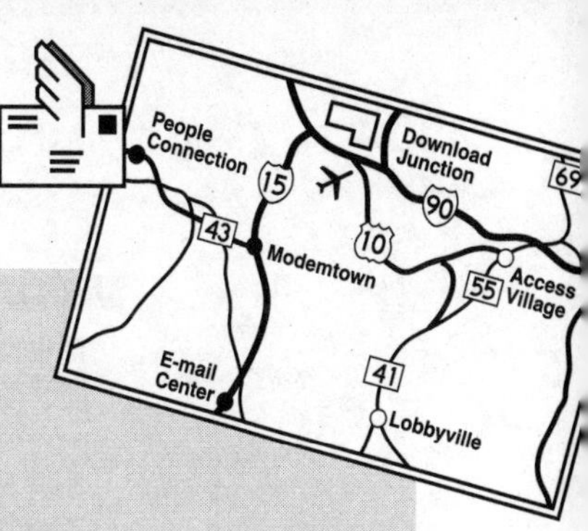

CHAPTER 9

Preferences

- General Preferences
- Toolbar Preferences
- Mail Preferences
- WWW Preferences
- Chat Preferences
- Download Preferences
- Graphics Viewing Preferences
- Passwords Preferences
- Automatic AOL
- Personal Filing Cabinet Preferences
- Spelling Preferences
- Font Preferences
- Language Preferences
- Buddy List Preferences

Ask 10 people how they use America Online and you'll probably get 10 different answers. One may tell you how they compose e-mail while waiting in clients' offices, turning off all America Online sounds so as not to disturb others. Another may reveal that they now navigate almost exclusively with keywords, disabling the display of the Channel screen at sign on to save a few extra seconds. And yet another may confess that they have set their font to Bauhaus 93 in a scalding shade of hot pink. We've even heard tell of a bicyclist who took America Online on the road with him, necessitating a particular and perhaps unique use of Automatic AOL options.

Whether you want to tone it down, speed it up, spin it around, or simply make it work best for you, America Online makes it possible. All of these things—and a number of others—are covered by America Online's member preferences. In fact, by our count there are over 100 distinct options you can set for your AOL software, each according to your whim and fancy. Preferences are yours and yours alone.

Begin by choosing Preferences from the My AOL icon on the toolbar. You don't have to be online to do this. Fourteen categories of preferences will appear in the form of the 14 buttons pictured in Figure 9-1; most of them can be set either offline or online.

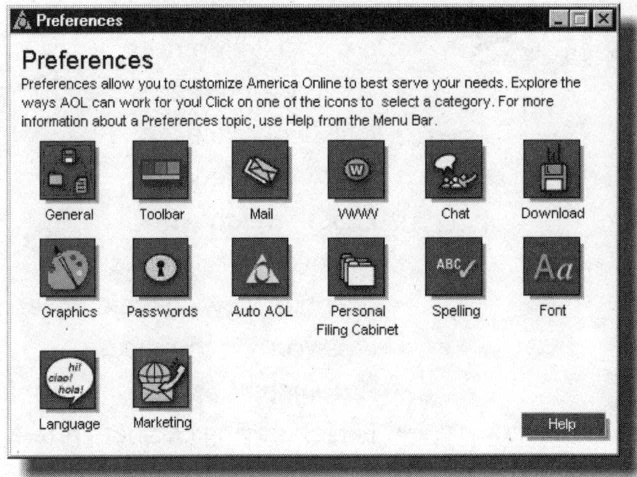

Figure 9-1: The 14 preference categories—and there's room for more. Click on any one of them to make changes.

We'll explore each of your options in the pages to come. Set aside your magnanimity and be picky, picky, picky. This is preferential treatment at its finest.

Tim Barwick

Tim Barwick is one of those people who doesn't measure success by the number of windows in his office. When we first met him in 1993, he occupied a fourth-floor office with palatial picture windows overlooking a deciduous Virginia woods. Squirrels scampered among Technicolor leaves. When we last saw Tim, he had moved his office to Reston, Virginia, where he had no exterior windows whatsoever and the only adornment was this sidebar, torn from the book and taped to his office door.

Tim doesn't care about the windows. He's a software guy. The only windows software guys worry about come from Microsoft. In fact, Tim's *the* software guy at AOL. When it comes to AOL's client software, Tim calls the shots.

And Tim likes preferences. He measures software quality by its preferences. "Good software," Tim says in his trademark British accent, "accommodates the user, not the other way around."

Consequently, the latest AOL client offers over 100 preferences and we've had to devote an entire chapter to the subject. We've used this software for five years now and it's infinitely better than it ever was, due primarily to Tim Barwick's penchant for preferences. Thanks, Tim. And we're sorry about the windows....

General Preferences

Control over sounds, text, and Network News are kept under General Preferences. Click on the My AOL icon on the toolbar, then choose Preferences. When the Preferences window opens, choose General Preferences (see Figure 9-2). There are a number of controls here. Here's what each one does:

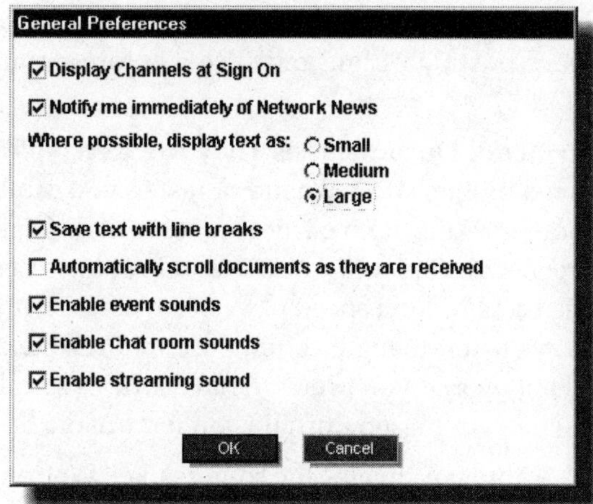

Figure 9-2: The General Preferences window provides control over the most frequently changed options in the program.

- **Display Channels at Sign On.** Shows the Channels window when you first come online. If you don't use the Channels window to navigate America Online, you may prefer to turn this option off. (On is the default setting.)
- **Notify Me Immediately of Network News.** Turns on the Network News announcements that flash across your screen occasionally, such as when America Online is about to go down for regular maintenance. You don't need to do anything to get these messages—they automatically appear on your screen, and they don't interrupt what you're doing. If you would prefer not to receive these messages while you're online, turn off this option. (On is the default setting.)
- **Where Possible, Display Text As.** Provides control over the size of most text that's received online. If you're using an SVGA monitor or a large monitor, incoming text may be too small for you to read. Some people have trouble reading small text (as does Jennifer: note that her text is set to Large in Figure 9-2 so it isn't lost on her larger-than-normal screen). No matter what causes the problem, this control offers the fix. (The default is Medium.)

- **Save Text With Line Breaks.** Gives you the option of curtailing the software's habit of adding a line break (also known as a *hard return*) at the end of each line. Although there are special conditions under which you might need line breaks at the end of each line (some DOS word processors require it, for example), text shouldn't have breaks at the end of each line unless you insert one yourself with the Return key on your keyboard. Disabling this function is useful if you want to type a reply to a message board posting offline and save it before signing on to post. (On is the default.)
- **Automatically Scroll Documents as They Are Received.** Scrolls articles as they are received online. At 2400 baud or faster, you can't read this fast, so scrolling incoming text is of no particular value at this speed or faster. It makes the screen a busy place to watch, and in some cases may actually slow down the transmission speed of text transfers. That's why the default is Off. It's always better to log incoming text and read text like this after you sign off. However, if you prefer to have articles scroll as they are received, for whatever reason, turn this preference on.
- **Enable Event Sounds.** Activates the sounds like "Welcome" when you sign on and "You have mail" when mail is waiting for you. If your machine can play these sounds (some machines can't—read Chapter 7, "Chat," for details on this subject) and you don't want to hear them, turn this control off. (On is the default.)
- **Enable Chat Room Sounds.** Activates member-sent sounds in chat rooms. Some chat rooms are especially sound oriented (see Chapter 7 for a discussion of chat rooms). Try LaPub for an example. These people love to laugh out loud and slap one another on the back—quite aurally. To hear these sounds, you must have them installed on your machine, your machine must be sound compatible, and you must leave this preference turned on. (On is the default.)
- **Disable Streaming Sound.** Gives you the option of turning off the sound that accompanies some graphics online. Graphics that have accompanying music and/or voices will download the sound data to your computer as the graphic renders. This can be slow-going for some older computers, though America Online has already anticipated this by automatically disabling it for members connecting at speeds below 9600 baud. As long as your computer can handle it, you'll probably want to keep this enabled so you don't miss one of the newer features of the AOL software. (On is the default).

Toolbar Preferences

For many, the toolbar (the row of buttons usually found at the top of your screen) is an invaluable navigational aid for America Online. And as such, some customization is only natural (see Figure 9-3). Click the Toolbar icon in the Preferences window and follow along as we discuss each of the toolbar commands.

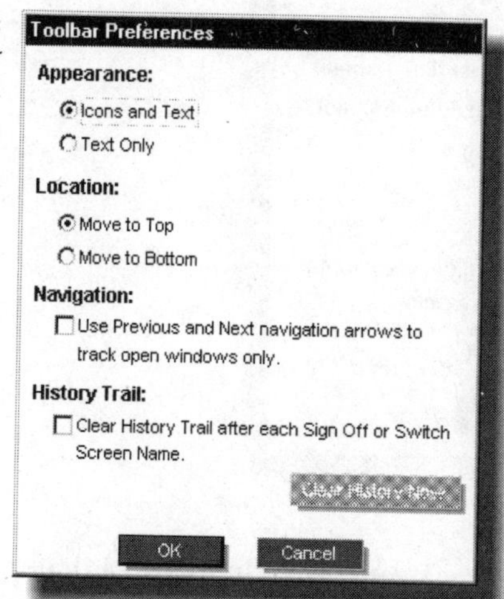

Figure 9-3: Keep track of your toolbar with options befitting a master craftsman.

- **Appearance.** Lets you streamline the toolbar for more screen space. Keep the default *Icons and Text* enabled for the full effect, or change it to *Text Only* to see the icons as labels only (all functionality remains).
- **Location.** Allows you to reposition the toolbar between the top of the screen (keep the default *Move to Top* enabled) and the bottom of the screen (*Move to Bottom*).
- **Navigation.** Gives you the option of using the *Previous and Next navigation arrows to track open windows only* rather than all windows you've visited, including those you've already closed. We suggest you enable this option—if you've closed a window, you probably won't want to be bothered with it again. You can always select it from your history list to return if you want (your history list is available when you click the down arrow next to the address box). (Off is the default.)
- **History Trail.** Offers the convenience of cleaning up behind you. The toolbar keeps a history of places you've visited visible and accessible to anyone using your software. If you don't want others to know where you've been, enable the *Clear the History Trail After Each Sign Off or Switch Screen Name* option. (Off is the default.)

Mail Preferences

Electronic mail is an important part of America Online (e-mail is discussed in Chapter 3). Here are the preferences that apply to your e-mail (see Figure 9-4).

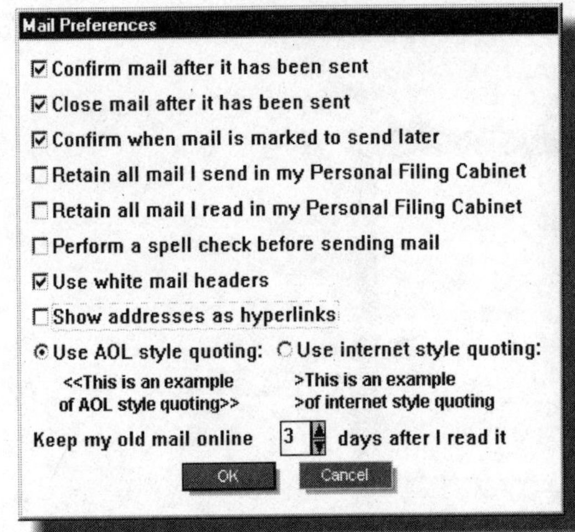

Figure 9-4: The Mail Preferences offer control over mail sent and received.

- **Confirm Mail After It Has Been Sent.** Gives you a dialog box after your mail has been sent. If you send a lot of mail, you may prefer to turn this preference off. (The default is On.)
- **Close Mail After It Has Been Sent.** Closes the e-mail window after you've sent mail to the recipient. If you would like to keep a document you've already sent open on your screen, turn this preference off. (The default is On.)
- **Confirm When Mail Is Marked to Send Later.** Gives you a dialog box after you click the Send Later button on a piece of mail letting you know that the mail has indeed been marked to send later. Again, if you send a lot of mail, you may prefer to turn this preference off. (The default is On.)
- **Retain All Mail I Send in My Personal Filing Cabinet.** Keeps a copy of the mail you send on your hard disk (the Personal Filing Cabinet is discussed in Chapter 3). This is useful if you want to keep a permanent record of your mail. Note: The Sent Mail command under the Mail Center icon accesses the mail that AOL holds for you on their hard disks at

headquarters. This is a courtesy, and the amount of mail held there is variable. Only your Personal Filing Cabinet is capable of automatically storing your mail indefinitely. (The default is Off.)

- **Retain All Mail I Read in My Personal Filing Cabinet.** Keeps a copy of the mail you have read on your hard disk. Be careful: under certain conditions, this can balloon the size of your Personal Filing Cabinet on your hard disk. If you subscribe to Internet mailing lists, for example, your Personal Filing Cabinet could grow in size very quickly. (The default is Off.)
- **Perform a Spell Check Before Sending Mail.** Checks your mail's text for spelling errors before it is sent. If you aren't a good speller or want to be sure that mail goes out looking its very best, enable this preference. (The default is Off.)
- **Use White Mail Headers.** Lets you see an e-mail's routing information (subject, date, sender, recipient) with a white background. If you disable this option, this information will appear with a shaded background. Disable this option if you like to see the obvious difference between routing information and content. (The default is On.)
- **Show Addresses as Hyperlinks.** Displays the e-mail addresses of the sender and recipient(s) as hyperlinks, allowing you to simply click on their names for individual replies. Enable this option if find yourself replying to specific individuals often. (The default is Off.)
- **Use AOL Style Quoting** and **Use Internet Style Quoting.** Allows you to toggle between AOL's style of quoting text (<< and >> around the text) or the Internet's style (> in front of each line only). If you frequently send e-mail across the Internet, you may prefer Internet style. (The default is AOL style.)
- **Keep My Old Mail Online *X* Days After I Read It.** Lets you set the length of time read mail will remain accessible (you can access it with the Old Mail command under the Mail Center icon). You can go as high as 7 days and as low as 1 day. If you like the security of knowing your mail is available for a while, increase the length of time. If you would prefer mail be removed shortly after you read it for enhanced privacy or simplicity, lower the number. Note that if you increase the number of days, the missing mail will not reappear—the change applies only to future mail. (The default is 3 days.)

WWW Preferences

The Microsoft Internet Explorer Web browser may be fully integrated into your AOL software, but it has enough features to qualify as the standalone application it is. Like all good software, it can be configured to your liking (see Figure 9-5). Keep in mind that these preferences should be set before you enter the Web, and that like most of America Online's preferences, you can set them whether you're online or off.

The interface for these preferences is currently under development, as is the number of preferences for which you'll be provided control. Don't be surprised if they have changed by the time you read this. Although the specifics might change, the general purpose of the commands will remain the same. Each one is discussed in the following sections.

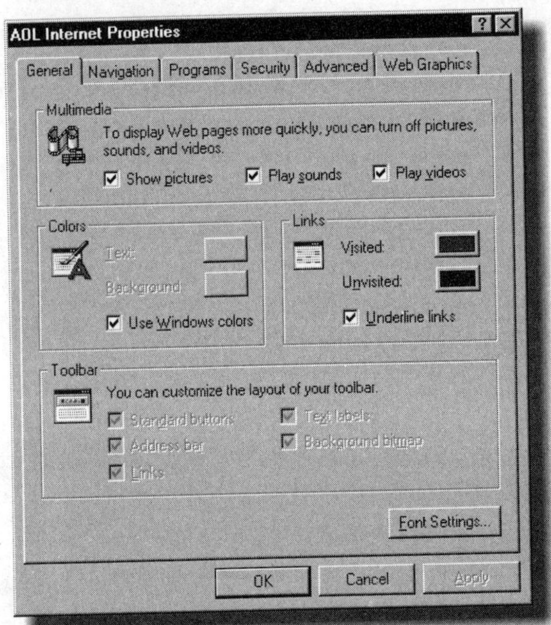

Figure 9-5: The AOL Internet Properties window provides a plethora of preferences.

General Preferences

- **Show Pictures, Play Sounds,** and **Play Videos.** Shows graphics, sounds, and videos respectively when enabled (the default) and hides them when disabled. Turn them off if you seek faster connections.

- **Colors.** Allows you to set the text and background colors shown in Web pages. We strongly suggest you use the default colors for your computer.
- **Links.** Controls how visited and unvisited hyperlinks appear. The defaults are usually the best.
- **Toolbar.** The standard Microsoft Internet Explorer toolbar is not used in this integration, thus the *Toolbar* option is not available.
- **Font Settings.** Lets you designate the font used in Web pages.

Navigation Preferences

- **Customize.** Allows you to designate your start page (the page at which you'd like to start when you first enter the Web or when you click the small house icon on your toolbar). Change this to another URL address if you'd like to begin at that page instead. (The default setting is the address for AOL's own Web site.)
- **History.** Lets you designate the size of your browser's cache, which holds the most recent pages and graphics you've accessed from the Web. There's a great value here: if, for example, you return to a page that you've visited recently, the browser will find the page in its cache—on your hard disk—and retrieve it from there rather than taking the time to go "out on the Web" for the information. Local access is *much* faster. The preference allows you to set the amount of hard disk space you want to allocate for the cache. Start with the default if you have that amount of space to spare. If you frequently visit a number of different sites, this number might be too low—something you'll know when frequently visited sites' pages have to be downloaded each time they're visited. If you only visit a site or two on a regular basis, try decreasing this value.
- **Clear History.** Removes all pages that have been saved on your hard disk. You may wish to enable this option if you want to revisit those pages and have them update with new information or if Web pages seem to display very slowly.

Program Preferences

- **Mail and News options.** Disabled for this version of the browser.
- **Viewers.** Lets you designate which viewer application(s) will be used when you try to open files from the Internet.

Security Preferences

- **Content Advisor.** Helps control what content can be viewed, a particularly useful feature for parents.
- **Certificates.** Helps you authenticate specific sites.
- **Active Content.** Lets you choose what type of software Web sites can download and run, such as ActiveX and Java. You may want to disable these options for security. (The default is On for all.)
- **Safety Level.** Allows you to set the security level of your Web browser. Web sites often send information to your hard disk. Usually data like this is benign and fundamental to the viewing of the associated page, but downloaded data can contain a computer virus. The *High* safety level setting simply avoids all unsafe situations, *Medium* will notify you of potentially unsafe situations and let you make your own choice (the default), and *None* will not notify you of any possibly unsafe situations. (For further discussion of downloaded data, see the Martha's Cookies sidebar in this chapter.)

Advanced Preferences

- **Warnings.** Lets you select what type of things you'd like the browser to look out for and warn you about. You may want to disable some of these options, though we suggest you enable *Warn Before Accepting "Cookies"* until you are more experienced. See the "Martha's Cookies" sidebar for more information on this topic.
- **Temporary Internet Files.** Your browser stores Web pages as it encounters them on the assumption that you visit the same pages regularly. By saving them on your hard disk, your browser doesn't have to download the page each time you visit. This preference lets you change how often newer versions of these files are saved, how much disk space is used to store them, and where they are kept. *Settings* also lets you clear the browser's cache by deleting them—when you need the disk space, for example, or when you want to force the browser to reload all Web pages it encounters.

- A variety of options at the bottom are available for advanced users. For beginners, the defaults will serve you well.

Martha's Cookies

Sometimes, Web sites need to know a bit about you. Even though it might not seem so at first, it's a reasonable requirement. Let's say you visit Martha Stewart's Web site often at **http://www.marthastewart.com**. This site is rampant with cookies (appropriate, we suppose, for a cookbook author). Here's an example: Martha's site requires a membership and a password. When you visit the site, it needs to know if you're a member or a first-time visitor. Each is treated differently: it wouldn't do for the site to ask for a password from a first-time visitor.

How does marthastewart.com know if you've visited before? It plants a cookie on your hard disk—a benign string of characters that are meaningless to anyone and anything but marthastewart.com—when you first become a member. Every time you visit after that, Martha's Web site looks for that cookie. If the cookie is found, marthastewart.com assumes you're a member and asks for your password. If there's no cookie, a first-time visitor routine is invoked.

So that's what a cookie is: usually a short (rarely more than 100 bytes) string of seemingly nonsensical (but unique and identifiable) characters, stored on your hard disk by a Web site, for that site's use whenever you visit.

Most cookies are benign, but by definition, receipt of a cookie means remote software wants to put something on your hard disk. The request could portend a virus. That's why the browser intercepts cookies and asks you about them.

What should you do when you encounter a cookie? It's really a matter of knowing the site that's making the request. If marthastewart.com wants to put a cookie on your hard disk, you can be pretty sure it's benign. But if the request comes from a site you know little about, it could pay to be wary. If you reject a cookie, it won't hurt anything. You can always accept it later.

Web Graphics

- **Use Compressed Graphics.** Gives you a choice in how you'd like to view the graphics in Web pages. If you prefer speed over scenery, keep this option enabled. Keep in mind that the Use Compressed Graphics option will produce saved images (if you elect to save them or if you view them in your Temporary Internet Files collection) in a special .art format that can only be opened by your AOL software but not with other applications. To save a graphic in more traditional formats—PICT, .bmp, .gif, or .jpg—simply disable this option. To see the Web in its full glory (if you don't mind waiting a little longer), again disable this option and make sure the *Show Pictures* option under General is enabled. (The default is On.) Keep in mind that "compressed graphics" can sometimes cause problems with complex Web images, so if you see something that doesn't quite look right, turn this preference off, clear your cache (see "Temporary Internet files," earlier in this chapter), and reload the Web page.

Chat Preferences

If you're fond of chat rooms, look these preferences over carefully (see Figure 9-6; chat rooms are discussed in Chapter 7).

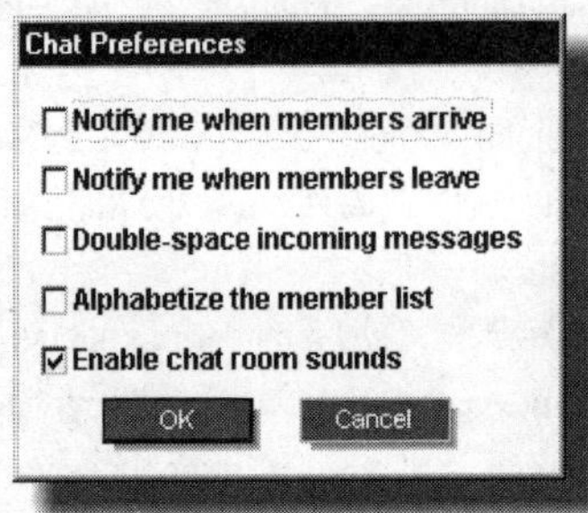

Figure 9-6: The Chat Preferences provide control over your chat room environment.

- **Notify Me When Members Arrive.** Causes the OnlineHost to place a line in your chat room window announcing the entrance of every arriving member. Hosts and Guides love this feature, and it's helpful for all of us when we're in a room that doesn't have a lot of comings and goings. If the members in a room are transitory—as people in lobbies, for instance, tend to be—you will probably want to leave this preference off. (The default is Off.)

- **Notify Me When Members Leave.** Same as the preceding preference, except the notification is provided when the member leaves, rather than arrives in, the room. Again, it's helpful for hosts and Guides. (The default is Off.)
- **Double-Space Incoming Messages.** Makes incoming messages easier to read. It also halves the amount of conversation that's displayed on your screen at any one time. It's a compromise, but the decision is yours. (The default is Off.)
- **Alphabetize the Member List.** Offers you the choice of viewing the member list (the little scroll box of member names in the upper right corner of chat windows) in alphabetical order or in the order in which members arrive in the chat room. If you want to watch comings and goings (and the Notify preferences are turned off), leave this preference turned off. If you tend to refer to the list often—perhaps to look up the profiles of or send Instant Messages to other members in the room—alphabetizing it may help. (The default is Off.)
- **Enable Chat Room Sounds.** Simply a second offering of the preference discussed earlier. It's listed under the General Preferences (see Figure 9-2) as well. You may turn it on or off in either place—the change will be made for you in both places. (The default is On.)

Download Preferences

If you do much downloading, you should (1) use the Download Manager and (2) examine the preferences listed on the next page (Figure 9-7 shows the Download Preferences dialog box, downloading is discussed in Chapter 6, and the Download Manager is discussed in Chapter 8).

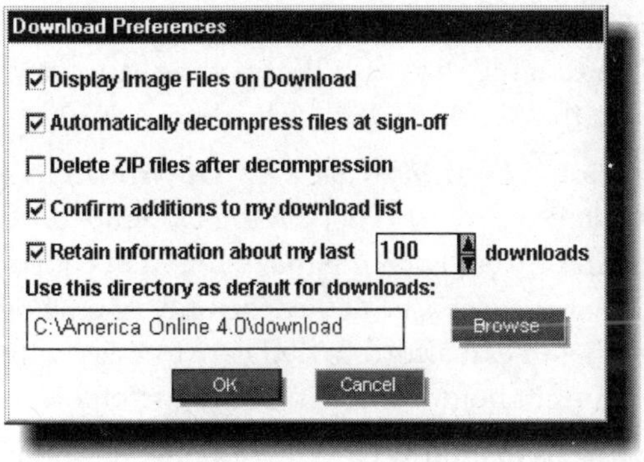

Figure 9-7: The Download Preferences dialog box provides control over your downloading configuration.

- **Display Image Files on Download.** Allows you to view most graphics as they're received. Viewing them online allows you to abort the download if you don't like (or need) what you see. It's best to leave this preference on unless your computer is very low on memory or very slow. (On is the default.)
- **Automatically Decompress Files at Sign-Off.** Uses AOL's built-in version of WinZip (for the PC) or StuffIt (for the Mac) to decompress any compressed files you have downloaded. America Online automatically decompresses these files when you sign off. If you would prefer that they not be decompressed, turn this preference off. If you download to a floppy, you will want to turn this preference off. (On is the default.)
- **Delete ZIP (or StuffIt) Files After Decompression.** Removes the archive from your disk after it's decompressed. Since many of us prefer to store the archive as a form of backup, this option defaults to the Off condition.
- **Confirm Additions to My Download List.** Causes the dialog box pictured in Figure 9-8 to appear whenever you add a file to your queue of files to be downloaded.

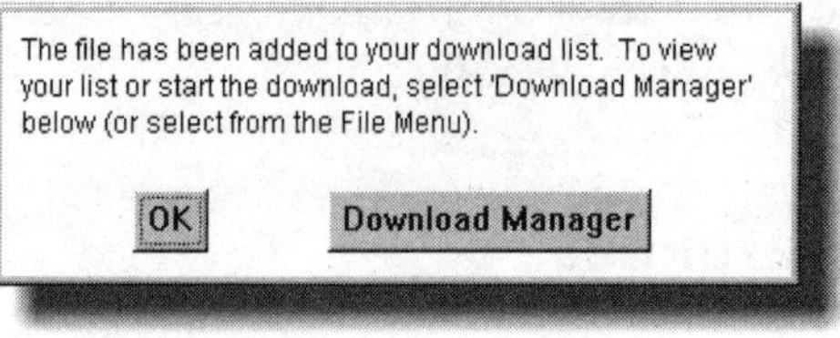
The file has been added to your download list. To view your list or start the download, select 'Download Manager' below (or select from the File Menu).
OK
Download Manager

Figure 9-8: AOL displays this dialog box whenever you add a file to your download queue. If you don't want to bother with it, turn the appropriate preference off.

This dialog box is a convenience if you like to visit the Download Manager every time you add a file to its list. It's an annoyance if you do not. If it annoys you, turn the preference off. (The default is On.)

- **Retain Information About My Last *XXX* Downloads.** Determines how many files are listed when you click on the Download Manager's Show Files Downloaded button. Each file that's retained consumes about 2K of your hard disk's storage space. You're the only one who knows how much of your hard disk you can afford to dedicate to this feature, so give this number some thought before changing it. (The default is 100 files.)
- **Use This Directory as Default For Downloads.** Lets you specify where you want to save downloaded files. You can manually type in a new directory, or you choose one using the Browse button. (The America Online 4.0 "download" directory is the default.)

Graphics Viewing Preferences

The Graphics Viewing Preferences pertain to the online viewing of graphics as they're received (see Figure 9-9; downloading graphics and the online graphics viewers are discussed in Chapter 6).

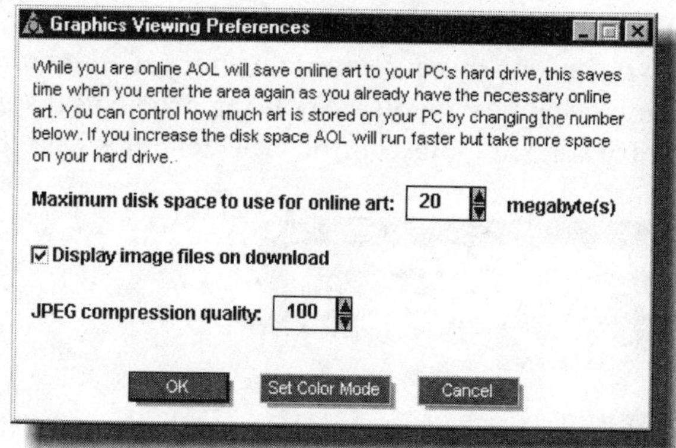

Figure 9-9: The Graphics Viewing Preferences provide control over graphics that are received online.

- **Maximum Disk Space to Use for Online Art.** Controls the size of the file that holds the graphics that adorn the windows you see online. If you visit a lot of places—exploratory journeys are notorious for this—your online art database can become huge. This not only squanders disk space, it also slows down America Online's performance. Twenty megabytes is about right if you have that amount of hard-disk space to spare. Use a smaller setting if you don't.
- **Display Image Files on Download.** A second offering of the preference discussed earlier in "Download Preferences" (see Figure 9-7). Again, this preference allows you to view most graphics as they're downloaded. Changing the preference here will change it under the Download Preferences as well. (On is the default.)
- **JPEG Compression Quality.** Allows you to set the rate of compression for JPEG graphics as they're received. JPEG is actually a compression method rather than a graphic format. It's a *lossy* compression method, meaning that some of the graphic's detail is lost when it's saved in the JPEG format. The "compression quality" number in Figure 9-9 ranges from 1 to 100. The higher this number, the less data is lost and the better quality the image is when you save a graphic using the JPEG method. Smaller compression quality numbers cause more data to be lost and image quality to be diminished. On the other hand, small compression quality figures mean smaller files. What's best? We say leave this number set to 100 unless you

are low on disk space or don't mind the quality loss. Always perform a test JPEG save before you commit a graphic to a lower number; once a graphic is saved, there's no going back. (The default is 100.)

- **Set Color Mode.** Available through the button on the bottom of the window; gives you the option of choosing the correct number of colors that your monitor can display (see Figure 9-10). Normally, America Online can determine this automatically, but not all monitors accurately report their capabilities. If you are noticing problems displaying images, you might try adjusting this control. (The default is Detect Automatically.)

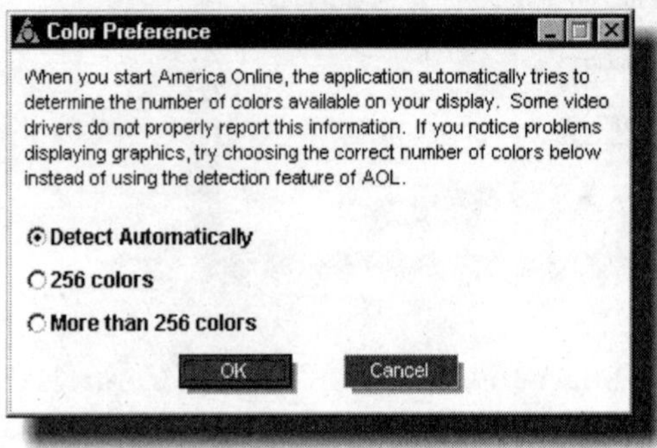

Figure 9-10: The Color Preference gives control over the number of colors AOL displays. Leave this at Detect Automatically unless you are experiencing problems.

Passwords Preferences

Passwords keep other people from using your account and peeking in your files when you're not around. Once a password is stored, anyone using the machine on which it is stored can sign on and spend hours online, at your expense.

On the other hand, there are those of us for whom that potential simply doesn't exist. Perhaps you lock your computer when you're away, or the other people in your office or home are trustworthy beyond reproach. Tom signs on 5 or 10 times a day, and his computer is in his studio, which is sanctified ground. Typing his password 5 or 10 times a day is not only unnecessary, it's counterproductive. For this reason, he stores his password (Figure 9-11) and never has to type it in.

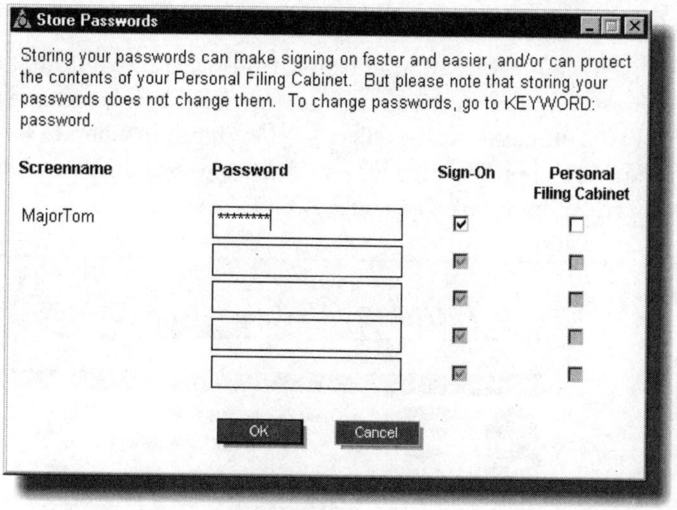

Figure 9-11: You can't read MajorTom's stored password. AOL displays only asterisks. The password, nonetheless, is there, and Tom doesn't have to type it in when he signs on.

Store Passwords

Storing your passwords can make signing on faster and easier, and/or can protect the contents of your Personal Filing Cabinet. But please note that storing your passwords does not change them. To change passwords, go to KEYWORD: password.

Screenname	Password	Sign-On	Personal Filing Cabinet
MajorTom	********	☑	☐

OK Cancel

The two columns beside the passwords let you designate what the password can (and cannot) be used for. When the *Sign-On* option is enabled, your stored password will be used for signing on only, which allows you to sign on quicker. Conversely, when the *Personal Filing Cabinet* option is enabled, AOL uses your password to protect its contents, requiring that anyone attempting to access your Personal Filing Cabinet type the password first. Enabling the first option makes access to AOL easier but less secure, while enabling the second makes access to your Personal Filing Cabinet harder and more secure. You can enable just one or both based on your needs.

Use the Sign-On option with care! America Online shows no pity when members call with unexpected bills run up by fellow office workers or members of the family. If there's a possibility that someone might access your account while you're away, don't utilize this feature. Finally, *never, ever, ever* use the stored password feature on a laptop installation. If someone is low enough to make off with your portable, they will undoubtedly be happy to run up a large bill at your expense. (The default is Off.)

Automatic AOL

Auto AOL (short for Automatic AOL) allows you to automatically send and receive mail and postings as well as download files you have marked for later retrieval. Automatic AOL is discussed in depth in Chapter 8, "Working Offline." These preferences let you designate activities, set schedules, and select screen names (see Figure 9-12).

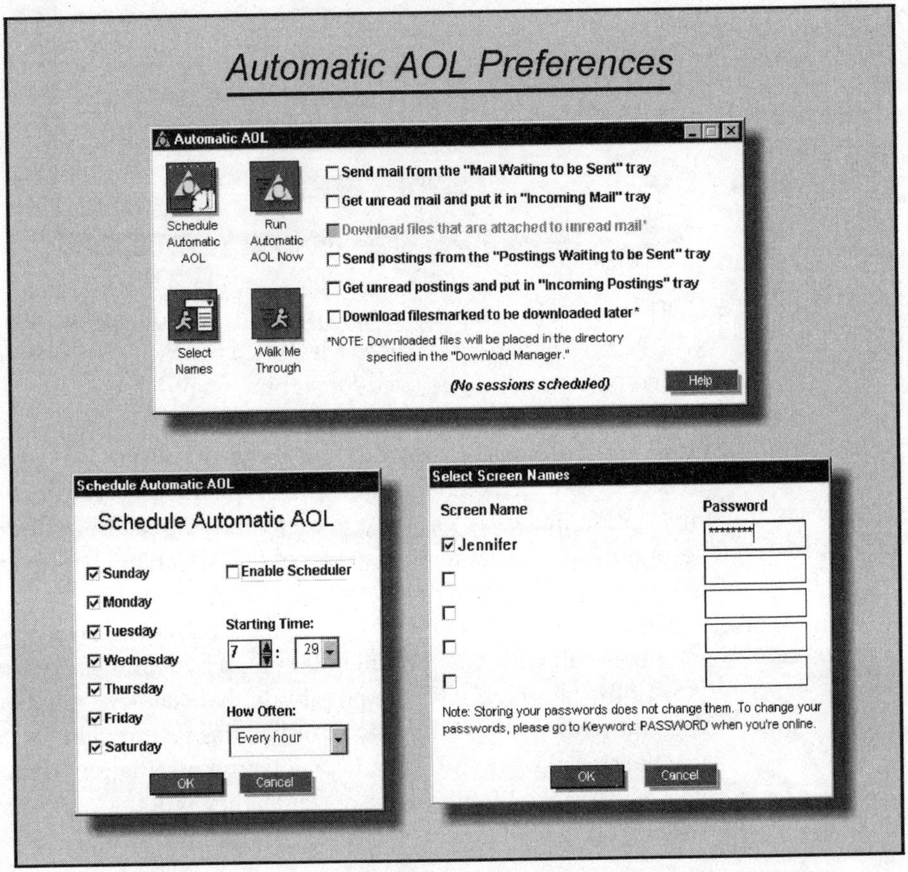

Figure 9-12: Set up the automatic transmission and retrieval feature with Automatic AOL preferences.

Automatic AOL Main Preferences

These preferences are found on the first window you see after clicking Auto AOL on the Preferences screen:

- **Send Mail From the "Mail Waiting to Be Sent" Tray.** Instructs Automatic AOL to send all mail marked to be sent later for the screen names you've selected under the Select Names button (described later). (The default is Off.)
- **Get Unread Mail and Put in the "Incoming Mail" Tray.** Directs Automatic AOL to read and save all new mail and file it in the Incoming/Saved Mail folder within your Personal Filing Cabinet. Again, only mail sent to the screen names you've designated for Automatic AOL will be retrieved. (The default is Off.)
- **Download Files That Are Attached to Unread Mail.** Instructs Automatic AOL to download all files that are encountered while reading your new mail. You may wish to disable this preference if you prefer to check that the file is one you want first. Note: All downloaded files will be placed in the directory specified in your Download Preferences described earlier. (The default is Off, and this option is not available until you've enabled the preceding one.)
- **Send Postings From the "Postings Waiting to Be Sent" Tray.** Tells Automatic AOL to send all message board and newsgroup postings composed and marked to be posted later for the screen names you've selected. (The default is Off.)
- **Get Unread Postings and Put in the "Incoming Postings" Tray.** Directs Automatic AOL to read and save all new postings from your selected message boards and newsgroups and file them in the Incoming/Saved Postings folder within your Personal Filing Cabinet. (The default is Off.)
- **Download Files Marked to Be Downloaded Later.** Tells Automatic AOL to download all files you have marked in your Download Manager. Note: Again, all downloaded files will be placed in the directory you specified in your Download Preferences. (The default is Off.)

Automatic AOL Scheduling Preferences

These preferences are accessible under the Schedule Automatic AOL button on the Automatic AOL Preferences window:

- **Day of the Week.** Allows you to choose any or all of the days you'd like Automatic AOL to run. (Default is all days.)
- **Enable Scheduler.** Turns on the scheduler. You must enable this option if you wish Automatic AOL to do an unattended session on the days and times you've set. (The default is Off.)
- **Starting Time.** Lets you select when your unattended Automatic AOL sessions will begin. You can specify any hour, but you are limited to only two possible starting points within each hour to avoid stress on the system. (The default varies.)
- **How Often.** Allows you to set the frequency at which you want Automatic AOL to sign on and perform its operations. Once a day is usually enough for most folks. Note: Your computer must be turned on in order for Automatic AOL to sign on. (The default is every hour.)

Automatic AOL Screen Name Preferences

These preferences are available under the Select Names button on the Automatic AOL Preferences window. Select Screen Names allows you to enable the screen name(s) you want Automatic AOL to use and enter the password(s) for each screen name. Note that your password isn't displayed as you type; asterisks representing each letter in your password appear instead.

Personal Filing Cabinet Preferences

The Personal Filing Cabinet (PFC) organizes your Favorite Places, e-mail, and newsgroup messages, among other things. As it stores some important items, preferences are provided to protect against accidental deletion. Other preferences control its size and organization (see Figure 9-13), as explained in the following list.

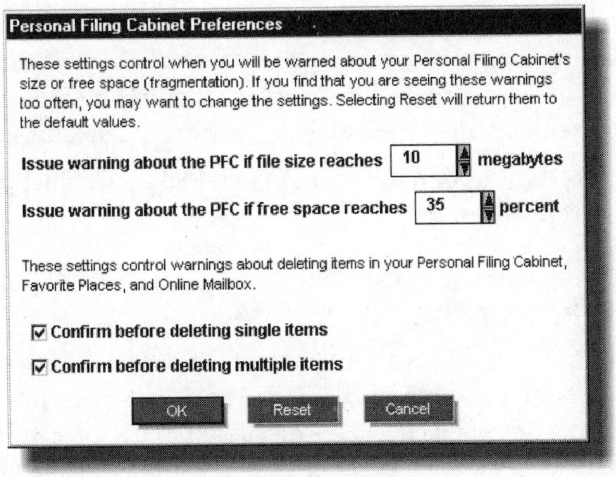

Figure 9-13: The Personal Filing Cabinet Preferences allow you to control the behavior and size of your Personal Filing Cabinet.

Personal Filing Cabinet Preferences

These settings control when you will be warned about your Personal Filing Cabinet's size or free space (fragmentation). If you find that you are seeing these warnings too often, you may want to change the settings. Selecting Reset will return them to the default values.

Issue warning about the PFC if file size reaches 10 megabytes

Issue warning about the PFC if free space reaches 35 percent

These settings control warnings about deleting items in your Personal Filing Cabinet, Favorite Places, and Online Mailbox.

☑ Confirm before deleting single items

☑ Confirm before deleting multiple items

OK Reset Cancel

- **Issue Warning About the PFC if File Size Reaches *XX* Megabytes.** Triggers the warning similar to that pictured in Figure 9-13 whenever the size of your Personal Filing Cabinet reaches the specified value. Large PFC files slow down your software, especially when you start the AOL software or change screen names. The smaller you set this value, the more often you will receive warnings (assuming you're using your Personal Filing Cabinet in the first place). If your software takes an unusually long time to start, reduce this value. The default value is 10 megabytes.
- **Issue Warning About the PFC if Free Space Reaches *XX* Percent.** Triggers a message whenever your PFC needs to be compacted. Free space will occur whenever you delete an entry or a number of entries from the PFC. Free space is cumulative, and if it exceeds the value shown in Figure 9-13, you'll be notified. It's a simple matter to compact your Personal Filing Cabinet, and you can do it while you're offline (compacting the Personal Filing Cabinet is discussed in Chapter 3). The default value is 35 percent.
- **Confirm Before Deleting Single Items.** Allows you to turn on or off the confirmation notice when deleting an item. You may wish to turn this on if you're concerned about accidentally deleting something important. (The default setting is On.)

- **Confirm Before Deleting Multiple Items.** Gives you the option of enabling or disabling the confirmation notice when deleting two or more items. Unless you delete multiple items frequently, it is best to keep this on in case you accidentally select more than one item. (The default setting is On.)

Note: Password protection for your Personal Filing Cabinet is set under the Passwords Preferences.

Spelling Preferences

The built-in spell checker is a convenient feature that allows you to check the spelling and punctuation of your text in e-mail, postings, Instant Messages, and chat rooms (the spell checker is discussed in Chapter 3, "Electronic Mail & the Personal Filing Cabinet"). The spell checker is available under the Edit menu when you have a document open or from within a new mail window when you select Compose Mail from the Mail Center icon. Consult Figure 9-14 as we discuss the preferences listed below.

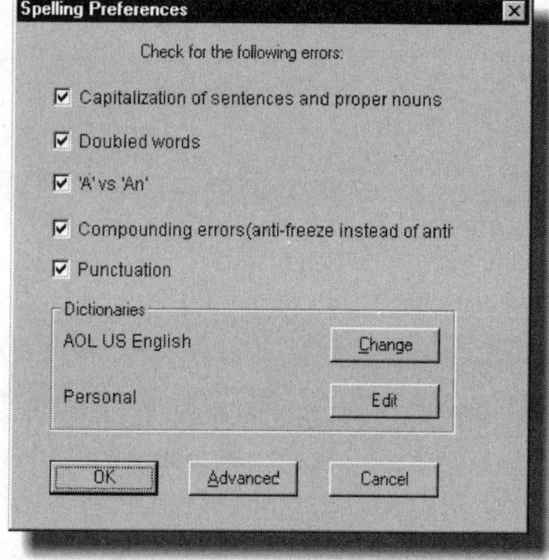

Figure 9-14: Spelling Preferences provide control over America Online's built-in spell checker.

- **Capitalization of Sentences and Proper Nouns.** Flags the initial letter of sentences and proper nouns that are lowercase when they should be capitalized. (The default is On.)
- **Doubled Words.** Watches for two identical words in succession and will delete the second occurrence for you if found, with the exception of legitimate doubled words. (The default is On.)

- **'A' vs. 'An'.** Flags the article *a* to *an* when it precedes a vowel (e.g., "an apple") and vice versa when it precedes a consonant (e.g., "a doctor"). (The default is On.)
- **Compounding Errors.** Checks all compound words (those with hyphens) for errors, such as *anti-freeze* or *spell-checker*, neither of which should be compound words. (The default is On.)
- **Punctuation.** Flags general punctuation mistakes, such as the incorrect placement of commas and the inappropriate punctuation of parentheses or quotations. (The default is On.)
- **Dictionaries.** Allows you to select a different dictionary as well as edit your personal dictionary, which you add to each time you ask the spell checker to "learn" something. (The default dictionary is U.S. English.)
- **Advanced Spelling Preferences.** Offers even more spelling, punctuation, and grammar error checks. (The default for all advanced preferences is On.)

Font Preferences

The Font Preferences allow you to change your preference for the font, size, color, and style of your text online. For example, if you have difficulty reading online text, you may be more comfortable with a larger size or even a different font. You can select any font you have installed on your computer, as long as it's TrueType. AOL 4.0 won't support PostScript fonts, though it can display them. The choices you make will apply to all your text. Consult Figure 9-15 as we discuss the font preferences.

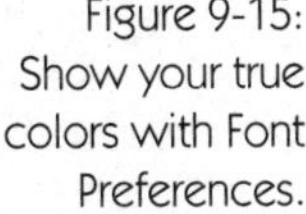

Figure 9-15: Show your true colors with Font Preferences.

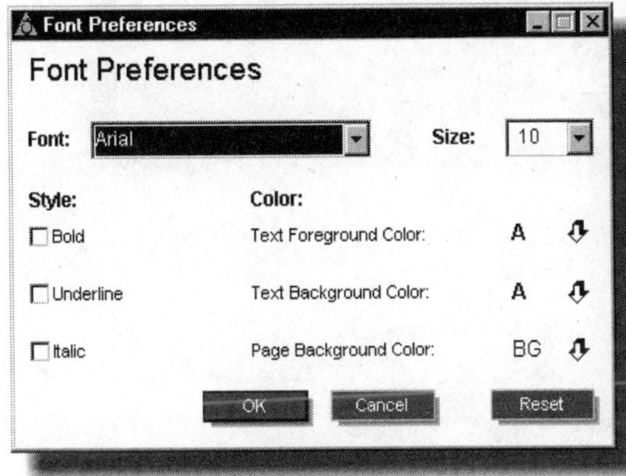

- **Font.** Sets the fonts you'd like to use. Again, any TrueType font installed on your computer can be selected here.
- **Size.** Sets the size you'd like, ranging from 8 (quite small) to 72 (very large). (The default is 10.)
- **Style.** Changes the text style to *Bold, Underline, Italic,* or any combination. We advise against any style that will make your text difficult for others to read. (The defaults are Off.)
- **Color.** Sets the text foreground, text background, and page background colors. If the standard black on white doesn't suit you, experiment with this preference to find a combination that does. Use the small down arrows next to each color option to choose a new color.

Language Preferences

Language Preferences allow you to select any additional languages you may want to use while on America Online (no, this isn't a universal translator). Simply select it from the column on the left and click the Add button (see Figure 9-16). Once selected, your language(s) will appear in the Language menus of windows where language is significant.

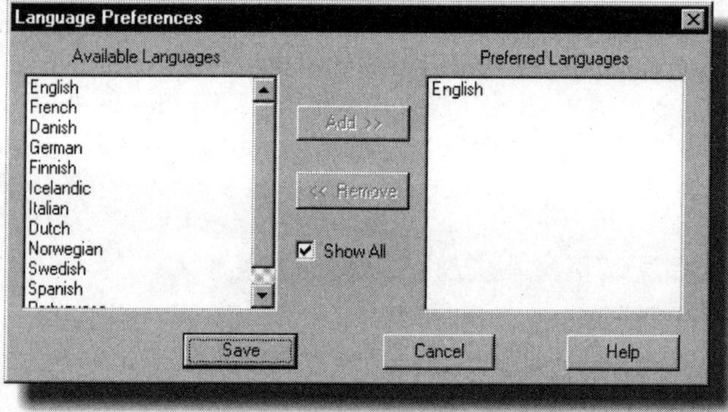

Figure 9-16: Language Preferences let you designate the languages you use online.

Marketing Preferences

Marketing Preferences let you control the types of offers you'd like to receive as a member of America Online, if any at all. As the online industry is still a moving target, don't be surprised if these preferences change in the near future. Consult Figure 9-17 as we discuss the preferences in the list below.

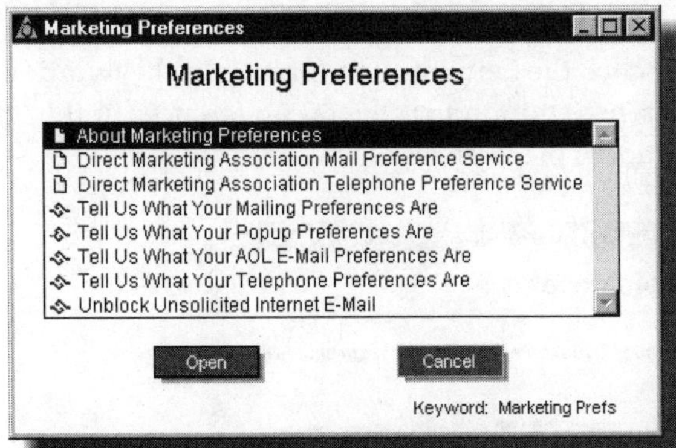

Figure 9-17: Add and remove yourself from lists with Marketing Preferences.

- **Mailing Preferences.** Let you communicate your interests to America Online should they share their mailing list with other companies. If you'd rather not receive mailings from other companies or America Online, you can designate either or both here. (The default is to receive mailings.)
- **Pop-up Preferences.** Also let you communicate your interests to America Online for the special "pop-up" offers that sometimes appear on your screen immediately after you sign on. You can elect to limit these product offers as well. (The default is to receive pop-ups.)
- **E-Mail Preferences.** Let you designate interest in e-mailed offers as well as turn them off. (The default is to receive e-mail offers.)
- **Telephone Preferences.** Relate to offers by phone, with the same options as those just listed. (The default is to receive phone offers.)
- **Unblock Unsolicited E-Mail.** Lets you begin receiving all the junk mail that America Online filters out for members by default. Unless you really wants scads of unsolicited mail, we don't recommend you enable this option. (The default is Off.)

Buddy List Preferences

Buddy Lists allow you to keep a list of friends or colleagues and then find out if they are online at the click of a button (Buddy Lists are discussed in Chapter 7). It's a convenient feature, and equally convenient are the controls America Online gives you to set up this feature to suit your needs. You cannot access Buddy List Preferences from the Preferences dialog, and you can't access them unless you're online. Instead, select Buddy Lists from the My AOL icon, click the Setup button (or just use keyword: **Buddy**), and then click the Preferences button for general preferences or the Privacy Preferences for additional preferences.

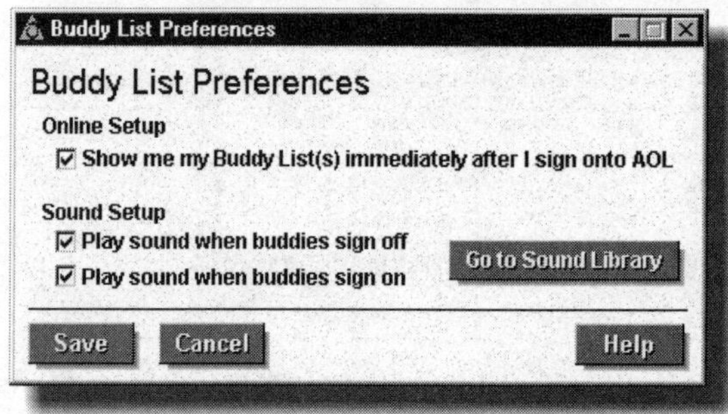

Figure 9-18: Buddy List Preferences provide control over America Online's Buddy List feature.

General Preferences

The General Preferences are preferences that apply to the Buddy List feature independently of the Buddy List privacy preferences, which are discussed next. General preferences have to do with the display of your Buddy List window and its associated sounds.

- **Show Me My Buddy List(s) Immediately After I Sign Onto AOL.** Displays your Buddy Lists automatically when you first connect to America Online. If this preference is off, you will have to issue the Buddy List command (from the My AOL icon) before America Online will monitor the comings and goings of your buddies for you. (The default setting is On.)
- **Play Sound When Buddies Sign On.** Gives you an aural alert any time someone in one of your Buddy Lists logs on to AOL. This keeps you from having to constantly check the Buddy List window.
- **Play Sound When Buddies Sign Off.** Exactly the opposite of the preceding option, noisily notifying you that one of your buddies has taken off.

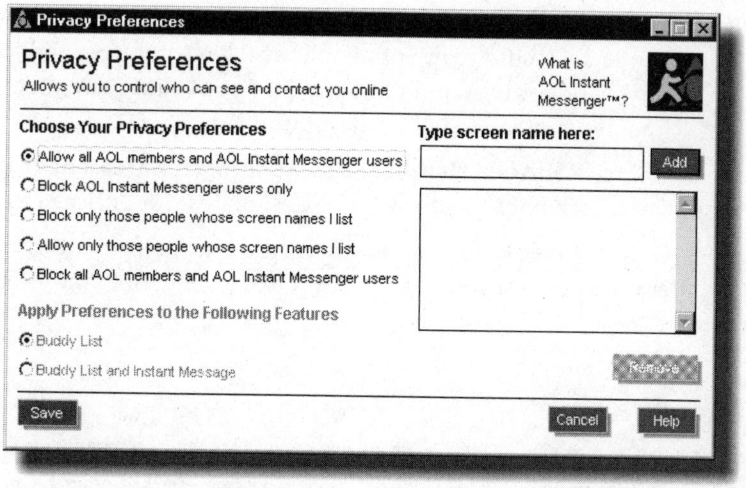

Figure 9-19: Don't want to be a buddy? Here's where you can declare yourself off limits to other people's Buddy Lists.

Privacy Preferences

Privacy Preferences determine two things: (1) who can add *your* screen name to *their* Buddy List (set with the first *Buddy List* option at the bottom of Figure 9-19) and (2) who may list you as a buddy *as well as* contact you via Instant Message (set with the second *Buddy List and Instant Message* option, also at the bottom of Figure 9-19). Blocking people from adding you to their Buddy List also prevents them from sending you Buddy Chat invitations as well as finding you when they select the Locate Member Online command from the People icon in the toolbar. Blocking Instant Messages means others cannot send them to you (if they try, they will be notified that you aren't currently signed on), and you cannot send them to those you've blocked. You may choose one of these two privacy options, along with one of the following five people options:

- **Allow All AOL Members and AOL Instant Messenger Users.** Lets everyone see and contact you. This preference does not distinguish between the two Buddy List privacy options. Allowing all people means allowing all options as well.
- **Block AOL Instant Messenger Users Only.** Blocks those who use AOL Instant Messenger (on the Internet) from seeing you or from both seeing and contacting you.
- **Block Only Those People Whose Screen Names I List.** Prevents a specific group of people from seeing you or both seeing and contacting you. To designate them, type their screen names in the box and click Add.

- **Allow Only Those People Whose Screen Names I List.** Allows you to enter a specific group of people who have your permission to list your name or both list and contact you. Again, designate them by typing their names and clicking the Add button.
- **Block All AOL Members and AOL Instant Messenger Users.** Does exactly what it says—you can designate it for either privacy option.

Be sure to click the Save button in the lower left-hand corner of the window after making your selections or the changes will not take effect.

MacPreferences

Preference is what having a Mac is all about, according to Jennifer. America Online doesn't skimp on preferences either, particularly not on the Macintosh. Mac AOL offers fifteen preference categories; most correspond to those we've described for Windows. Additional preferences are: Helpers, AOL Link, and Speech. We're missing the Graphics preference (options are available in other preferences, however) and Marketing (which is available at keywords: **Marketing Prefs**). The preferences that differ between the Mac and PC versions of AOL are described in the following paragraphs.

General Preferences on the Mac look significantly different than they do on Windows. Of the preferences that are missing, several are not needed due to the elegance of the Mac's programming (such as Save Text With Line Breaks). You can enable chat room sounds under the Chat Preferences.

Mail Preferences are virtually identical, aside from some wording differences. An option exclusive to Mac members is Use White Mail Headers, which allows you to see the preliminary information in e-mail (subject, sender, recipients, date) with a white background instead of a gray background (the default).

Filing Cabinet Preferences can be set to delete items in various locations automatically, from one week to one year after arrival. You are encouraged to use these automatic deletion features, especially for the list of downloaded files and offline newsgroups that you don't generally want to keep for long anyway. Not only does this delete old files, but it automatically "compacts" your Personal Filing Cabinet to keep it smaller and faster. In fact, Jennifer recommends you also manually compact your Personal Filing Cabinet once a month or so—you'll find this option at the bottom of the window.

Font Preferences on the Mac allow you to set different formats for writing mail and for chat, unlike in Windows, where the same choice must be made for both.

Helpers Preferences let you modify and expand the support for Web pages and other multimedia files containing special encoded data. AOL decodes most of this special information automatically, but you have the option of using a separate application to view or open it.

AOL Link gives you the ability to use other Internet applications (such as Netscape) over the AOL connection, as well as allowing you to configure AOL Link if you use an Internet Service Provider. The Use AOL Link When Connecting With A Modem option checks to make sure your Mac is configured to use AOL Link; if it is not, it will do so automatically. The Manual Configuration options let you set or restore your settings as needed.

Toolbar Preferences offer the option of entirely unanchoring the toolbar and letting it "float" on our screen. You can also remove any customized icons you may have added to the toolbar.

Speech Preferences enable AOL to read online text for you, using Apple's built-in speech manager. Here you can select the voice, rate, and pitch, then try out your settings with the Test button (Jennifer's favorite is Deranged on Slow and Low; try it and you'll see why). The Speak Button Under Cursor... option lets you choose a key to press when you want to hear the name of a button; just hold down that key, move your cursor over the button in question, and click. Talking Chat Rooms Preferences let you listen to text in chat rooms.

Moving On

Explore these preferences. Alter every one of them and live with the changes for a week. You may discover something you didn't know about yourself! It can pay to be persnickety.

Now it's time for some rewards. You've learned how to do almost everything with your client software, now it's time to get out there and—as Nike would say—just do it. "But where shall I go?" you ask. Read on. We're about to make some suggestions.

CHAPTER 10

Destinations

- Staying Informed
- The Computing Channel
- Amusements
- The Personal Finance Channel
- The Research & Learn Channel
- The Health Channel
- The Shopping Channel

If you've been reading this book from beginning to end, you have your America Online black belt now. You can download files, surf the Internet, and chat it up with the best of them. You know more than most people know about AOL, even if you've never been online.

Now it's time for your reward. On the next few pages, we want to show you some of the remarkable online destinations AOL has to offer. These are the riches of Solomon, and like a truly wealthy person, your riches are yours to enjoy every day.

Staying Informed

In the beginning of the information age, people got their news from newspapers. At best, newspapers offered the news once a day—a small inconvenience considering the limited expectations of the public in those days. Radio emerged 70 years ago, offering immediate "on-the-scene" coverage. But there were no pictures, and if you weren't listening when the news was broadcast, you missed it. Forty years ago, television brought pictures, but even today you're at the mercy of TV scheduling if you want the latest news.

What if you had access to the most up-to-date news and information all the time—exactly when and how you wanted it? What if you could see the pictures and hear the sounds while you're seated in front of your computer? The emergence of the News Channel (see Figure 10-1) as one of AOL's most popular destinations is testament to the synergy of medium and message.

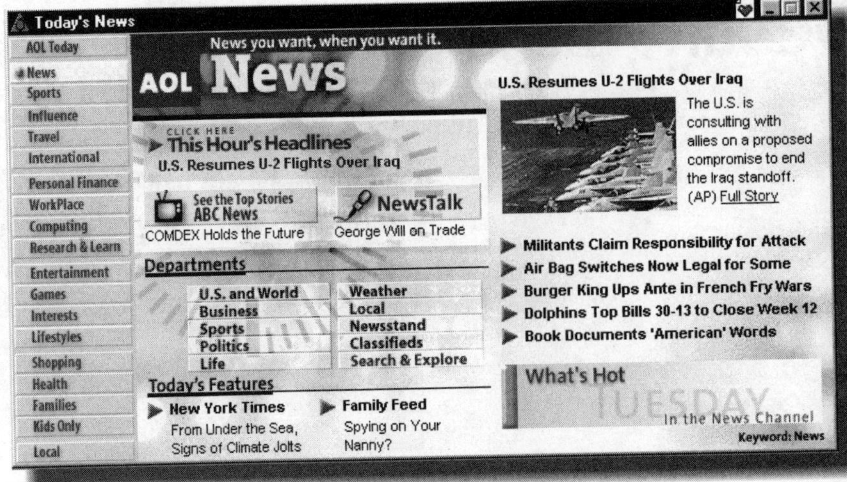

Figure 10-1: The News Channel connects you with an arsenal of information resources that are continually updated and maintained.

Know Your Tools

Before we go much further, we need to discuss some of the tools available to you as you browse the information resources available on AOL. You'll want to save some of the material you see, or print it, or specify the scope of your wanderings. Here's how it's done.

Saving Articles

Whenever an article appears on your screen in the frontmost window, it's available to be saved on your hard drive or a diskette. To save an article (news or otherwise—we're talking about any article, at any time), just choose Save from the File menu. You'll see a standard Save As dialog box where you can assign the article a name and file location.

Saved articles are pure text and can be opened with any word processor. (Hint: If you're using Windows, use the .txt filename extension so the material you save offers the most compatibility with any software you might use, such as a word processor or Windows Notepad.) You can use AOL's software to open any articles saved this way—whether you're online or off—by choosing Open from the File menu.

Printing Articles

You can print any article that appears in AOL's frontmost window. Using the File menu, choose Print and you'll see your computer's standard print dialog box. Make any necessary changes to the print configuration and click OK. America Online will print the article to your computer's currently selected printer. When you print directly like this, you won't have much control over the formatting of the printed page; if you want that kind of control, open the article with your word processor after you've saved it to your hard drive.

Keeping a Log

While AOL's news articles are informative, invaluable, and often fascinating, reading them online is not. We prefer to absorb information like that at our leisure, when the online clock isn't running.

The solution is found in AOL's Log Manager. When a log is turned on, all text appearing on your screen is recorded on your disk. An online session can get a bit hectic. Your memory of it might need some nudging once you've signed off. If you have a log file to refer to, you'll never forget where you've been or what you read. A log, like a flashlight, is available only if you need it but essential when you do.

Now that we've reread the preceding paragraph, we feel compelled to make a disclaimer: some things offer their own saving routines (World Wide Web pages—discussed in Chapter 4, "Using the Internet"—are a good example); others may have to be copied and pasted into a new document for saving. Generally, the logging feature is used for articles—AOL text files—so that they can be saved for later review.

To start a log: while you're online, click the My Files icon on the toolbar and choose Log Manager from the resulting menu. In the Logging window, open a Session Log by clicking the Open Log button in the lower part of the window. AOL will display a standard file-open dialog box complete with a suggested filename and location (see Figure 10-2). Make any filename/location changes you want and click Save. From then on, all the text you see onscreen will be saved on your disk.

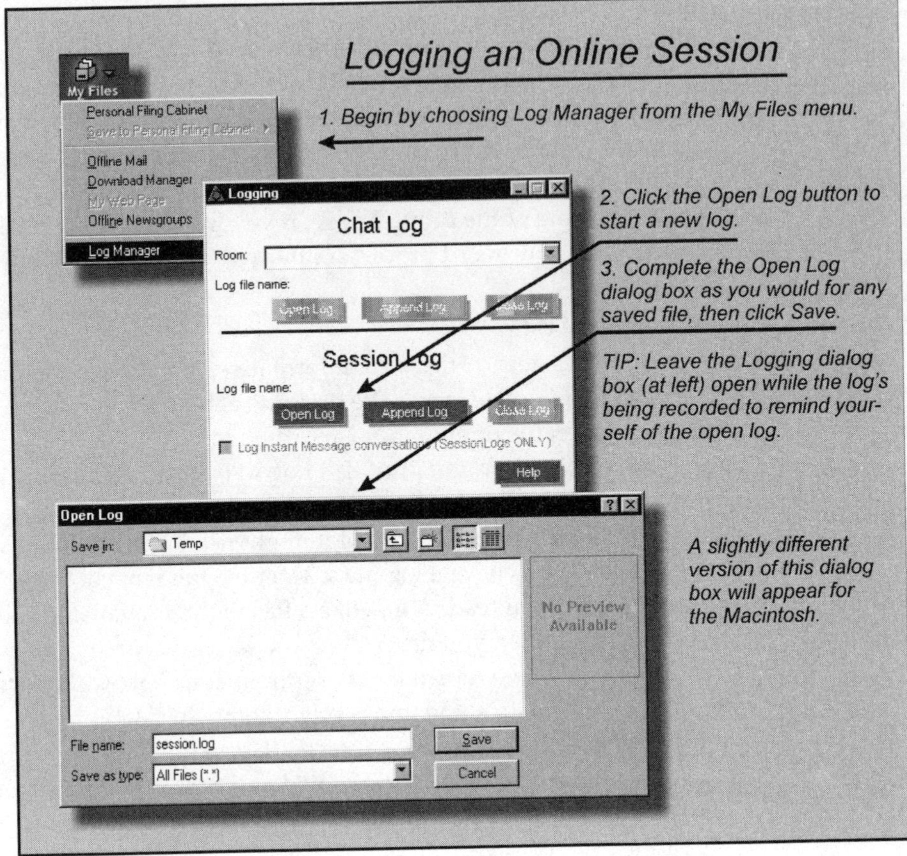

Figure 10-2: Log files capture and save onscreen activity to disk for later review.

If you look carefully at the center window in Figure 10-2, you will note two types of logs. The Session log is the one that captures articles like those discussed in this chapter; it doesn't capture chats and instant messages (we discuss those in Chapter 7).

A Few Notes About Logs

Logs are deceiving: at first they seem simple, but their potential is staggering—especially their potential for size. Here are a few notes to help you manage them.

- To capture the complete article in your log, you must double-click (open) the article's headline while you're online (and while logging is enabled, of course) and allow AOL to finish the transmission of the article to your computer (be sure it's complete: if the More button is active, then there's more to follow). When the hourglass cursor changes back to the arrow cursor, transmission is complete. You don't have to read it online—you don't even have to scroll to the end of it—you just have to receive it in its entirety.
- Log files can be as large as you want them to be, but they can grow quickly if you don't pay attention. Monitor your activity online while a log file is open as you would monitor your fuel gauge while traveling through Death Valley.
- You can always close the log or append an existing one by using the buttons in the Logging window (refer again to Figure 10-2). This is handy when you want to turn your log on and off; you can use the Close and Append buttons as you would the pause button on a tape recorder, capturing the material you want and excluding what you don't want. The Logging window works while you're offline as well, so you can start a log even before you sign on. You'll never miss a thing that way.

Searching the News

Look again at Figure 10-1. Do you see the button marked Search & Explore? This is an extremely powerful tool. It's powerful because it searches not only world news but also news about business, entertainment, sports, and even weather. If you know of a subject that's in the news and you want to know more, click this button (see Figure 10-3).

Figure 10-3: Using the criterion: "Virus," we receive 270 "hits" in an America Online news search. By specifying "Computer Virus," we narrow our search to only 99 hits. Review Chapter 5 for more information about searches.

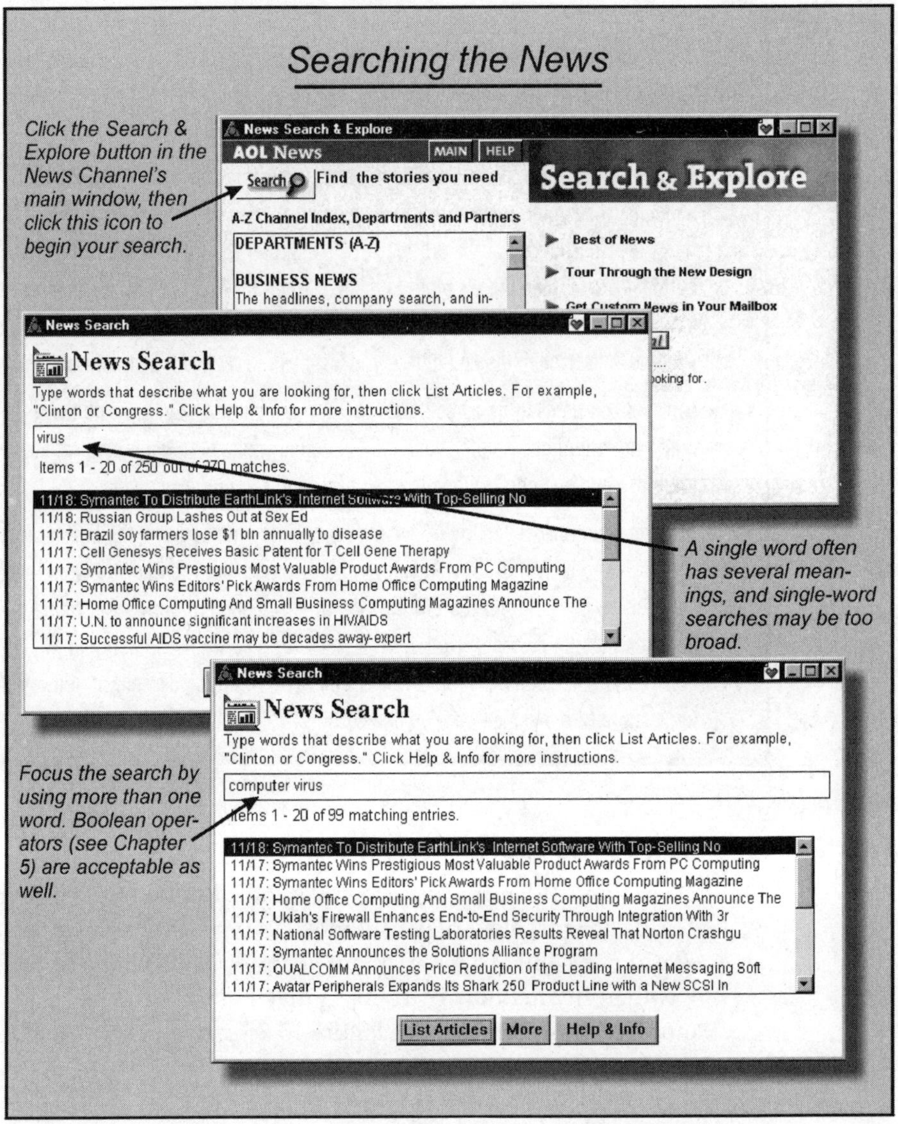

Searching the News

Click the Search & Explore button in the News Channel's main window, then click this icon to begin your search.

News Search & Explore
AOL News MAIN HELP
Search Find the stories you need
Search & Explore
A-Z Channel Index, Departments and Partners
DEPARTMENTS (A-Z)
BUSINESS NEWS
The headlines, company search, and in-
Best of News
Tour Through the New Design
Get Custom News in Your Mailbox

News Search
News Search
Type words that describe what you are looking for, then click List Articles. For example, "Clinton or Congress." Click Help & Info for more instructions.
virus
Items 1 - 20 of 250 out of 270 matches.
11/18: Symantec To Distribute EarthLink's Internet Software With Top-Selling No
11/18: Russian Group Lashes Out at Sex Ed
11/17: Brazil soy farmers lose $1 bln annually to disease
11/17: Cell Genesys Receives Basic Patent for T Cell Gene Therapy
11/17: Symantec Wins Prestigious Most Valuable Product Awards From PC Computing
11/17: Symantec Wins Editors' Pick Awards From Home Office Computing Magazine
11/17: Home Office Computing And Small Business Computing Magazines Announce The
11/17: U.N. to announce significant increases in HIV/AIDS
11/17: Successful AIDS vaccine may be decades away-expert

A single word often has several meanings, and single-word searches may be too broad.

News Search
News Search
Type words that describe what you are looking for, then click List Articles. For example, "Clinton or Congress." Click Help & Info for more instructions.
computer virus
Items 1 - 20 of 99 matching entries.
11/18: Symantec To Distribute EarthLink's Internet Software With Top-Selling No
11/17: Symantec Wins Prestigious Most Valuable Product Awards From PC Computing
11/17: Symantec Wins Editors' Pick Awards From Home Office Computing Magazine
11/17: Home Office Computing And Small Business Computing Magazines Announce The
11/17: Ukiah's Firewall Enhances End-to-End Security Through Integration With 3r
11/17: National Software Testing Laboratories Results Reveal That Norton Crashgu
11/17: Symantec Announces the Solutions Alliance Program
11/17: QUALCOMM Announces Price Reduction of the Leading Internet Messaging Soft
11/17: Avatar Peripherals Expands Its Shark 250 Product Line with a New SCSI In
List Articles | More | Help & Info

Focus the search by using more than one word. Boolean operators (see Chapter 5) are acceptable as well.

The News Delivered to Your Door

A feature called News Profiles searches AOL's many news sources for articles that match your interests and sends them to you as e-mail (see Figure 10-4). Instead of making you search for the news yourself, News Profiles puts it all in one place, so your news is waiting for you as soon as you sign on.

You're not charged for this service, and once you create your "news profiles"—once you tell AOL what kind of news stories interest you—the process is entirely automatic. Find out more at keywords: **News Profiles.**

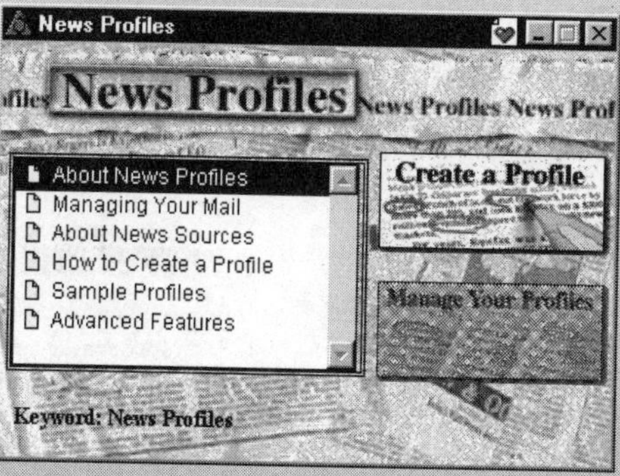

Figure 10-4: The News Profiles feature finds news of interest to you, automatically.

The News Channel's Newsstand

If the immediacy of the News Channel is the online analog to television, the News Channel's Newsstand compares with the magazine section at the library. The main difference is that it offers a distinctly different, but profoundly significant, journalistic advantage: capacity.

Most magazine readers value the printed medium; but if you're like us, you've given up on filing past issues. After a few months, we just recycle most of our magazines. And all too often, after we dispose of them we decide to review something we saw in an issue that's now gone.

We have good news, periodical patrons: the Newsstand is AOL's answer to the problem of that stack of magazines in the garage. It's a place where you can read current issues, save articles, download files, and even talk to the editors online. Perhaps best of all, the Newsstand is not only horizontally comprehensive (lots of publications), it's vertically comprehensive as well (most back issues are searchable). Chances are, if you search for a subject of interest, it's there. That's what we mean by the benefits of capacity (Figure 10-5).

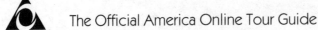

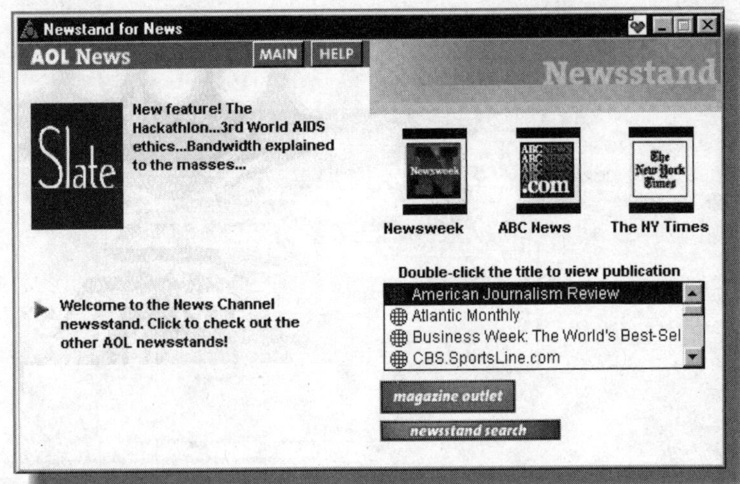

Figure 10-5: The News Channel's Newsstand gathers all of AOL's online magazines into one central location. Click the Newsstand button in the News Channel window to get there.

The magazines listed with the newsstand are all searchable, as you might assume, but there's more. You might assume that each magazine can be searched (and you'd be right), but they're searchable collectively as well. A search using the word "catcher" might just as well find a match in The Sporting News as it would in a Salinger essay in *George* magazine.

Sports & Weather

We pay sports and weather their dues in Chapter 5. Be sure to read that chapter, not only for these two subjects, but also to learn about finding information of all sorts on AOL and the Web.

The Computing Channel

You can get computer programs, drivers, fonts, graphics, sounds, movies, accessories—even the computers themselves—here on AOL. And with the exception of the hardware, it's all available at nothing more than the cost of your normal connect time and an occasional shareware fee.

In fact, even if you're not a Macintosh maniac or a Windows weirdo, you'll spend a lot of time with AOL's computing resources. There are thousands of files available—fonts and graphics in particular—that will appeal to even the casual user. And if you need help with either your computer or the software you run on it, AOL is ready to oblige. There are stimulating forums here, ranging from the fundamental to the existential. This place is as rife with opportunity as a sunny Saturday in August, and you can enjoy it any day of the year.

Almost everything we're about to discuss falls under the custody of the Computing Channel (see Figure 10-6). You'll find the Computing Channel on the Channels window, or click the Channels icon on the toolbar.

Figure 10-6: At AOL, the Computing Channel serves as the headwaters for almost everything having to do with computers.

The resources offered by this channel are so vast that we've had to divide them up and present them in various chapters of this book. You'll find a discussion of the Computing forums, for example, in Chapter 7, "Chat." Many of the Computing Channel's help resources are discussed in Chapter 2, "The Abecedarium," and the process of downloading its files is described in Chapter 6, "Transferring Files."

Live Events

A unique benefit offered by the online community is real-time conferencing. Although this subject is discussed in Chapter 7, it warrants special mention here. Perhaps you've noticed already: people who use computers are never shy when the topic of discussion turns to computing. We have more opinions about computers than Andy Rooney has about politics.

Live computing events occur each week. Many feature celebrities, others feature a computer company representative, and others bring a noted columnist or writer to the stage. Don't confuse these events with one-way media like television or magazines: they are interactive discussions, and you, the member, are as much a part of them as the guest. Where else could you sit down and chat with Bill Gates or Steve Wozniak?

Keeping up with the schedule of these appearances, however, is like keeping up with a television schedule. We need some kind of "channel listing" of upcoming live events, and it's available in the Computing Channel's Event Schedule window (keywords: **Live Computing**; see Figure 10-7).

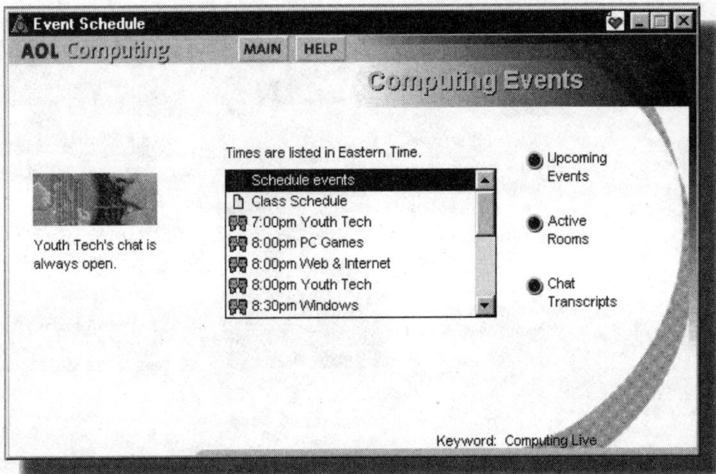

Figure 10-7: The Event Schedule is your guide to upcoming live computing events on AOL.

At Your Doorstep

Just like subscribing to *TV Guide*, you can receive notifications of upcoming live events via e-mail. The people at AOL will send you a notice every week listing all of the events scheduled for the following week, including their start times and keywords.

Unlike *TV Guide*, the service is free. Just send e-mail to the screen name MailEvents. Ask to be placed on the list of upcoming computing events. They'll take care of the rest.

Computing Newsstand

You simply cannot find a computer magazine that doesn't participate in the online medium in some way. In fact, almost every magazine offers an e-mail address. With magazines, an online presence is a conditioned reflex. Magazines aren't the only computing medium that has discovered the online community—television, radio, newspapers, books; they all offer a presence in some way or other, many on AOL.

The Computing Newsstand is a clearinghouse for all media online that relate to computing (see Figure 10-8). Here's where you'll find all of AOL's online magazines and radio features, plus links to the most popular computing-media Web sites.

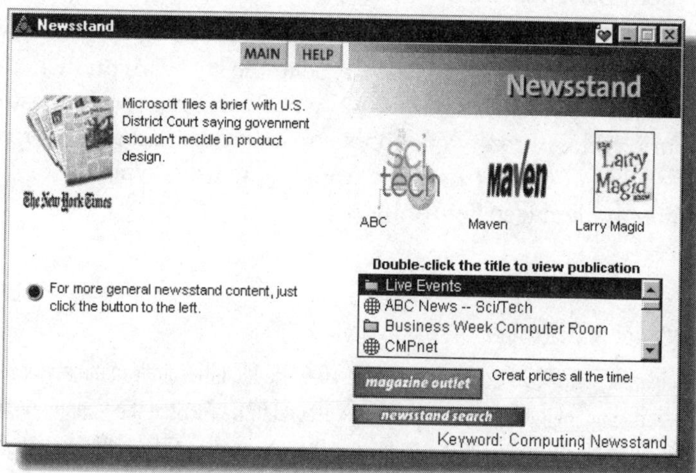

Figure 10-8: Use the keywords: **Computing Newsstand** to access all of the computing media resources from one central location.

Keyword Tricks

If you take the time to thumb through Appendix B of this book, you'll see that AOL's list of keywords is epic, and more are being added every day.

Let's say you want to go to the *New York Times* online area. Actually, its online name is @times, but you've forgotten that. Don't fret: try the keywords: **New York**, or **Times**, or **NYC**, or **NYTimes**—they'll all get you there.

This tip doesn't just apply to the *Times*, nor does it just apply to the computer-related online magazines mentioned in the text; it applies to almost every area online. Forget the keyword? Press Ctrl+K or Command+K, and then type in almost anything that describes where you want to go. What's to lose? The worst that can happen is that you'll get an "Invalid Keyword" error.

Thanks to Sean Stallings (who uses a HAL 9000 for his online travels) for this tip.

The Computing Company Connection

Computer users often need help with hardware or software, which leads us directly into a discussion of the Computing Company Connection. There are a number of ways to solve problems with your computer:

- Worry at the problem, trying solutions as they come to mind. This might take a week.
- Look up the solution in the manual (if you can remember where you put it). This usually takes half a day.
- Call the publisher or manufacturer—which can involve 20 minutes on hold (listening to a bad radio station playing commercials for stores in a city 3,000 miles away) and then several days waiting for someone to return your call.

Or you can sign on to AOL, type in the software publisher's keyword (or the hardware manufacturer's keyword), and post your question. Within 24 hours, you will receive not only a response from the vendor you're trying to reach, but also helpful advice from fellow users who have experienced the same problem (see Figure 10-9).

No Place for Vilification

Look again at SgSpk6785's question in Figure 10-9. He identifies the complexity of his problem, including methods he's using to work around it. He resisted the temptation to take out his frustration on the manufacturer. Instead, he is concise, specific, and nonantagonistic.

Prepare your question in advance, before you sign on. Include the hardware brand name, software version number, system configuration—those kinds of things. Spend a few moments checking your message for clarity, brevity, and courtesy. Sign on and post your message only after it has passed this kind of scrutiny. You can prepare a message offline, away from a message board, by choosing New from the File menu. After you have prepared the message, select it all and copy it. Now sign on and find the message board you want; then paste your message into the form used for posting messages on the board. The Select All, Copy, and Paste commands are all under the Edit menu.

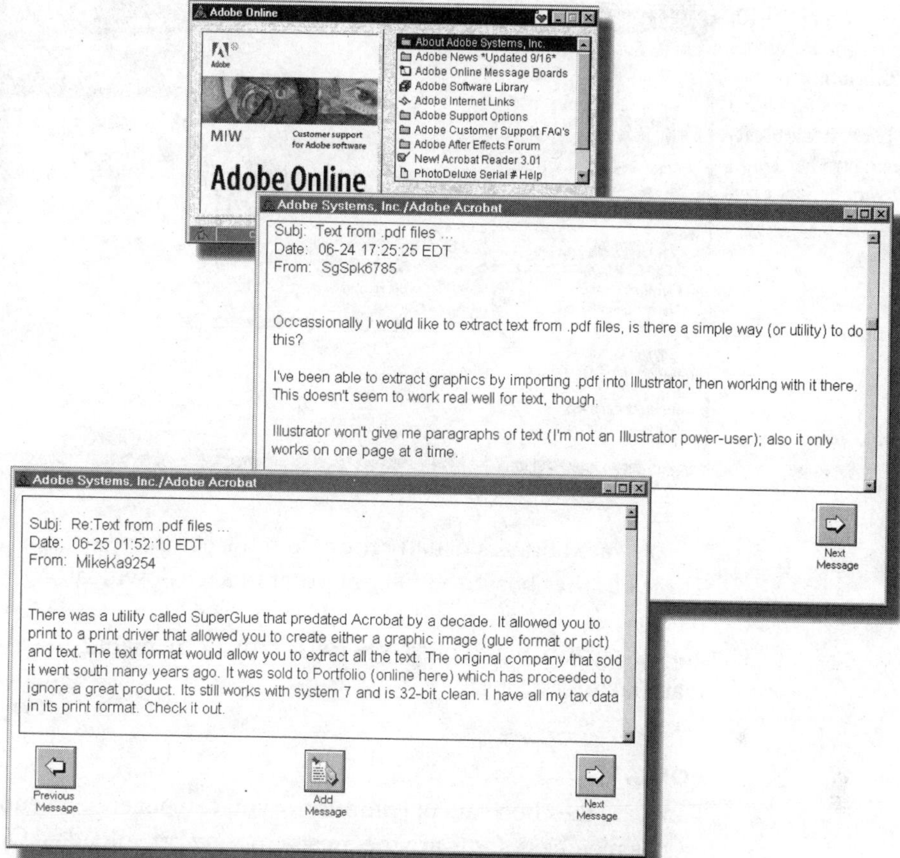

Figure 10-9: No waiting on hold: Post your question online and read a response at your convenience a few hours later.

The service that provides this help is AOL's computing companies area shown in Figure 10-10 (use the keyword: **Companies**). Hundreds of vendors currently maintain message boards on AOL, and each vendor checks its board at least once a day. Not only is excellent vendor support found here, but also peer support, libraries of accessories and updates, announcements from the industry, and tips from other users.

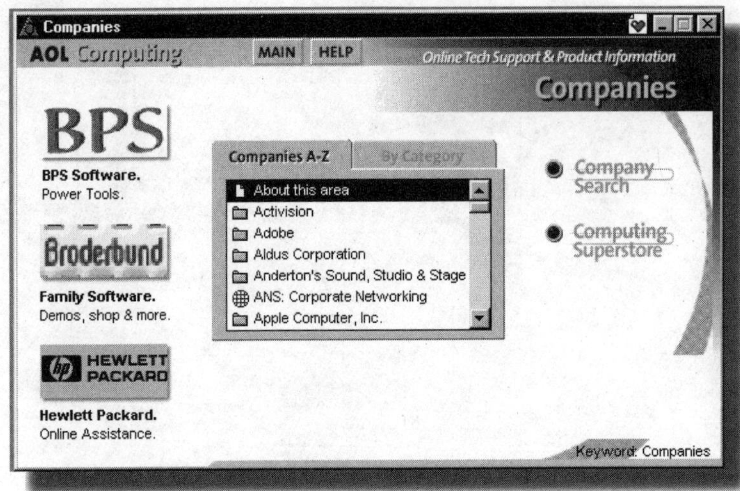

Figure 10-10: The keyword: **Companies** is your direct route to hundreds of software and hardware manufacturers.

Software libraries usually round out the company support area online. These libraries boast a variety of programs for downloading, including patches, demo versions, diagnostic tools, and hardware and software drivers—programs that would otherwise only be available directly from software manufacturers.

Fonts

Fonts are the chocolate of computing: you can never have enough. To many of AOL's members, fonts are the most tempting downloads AOL offers. They're relatively small (most download in less than a minute at 28.8 Kbps) and inexpensive. Most of these fonts are shareware or freeware; the shareware fees rarely exceed $15. Best of all, they enhance your documents with personality and individuality, like icing on a cake. Chocolate icing, of course. *Yum!*

Windows fonts come in two flavors: TrueType and PostScript (the Desktop and Web Publishing Forum—keyword: **PCDWPF** for the PC or keyword: **MacDTP** for the Mac, where you'll find vast libraries of fonts—calls these ATM fonts). Most general users seem to prefer TrueType, though desktop publishers prefer PostScript. Neither group could ask for much more than the extensive Application Forum offerings. Researching this chapter, we found more than 190 PostScript Windows fonts online. We didn't bother to count the TrueType ones, but there were just as many, or more. In addition, a number of Macintosh-to-Windows font converters were available, which means the entire Macintosh desktop publishing font library (keyword: **MacDTP**) is accessible as well. We're talking about thousands of fonts here. See Figure 10-11 for an example.

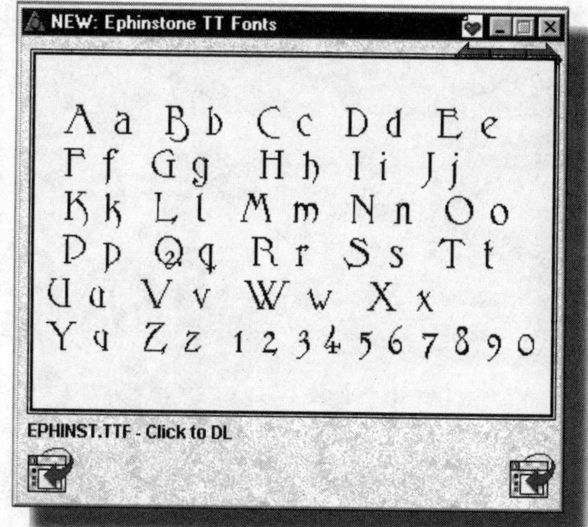

Figure 10-11: The Desktop & Web Publishing Forum (keyword: **DWP**) offers a "Font Petting Zoo" where you can see fonts before they're downloaded.

Amusements

So far we've discussed things like the Computing Channel, the Internet, managing mail, and transferring files. That's all necessary information, but what if we want to have some fun? We're here partly for the fun of it, after all. What's in it for us?

The answer is plenty. As evidence, we offer some amusements: diversions, divertissements—places where fun is foremost and duty is disenfranchised. Loosen your tie. Kick off your shoes. Admit intemperance into your life. The night's young.

The Games Channel

There's a world of game lovers who find the game-playing arena online to be their hermitage, the place where games are paramount and challenges abound. It's here that knights slay dragons, space voyagers conquer aliens, and residents of the late 20th century scratch their heads in bewilderment. You owe it to yourself to try an online game if you never have: the challenge of playing with human opponents—unseen and unknown—is unmatched by any other. And if you get hooked, the Games Channel at AOL stands ready to nourish your obsession. For some of the gaming areas available online, consult Figure 10-12.

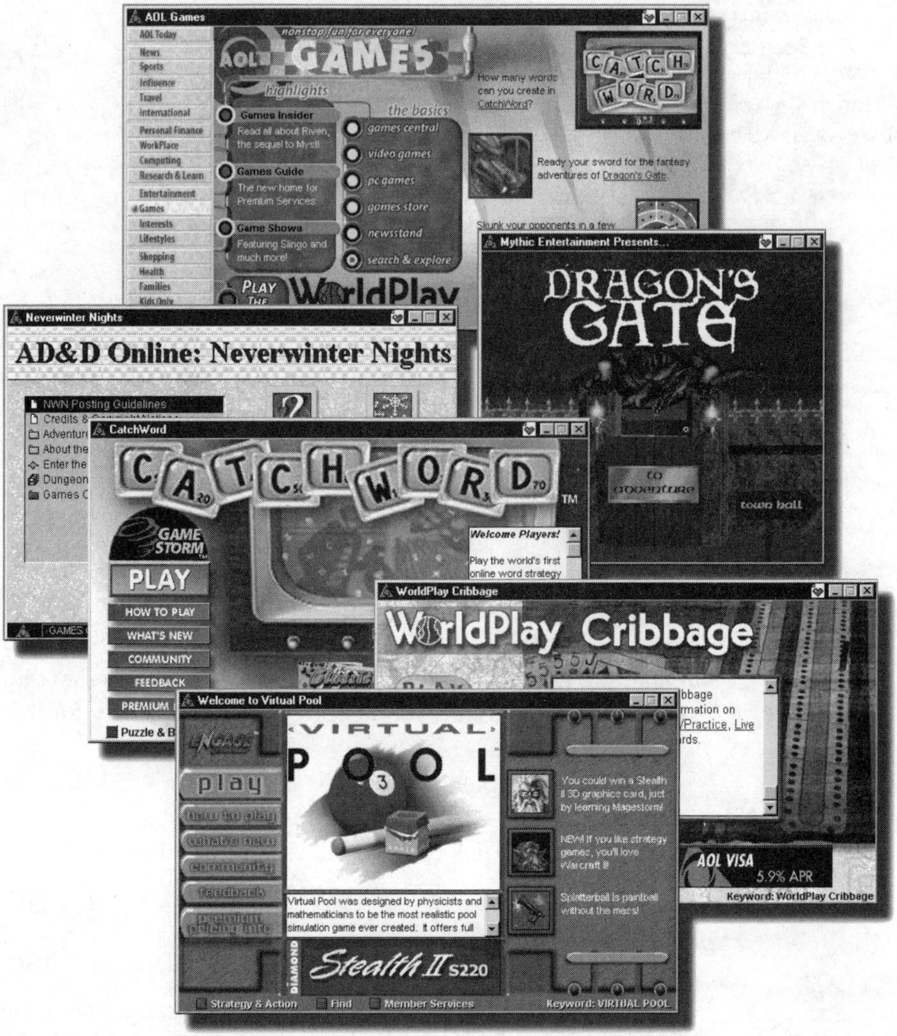

Figure 10-12: Some of the games pictured here are "premium" areas within AOL: there's an hourly charge for their use. Most games, however, carry no surcharges. Just visit the Games Channel at keyword: **Games**.

WorldPlay Games

AOL's crème de la crème of online games is found at the keywords: **WorldPlay Games**. Here you'll find single- and multi-player games rich in color, texture, and excitement. WorldPlay offers adventure, strategy, action, classic card, puzzle, and board games, including Whist, Spades, Legends of Kesmai, Hearts, Cribbage, and Air Warrior—and at least 20 more. If you're a game player, be sure to give WorldPlay a try.

The Entertainment Channel

We've made a number of online friends over the years, and we've developed ongoing philosophical discussions with a few of them. It's our brain food, and we enjoy it.

The other day we were discussing some of the significant changes in the American lifestyle over the past 100 years. Our conclusion: three major developments have changed that lifestyle forever: (1) the automobile, (2) the computer, and (3) the media.

That last development is the one that brings us to the subject at hand: Entertainment. Imagine entertainment when there were no movies, no videos, no television, no magazines, and very few books. What did people do with their time? They certainly couldn't hang around AOL's Entertainment Channel.

That opportunity, it would appear, is uniquely ours. And it's one you're not going to want to miss. This place is rife with the spangles of technoglitter.

Media Reviews

You'll find a number of media reviews online, including reviews of film, music, video, literature, and the Internet. Hollywood Online (keyword: **Hollywood**) is one; the *New York Times* (keyword: **@Times**) and NetGuide (keyword: **NetGuide**) are a couple of others.

Arts & Leisure (keyword: **Arts**) discusses art and literature; Home Video (keywords: **Home Video**) reviews video releases; SPINonline (keyword: **SPIN**) reviews music; and the keywords: **Movie Reviews** calls up a number of reviewers from a variety of renowned media (see Figure 10-13). Try each of these services; it's the only way to find the reviewers whose preferences match yours.

Figure 10-13: A sampling of the reviews (and reviewers) available online.

Entertainment Asylum

Entertainment Asylum is a complete online entertainment community, your one-stop site to interact in real time with celebrities, get all the latest Hollywood gossip, news and commentary, participate in live events and interviews, and locate special movie genres. Brainchild of the late Brandon Tartikoff, the legendary creator of brilliant television programming, Entertainment Asylum is a dynamic site filled with stars, information, and cutting edge technology. If you enjoy entertainment (don't we all?), use the keyword: **Asylum** to feed your fetish.

Books

The Books area (see Figure 10-14) is your jumping-off point for book reviews and bookstores. Be sure to check out Barnes and Noble, where every hardcover book is discounted 30 percent and over a million titles are in stock.

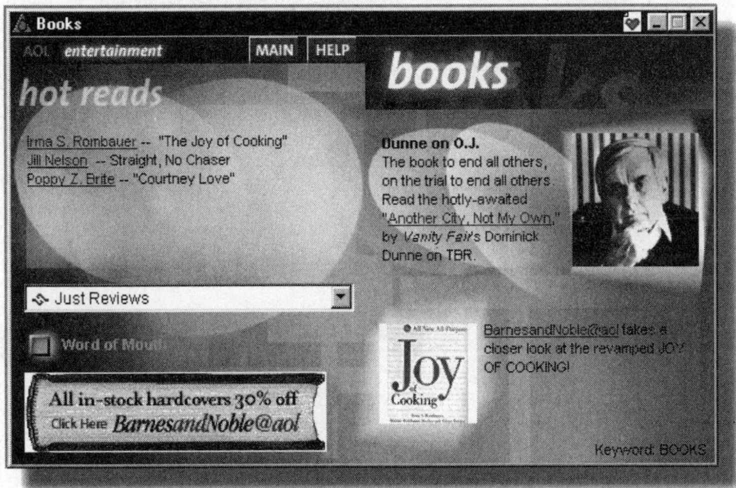

Figure 10-14: You'll find book reviews and booksellers at keyword: **Books**.

Don't forget Café Booka (keywords: **Cafe Booka**). When we last visited, there were 120 book-discussion groups, totaling over 9,000 members. Peer reviews are often the most incisive of all.

Cartoons

Let's take a little survey. What's the first section you read when you pick up the Sunday paper? If you're like us, you read "the funnies" before anything else. Often they're the *only* thing we read, depending on how dreary the world has been that week.

America Online is particularly rich in cartoons (see Figure 10-15), and you don't have to wait until Sunday morning to enjoy them. A number of nationally acclaimed cartoonists contribute to AOL each week. They include the following:

- Scott Adams's comic strip "Dilbert," reaching more than 30 million newspaper readers in 9 countries. "Dilbert" was the first syndicated comic strip to appear online, where fans have initiated more than 30,000 comic downloads monthly and generated over 50,000 e-mail messages. "Dilbert" is at keyword: **Dilbert**.
- The Comic Strip Centennial, where you can learn about the history of one of the very few art forms "born in the U.S.A." This area is presented in cooperation with the Newspaper Features Council in honor of the 100th anniversary of the birth of the comics, and it includes exhibits from the Library of Congress and the U.S. Postal Service (use the keywords: **Comic Strips**).
- The Cartoon Network, with its own forum of 'toons and comments, at keyword: **Cartoon**.
- AOL Out of Line from ABC, where you supply the caption and win prizes, at keyword: **AOOL**, and DC Comics, at keywords: **DC Comics**.

Figure 10-15: Cartoons abound at keyword: **Funnies**.

Columnists & Features Online

Columnists & Features Online is the best way to read provocative newspaper columnists and communicate with them online (see Figure 10-16).

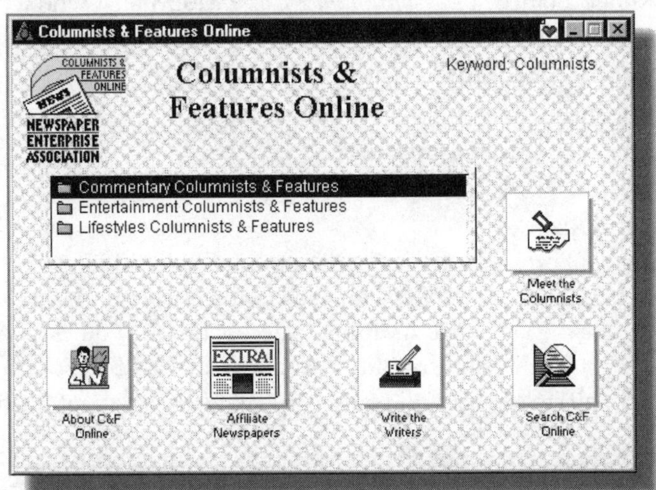

Figure 10-16: Columnists & Features Online offers current material as well as an extensive searchable library. Use the keyword: **Columnists**.

The Newspaper Enterprise Association (NEA) syndicates distinguished writers and political columnists, including the 29 (a number that's sure to grow) featured on AOL, to newspapers nationwide.

The text of each column appears the same day it is released to the newspapers and remains online for a week. After that, past columns are posted in the library. Use standard AOL criteria to search them. Some of the columnists include the following:

- Hodding Carter, the State Department spokesman for Jimmy Carter's administration, offering sharp opinions on today's issues from the perspective of a respected insider and noted partisan of strong, active government.
- Nat Hentoff, one of the foremost authorities on the First Amendment. Hentoff's column, which appears in the *Washington Post*, examines how legislative decisions affect our basic freedoms to speak, write, think, and assemble.
- George Plagenz, an ordained minister and news veteran who writes "Saints and Sinners," a personal look at family values and spiritual issues.
- Ian Shoales, a popular humor columnist from National Public Radio and the *San Francisco Examiner*, known for his amusing social commentary.

- "Environment," by J.D. Hair, who is the president of the National Wildlife Federation. Hair offers insightful reports and timely accounts of current environmental concerns, covering all aspects of natural resource protection.
- Robert Bianco, a *Pittsburgh Post-Gazette* journalist who writes "Home Video," up-to-the-minute reviews of home video releases.
- Astrologer Bernice Bedeosal, the author of "Astrograph." What's in the stars for you? You'll find it in "Astrograph," one of the most popular astrology columns in America.

Horoscopes

Mention of Bernice Bedeosal's "Astrograph" column reminds us of Astronet, where you'll find horoscopes for each of the astrological signs every day (Figure 10-17). Use the keyword: **Astronet** to access this area quickly. And if you'd like something a little more specific, stop by the Crystal Ball Forum (keywords: **Crystal Ball**) to see what the tarot cards have to say about the future.

Figure 10-17: Stop by Astronet every day; consult the stars before you do anything rash.

Entertainment Weekly Online

Entertainment Weekly Online (keyword: **EW**) brings AOL subscribers the full text of *Entertainment Weekly* magazine each week: feature stories and reviews of movies, TV, music, books, videos, and multimedia.

That's the official line, but if you're an *Entertainment Weekly* reader, you know there's much more to the magazine than that. Just this week we dropped in and caught Mary Makarushka's encore piece about Jim Croce. *Rolling Stone* noted that the critics were content to consign him to the status of a likable nonentity, yet "Time in a Bottle" is still one of our favorite songs of all time, and Makarushka agrees. There's insightful, contemporary journalism here (see Figure 10-18).

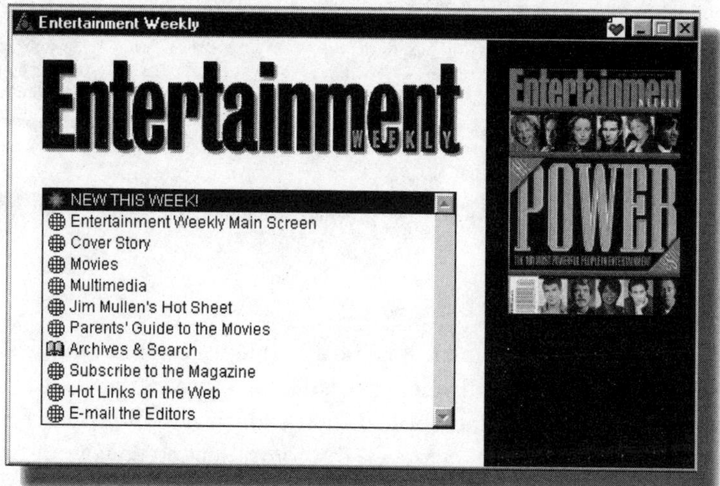

Figure 10-18: Entertainment Weekly Online not only offers the full text of the magazine each week, but you can chat with staffers and participate in guest events.

The Travel Channel

Who hasn't indulged in an "If I had a million dollars . . ." fantasy? Our favorite is travel: South America, the British Isles, a cruise, the Orient Express . . . . Heck, we'd be happy if someone just gave us a ticket to Tucumcari.

Of course, fantasies require money. That's why they're fantasies. If you want money-optional indulgences, try AOL's Travel Channel (keyword: **Travel**). Not only can you indulge your fantasies here, you can actually fulfill them as well. You can find exceptional travel bargains; book airline, car, and hotel reservations; consult with other travelers before you depart. They say there are only two types of people in the world: those who are on vacation and those who wish they were. The Travel Channel serves both types (Figure 10-19).

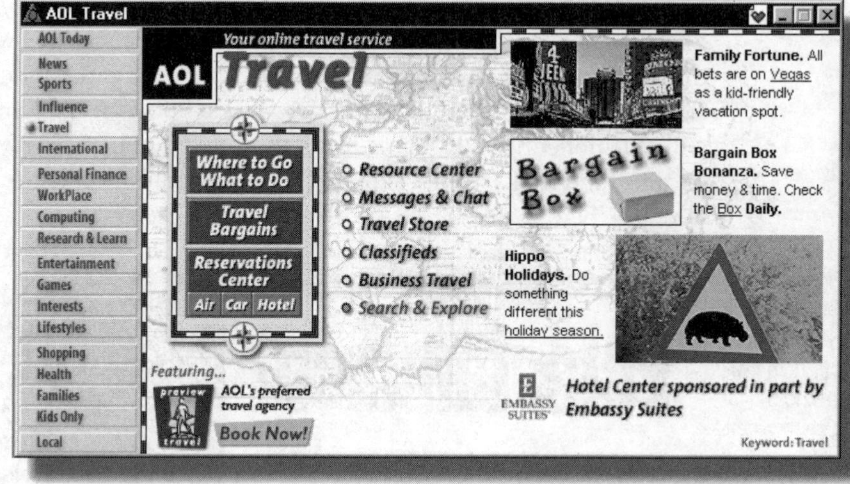

Figure 10-19: The Travel Channel is the place for anything that has to do with travel, including destination reviews, spectacular packages, and travel agency services.

Preview Travel

Perhaps one of the most specific advantages offered online is the ability to shop for your own airline reservations. For years, travel agents have peered at computer screens and applied their expertise to interpret cryptic displays for tyro travelers. Now, however, the computer screen is your own; the display is graphical and precise; you can examine the alternatives yourself and make your own decisions; you can even book the reservations from your keyboard (see Figure 10-20). Now, you can travel on your own terms.

Figure 10-20: Select your itinerary and make your own reservations at keywords: **Preview Travel**.

The Independent Traveler

As long as we're in a traveling mood, let's check out the Independent Traveler. Articles, message boards, a resource center, and a library offer a wealth of information and tips for the domestic or world traveler (see Figure 10-21).

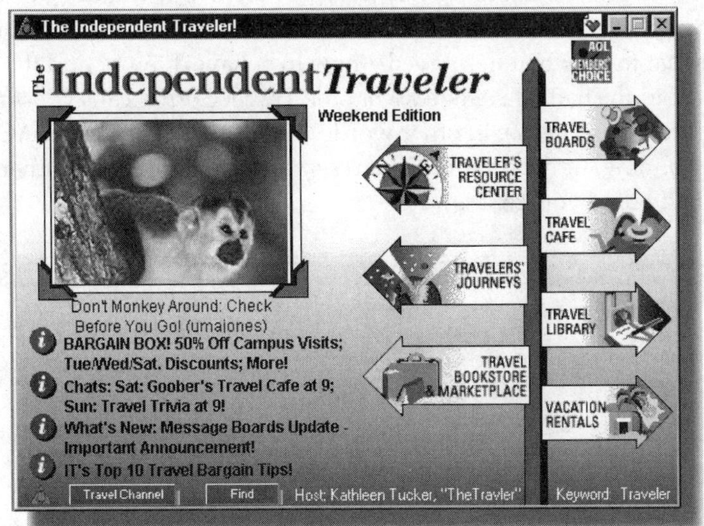

Figure 10-21: The Independent Traveler (keyword: **Traveler**) offers not only expert advice, but also the experience of traveling peers—perhaps the best advice of all.

Are you looking for a romantic hideaway for your getaway weekend? Check the cruise message board. If you're looking for the best itinerary for your train trip through Europe, check the World Traveler message board. If you're traveling overseas, check out the U.S. State Department Travel Advisories and the Forum's special events with travel experts. In-depth articles cover topics such as "How to find hotel discounts" and "Should I buy trip cancellation insurance?"

Travel plans, perhaps above all else, benefit from peer support. The Independent Traveler is where you can solicit the advice of peers and pros alike. No travel plans are complete until you talk to those who have been there. For this purpose, check the Independent Traveler's message boards. Lots of people travel, and most who do like to talk about it. Their comments are candid and relevant, and because it's a message board, everything is current.

The Travel Corner

Arnie Weissmann began planning for an around-the-world journey in the early 1980s. To his dismay, he couldn't find information about his destinations. He knew how he was traveling, he knew what his costs were going to be, he knew what to pack and how to dress. But what he needed were friends, chaperones familiar with his destinations who could tell him where to go and what to do when he arrived—how to behave, how to find the good stuff and avoid the bad. He needed what the Travel Corner calls "destination profiles" (see Figure 10-22). In other words, other travel features on AOL concentrate on planning, transportation, and reservations. The Travel Corner focuses on what to do once you get there.

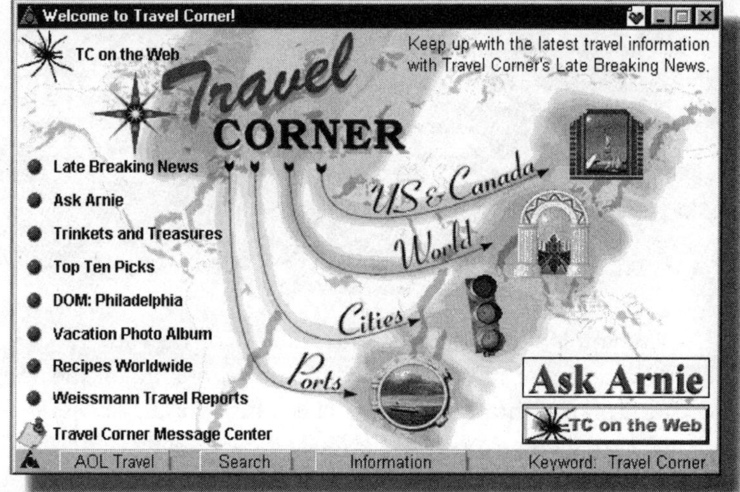

Figure 10-22: The Travel Corner offers destination information for thousands of locations around the world at keywords: **Travel Corner**.

Your Wallet Is Safe at AOL

All this talk about travel agencies, renting cars, and booking airline tickets may make you a little squeamish: "Does my AOL membership obligate me for anything beyond the standard monthly fee and connect charges?" No, not at all. All the additional-expense items we've discussed in this chapter are voluntary—not requisite to membership in AOL. This is the Travel Channel, after all, and most travel is discretionary—and an additional expense.

ExpressNet

ExpressNet from American Express (see Figure 10-23) offers a comprehensive online resource for American Express cardholders. Using a password, you can query the status of your American Express account, including all billed and unbilled charges. You can download billing details to your computer for use with Quicken, Managing Your Money for Windows, and Kiplinger's Simply Money software. By providing American Express with your checking-account information, you can even pay your American Express bill online!

Figure 10-23: ExpressNet offers an extensive array of services for American Express cardholders.

ExpressNet members (there's no charge, though you must have an American Express card) also have access to the following:

- The American Express Travel Service for airline, hotel, and car rental reservations.
- The ExpressNet Shopping Service, where every purchase builds bonus miles in the American Express Membership Miles feature.
- A database of the special discounts and value-added offers exclusively available to American Express Cardmembers.

There's more, but you have to have an American Express card to access all of the features ExpressNet has to offer. Naturally, you can apply for a card online—just use the keyword: **ExpressNet**.

Other Travel Services Online

Space limitations simply don't permit us to explore the entirety of the Travel Channel. Still, we'd be remiss if we didn't mention at least some of the other major travel areas offered by AOL. If you've ever thought about taking an ocean cruise, discover Cruise Critic (keywords: **Cruise Critic**), an online cruise guide with in-depth, candid reviews of cruise ships and cruises. You'll find the latest cruise bargains, cruise tips, reviews of more than 100 ships—plus the advice of your fellow AOL cruisers. If you're planning a vacation at a bed and breakfast, Pamela Lanier's Bed & Breakfast area (keywords: **Bed & Breakfast**) is where you'll find everything you need. If you're the outdoors type, then the Outdoor Adventure Online area (keyword: **OAO**) will get you where you want to go. For the bargain minded, AOL has the Traveler's Advantage area (keywords: **Traveler's Advantage**). And finally, there's complete access to the Internet, where even more travel opportunities and interests await.

Music

We tend to think of the online medium as one that's primarily textual, with a few graphics for window dressing. That perception isn't far off the mark, but the mark is a moving target. The online medium of today bears little resemblance to what we'll be using tomorrow. We are the pioneers. Future generations will remember us as we remember the pony express riders back in the days when mail was carried on horseback.

Perhaps the most profound change will occur in the music business (see the sidebar, "Thea McCue"). Music recording technology is already almost exclusively digital; even some musical instruments are digital. Digital is the language of computers. It's only a matter of time before digital music and your computer are wedded via the online medium.

In 1969 Tom camped across from the launch site of *Apollo 11*, the first rocket to land a man on the moon. The night before launch, the anticipation among the people gathered there was electric. Something big was about to happen and they were all there to see it. AOL's Music area (see Figure 10-24) is like that. It is home to some of the most creative people in mass communications—people drawn to both music and the online medium. They're camped out here, waiting for Something Big. If you want to be there when it happens, visit the Music area (keyword: **Music)** often.

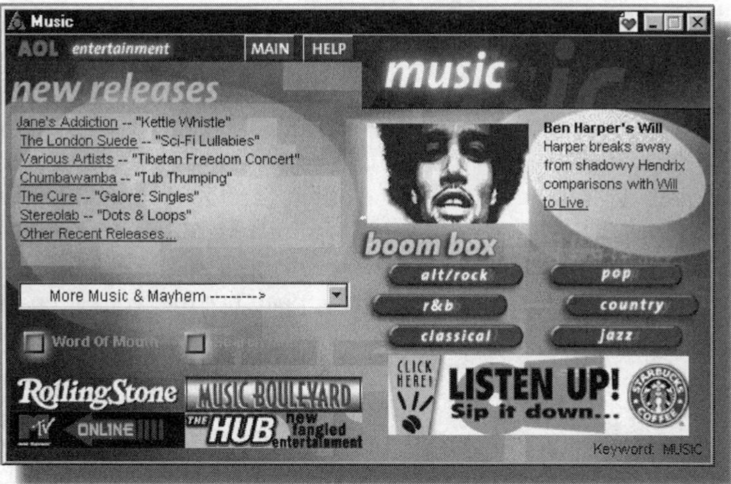

Figure 10-24: The Music area is the conductor's podium for all things musical on AOL. If you enjoy music—be it classical, hip-hop, or anything in between—use the keyword: **Music** every time you sign on.

Thea McCue

Thea McCue is an account coordinator for AOL, and her purview is MusicSpace. Like many of the members of AOL's creative staff, her job is not only to manage the day-to-day operation of her area, but to stay an appropriate distance ahead of it as well.

In perhaps five years, when "the bandwidth" opens up and we're all able to connect to AOL at, say, 256 Kbps—a megabyte every 10 seconds—Thea foresees a MusicSpace that's considerably different from the one that exists today. "Music producers today are at the mercy of the broadcast media; if radio stations don't play it, if MTV or VH1 doesn't run the video, the music dies." The consumer, in other words, sees and hears new music only after it has passed through the broadcast media's filters—hardly an unbiased selection.

In five years you might be listening to music—perhaps even watching videos—that you've downloaded from Thea's libraries. These libraries will offer all of the new music that's available, not a subset passed through a filter. You'll listen to it when you want and it will be digital quality—the same as CDs today. AOL will keep track of the downloads—just as they do today—and those selections with large download numbers will become hits. Feedback from listener to artist will be direct via message boards and download numbers. You might even furnish your credit card number and have AOL download the entire album to your writable CD-ROM. Consumer and producer will share a distribution channel that's equitable and immediate.

Music is a personal thing. This scenario will not only complement that intimacy, it will promote it. There are changes ahead, and many of them will be for the better.

MTV Online

Irreverent as the Dead Kennedys and as subtle as Jim Carrey, MTV can be expected to provide irrepressible online content, and they do. Significantly, MTV Online (keyword: **MTVO**) offers exclusive content to AOL members, in the X-clusive area. Here's you'll find Video Snacks, Rock n Jock, Loveline, the MTV Yak, and Krank, among others. You'll not only hear the music, you'll see it as well: QuickTime videos abound at MTV, as you would expect.

Interestingly, MTV's "home page" greeting screen (see Figure 10-25) is sedate and textual. Don't let its appearance fool you. Keep clicking those links!

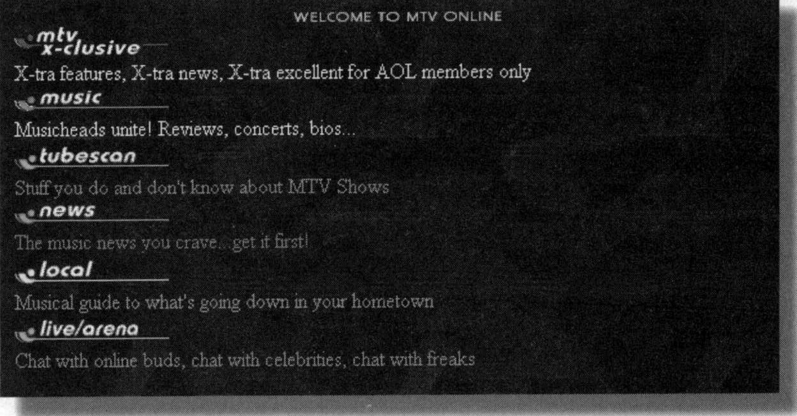

Figure 10-25: Don't let its sedate appearance fool you: MTV Online is about as reverent as a fraternity house on a Saturday night in June.

Even if you can't make sense of what's going on at MTV Online, the place flaunts the best eye candy that's available online. Be sure your color is turned on!

VH1

Shall we mellow the demographic somewhat? On cable, VH1's appeal is to a slightly older market than MTV's, with artists such as Emmylou Harris, Billy Joel, k.d. lang, and Mariah Carey. The same can be said of VH1's online offering (see Figure 10-26).

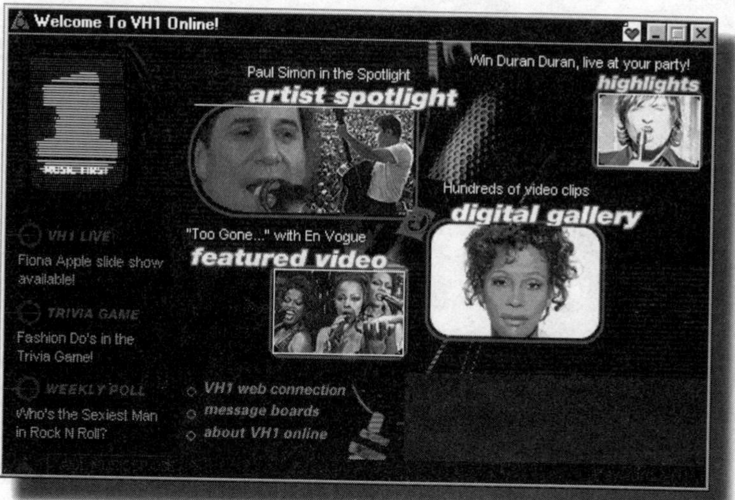

Figure 10-26: VH1 Online spotlights music, of course, and much of it is downloadable. VH1 is a compelling multimedia resource that's available now at keyword: **VH1**.

The Corner Tavern

Anyone who has attended the showing of a good film in a full theater knows that most people prefer their entertainment in the company of other people. We go to the movies not just to see the film, but to see the film in the company of others. We laugh more at sitcoms when we're not alone. We travel to the corner tavern for *Monday Night Football* so that we can comment to one another while the game is in progress.

It comes as no surprise to the people at AOL, then, to learn that there's a significant coincidence between message board usage and broadcast television. Visit the MTV Arena someday while your TV is tuned to the MTV channel, on a weekday after school has let out. Chances are, the discussion will coincide with the events onscreen. The same can be said of the *Melrose Place* board—though peak activity might occur just after an episode ends—or, indeed, *Monday Night Football*. It's a peculiar but quantifiable phenomenon. Someone should write a thesis.

MusicSpace Message Center

The MusicSpace Message Center is the Big Daddy of all of the message boards on AOL. It's one of the busiest places you'll find anywhere online—it requires a staff of almost 20 people—and because of its size, there's bound to be a music category that suits your needs.

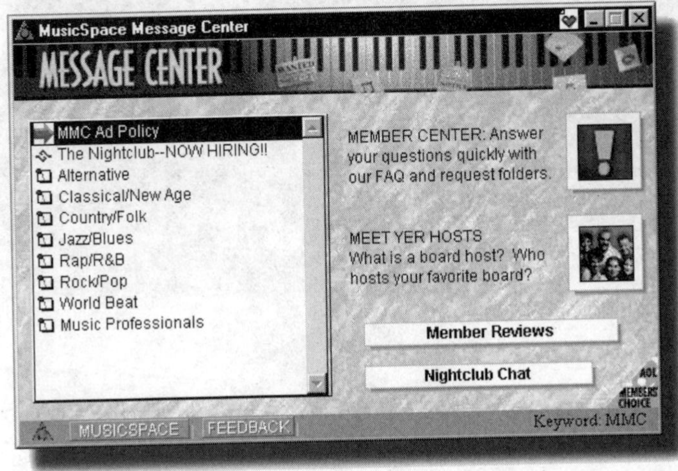

Figure 10-27: The MusicSpace Message Center is the place for you to exchange views and queries about music of all forms.

Figure 10-27 hardly does the MusicSpace Message Center justice. Each of the broad categories appearing in the illustration contains scores—sometimes hundreds—of individual folders. The Rock/Pop category, for example, offers over 280 boards, discussing topics from ABBA to Zappa.

The Message Center's success is, most likely, attributable to its attitude. The Center's focus is fans, not the media, and the participants appreciate the lack of industry intrusion. If you like music and you want to talk with others who like music, use the keyword: **MMC** and become involved with the MusicSpace Message Center.

SPINonline

As you would expect from the people who produce *SPIN* magazine, SPINonline offers creative irreverence and verbal spaghetti. It's all in fun, and every corner of the online medium is exposed along the way. These guys push the envelope (see Figure 10-28).

Figure 10-28: Sound Bytes, Down Lode, Heavy Rotation, and the Digital Rec Room—they're all waiting to be explored at keyword: **SPIN**.

WEB TopStops

AOL's MusicWeb (Figure 10-29) is your jumping-off point to music sites on the Web. Be sure to try the Virtual JukeBox, where you'll find full-length previews of upcoming (or just-released) hits, in stereo, and streamed (no downloading!) using RealAudio Technology.

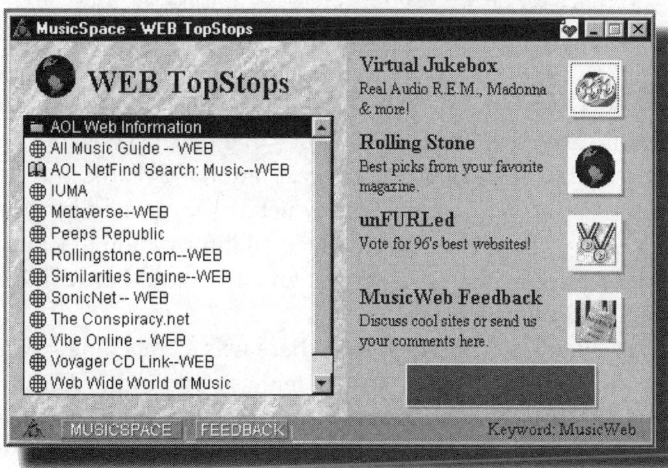

Figure 10-29: AOL's WEB TopStops brings order to the chaos of music Web sites at keyword: **MusicWeb**.

Warner Brothers Records Online

As you would expect, Warner/Reprise online exists to keep fans informed about artists on the Warner Brothers family of labels (see Figure 10-30). You'll find music industry news here, too, and a kaleidoscope of multimedia files, including an extensive library of videos.

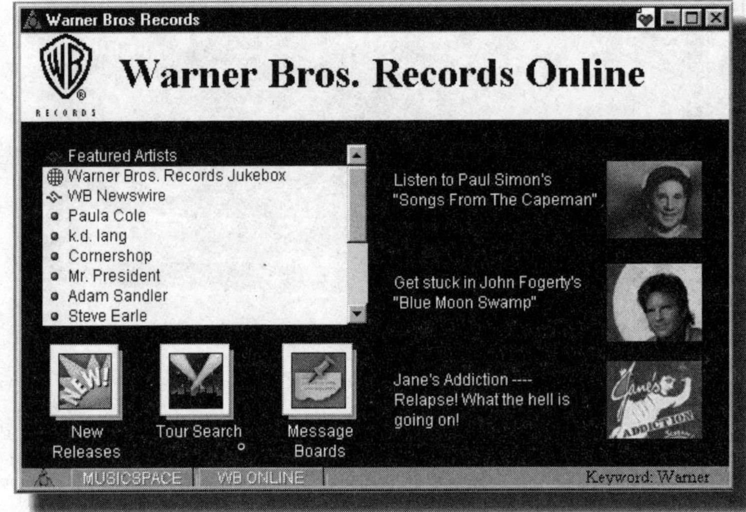

Figure 10-30: The Warner Brothers area (keyword: **Warner**) offers news and multimedia files for minstrels, contrapuntists, syncopators, kapellmeisters, and troubadours alike.

And that—as Porky used to say—is all, folks!

The Personal Finance Channel

Have you ever seen those little radios that pick up weather reports? We use one every day. It's tuned to the local National Oceanic and Atmospheric Administration (NOAA) station, which broadcasts nothing but the weather, 24 hours a day. These gadgets are the ideal information machine: always current, always available, and nearly free. Now if we could only find a similar source for financial information.

Aha! What about AOL? If ever there was a "machine" for instant financial news, America Online is it. Unlike television or radio, AOL's market information (Figure 10-31) is available whenever you want it; there's no waiting for the six o'clock news or suffering through three stories (and four commercials) that you don't want to hear. Unlike newspapers, AOL's financial news is always current. It's not this morning's news; it's this *minute's* news. It's current, it's always available, and it's almost free.

Does Ted Turner know about this?

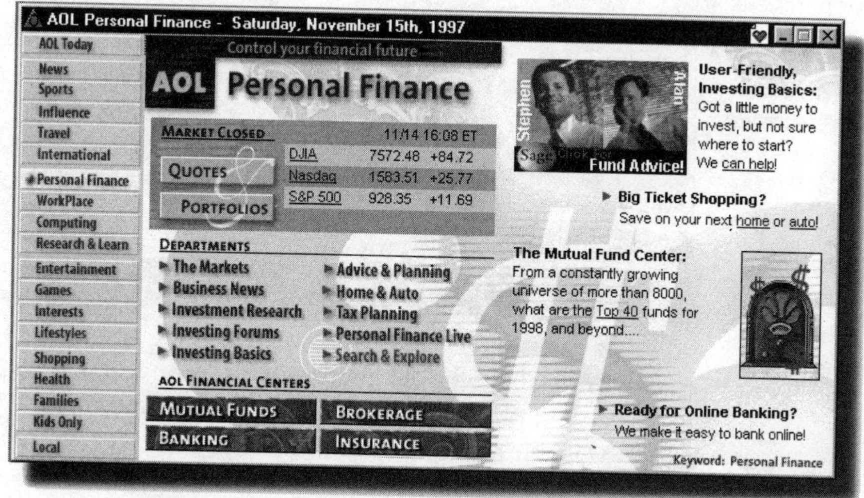

Figure 10-31: The Personal Finance Channel is both your source and your medium for personal investment. Use the keywords: **Personal Finance**.

Quotes & Portfolios

A portfolio of investments is a fascinating thing to follow and nourish, even if it's only make-believe. And if you want to add some real punch to it, AOL offers a brokerage service. You can invest real money in real issues and realize real gains (or real losses).

Getting a Quote

Whether you intend to invest real cash or just funny money, a portfolio of investments is a fascinating thing to follow. Of course, before you can follow a portfolio, you have to make some investments. In Figure 10-32, we have used the keyword: **Quotes** to discover the selling price for America Online, which trades on the New York Stock Exchange as, naturally, AOL.

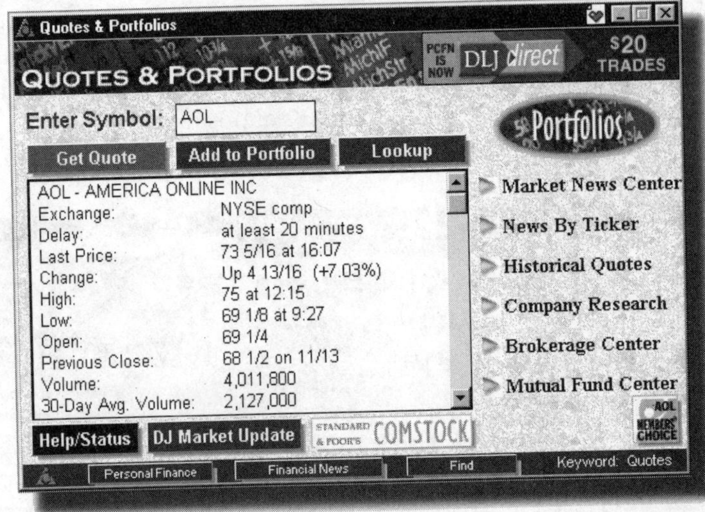

Figure 10-32: America Online might be our dream investment. Note that we can receive news, historical information (graphs, in particular), and background information on the issue, all from this screen.

Now we need to seek out a broker to handle our transaction. Specifically, we'll have to open an account with one of the online brokers. There are eight of them available at AOL: DLJdirect, Fidelity, E*Trade, Waterhouse, Schwab, Ameritrade, Accutrade, and SureTrade. Each has advantages over the others, and each has its disadvantages as well. Research is required, but fortunately, it's all available at the Brokerage Center (Figure 10-33).

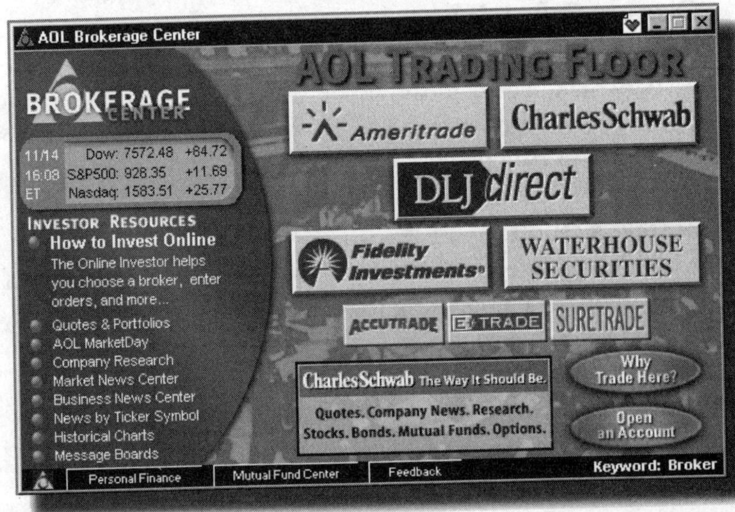

Figure 10-33: Eight brokers await you at keyword: **Broker**. Do your research, then pick the one that suits your investment style best.

We hasten to mention again that you don't *have* to purchase investments in order to open a portfolio. You can have a "conservative" portfolio, a "wild and crazy" portfolio, a portfolio of just high-tech stocks—as many as 20 portfolios, each with as many as 100 issues, and not a one of them has to be real.

But when you *are* ready to invest, one of the brokers pictured in Figure 10-33 stands ready to serve you.

Real money or funny money, when you invest, be sure to record the investment in your portfolio. Figure 10-34 shows our one-issue portfolio three years after we bought into America Online. Not a bad return for a three-year investment.

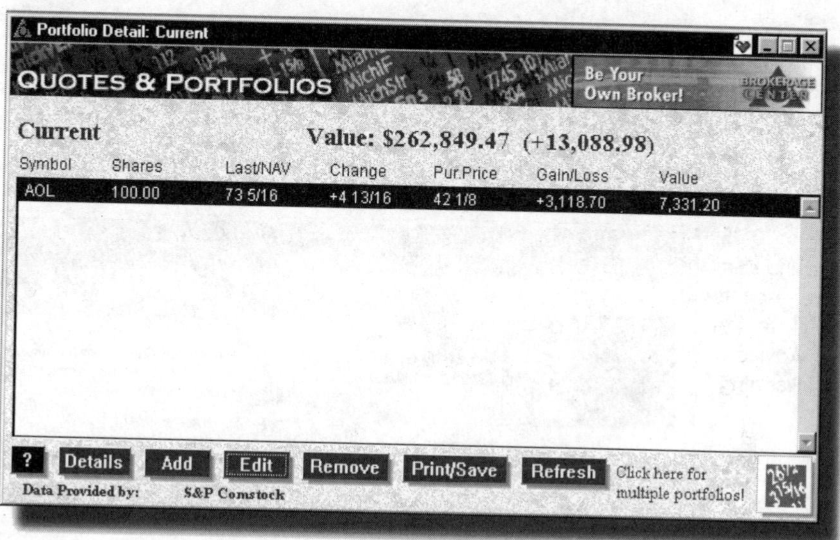

Figure 10-34: Our $4,200 AOL investment is now worth $7,300—a 74 percent increase in 3 years. If only they were all like this!

The Quotes & Portfolios area of the Personal Finance Channel is a comprehensive financial information service equaled by few others in the telecommunications industry and available on AOL without surcharge. America Online is connected to the financial centers of the world via high-speed data lines and provides financial information that is updated continuously during market hours—usually about 15 minutes behind the action.

Printing & Saving Your Portfolio

The Print/Save button at the bottom of Figure 10-34 prints the data displayed in the Quotes & Portfolios window, as you would expect.

Few people are aware, however, that by clicking the Print/Save button, you can also save your portfolio for advanced analysis by spreadsheet and database programs.

The File | Save command is disabled when the primary Quotes & Portfolios window is displayed, but when you click its Print/Save button, the contents of the window are reformatted (in Courier, for printing) and the Save command is enabled. Your portfolio data will be saved as a text file that many programs—word processing and spreadsheet in particular—can interpret. Microsoft's Excel spreadsheet can even resolve the mixed fractions and decimals in the Last/NAV column.

Advice & Planning

We're not going to overwhelm you with a comprehensive introduction to AOL's financial features, but there is one more area that warrants special mention: Advice & Planning (see Figure 10-35).

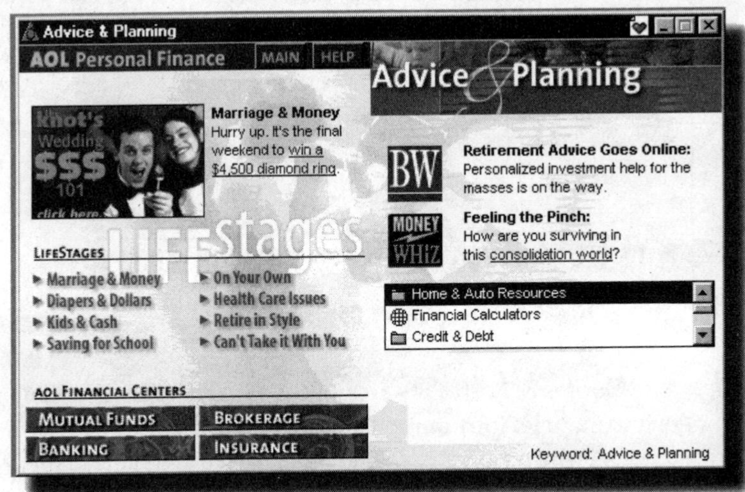

Figure 10-35: Advice and Planning on all aspects of your life at keywords: **Advice & Planning**.

You can see what's available by looking closely at Figure 10-35: Marriage & Money, Diapers & Dollars, Kids & Cash, Health Care, Automobiles, Credit & Debt, Women & Money, Retirement—it's all there, free for the taking.

Live Charts

The financial market is a moving target. Trying to take aim at it by observing a static chart is like trying to shoot skeet with a cannon: impressive to behold, but hardly nimble enough for the job.

That's why AOL provides "live" charts for your observation of financial activity. Use the keyword: **MNC** (to call up the Market News Center). When the chart appears, leave it on your screen; it'll be automatically updated every few minutes (see Figure 10-36). Explore the buttons on this screen; there are plenty more charts where the first one came from.

Figure 10-36: AOL's live charting feature provides 28 animated looks at market activity as it happens, all day long. Use the keyword: **MNC**.

The Research & Learn Channel

Our dictionary defines the word *inquisitive* as "inclined to investigate; eager for knowledge." While the online medium's chat, e-mail, and files for downloading receive the lion's share of media attention, and while they might be the enticements that lured many of us here in the first place, we soon discover that the true value of the medium is personal enrichment via the pursuit of knowledge. Nothing can compare to the online medium's seemingly limitless

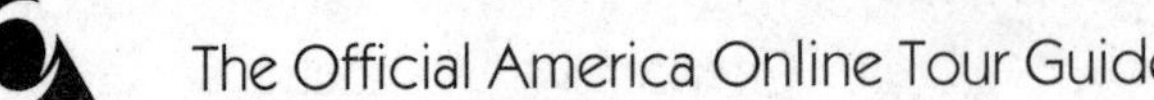

variety, hair-trigger immediacy, and extensive multimedia capabilities. If you're "eager for knowledge," the Research & Learn Channel is your citadel (see Figure 10-37). Use the keywords: **Research & Learn**, or click on the channel's button on the Channels screen.

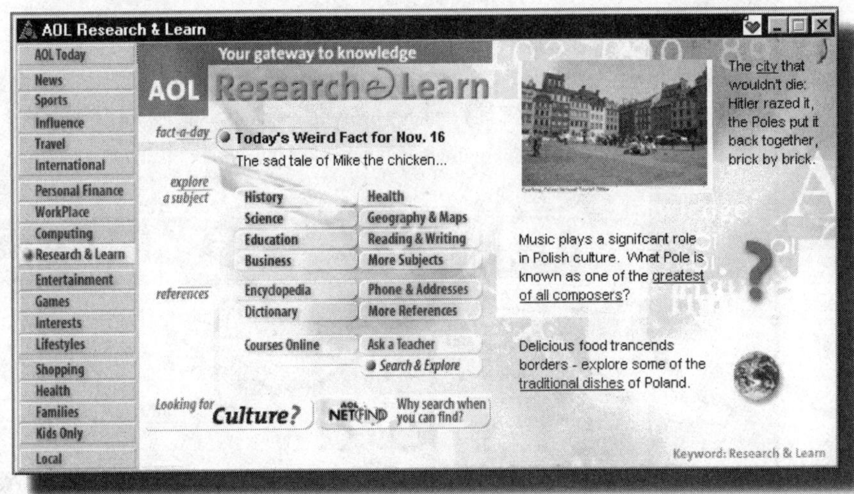

Figure 10-37: Alvin Toffler, author of *Future Shock*, once said that ". . . knowledge is the most democratic source of power," referring, perhaps, to its accessibility. The Research & Learn Channel brings an infinite resource directly to your PC that can increase your knowledge and thus your power. Use the keywords: **Research & Learn** to investigate.

The print medium—home to reference works for centuries—is losing its predominance. Large volumes containing thousands of pages are simply too inconvenient, too wasteful of natural resources, and too unwieldy to meet the push-button demands of the electronic information age.

A printed encyclopedia, for example, made sense 60 years ago, but to describe every aspect of today's society—especially today's technological society—a comprehensive encyclopedia would have to fill a room, not a shelf. Even if you had the room, you would hesitate to use the thing: searching—especially cross-referencing—would be too tedious; information would probably be out-of-date by the time it was printed (and certainly by the time you had it paid for); and the perpetual revisions would make indexing a nightmare.

Forget the printed encyclopedia. Forget the room to house it. Forget the payments and revisions. Turn on your computer, punch up AOL, and click the Learning & Reference button on the Channels screen. It's all here, it's all topical, it's all affordable. And not a single tree fell to make it possible.

Compton's NewMedia Forum

Four years ago, the keyword: **Comptons** brought you a rather plain presentation of *Compton's Encyclopedia*. It was an admirable resource—more than 9,000,000 words, 5,274 full-length articles, 29,322 capsule articles, 63,503 index entries—and it won the Critics' Choice award for the best education program as well as top honors at the 1991 Software Publisher's Association awards ceremony. But it remained primarily textual, a vestige of its print heritage; hardly a sterling example of the online medium.

That, of course, was in the days of 1200 baud modems and 16-color displays. Today, things have changed, including the Compton's NewMedia Forum (see Figure 10-38).

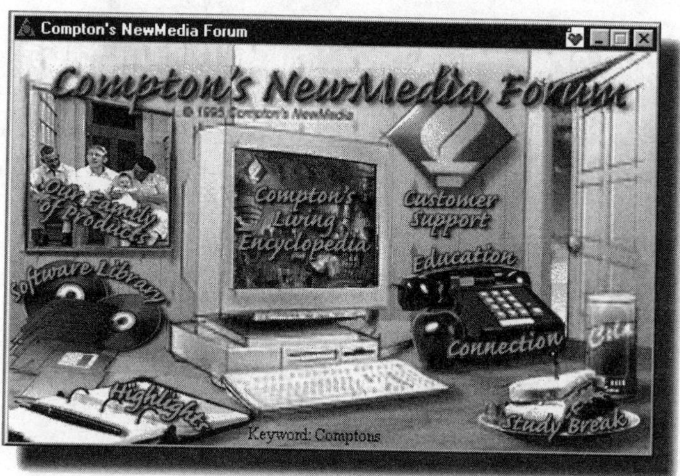

Figure 10-38: Compton's NewMedia Forum offers a newly enhanced multimedia encyclopedia and a growing array of support services.

> **Encyclopedic Potential**
>
> Compton's isn't the only encyclopedia available online. Look also for the *Columbia Concise Encyclopedia* (keyword: **CCE**) and the *Grolier Multimedia Encyclopedia*, at keyword: **Grolier**.

Merriam-Webster

Speaking of antiquated media, another has just come to our attention: the ubiquitous dictionary. Quickly now, name the first dictionary that comes to mind. Chances are, you said Webster's (actually, it's *Merriam-Webster* now), and that's just what AOL has to offer (see Figure 10-39).

Figure 10-39: Merriam-Webster not only obligingly places its complete dictionary online, it also includes a thesaurus and its delightful Word Histories lexicon.

Like the encyclopedia, the dictionary is perfectly served by the machinery of the online medium. So is the thesaurus, which Merriam-Webster also offers online. AOL's machines search Merriam-Webster's references with speed and accuracy, returning not only definitions, pronunciations, and synonyms, but fascinating information about the etymology of words—especially if you choose to consult Word Histories, Merriam-Webster's nutriment for the bibliophile appetite. You'll find all the Merriam-Webster offerings at the keywords: **Merriam-Webster**.

Nolo Press Self-Help Law Center

Twenty-five years ago, two former legal aid lawyers, dissatisfied with the lack of affordable legal information and advice available to the public, began writing understandable, easy-to-use, self-help law books. Legal kits, software, and tapes all followed, but the purpose has never changed: to take the mystery out of law and make it accessible to Everyman.

Since they were already involved in print, audio, and video publications, it seemed only natural that Nolo Press would commit to the online medium as well, and they've done just that with their Nolo Press Self-Help Law Center at keyword: **Nolo** (see Figure 10-40).

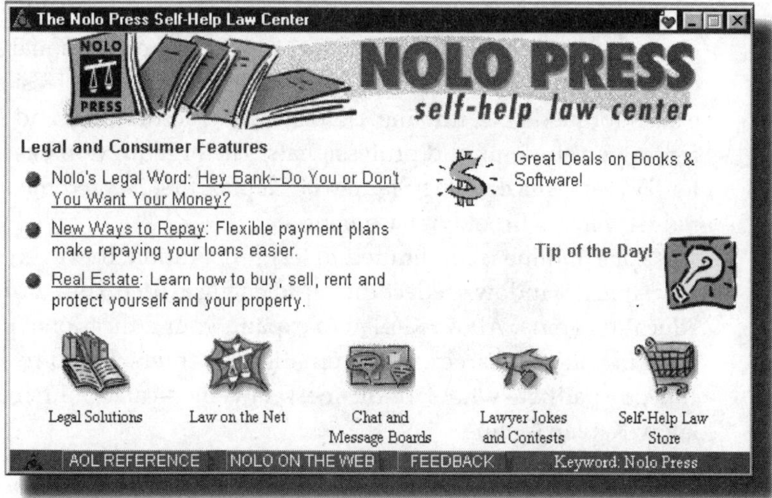

Figure 10-40: Look to the Nolo Law Center for legal self-help.

Kaplan Online

AOL offers a number of resources for the student, a few of which we'll discuss next. One of them is a resource that's specifically intended to help students get into college, and its name is Kaplan Online (see Figure 10-41).

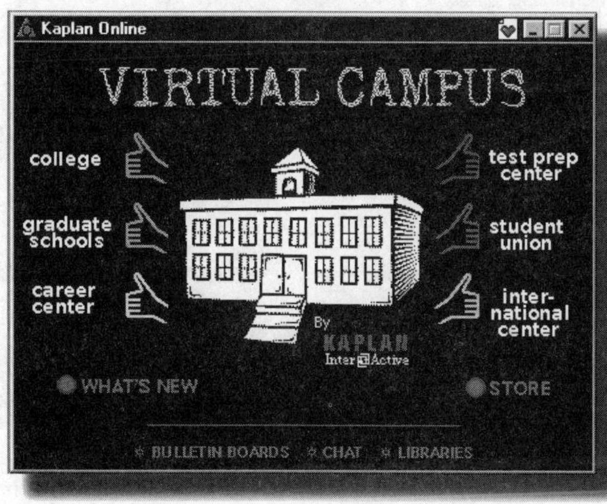

Figure 10-41: Kaplan Online offers sample test questions, examples of how to prepare for the test, a countdown to the test day—even what to do after the test. Best of all, there's no charge. It's all available at keyword: **Kaplan**.

Kaplan offers courses for over 30 standardized tests: college admissions exams, such as the SAT and ACT; graduate and professional school entrance exams, such as the GMAT, GRE, LSAT, and MCAT; professional licensing exams for medicine, nursing, dentistry, and accounting; and specialized exams for foreign students and professionals. The organization has been doing this for 55 years, since young Stanley H. Kaplan first created the test preparation industry in his Brooklyn basement.

Kaplan Online is not limited to test preparation, however, and its recently redesigned windows reflect the rapid changes occurring throughout the education arena. Allow Kaplan to expand your educational perspectives by checking out the Career and International Centers. If you're about to enter college, graduate school, or business, law, medical, or nursing school, get to know Kaplan Online.

The Gonyea Online Career Center

Let's see, now: we've helped you select a college and even helped you prepare for entry, and now that you've graduated, it's time to find a job. We can help with that too, in the form of the Gonyea Online Career Center (see Figure 10-42).

Figure 10-42: The Gonyea Online Career Center is the first electronic career and employment guidance agency in America. Use the keywords: **Career Center**.

Dan Gonyea's Online Career Center offers career counseling, articles on hiring trends, libraries of résumé and employment letter templates, profiles of those elusive home computing business opportunities, and a database of employer contacts. There's information on over 200 occupations—job descriptions, entrance qualifications, salaries, future prospects, and working conditions—in the occupational profiles database, and there's help-wanted and employment agency databases as well. You can even list your professional skills in the Career Center's talent database. If you're looking for work, this place is a gold mine of opportunity.

Ask-a-Teacher

Perhaps we're ahead of ourselves. You might not be in the job market yet. Lots of AOL members are still students. For students, Ask-a-Teacher (keywords: **Ask-a-Teacher**) offers tutoring, help with homework, or assistance in polishing skills that have become rusty. In particular, this is the place to find teachers—teachers who are online and dedicated to the pursuit of academic goals (see Figure 10-43).

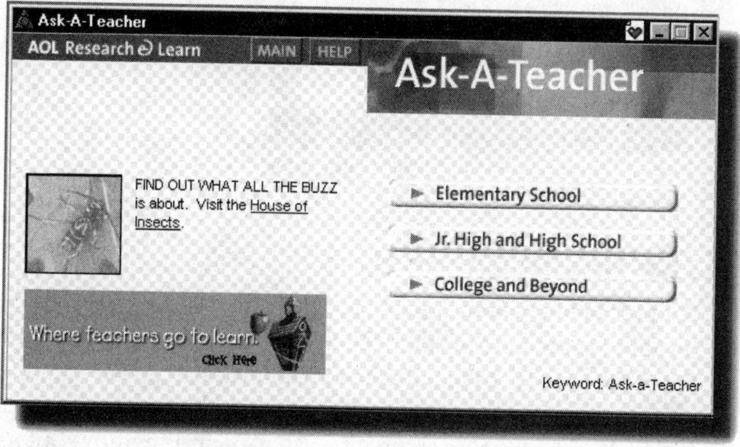

Figure 10-43: The Ask-a-Teacher area is where students can find teachers and other professionals who will help them with their schoolwork.

College Board Online

Founded in 1900, the College Board is a national, nonprofit association of more than 2,500 institutions and schools, systems, organizations, and agencies serving both higher and secondary education. The College Board assists students moving from high school to college with services that include guidance, admissions, placement, credit by examination, and financial aid. In addition, the board is chartered to sponsor research, provide a forum to discuss common problems of secondary and higher education, and address questions of educational standards.

Which is a mouthful. What it means is that the College Board Online (keywords: **College Board**) is an invaluable service to the student faced with all the college-related questions: Where should I go? How much will it cost? What are the admission requirements? What are my chances of being accepted? (See Figure 10-44.)

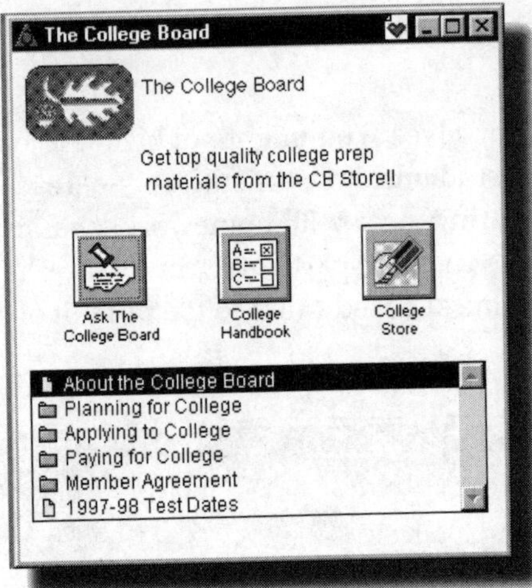

Figure 10-44: The College Board Online (keywords: **College Board**) is invaluable for the student contemplating a college education.

The Health Channel

For at least the last hundred years, health care decisions have been solely the province of doctors, modern society's scientific experts on the machinery of the human body. In real life and in countless television and film productions, patients have traditionally played passive rather than active roles in the management of their personal health care and therapy. But as the end of the century approaches, deep and significant changes are afoot in the definition and delivery of complete health care, many of which offer patients greatly increased participation, understanding, and compassion—not to mention renewed status as human beings.

America Online's noteworthy contribution to this trend is found at the Health Channel, an online compendium of medical networks and resources that has no peer elsewhere online. If a single example were to be requested as to the benefits of the online medium, the Health Channel (see Figure 10-45) would be an excellent choice.

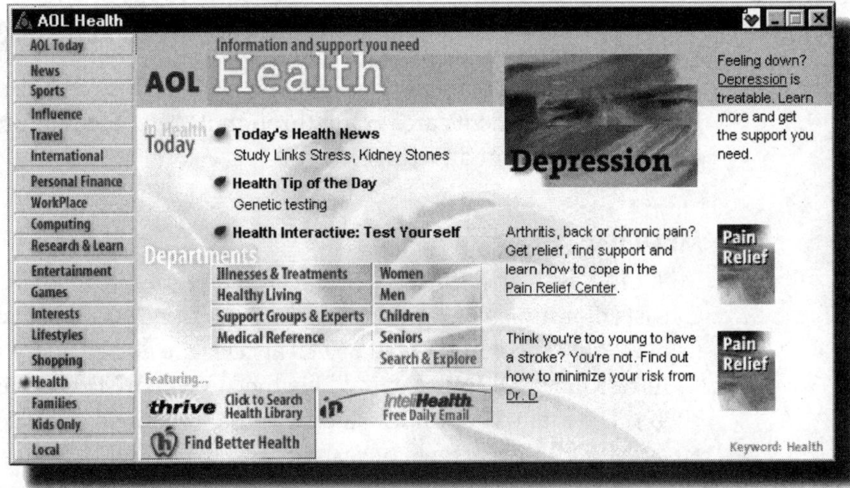

Figure 10-45: The Health Channel stands ready to help you with every aspect of your well-being.

Illnesses & Treatments

A perfect example of how you can take an active role in your health care is the Illnesses & Treatments area at keyword: **Illness** (see Figure 10-46).

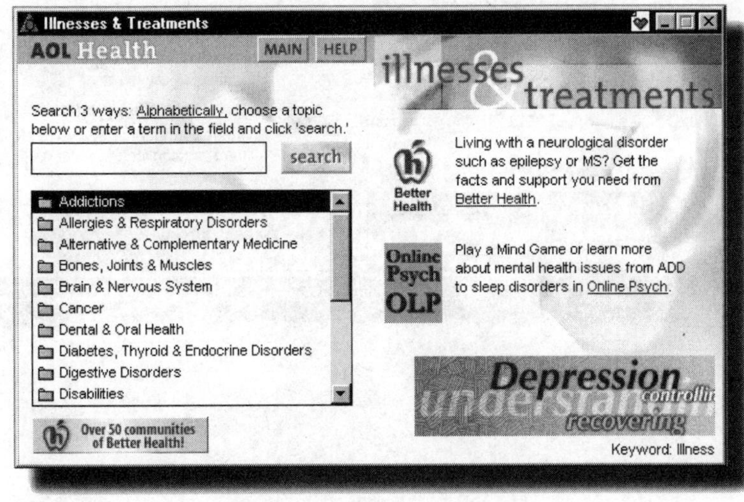

Figure 10-46: Do you have a health problem but you're not quite ready to visit a doctor? Visit the Illnesses & Treatments area with a description of your ailment. Hundreds of resources are referenced here.

The Illnesses & Treatments area references hundreds of resources, both at AOL and on the Web—an aggregation that's growing every day. Simply type in a few words describing your ailment, click the Search button, and let the Illnesses & Treatments area comb through its references to provide a listing of those perfectly suited to you.

MEDLINE

MEDLINE is the health-care industry's bibliographic medical database. It consists of millions of records and abstracts from over 3,500 medical journals from all over the world—and 35,000 articles are added every month.

Access to MEDLINE is gained via the keyword: **MEDLINE** (see Figure 10-47). The main MEDLINE window leads directly to several incredibly rich areas: MEDLINE's arsenal of search tools, the MEDLINE Message Board, the Better Health and Medical Forum, and the Personal Empowerment Network.

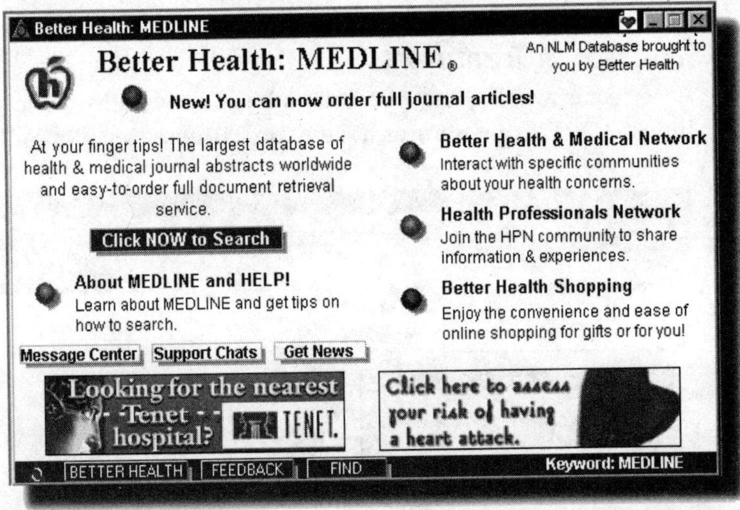

Figure 10-47: No longer the exclusive province of medical professionals, MEDLINE is your health information gateway to medical research, organizations, and health-related groups.

MEDLINE is one of the few areas on AOL where you'll incur extra charges if you pursue your query to its fullest extent. A MEDLINE search will produce a number of abstracts (summaries of journal articles) for you to consider. When you find an article you'd like to read, you'll have to order it from MEDLINE. There's a charge for this, but then again, everyone—doctors, nurses, researchers—pays the same amount.

The Shopping Channel

This section is your guide to a new generation of shopping—indeed, a new definition of buying and selling that is being written even as you read these words.

Electronic marketing is in its infancy. As you explore, remember that what you will find is important, not only for the products and marketing models available now, but also as a prediction of product selection and store location of the future.

The AOL Store

Electronic commerce has become big business. By the holiday season of 1997, e-commerce was vying for a double-digit slice of the retail marketplace, and rightfully so: shopping with your computer is not only convenient, the transactions are secure, and the order processing is almost instantaneous.

The AOL Store advances electronic commerce one more step up the ladder of convenience: this isn't really a store; it's not even an electronic store. It's a mall. The AOL Store is actually a collection of shops: the Hardware Shop, the Software Shop, the Modem Shop, the Digital Shop, the Book Shop, and the Logo Shop (see Figure 10-48). Each one offers the most popular products of its genre, all popularly priced, and all conveniently catalogued at the keywords: **AOL Store**.

Figure 10-48: Show your pride in America Online! Browse AOL using your new Modem-Shop modem while you sip coffee from your Logo-Shop AOL mug.

1-800-FLOWERS

It's easy to forget that communication is much more than words. No matter the occasion, situation, or location, one of the most pleasant and touching messages you can send is the gift of flowers, a task made simple by entering keyword: **Flowers**. (See Figure 10-49.)

You'll find seasonal and holiday suggestions for fresh cut flowers as well as event and gift items including chocolates, cakes, centerpieces, gift baskets, wreaths, dried flower arrangements, and even a gift reminder service. You'll find it all at keyword: **Flowers**.

Figure 10-49: The world's premier florist and gift shop: 1-800-FLOWERS.

Hallmark Connections

How many times has a birthday or anniversary slipped your mind until it was nearly upon you? What do you do? You could stop what you're doing, jump in your car, drive to a store, and get a card, but who has that kind of time these days? Well, Hallmark Connections is here to change all of that (see Figure 10-50).

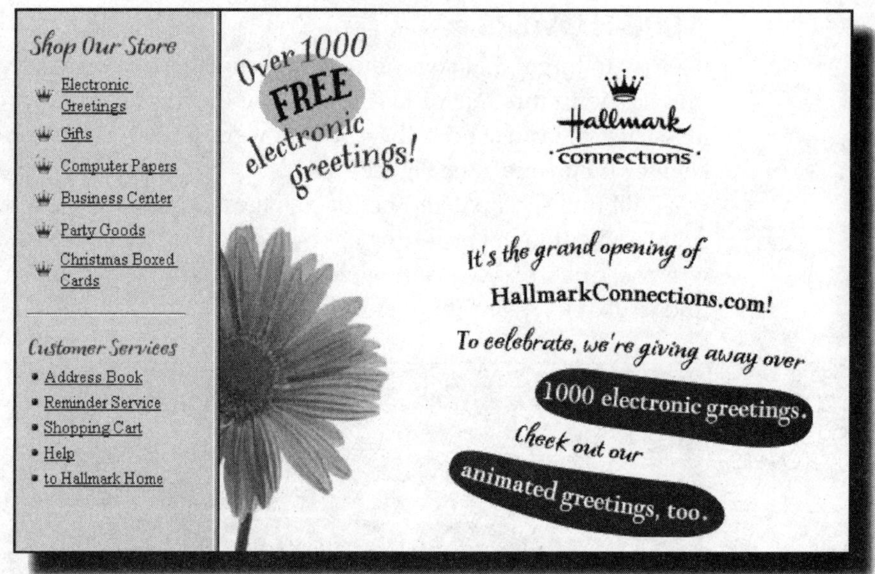

Figure 10-50: Hallmark Connections—when you care enough to send the very best (but don't want to drive to the store . . .).

The area is organized much like a real-world card department in any store you might visit. You can choose from seven departments with cards ranging from seasonal to business greetings. Once you've selected a card department, AOL will either ask you to narrow your search a bit further or show you a list of available cards within your chosen department. Once you select a particular card, you'll be able to see what it actually looks like.

You'll also be able to personalize your card by supplying the recipient's name (or other information as indicated) as well as your own closing message and name. The cards will be printed on recycled paper, and your closing message and name will be printed in a scripted font to simulate a signature. Your card will then be mailed to any address in the United States—either within 48 hours of your order or at any time you choose.

Eddie Bauer

Considering its humble beginnings 75 years ago in a small downtown Seattle store, Eddie Bauer has become one of America's most innovative retailers, with over 400 stores in 3 countries, a CD-ROM, and now, an online presence on AOL (see Figure 10-51).

In addition to Eddie Bauer's traditional line of exceptional products with a casual attitude, the keywords: **Eddie Bauer** also take you to the Eddie Bauer/ Global ReLeaf Tree Project, a program designed to plant healthy, native trees in eight reforestation sites in North America. All you do is click the order button and Eddie Bauer plants a one- to two-year-old tree on your behalf for each dollar you donate and matches your donation.

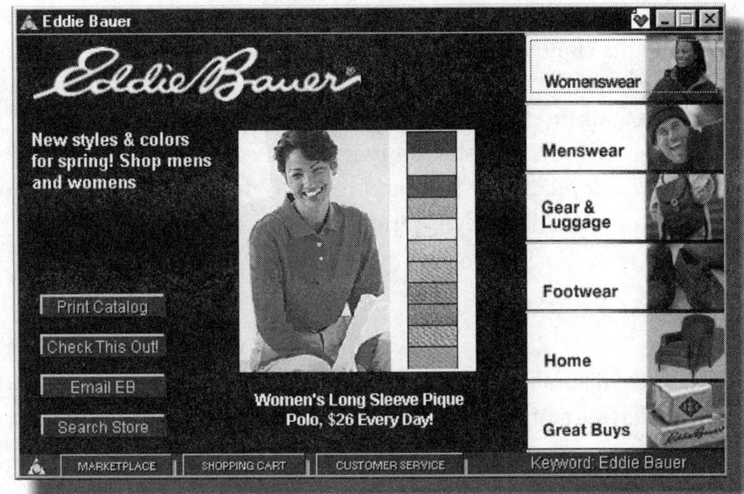

Figure 10-51: The greenest commercial destination online, Eddie Bauer offers clothing, field accessories, products for the home, and the Eddie Bauer/Global ReLeaf Tree Project. Use the keywords: **Eddie Bauer**, of course!

Eddie Bauer and The Global ReLeaf project have planted over 300,000 trees to date.

One Hanes Place

One Hanes Place (see Figure 10-52) is also a new addition to AOL. The Main Store at One Hanes Place is stocked with great everyday values on fashion legwear, intimate apparel, and activewear as well as brand-name basics. You'll save up to 50 percent on Hanes, L'eggs, Bali, Playtex, Hanes Her Way, Champion, Just My Size, and Color Me Natural products.

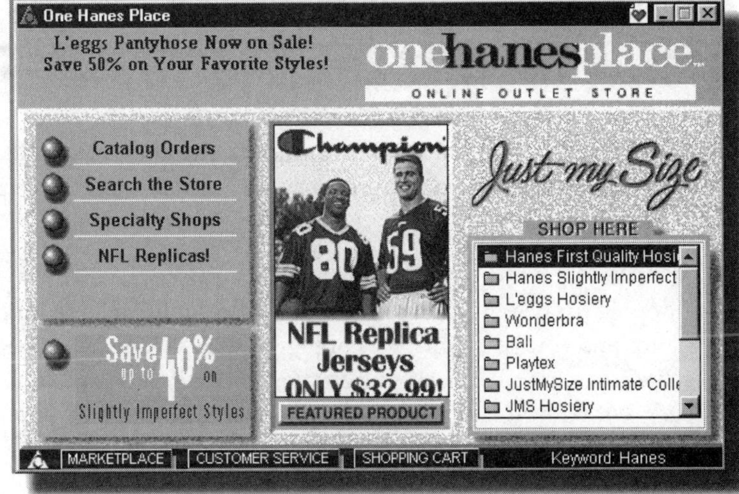

Figure 10-52: The One Hanes Place Main Store and the Olympic Shop "store within a store."

The Olympic Shop at One Hanes Place is a "store within a store." Champion and Hanes were two of the sponsors of the 1996 Centennial Olympic Games in Atlanta. The Olympic Shop is where you can find authentic apparel from Champion and officially licensed apparel from Hanes. This shop was created with the whole family in mind—its inventory includes everything from Olympic printed apparel (collectible stuff!) to Looney Tunes goodies. Take a look around by typing the keyword: **Hanes**.

Tower Records

When Tower Records went online, Tom went to heaven. He's a music junkie—CDs are his habit—and without a weekly fix he's petulant and sullen (ask Jennifer!). Imagine his delight, then, when Tower offered him the ability to shop for music without having to leave his keyboard! (See Figure 10-53.)

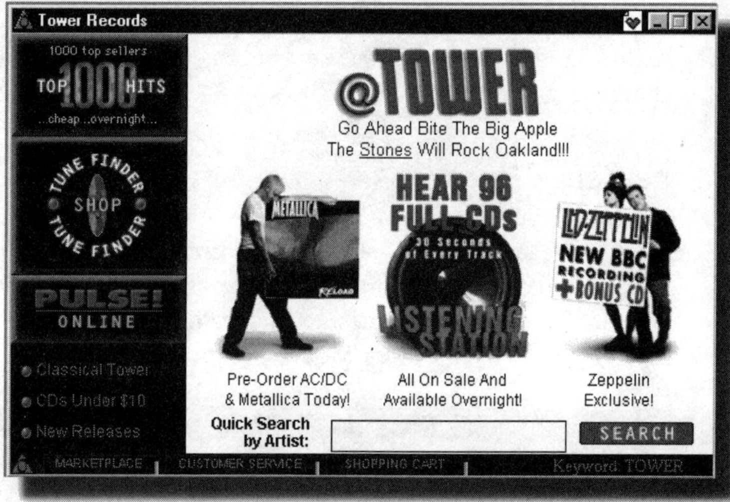

Figure 10-53: Tower Records offers sustenance for the musically malnourished.

Perhaps most significantly, the online version of Tower Records allows you to *listen* to excerpts of certain recordings. Just click the Listening Station icon.

Health & Vitamin Express

Shopping for health care products can be as confusing as a foreign language. Claims and counterclaims, lists of ingredients as long as an IRS "clarification"—we've sometimes left health care stores as bewildered as a hound with hay fever. But with AOL's help, it doesn't have to be that way (see Figure 10-54).

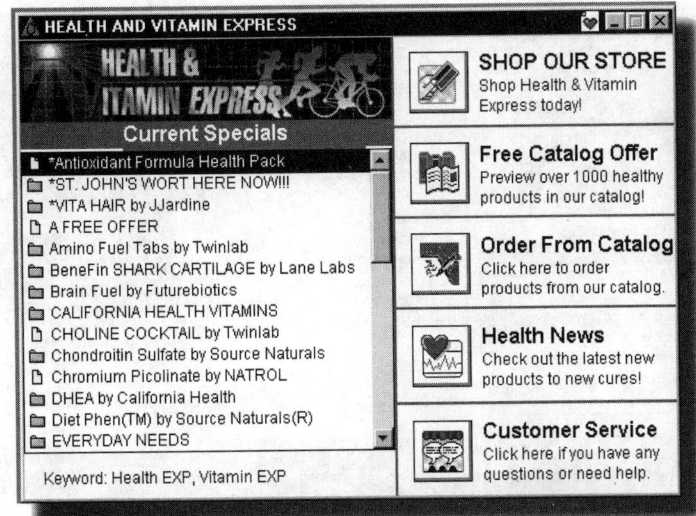

Figure 10-54: Health & Vitamin Express offers health care products—and consultation too.

The people at Health & Vitamin Express (keywords: **Health EXP**) understand that health care can be complex and confusing, so they offer what any good store should offer: a comprehensive product array, low prices, and good information that's available for free. You can leave a message online and return later for a reply, or you can call their toll-free hotline for an immediate consultation about your individual needs and the products that can best meet those needs. And once you've determined what you're looking for, chances are very good you'll find it at Health & Vitamin Express at 10 to 15 percent off regular prices.

Shoppers' Advantage

Speaking of browsing, millions of people browse Shoppers' Advantage every day. This is a little like the shopping "clubs" that have sprouted up nationwide: you pay a small annual membership fee and you're rewarded with a warehouse full of products, attractively priced, in stock, and ready for shipment. Shoppers' Advantage not only adds the convenience of online shopping (no crowds, no parking lots, no waiting), it guarantees the lowest prices anywhere or it will refund the difference. Now that's a powerful package! (See Figure 10-55.)

Figure 10-55: You can browse the store whether or not you're a member of Shoppers' Advantage—a significant advantage over local shopping clubs—and you can enroll online at any time.

The Sharper Image

For many of us, life is not complete without a Sharper Image Catalog. This is the ultimate toy store for children over 20, where technology perfects the art of living, courtesy of hundreds of products, each as compelling as a Popsicle in August.

There's a free customer service number (800-344-5555) and a 60-day return guarantee. There's a 60-day price protection plan too: if you see the same product advertised for less, The Sharper Image will refund the difference (see Figure 10-56).

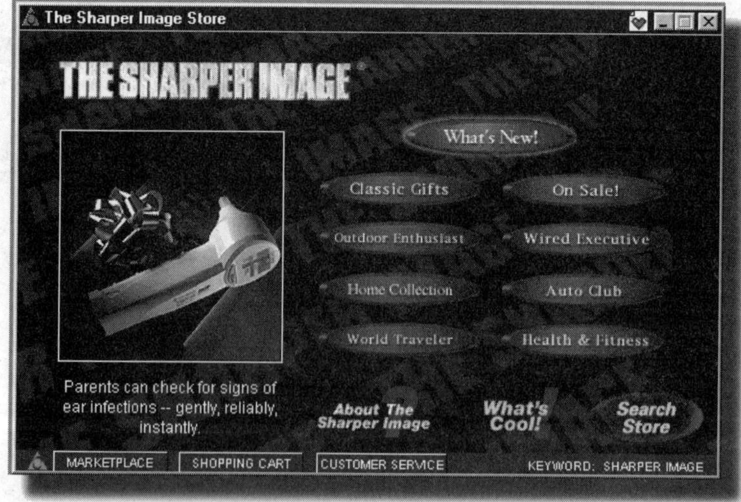

Figure 10-56: Use the keywords: **Sharper Image** for access to products to enhance your life, improve your health, and help the environment.

atOnce Software

Only a few years ago, an A-to-Z list of computer software would have been short and missing more than a few letters of the alphabet. Today that's all changed, and perusing software titles and capabilities is more like confronting the inventory of an entire library. Wouldn't it be nice if, like the library's catalog system, there was a place where a comprehensive, detailed list of software information could be found?

Such a place does exist, and you need look no further than AOL's atOnce Software (see Figure 10-57). Here you'll find thousands of software titles nestled in a database that's much easier to explore and contains much more information than your local library's book catalogue. If you're looking for software, or information on software, this is a great place to start. Just use the keyword: **atOnce**.

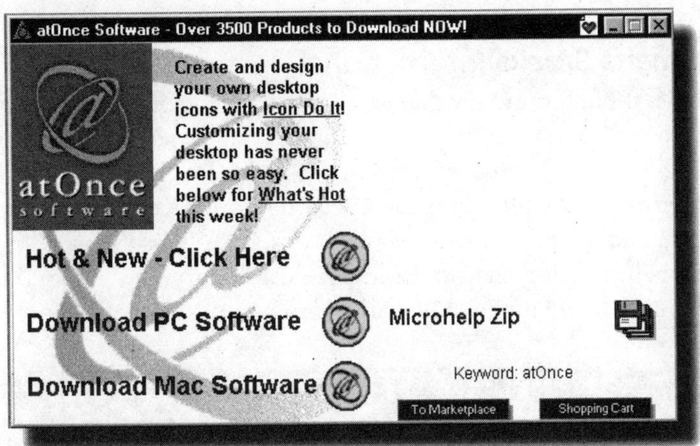

Figure 10-57: Looking for software information? The place to start is atOnce Software.

KidSoft Super Store

The KidSoft Super Store is the "kids" version of the atOnce Mail Order Store: a source for prescreened quality software just for children, with special emphasis on learning software (see Figure 10-58). You'll find software that focuses on reading, math, spelling, music, creativity/art, geography, reference, and much more, some featuring well-known names such as Mario, Putt-Putt, the Science Sleuths, Dr. Seuss, the Lion King, and Carmen Sandiego. And to make things easy as pie, you can search by age grouping, software title, or category to find descriptions and sample screens.

Figure 10-58: The KidSoft SuperStore: a software store just for kids.

Omaha Steaks International

Even though rampant change is a given in the online medium, some online discoveries tend to surprise more than others, such as food service businesses in general and Omaha Steaks in particular (see Figure 10-59). Omaha Steaks International's reputation as a premium purveyor of steaks, meats, and other gourmet foods spans 75 years, 8 states, and 28 locations, with its mail order branch claiming an astonishing 44-year history. So at second glance, Omaha Steaks's move to the online arena is a completely natural progression.

Figure 10-59: From Omaha, Nebraska, and the heart of cattle country direct to your door, Omaha Steaks's internationally recognized meats, seafood, and desserts are available now at keyword: **Omaha**.

Omaha Steaks's mission is the delivery of the very best beef, poultry, pork, veal, lamb, seafood, and desserts to your Omaha Steaks table, or to your front door. If your epicurean interests are creative, you'll also find proven, delicious recipes from the nation's heartland. And don't forget to check out Omaha Steaks's Chocolate Ecstasy Cake and triple-trimmed filet mignons in the Specialties area. Are you hungry now? Just use the keyword: **Omaha**.

Caffe Starbucks

After all this talk of shopping, you're probably ready for a good cup of coffee, right? Then you should not be surprised to find that Starbucks, one of the premier suppliers of gourmet coffees, is as close as AOL and the keyword: **Starbucks**. Being a top coffee contender is no mean feat in the northwest, where a request for a "double-skinny-mocha-decaf" is received with utter aplomb. And now you can join in the coffee revolution no matter where you live (see Figure 10-60).

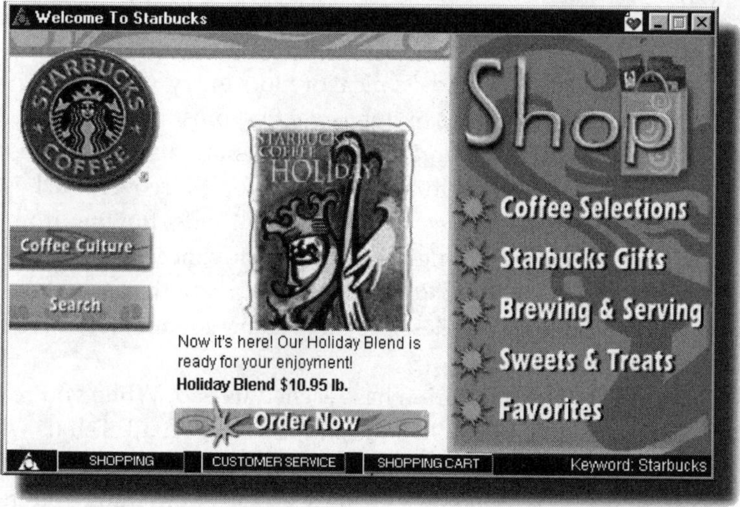

Figure 10-60: Coffee advice, coffee philosophy, coffee cups, even regular coffee deliveries—Starbucks is your one-stop coffee resource.

No discussion of coffee would be complete without mention of the myriad delectables that can transform a superior coffee break into an extraordinary culinary experience. Just click the Sweets and Treats button and unleash your imagination.

MacDestinations

Speaking of sweets and treats, destinations on the Mac are as good as they get. Jennifer reports that virtually every one of the destinations we've detailed in this chapter is identical on the Mac. The only differences appear when you go to the Computing Channel; the Mac has its own set of forums, designed by and for Mac aficionados. For example, rather than a "font petting zoo," you'll find a "Fontorium" (at keyword: **MacDTP**). And, of course, there are some special Mac destinations, like the Apple on AOL forum at keyword: **Apple**.

To log text in windows (not chat or Instant Messages) on the Mac, open a System log in your Log Manager. Chat and Instant Messages can be captured with their own logs, also accessible via the Log Manager.

That's it! If you discover something Jennifer missed and would like some help understanding how it works, send her mail at screen name "Jennifer". Her Mac is always at the ready.

Everybody Out of the Bus!

Our tour has concluded. Typical of tours everywhere, ours has been an abridgment, a synopsis of things we find most interesting about AOL. You will find your own favorites, and in so doing discover things that we not only didn't mention but didn't know ourselves. Moreover, AOL is a moving target: like most online services, AOL is almost fluid—flowing from opportunity to opportunity, conforming to trends and advances, relentlessly expanding to fill new voids. We'll try to keep up, and no doubt there will be another edition of this book someday to describe an even bigger and better AOL than the one we know today.

Meanwhile, this edition has reached its end. While you're waiting for the next one, sign on to AOL and send us some e-mail. Tell us what you want included (or excluded) in the next edition. Tell us what you liked or disliked about this book. Send us logs, files, articles—anything you think might complement *The Official America Online Tour Guide*. We look forward to hearing from you.

Jennifer Watson (Jennifer)
Tom Lichty (MajorTom)

Appendix A

Making the Connection

If you have never used America Online—if you have never even installed the software—this chapter is for you. It's written for novices—those who hold disks in their sweaty palms and wonder if they are stalwart enough to connect their PCs to the outside world.

If you *have* used America Online—if you already have an account and a password—read on. We'll tell you when it's appropriate to skip the new member material in this chapter and what page to turn to.

Things You'll Need

Let's take inventory here. There are a few things you need before you can connect with America Online. You may already have them, but let's be sure.

The Computer

This appendix describes installation of the AOL Windows client software, and is appropriate for either AOL for Windows 3.1 or AOL for Windows 95. As this book went to press, the Macintosh version of the AOL installation routine was not available. However, we have been assured that the differences will be few: Macintosh users should feel free to use this appendix for assistance in installing the software, though the instructions in this appendix should not be followed verbatum.

You will need at least 8 megabytes of RAM (random access memory): this is the minimum requirement for running Windows 95 regardless of what the specifications say; if you can afford it, get at least 16MB—you'll appreciate the difference in all your Windows programs' performance. You'll also need a hard disk with about 28MB of free space—even more if you plan to use the Web browser's cache. You will also need a CD-ROM drive. If you need the software on a medium other than the one you have, call 800-827-6364.

The Fine Print

The minimum required disk space is for the installation of the software only. America Online offers a disk-based cache feature (for use with the World Wide Web) that speeds the presentation of Web pages. The speed gain is so significant that anyone planning to use the Web should also plan to use the cache.

If you do plan to use the cache, assume you will need to allocate at least 5 percent of your hard disk—more if it's available. The World Wide Web and other Internet features are discussed in Chapter 4.

Your AOL software also offers a Personal Filing Cabinet, where you can store your electronic mail, and Favorite Places (the Personal Filing Cabinet and e-mail are discussed in Chapter 3; the Favorite Places feature is discussed in Chapter 5). If you intend to use the Personal Filing Cabinet, add another 5MB of hard disk space to the minimum requirement.

In other words, for a full installation, you will need 8MB for the software, 5 percent of your disk's capacity—we'll call it 25MB—for the browser's cache, and 5MB for the Personal Filing Cabinet. That's a total of 38MB—ample room for America Online to roam.

Finally, a display system capable of displaying 256 colors is recommended. Your AOL software works with 16-color systems, but the presentation of the service is optimized for 256 colors or more. Refer to your Windows manual (or the manual for your video display adapter, if one is installed as an option) for information on how to change the number of colors your system displays.

We digressed. Essentially, any Windows-compatible machine will do. If yours isn't the latest model—if it doesn't have 435 horsepower and fuel injection and a 5-speed transmission—don't worry.

The Telephone Line

You need access to a telephone line. Your standard residential phone line is fine. A multiline business telephone might be more of a challenge. What's really important is that your telephone plugs into a modular telephone jack (called an *RJ-11* jack, if you care about that sort of thing). It's the one with the square hole—measuring about a quarter inch—on one side.

Whenever you're online, your telephone is out of commission for normal use. If you try to make a voice call using an extension phone on the same line, it's as if you picked up the phone and someone else was having a conversation—except that you'll *never* want to eavesdrop on an America Online session; the screeching sound that modems make when communicating with each other is about as pleasant as fingernails on a blackboard—and about as intelligible.

The Modem

A modem (short for *mo*dulator/*dem*odulator) is a device that converts computer data into audible tones that the telephone system can transmit. Modems are required at both ends of the line; America Online has a number of them at their end as well.

Modems are rated according to their data-transmission speed. If you're shopping for a modem, get one rated at 56 kilobits per second ("56 Kbps") if you can. Modems rated at 56 Kbps are fast and are capable of extracting every bit of performance America Online has to offer. (If America Online doesn't offer 56 Kbps capability in your area when you read this, be patient. It's probably in the works.) On the other hand, high-speed modems really only strut their stuff when you're browsing the World Wide Web or downloading files (discussed in Chapters 4 and 6, respectively). In other words, a 14.4 kilobaud modem might satisfy your needs if all you really want to do is exchange electronic mail. That's all Tom has on his old laptop, for example. A 14.4 kilobaud modem, however, should be considered the minimum, if you can find one at all.

We prefer modems with speakers and lights. Lights, of course, are only found on external modems, and external modems typically require an available serial port. If you have an internal modem, you won't need an available serial port (and you won't have any lights to watch). Tom's modem has six or seven lights. He doesn't understand most of them, but they look important. The one marked RD (receiving data) is worth watching when you are transferring a file (we discuss file downloading in Chapter 6). It should stay on almost continuously. If, during a file transfer, your RD light is off more than it's on, you've either got a noisy phone line or the system is extremely busy. Whatever the cause, it's best to halt the file transfer (America Online always leaves a Finish Later button on the screen for that purpose) and resume it another time. That's why we advise buying a modem with lights: if you don't have them, how can you tell what's going on?

A number of PCs now offer internal modems: modems inside the PC itself. If you have an internal modem, you won't tie up a communications port on the back of your PC (leaving it available for some other purpose), but you won't have any lights to watch either. Life is full of compromises.

Baud Rates

The term *baud rate* refers to the signaling rate, or the number of times per second the signal changes. Don't confuse the baud rate with *bits per second* (bps)—they're not the same thing. By using modern electronic wizardry, today's modems can transmit 2, 3, or 4 bits with each change of signal, increasing the speed of data transfer considerably. Because it takes 8 bits to make a byte—the amount of data required to describe a single character of text—a modem rated at 56K can theoretically transfer 7,000 bytes per second.

Alas, the world is an imperfect place—especially the world of phone lines. If there's static or interference of any kind on the line, data transmission is garbled. And even one misplaced bit can destroy the integrity of an entire file. To address the problem, America Online validates the integrity of received data. In plain English, this means that America Online sends a packet of information (a couple of seconds' worth) to your PC and then waits for the PC to say, "I got that, and it's okay," before it sends the next packet. Validation like this means things run a little slower than they would without validation, but it's necessary. We're probably down to a minimum of 5,000 characters per second once we factor in the time it takes to accommodate data validation.

Then there's noise. You've heard it: static on the line. If you think it interferes with voice communication, it's murder on data. Often your PC says, "That packet was no good—send it again," and America Online complies. The reliability of any particular telephone connection is capricious. Some are better than others. Noise, however, is a definite factor, and packets have to be resent once in a while. Now we're probably down to a minimum of 4,000 characters per second on a good telephone line on a good day—which is still over 45 lines of text per second at 56K.

In other words, a 56K modem isn't 24 times faster than a 2400 bps model, and a 9600 bps modem isn't 4 times faster than one rated at 2400 bps. On the other hand, a 56K modem doesn't cost 24 times as much as a 2400 bps model. What we're trying to say is, in terms of baud per buck, 56K is your best buy.

If your modem is of the external variety, it will need power of some kind. Some external modems use batteries, but most use AC power and plug into the wall. Be sure an outlet is available.

Most important, be sure you have the proper cables. For an external modem, you need two cables: one to connect the modem to the PC and another one to connect the modem to the phone jack. The modem-to-phone-jack cable bundled with many modems rarely exceeds 6 feet. If the distance between your modem and your phone jack exceeds that distance, you can buy an extension cable at a phone, electronics, or hardware store. Extension cables are standardized and are inexpensive.

Few external modems include a PC-to-modem cable. You probably will have to purchase one if you're buying an external modem. Check your modem's manual to see if your modem requires a hardware-handshaking (high-speed) cable. If it does, it's essential that you use one, as it will provide a more reliable connection at top speed.

You might also need to make some provision for using your phone on the same line when you're not online. It's less complicated if the modem has a jack for your phone. In that case, you can plug the modem into the phone jack, then plug the phone into the modem. The jacks on the back of the modem should be marked for this. Note: You will *not* be able to use your modem and your phone simultaneously; it's one or the other.

If your modem is internal, or if your external modem only has a single jack and you want to continue using your phone as well as your modem on the same line, you might also want to invest in a modular splitter, which plugs into the phone jack on your wall and makes two jacks out of one. You plug your phone into one of the splitter's jacks and your modem into the other. Plugging both devices into the same jack won't interfere with everyday telephone communications; incoming calls will continue to go to your phone, just as they did before. You should be able to find a splitter at a phone, electronics, or hardware store for less than $3.

The best solution, of course, is to get a second telephone line for your modem. Contact your telephone company to explore the potential.

If all this sounds like a lot of wires to keep track of and you have trouble plugging in a toaster, don't worry. Most modems come with good instructions, and the components are such that you can't connect anything backward. Just follow the instructions and you'll be all right.

The Money

Before you sign on to America Online for the first time, there's something else you'll need: money. America Online wants to know how you plan to pay the balance on your account each month. Cash won't do. Instead, you can provide a credit card number: VISA, MasterCard, American Express, or Discover Card are all acceptable. So are certain bank debit cards. Or have your checkbook handy; America Online can have your bank automatically transfer the funds each month if you provide the necessary numbers.

The Screen Name

We're almost ready, but right now we want you to get all other thoughts out of your mind and decide what you want to call yourself. Every America Online member has a unique screen name. Screen names are how America Online tells us apart from each other. You must have one, and it has to be different from everybody else's.

A screen name must consist of from 3 to 10 characters—letters, or letters and numbers. Punctuation and spaces are not acceptable. Millions of people use America Online, and they all have screen names of 10 or fewer characters. Chances are, the screen name you want most is taken, so have a number of alternates ready ahead of time and prepare yourself for disappointment. Hardly anyone ever gets his or her first choice. Jennifer was extremely lucky to get her first name as her screen name. Unless you have a very rare name, you can bet someone else has already grabbed it.

Though screen names aren't case sensitive—you can address mail to majortom or MajorTom or MAJORTOM, and it will still get to Tom—they always appear onscreen the way they were first entered. Tom first entered his screen name, for example, as MajorTom. If you send mail to majortom, he will see MajorTom on the To line of his incoming mail. He's MajorTom in chat rooms and Instant Messages as well. Keep this in mind as you enter your screen name for the first time, and capitalize your screen name as you want others to see it.

There's no going back, by the way. Once America Online accepts your initial screen name, it's yours as long as you remain a member. Though your account can have as many as five screen names (to accommodate other people in your family or your alter egos), your initial screen name is the one America Online uses to establish and verify your identity. For this reason, your initial screen name can't be changed. Be prepared with a zinger (and a half-dozen alternates), otherwise, America Online will assign you something like TomLi5437, and you'll forever be known by that name. People have a hard time relating to a name like that.

MajorTom

Tom worked his way through college as a traffic reporter for an Oregon radio station. He was both reporter and pilot. It was a great job: perfect hours for a student, easy work, and unlimited access to a flashy plane. It didn't pay much, but somehow that wasn't important—not in the halcyon days of bachelorhood.

Though this is sure to date him, David Bowie was an ascending force on the music scene in those days. Impertinent, perhaps—a little too androgynous and scandalous for the conservative element of the Nixon era—but definitely a hit-maker. Tom's station played Bowie. On his first day, the morning show disk jockey switched on his microphone and hailed, "Ground Control to Major Tom"—a line from Bowie's Space Oddity—to get his attention. The name stuck. He was known as Major Tom from then on.

When the time came for him to pick his screen name years ago, America Online suggested TomLi5437 and he balked. "How about just plain Tom?" he asked. It's in use, America Online replied. He tried four others, and America Online continued to remind him of his lack of imagination. In desperation he tried MajorTom and America Online accepted it. Once an initial screen name is accepted, that's it. He's MajorTom on America Online now and will be forever more.

The Password

Oh yes, you need a password. Without a password, anyone who knows your screen name can log on using your name and have a heyday on your nickel. Passwords must be from four to eight characters in length, and any combination of letters, or letters and numbers, is acceptable. (As is the case with screen names, punctuation and spaces aren't allowed in passwords.) You will enter your password every time you sign on, so choose something fairly easy to remember—something that's not a finger-twister to type—but something hard enough that others won't get it. It should be different from your screen name, phone number, Social Security number, address, or real name—something no one else would ever guess, even if they know you well. Avoid words you could find in a dictionary as well.

A Case for Elaborate Passwords

In his book *The Cuckoo's Egg,* Cliff Stoll describes computer hackers' methods for breaking passwords. Since most computers already have a dictionary on disk—all spell checkers use dictionaries—the hackers simply program their computers to try every word in the dictionary as a password. It sounds laborious, but computers don't mind.

Read this carefully: *No one from America Online will ever ask you for your password.* This is another hacker's ruse: lurking in America Online's dark corners, hackers troll for new members. When they spot someone they think is new, they'll send e-mail or an Instant Message (a real-time message that pops onto your screen) masquerading as an America Online employee. They'll say they're verifying billing records, or something like that, and ask for your password—this is referred to as *phishing. Don't reply!* Instead, make a note of the perpetrator's screen name, then use the keyword: **TOS** (it's free) to access the Terms of Service and determine what you should do next.

In other words, we're making a case for elaborate passwords here. Don't make it personal, don't use your Social Security number, don't write it down, select something that's not in a dictionary, and never, ever give out your password to *anyone.* This is important.

Installing the Software

Finally, we're ready to get our hands dirty. Don't fret: installing the AOL software is a straightforward process. An installation program does all the work for you.

Insert the CD into your CD-ROM drive. Connect your modem to your PC and turn it on. Refer to your modem's instruction manual if you're not sure how to connect it. The modem doesn't have to be connected in order to install the software, but the assumptions the installer program makes about your hardware will be more accurate if it is. It is also recommended that you avoid running other applications while you're installing America Online.

Start Windows 95 and choose Run from the Start menu. Type **D:\Setup** (if your CD-ROM drive isn't drive D:, substitute the appropriate letter designation) and click OK. Eventually, the installer program's Welcome screen will appear (see Figure A-1).

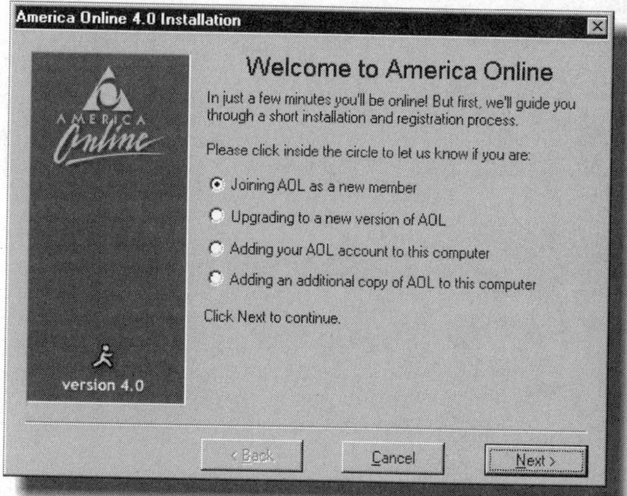

Figure A-1: The Installer program's Welcome screen is displayed when the installer is loaded and ready to run.

The installer will first ask you to indicate if you are a new member, if you're upgrading to the new software, if you're adding your AOL account to your computer, or just adding another copy of the software. New members will want to first option (the default). Once you've made your choice, click the Next button.

A few minutes might pass as the installer determines the best way to install your software. It's looking at the amount of space on your hard disk. It's also looking for an earlier version of the AOL software on your disk. We'll discuss that potential later. The system examination process can take a while. Don't let it worry you: the installer isn't making any changes to your machine during this time.

The installer program assumes that you want to install the software in a C:\America Online 4.0 directory on your hard disk. (Note: We're using an early release of the software. The name of this directory could change by the time you read this. The point is, the new directory name will probably be unique, and it won't be the same as the name of the directory that's associated with the earlier version of America Online that you've been using.) If you want to have the program installed in a different subdirectory, either type over the existing path or click the Choose Directory button (shown in Figure A-2), find the one you want, then click OK. Be sure to include the drive letter and full path. Note: You need not create the directory—whatever it is—prior to installation. The installer program creates the directory if it doesn't already exist.

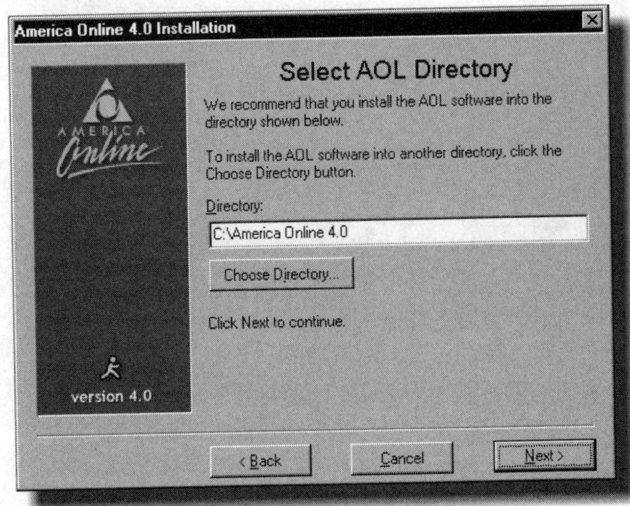

Figure A-2: Accept the directory provided or change the path (including the drive letter if necessary) as you see fit.

Once you click Figure A-2's Next button, the installer program will ask if you want to launch America Online each time you start your computer. You can also choose to have a shortcut added to your Microsoft Office toolbar if you have Microsoft Office installed. Choose the one(s) that you prefer (or none at all) and click Next.

Now you're almost ready to install the software itself. The program will let you know exactly how much free space is needed (as well as how much you have). If the required amount of space is larger than your available space, you'll need to free up space on your hard drive before continuing. If you have the space, click Next, and then watch the installer program do its work. This takes a couple of minutes. As it's working, a progress indicator keeps you abreast of the program's progress (see the center window in Figure A-3) and information about your new software is splashed on your screen. When the installation process is complete, America Online offers a Quick Reference Guide you can either read or print (or both)—it provides help with the rest of the setup and registration process plus plenty of helpful hints (bottom window of Figure A-3). When you're ready, click Finish.

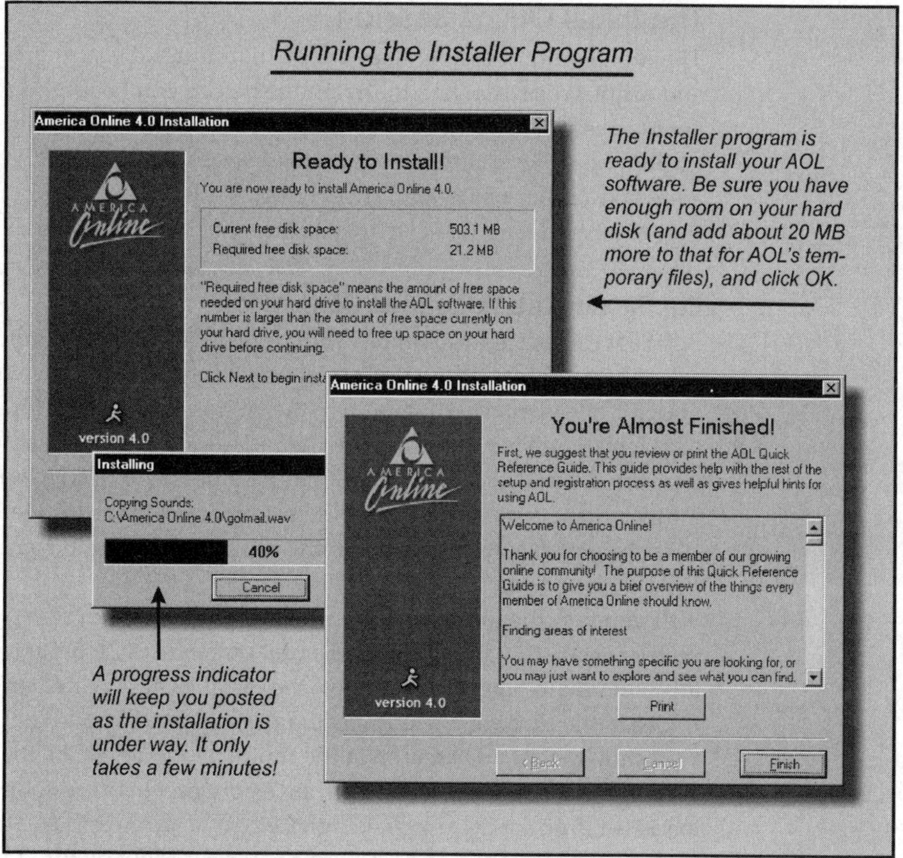

Figure A-3: Installation of the America Online software takes only a few minutes.

There. You've done it. You've installed the software, and you're ready to sign on (go ahead and click Yes when asked if you want to sign on). Eject the disk and put it in a safe place. Then let's get on with it.

Existing members, note: The upcoming pages discuss finding local phone numbers and declaring a billing method—matters that don't concern you. Please turn to the section titled "Upgrading" on page 439 of this appendix to continue your upgrade.

The Initial Online Session

The initial online session takes about 15 minutes. Be sure you have the time and uninterrupted access to the phone before you begin. You needn't worry about money: though you'll be online for a while, the setup process is accomplished on America Online's dime, not yours. You needn't worry if you make a mistake either; plenty of Cancel buttons are offered during the initial session. If you get cold feet, you can always hang up and start over.

Configuring the Telephone Connection

Before it can successfully make the connection, America Online needs to know a number of things about your telephone. It needs to know whether you have Touch-Tone or rotary dialing, whether it needs to dial a 9 (or something else) to reach an outside line, and whether a 1 should be dialed before the 800 number. Canadian and international members will need to supply additional information. Your modem should be connected to the phone line and to your PC before you sign on and begin the initial online session, and everything should be turned on.

If you told the installer program that you wanted to sign on after it completed installation, you'll be at the first screen of AOL Setup already (see the top window in Figure A-4). If not, the installer has created an America Online folder in the directory you indicated during installation. That folder is probably showing on your screen at the moment. Double-click the AOL icon to begin. The AOL Setup screen will probably greet you as soon as the software loads—if it does not, just click Sign On.

If you began automatic setup in the top window pictured in Figure A-4—something we recommend—you'll see Figure A-4's second window. Setup is now looking for the communications port to which your modem is attached and the modem itself.

A third screen will display your connection choices (see the third screen in Figure A-4). Again, the assumptions displayed here are the result of the Setup program's investigation routines. Choose the connection you want to use, or click Change Connection to make any necessary changes to the contents of this window. Here's a tip: Even if your modem is Hayes compatible, select your modem brand and model from the list. Specificity pays under these circumstances. When ready, click Next.

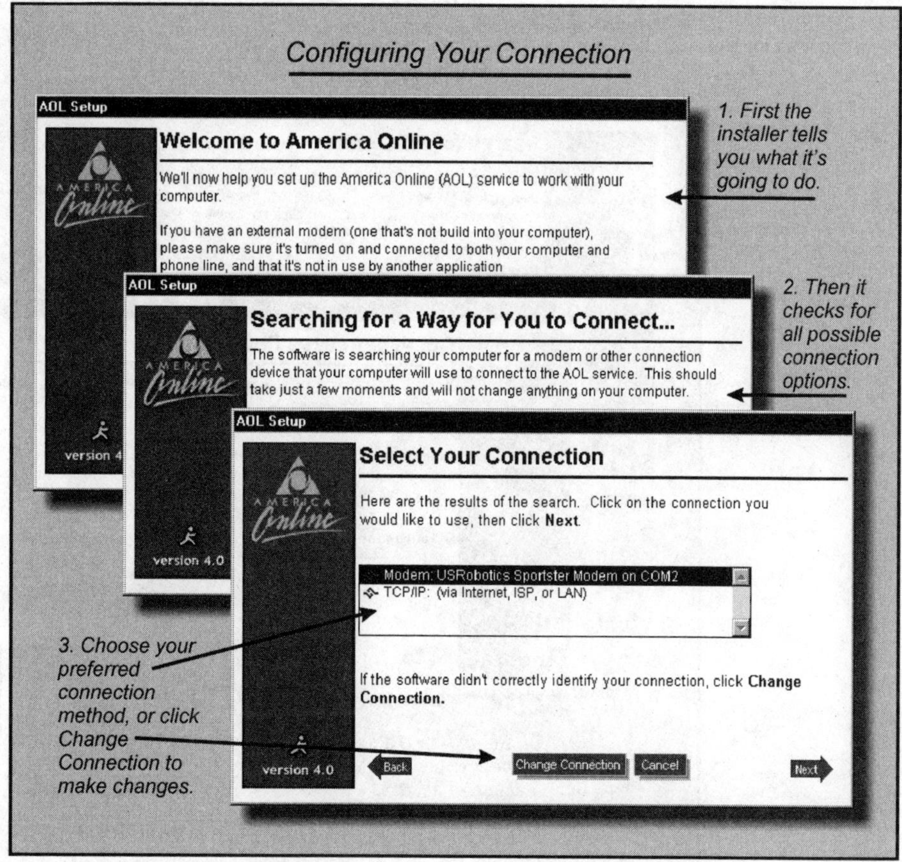

Figure A-4: Read these screens carefully, make changes if they're necessary, and take advantage of the opportunity to specify your modem.

Now AOL Setup needs to find access numbers for you. To do that, it needs to know where you are. It finds that out by requesting your local area code (see the top window of Figure A-5). Type it in and click Next. A second window will appear with dialing options. Choose those that apply and click Next. Now Setup dials an 800 number to find a local access number for you. You will be able to monitor the call's progress by watching the window pictured at the bottom of Figure A-5. Once you see the message that says, "Connected at *XXXX* baud" (the baud rate is determined by the speed of your modem and the quality of your telephone line at the moment), you can be sure your PC and modem are communicating properly. You can be sure that your modem and the telephone system are connected. If the AOL software found anything amiss prior to this point, it would have notified you and suggested solutions.

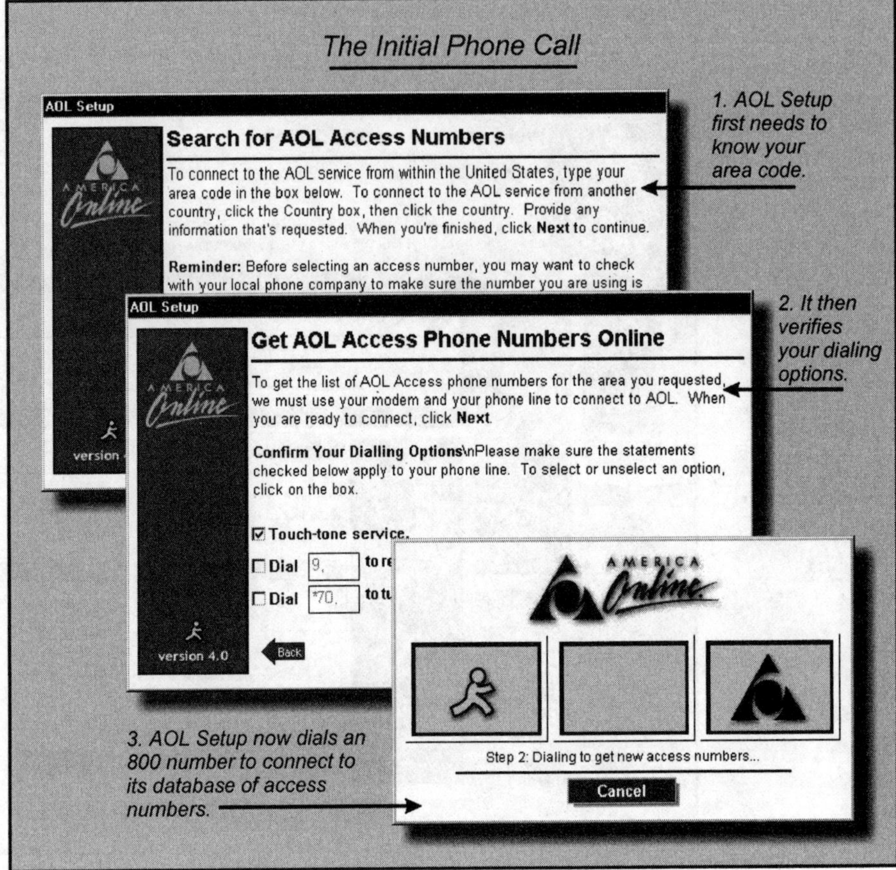

Figure A-5: America Online verifies your dialing information and then dials an 800 number for the initial connection.

Isolating Connection Errors

Though they rarely do, things can go wrong during the connect process. The problem could be at your end (e.g., the modem or the phone lines), or it could be at America Online's end. You'll know that the problem is at your end if you don't hear a dial tone (assuming your modem has a speaker) before your modem begins dialing. If you hear the dial tone, the dialing sequence, and the screeching sound that modems make when they connect, you'll know everything is okay all the way to the common carrier (long-distance service) you're using. If your connection fails during the initial connect process, don't panic. Wait a few minutes and try again. If it fails a second time, call AOL Technical Support at 800-827-6364.

Selecting Your Local Access Numbers

Now you're connected, and America Online is eager to say hello. Its initial greeting is friendly, if a bit prosaic (see the top window in Figure A-6). Its singular interest right now is to find some local access numbers for you. Using your area code, America Online consults its database of local access numbers and produces a list of those nearest you. Look over the list carefully. The phone number at the top of the list isn't necessarily the one closest to you. Also, note the baud rates listed (i.e., 14.4, 28.8, and 36.6). You can select any number with a baud rate that's as fast as your modem or faster. Click the More Info button to get further details on each of the available numbers.

Figure A-6: America Online asks you to select at least two local numbers for access to the service.

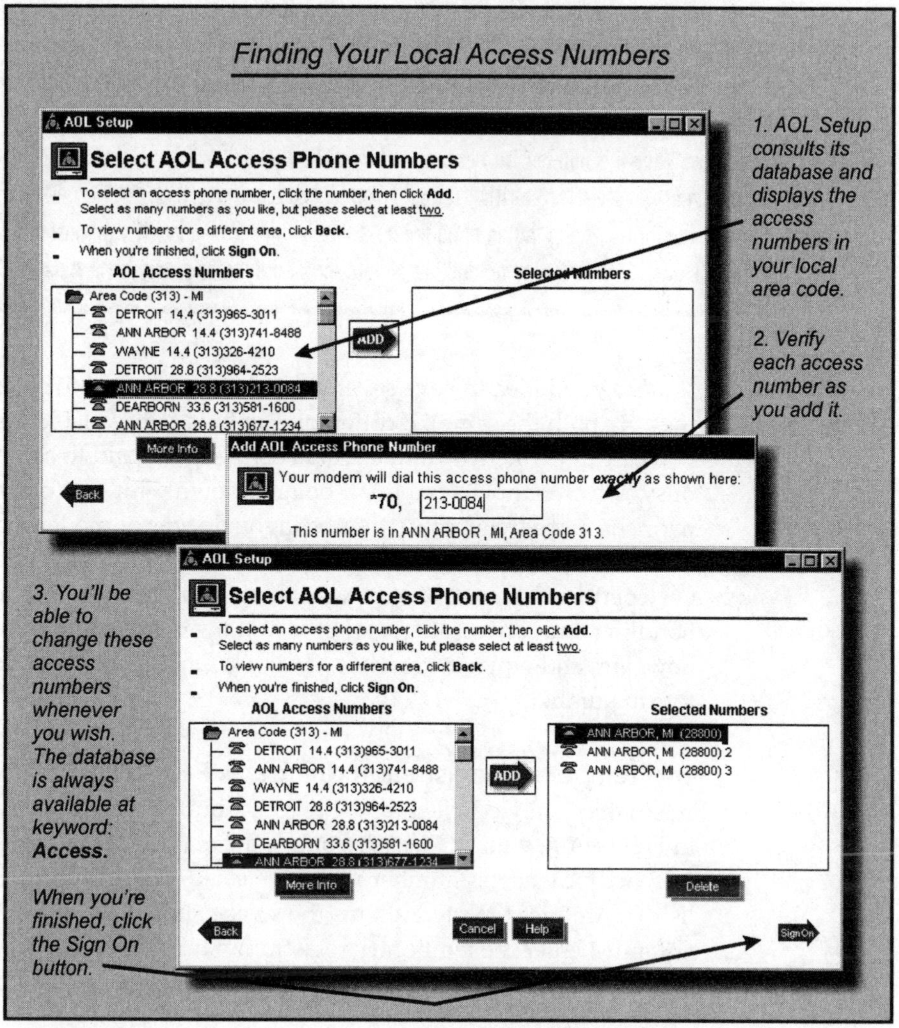

Finding Your Local Access Numbers

AOL Setup

Select AOL Access Phone Numbers

- To select an access phone number, click the number, then click **Add**. Select as many numbers as you like, but please select at least two.
- To view numbers for a different area, click **Back**.
- When you're finished, click **Sign On**.

AOL Access Numbers — **Selected Numbers**

Area Code (313) - MI
DETROIT 14.4 (313)965-3011
ANN ARBOR 14.4 (313)741-8488
WAYNE 14.4 (313)326-4210
DETROIT 28.8 (313)964-2523
ANN ARBOR 28.8 (313)213-0084
DEARBORN 33.6 (313)581-1600
ANN ARBOR 28.8 (313)677-1234

ADD — More Info — Back

1. AOL Setup consults its database and displays the access numbers in your local area code.

2. Verify each access number as you add it.

Add AOL Access Phone Number

Your modem will dial this access phone number ***exactly*** as shown here:

***70,** 213-0084

This number is in ANN ARBOR, MI, Area Code 313.

AOL Setup

Select AOL Access Phone Numbers

- To select an access phone number, click the number, then click **Add**. Select as many numbers as you like, but please select at least two.
- To view numbers for a different area, click **Back**.
- When you're finished, click **Sign On**.

AOL Access Numbers — **Selected Numbers**

Area Code (313) - MI
DETROIT 14.4 (313)965-3011
ANN ARBOR 14.4 (313)741-8488
WAYNE 14.4 (313)326-4210
DETROIT 28.8 (313)964-2523
ANN ARBOR 28.8 (313)213-0084
DEARBORN 33.6 (313)581-1600
ANN ARBOR 28.8 (313)677-1234

ANN ARBOR, MI (28800)
ANN ARBOR, MI (28800) 2
ANN ARBOR, MI (28800) 3

ADD — More Info — Delete — Back — Cancel — Help — Sign On

*3. You'll be able to change these access numbers whenever you wish. The database is always available at keyword: **Access.***

When you're finished, click the Sign On button.

If there isn't a local number listed for your area—that is, if you have to dial a 1 before your access number in order to complete the call—you might have to pay long-distance charges to your telephone company in order to connect to America Online. (There's an alternative: read the sidebar, "The Other 800 Number.") Once the initial sign-on process concludes and you're online, use the keyword: **Access** and investigate America Online's database of access numbers regularly. You may find a number there after all.

The Other 800 Number

America Online actually offers two 800 numbers. The first is the one the Setup program consults when it's searching for access numbers in your area. The second 800 number is there to save you money. To serve members who live in remote communities, America Online has established this 800 number for access from anywhere in the contiguous United States. While this number isn't exactly toll free, the charge for its use is considerably less than most long-distance tariffs. (It might also be less expensive than paying a hotel for its local-call tariff—keep that in mind the next time you're traveling.) If you must dial 1 to reach America Online, sign on and investigate the 800 number at keyword: **Access**.

It's a good idea to have several numbers (you need to enter two, even if they are both the same). If different numbers are available, select as many as you can and America Online will keep them on hand to call if the first one is busy (which happens rarely) or bogged down with a lot of traffic (which happens more frequently). Interestingly, dozens of modems can use the same number at the same time by splitting their usage into tiny packets. This is all very perplexing to those of us who think of phone numbers as capable of handling one conversation at a time, but it's nonetheless true. There is a limit, however, and when it's reached, America Online tries the second or third or fourth number.

The Temporary Registration Number & Password

Assuming you've clicked on the Sign On button shown in the bottom window in Figure A-6, your PC will disconnect from the 800 number and dial the primary local access number you've selected. Once the connection is reestablished, America Online presents the screen shown in Figure A-7. This is where you must enter the temporary registration number and password you received with your start-up kit. These are the temporary equivalents of the permanent screen name and password you'll soon establish. Enter the words and numbers carefully; they're usually nonsensical and difficult to type without error.

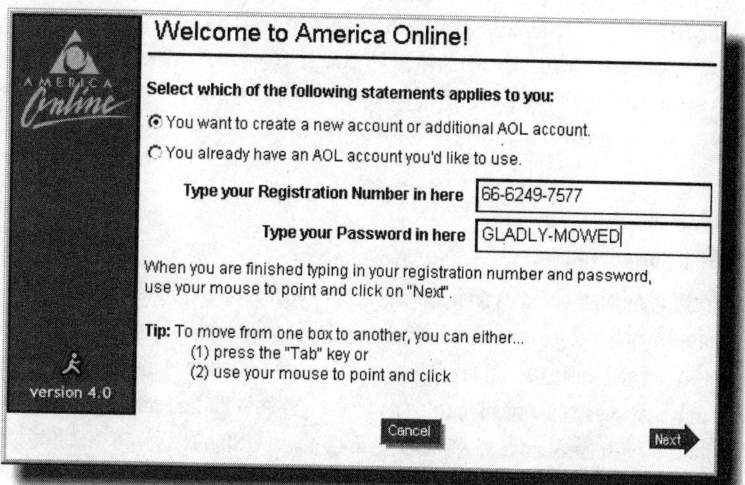

Figure A-7: Enter your registration number and password here. Be sure to type them exactly as they appear on your certificate or label. (Don't try to use the one in the picture—it won't work!)

Your Name & Address

When you click the Next button shown in Figure A-7, America Online asks you for some personal information (see Figure A-8).

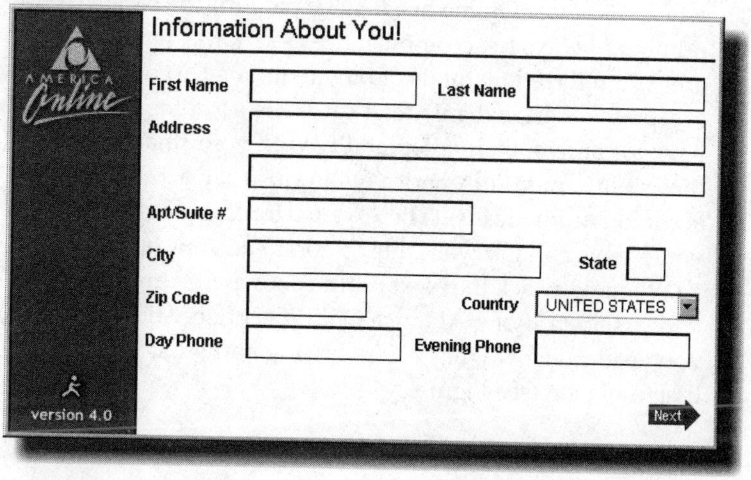

Figure A-8: Provide your name, address, and phone number(s).

America Online uses this information to communicate with you offline. Although America Online never bills members directly (we'll discuss money in a moment), and though this information is not available online to other members, the America Online staff occasionally does need to contact you offline, and they use this information to do so. They might want to send you a disk containing an upgrade to the software, or perhaps you've ordered something from them (this book, for example) that needs to be mailed. That's what this information is for.

Your Phone Number

Your phone number becomes an important part of your record at America Online—not because anyone at America Online intends to call you (although they might), but because America Online's Customer Service Department uses this number to identify you whenever you call. Should you ever need to call, one of the first questions Customer Service may ask is, What's your phone number? It's unique, after all, so Customer Service uses it to look up your records. It's an efficient method, but only if you provide the number accurately during your initial sign-on.

Providing Your Billing Information

Let's be up-front about it: America Online is a business run for profit. In other words, America Online needs to be paid for the service it provides. It offers a number of ways to accomplish this. VISA, MasterCard, and American Express are the preferred methods of payment. The Discover/Novus card also is acceptable. Certain bank debit cards are acceptable as well, although you will have to confirm their acceptability with your financial institution. If none of these work for you, America Online also can arrange to debit your checking account automatically. (There's a fee for this—more than a credit card costs you—so you might want this option to be your last resort.)

When you click the Next button shown in Figure A-8, another screen appears, identifying America Online's connect-time rates. Read it carefully—you need to know what you're buying and what it's costing you, after all—then move on (see Figure A-9).

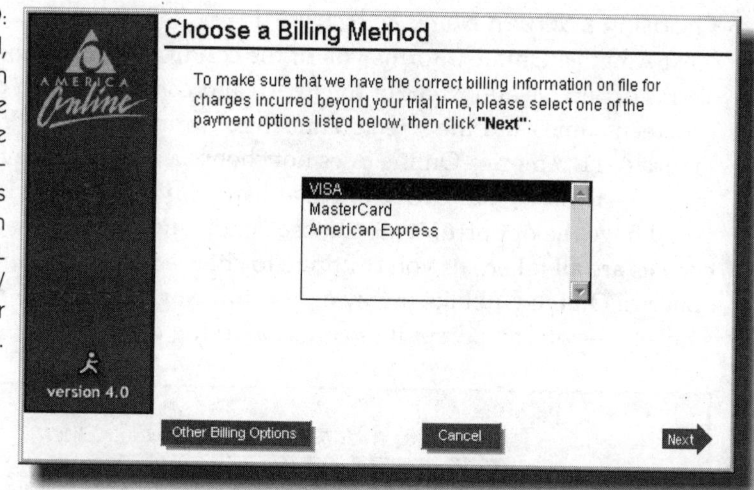

Figure A-9: VISA, MasterCard, and American Express cards are welcome, and the Other Billing Options button leads to information about using an AOL VISA, Discover/Novus card, or checking account.

Figure A-10 shows an example of the billing information screen that lies under the options pictured in Figure A-9. This is the VISA form, but the forms for the other cards are about the same.

Billing Information

By providing the following account information, I hereby authorize America Online to debit my account for any charges I incur in excess of my free trial period.

Please fill out the account information below, following the example for: VISA

Card Number: 0123-4567-9001-2345 **Exp. Date**: 08 99 **Bank Name**: First Virginia Bank

Card Number

Exp. Date **Month** **Year**

Bank Name

Please indicate whether this is a debit or credit card: Credit Debit

Finally, type in your name - exactly as it appears on your card:

First Name and MI **Last Name**

AMERICA Online

version 4.0

Payment Options Cancel Next

Figure A-10: The VISA form is about the same as the one for MasterCard, American Express, or the Discover/Novus card. Use the number formats described.

When you click the Next button shown in Figure A-10, you are asked to verify your billing information. Be sure the address given here is the same as the one that appears on your credit card or bank statement. Make any changes necessary and click the Next button.

Choosing a Screen Name & Password

Next America Online informs you of the conditions of membership (the Terms of Service and Rules of the Road) and concludes with the significance of screen names and the screen name input form pictured at the top of Figure A-11. America Online does not choose a screen name for you—an incentive to have your own choices at hand. If your first choice was taken, you'll have the opportunity to choose again (and again and again if your choices are all taken). If you continue to choose names that are taken, America Online will take mercy on you and suggest a name for you that is available—you can accept it or continue trying other ones.

Figure A-11: Conclude the registration process by entering your screen name and password.

Choosing a Screen Name and Password

Choosing Your Screen Name

All AOL members have an online identity--a screen name--that also serves as your e-mail address. You can have as many as five screen names, but the one you choose now is your "master" screen name and cannot be changed.

Online you're known by your screen name, so pick a good one! You can base it on your real name, your job, your hobby--anything that appropriately identifies you. Just remember these three guidelines:

(1) It needs to be 3 to 8 characters long.
(2) It can be a mix of letters, numbers, and spaces.
(3) It must start with a capital letter.

You may want to avoid using ALL CAPITAL LETTERS because that's how shouting is indicated online (and everyone know's it's impolite to shout!).

Please type in your choice for a screen name here, then click "Next."

Next

AMERICA Online version 4.0

1. Provide a screen name between three and eight alphanumeric characters here.

Choose Your Password

Each time you sign on to America Online, you'll need to type in a password.

Never give your password to anyone, because anyone who has it has access to your account. You should guard your password as you would guard the PIN to your ATM card. **Remember: AOL employees will never ask you for your password.**

When choosing your password, remember these guidelines:
* Make it easy for you to remember, but hard for others to guess.
* Do not use your real name, family member's name, or other obvious words.
* Make it 4 to 8 characters long (use letters and numbers only).

Please type your password twice (once in each box), then click "Next."
To ensure confidentiality, it will not appear when you type it.

******** ********

Next

AMERICA Online version 4.0

Choose a password that's easy for you to remember and hard for others to guess. Enter it carefully (you won't see what you type).

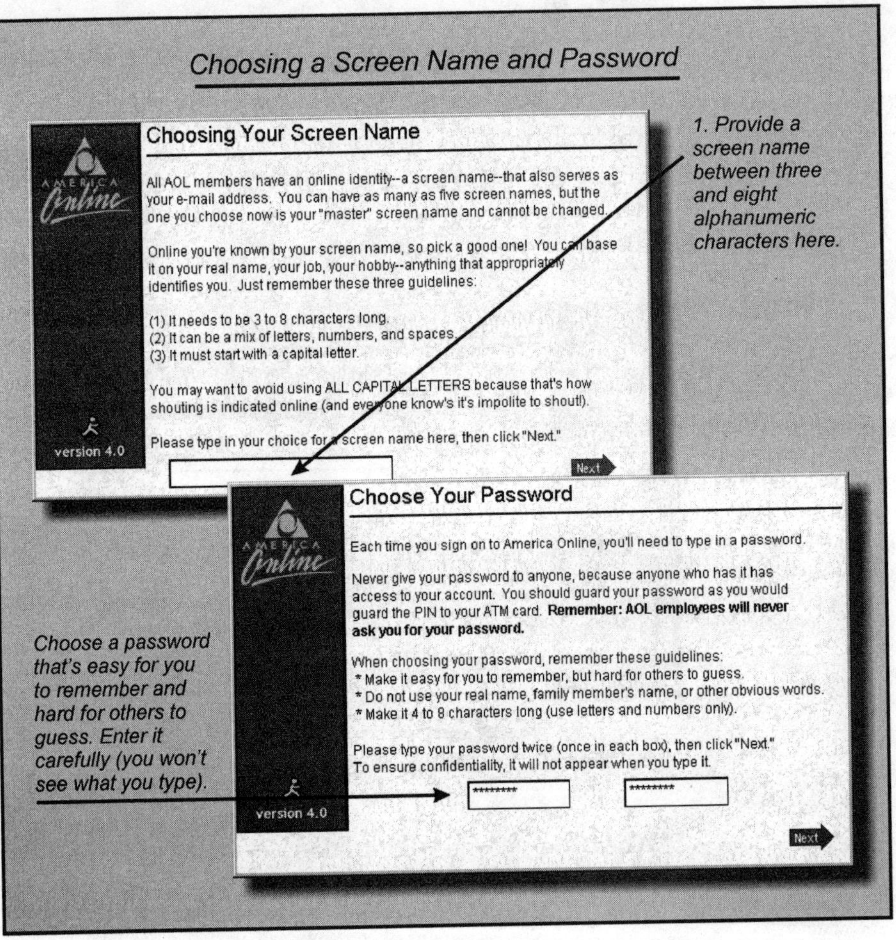

Note that the characters of your password don't appear on your screen as you type them. Substituting asterisks for the letters of your password is a standard security precaution—you never know who's looking over your shoulder. America Online asks you to enter your password twice to be sure you didn't mistype it the first time.

Upgrading

Like all good things, the America Online software is continually improving. You can always download the latest copy of the software online at keyword: **Upgrade**. In fact, you may want to stop in there to verify that you have the latest version of software. You can check to see what version you are currently running by choosing About America Online from the Help menu.

If you are already an America Online member and you're installing an updated version of the software, here are a couple of tricks that will expedite the process.

Use Your Existing Account Information

Be sure you're signed off and you have quit your AOL software. Do *not* remove the outdated AOL software from your hard disk. The C:\America Online 3.0 directory (or earlier) contains a bounty of account information that you probably want to retain: preferences, the Personal Filing Cabinet, your Web cache, Parental Controls, and Favorite Places. This information can all be transferred to your new software *if* you leave the outdated software on your disk until the upgrading process has concluded.

Now follow the steps detailed in "Installing the Software" earlier in this appendix. Be sure to choose the Upgrading to a New Version of AOL option that appears in Figure A-1 to verify that the Setup program found the existing copy of your AOL software.

Unless you tell it otherwise, the installer program will install the new software in a directory named C:\America Online 4.0. Change the directory name if you wish, but *do not overwrite your existing AOL software.* This implies that you will temporarily have to have enough room on your hard disk for two America Online installations until you're ready to delete the old one.

Follow the abbreviated instructions in Figures A-2 through A-6. Though there are ways to bypass the local-number lookup routine, let the installer program jump through its hoops: you might find a new local access number in the process, and it might be better than the one(s) you've been using.

When you come to the AOL Setup welcome screen pictured in Figure A-7, indicate that you already have an AOL account you'd like to use; then enter your existing screen name and password where indicated. The setup routine will conclude and you'll drop into America Online as if you'd signed on normally. When you do, check your preferences, Personal Filing Cabinet, and Favorite Places to verify that information has been retained from your old software.

Delete Your Old Software

Once you've signed off, use Windows' uninstall utility to erase any old, unwanted copies of AOL. To do this, Click the Start button, go to Settings, then Control Panel (or simply hit Windows+C if you have one of the newer keyboards). Double-click "Add/Remove Programs," then double-click the entry for America Online. The uninstaller will launch and identify all copies of AOL installed on your computer. You can then use the uninstaller to remove one or more of them (the most recently installed copy is listed first, so you probably don't want to erase it). This will free up considerable space on your hard disk and prevent you from accidentally invoking your old software when you next sign on—a common error. Your new AOL software will appear on your Start menu; invoke the program from there. AOL 4.0 also puts an icon on your desktop and in the system tray, so you won't ever lose the program. If you use Internet Explorer 4.0 and have the "Web-enabled" desktop, AOL 4.0 will also put its icon in the new "Quick Launch" toolbar.

Where to Go from Here

Once you're online, you have the entire America Online universe to explore. The thought is at once enticing and overwhelming. Here's what we suggest: if you're new, spend a half hour wandering around aimlessly. You have quite a bit of free connect time coming, so you don't have to worry about money. Enter the keyword: **Hot** into the space in the toolbar and click Go to see what's hot online this month. Use the keyword: **Internet** to find an Internet feature that interests you; then, without any particular agenda, explore that feature and perhaps one other.

During this initial session, don't try to absorb the entire contents of America Online or the Internet. Rather, wander aimlessly, getting a feeling for the nature of the online universe. America Online's interface takes practically no getting used to: just enjoy yourself.

After a half hour or so, you might want to sign off. Choose Sign Off from the Sign Off menu. Once the dust settles, turn to the chapter in this book that describes a feature you just visited. Read that chapter, then sign back on and explore those features again. See if you can find the things we described in the chapter. Spend another half hour at this.

Now you're on your own. Explore another department if you wish, or turn to Chapter 3, "Electronic Mail & the Personal Filing Cabinet," and learn how to send mail to somebody. You'll probably get a response in a few days. People at America Online are very friendly. It really *is* a community.

Appendix B

Keywords

Keywords are the fastest way to get from one place to another on America Online. To go to a specific forum or Area, you just type the keyword into the entry box on the toolbar and click Go. You can also bring up a special Keyword window by clicking the Keyword button on the toolbar, by selecting Go To Keyword from the Favorites icon (which is also in the toolbar), or by using Ctrl+K (PC) or Command+K (Mac).

Of course, you need to know the keyword before you can enter it. The most current list of keywords is always available by using (what else?) keyword: **Keywords**. It's a long list, and because of its length, you might have trouble finding the keyword you're after by consulting it online. (Printing is an option.)

Allow us to suggest two alternatives: (1) Bring up the keyword window (Ctrl+K or Command+K), enter a description of what you're after, then click the Search button in the Keyword window (instead of the Go button). This invokes AOL Find, a searchable database of services offered by America Online (and it's discussed in Chapter 5, "Finding Stuff"). Because it's searchable, using the Keyword window is a faster method of locating an online Area than reading through the list of keywords, and AOL Find always lists keywords when they're available. (2) Use the list of keywords that appears in this appendix. They're alphabetical by keyword. They may save you the trouble of printing a keyword list of your own.

Keyword Tips

The three little keyword tips below may be of help to you:

- Like screen names, keywords are neither case sensitive nor space sensitive; **aolfind** works just as well as **AOL Find**.
- Many of America Online's Areas identify their associated keywords in their primary window somewhere. Look for them.
- If you find an Area you think you'll visit again often, click the little heart icon on the title bar of that Area's window. This will add the location to your Favorite Places list where you can organize and access it conveniently. The Favorite Places feature is discussed in Chapter 5, "Finding Stuff."

The keyword list below was compiled by Jennifer in November 1997. Please e-mail changes or additions to her (screen name: **Jennifer**), as she maintains a list on a continuing basis.

Entries with asterisks are in the unlimited usage Area. Entries that are platform dependent (those that are only available to members using specific types of computers) are indicated as such. Those keywords that lead directly to World Wide Web (WWW) sites are also indicated.

Alphabetical by Keyword

Keyword	Area
:)	Grateful Dead Forum
:-)	The Friendly Face
;)	Hecklers Online
;-D	Virtual Christian Humor
<><	Christianity Online
?	Discover America Online (New Member Area)
@ACTIVE SPORTS	Thrive@Active Sports
@AOL LIVE	AOL Live Auditorium
@BOWL	The Bowl Auditorium
@CAFE	AOL Live Chat Cafe
@COLISEUM	The Coliseum Auditorium
@CYBER RAP	Cyber Rap Auditorium
@CYBERPLEX	Cyberplex Auditorium
@DCRELIGION	DC Religion
@DOME	The Grandstand: Meeting Hall Auditorium
@EATS	Thrive@AOL: Eats
@EATS EXPERTS	Thrive@AOL: Ask The Experts
@EATS TALK	Thrive@AOL: Talk
@FITNESS	Thrive@AOL: Shape
@GLOBE	The Globe Auditorium
@HEALTH	Thrive@AOL: Health
@HEALTH EXPERTS	Thrive@AOL: Ask the Experts
@HEALTH LIVE	Thrive@AOL: Chat and Auditorium Events
@HEALTHY LIVING	Thrive@AOL: Health
@INC LIVE	Inc Live Conference Room
@LOVE	Thrive@Love
@MARKETPLACE	Thrive Marketplace
@NEWSROOM	The News Room
@ODEON	The Odeon
@OUTDOORS	Thrive@Outdoors
@RELIGION	Digital City Religion
@ROTUNDA	Computing & Software Rotunda Auditorium

@SEX	Thrive@Sex
@SEXEXPERTS	Thrive Experts
@SEXTALK	Thrive Talk
@SHAPEEXPERTS	Thrive Experts
@SHAPELIVE	Thrive Live
@SPORTSFAN	SportsFan Radio Network
@TCB	Community Building
@THEMOVIES	Movie
@THENEWSROOM	The News Room
@TIMES	New York Times Online
@TIMESCHAT	New York Times Scheduled Chat Events
@TOWER	Tower Records
@WASHRELIGION	DC Religion
3	Upgrade to Latest Version
17	Seventeen Magazine Online
800	AT&T 800 Directory Web Site
1060	KYW Newsradio
1776	AOL's Revolutionary War Forum
9600	Modems and Connections*
90210	90210 Wednesdays
.NET	UK Internet Magazine
OS 8	Mac System 8
1 800 BATTERIES	1-800-Batteries
1 800 FLOWERS	1-800-Flowers
1 YEAR PRIME	1-Year Subscription to PrimeHost
1-800-98-PERFUME	Secure Super Shopper
106 JAMZ	Digital City Chicago: V103 Online
12 STEP	Addictions and Recovery Forum
128 BROWSER	Browser Update for WAOL 3.0
1996 YEAR IN REVIEW	Year
1ST HAWAIIAN	First Hawaiian Bank
1ST SITE	Premiere Introductory Service
21 CT	21st Century Teachers Welcome
21 ONLINE	Century 21 Online
2MARKET	Marketplace Gift Valet
2ND CHANCE	Your Second Chance
3-D	3D Forum
3.0 TOUR	AOL 3.0 Upgrade Tour* [Platform dependent]
3D REALMS	Apogee/3D Realms Support Center
3D SIG	3D Special Interest Group
3D STUDIO	3D Studio
40BROWSER	MMBrowser 40 bit TOD
49ERS	49ers
4DDA ENTRY	Mac Business Forum [MAOL only]
4MERCY	For Mercy Online
4STAR	Chef's Catalog Store
50 STATES	The Fifty States
5280MAG	Denver Entertainment, Dining and Nightlife
76ERS	Pro Basketball
777-FILM	MovieLink
7TH LEVEL	Seventh Level Software
800 DIRECTORY	AT&T 800 Directory Web Site
800 FLOWERS	1-800-Flowers
800NUMBER	AOL's 800 number
91XFM	Digital City San Diego 91x
94CHAMPS	Expos Team Club
96ROCK	WKLS - 96 Rock Atlanta
98PERFUME	Secure Super Shopper
A&A	Axis and Allies Club
A&B	Simon & Schuster College Online
A&E ONQ	onQ: Arts & Entertainment
A'S	Major League Baseball Team: Oakland Athletics
A/C CONTRACTOR	Contractor's Community - AOL's Your Business
AA	AA Online (Alcoholics Anonymous)
AA MEET	AA Online: Meeting Schedule
AAA	AAA Online
AAA STORE	AAA Store
AAC	Academic Assistance Center
AAII	American Association of Individual Investors
AARDVARK	Aardvark Pet Supplies
AARDYS SPECIALS	Aardvark Aardy's Specials
AARP	American Association of Retired People
AB.COM	Rockwell Automation
ABC	ABC Online
ABC AUDITORIUM	ABC Online Auditorium
ABC AUTO	ABC Auto Racing
ABC BELMONT STAKES	Belmont Stakes
ABC BETA	ABC Test Tube
ABC CBB	ABC College Basketball
ABC CFB	ABC Sports College Football
ABC CLASS	The ABC Classroom
ABC CLUELESS	ABC Clueless
ABC COLLEGE BASKETBALL	ABC College Basketball
ABC COLLEGE FOOTBALL	ABC Sports College Football
ABC CROWN	VISA Triple Crown Challenge
ABC DANGEROUS MINDS	ABC Dangerous Minds
ABC DAYTIME	ABC Daytime/Soapline
ABC ENTERTAINMENT	ABC Prime Time

ABC EVENTS	ABC Online Auditorium
ABC EXCLUSIVES	ABC News Live on AOL
ABC FIGURE SKATING	ABC Sports Figure Skating
ABC FOOTBALL	ABC Sports College Football
ABC GMA	ABC Good Morning America
ABC GOLF	ABC Golf
ABC GUESTS	ABC Online Auditorium
ABC HORSING	ABC Horsing
ABC INDY 500	ABC Sports Indy 500
ABC JOKES	JOKES!etc.
ABC KIDS	ABC Kidzine
ABC LIVE	ABC Live Chat and Auditorium Event
ABC LOVE	ABC Love Online
ABC MNF	ABC Sports Monday Night Football
ABC NEWS	ABC News On Demand
ABC NEWS.COM	ABC News.com
ABC NYPD BLUES	ABC NYPD Blues
ABC POLLS	ABC Polls
ABC PREAKNESS	ABC Preakness
ABC PRIME TIME	ABC Prime Time
ABC RACING	ABC Auto Racing
ABC SABRINA	ABC Sabrina
ABC SHOWS	ABC Online: Stars and Shows
ABC SOCCER	ABC Soccer
ABC SPIN CITY	ABC Spin City
ABC SPORTS	ABC Sports
ABC SPORTS KENTUCKY DERBY	Kentucky Derby
ABC SPORTS STORE	ABC Sports Store
ABC STARS	ABC Online: Stars and Shows
ABC STATION	ABC Online: Stations
ABC STORE	ABC Store
ABC TEST TUBE	ABC Test Tube
ABC TOOLBOX	ABC Tool Box
ABC TRACK	ABC Track
ABC TRIPLE	VISA Triple Crown Challenge
ABC TV	ABC Primetime
ABC VIDEO	ABC Online: Video Store
ABC WOMEN	ABC Sports Women's Sports
ABCDS OF LEARNING	Hoffman and Associates Inc.
ABERDEEN	Digital City Aberdeen
ABERDEEN EOL	Scotland Events Online
ABI YELLOW PAGES	Business Yellow Pages
ABM	Adventures by Mail
ABOUT WORK	About Work
ABOUTWORK	Punch in to About Work!
ABOVE THE RIM	NESN Basketball
ABX	AOL Business Research
ACC CARING ORGS	Community Resources
ACC CHAT	ACC: Chats
ACCESS	Accessing America Online*
ACCESSORIES	Third Party and Offline Applications
ACCORDING TO BOB	Company Research Message Boards
ACCOUNT	AOL Rewards
ACCOUNTANT	Accounting Community
ACCUTRADE	Accutrade
ACLU	American Civil Liberties Union
ACLU BOARDS	ACLU: Message Boards
ACOA	Alcoholics Anonymous Online
ACOC	Atlanta Chamber of Commerce
ACS	American Cancer Society
ACTING	The Casting Forum
ACTION GAMES	Antagonist Inc.
ACTIVE SPORTS	Active Sports
ACTIVISION	Activision Inc.
ACUBED	America-3: The Women's Team
AD	Athlete Direct
AD AUTO RACING	Athlete Direct Auto Racing
AD BASE	Athlete Direct Baseball
AD BASKETBALL	AD Hoops
AD BOXING	Athlete Direct Boxing
AD FOOD	Athlete Direct - Food
AD FOOTBALL	Athlete Direct Football
AD JOCKEY	Athlete Direct Jockeys
AD LIFESTYLES	Athlete Direct - Lifestyles
AD MOVIES	Athlete Direct - Movies
AD MUSIC	Athlete Direct - Music
AD PLAYOFFS	Athlete Direct Playoffs
AD POTPOURRI	Athlete Direct - Potpourri
AD SIG	Advertising Special Interest Group
AD TENNIS	Athlete Direct Tennis
AD SOCCER	Athlete Direct Soccer
AD TRAVEL	Athlete Direct - Travel
ADAM CAROLLA	MTV Online: LoveLine
ADAMS	Cindy Adams: Queen of Gourmet Gossip
ADAR	Athlete Direct Auto Racing
ADDICTION	Addictions and Recovery Forum
ADDONS	BPS Software
ADDRESS	Billing Information and Changes

ADDRESS INFO	Orientation Feature
ADF	Athlete Direct Football
ADHD	Attention Deficit Disorder
ADOBE	Adobe Online
ADOBE.COM	Adobe Systems Incorporated [WWW site]
ADOPTION	Adoption Forum
ADP	Athlete Direct Playoffs
ADRENALINE	Adrenaline Alli
ADSIG	Advertising SIG AOL UK
ADVENTURES BY MAIL	Adventures by Mail
ADVENTURESSF	Digital City San Francisco Adv
ADVERTISEWITHUS	AOL NetFind Advertising Link
ADVERTISING	Advertising Special Interest Group
ADVICE	Advice & Tips
AECSIG	P.L.A.C.E.S. Forum
AEFD	American Express Financial Direct
AEGIS	onQ: Transgender Organizations
AEROBICS	Health
AERONAUTICS	Aviation & Aeronautics
AEROSPACE	The Defense & Aerospace Community
AF'S SECRET BARGAINS	Arthur Frommer's Secret Bargains
AF.COM	Atlantic Financial [WWW site]
AFGHANISTAN	Afghanistan
AFI	American Finance and Investment
AFRICA	Afrocentric Culture
AFRICAN AMERICAN	Hobby Central: Communities
AFRICAN AMERICAN ART	Black Art
AFRICAN AMERICANS	Blacks
AFROCENTRIC	Afrocentric Culture
AFT	American Federation of Teachers
AFTEREFFECTS	Adobe After Effects
AFTERWARDS	Afterwards Cafe
AGGIES	AOL College Football
AGGRESSIVE SKATING	Inline/Aggressive/Roller Skating
AGGROSKATE	Aggressive Inline Skating MiniForum
AGIF	Animated GIF Resource Center
AGNOSTIC	Atheism-Agnosticism Forum
AGOL	Assemblies of God Online
AHCF	American Home Cooking Forum
AHH	Alternatives: Health & Healing
AHL	National Hockey League
AHS	American Hiking Society
AI INC	Hecklers Online: Antagonistic Trivia
AIDS	AIDS and HIV Resource Center
AIDS DAILY	AIDS Daily Summary
AIDS ONQ	onQ: Positive Living with HIV/AIDS
AIDS QUILT	AIDS Memorial
AIDS WEB	AIDS Web
AIDS&HIV	AIDS & HIV Screen
AIDSLINE	AIDS Line
AIDSONQ	HIV onQ
AINTREE	The Martell British Grand National
AINTS	Saints
AIQ	AIQ Systems
AIR WARRIOR	Air Warrior
AIRCRAFT	Flying Magazine
AIRFARE	Preview Travel
AIRFORCE	Military City Online
AIRMAIL.COM	Internet America Website
AIRPLANE	Aviation Forum
AIRWEVENTS	Air Warrior Events
AJGA	American Junior Golf Association
ALA	America Lung Association
ALA TEEN	AA Online (Alcoholics Anonymous)
ALABAMA	Digital Cities: South
ALANON	Alcoholics Anonymous Online
ALARM	Consumer Electronics
ALBANIA	Albania
ALBANY DC	Digital Cities: Albany NY
ALCOHOL	Addictions and Recovery Forum
ALDUS	Adobe Systems Inc.
ALF	American Leadership Forum
ALGERIA	Algeria
ALISSA	WB 17 - Warner TV
ALL MY CHILDREN	ABC Daytime/Soapline
ALL SPORTS	AllSport
ALL STAR	MLB All-Star Ballot
ALLE JEWELRY	Alle Fine Jewelry
ALLERGIES	Allergies and Asthma
ALLI	Alli
ALLI	Adrenaline Alli
ALLIED PILOTS	APA Online
ALLSPORT	AllSport
ALLSTAR FAN CENTRAL	All Star Fan Central
ALLSTAR GAME	All Star Fan Central
ALLSTATE	Allstate: Lincoln Benefit Life
ALPHA TECH	Alpha Software Corporation
ALPT	The Grandstand's Simulation Golf

ALPTLS	ALPT LS League
ALTAMIRA	Canadian Mutual Fund
ALTERNATIVE	MusicSpace: Alternative Music Forum
ALTERNATIVE DISNEY	Unofficial Guide to Walt Disney World
ALTERNATIVE MEDICINE	Alternative Medicine Forum
ALTERNATIVE MEDICINE WEB	Alternative Medicine Internet Sites
ALTERNATIVE WDW	Unofficial Guide to Walt Disney World
ALTERNATIVES	Alternatives: Health & Healing
ALTMED	Alternative Medicine
ALUMNI	Alumni Hall
ALYSIS	Alysis Software
AM CANCER SOCIETY	American Cancer Society
AMASSEMBLY	American Assembly
AMATEUR RADIO	Entertainment's Radio Forum
AMAZING	Amazing Trivia Game
AMAZON.COM	Thrive Amazon
AMBASSADOR	Ambassador
AMC WEB SITES	AOL Members' choice Web Sites
AMELIA ISLAND	Amelia Island - Destination Florida
AMENDMENT 2	GLCF's Amendement 2 Central
AMER GREET.COM	American Greetings Web Site
AMER STOCK EXCHANGE	American Stock Exchange
AMERICA DESUD	South America
AMERICA ONLINE	Discover America Online (New Member Area)
AMERICA ONLINE STORE	America Online Store
AMERICA ONLINE STORE	AOL Products Center
AMERICA OUT OF LINE	ABC Online: America Out Of Line
AMERICA'S FUTURE	President's Summit
AMERICA3	America-3: The Women's Team
AMERICAN ART	NMAA Online
AMERICAN ASSEMBLY	American Assembly
AMERICAN DIABETES	American Diabetes
AMERICAN DIALOGUE	American Dialogue
AMERICAN DREAM	Your Business: The Dream
AMERICAN EXPRESS	ExpressNet (American Express)
AMERICAN FINANCE	American Finance and Investment
AMERICAN GREET.COM	American Greetings
AMERICAN GREETINGS	American Greetings Store
AMERICAN HIKING SOCIETY	American Hiking Society
AMERICAN INDIAN	Hobby Central: Communities
AMERICAN LUNG	American Lung Association
AMERICAN OUT OF LINE	ABC - America(n) Out of Line
AMERICAN PHOTO	American Photo Syndicate Inc. [WWW site]
AMERICAN PHOTO	American Photo [WWW site]
AMERICAN REVOLUTION	AOL's Revolutionary War Forum
AMERICAN WOODWORKER	American Woodworker Online
AMERICAN-PHOTO.COM	American Photo Syndicate Inc. [WWW site]
AMERICON	America Online Gaming Conference
AMEX	ExpressNet (American Express)
AMEX ART	ExpressNet Art Download*
AMEX CARD	ExpressNet: Cards
AMEX CHECKS	ExpressNet: Cheques Online
AMEX OFFERS	ExpressNet: Special Offers & Events
AMEX RES	ExpressNet: Travel Reservations
AMNESTY	Amnesty International
AMOR	Love@AOL
AMSTERDAM	Time Out's Guide to Amsterdam
AMUG	Apple Macintosh Users Group (AMUG) [WWW site]
AMY GRANT	Christianity Online's Friends of Amy Grant
ANAHEIM ANGELS	California Angels
ANAWAVE	Anawave Software [WWW site]
ANDERS	Anders CD-ROM Guide
ANDERSONVILLE	Andersonville
ANDERTON	Craig Anderton's Sound Studio & Stage
ANDORRA	Andorra
ANDY PARGH	Andy Pargh/The Gadget Guru
ANGELFIRE	Angelfire Communications [WWW site]
ANGELS	Major League Baseball Team: California Angels
ANGLEFIRE.COM	Angelfire Website
ANGLER	Fishing Broadcast Network
ANGLIA	Anglia
ANGLIA O & A	Anglia O & A
ANGLIACHAT	Anglia Chat
ANGLIALEARNING	Anglia Learning
ANGLIAPLAYGROUND	Anglia Playground
ANGLIATEACHERS	Anglia Teachers
ANGOLA	Angola
ANIMA	Anima Selections
ANIMAL	Pet Care Forum
ANIMAL TRACKS	Digital City Twin Cities: Animal Tracks Insider
ANIMANIAC	Animaniacs
ANIMATED GIF	Animated GIF Resource Center
ANIMATION	Graphic Forum [Platform dependent]
ANIMATION SHOW	Animation Show
ANIME	Wizard World -or- Japanimation Station
ANNUAL PLAN	Annual AOL Subscription Plans

ANNUAL PRIME HOST	1 Year Subscription to PrimeHost
ANNUAL REPORTS	PC Financial Network: Annual Reports
ANNUAL VALUE	Annual Value Plan E-mail
ANON	Overeaters Anonymous - Philly
ANOREXIA	Eating Disorders
ANOTHER CO	Another Company
ANS	ANS [WWW site]
ANSWER	Parent Soup: Ask the Experts
ANTAG	Hecklers Online: Antagonistic Trivia
ANTHEM	National Anthems of the World
ANTHILL	The ANT Hill
ANTICS	Digital Twin Cities Antics Insider
ANTIGUA&BARBUDA	Antigua & Barbuda
ANTIQUE	Collector's Corner Exchange
ANTIVIRUS	The Virus Experts
ANTONYMS	Merriam-Webster Thesaurus
ANTPC	Antagonist, Inc. PC Games
ANTTRIVIA	Antagonist Trivia
ANYWHERE	AOL Mystery Tour
AOL ANNUAL PLAN	Annual AOL Subscription Plans
AOL AUTO CENTER	AOL Auto Center
AOL AUTODIALER	The AOL Autodialer
AOL BEGINNERS	Help Desk [Platform dependent]
AOL BIKE	AOL Bike
AOL BUSINESS DIRECTORY	AOL Business Directory [WWW site]
AOL CANADA	AOL Canada
AOL CARD	AOL Visa Card
AOL CHORUS	Culture Finder AOL Chorus
AOL CLASSIFIED	AOL Classifieds Online
AOL COMICS	Comic Books
AOL CRUISE	AOL Member Cruise
AOL DEAD	AOL Live Auditorium
AOL DIAG	AOL Diagnostic Tool
AOL DIGITAL SHOP	AOL Store Digital Shop
AOL EDUCATION	AOL Education
AOL ELSEWHERE	International Access
AOL FAMILIES	AOL Families
AOL FIND	AOL Find
AOL FRANCE	International Channel
AOL FULL DISCLOSURE	AOL's Full Disclosure for Investors
AOL GIFT	AOL Gift Certificates
AOL GUARANTEE	AOL Cybershopping Guarantee
AOL HOME PAGE	AOL's Home Page on the Web
AOL INSIDER	AOL Insider
AOL INTERNATIONAL	International Channel
AOL IR	AOL's Full Disclosure for Investors
AOL ISRAEL	AOL Israel
AOL LEGAL	Legal Areas
AOL LINK	Using AOL Link
AOL LIVE	AOL Live!
AOL LIVE GAMES	AOL Live Games
AOL LIVE NEWSLETTER	AOL Live's Newsletter
AOL LIVE!	The Auditorium
AOL LOGO	AOL Store Logo Apparel Shop
AOL MAX	Family Computing Forum: Maximum AOL
AOL MEDIA	America Online Media Space
AOL MEMBER CRUISE	AOL Member Cruise
AOL MEMBER SURVEY	AOL Survey
AOL MFC	AOL Mutual Fund Center
AOL MOVIES	@the.movies
AOL MUTUAL FUND CENTER	Mutual Fund Center
AOL NETFIND	AOL NetFind
AOL NETFIND TIPS	AOL Netfind: NetFind Tips
AOL ONLINE AUCTION	AOL Online Auctions
AOL PAGE	AOL Pagers
AOL POINTS	AOL Rewards
AOL POWERPAC	PowerPac
AOL PREVIEW	Upgrade to the latest version of AOL* [Platform dependent]
AOL PRODUCTS	America Online Store
AOL REDIALER	The AOL Autodialer
AOL REWARDS	AOL Rewards
AOL ROADTRIP	AOL Roadtrips
AOL SCUBA	AOL Scuba
AOL SECRETS	AOL Secrets
AOL SOFTWARE SHOP	AOL Software Shop
AOL SOUND	AOL Sound
AOL SPORTS LIVE	AOL Sports Live
AOL STORE	America Online Store
AOL STORE DIGITAL SH	AOL Store Digital Shop
AOL STORY	AOL Stories
AOL SURVEY	AOL Survey
AOL TICKER	Today's News Ticker
AOL TIPS	Family Computing Forum: Tip of the Day
AOL TODAY	On AOL Today
AOL TOUR	Tutorial
AOL UK LIVE	Live Events on AOL UK
AOL VISA	AOL Visa Card

AOL VOTER TRAX	AOL Politics' Voter Trax
AOL W	AOL Headquarters Weather
AOL WEB	AOL's Home Page on the Web [WWW site]
AOL WORLD	International Channel
AOL'S HOME PAGE	AOL's Home Page on the Web [WWW site]
AOL.COM	www.aol.com [WWW site]
AOLGLOBALNET	AOLGLOBALnet International Access*
AOLI	AOL Insider
AOLNET	Local Access Numbers
AOLPLUGINS	Multimedia Showcase
AOLSEWHERE	International Access
AOOL	ABC Online: America Out Of Line
AOP	Association of Online Professionals
AOTW	Artists on America Online
AP	AOL Accounts Payable
APA	APA Online
APARTMENT LOCATOR	Apartment Connection
APARTMENTS PLUS	Visual Properties
APPAREL	Your Business: Apparel Community
APPLE	Apple/Macintosh Forums
APPLE BIZ	Apple Business Consortium
APPLE CAFE	Apple Cafe Chatroom
APPLE COMMUNITY	Apple's Community Live Area
APPLE COMPUTER	Apple Computer Inc.
APPLE DIRECTORY	Apple's Directory Area
APPLE INFO	Apple's Info Center
APPLE SCRIPT	AppleScript Resource Center
APPLE UPDATE	Apple System 7.x Update
APPLE.COM	Apple Computer [WWW site]
APPLIANCEREPAIR	Appliance Dealers, Service & Repair - AOL's Your Business
APPLICATIONS	Business/Applications Forum [Platform dependent]
APRIL 15	International Channel Taxes Area
APRIL FOOL	AOL's April Fool Area [May disappear without notice]
APTCONNECTION	Apartment Connection
AQUARIUM	Pet Care Forum
AQUARIUMS	Zoos and Aquariums
AQUARIUS	AOL UK: Astrology
ARABIC	International Channel Middle East
ARCHAEOLOGY	Archaeology Forum
ARCHIE	WAIS/Gopher Preview
ARCHITECT	Your Business: Architects & Architecture Community

ARCHITECTURE	Home Magazine Online
ARCHIVE PHOTOS	Archive
ARCHY	Archaeology Forum
ARCTIC	Arctic Journal Polar Expeditions
ARDVARK	Aardvark Pet Supplies
ARDYS SPECIALS	Aardvark Aardy's Specials
ARENA	The Coliseum / Arena
ARFA	American Running & Fitness Association
ARGENTINA	Argentina
ARIES	Air Warrior
ARIZONA	Arizona Central
ARIZONA STATE	Arizona State
ARIZONACLASSIFIEDS	AZ Classifieds
ARKANSAS	50 States
ARMENIA	Armenia
ARMY	Military City Online
ARNIE	Ask Arnie about Travel
AROUND THE HORN	NESN: New England Baseball
ART	Graphic Forum [Platform dependent]
ART BELL	Parascope: Art Bell
ARTHRITIS	Pain Relief Center: Arthritis
ARTHRITISMONTH	National Arthritis Month
ARTHUR FROMMER	Arthur Frommer's Secret Bargains
ARTIST	Artists on America Online
ARTIST GRAPHICS	Artist Graphics
ARTIST SPOTLIGHT	Artist's Spotlight Center
ARTISTIC SKATING	Artistic Roller Skating MiniForum
ARTISTS	Artists on America Online
ARTISTS & GALLERIES	Your Business: Artists & Galleries Community
ARTISTS SPOTLIGHT	Artist's Spotlight Center
ARTISTUNDERGROUND	Artist Underground Music Area
ARTREFERENCE	Art and Music Reference
ARTS	Afterwards Cafe
ARTS ONQ	onQ: Arts & Entertainment
ARTS&CRAFT	Art and Craft
ARTSGUIDE	UK Arts & Days Out Guide
ARTSHOPPER	Image Exchange Art Shopper
ARTSHOPPING	Image Exchange Marketplace
ARTSKATE	Artistic Roller Skating MiniForum
ARTSONQ	Arts & Entertainment
ARTSPEAK	The Hub: ArtSpeak
ARTTALK	Image Exchange Art Talk
ARTWEB	ArtWeb
ARTWORKSHOP	Current: workshop (add)

ARUBA	Aruba
ARVADANEWS	DCD News and Information
ASC TECH	Alpha Software Corporation
ASE	American Stock Exchange
ASFL	The Grandstand: Simulation Football
ASFM	Atlanta Sports and Fitness Magazine
ASIA	International Channel's Asian Cont
ASIANAMERICAN	Channel A
ASK A DOC	Physician On Call
ASK A RABBI	Ask A Rabbi
ASK AOL	Member Services*
ASK DELILAH	Sex Expert - Thrive
ASK ERIC	AskERIC
ASK GAYE	Ask Gaye
ASK JOAN	Thrive - Meet Joan
ASK MICHELE	Ask Michele
ASK MPD	Ask MPD
ASK NANCY	Parenting Online's Ask Nancy Snyderman
ASK PEGGY	Ask Peggy
ASK SERENA	Weekly World News
ASK STAFF	Questions*
ASK THE EXPERT	Ask the Expert
ASK TODD	The Image Exchange: Ask Todd Art
ASL	ASL Club
ASP	Association of Shareware Professionals
ASP AUTHORS	Association of Shareware Professional Authors
ASSEMBLY	Development Forum [Platform dependent]
ASSESS YOURHEALTH	Assesses Your Health Area
ASSN ONLINE PROF	Association of Online Professionals
AST	AST Support Forum
ASTHMA	Allergies and Asthma
ASTROLOGERSFUND	Astrologers Fund
ASTRONET	Astronet
ASTRONOMY	Astronomy Club
ASTROS	Major League Baseball Team: Houston Astros
ASWD PUBLIC	Association for Software Design
AT ONCE	atOnce Software
AT TIMES	@times/The New York Times Online
AT&T	AT&T Wireless Service
AT&T	AT&T
ATAGONISTS	Hecklers Online: Antagonistic Trivia
ATHEISM	Atheism-Agnosticism Forum
ATHLETE DIRECT	Athlete Direct
ATHLETEDIRECTFOOTBALL	Athlete Direct Football Area
ATHLETEDIRECTTENNIS	Athlete Direct Tennis
ATHLETICS	Major League Baseball Team: Oakland Athletics
ATHOMENN	Gay Area within NetNoir
ATL COMM	Digital City Atlanta: Community
ATL FUN	Digital City Atlanta: Fun
ATL MARKET	Digital City Atlanta: Marketplace
ATL NEWS	Digital City Atlanta: News
ATL PEOPLE	Digital City Atlanta: People
ATLANTA ART	Atlanta Museums and Galleries
ATLANTA BANK	Atlanta Internet B@nk: A Service of Carolina First Bank
ATLANTA BEER	Atlanta Beer Haus
ATLANTA BRAVES	Major League Baseball Team: Atlanta Braves
ATLANTA CAR	Atlanta Auto Mart
ATLANTA CBS	WGNX-TV Channel 46
ATLANTA CHAMBER	Atlanta Chamber of Commerce
ATLANTA COMM	Atlanta Comm
ATLANTA EMPLOYMENT	Atlanta Jobs Now
ATLANTA FUN	Atlanta Fun
ATLANTA HEALTH	Digital City Atlanta Health
ATLANTA JOB	Atlanta Jobs Now
ATLANTA KIDS SAFE	Digital City Atlanta Kids Safe
ATLANTA LEISURE	Atlanta Leisure
ATLANTA LOAF	Creative Loafing
ATLANTA MARKET	Atlanta Market
ATLANTA MUSEUM	Atlanta Museums and Galleries
ATLANTA NEWS	Atlanta News
ATLANTA OMNI	The Omni
ATLANTA PEOPLE	Atlanta People
ATLANTA REAL ESTATE	Atlanta Real Estate
ATLANTA SPORTS	Digital City Atlanta Sports
ATLANTA SPORTS MAG	Atlanta Sports and Fitness Magazine
ATLANTA THEATER	Atlanta Theater Weekly
ATLANTIC FINANCIAL	Atlantic Financial [WWW site]
ATLANTICCITY	Digital City Philadelphia
ATLANTICFINANCIAL	Atlantic Financial Website
ATLAS	Reference Channel Maps
ATL CHAMBER	Atlanta Chamber of Commerce
ATL CHAT	Atlanta Chat Room
ATL HEALTH	Digital City Atlanta Health
ATL LEISURE	Atlanta Business
ATL MUSEUMS	Atlanta Museums and Galleries
ATL SPORTS	Digital City Atlanta Sports
ATL THEATER WEEKLY	Atlanta Theater Weekly

ATLUS	Atlus Software
ATONCE	atOnce Software
ATONCE DOWNLOAD	atOnce Download
AT RELIGION	Digital City Religion
ATTENTION DEFICIT DISORDER	Learning Disabilities and Special Needs
ATTICUS	Atticus Software
ATTORNEY	Your Business Legal Professionals Company
AU	Artist Underground Music Area
AUBURN	Auburn
AUCTION	AOL Online Auctions
AUDITORIUM	AOL Live!
AUG	User Group Forum
AUMUSIC	Artist Underground Music Area
AUSSIE	The Oz Channel
AUSTRALIA	Australia
AUSTRIA	Austria
AUTHOR	Book Discussions and Chat
AUTO	Auto
AUTO BY TEL	Auto-By Tel, Online Car Shopping
AUTO DISCOUNTS	AutoVantage
AUTO RACING	AOL Auto Racing
AUTO SOUND	Consumer Electronics
AUTOCAD	CAD Resource Center
AUTOCENTER	AOL Auto Center
AUTODESK	Autodesk
AUTODIALER	The AOL Autodialer
AUTOEXEC	Tune Up Your PC
AUTOFINDER	DC Hampton Roads Autofinder
AUTOHELP	Ask the Expert
AUTOMART	Digital City Philadelphia Automart
AUTOMOTIVE	Wheels
AUTOMOTIVE SERVICE	Your Business: Automotive Services Community
AUTORACING	Autoracing
AUTOREPAIR	Automotive Service
AUTOS	Auto Selections
AUTOSERVICE	Automotive Service
AUTOSPORT	Autosport Magazine
AUTOVANTAGE	AutoVantage
AUTOWEB	Autovantage Web
AV FORUM	Aviation Forum
AVALANCHE	Colorado Avalanche
AVEDASPA	Oxford/Aveda Spa at Oxford Hotel, Denver CO
AVIATION	Aviation Forum
AVID	Avid Technology
AVON	Avon
AVONCRUSADE	Avon's Awareness Crusade Online
AVONOPINION	AOL Rewards/ AVON
AW	About Work
AW ENTREPRENEURS	About Work: Entrepreneurs
AW FIRST JOBS	About Work: First Jobs
AW CHAT	Air Warrior Events
AWAD	Awad
AWAKE EYE	Awakened Eye Special Interest Group
AWAYFRIEND	International Channel: Sign on a Friend
AWC	AWC Club
AWENTREPRENEUR	about work (c)
AWGUTINSTINCT	About Work Gut Instinct
AXIS	Axis and Allies Club
AZ ALT	Arizona Central: ALT.
AZ ASU	Arizona Central: Sports
AZ AT EASE	Arizona Central: At Ease
AZ BEST	Arizona Central: The Best
AZ BIZ	Arizona Central: Small Business
AZ BUSINESS	Arizona Central: Your Money
AZ CACTUS	Arizona Central: Cactus League (Classifieds)
AZ CALENDARS	Arizona Central: Plan on It
AZ CARDINALS	Arizona Central: Sports
AZ CAROUSING	Arizona Central: Carousing
AZ CENTRAL	Arizona Central
AZ COMMUNITY	Arizona Central: Your Community
AZ COMPUTERS	Arizona Central: Computers
AZ CONCERTS	Arizona Central: Carousing
AZ DESTINATIONS	Arizona Central: Destinations
AZ DIAMONDBACKS	Arizona Central: Sports
AZ DINING	Arizona Central: Dining
AZ EDITORIALS	Arizona Central: Sound Off
AZ GOLF	Arizona Central: Golf
AZ HIGH SCHOOLS	Arizona Central: Preps
AZ HOME	Arizona Central: House/Home
AZ KTAR	Arizona Central: KTAR Talk Radio
AZ LIFE	Arizona Central: Your Life
AZ MONEY	Arizona Central: Your Money
AZ MOVIES	Arizona Central: Films
AZ NEWS	Arizona Central: Newsline
AZ NEWSLINE	Arizona Central: Newsline
AZ PHOTOS	Arizona Central: Photos
AZ SCHOOLS	Arizona Central: Schools
AZ SCOREBOARD	Arizona Central: Scoreboard

AZ SMALL BUSINESS	Arizona Central: Small Business
AZ SOUNDOFF	Arizona Central: Sound Off
AZ SPORTS	Arizona Central: Sports
AZ STARDUST	Arizona Central: Stardust
AZ SUNS	Arizona Central: Sports
AZ TRAVEL	Arizona Central: Destinations
AZ TV	Arizona Central: Couching
AZ U OF A	Arizona Central: Sports
AZ VOLUNTEERS	Arizona Central: Volunteers
AZERBAIJAN	Azerbaijan
AZ INFO	Arizona Information
B&B	Bed & Breakfast U.S.A.
B&N	Barnes & Noble Booksellers
BA	Bank of America
BABY	AOL Families: Babies
BABY BOOMER	Baby Boomers Area
BABY NAME	Parent Soup: Baby Names
BABYLON 5	Babylon 5
BAC Chat	Bay Area California Chat Room
BACK PAIN	Pain Relief Center
BACK TO SCHOOL	Back to School [May disappear without notice]
BACKGAMMON	Backgammon [WAOL 95 Only]
BACKPACKER	Backpacker Magazine
BADGERS	AOL College Football
BAFTAS	Baftas
BAHA'I	Baha'i Faith Forum
BAIR	James Bair Software
BALANCE	AOL Rewards
BALANCE SHEET	Disclosure's Financial Statements
BALI	One Hanes Place
BALKAN	Balkan Operation Joint Endeavor
BALLOON	1-800-FLOWERS: Balloon Boutique
BALTIMORE ORIOLES	Major League Baseball Team: Baltimore Orioles
BANK	Banking Center
BANK AMERICA	Bank of America
BANK@HOME	Union Bank of California Online
BANK OF STOCKTON	Bank of Stockton
BANK RATE	BRM Data Center
BANKING CENTER	Banking Center
BANKNOW	BankNOW
BANKS	Online Banking Center
BAR	Taverns: Pubs & Bars
BARGAINS	Checkbook Bargains
BARRONS	Barrons Booknotes
BASEBALL	AOL Baseball
BASEBALL DAILY	Baseball Daily by Extreme Fans
BASIC	Development Forum [Platform dependent]
BASKETBALL	NBA Basketball
BASKETBALL TRIVIA	NTN Basketball Trivia
BASS	BASS Tickets
BATMAN	DC Comics Online
BATTLETECH	Multiplayer BattleTech
BAY AREA CALIFORNIA	Bay Area California
BAYWATCH FRAGRANCE	Baywatch Fragrance
BB	Black Bayou
BBS	BBS Corner
BC	Book Central
BC BOARDS	Book Central: Message Boards
BC BOOKSHELVES	Book Central: Book and Author Information
BCREEK	Blackberry Creek
BD	Extreme Fans: Baseball Daily
BEARS	Chicago Bears Football Coverage
BEATCO	Beaty & Company
BEATY	Company Research Message Boards
BEAUTIFUL COOKING	The World of Beautiful Cooking
BEAVERS	Beavers: Canadian Humour With Bite
BED AND BATH	Cybershop
BEDTIME STORY	A Bedtime Story
BEE	BeeSoft
BEEPER	Consumer Electronics
BEGINNER	Help Desk [Platform dependent]
BEHIND THE SCENES	NetGuide: Behind the Scenes
BELGIUM	Belgium
BERGER	The Berger Funds
BERKSYS	Berkeley Systems
BEST OF AOL	Best of America Online Showcase
BEST TIPS	Top Tips for AOL
BETA APPLY	Beta Test Application Area [May disappear without notice]
BETHEL	Bethel College and Seminary
BETTER HEALTH	Better Health & Medical Forum
BETTER HEALTH BOOKS	Better Health Bookstore
BETTER HEART HEALTH	Better Heart Health
BETTER LIVING	Ideas for Better Living
BEYOND	Beyond Inc.
BHH	Better Heart Health
BIBLE	Religion & Beliefs: Christianity
BIC MAG	Bicycling Magazine

BICYCLE DEALERS	Your Business: Bicycle Dealers Community
BIDDLE	Christianity Online: Brother Biddle
BIG TWIN	Big Twin Online: The All-Harley Magazine
BIG YELLOW	Big Yellow Online Yellow Pages [WWW site]
BIGBOOK	BigBook (Internet yellow pages) [WWW site]
BIGBOOK.COM	BigBook [WWW site]
BIGHORN	Bighorn Computer Services [WWW site]
BIKEBRATS	onQ: BikeBrats [WWW site]
BIKENET	The Bicycle Network
BILLING	Accounts and Billing*
BINGO ZONE	Bingo Zone [WWW site]
BIOLOGY	Simon & Schuster Online: Biology Dept.
BIOSCAN	OPTIMAS Corporation
BIOTECH	Your Business: Biotechnology Community
BIRDING	Bird Watching
BIRDWATCHER	Birdwatchers
BISEXUAL	Gay & Lesbian
BIZ	The Entertainment Biz
BIZ WEEK	Business Week Online
BL	Buddy Lists
BLACK HISTORY	Black History Month [May disappear without notice]
BLACK VOICES	Orlando Sentinel Online: Black Voices
BLACKHAWKS	NHL Hockey
BLIND	DisABILITIES Forum
BLIZZARD ENT	Blizzard Entertainment
BLOC DEVELOPMENT	TIGERDirect Inc.
BLOCKBUSTER	Blockbuster Music's Online Store
BLUE JAYS	Major League Baseball Team: Toronto Blue Jays
BLUE RIBBON	Blue Ribbon Soundworks
BOARDSAILING	Sailing Forum
BOAT	Boating Online
BOAT DEALERS	Your Business: Boat Dealer Community
BOATING	Boating Selections
BOATS	The Exchange
BOB BEATY	Company Research Message Boards
BOB'S FITNESS	Bob's Summer Fitness Challenge
BOBB	Company Research Message Boards
BODYBUILDING	AOL Weightlifting & Bodybuilding
BOFA	Bank of America
BONJOUR PARIS	Bonjour Paris
BOOK	Books & Writing
BOOK DEALERS	Your Business: Book Dealers Community
BOOK NOOK	The Book Nook
BOOK REPORT	The Book Report
BOOK SHOP	AOL Book Shop
BOOKNOTES	Barrons Booknotes
BOOKS	Books & Writing
BOOKS & CULTURE	Christian Books & Culture
BOOKS ON BREAK	Just Books!
BOSNIA	Balkan Operation Joint Endeavor
BOSOX	Major League Baseball Team: Boston Red Sox
BOSTON	Digital Cities: Boston MA
BOSTON BRUINS	NESN: New England Hockey
BOSTON CELTICS	NESN: New England Basktetball
BOSTON GLOBE	Boston Globe [WWW site]
BOSTON RED SOX	Major League Baseball Team: Boston Red Sox
@BOWL	The Bowl Auditorium
BOWL	AOL Live!
BOWL GAME	Fool Bowl
BOWL GAMES	NCAA Football Bowl Info
BOWLING	The Grandstand: Other Sports
BOXER JAM	Boxer*Jam Gameshows [WAOL only]
BOXING	Sports Channel
BP MARKETPLACE	Backpacker Online's Marketplace
BPS SOFTWARE	BPS Software
BRAINBUSTER	NTN's Brainbuster Trivia
BRAINSTORM	Brainstorm Products
BRAINSTORMS	Brainstorms Store
BREAKAWAY	Focus on Family: Breakaway Magazine
BREWERS	Major League Baseball Team: Milwaukee Brewers
BRIDGES	The Hub: Even More Bridges of Madison County
BRIT SCI FI	British Science Fiction Online
BROADBAND	AOL's Cable Center
BRODERBUND	Broderbund
BROKERAGE	PC Financial Network: Brokerage Center
BRONCOS	Denver Broncos Football Coverage
BROTHER BIDDLE	Christianity Online: Brother Biddle
BROWSER FIX	Upgrade to the latest version of AOL*
BRUINS	NHL Hockey
BRUINS HOCKEY	NESN: New England Hockey
BUCKEYES	AOL College Football
BUCKS	Pro Basketball
BUCS	Major League Baseball Team: Pittsburgh Pirates
BUDDHISM	The Buddhism Forum
BUDDY VIEW	Buddy View
BUFFALOES	AOL College Football
BUILDERS	Your Business: Construction Community

BULGARIA	Bulgaria
BULL MOOSE	Bull Moose Tavern
BULLETS	Pro Basketball
BULLS	Pro Basketball
BURUNDI	Burundi
BUSINESS	Business News Area
BUSINESS FORUM	Applications/Business Forum [Platform dependent]
BUSINESS INSIDER	The Business Insider
BUSINESS LUNCH	Your Business Lunch
BUSINESS NEWS	Business News Area
BUSINESS OWNERS TOOLS	CCH Business Owners' Toolkit
BUSINESS RANKINGS	Business Rankings
BUSINESS SCHOOL	Kaplan Online -or- The Princeton Review
BUSINESS SENSE	Business Sense
BUSINESS STRATEGIES	Business Strategies Forum
BUSINESS TRAVELER	Business Traveler
BUSINESS WEEK	Business Week Online
BUZZSAW	Buzzsaw
BV	Buddy View
BV CHAT	Orlando Sentinel Online: Black Voices' Chat
BV GAY	Black Voices: Ebony Gay & Lesbian
BW ONLINE	Business Week Online
BW SEARCH	Business Week: Search
BYTE BY BYTE	Byte By Byte Corporation
C CHAT	Today in Computing [Platform dependent]
CABLE	AOL's Cable Center
CAD	CAD Resource Center
CADILLAC	Cadillac WWW Home Page
CAFE BOOKA	Book Central: Cafe Booka Reading Groups
CAFFE STARBUCKS	Caffe Starbucks
CALENDAR GIRLS	The Hub: Calendar Girls
CALIFORNIA	Digital Cities: West
CALIFORNIA ANGELS	Major League Baseball Team: California Angels
CALL AOL	Call AOL: Telephone Support
CAMERA	Photography Selections
CAMEROON	Cameroon
CAMPUS	Online Campus
CAMPUS LIFE	Campus Life Magazine
CANADA	AOL Canada
CANADA CHAT	AOL Canada: Chat
CANADA INTERNET	AOL Canada Internet Channel
CANADIENS	NHL Hockey
CANCEL	Cancel Account*

CANCER	Cancer Forum
CANUKS	NHL Hockey
CAPITALS	Washington Capitals
CAPRICORN	AOL UK: Astrology
CAPS	Washington Capitals
CAR AND DRIVER	Car and Driver Magazine
CAR INFO	AutoVantage: New Car Summary
CAR PHOTOS	Wheels Exchange
CARD	AOL Visa Card
CARDINALS	Major League Baseball Team: St. Louis Cardinals
CARDOMATIC	Card-o-Matic
CARDS	Card Selections
CAREER	Career Selections
CAREERPATH	Careerpath [WWW site]
CAROLE 2000	Astronet
CARTOON NETWORK WORLD	Cartoon Network World
CARTOONS	The Cartoons Forum
CASINO	RabbitJack's Casino
CASINO POKER	Kesmai's Casino Poker
CASTING	Casting Central
CASTLES 2	Castles II [WAOL 3.0 only]
CATERING	Your Business: Catering Community
CATHOLIC	Catholic Community
CATHOLIC NEWS	Catholic News Service
CATHOLIC REPORTER	National Catholic Reporter
CAVALIERS	Cleveland Cavaliers Basketball
CB	College Board
CBD	Commerce Business Daily
CBS	CBS Eye on the Net [WWW site]
CC	Computing Company Connection
CC BIZ	Company Connection: Business
CC DEV	Company Connection: Development
CC ED	Company Connection: Education
CC GRAFIX	Company Connection: Graphics/Presentation
CC HARD	Company Connection: Hardware
CC MMEDIA	Company Connection: Multimedia
CC MUSIC	Company Connection: Music
CC TELECOM	Company Connection: Telecom/Networking
CC UTIL	Company Connection: Utilities
CCA	Craig Crossman's Computer America
CCB	Digital City Chicago: Crain's Chicago Business
CCC	Computing Company Connection
CCC BIZ	Company Connection: Business
CCC ED	Company Connection: Education

CCC GAMES	Company Connection: Games
CCC GRAPHICS	Company Connection: Graphics/Presentation
CCE	Columbia Encyclopedia
CCGF	Collectible Card Games Forum
CCH	CCH Business Owners' Toolkit
CDN	AOL Canada
CDNOW	CDnow [WWW site]
CE	Consumer Electronics
CEC	Christian Education Center
CEL	Japanimation Station
CELEBRITY CIRCLE	Oldsmobile/Celebrity Circle
CELL PHONE	Your Business: Cell Phone Community
CELLULAR	Consumer Electronics
CELTICS	NESN: New England Basketball
CELTS	Pro Basketball
CENSUS	U.S. Census Bureau [WWW site]
CENTER STAGE	AOL Live!
CENTURA	Centura Bank
CEP	Council on Economic Priorities
CF	CultureFinder
CFB	AOL College Football
CH	Christian History Magazine
CHAMPION	One Hanes Place
CHANGE PASSWORD	Change your password*
CHANGE PROFILE	Edit your member profile
CHANNEL	AOL Channels
CHANNEL 1	Channel One Network Online
CHANNEL 17	Digital City Philadelphia: WPHL Channel 17
CHANNEL 46	Digital City Atlanta: WGNX Channel 46
CHANNEL 56	Digital City Boston: WLVI Channel 56
CHANNEL A	Asia Magazine
CHANNEL ONE	Channel One Network Online
CHANNELS	AOL Channels
CHARTER	Charter Schools Forum
CHARTOMATIC	Chart-O-Matic: Auto Stock Charting
CHASE	Chase Manhattan Bank
CHAT	People Connection
CHAT SHACK	The Hub: Chat Shack
CHATTER	People Connection Newsletter
CHEAP THRILLS	Trendzine: Cheap Thrills
CHEERLEADING	The Grandstand: Cheerleading Area
CHEFS CATALOG	Chef's Catalog
CHEFS CLOTHING	Professional Cutlery Direct
CHESS	Strategy & Wargaming Forum
CHEVROLET	Chevrolet
CHICAGO	Digital City Chicago
CHICAGO CHAT	Digital City Chicago: Chat/Forums
CHICAGO COMPUTING	Digital City Chicago: Computing Guide
CHICAGO CUBS	Major League Baseball Team: Chicago Cubs
CHICAGO MARKETPLACE	Digital City Chicago: Marketplace
CHICAGO NEWS	Digital City Chicago: News, Business & Weather
CHICAGO RADIO AND TV	Digital City Chicago: Radio and TV
CHICAGO SCI FI	Digital City Chicago: Sci-Fi Forum
CHICAGO SPORTS	Digital City Chicago: Sports
CHICAGO SYMPHONY	Chicago Symphony Orchestra Online
CHICAGO TICKET	Digital City Chicago: Ticketmaster
CHICAGO TRIBUNE	Chicago Tribune
CHICAGO VISITOR	Digital City Chicago: Visiting
CHICAGO WEATHER	Digital City Chicago: Weather
CHILD CARE	The Child & Elder Care Community
CHILD CARE	Your Business: Child Care Community
CHILD SAFETY	Child Safety on the Information Highway
CHILDREN	Cybershop
CHILDREN'S HEALTH	Children's Health Forum
CHOCOLATIER	Godiva Chocolatier
CHOOSE A SPORT	Choose a Sport on AOL
CHOOSE OR LOSE	MTV Online: Choose or Lose
CHRIST	Christianity Online
CHRISTIAN	Religion & Ethics Forum
CHRISTIAN COLLEGES	Christian College Guide
CHRISTIAN CONNECTION	Christianity Online: Chat & Live Events
CHRISTIAN EDUCATION	Christian Education Center
CHRISTIAN FAMILY	Christianity Online: Marriage/Family Forum
CHRISTIAN HISTORY	Christian History Magazine
CHRISTIAN KID	Christianity Online: Kids of the Kingdom
CHRISTIAN MEDIA	Christian Media Source
CHRISTIAN MEN	Christianity Online: Men's Fellowship
CHRISTIAN MUSIC	Christianity Online: Music & Media
CHRISTIAN PRODUCTS	Christian Products Center
CHRISTIAN READER	Christian Reader
CHRISTIAN SINGLES	Christianity Online: Singles
CHRISTIAN WOMAN	Christianity Online: Women to Women
CHRISTIANITY	Christianity Online
CHRISTIANITY TODAY	Christianity Today
CHROL RESOURCES	Christian Resource Center
CHURCH LEADERS	Christianity Online: Church Leaders Network
CICC	The Grandstand: Simulation Auto Racing
CIGAR	Food & Drink Network

CINCINNATI REDS	Major League Baseball Team: Cincinnati Reds
CITIBANK	The Apple Citibank Visa Card
CITY.NET	Excite City.Net [WWW site]
CITY WEB	City Web
CIVIL WAR	The Civil War Forum
CIVIL WAR JOURNAL	The History Channel: Civil War Journal
CL	Campus Life Magazine
CLARIS	Claris
CLARK	Digital DeLeon
CLARK DELEON	Digital City Philadelphia: Clark DeLeon
CLASSICAL	Classical Music Forum
CLASSICAL MUSIC	CultureFinder
CLASSIFIED	AOL Classifieds Online
CLASSIFIEDS ONQ	onQ: Classifieds
CLEAN UP	Spring Cleanup [May disappear without notice]
CLEANING	Your Business: Cleaning and Janitorial Community
CLEARANCE	The Fragrance Counter: Clearance Counter
CLEVELAND	Digital Cities: Cleveland OH
CLEVELAND INDIANS	Major League Baseball Team: Cleveland Indians
CLICK & GO	Click & Go: On The Road To The Next AOL
CLICKER	The Hub Clicker
CLIPS	Digital City Los Angeles: Sports
CLN	Christianity Online: Church Leaders Network
CLOCK	Time of day and length of time online
CLUB KIDSOFT	Club KidSoft
CLUELESS	Paramount's Clueless TV Show
CM	Christian Ministries Center
CMC	Creative Musician's Coalition
CMS	Christian Media Source
CNFA	The Grandstand: Simulation Football
CNN.COM	CNN Interactive [WWW site]
CNNFN.COM	CNNfn: The Financial Network [WWW site]
CNS	Catholic News Service
CNW	Cartoon Network World
CO ASSOCIATIONS	Christianity Online: Associations & Interests
CO CLASSIFIEDS	Christianity Online: Classifieds
CO FAMILY	Christianity Online: Marriage/Family Forum
CO HOLIDAY	Christianity Online: Holidays and Contests
CO LIVE	Christianity Online: Chat & Live Events
CO NEWS	Christianity Online: Newsstand
CO SENIORS	Christianity Online: Seniors Connection
CO SINGLE	Christianity Online: Singles
CO STUDENT	Christianity Online: Campus Life's Student Hangout

CO SW	Christianity Online: Software Store
COBB	The Cobb Group Online
COGS	Christianity Online: Global Stewardship
COIN-OP	Your Business: Vending Machine Community
COINS	The Exchange
COL CHAT	Digital City Chicago: Chat/Forums
COL EDUCATION	Digital City Chicago: Education Forum
COL ENTERTAINMENT	Chicago Tribune: Local Entertainment Guide
COL FILES	Digital City Chicago: Libraries
COL GOVT	Chicago Tribune: Election '96
COL TRAFFIC	Chicago Tribune: Traffic Updates
COLISEUM	AOL Live!
@COLISEUM	The Coliseum Auditorium
COLLECT	Collectibles Online
COLLECT CARDS	Collectible Card Games Forum
COLLECTING	Wizard World
COLLECTOR	The Exchange
COLLEGE	College Selections
COLLEGE BOARD	College Board
COLLEGE FOOTBALL	AOL College Football
COLLEGE HOOPS	Extreme Fans: College Hoops
COLLEGE ONLINE	Simon & Schuster College Online
COLLEGIATE	Merriam-Webster's Collegiate Dictionary
COLOGNE	The Fragrance Counter
COLOR IMAGING	Advanced Color Imaging Forum
COLOR WEATHERMAPS	Main Weather Area
COLORADO	Digital City West
COLORADO ROCKIES	Major League Baseball Team: Colorado Rockies
COLUMBIA	Columbia Encyclopedia
COLUMBIANET	Columbia's Health Today
COM FED BANK	Commercial Federal Bank
COMEDY	The Comedy Pub
COMIC STRIP	Comic Strip Centennial
COMICS	Comics Selection
COMING OUT	onQ: Coming Out
COMMANDO	Kim Komando's Komputer Clinic
COMMERCE	Commerce Bank
COMMUNICATIONS	Communications Forum [Platform dependent]
COMMUNITIES	Hobby Central: Communities
COMMUNITY	AOL Community Matters!
COMMUNITY CENTER	People Connection Community Center
COMMUNITY UPDATE	Community Update Letter*
COMP LIVE	Today's in Computers & Software [Platform dependent]

COMP SITES	Computing Internet Sites
COMP SPOT	What's Hot in Computing & Software [Platform dependent]
COMPANY NEWS	Company News
COMPANY PROFILES	Hoover's Handbook of Company Profiles
COMPANY RESEARCH	Company Research
COMPAQ	Compaq
COMPASS	Compass Bank
COMPASS.COM	Compass Mall [WWW site]
COMPOSER	Composer's Coffeehouse
COMPTONS	Compton's NewMedia Forum
COMPTONS ENCYCLOPEDIA	Compton's Living Encyclopedia
COMPTONS SOFTWARE	Compton's Software Library
COMPUADD	CompuAdd
COMPUKIDS	Compukids
COMPUSTORE	Shopper's Advantage Online
COMPUTER AMERICA	Craig Crossman's Computer America
COMPUTER GAMES	Hecklers Online
COMPUTER LAW	CyberLaw/Cyberlex
COMPUTER LIFE	Computer Life Magazine
COMPUTER PERIPHERALS	Computer Peripherals Inc.
COMPUTER SERVICE	Your Business: Computer Service Community
COMPUTER TERMS	Dictionary of Computer Terms
COMPUTING	Computing Channel [Platform dependent]
COMPUTING NEWS	Computing News [MAOL only]
COMPUTING SITES	Computing Internet Sites
COMPUTING SUPERSTORE	Computing Superstore
CONCERTS	MusicSpace: Concerts
CONFERENCE	Computing Forum Chats and Conferences
CONFIG	Tune Up Your PC
CONGRESSIONAL	Congressional Quarterly
CONNECTICUT	Digital Cities: Northeast
CONNECTING	Accessing America Online*
CONNECTION	PC Dads
CONNECTIX	Connectix
CONSULTING	Your Business: Consulting Community
CONSUMER ELECTRONICS	Consumer Electronics
CONSUMER REPORTS	Consumer Reports
CONTACTS	Employer Contacts Database
CONTEST	AOL Contest Area
CONTRACTOR	Your Business: Contractor's Community
COOKBOOK	Celebrity Cookbook
COOKING	Everything Edible!
COOKING CLUB	Cooking Club
COPYING	Your Business: Duplicator's Community
CORBIS	Corbis Media
CORCORAN	Corcoran School of Art
COREL	Corel Special Interest Group
CORESTATES	Core States Bank & NJ National Bank
CORKSCREWED	Corkscrewed Online
CORNHUSKERS	AOL College Football
CORPORATE PROFILES	Hoover's Handbook of Company Profiles
COSM	Christianity Online: Seniors Connection
COSTAR	CoStar
COSTUMES	Your Business: Costume Supply Community
COUNTDOWN	NTN Trivia
COUNTRIES	The World
COUNTRY	Country Music Forum
COURSES	Online Courses
COURT TV	Court TV's Law Center
COURTROOM TELEVISION	Court TV's Law Center
COWBOYS	Dallas Cowboys Football Coverage
COWLES	Cowles/SIMBA Media Information Network
COYOTES	NHL Hockey
CQ	Congressional Quarterly
CR	Christian Reader
CRAFTS	Craft Selections
CRAFTS MAGAZINE	Crafts Magazine
CRAIG CROSSMAN	Craig Crossman's Computer America
CRAIN'S	Digital City Chicago: Crain's Chicago Business
CRAIN'S SMALL BIZ	Crain's Small Business
CRAZY HORSE	Rockline Online
CREATIVE WONDERS	Creative Wonders
CREDIT	Credit Request Form for connect problems*
CRESTAR	Crestar Bank
CRIMSON TIDE	AOL College Football
CRITIC	Critic's Choice
CROATIA	Croatia
CROSSMAN	Craig Crossman's Computer America
CROSSWORD	The New York Times Crosswords
CRUISE CRITIC	Cruise Critic
CRYSTAL	Crystal Dynamics
CRYSTAL BALL	The Crystal Ball Forum
CS HOT	What's Hot in Computing & Software [Platform dependent]
CSB	Crain's Small Business
CSPAN	C-SPAN
CSPAN CLASS	C-SPAN in the Classroom

CT	Christianity Today
CUBS	Major League Baseball Team: Chicago Cubs
CULTUREFINDER	CultureFinder
CURRICULUM	Assoc. for Supervisor & Curriculum Development
CURVE	PlaNetOut: Curve Magazine
CURVE STORE	PlaNetOut: Curve Store
CUSTOMER SERVICE	Member Services*
CUTTING EDGE	NESN: New England Hockey
CW	Cycle World Online
CWUG	ClarisWorks User Group
CYBER 24	24 Hours in Cyberspace
CYBER BABE	Cyber Babes Calendar
@CYBER RAP	Cyber Rap Auditorium
CYBERCAMP	Summer Cyber Camp
CYBERCOMIC	Marvel Online
CYBERCON	CyberCon Chicago
CYBERLAW	CyberLaw/CyberLex
CYBERLOVE & LAUGHTER	Cyberlove & Laughter
@CYBERPLEX	Cyberplex Auditorium
CYBERSALON	Cybersalon
CYBERSERIALS	Cyberserials
CYBERSHOP	Cybershop
CYBERSPORTS	The Grandstand: Fantasy & Simulation Leagues
CYBERSTOCK	Hoover's Cyberstocks [WWW site]
CYBERSTRIKE	Cyberstrike [WAOL 3.0 only]
CYBERZINES	Digizine Sites on the Web
CYCLE WORLD	Cycle World Online
CYMRU	Virtual Wales
CZECH REPUBLIC	Czech Republic
;-D	Virtual Christian Humor
DAD	AOL Families
DAILY FIX	The Daily Fix
DAILY LIVING	Daily Living
DAILY Q	The Daily Q Trivia
DALLAS	Digital Cities: Dallas/Ft. Worth TX
DAN HURLEY	Amazing Instant Novelist
DANCE	Dance SelEctions
DARK SHADOWS	Dark Shadows Online
DATABASE	Database Support Special Interest Group
DATADESK	Datadesk
DATAPACK	DataPak Software
DAVID LETTERMAN	Dave Letterman's Late Show Online
DAY ONE	ABC News InFocus
DC	Digital City -or- DC Comics
DC CHAT	DC Comics Online: Chat Rooms
DC COMICS	DC Comics Online
DC EVENT	Digital City: The Event Source
DC FUN	Digital City: Entertainment
DC HOMES	Digital City Washington: Homes
DC JOIN	Register as a Digital Citizen
DC MARKETPLACE	Digital City: Marketplace
DC MIDATLANTIC	Digital Cities: Mid-Atlantic
DC MIDWEST	Digital Cities: Midwest
DC NEWS	Digital City: News/Weather
DC NORTHEAST	Digital Cities: Northeast
DC NORTHWEST	Digital Cities: Northwest
DC PEOPLE	Digital City: People
DC REAL ESTATE	Digital City Washington: Real Estate
DC SOUTH	Digital Cities: South
DC SPORTS	Digital City: Sports
DC WEB	City Web
DC WEST	Digital Cities: West
DCITY NATIONAL	Digital City
DCL	Dictionary of Cultural Literacy
DCWP	Digital Cities: White Pages
DEAD END	The Dead End of the Internet
DEAF	Deaf & Hard of Hearing Forum
DEAR DOTTI	Weekly World News
DEC	Digital Equipment Corporation
DECISION POINT	Decision Point Forum
DECORATING	Home Magazine Online
DEFENSE CONTRACTING	Your Business: Defense Contractor's Community
DEJANEWS	DejaNews: The Source for Internet Newsgroups [WWW site]
DELAWARE	Digital Cities: Mid-Atlantic
DELEON	Digital DeLeon
DELIGHTS	Howdy from America Online!
DELL	Dell Computer Corporation
DELPHI	Delphi Resource Center
DELRINA	Symantec
DELTA POINT	Delta Point
DELTA TAO	Delta Tao
DEMOCRAT	Democratic Party Online
DENEBA	Deneba Software
DENGO	Sun-Sentinel: Next Generation Online
DENMARK	Denmark
DENOMINATION	Religion & Ethics Forum
DENTAL CLAIMS	Your Business: Dental Claims Community

DENVER	Digital Cities: Denver CO
DEPARTMENT 56	Department 56 Collecting
DEPARTMENT STORE	Your Business: Department Store Community
DEPENDENCY	Dependency and Recovery Issues
DEPIXION	InToon with the News
DEPT 56	Department 56 Collecting
DERBY	Digital Cities: UK: Derby
DERRY	Digital Cities: UK: Derry
DESIGN SIG	Design Special Interest Group
DESK REFERENCE	New York Public Library Desk Reference
DESKMATE	DeskMate
DESKTOP PUBLISHING	Desktop and Web Publishing Area [Platform dependent]
DESTINATION EUROPE	Destination Europe
DETROIT	Digital Cities: Detroit
DETROIT TIGERS	Major League Baseball Team: Detroit Tigers
DEV	Development Forum [Platform dependent]
DEV STUDIO	Developer's Studio
DEVILS	NHL Hockey
DF	The Daily Fix
DF OUT	Destination Florida: Outdoors
DF PARKS	Destination Florida: Attractions
DF SPACE	Destination Florida: Space Coast
DF TICKET	Destination Florida: Ticketmaster
DFG	Doug Forsythe Gallery
DG	Hecklers Online: Digital Graffiti
DI	Disney Interactive
DIABETES	American Diabetes Association
DIAL	Dial/Data
DIALOGUE	American Dialogue
DICTIONARY	Dictionary Selections
DIGCPERSONALS	Digital City Personals
DIGITAL CITY JOIN	Register as a Digital Citizen
DIGITAL DELEON	Digital City Philadelphia: Clark DeLeon
DIGITAL IMAGING	Digital Imaging Resource Center
DIGITAL WORLDS	Digital Worlds
DIGITAL YELLOW	Digital Cities: Yellow Pages [WWW site]
DIGITS	Web Counter [WWW site]
DIGIZINES	Digizine Sites on the Web
DILBERT	Dilbert Comics
DINE OUT	Dinner On Us Club
DINER CREW	The Web Diner
DIRECTORY	Member Directory
DISABILITY	DisABILITIES Forum
DISCLOSURE	Disclosure Incorporated
DISCOVER AOL	Discover America Online (New Member Area)
DISCOVERY	The Discovery Channel
DISCOVERY.COM	Discovery Channel Online [WWW site]
DISCOVERY ED	The Discovery Channel: Education
DISNEY	Disney Services
DISNEY.COM.LOW	Disney.com Sneak Preview
DISNEY INTERACTIVE	Disney Interactive
DISNEY JOBS	Disney Jobs
DISNEY MAGAZINE	Disney Adventures Magazine
DISNEY STORE	Disney Store Online
DISPLAY DOCTOR	SciTech Software
DIVA	Soap Opera Digest
DJ	Don Johnston Inc.
DJBC	Dow Jones Business Center
DNC	Democratic Party Online
DO IT YOURSELF	HouseNet
DO SOMETHING	Do Something!
DOCL	Dictionary of Cultural Literacy
DOCTOR WHO	Doctor Who Online
DODGE	Dodge Truck [Web Site]
DODGERS	Major League Baseball Team: Los Angeles Dodgers
@DOME	The Grandstand: Meeting Hall auditorium
DON'T CLICK HERE	Don't Click Here
DONT MISS	Directory of Services
DOS 6	MS-DOS 6.0 Resource Center
DOU	Dinner On Us Club
DOW JONES	Dow Jones Business Center
DOWNLOAD	Software Center [Platform dependent]
DOWNLOAD 101	Download Help*
DOWNLOAD CREDIT	Credit Request Form for connect problems*
DOWNLOAD GAMES	Download Online Games* [WAOL and GAOL only]
DOWNLOAD HELP	Download Help*
DOWNLOADING	Software Center [Platform dependent]
DOWNTOWN MSG	Downtown AOL Message Boards
DP	Decision Point Forum
DR D	Dr. D Talks About
DR GAMEWIZ	Dr Gamewiz Online
DR JUDY	The Hub: Sex Talk wtih Dr. Judy
DR KATE	Answers by Dr. Kate
DR MCCALL	Examining Your Doctor
DR WHO	Doctor Who Online

DREALMS	DragonRealms
DREAM SHOW	The Hub: Dream Show
DREAM WORLD NEWS	The Hub: Dream World News
DRESSAGE	Horse Forum's Dressage MiniForum
DREW CAREY	Drew Carey Show
DREYFUS	Dreyfus Online Investment Center
DROWNED GOD	Drowned God
DRUGS	Addictions and Recovery Forum
DRUM	Drum Magazine
DRUM CIRCLE	Grateful Dead: The Drum Circle
DTP	Desktop and Web Publishing Area [Platform dependent]
DUBLCLICK	Dubl-Click Software
DUCKS	NHL Hockey
DVORAK	Software Hardtalk with John C. Dvorak
DWP	Desktop & Web Publishing [Platform dependent]
DYNOTECH	DynoTech Software
E!	E! Entertainment Television
E	Entertainment Channel
E HELP	Entertainment Channel Help Desk
E INDUSTRY	The Industry: Entertainment News
E LIBRARY	Research Zone
E STORE	Entertainment Channel Store
E WEB	WebEntertainment
E-MAIL	Mail Center
E-MAIL HELP	net.help: E-mail Help
E-ZONE	Your Business
EAGLE	Eagle Home Page
EAGLES	Philadelphia Eagles Football Coverage
EAGLES ONLINE	Philadelphia Eagles Online
EARLY ED	Preschool/Early Childhood SIG
EAS	Entertainment Advantage Store
EATING DISORDERS	Thrive@AOL: Eats
@EATS EXPERTS	Thrive@AOL: Ask The Experts
@EATS LIVE	Thrive@AOL: Chat and Auditorium Events
ECHAT	Entertainment Chat
ECOTOURISM	Backpacker Magazine
ED	Digital City's Emotion Detector
ED ANGER	Weekly World News
EDDIE BAUER	Eddie Bauer
EDELSTEIN	Fred Edelstein's Pro Football Insider
EDGAR	Disclosure's EdgarPlus
EDGE	Company Research
EDIBLE	Everything Edible!
EDIT PROFILE	Edit your member profile
EDMARK	Edmark Technologies
EDMUNDS	Edmund's Automobile Buyer's Guides Web site [WWW site]
EDTECH	Assoc. for Supervisor & Curriculum Development
EDUCATION	Research & Learn Channel
EDUCATION CONNECTION	Compton's Education Connection
EF	Extreme Fans
EF PRO HOOPS	Extreme Fans: Pro Hoops
EFCF	Extreme Fans: College Football
EFORUM	Environmental Forum
EFPRO	EFPRO - Extreme Fans: Pro Football
EGG	Electronic Gourmet Guide
EGYPT	Egypt
ELECTION HANDBOOK	Student's Election Handbook
ELECTRIC IMAGE	Electric Image
ELECTRONIC LIBRARY	Research Zone
ELECTRONIC NEWS	The Electronic Newsstand [WWW site]
ELECTRONIC PUBLISHING	Desktop & Web Publishing [Platform dependent]
ELI CONTEST	Eli's Cheesecakes Contest
ELIGIBLE	Love@AOL: Eligible Magazine
ELIS CHEESECAKES	Eli's Cheesecakes
ELLE	Elle Magazine Online
ELLE.COM	ELLE [WWW site]
ELMER	Elmer Customer Link Web Site
ELVIS	Weekly World News
EMAIL	Mail Center
EMAIL ADDRESS	EMail Address (directory) [WWW site]
EMALL	Orlando Sentinel Online: E-Mall
EMBROIDERY BUSINESS	Your Business: Embroidery Community
EMERGENCY	Public Safety Center
EMIGRE	Emigre Fonts
EMPOWERMENT	Personal Empowerment Network
ENCYCLOPEDIA	Enclopedias
ENERGY	Your Business: Energy & Oil Industry Community
ENGINEER	Your Business: Engineering Community
ENGLISH	Simon & Schuster Online: English Dept.
ENIGMA	Virgin Records: Enigma
ENT INDUSTRY	The Industry: Entertainment News
ENT SPOT	What's Hot in Entertainment
ENT STORE	Entertainment Channel Store
ENTERPRISE	AOL Enterprise
ENTERTAIN WEB	WebEntertainment
ENTERTAINMENT CHAT	Entertainment Chat

ENTERTAINMENT NEWS	Entertainment News
ENTERTAINMENT NEWSLETTER	Peek: The Entertainment Channel Newsletter
ENTERTAINMENT WEEKLY	Entertainment Weekly
ENVIRO	Your Business: Environmental Services Community
ENVIRONMENT	Environment Forum
ENVIRONMENTAL ED	Earth Day / Environment
EPARTNERS	Electronic Partnerships
EPICURIOUS	Epicurious Food and Travel [WWW site]
EPUB	Desktop & Web Publishing [Platform dependent]
EQUIBASE	Horse Racing
EQUINE	Pet Care Forum
EQUIS	Equis International
ER	ER Forum
ESH	Electronic Schoolhouse
ESPN	ESPNET SportsZone [WWW site]
ETEXT	PDA's Palmtop Paperbacks!
ETF	Mac Education & Technology Forum
ETHERIDGE	Melissa Etheridge Information
ETHICS	Ethics & Values
ETRADE	How to Use StockLink & Gateway Host
EUN	Electronic University Network
EUROPE	Europe Selections
EVA	Evita!
EVENINGS WITH EVA	Evenings with Eva
EVENT	Today's Events in AOL Live!
EVENT PLANNING	Your Business: Event Planning Community
EVENTS	Today's Events in AOL Live!
EXAM PREP	Exam Prep Center
EXCITE	excite Web Search [WWW site]
EXERCISE	Fitness Forum
EXPERT PAD	PDA/Palmtop Forum
EXPOS	Major League Baseball Team: Montreal Expos
EXPRESS NET	ExpressNet (American Express)
EXPRESSNET ART	ExpressNet Art Download*
EXTRA	EXTRA Online
EXTREME FANS	Extreme Fans
EZINE	PDA's Palmtop Paperbacks!
EZINES	Digizine Sites on the Web
EZONE	Your Business
F1	iRACE
FABFACTS	Fabulous Facts
FAG	PlaNetOut
FAITH	Religion & Beliefs
FALCONS	Atlanta Falcons Football Coverage
FALL TV SHOWS	Lost & Found TV Shows
FAM HOT	What's Hot in AOL Families
FAM M2M	AOL Families: Member to Member
FAMILY	Families Channel
FAMILY COMPUTING	Family Computing Resource Center
FAMILY INFOSOURCE	Family InfoSource
FAMILY LIFE	Family Life Magazine Online
FAMILY ONQ	onQ: Home & Family
FAMILY PC	FamilyPC Online
FAMILY ROOM	Family Computing Forum: Online Family
FAMILY SOFTWARE	Family Software
FAMILY TRAVEL	Family Travel Selections
FAMILY TRAVEL NETWORK	Family Travel Network
FAMILY TREE	Family Tree Maker Online [WWW site]
FAMILY TREE MAKER	Family Tree Maker Online
FAN CENTRAL	NCAA Fan Central
FANTASY	Fictional Realm
FANTASY BASEBALL	The Grandstand: Fantasy Baseball
FANTASY BASKETBALL	The Grandstand: Fantasy Basketball
FANTASY FOOTBALL	The Grandstand: Fantasy Football
FANTASY HOCKEY	The Grandstand: Fantasy Hockey
FANTASY LEAGUE	The Grandstand: Fantasy & Simulation Leagues
FAO SCHWARZ	F.A.O. Schwarz
FARALLON	Farallon
FARM AID	Official Farm Aid '96 [May disappear without notice]
FARMING	Your Business: Farming Community
FASHION FREAK	Trendzine: Ask Fashion Freak
FAVORITE FLICKS	Favorite Flicks!
FBN	Fishing Broadcast Network
FC TIPS	Family Computing Forum: Tip of the Day
FCF	Family Computing Forum
FCNBD	First Chicago NBD Online
FD	AOL's Full Disclosure for Investors
FDN	Food & Drink Network
FEDERATION	Federation
FEEDBACK	Member Services*
FELLINI	La Dolce Vita
FERNDALE	Ferndale
FFGF	Free-Form Gaming Forum
FICTIONAL REALM	Fictional Realm
FID AT WORK	Fidelity Online's Working Area
FID FUNDS	Fidelity Online's Funds Area

FID GUIDE	Fidelity Online's Guide Area
FID NEWS	Fidelity Online's Newsworthy Area
FID PLAN	Fidelity Online's Planning Area
FIDELITY	Fidelity Online Investments Center
FIESTA	Hispanic Heritage
FIGHTING IRISH	AOL College Football
FIGURE SKATING	ABC Sports Figure Skating
FILE	Software Center [Platform dependent]
FILE SEARCH	Search Database of Files and atOnce Software Search [Platform dependent]
FILEMAKER	The Filemaker Pro Resource Center
FILM STUDIOS	MovieVisions
FINANCE	Personal Finance Channel
FINANCIAL	Your Business: Financial Services Community
FINANCIAL ASTROLOGY	Astronet
FINANCIAL PLANNING	MoneyWhiz
FINANCIALS	Disclosure's Financial Statements
FIND	AOL Find
FINLAND	Finland
FIREFLY	Firefly Network Inc. (Music and Movies) [WWW site]
FIRST CHICAGO ONLINE	First Chicago Online
FIRST HAWAIIAN BANK	First Hawaiian Bank
FIRST TRACKS	Transworld SNOWboarding
FIRST WIFE	The Club for First Wives
FISHING	Boating Online
FITNESS	Fitness Forum
FLASH	Mad About Music
FLIGHT SIM	Flight Sim Resource Center
FLINT DCITY	Digital Cities: Flint
FLORIDA	Destination Florida
FLORIDA KEYS	The Florida Keys
FLORIDA MARLINS	Major League Baseball Team: Florida Marlins
FLOWER	Your Business: Florist Community
FLY	Aviation Forum
FLY FISHING	Fly-Fishing Broadcast Network
FLYERS	NHL Hockey
FLYING MAGAZINE	Flying Magazine
FOA	Christianity Online's Friends of Amy Grant
FOCUS ENHANCEMENTS	Focus Enhancements
FOG	Fellowship of Online Gamers/RPGA Network
FOLKWAYS	Folklife & Folkways
FOOD LOVER	Electronic Gourmet Guide: Food Lovers Directory
FOOD SERVICE	Your Business: Food Service Community
FOOL	The Motley Fool: Finance & Folly
FOOL AERO	Motley Fool: Aero
FOOL BIO	Motley Fool: Biotechnology
FOOL DOME	Motley Fool: The Fool Dome
FOOL FOOD	Motley Fool: Food
FOOL HARD	Motley Fool: Hardware
FOOL HEALTH	Motley Fool: Health
FOOL MART	Motley Fool: FoolMart
FOOL NET	Motley Fool: Networking
FOOL OIL	Motley Fool: Oilfield Services
FOOL PAPER	Motley Fool: Paper & Trees
FOOL RAILS	Motley Fool: Railroads
FOOL SOFT	Motley Fool: Software
FOOL TECH	Motley Fool: Storage Tech
FOOL UTIL	Motley Fool: Utilities
FOOLISH	The Motley Fool: Finance & Folly
FOOTBALL	AOL Football
FOREIGN	International Cafe
FORESTRY	Your Business: Forestry Community
FORMZ	auto*des*sys Inc.
FORTNER	Fortner Research
FORUM	Computing Channel [Platform dependent]
FOSSIL	Fossil Watches and More
FOUND TV	Lost & Found TV Shows
FOUR RESOURCES	AT&T Home Business Resources
FOUR11	Four11 Directory Services [WWW site]
FRACTAL	Fractal Design
FRANCE	International Channel
FRANCHISE	Your Business: Franchising Community
FRASIER	Frasier Tuesdays
FREELANCE	Freelance Artists Special Interest Group
FREEMAIL	FreeMail Inc.
FREESHOP ONLINE	The FreeShop Online
FREETHOUGHT	Freethought Forum
FRENCH OPEN	French Open [May disappear without notice]
FRENCH TEST	France Beta Test* [May disappear without notice]
FREQUENT FLYER	Inside Flyer
FRESHWATER FISHING	Fishing Broadcast Network
FRESNO DCITY	Digital Cities: Fresno/Visalia CA
FRIEND	Sign on a friend to AOL*
FRIEND IN FRANCE	France Beta Test* [May disappear without notice]
FRIENDLY FACE	The Friendly Face
FROMMER	Frommer's City Guides
FRONT PAGE	Microsoft Internet Resource Center

FRONTIERS	Scientific American Frontiers
FSFCA	Fantasy & Science Fiction Creative Artists
FT LAUDERDALE DIGC	Digital Cities: Miami/Ft. Lauderdale
FT MYERS DCITY	Digital Cities: Ft. Myers/Naples FL
FT WORTH	Digital Cities: Dallas/Ft. Worth
FTP	Internet FTP
FTP HELP	net.help: FTP Help
FULL DISCLOSURE	AOL's Full Disclosure for Investors
FUN PARKS	Travel America
FUNB	First Union National Bank
FUNDS	Morningstar Mutual Funds
FUNDWORKS	Fundworks Investors' Center
FUNERAL	Your Business: Funeral Directors Community
FUNNIES	The Funny Pages
FURNITURE	Furniture Selections: American Woodworker -or- Home Magazine Online
FUTURE	Can you believe what's possible these days?
FUTURE LABS	Future Labs Inc.
FUZZY	The Hub: Fuzzy Memories
FW	Fundworks Investors' Center
GA TECH	Georgia Institute of Technology [WWW site]
GADGET GURU	Andy Pargh/The Gadget Guru
GALLERY	Portrait Gallery
GAME	Games Channel
GAME BASE	Game Base
GAME DESIGN	Game Designers Forum
GAME SITES	WWW Game Sites
GAMEPLAYERS	ULTRA Game Players [WWW site]
GAMEPRO	GamePro Online
GAMES DOWNLOAD	Download Online Games* [WAOL and GAOL only]
GAMES FORUM	Games Forum [Platform dependent]
GAMES PARLOR	Games Parlor
GAMESPOT	GameSpot [WWW site]
GAMEWIZ	Dr. Gamewiz Online
GAMEWIZ FILE	Dr Gamewiz: File Libraries
GAMING	Online Gaming Forums
GARDEN	Gardening Online Selections
GARDEN.COM	Garden Escape [WWW site]
GARDEN ESCAPE	Garden Escape
GARDEN ONQ	onQ: Garden
GARDENER	Your Business: Gardening Community
GARDENING	Gardening Online Selections
GATEWAY 2000	Gateway 2000 Inc.
GATEWAY2000.COM	Gateway 2000 [WWW site]
GATORS	AOL College Football
GAY BOARDS	onQ: Boards
GAY BOOKS	Lambda Rising Bookstore Online
GAY CHAT	onQ: Chat
GAY MARRIAGE	onQ: Marriage
GAY NEWS	onQ: News
GAY ORG	onQ: Organizations
GAY TRAVEL	onQ: Travel
GAY TRIVIA	onQ: Gaymeland
GAY YOUTH	onQ: Youth
GAYMELAND	onQ: Gaymeland
GAZEBO	onQ: Transgender Chats
GBL	The Grandstand: Simulation Baseball
GC ACTION	Games Channel: Action
GC CLASSIC	Games Channel: Classic Games
GC CONTESTS	Games Channel: Contests
GC HOT	What's Hot in AOL Games
GC INFO	Games Channel: Gaming Information
GC KNOWLEDGE	Games Channel: Knowledge Games
GC NEWS	Games Channel: News
GC PERSONA	Games Channel: Persona Games
GC RPG	Games Channel: Role Playing Games
GC SIMULATION	Games Channel: Simulation Games
GC SPORTS	Games Channel: Sports Games
GC STRATEGY	Games Channel: Strategy Games
GCFL	The Grandstand: Simulation Football
GCS	Gaming Company Support
GD STORE	Grateful Dead Forum Store
GDT SOFTWORKS	GDT Softworks Inc.
GEMINI	AOL UK: Astrology
GENEALOGY	Genealogy Forum
GENERAL AVIATION	Aviation Forum
GENERAL HOSPITAL	ABC Daytime/Soapline
GENERAL MAGIC	General Magic
GENIE EASY	Astronet
GEO SDK	Geoworks Development
GEORGE ONLINE	George Online
GERALDO	The Geraldo Show
GERMANY	International Channel
GERTIE	Mercury Center Trivia
GET 2.7	AOL 2.7 for Macintosh*
GG	Global Gourmet

Keyword	Description
GIANTS	Major League Baseball Team: San Francisco Giants
GIF	Graphics Forum [Platform dependent]
GIF CONVERTER	GIF Converter
GIFT	Marketplace Gift Valet
GIFT CERTIFICATE	AOL Gift Certificates
GIFT EXPERT	Ask the Marketplace Gift Experts
GIFT REMINDER	Gift Reminder
GIFT SHOPS	Your Business: Gift Shop Community
GIFT VALET	Marketplace Gift Valet
GIFTED	Giftedness Forum
GIGABYTES	The Hub: Gigabytes Island
GIRLJOCK	GirlJock Magazine Online
GIX	Gaming Information Exchange
GLCF	onQ
GLCF H2H	onQ: Relationships
GLCF QUILT	AIDS Memorial
GLCF WOMAN	onQ: Women's Space
GLENNA	Glenna's Garden: Cancer Support
GLOBAL	Global Village Communication
GLOBAL CITIZEN	ExpressNet: Global Citizen
GLOBAL DINER	Global Gourmet: Chat Rooms
GLOBAL GOURMET	Global Gourmet
GLOBAL STEWARDSHIP	Christianity Online: Global Stewardship
GLOBAL VILLAGE	Global Village Communication
GLOBALNET	AOLGLOBALnet International Access*
GLOBE	AOL Live!
@GLOBE	The Globe Auditorium
GLOSSARY	America Online Glossary*
GM	General Motors Web Site
GMAT	Kaplan Online -or- The Princeton Review
GMS CORNER	The GM's Corner
GN	GrittyNews
GO FLORIDA	Destination Florida [WWW site]
GOALS 200	Goals 2000: National Education Act
GODIVA	Godiva Chocolatiers
GOLF	AOL Golf Area
GOLF AMERICA	Golfing Forum
GOLF DATA	GolfCentral
GOLFIS	Golfis Forum
GONER TV	Lost & Found TV Shows
GOOD LIFE	Your Good Life
GOOD MORNING AMERICA	ABC Good Morning America
GOP	Republican National Committee
GOPHER	Internet Gopher
GOPHER HELP	net.help: Gopher Help
GORE	Democratic Party Online
GOURMET FOOD	Cybershop
GPF	GPF Help
GRANDSTAND	The Grandstand
GRAPHIC	Graphic Simulations
GRAPHIC ARTS	Graphic Arts & CAD Forum [Platform dependent]
GRAPHIC DESIGN	Design Special Interest Group
GREAT DEBATE	The Great Debate
GREAT OUTDOORS	Great Outdoors
GREECE	Greece
GREENHOUSE	AOL Greenhouse
GRITTY NEWS	GrittyNews
GRIZZLIES	Pro Basketball
GROCER	Your Business: Grocery Community
GROLIERS	Grolier's Encyclopedia
GROUPWARE	GroupWare Special Interest Group
GS ARTS	The Grandstand: Martial Arts (The Dojo)
GS AUTO	The Grandstand: Motor Sports (In The Pits)
GS BASEBALL	The Grandstand: Baseball (Dugout)
GS BASKETBALL	The Grandstand: Basketball (Off the Glass)
GS BOXING	The Grandstand: Boxing (Squared Circle)
GS COLLECTING	The Grandstand: Collecting (Sports Cards)
GS FOOTBALL	The Grandstand: Football (50 Yard Line)
GS GOLF	The Grandstand: Golf (On The Green)
GS HOCKEY	The Grandstand: Hockey (Blue Line)
GS HORSE	The Grandstand: Horse Sports & Racing Forum
GS MAG	GS+ Magazine
GS OTHER	The Grandstand: Other Sports (Whole 9 Yards)
GS SIDELINE	The Grandstand: Sideline
GS SOCCER	The Grandstand: Soccer (The Kop)
GS SOFTWARE	The Grandstand: Sports Software Headquarters
GS SPORTS TRIVIA	The Grandstand: Sports Trivia
GS SPORTSMART	The Grandstand: Sports Products (Sportsmart)
GS TENNIS	The Grandstand: Tennis
GS WINTER	The Grandstand: Winter Sports (The Chalet)
GS WRESTLING	The Grandstand: Wrestling (Squared Circle)
GS3	GemStone III
GSDL	The Grandstand: Simulation Basketball
GSFL	The Grandstand: Simulation Football
GSHL	The Grandstand: Simulation Hockey
GSS	Global Software Support
GST	GST Technology

GTR	Guitar Special Interest Group
GUAM	Guam
GUARANTEE	AOL Cybershopping Guarantee
GUCCI	Gucci Parfums Counter
GUERILLA MARKETING	Guerilla Marketing Online
GUESS	Guess Inc.
GUIDE PAGE	I Need Help!
GUITAR	Guitar Special Interest Group
GUITAR SIG	Guitar Special Interest Group
GUNS	The Exchange: Interests & Hobbies
GUNSMITH	Your Business: Gunsmith Community
GURU	Andy Pargh/The Gadget Guru
GV	Global Village Communication
GVC	MaxTech Corporation
GWA	The Grandstand: Simulation Wrestling
GWPI	The Hub: Global Worldwide Pictures International Ltd.
H&C	The Exchange: Home & Careers
H2H	onQ: Relationships
HACHETTE	Hachette Filipacchi Magazines
HACIENDA	Channel One Network Online
HAIR	Hair Now!
HAIR & BEAUTY	Your Business: Hair & Beauty Community
HAIR NOW	Hair Now!
HALLMARK	Hallmark Connections
HALLOWEEN	Halloween Area [May disappear without notice]
HAM RADIO	Ham Radio Club
HAMMACHER	Hammacher Schlemmer
HANDLE	Add change or delete screen names
HANES	One Hanes Place
HAPPY NEW YEAR	New Years@AOL [May disappear without notice]
HARDWARE	Hardware Forum [Platform dependent]
HARLEY	Big Twin Online: The All-Harley Magazine
HARPOON	Harpoon Online [WAOL 3.0 only]
HAWKEYES	AOL College Football
HAWKS	Pro Basketball
HBS PUB	Harvard Business School Publishing
HEADACHES	Pain Relief Center: Headaches
HEADHUNTER	Motley Fool: Ask the Headhunter
HEADLINES	News Channel
HEALTH	Health Channel
@HEALTH	Thrive@AOL: Health
HEALTH CARE	Your Business: Health Care Community
HEALTH EXP	Health and Vitamin Express
@HEALTH EXPERTS	Thrive@AOL: Ask The Experts
HEALTH EXPRESS	Health and Vitamin Express
HEALTH FOCUS	Health Focus
HEALTH LIVE	Health Speakers and Support Groups
@HEALTH LIVE	Thrive@AOL: Chat and Auditorium Events
HEALTH MAGAZINE	Health Magazine
HEALTH RESOURCES	Health Resources
HEALTH WEB	Health Web Sites
HEART	Better Heart Health
HEART TO HEART	onQ: Relationships
HEBREW	Judaism Forum
HECKLER	Hecklers Online
HECKLERS CLUBS	Hecklers Online: Clubs
HEDGEHOG	People Connection Plaza
HELP	Member Services*
HELP DESK	Help Desk [Platform dependent]
HELP FORUM	Help Desks [Mac or PC]
HELP OKC	Help Heal Oklahoma City
HELP WANTED	Help Wanted Ads
HEM	Home Education Magazine
HERITAGE FOUNDATION	Heritage Foundation
HFC	Highlights for Children
HFC STORE	Highlights for Children Catalog
HFM MAGNET WORK	Hachette Filipacchi Magazines
HH	House & Home Area
HH KIDS	Homework Help for Kids
HH TEENS	Homework Help for Teens
HICKORY FARMS	Hickory Farms
HIGH SPEED	Modems and Connections*
HIGHLANDER	Highlander Online
HIGHLIGHTS	Highlights for Children
HIGHLIGHTS CATALOG	Highlights for Children Catalog
HIKER	Backpacker Magazine
HINDU	The Hinduism Forum
HISPANIC	Hispanic Selections
HISPANIC ONLINE	HISPANIC Online
HISTORICAL QUOTES	Historical Stock & Fund Quotes
HISTORY	History Area
HISTORY CHANNEL	The History Channel
HITCHHIKER	The Hub: John the Hitchhiker
HIV	AIDS and HIV Resource Center
HIV ONQ	onQ: Positive Living with HIV/AIDS
HMCURRENT	Health Magazine's Current Area
HMFITNESS	Health Magazine's Fitness Area

HMFOOD	Health Magazine's Food Area
HMRELATIONSHIPS	Health Magazine's Relationships Area
HMREMEDIES	Health Magazine's Remedies Area
HOBBY	Hobby Central
HOBBY SHOP	Your Business: Hobby Shop Community
HOC	Home Office Computing Magazine
HOCKEY	Hockey
HOCKEY TRIVIA	ABC Hockey Trivia
HOGS	Extreme Fans Arkansas Team Club
HOKIES	AOL College Football
HOLIDAY	Holidays@AOL [May disappear without notice]
HOLIDAY MOVIES	Holiday Movies [May disappear without notice]
HOLIDAY ONQ	onQ: Holidays
HOLLYWOOD	Hollywood Online
HOLLYWOOD NEWS	Hollywood Online: News
HOLLYWOOD PRO	The Biz!
HOLYLAND	Isr@el Interactive
HOME	House & Home
HOME AT AOL	AOL Home Tour
HOME AUDIO	Consumer Electronics
HOME BANKING	Bank of America
HOME DESIGN	Home Magazine Online
HOME IMPROVEMENT	House and Home
HOME OFFICE	Home Office Computing Magazine
HOME ONQ	onQ: Home & Family
HOME OWNER	Homeowner's Forum
HOME PAGE	Personal Publisher
HOME PAGE CONTEST	Home Page Contest
HOME PC	HomePC Magazine
HOME THEATER	Stereo Review Online
HOME VIDEO	Home Video
HOMEARTS	HomeArts Network [WWW site]
HOMER	Homer's Page at The Odyssey Project
HOMES	Homes & Land Electronic Magazine [WWW site]
HOMESCHOOL	Homeschooling Forum
HOMEWORK	Homework Area
HOMOSEXUAL	Gay & Lesbian
HONG KONG	Hong Kong
HOOPS	NCAA Hoops [May disappear without notice]
HOOPS BOARDS	Extreme Fans: Message Boards
HOOPS TRIVIA	NTN Basketball Trivia
HOOSIERS	AOL College Football
HOOVER'S	Hoover's Business Resources
HOOVERS UPDATES	Hoover's Company Masterlist
HORNETS	Pro Basketball
HOROSCOPE	Horoscopes
HORROR	Fictional Realm
HORSE	The Horse Forum
HORSE RACING	The Grandstand: Horse Sports & Racing Forum
HORSES	The Horse Forum
HOSPITALITY	Hospitality Services
HOT AIR	Global Challenger Balloon Race
HOT ENT	What's Hot in Entertainment
HOT FILES	Hot Mac Files of the Day
HOT GAMES	What's Hot in AOL Games
HOT HEALTH	What's Hot in Health
HOT MAC	What's Hot in Mac Computing
HOT NEWS	Hot News
HOT REF	Hot Reference
HOT SOFTWARE	Hot Mac Software
HOT SPORTS	What's Hot in Sports
HOT SPOT	MTV Online: Hot Spot
HOT TODAY	What's Hot Today!
HOT TOPICS	Hot Topics
HOT TRAVEL	What's Hot in Travel
HOTBED	Love@AOL: Hotbed
HOTLANTA	Digital Cities: Atlanta
HOTLINE	Member Services*
HOTWIRED	HotWired [WWW site]
HOUSE OF BLUES	House of Blues Online [WWW site]
HOUSE OF STYLE	House of Style
HOUSENET	HouseNet
HOUSEWARES	Cybershop
HOUSTON	Digital Cities: Houston
HOUSTON ASTROS	Major League Baseball Team: Houston Astros
HOW TO	Top Tips for AOL
HOWARD STERN	Digital City Philadelphia: Howard Stern
HOWDY	Howdy from America Online!
HP	Hewlett-Packard
HP.COM	Hewlett-Packard [WWW site]
HP FAX	Hewlett-Packard: Fax Products
HP FILES	Hewlett-Packard: Support Information Files
HP HOME	Hewlett-Packard: Home Products Information
HP MULTI	Hewlett-Packard: Multifunction Products
HP PLOT	Hewlett-Packard: Plotter Products
HP PRN	Hewlett-Packard: Printer Products
HP SCAN	Hewlett-Packard: Scanner Products
HP SCSI	Hewlett-Packard: SCSI Products

HP SERVER	Hewlett-Packard: Server Products
HP STORE	Hewlett-Packard: Information Storage Products
HP VECTRA	Hewlett-Packard: Vectra Products
HQ	Company Research
HQFAX	HTF Consulting
HRS	Better Health & Medical Forum
HSC	MetaTools Inc.
HTS	Home Team Sports
HTTP	What is http?
HUB	The Hub
HUB CHAT	The Hub: Chat
HUB INDEX	The Hub: Index
HUGE CLICKER	The Hub Clicker
HULL	Digital Cities: UK: Hull
HUMAN SEXUALITY	Simon & Schuster Online: Human Sexuality Dept.
HUMANISM	Humanism-Unitarianism Forum
HUMOR	The Comedy Pub
HUNGARY	Hungary
HURLEY	Amazing Instant Novelist
HURRICANE	Tropical Storm and Hurricane Info
HURRICANES	AOL College Football
HYPERCARD	Mac HyperCard & Scripting Forum
HYPERLINK	Learning AOL: Using Hyperlinks
HYPR	Hypractv8 with Thomas Dolby
HYW	Hundred Years War
I NEED HELP	I Need Help!
IA	Warner Bros. Insomniacs Asylum
IBD	Investor's Business Daily
IBIZ	InBusiness
IBM	IBM Forum
IBM.COM	International Business Machines Corp. [WWW site]
IBM ONLINE	IBM Online HelpCenter
IBM OS2	OS/2 Forum
IC	Internet Connection
IC HILITES	IC Hilites
ICA	Digital City Boston: Institute of Contemporary Art
ICC	Internet Chess Club
ICELAND	Iceland
ICTLEP	onQ: Transgender Organizations
IDAHO	Digital Cities: Midwest
IDEAS FOR BETTER LIVING	Ideas for Better Living
IDITAROD	Iditarod Trail Sled Dog Race
IDSOFTWARE	Id Softare Inc. [WWW site]
IFGE	onQ: Transgender Organizations
IG ONLINE	Intelligent Gamer Online
IGOLF	iGolf
IGS	Internet Graphics
IGUIDE	iGUIDE: The Internet Entertainment Guide [WWW site]
ILLINI	AOL College Football
ILLINOIS	Digital Cities: Midwest
ILLUSTRATOR	Mac Graphics Illustrator Special Interest Group
IMAGE	Image Exchange
IMAGE DESIGN	Your Business: Image Design Community
IMAGING	Advanced Color Imaging Forum
IMH	Issues in Mental Health
IMMIGRATION	Genealogy Forum
IMMIGRATION	Tell Us Your Story
IN	Investors' Network
INBUSINESS	InBusiness
INC.	Inc. Magazine
@INC LIVE	Inc Live Conference Room
INCOME STATEMENT	Disclosure's Financial Statements
INCORPORATE	Incorporate now!
INDIA	India
INDIANA	Digital Cities: Midwest
INDIANA UNIVERSITY	Indiana University [WWW site]
INDIANS	Major League Baseball Team: Cleveland Indians
INDIE MOVIES	Hollywood Online: Independent Films
INDIEFILM	ABC Online: iLINE Indie Films
INDUSTRIAL EQUIPMENT	Your Business: Industrial Equipment Community
INDUSTRIES	Your Business: Industries & Niches
INDUSTRY CONNECTION	Computing Company Connection
INDUSTRY PROFILES	Hoover's Industry Profiles
INDY 500	Indianapolis 500
INET CHAT	Internet Chat
INET EMAIL	Internet E-mail
INET EXCHANGE	Internet Exchange
INET MAGS	Internet Computing Magazines
INET ORGS	Internet Organizations
INFINITI	Infiniti Online
INFLUENCE	Influence Channel
INFO SHOP	Member Services*
INFODEPOT	Chena Software
INFORMATION PROVIDER	Information Provider Resource Center
INFORMED PARENT	Princeton Review Informed Parent
INFOSOURCE	Family InfoSource

INLINE SKATING	Inline/Aggressive/Roller Skating
INN	INNsider's Forum
INSIDE FLYER	Inside Flyer
INSIDE MEDIA	Cowles/SIMBA Media Information Network
INSIDER	AOL Insider
INSOMNIACS	Warner Bros. Insomniacs Asylum
INSTANT ARTIST	Print Artist Special Interest Group
INSTANT MESSENGER	AOL Instant Messenger
INSTANT NOVELIST	Amazing Instant Novelist
INSULATION	Owens Corning
INSURANCE	MoneyWhiz
INSURANCE INDUSTRY	Your Business: Insurance Community
INTEL	PC Dads
INTEL.COM	Intel Corporation [WWW site]
INTELLICAST	MSNBC Weather by Intellicast [WWW site]
INTELLIGENT GAMER	Intelligent Gamer Online
INTERCON	InterCon Systems Corporation
INTEREST	AOL Interests Channel
INTERFAITH	Interfaith Forum
INTERIOR DECORATOR	Your Business: Interior Decorator Community
INTERIOR DESIGN	Home Magazine Online
INTERNATIONAL	International Channel
INTERNATIONAL ACCESS	International Access
INTERNATIONAL CAFE	International Cafe
INTERNATIONAL LOVE	Passport to Love
INTERNATIONAL TAXES	International Taxes
INTERNATIONAL TRADE	Your Business: International Trade Community
INTERNET	Internet Connection
INTERNET AMERICA	Internet America [WWW site]
INTERNET BIZ	InBusiness
INTERNET CHAT	Internet Chat
INTERNET EMAIL	Internet E-mail
INTERNET EXCHANGE	Internet Exchange
INTERNET GRAPHICS	Internet Graphics
INTERNET MAGS	Internet Computing Magazines
INTERNET MOVIE DATABASE	The Internet Movie Database [WWW site]
INTERNET NEWS	Internet Newsstand
INTERNET ORGS	Internet Organizations
INTERNET QUESTIONS	Internet Questions*
INTERNETFIND	AOL NetFind
INTERSEXED	onQ: Transgender Community Forum
INTL ACCESS	International Access
INTL LOVE	Passport to Love
INTL TAXES	International Taxes

INTOON	InToon with the News
INTUIT	Intuit Inc.
INVEST	Investors' Network
INVESTMENT LINGO	Investment Lingo
INVESTOR RELATIONS	AOL's Full Disclosure for Investors
INVESTOR'S DAILY	Investor's Business Daily
IOM	National Academy of Science Online
IOMEGA	Iomega Corporation
IOWA	Digital Cities: Midwest
IP	Information Provider Resource Center
IPA	Advanced Color Imaging Forum
IPG	BPS Software
IPO CENTRAL	IPO Central
IR	AOL's Full Disclosure for Investors
IRACE	iRACE
IRELAND	Ireland
ISKI	iSKI
ISL	MacMillan Information SuperLibrary
ISLAM	Islamic Resources
ISLANDERS	NHL Hockey
ISR@EL	Isr@el Interactive
ISRAEL	Israel
ITALY	Italy
IVANHOE	Medical Breakthroughs reported by Ivanhoe Broadcast News Inc. [WWW site]
IVILLAGE	Parent Soup
JAID	Jaid Uncensored
JAMANCUSO	Shopologist
JAPAN	International Channel
JAPANIMATION	Japanimation Station
JAVA	JAVA InfoCenter
JAYHAWKS	AOL College Football
JAYS	Major League Baseball Team: Toronto Blue Jays
JAZZ	Jazz Music Forum
JCOL	Jewish.COMMunity
JCP	JCPenney
JENNY FLAME	The Comedy Pub
JERUSALEM	AOL's Seven Stop Tour of Jerusalem [May disappear without notice]
JET	Aviation Forum
JEWELER	Your Business: Jewelers' Community
JEWISH ART	Jewish Arts
JEWISH BOARDS	Jewish Message Boards
JEWISH CHAT	Jewish Chat Room

JEWISH COM	Jewish.COMMunity
JEWISH DOWNLOADS	Jewish File Downloads
JEWISH EDUCATION	Jewish Education
JEWISH FAMILY	Jewish Family & Personal
JEWISH FOOD	Jewish Food
JEWISH HOLIDAY	Jewish Holidays
JEWISH NEWS	Jewish News
JEWISH SINGLES	Jewish Singles
JEWISH STORE	Jewish Store
JEWISH YOUTH	Jewish Youth
JJ	Justice with Jacobs
JOB	MoneyWhiz
JOE TORRE	The Book Report: Joe Torre, Chasing the Dream
JOEL SIEGEL	ABC Good Morning America
JOHN GRAY	Men Are From Mars
JOIN DC	Register as a Digital Citizen
JORDAN	Jordan
JPEG	Graphics Forum [Platform dependent]
JUDAISM	Judaism Forum
JUICY CHAT	The Hub: Juicy Chat
JUMBO	JUMBO! (Shareware and Freeware libraries) [WWW site]
JUST DO IT	Computer Life Magazine
KAAL TV	ABC Online: KAAL-TV in Rochester MN
KABC TV	ABC Online: KABC-TV in Los Angeles CA
KAIT TV	ABC Online: KAIT-TV in Jonesboro AR
KAKE TV	ABC Online: KAKE-TV in Wichita KS
KANSAS	Digital Cities: Midwest
KANSAS CITY ROYALS	Major League Baseball Team: Kansas City Royals
KAPLAN	Kaplan Online
KAPLAN SUPPORT	Kaplan InterActive Software Support
KARATE	The Grandstand: Martial Arts (The Dojo)
KARROS	Eric Karros Kronikles
KATE	Answers by Dr. Kate
KAUFMANN	The Kaufmann Fund
KAZAKHSTAN	Kazakhstan
KCRW	Digital City Los Angeles: KCRW 89.9 FM
KEEFE	InToon with the News
KENNELS	Your Business: Pet Store Community
KENS GUIDE	The Hub: Ken's Guide to the Bible
KENT MARSH	Kent*Marsh
KENTUCKY	Digital Cities: Midwest
KESMAI	Air Warrior
KESQ TV	ABC Online: KESQ-TV in Palm Springs CA
KEWL GRAFFITI	gRaFfItI
KEYWORD	Keyword List Area
KEZI TV	ABC Online: KEZI-TV in Eugene OR
KFSN TV	ABC Online: KFSN-TV in Fresno CA
KGO	KGO - San Francisco Newstalk AM 810
KGO TV	ABC Online: KGO-TV in San Francisco CA
KGTV TV	ABC Online: KGTV-TV in San Diego CA
KGUN TV	ABC Online: KGUN-TV in Tucson AZ
KHBS TV	ABC Online: KHBS/KHOG-TV in Fort Smith AR
KID DESK	Edmark Technologies
KID MOVIES	Hollywood Online: Kids Corner
KID SPORTS	New England Cable Network: Sports for Kids
KID STUFF	Gift Valet: New Babies & Kids
KID TRAVEL	Family Travel Network
KIDCARE	KidCare
KIDS CHOICE	Nickelodeon: Kids' Choice Awards
KIDS DICTIONARY	Merriam-Webster's Kids Dictionary
KIDS FIND	AOL NetFind for Kids
KIDS OUT	Kids Out: London's Family Events Guide
KIDS PAGE	I Need Help! (for kids)
KIDS QUEST	The Quest CD-ROM Companion to AOL's Kids Only Channel
KIDS WB	Kids' Warner Brothers Online
KIDS WEB	Kid's Top Internet Sites
KIDSOFT	Club KidSoft
KIDSOFT STORE	KidSoft Superstore
KIDZINE	ABC Kidzine
KIFI TV	ABC Online: KIFI-TV in Idaho Falls ID
KING	Martin Luther King
KING OF THE BEACH	AVP Pro Beach Volleyball
KINGS	NHL Hockey
KIPLINGER	Block Financial Software Support
KIVI TV	ABC Online: KIVI-TV in Boise ID
KMBC TV	ABC Online: KMBC-TV in Kansas City MO
KMGH TV	ABC Online: KMGH-TV in Denver CO
KMIZ TV	ABC Online: KMIZ-TV in Columbia MO
KNICKS	Pro Basketball
KNITTING	Needlecrafts/Sewing Center
KNOT	The Knot: Weddings
KNOWLEDGE BASE	Microsoft Knowledge Base
KNTV TV	ABC Online: KNTV-TV in San Jose CA
KNXV TV	ABC Online: KNXV-TV in Phoenix AZ
KO	Kids Only Channel
KO CENTRAL	Kids Only: Central

KO CHAT	Kids Only: Chat Rooms
KO CLUBS	Kids Only: Clubs
KO CREATE	Kids Only: Create
KO FAME	Kids Only: Hall of Fame
KO GAMES	Kids Only: Games
KO GET INVOLVED	Kids Only: Get Involved
KO HOT	Kids Only: What's Hot
KO NEWS	Kids Only: News
KO SPEAK	Kids Only: Speak Out
KO SPORTS	Kids Only: Sports
KO SS	Kids Only: Shows + Stars
KO SUPERSTARS	Kids Only: Superstars
KOAT TV	ABC Online: KOAT-TV in Albuquerque NM
KOB	AVP Pro Beach Volleyball
KOCO TV	ABC Online: KOCO-TV in Oklahoma OK
KODAK	Kodak Photography Forum
KODAK WEB	Kodak Web Site
KODE TV	ABC Online: KODE-TV in Joplin MO
KOMANDO	Kim Komando's Komputer Clinic
KONSPIRACY	The Hub: Konspiracy Korner
KOREA	Korea
KPT	MetaTools Inc.
KQTV TV	ABC Online: KQTV-TV in St. Joseph MO
KRAMER	Astronet
KRANK	MTV Online: Krank
KTBS TV	ABC Online: KTBS-TV in Shreveport LA
KTKA TV	ABC Online: KTKA-TV in Topeka KS
KTRK TV	ABC Online: KTRK-TV in Houston TX
KTVX TV	ABC Online: KTVX-TV in Salt Lake City UT
KTXS TV	ABC Online: KTXS-TV in Abilene TX
KURZWEIL	Kurzweil Music Systems
KVIA TV	ABC Online: KVIA-TV in El Paso TX
KVUE TV	ABC Online: KVUE-TV in Austin TX
KWM WEB	Korean War Memorial Home Page
KYW1060	KYW News Radio 1060
L'EGGS	One Hanes Place
LA	Digital Cities: Los Angeles
LA ADVICE	Online Alice: Digital City LA's Advice Expert!
LA ANIMATION	LA Animation Fest
LA ANNEX	The Learning Annex
LA APARTMENTS	Digital City LA Rental Connection
LA ATTRACTIONS	Los Angles Tourism
LA AUTO	Los Angeles AutoMart: Where Angelenos Shop!
LA BREW PUB	SoCal Brew Pubs & the People that Love Them
LA BUSINESS DIRECTORY	Los Angeles Business Directory
LA CHAT	LA People
LA CITIES	Los Angeles Cities
LA CLASSIFIED	Los Angeles Classifieds
LA CLIP	LA Clippers
LA COMM	Digital City Los Angeles: Community
LA COMMUNITIES	Los Angeles Communities
LA COMPUTER CURRENTS	Computer Currents
LA DINING	Digital City Los Angeles: Dining
LA DIRECTORY	Los Angeles Business Directory
LA DOLCE VITA	La Dolce Vita
LA EDUCATION	Los Angeles Communities
LA ENTERTAINMENT	Los Angeles Entertainment
LA EVENTS	Los Angeles Events, Offline and On!
LA GALAXY	Los Angeles Galaxy
LA GAY	onQ: Los Angeles
LA IOCA	HLCA
LA JEWISH	Jewish Community Los Angeles
LA JEWISH SINGLES	Los Angeles Jewish Singles
LA KINGS	Los Angeles Kings
LA LEARNING	The Learning Annex
LA MARATHON	Los Angeles Marathon
LA MARKET	Los Angeles Marketplace
LA MASTER PLAN	Los Angeles Master Planner
LA MOVIES	Los Angeles Movies
LA NEWS	Digital City Los Angeles: News & Weather
LA NIGHTS	LA Nights Cyber Comic
LA PEOPLE	Digital City Los Angeles: People
LA PERSONALS	LA Personals
LA PHONE	Los Angeles Business Directory
LA POP	LA Pop: LA's Source for Pop Culture
LA RENTALS	Digital City LA Rental Connection
LA SINGLE	LA Personals
LA SOCCER	LASoccer (c)
LA SPORTS	Los Angeles Sports
LA STORES	Los Angeles Marketplace
LA TEENS	Digital City LA's Teen Area
LA TIMES.COM	Los Angeles Times [WWW site]
LA TOUR	Digital City Los Angeles: City Tour
LA TOURISM	Los Angeles Tourism
LA TV	TV Navigator Los Angeles
LA VACATION RENTALS	Vacation Destinations & Rentals for California Traveler
LA WEATHER	Digital City Los Angeles: News & Weather

LA WEEKLY	LA Weekly Magazine
LA WHITE PAGES	Los Angeles Business Directory
LAB	The Lab
LABELS	MusicSpace: Record Labels
LACROSSE	The Lacrosse Forum
LAKERS	LA Lakers Basketball
LAKEWOOD NEWS	Digital City Denver: News and Information
LAMBDA	Lambda Rising Bookstore Online
LANCASTER EOL	North West Events Online
LANCH	Colorado Avalanche Hockey
LANDS' END	Lands' End Store
LANDSCAPE	WorkPlace: Landscaping & Gardening Community
LANDSCAPING	Home Magazine Online
LANGUAGE GAME	International Channel Word Games
LANGUAGE REFERENCE	Literature Reference
LANGUAGE SYS	Fortner Research
LANIER	Lanier Family Travel Guides
LAOS	Laos
LAPTOP	PowerBook Resource Center
LAPUB	LaPub
LAREDO	The Laredo National Bank
LAS VEGAS	Digital City: Las Vegas
LAS VEGAS GUIDE	Unofficial Guide to Las Vegas
LAS VEGAS NV	Las Vegas
LASER CENTER	The Laser Center
LAST SHOT	EF Last Shot
LATE SHOW	Dave Letterman's Late Show Online
LATINA TAG TEAM	The Latina Tag Team
LATINO	HISPANIC Online
LATINO CHAT	HISPANIC Online Chat
LATINO NET	LatinoNet
LATVIA	Latvia
LAUNCH PAD	Launch Pad
LAURA RAPOSA	Boston Herald: Gossip Gals
LAVACATION	Los Angles Tourism
LAW	Research & Learn: Law & Government
LAW CENTER	Court TV's Law Center
LAW NET	Nolo Press: Law on the Net
LAW PROFESSIONAL	Your Business Legal Professionals
LAW REFERENCE	Government Reference
LAW SCHOOL	Kaplan Online -or- The Princeton Review
LAWN & GARDEN	Landscaping & Gardening Community: AOL's Your Business
LAWYER	Nolo Press Self-Help Law Center
LAWYERS	AOL Workplace: Legal Professionals
LAX	The Lacrosse Forum
LBL	Allstate: Lincoln Benefit Life
LC ABC	ABC Online: Lois & Clark
LC HOT	What's Hot in Learning & Culture
LC STORE	Learning & Culture Store
LCI	London Calling Home Page
LCI CLUBS	London Calling Clubs Area
LCI GIGS	London Calling Gigs Area
LCI LIFE	London Calling Life Area
LCI LIVE	London Calling Live on AOL
LCS	LCS Guide to Hockey
LD HELP	Long Distance Help Area
LE BEC FIN	George Perrier's LeBec-Fin
LE COQ SPROTIF	LCS Guide to Hockey
LEADERSHIP	Leadership Journal
LEADING EDGE	Leading Edge
LEAFS	Toronto Maple Leafs
LEARN	Research & Learn Channel
LEARN AOL	Learn to Use America Online
LEARN AUTO AOL	Orientation Feature
LEARN CHAT	Discover AOL - Chat & Auditoriums
LEARN DOWNLOAD	Discover AOL - Downloading
LEARN E-MAIL	Discover AOL - E-mail
LEARN FAVORITE PLACES	Orientation Feature
LEARN FIND	Discover AOL - Findings
LEARN FINDING	Learn AOL - MAC Find
LEARN FINDING PEOPLE	LEARN HOW
LEARN GAMES	LEARN HOW
LEARN HYPERLINK	Using Hyperlinks in E-mail and IMs
LEARN IM	Learn IM
LEARN INTERNET	Learn AOL MAC Internet
LEARN KEYWORDS	Orientation Feature
LEARN MASSAGE	Georgetown Bodyworks
LEARN MEETING PEOPLE	LEARN HOW
LEARN MESSAGE BOARDS	Discover AOL - Message Boards
LEARN NAVIGATION	Discover AOL - Getting Around
LEARN NEWS GROUPS	Orientation Feature
LEARN NEWS PROFILES	LEARN HOW
LEARN PARENT	Learn Parental Controls
LEARN PEOPLE	Learn People Connection
LEARN PP	Learn Personal Publisher
LEARN PUBLISHER	LEARN HOW
LEARN QUOTES	LEARN HOW
LEARN RICH TEXT	LEARN HOW

LEARNING	Research & Learn Channel
LEARNING DISORDERS	Learning & Development Disorders
LEARNING POLL	Learning Poll
LEATHER ONQ	onQ
LEATHER SOULS	PlanetOut Leather Community
LEBANON	Lebanon
LEEDS	Digital City: Leeds
LEEDS EOL	Leeds Events Online
LEGAL	Online Legal Areas
LEGAL INFORMATION NET	Lin
LEGAL NOTICE	Special Notice
LEGAL PRO	Counsel Connect
LEGAL PROFESSIONAL	Your Business Legal Professionals
LEGAL SIG	Legal Information Network
LEGENDS	Legends of Kesmai
LEICESTER	Digital City Leicester
LEISURE ATLANTA	Atlanta Leisure
LENS	Lens Express
LEO	AOL UK: Astrology
LEPRECHAUN	Irish Heritage
LESBIAN	Gay & Lesbian Community Forum
LESBIAN & GAY RIGHTS	Human Rights Campaign (Gay & Lesbian Rights Area)
LESBIAN BUSINESS	Business onQ
LESBIAN CHAT	onQ: Chat
LESBIAN ENTERTAINMENT	onQ: Arts & Entertainment
LESBIAN HOMES	onQ: Home & Garden
LESBIAN MARRIAGE	Marriage
LESBIAN MUSIC	Women's Space - Music Area
LESBIAN NEWS	onQ: News
LESBIAN ORG	onQ: Organizations
LESBIAN POLITICS	In the News onQ
LESBIAN SF	Digital City San Francisco Gay Community
LESBIAN TRAVEL	onQ: Travel
LESBIAN TRIVIA	onQ: Gaymeland
LESBIAN UK	Utopia
LESBIAN YOUTH	onQ: Youth
LESLEY	Lesley College SIG
LESOTHO	Lesotho
LETTER	Community Updates From Steve Case*
LEWISVILLE	Lewisville Leader Newspaper
LEXIS NEXIS 123	Lexis-Nexis 123
LFF	London Film Festival
LIB ONQ	onQ: Libraries
LIBERIA	Liberia
LIBERTARIAN	Libertarian Party Forum
LIBERTY BELL	Digital City Philadelphia: Walking Tour
LIBERTYBELLE	Digital City Philadelphia: Liberty Belle Cruises
LIBRA	AOL UK: Astrology
LIBRARIES	Software Center [Platform dependent]
LIBRARIES ONQ	onQ: Libraries
LIBS	Software Center [Platform dependent]
LIBYA	Libya
LIECHTENSTEIN	Liechtenstein
LIFE	Computer Life Magazine
LIFE ON MARS	Learning & Culture Life on Mars
LIFETIME	Lifetime Television for Women
LIFTING	AOL Weightlifting and Bodybuilding
LIGHTNING	Tampa Bay Lightning Hockey
LILLIAN	Lillian Vernon
LIN	Legal Information Network
LINCOLN	Digital City: Lincoln
LINCOLN BENEFIT LIFE	Allstate: Lincoln Benefit Life
LINCOLN EOL	Midlands Events Online
LINEUP4	AOL Classic Java Games
LINGO	Investment Lingo
LINK EXCHANGE	The Internet Link Exchange (free WWW advertising) [WWW site]
LINKEXCHANGE.COM	Link Exchange Website
LINN	LinnSoftware
LINUX	Linux Info
LIONEL	Model Trains
LIONS	Detroit Lions Football Coverage
LIP LOUNGE	HUB Lip Lounge
LIQUOR STORE	Liquor Stores & Suppliers Community - AOL's Your Business
LIST GUY	NetGuide on AOL Listguy
LISTENUP	ListenUp Audio and Video
LISTSERV	Internet Mailing Lists
LISZT	Liszt: Searchable Directory of E-mail Discussion Groups [WWW site]
LISZT.COM	Liszt Website
LITERARY CRITICISM	Barron's Booknotes
LITERATURE LANGUAGE	Literature Reference
LITHUANIA	Lithuania
LIVE	AOL Live!
LIVE BUZZ	BackStage Buzz
LIVE EVENTS	Online Promotions
LIVE FEED	Feed Magazine

LIVE GIRL	The Hub
LIVE GUIDE	Live Guide Coming Attractions on AOL
LIVE REMOTE	Snowboarding Online
LIVE SPORTS	AOL Sports Live
LIVE!	AOL Live!
LIVE@THRIVE	Thrive@AOL: Chat and Auditorium Events
LIVERPOOL	Digital City Liverpool
LIVERPOOL EOL	Liverpool Events Online
LIVING HISTORY	The History Channel's Living History
LJ	Leadership Journal
LNB	Laredo National Bank
LOA ANGELES CURRENTS	Computer Currents
LOBBY	People Connection
LOCAL	Digital Cities Channel
LOCAL ACCESS	Local Access Numbers
LOCAL NEWSPAPERS	Newspapers Selection
LOCAL SPORTS	Local Sports
LOCAL WEATHER STATION	Wavy Weather
LOCKER ROOM	NTN Locker Room
LOGGING	The Forestry Community
LOGO SHOP	AOL Store Logo Apparel Shop
LOIS & CLARK	ABC Online: Lois & Clark
LOLLA	Lollapalooza
LON PRIDE	London Pride
LONDON	DLCity
LONDON ACOM	Digital City London: Accommodations
LONDON AIRPORTS	Digital City London: Transport
LONDON ART	Digital City London: Art
LONDON ARTS	Events Online - London Arts
LONDON ATTRACTIONS	Digital City London: Attractions
LONDON B&BS	Digital City London: Accommodations
LONDON BUSINESS	Business Travel Guide to London, England
LONDON CABS	Digital City London: Transport
LONDON CALENDAR	Digital City London: Calendar
LONDON CALLING	London Calling Home Page
LONDON CHAT	DLChat
LONDON CHURCHES	Digital City London: Attractions
LONDON CINEMA	Digital City London: Cinema
LONDON CITY GUIDE	DLGuide
LONDON CLASSICAL	Digital City London: Classical
LONDON CLUBS	Digital City London: Clubs
LONDON COLLEGES	Digital City London: Education
LONDON COMEDY	Digital City London: Comedy
LONDON DANCE	Digital City London: Dance
LONDON DRINKS	London Drinking Guide
LONDON EDUCATION	Digital City London: Education
LONDON EOL	Events Online - London
LONDON EVENTS	Digital City London: Calendar
LONDON FEEDBACK	London Feedback
LONDON FESTIVAL	City of London Festival Guide
LONDON FOOD	DLFood
LONDON GAY	Digital City London: Gay
LONDON GUIDE	DLGuide
LONDON HOTELS	Digital City London: Accommodations
LONDON INDEX	London Index
LONDON INFO	Digital City London: Information
LONDON KIDS	Digital City London: Kids
LONDON MAPS	London Maps
LONDON MUSEUMS	Museums in London
LONDON MUSIC	Events Online - London Music
LONDON NEWS	DLNews
LONDON PERSONALS	DLPersonals
LONDON POLL	London Surveys
LONDON PRIDE	London Lesbian & Gay Pride
LONDON RESTAURANTS	DLFood
LONDON REVIEWS	London Events & Reviews
LONDON SCHOOLS	Digital City London: Education
LONDON SEARCH	London Search
LONDON SHOPS	Digital City London: Shopping
LONDON SIGHTS	Digital City London: Attractions
LONDON SPORT	Digital City London: Sport
LONDON SURVEY	London Surveys
LONDON SURVIVAL	Digital City London: Survival
LONDON THEATRE	Digital City London: Theatre
LONDON TOUR	Digital City London: Attractions
LONDON TRAINS	Digital City London: Transport
LONDON TV	Digital City London: Television
LONDON UNDERGROUND	London Underground
LONDON UNIS	Digital City London: Education
LONDON VENUES	Digital City London: Venues
LONDON WEATHER	London Weather
LONDON WEB	DLWeb
LONDONDERRY	Digital City: Londonderry
LONELY PLANET	Lonely Planet Travel Area
LONELY PLANET SEARCH	Lonely Planet Search
LONG BEACH	Los Angles Cities
LONG DISTANCE HELP	Long Distance Help Area
LONGHORNS	AOL College Football

LOOK SOFTWARE	The Virus Experts
LOOK UP	Look Up! [WWW site]
LOS ANGELES	Digital Cities: Los Angeles
LOS ANGELES CHAT	LA People
LOS ANGELES CLIPPERS	LA Clip (c)
LOS ANGELES DINING	Digital City Los Angeles: Dining
LOS ANGELES DODGERS	Major League Baseball Team: Los Angeles Dodgers
LOS ANGELES EVENTS	Los Angeles Events, Offline and On!
LOS ANGELES GALAXY	Los Angeles Galaxy
LOS ANGELES KIDS	Digital City Los Angeles: Kids
LOS ANGELES KINGS	Los Angeles Kings
LOS ANGELES LAKERS	LA Lakers Basketball
LOS ANGELES MARATHON	Los Angeles Marathon
LOS ANGELES MOVIE	Los Angeles Movies
LOS ANGELES NEWS	LA News
LOS ANGELES NIGHTS	LA Nights Cyber Comic
LOS ANGELES PEOPLE	LA People
LOS ANGELES SINGLES	LA Personals
LOS ANGELES SOCCER	Digital City Los Angeles: Sports
LOS ANGELES SPORTS	Digital City Los Angeles: Sports
LOS ANGELES TRAVEL	Los Angeles Tourism
LOS ANGELES TV	TV Navigator Los Angeles
LOST TV	Lost & Found TV Shows
LOTTERY	Lotteries
LOTUS	Lotus Notes Resource Center
LOTUS 123	PC Spreadsheet Computing Forum
LOTUS NOTE	Lotus Notes Resource Center
LOUISIANA	50 States
LOUISIANA STATE	Louisiana State
LOVE	Romance Channel
LOVE FILES	The Love Files
LOVE LINE	Love@AOL
LOVE ONLINE	ABC Love Online
LOVE ONQ	Relationship
LOVE PROFILE	Love@AOL Profile Form
LOVE SHACK	The Love Shack
LOVE SHOP	The Love Shop
LOVE TOWN	DC Personals
LOVE@1ST SITE	Premiere Introductory Service
LOW FARE	FareWars
LOWE	Backpaker Magazine Marketplace
LP	Lonely Planet Travel Area
LPS	Lonely Planet Search
LS&I	Lifestyles & Interests
LSAT	Kaplan Online -or- The Princeton Review
LSI	Lifestyles & Interests
LSI CHAT	Club Chat
LSI FEEDBACK	LSI Feedback FDM
LSI HOT	C&I HOT
LSI STORE	Life, Styles & Interests Store
LSU	Louisiana State
LTT	Digital City San Diego: The Latina Tag Team
LUCAS	LucasArts Games
LUGE	my sport->luge (c)
LUNAR SCOPES	DjunaVerse
LUNCH BYTES	Jim Ayers' witty take on life. Published by lunchtime every day.
LUNG DISORDERS	Lung and Respiratory Screen
LUV HUB	Tease: The HUB
LUXEMBORG	Luxemborg
LYNN VARGAS	Vargas Designs
LYNX AIRWAYS	Virtual Airlines
M AND T BANK	Manufacturers & Traders Trust Company
M SQUARE	Maple Square - Canada's Internet Directory
M ZONE	Multimedia Zone
M&T	M&T Banks
M'S	Seattle Mariners
M-W DICTIONARY	Merriam-Webster's Collegiate Dictionary
M1	ABC Online: Murder One Show
MAC	Macintosh Computing & Software
MAC 0S 8	Mac System 8
MAC APPS	Mac Business/Applications Forum
MAC ART	Graphic Art & CAD Forum [MAOL only]
MAC AV SC	Mac Animation and Video
MAC BF SC	Mac Business and Finance
MAC BIBLE	The Macintosh Bible/Peachpit Forum
MAC BUSINESS	Macintosh Business & Home Office Forum
MAC CAD	Mac Graphic Art & CAD Forum
MAC CHAT	Today's in Computers & Software [Platform dependent]
MAC CHATS	Mac Computing Forums: Chats and Conferences
MAC COMMUNICATION	Mac Communications and Networking Forum
MAC COMPUTING	Macintosh Computing & Software
MAC DESKTOP	Mac Desktop Publishing/WP Forum
MAC DESKTOP VIDEO	Macintosh Multimedia
MAC DEVELOPMENT	Macintosh Developers Forum
MAC DP SC	Mac Desktop Publishing

MAC DTP	Mac Desktop Publishing/WP Forum
MAC DV SC	Mac Development and Programming
MAC DWP	MACDWP
MAC ED SC	Mac Education and Reference
MAC EDUCATION	Mac Education & Technology Forum
MAC ESSENTIAL	Mac Essentials
MAC ESSENTIALS	Macintosh Essential Utilities
MAC FAQ	Mac Utilities FAQ Resource Center
MAC FORMAT	MacFormat Magazine
MAC FU SC	Mac Fun and Games
MAC GAME	Mac Games & Entertainment Forum
MAC GR SC	Mac Graphics
MAC GRAPHICS	Mac Graphic Art & CAD Forum
MAC HARDWARE	Mac Hardware Forum
MAC HELP	Mac Help Desk
MAC HO SC	Mac Home and Hobby
MAC HOME	Mac Home Journal
MAC HOT	What's Hot in Mac Computing [Platform dependent]
MAC HOT FILES	Mac and PC Forum NewFiles
MAC HYPERCARD	Mac HyperCard & Scripting Forum
MAC IN SC	Mac Internet
MAC LIBRARIES	Mac Software Center
MAC LIVE A	Mac Tech Live A
MAC LIVE B	Mac Tech Live B
MAC MARVEL	Marvel Chat Room
MAC MS SC	Mac Music and Sound
MAC MULTIMEDIA	Mac Desktop Video & Multimedia Forum
MAC MULTIMEDIA TOOL	mmm tool
MAC MUSIC	Mac Music & Sound Forum
MAC NEW FILES	Mac New Files
MAC NEWS	Mac Computing News & Newsletters
MAC NT SC	Mac Networking and Telecom
MAC OFFICE	Mac Business/Applications Forum
MAC OS	Mac Operating Systems Forum
MAC PRESCHOOL	Preschool
MAC PRESS	Mac News
MAC PROGRAMMING	Macintosh Developers Forum
MAC QUICKFIND	File Search
MAC SCITECH	MacSciTech Forum
MAC SOFTWARE	Mac Software Center
MAC SOUND	Mac Music & Sound Forum
MAC SOUND TOOL	MMStool
MAC SPEAKERZ	True Image Audio
MAC SUMMER	Mac Computing Forums: Summer [May disappear without notice]
MAC TIPS	Family Computing Forum: Tip of the Day
MAC TODAY	Mac Today Magazine
MAC TOOLBOX	Mac Toolbox
MAC UPDATE	MAS Update
MAC UT SC	Mac Utilities and Tools
MAC UTILITIES	Mac Utilities Forum
MAC VID	Mac Desktop Video & Multimedia Forum
MAC VIDEO	MVD
MAC VIRUS	Mac Virus Information Center
MAC WP	Mac Desktop Publishing/WP Forum
MACEDONIA	Macedonia
MACH IT	Global Gourmet: Match-It Game
MACHESTER EOL	North West Events Online
MACHINERY	Your Business: Machinery Community
MACINTAX	Parsons Technology
MACINTOSH BIBLE	The Macintosh Bible/Peachpit Forum
MACINTOSH NEWS	Mac News
MACKEREL	Owl Magazine: Mighty Mites
MACMILLAN	MacMillan Information SuperLibrary
MACRO	Affinity Microsystems
MACRO INT	Macro International
MACROMEDIA	Macromedia, Inc.
MACROMEDIA.COM	Macromedia [WWW site]
MACROMIND	Macromedia, Inc.
MACUSER	MacUser Magazine
MACWORLD	MacWorld Magazine
MAD	DC Comics Online
MAD ABOUT	Mad About You Fan Forum
MAD MAGAZINE	DC Comics Online
MAD WORLD	Today's News: It's a Mad, Mad World
MADA	MacApp Developers Association
MADAGASCAR	Madagascar
MADAME ADAMS	Cindy Adams
MADRID	Time Out Travel Guide to Madrid, Spain
MAG OUT	AOL Magazine Outlet Store
MAG RACK	Magazine Rack
MAGAZINE	new: magazine referee
MAGAZINE OUTLET	AOL Magazine Outlet Store
MAGAZINE RACK	Computing Magazine Rack
MAGAZINES	The Newsstand
MAGE	Multi-playerAction Game
MAGELLAN	Magellan Internet Guide [WWW site]

MAGELLAN.COM	Magellan Website
MAGIC KINGDOM	Walt Disney World
MAGIC LINK	Sony Magic Link
MAGIC ONLINE	Digital City Denver: Magic Online
MAGICK	Pagan Religions & Occult Sciences
MAGTOUR	MagTour
MAGYARORSZAG	Hungary
MAIDS	Cleaners & Janitors - AOL's Your Business
MAIL	Mail Center
MAIL CONTROLS	Mail Controls
MAIL GATEWAY	Mail Gateway
MAIL HELP	net.help: E-mail Help
MAIL ORDER	Your Business: Mail Order Community
MAIL PW	Mailbox Password
MAIL SERVICE	Your Business: Mail Service Community
MAILING LIST	Internet Mailing Lists
MAILING LIST HELP	net.help: Mailing List Help
MAIN STREET	Main Street
MAIN US	AOL US Channel
MAINE	Digital Cities: Northeast
MAJORDOMO	Internet Mailing Lists
MAKE FRIENDS	LEARN HOW
MAKEDNIJA	Macedonia
MALAWI	Malawi
MALAYSIA	Malaysia
MALDIVES	Maldives
MALE ONQ	onQ
MALI	Mali
MALIBU	Los Angles Cities
MALL	Shopping Channel
MALTA	Malta
MAM	Mad About Music
MAMA'S CUCINA	Mama's Cucina by Ragu
MANCHESTER	Digital City Manchester
MANGA	Wizard World/PDA/Palmtop Forum
MANGO MARKET	Destination Florida - Mango Market Store
MANHATTAN GRAPHICS	Manhattan Graphics
MANNIX	Boston Herald: Mannix
MANUFACTURE	Your Business: Manufacture Community
MAP	Maps: U.S. & World
MAPEL	Pangea Toy Network: ToyBuzz
MAPLE	Maple Square - Canada's Internet Directory
MAPLELEAFS	Toronto Maple Leafs
MAPQUEST	Mapquest (interactive mapping service) [WWW site]
MAPS	Maps: US & World
MARCH MADNESS STORE	March Madness Marketplace
MARGERY EAGAN	Boston Herald: Eagan
MARIANA	North Mariana
MARIETTA	Marietta Daily Journal Online
MARINARA	Papua New Guinea
MARINE	Boating Online
MARINE CORPS MARATHON	Marine Corps Marathon [May disappear without notice]
MARINERS	Major League Baseball Team: Seattle Mariners
MARINES	Military City Online
MARK SHIELDS	The Great Debate - Talk Politics
MARK SNYDER	Mark Snyder's Night Out!
MARKET MAIL	Marketplace Customer Service Email
MARKET MEDITATIONS	Market Meditations
MARKET NEWS	Market News Center
MARKET RESEARCH	American Dialogue
MARKETING PREFS	Marketing Preferences*
MARKETPLACE	Shopping Channel
MARKETPLACE GOODS	Marketplace Newsletter
MARKETPLACE HOLIDAY	Marketplace Holiday Village 1996
MARKETPLACE MAIL	Marketplace Customer Service E-mail
MARKETPLACE SALE	new: bargain
MARKETPLACE TOUR	Tour of the Stores/Tour of Marketplace
MARKETS	Market News Area
MARKETSCOPE	Standard and Poors: Mscope
MARLINS	Major League Baseball Team: Florida Marlins
MARQUETTE	Marquette Banks
MARRIAGE ONQ	onQ: Marriage
MARRIAGE PARTNERSHIP	Marriage Partnership Magazine
MARS	Mars@AOL (Mars Pathfinder Information) or Men Are From Mars
MARS ATTACK	Mars Attacks
MARS PATHFINDER	Mars Pathfinder Information
MARS TOKYO	Mars Tokyo's Visual Diary
MARS VENUS	Men Are From Mars
MARSHALL AUTO	Chesrown Autos, Denver CO
MARSHALL ISLANDS	Marshall Islands
MARTELL GRAND NATIONAL	The Martell British Grand National
MARTIAL ART	Martial Arts on AOL
MARTIAL ARTS	Hobby Central: Martial Arts
MARTIAL ARTS WORLDWIDE	Martial Arts Worldwide Network
MARTIN	Martin Luther King

MARTINI	Wineries
MARTINIQUE	Martinique
MARVEL	Marvel Comics Online
MARVEL KIDS	Marvel Online Kids Area
MARVEL STORE	Marvel Online Store
MARYC	Mary C
MARYLAND	Digital Cities: Mid-Atlantic
MARYLAND TERPS	Maryland Terps
MASSACHUSETTS	50 States
MASSAGE REFERRALS	International Massage Association
MASTER PLANNER LA	Los Angeles Master Planner
MASTERLIST	Hoover's Company MasterList
MASTYR	Scrye Magazine Online
MATCH	AOL Interest Profiles
MATCH COM	Match Website
MATCH IT	Global Gourmet: Match-It Game
MATCH YOUR INTEREST	Match Your Interests Main Screen
MATERNITY	Moms Online
MATH	National Academy of Science Online
MATH REFERENCE	Science and Math Reference
MATHEMATICS	Simon & Schuster Online: Mathematics Dept.
MATIN	Plateau Matin: l'actu au petit dejeuner
MATT	Matt Williams' Hot Corner - Baseball
MATTINGLY	CO News Commentaries
MAURITIUS	Muaritius
MAVEN	Business Week: Maven Computer Buying Guide
MAVERICKS	Pro Basketball
MAWN	Martial Arts Worldwide Network
MAWN CHAT	Chat Area for the MAW Network
MAWN ENT	Entertainment Area of the Martial Arts
MAWN REF	Reference Area of the Martial Arts
MAWN SD	Self Defense Area of the Martial Arts
MAWN SI	Self Improvement Area of the Martial Arts
MAWN TD	Training Area of the Martial Arts
MAX AOL	Family Computing Forum: Maximum AOL
MAX SAVINGS	OfficeMax Back to School
MAXELL	maxell->maxell (c)
MAXFIELD PARRISH	The Art of Maxfield Parrish Exhibit
MAXIMUM AOL	Maximum AOL
MAXIS	Maxis Support Forum
MAXTECH	MaxTech Corporation
MAYFEST	Digital City Glasgow: Mayfest
MAZOLA	Mazola
MBS	Macintosh Business & Home Office Forum
MC ADS	Mercury Center Advertising
MC CHAT	Mac Conferences
MC COMMUNICATION	Mercury Center Communication
MC LIBRARY	Mercury Center Newspaper Library
MC LIVING	Mercury Center Bay Area Living Area
MC MARATHON	Marine Corps Marathon
MC MARKET	Mercury Center Advertising
MC NEW	San Jose Mercury News [GAOL only]
MC NEWS	Mercury Center In the News Area
MC SPORTS	Mercury Center Sports Area
MC TRIVIA	Mercury Center Trivia
MCAFEE	McAfee Associates
MCAT	Kaplan Online -or- The Princeton Review
MCDONNELL DOUGLAS	McDonnell Douglas [WWW site]
MCGAW GRAPHICS	Bruce McGaw Graphics
MCINTIRE	University of Virginia Alumni/McIntire School of Commerce
MCKINNEY	Mckinney Messenger
MCL	Mystic Color Labs
MCM	Mac Communications and Networking Forum
MCO	Military City Online
MCO BASES	Military City Online Worldwide Military Installations Database
MCO BOSNIA	MCO Bosnia
MCO CIRC	MCO Subscriber Services
MCO COMM	Military City Online Communications
MCO EARLY	Early Bird Brief
MCO HQ	Military City Online Headquarters
MCO MAIN	MCO HQ
MCO MC	MCO Message Center
MCO PORT	MCOPORT
MCO SHOP	Military City Online Shop
MCO TOUR	Military City Online Tour
MCVEIGH	DC Denver & KWGN Channel 2 cover the McVeigh Trial
MDC.COM	McDonnell Douglas Website
MDJ	Marietta Daily Journal Online
MDP	Mac Desktop and Web Publishing Forum
MDV	Macintosh Developers Forum
ME TV	TV & Me
MEAT	Omaha Steaks
MECCA	International Channel Middle East
MED	Mac Education & Technology Forum
MEDALLION	Gold Medallion Winners
MEDIA & JOURNALISM	Your Business: Media and Journalism Community

MEDIA CABLE	Greater Media Cable Company
MEDIA CENTER	Library Media Center SIG
MEDIA INFORMATION	Cowles/SIMBA Media Information Network
MEDIA ONQ	Media onQ
MEDIA SPACE	AOL Media Space
MEDICAL	Your Business: Medical Services Community
MEDICAL BILLING	AOL's Your Business: Medical Billing & Claims Processing
MEDICAL CLAIMS	Your Business: Medical Claims Community
MEDICAL DICTIONARY	Merriam-Webster's Medical Dictionary
MEDICAL EXPERTS	Ask the Experts
MEDICAL PEARLS	Medical Pearls
MEDICAL SCHOOL	Kaplan Online -or- The Princeton Review
MEDICAL TRANSCRIPTION	AOL's Your Business: Medical Transcription Forum
MEDICINE	Health Channel
MEDIZINE	Medizine Pharmacists Network
MEDLINE	Medline
MEG	AOL Insider
MEGA NEWS	FamilyPC Online
MEGA SALE	new: bargain
MEGAHERTZ	Megahertz Corporation
MEISSNER	Meissner Chevrolet/Geo/Oldsmobile
MELISSA	Melissa Etheridge Information
MELLON	Mellon Bank
MEM CHOICE	AOL Member's Choice
MEM REWARDS	American Express/Membership Rewards
MEMBER COMMUNITY	Member Community
MEMBER DIRECTORY	Member Directory
MEMBER HOMEPAGE	Search Member Home Pages
MEMBER LEAGUES	Member Leagues
MEMBER PREFERENCES	My AOL
MEMBER PROFILE	Edit your member profile
MEMBER REWARD	AOL Rewards
MEMBER SERVICES	Member's Online Help
MEMBER SURVEY	Member Survey
MEMBERS	Member Directory
MEMBERS CHOICE	AOL Member's Choice
MEMBERS RIDES	Wheels Exchange
MEMBERSHIP REWARD	American Express/Membership Reward
MEMORIAL DAY	Memorial Day [May disappear without notice]
MEN ONQ	onQ: Men
MEN'S HEALTH	Men's Health Forum
MEN'S HEALTH WEB	Men's Health Internet Sites
MENTAL	Mental Health Forum
MENTAL HEALTH AWARENESS	Mental Health Awareness Month
MENTAL HEALTH WEB	Mental Health Internet Sites
MERCADO	Hispanic Online
MERCHANDISE	AOL Store
MESSAGE PAD	Newton Resource Center
MESSIAH	Messiah College
MET HOME	Metropolitan Home
METACREATIONS	HSC Software
METALLICA	Metallica Club
METASQUARES	Head-to-Head Strategy Game
METATOOLS	HSC Software
METRICOM	Metricom
METRO MUSIC	Metro Music
METRO TOURISTER	Digital City Twin Cities: Metro Tourist Insider
METROPLEX RELIGION	Dallas/Ft. Worth Religion
METROPOLITAN HOME	Metropolitan Home
METS	Major League Baseball Team: New York Mets
MEXICO	Mexico
MF	The Motley Fool: Finance & Folly
MF CENTER	Mutual Fund Center
MFC	AOL Mutual Fund Center
MFC CANADA	Canadian Mutual Fund Centre
MFC DEMO	Mutual Fund Center Transaction Dem
MFC LIVE	Mutual Fund Center Live
MFC VAULT	Mutual Fund Center: Vault
MFRC	Mutual Fund Center
MGM	Mac Games & Entertainment Forum
MHC	Mac HyperCard & Scripting Forum
MHM	Members Helping Members message board*
MHP CONTEST	Members Home Page Contest
MIAMI	Digital Cities: Miami/Ft. Lauderdale
MIAMI BLACK VOICES	South Florida Black Voices
MIAMI COMM	Digital City Miami: Community
MIAMI HEAT	Miami Heat
MIAMI NEWS	Digital City Miami: News & Weather
MIAMI PEOPLE	Digital City Miami: People
MIAMI TOUR	Digital City Miami: City Tour
MIC	Motorsports Information Central
MICHAEL FLATLEY	Rosie O'Donnell: Michael Flatley Lord of the Dance
MICHIGAN	Michigan Governor's Forum
MICHIGAN J FROG	The WB Network
MICHIGAN STATE	Michigan State
MICKEY	Mickey Starmaker (The Hub)

MICRON	Micron Electronics
MICRONESIA	International Channel
MICROSOFT	Microsoft Resource Center
MICROSOFT ACCESS	Microsoft Access User Group [German]
MICROSOFT INTERNET	Microsoft Internet Resource Center
MICROSOFT PUBLISHER	Microsoft Publisher Resource Center
MICROSOFT.COM	Microsoft Corporation [WWW site]
MIDDLE EAST	International Channel Middle East
MIDI	Music & Sound Forum [Platform dependent]
MIDLANDS EOL	Midlands Events Online
MIDWEST DIGC	Digital Cities: Midwest
MIGHTY DUCKS	NHL Hockey
MIGHTY MITES	Markerel Interactive Media
MIGRAINES	Pain Relief Center
MIKE KEEFE	Mike Keefe Editorial Cartoons
MILE-HIGH MAGAZINE	Denver Entertainment, Dining and Night Life
MILENNIUM	Millennium Forum
MILESTONE	DC Comics Online
MILFAM	Military Family Center
MILITARY	Military & Vets Club
MILITARY CITY	Military City Online
MILITARY FAMILY	Military Family Center
MILITARY HISTORY	Military History Forum
MILITARY ONQ	onQ: Military
MILLENNIUM	Millennium Forum
MILWAUKEE BREWERS	Major League Baseball Team: Milwaukee Brewers
MIME	Sending and Receiving MIME E-mail
MIND GAMES	OLP: games
MINING	Your Business: Mining Community
MINN COMM	Digital City Twin Cities: Community
MINN FUN	Digital City Twin Cities: Entertainment
MINN MARKET	Digital City Twin Cities: Marketplace
MINN NEWS	Digital City Twin Cities: News
MINN PEOPLE	Digital City Twin Cities: People
MINN SPORTS	Digital City Twin Cities: Sports
MINN TWINS	Major League Baseball Team: Minnesota Twins
MINN WEATHER	Digital City Twin Cities: News
MINNEAPOLIS	Digital Cities: Minneapolis/St. Paul
MINNEAPOLIS CHAT	Digital City Twin Cities: Chat Schedule
MINNEAPOLIS TOUR	Digital City Twin Cities: MN Living
MINNESOTA	Digital Cities: Midwest
MINWAX	Housenet Special Keyword
MIRABELLA	Mirabella Magazine
MIRROR LIVE	The Daily Mirror - Live
MISSING KIDS	Missing Kids
MISSION ORCHARD	Mission Orchards
MISSISSIPPI	Digital Cities: Southeast
MISSISSIPPI STATE	Mississippi State
MISSOURI	50 States
MISTER MOVIE	Digital City Philadelphia Presents
MITES	Markerel Interactive Media
MLB	Major League Baseball
MLB ALLSTAR	MLB All-Star Game
MLM	Multi-Level Marketing Online
MLS	AOL's Real Estate Center
MLS LIVE	The Grandstand: Major League Soccer
MM	PC Multimedia Forum
MM SEARCH	Multimedia Zone Search
MM SHOWCASE	Multimedia Showcase*
MM STORE	March Madness Marketplace
MM ZONE	Multimedia Zone
MMA	Metropolitan Museum of Art
MMC	Music Messaging Center
MMM	Mac Desktop Video & Multimedia Forum
MMR	Music Member Reviews
MMS TOOL	Sound & Midi Resource Center
MMZ S	MMZ Search
MN	Digital City Twin Cities: Presents Minnesota Online
MN EDGE	The Edge Online Newspaper
MN FILM BOARD	Digital City Twin Cities: Film Board
MN LIVING	Digital City Twin Cities: MN Living
MN MONTHLY	Digital City Minneapolis Presents Minnesota Monthly
MN SPORTS	Digital City Twin Cities: Sports
MNC	Market News Center
MNC BONDS	Market News Center Bonds
MNC CURRENCIES	Market News Center Currencies
MNC ECONOMY	Market News Center Economy
MNC INTERNATIONAL	Market New Center International
MNC STOCKS	Market News Center Stocks
MNC-XRAY	MNC X-ray
MNF	ABC Sports Monday Night Football
MOBIL USR	Megahertz Corporation
MOBILE	Mobile Office Online
MOBILECOMM	MobileComm - Paging & Personal Com
MOBILEMEDIA	MobileMedia
MOBILEWEB	Mobileweb
MOBILNET	GTE

MOD SQUAD	Mod Squad
MODEL	TopModel Online
MODEL PLANE	Model Planes
MODEL SCHOOL	Modeling School
MODEL SEARCH	Boss Models
MODEL TRAINS	Hobby Central: Model Trains
MODELING MANUAL	Model Manual
MODELS	Elle Magazine
MODEM	Modems and Connections*
MODEM SHOP	AOL Modem Shop
MODERN LIVES	The Hub: Modern Lives
MODESTO	Digital City: Sacramento
MOLDOVA	Moldova
MOLSON	Molson's
MOM ONLINE	Moms Online
MOM TRAVEL	Mother's Day Travel - Travel Channel
MONACO	Monaco
MONDAY NIGHT FOOTBALL	ABC Sports Monday Night Football
MONEY	Personal Finance Channel
MONEY FAQS	Personal Finance Advice
MONEY MATTERS	Washington's Money Matters
MONEY U	Ric Edelman - Your Financial Planner
MONEY WIZ	Real Life Main Screen
MONEYWISE	Moneywise Home Page
MONGOLIA	Mongolia
MONOGRAM	Personal Creations - Marketplace Merchant
MONSOON POWERLINK	Link to Monsoon Audio Area
MONSTER	The Monster Board (Career Hub) [WWW site]
MONSTER ISLAND	Adventures by Mail
MONSTER.COM	Monster Website
MONTANA	Digital Cities: Northwest
MONTESSORI	Montessori Schools
MONTREAL CANADIENS	Montreal Canadiens
MONTREAL EXPOS	Major League Baseball Team: Montreal Expos
MORALS	Ethics & Values
MORE GAMES	More Games
MORE SPORTS	More Sports
MORGAN DAVIS	Morgan Davis Group
MORNINGSTAR	Morningstar Mutual Funds
MOROCCO	Morocco
MOS UPDATE	Apple System 7.x Update
MOSIAC	Spiritual Mosiac
MOSLIM	Islamic Resources Area
MOTELS	Your Business: Hotel Community
MOTIVATIONAL	Success
MOTLEY	The Motley Fool: Finance & Folly
MOTORCYCLE	Wheels
MOTORCYCLING	Cycle World Online
MOTORSPORT	Motorsport '97 Online
MOTS CLES	AOL France Keyword List
MOUNT ST HELENS	Volcano Resources
MOUNT VERNON HONDA	Mount Vernon Honda
MOUNTAIN ASTROLOGY	Astronet
MOUNTAIN BIKE	Bicycling Magazine
MOUNTAIN BIKING	Mountain Biking - Active Sports
MOUNTAINEERS	AOL College Football
MOVERS	Your Business: Mover Community
MOVIE	AOL Entertainment: Movies
MOVIE ARCHIVES	Old Favorites
MOVIE CRITIC	Hype! You be the movie critic...
MOVIE CRITICS	Movie Reviews
MOVIE DB	Old Favorites
MOVIE FORUM	Movie Forums Area
MOVIE GUIDE	Hollywood Online: A-Z Movie Guide
MOVIE REPORTER	The Movie Reporter
MOVIE REVIEW DATABASE	Movie Review Database
MOVIE REVIEWS	Movie Reviews
MOVIE SHOWTIMES	@the.movies
MOVIE STAR	Image Exchange
MOVIE TIMES	Show Times - Web
MOVIE WEB	Movies on the Web
MOVIES	AOL Entertainment: Movies
MOVIES DB	Old Favorites
MOVIES IN TIME	The History Channel: Movies In Time
MOVIES LA	Los Angeles Movies
MOVIES TRIVIA	NTNMovies
MOVIEVISIONS	MovieVisions
MOVING SERVICES	Movers & Moving Services - AOL's Your Business Community
MOZAMBIQUE	Mozambique
MP DEAL	Marketplace Real Deals Newsletter
MPBT	Multiplayer Battletech
MPM	Marriage Partnership Magazine
MR MOVIE	Digital City Philadelphia Presents
MRC	IAS Multimedia Resource Center
MRC FAMILY	Novartis MRC Family Practice
MRC NEURO	Novartis MRC Neurology
MRC SALES	Novartis MRC Sales

MS	Maple Square - Canada's Internet Directory
MS ACCESS	MS Access Resource Center - US Version
MS BIZ	Your Business
MS DOS	DOS Forum
MS DOS 6	MS-DOS 6.0 Resource Center
MS EXCEL	PC Spreadsheet Computing Forum
MS INTERNET	Microsoft Internet Resource Center
MS PUB	Microsoft Publisher Resource Center
MS REQUESTS	Member Services Requests
MS SUPPORT	Microsoft Resource Center
MS WORKS	Microsoft Works Resource Center
MSBC	Your Business
MSCOPE	Standard & Poor's Marketscope
MSDL	SDL for MM Showcase
MSKB	Microsoft Knowledge Base
MSO	Macro International
MST	MacSciTech
MST3K	Mystery Science Theater 3000
MSTAR	Morningstar Mutual Fund Area
MSTLOGIN	MSTLogin
MSU.COM	MSU Website
MSWORD	Word for Windows Resource Center
MTC	Mac Communications Forum
MTPRODUCTIONS	San Francisco Lesbian Bars
MTV	MTV Online
MTV ARENA	Yack
MTV AWARDS	MTV Movie Awards
MTV BIOS	MTV Bios
MTV DAILY FIX	MTV Fix
MTV FAQ	MTV FAQ
MTV FRONT	MTV Main
MTV HOS	MTV House of Style
MTV MAIN	MTV Main
MTV MOVIES	MTV Movie Awards
MTV MUSIC	MTV Music
MTV NEWS	MTV News
MTV ONLINE	MTV Online
MTV PLUG	Plug
MTV PRIVATE	Your Own Private MTV
MTV SPRING BREAK	Spring Break
MTV TUBESCAN	Tube Scan
MTV VMAS	MTV Video Music Awards
MTV.COM	MTV Online [WWW site]
MTVD	Mars Tokyo's Visual Diary
MUARITIUS	Muaritius
MUCHM	MuchMusic Online
MULTI LEVEL MARKETING	Multi-Level Marketing Online
MULTIMEDIA	Multimedia Menu
MULTIMEDIA SEARCH	MMZ Search
MULTIMEDIA ZONE	Multimedia Zone
MULTIMEDIA FORUM	The Multimedia Zone
MULTIMEDIA SHOW	Multimedia Showcase
MULTIPLE SCLEROSIS	Multiple Sclerosis Forum
MUNDO	Mundo
MURDER 1	ABC Online: Murder One Show
MUS	Christianity Online: Music & Media
MUSCLE	Bones, Joints & Muscles Forum
MUSIC	MusicSpace
MUSIC & SOUND	Music and Sound Forum [Platform dependent]
MUSIC CHAT	Music Chat
MUSIC FAN	MusicSpace Fans & Followers
MUSIC GUIDE	UK Concert Guide
MUSIC HOT	What's Hot in Music
MUSIC HUB	HUB Music
MUSIC LABELS	Music Labels
MUSIC MESSAGE	Music Messaging Center
MUSIC MESSAGE BOARDS	Music Messaging Center
MUSIC NEWS	MTV Online: News
MUSIC PROGRAMMER	MusicProgrammer
MUSIC PROMO	What's Hot in Music
MUSIC REFERENCE	Art and Music Reference
MUSIC REVIEW	Music Member Reviews
MUSIC SPOT	Music Spotlight (Reward Town)
MUSIC STUDIO	The Studio
MUSIC STORE	Record, Tape & Disc Retailers - AOL's Your Business Community
MUSIC SUGGEST	MusicSpace Suggestions
MUSIC TALK	MusicSpace Communications
MUSIC TOOLS	Tools of the Trade
MUSIC TRAVEL	Concert and Music Festivals
MUSIC WEB	MusicSpace Web TopStops
MUSIC WEB FEEDBACK	MusicWeb Feedback
MUSICSPACE	MusicSpace
MUSICSPACE WEB	Cool Music Websites
MUSLIM	Islamic Resources
MUT	Mac Utilities Forum
MUT AWARD	Mac Shareware Awards [MAOL only]
MUTE	Mute

MUT TOOL	Mac Essentials
MUTUAL FUND	AOL Mutual Fund Center
MUTUAL FUND CENTER VAUL	Mutual Fund Center Vault
MUTUAL FUND LIVE	Mutual Fund Center Live
MUTUAL FUND PORTFOLIO	Mutual Fund Portfolio
MUTUTAL FUNDS CENTER	AOL Mutual Fund Center
MVC	Military & Vets Online
MVD	Mac Desktop Video & Multimedia Forum
MVD TOOL	Essential Multimedia Tools
MW EXPO	MacWorld Expo
MWISE	Moneywise Home Page
MWP	Mac Desktop and Web Publishing Forum
MW SOFTWARE	MW Software
MW THESAURUS	Merriam-Webster Thesaurus
MY AOL	My AOL
MY HOMEPAGE	Personal Publishing 2
MY PLACE	My Place (for FTP sites)
MY TV	It's TV & Me!
MYANMAR	Myanmar
MYI	Match Your Interests Main Screen
MYNDTALK	Online Psych: Myndtalk
MY PLACE HELP	My Place Help
MYRTLE	Dear Myrtle Daily Column
MY SPORT	MySport
MYST	Myst
MYSTERY	Fictional Realm
MYSTIC GARDENS	Mystic Gardens
MYSTICCOLORLAB	Mystic Color Lab
MYTHICA	Mythica
MZ	Multimedia Zone
N MARIANA ISLANDS	Northern Mariana Islands
N@N	Nick at Nite
N&B	Numerology & Beyond
NAEA	NAEA Tax Channel
NAGF	Non-Affiliated Gamers Forum
NAME	Add, change, or delete screen names
NANDO.NET	The Nando Times [WWW site]
NAPC	Employment Agency Database
NAPLES DCITY	Digital Cities: Ft. Myers/Naples FL
NAQP	National Association of Quick Printers Area
NAREE	AOL's Real Estate Desk
NAS	National Academy of Science Online
NASA	Space Exploration Online
NASA.GOV	National Aeronautics and Space Administration [WWW site]
NASCAR	AOL Auto Racing
NASCAR.COM	National Association for Stock Car and Auto Racing [WWW site]
NATIONAL PARENTING	The National Parenting Center
NATIONAL PARKS	Travel America
NATIVE AMERICAN	Hobby Central: Communities
NATURE	The Nature Conservancy
NAVIGATE	Top Tips for AOL
NAVISOFT	Navisoft
NAVY.MIL	NavyOnLine [WWW site]
NBA	Pro Basketball
NBA.COM	NBA.COM [WWW site]
NBC.COM	NBC.COM [WWW site]
NBR	The Nightly Business Report: Making $ense of It All
NC8	News Channel 8
NCR	National Catholic Reporter
NCT	Next Century Technologies
NEA	Accessing the NEA Public Forum*
NEA PUBLIC	National Education Association Public Forum
NEBRASKA	Digital Cities: Midwest
NEC	NEC Technologies
NECN	New England Cable News
NEIGHBORHOODS	USA Neighborhoods
NEOLOGIC	NeoLogic
NESN	New England Sports Network
NESN BASEBALL	NESN: New England Baseball
NESN BASKETBALL	NESN: New England Basketball
NESN FOOTBALL	NESN: New England Football
NESN HOCKEY	NESN: New England Hockey
NESN OUTDOORS	NESN Sports Circuit
NET	Internet Connection
.NET	.net: the Internet magazine
NET CHAT	Internet Chat
NET EXCHANGE	Internet Exchange
NET GAME	The Grandstand: Tennis
NET HELP	net.help
NET KNOW-HOW	NetGuide: Net Know-How
NET LIBRARY	Internet Software
NET NEWS	Internet Newsstand
NET ORGS	Internet Organizations
NET SOFTWARE	Internet Software
NET TODAY	NetGuide: The Net Today

NETFIND	AOL NetFind
NETGIRL	NetGirl
NETGIRL PERSONALS	NetGirl: Personals
NETGUIDE	NetGuide on AOL
NETGUIDELIVE	NetGuideLive: Your Daily Guide to the Internet [WWW site]
NETHERLANDS	Netherlands
NETNOIR	NetNoir
NETORGS	Net.Orgs
NETS	Pro Basketball
NETSCAPE	Netscape
NETSCAPE.COM	Netscape Communications Corporation [WWW site]
NETWORKING FORUM	Communications/Telecom/Networking Forum [Platform dependent]
NEVADA	Digital Cities: West
NEVERWINTER	AD&D Neverwinter Nights
NEW AGE	Religion & Ethics Forum
NEW AOL	Upgrade to the latest version of AOL* [Platform dependent]
NEW CAR	AutoVantage: New Car Summary
NEW ENGLAND CABLE	New England Cable News
NEW ENGLAND PATRIOTS	NESN: New England Football
NEW ERA	Tactic Software
NEW FILM	New Movie Releases
NEW GUINEA	Papua New Guinea
NEW HAMPSHIRE	Digital Cities: Northeast
NEW INTERESTS	New Interests
NEW LIFE	New Life Clinics
NEW MEMBER	Discover America Online (New Member Area)
NEW MEXICO	Digital Cities: West
NEW MOVIES	New Movie Releases
NEW ONQ	onQ: New
NEW PRICING	New Pricing*
NEW PRODUCT	New Product News
NEW PRODUCT SHOWCASE	New Product Showcase
NEW RELEASES	New Movie Releases
NEW WORLD	New World Computing
NEW YEAR	Have a Healthy New Year!
NEW YEARS	New Years@AOL [May disappear without notice]
NEW YORK METS	Major League Baseball Team: New York Mets
NEW YORK YANKEES	Major League Baseball Team: New York Yankees
NEW ZEALAND	New Zealand
NEWBIE	Discover America Online (New Member Area)
NEWPORT NEWS DCITY	Digital Cities: Newport News and Norfolk
NEWS	News Channel
NEWS 8	News Channel 8
NEWS LIBRARY	Mercury Center Newspaper Library
NEWS PROFILES	News Profiles
NEWS QUIZ	Chicago Tribune: News Quiz
NEWS SEARCH	Search News Articles
NEWS SENSATIONS	News Sensations
NEWS WATCH	Search News Articles
NEWSGROUP	Internet Usenet Newsgroup Area
NEWSGROUP HELP	net.help: Newsgroup Help
NEWSLETTER	Newsletter Subscriptions
NEWSLETTERS	Genealogy Forum
NEWSPAPER	Newspapers selection
NEWSPAPER LIBRARY	Mercury Center Newspaper Library
@NEWSROOM	The News Room Auditorium
NEWSSTAND	The Newsstand
NEWSTICKER	AOL NewsTicker
NEWSWEEK	Newsweek Magazine
NEWSWIRE	Newswire
NEWT GINGRICH	Eye on the Newt
NEWTON	Newton Resource Center
NEWTON BOOK	PDA/Palmtop Forum
NFL	Team NFL
NFL DRAFT	NFL Draft
NGLTF	Nation Gay & Lesbian Task Force
NHL	Hockey
NICHE	Your Business: Industries & Niches
NICK	Nickelodeon Selections
NICKELODEON	Nickelodeon Online
NIGERIA	Nigeria
NINTENDO.COM	Nintendo.com [WWW site]
NITTANY LIONS	AOL College Football
NLC	New Life Clinics
NMAA	National Museum of American Art
NMAH	National Museum of American History
NNFY	National Network for Youth
NOBLE	Barnes & Noble Bookseller
NOLO	Nolo Press' Self-Help Law Center
NOMADIC	Nomadic Computing Discussion SIG
NORFOLK DCITY	Digital Cities: Newport News and Norfolk
NORTH CAROLINA	Digital Cities: Southeast
NORTH DAKOTA	Digital Cities: Midwest
NORTHEAST	Digital Cities: Northeast
NORTON	Symantec

NORWAY	Norway
NOTEBOOK	PowerBook Resource Center
NOVELL	Novell Desktop Systems
NOVELL.COM	Novell Inc. [WWW site]
NPC	The National Parenting Center
NPCA	America's National Parks
NPR	National Public Radio Outreach
NPS	New Product Showcase
NS	News Sensations
NSS	Space Exploration Online
NTN HOCKEY TRIVIA	ABC Hockey Trivia
NTN HOOPS TRIVIA	NTN Basketball Trivia
NTN PLAYBOOK	NTN Playbook
NTN TRIVIA	NTN Trivia
NUGGETS	Pro Basketball
NUL	National Urban League
NUMBERS	Accessing America Online*
NUMEROLOGY	Numerology & Beyond
NUTRITION	Nutrition Forum
NW	Newsweek Magazine
NWFL	The Grandstand: Simulation Football
NWN	AD&D Neverwinter Nights
NY PUBLIC LIBRARY	New York Public Library Desk Reference
NY TIMES	@times/The New York Times Online
NY TIMES.COM	New York Times on the Web [WWW site]
NYPL	New York Public Library Desk Reference
NYT CROSSWORD	The New York Times Crosswords
O'S	Major League Baseball Team: Baltimore Orioles
OAKLAND A'S	Major League Baseball Team: Oakland Athletics
OAO	Outdoor Adventures Online
OBJECT FACTORY	Object Factory
OC	Owens Corning
OCTOBERFEST	Oktoberfest: German Heritage Month
ODDS	Sports Odds
ODEON	AOL Live!
@ODEON	The Odeon Auditorium
ODONNELL	Rosie O'Donnell Online
ODYSSEY	The Odyssey Project
OFFICEMAX	OfficeMax Online
OFS	Online Financial Services
OGF	Online Gaming Forums
OI	The Online Investor
OIL	Your Business: Energy & Oil Industry Community
OILERS	Houston Oilers Football Coverage
OKLAHOMA	Digital Cities: Southwest
OKLAHOMA BOMBING	Oklahoma City Bombing
OKTOBERFEST	Oktoberfest: German Heritage Month
OLD DOMINION	Virginia Forum
OLD FAVES	Favorite Flicks
OLDS	Oldsmobile/Celebrity Circle
OLI	The Online Investor
OLP	Psych Online
OLYMPIC SHOP	The Olympic Shop
OMAHA STEAKS	Omaha Steaks
OMEGA	Omega Research
OMNI	OMNI Magazine Online
OMNI GO	Hewlett-Packard Omni Go 100
ON AOL TODAY	On AOL Today
ON HOOPS	On Hoops Basketball (Web Page)
ONE LIFE TO LIVE	ABC Daytime/Soapline
ONE SOURCE	Columbia's Health Today
ONE STOP INFO SHOP	Member Services*
ONE WORLD	Preview Travel
ONLINE CAMPUS	Online Campus
ONLINE CLOCK	Time of day and length of time online
ONLINE DRIVE	NTN Fantasy Baseball: Online Drive
ONLINE FAMILY	Family Computing Forum: Online Family
ONLINE GAMING	Online Gaming Forums
ONLINE INVESTOR	The Online Investor
ONLINE ORIGINALS	Online Originals
ONLINE PSYCH	Psych Online
ONLY ON AOL	Only On AOL
ONQ	onQ
ONQ LEATHER	Leather onQ
ONQ NEWS	onQ: News
ONQ TRAVEL	onQ: Travel
OPERA	Afterwards Cafe
OPINION PLACE	Opinion Place
OPP	Other People's Problems
OPRAH	Get Movin' with Oprah
OPTIMA	Optima Technology
OPTIMAS	OPTIMAS Corporation
ORANGEMEN	AOL College Football
ORIENTATION	Discover America Online (New Member Area)
ORIGINALS	Online Originals
ORIOLES	Major League Baseball Team: Baltimore Orioles
ORL CHAT	Digital City Orlando: Chat Room
ORLANDO MAGIC	Pro Basketball

OS2	OS/2 Forum
OSCARS	The Daily Fix
OSKAR'S	Oskar's Magazine
OSO	Orlando Sentinel Online
OSO AUTO	Orlando Sentinel Online: Autos
OSO BEACH	Orlando Sentinel Online: Beach
OSO BLACK	Orlando Sentinel Online: Black Voices
OSO BUSINESS	Orlando Sentinel Online: Business
OSO CHAT	Orlando Sentinel Online: Chat
OSO CLASSIFIEDS	Orlando Sentinel Online: Classified Ads
OSO COLLEGE FB	Orlando Sentinel Online: College Football
OSO DOWNLOAD	Orlando Sentinel Online: Download Libraries
OSO E-MALL	Orlando Sentinel Online: E-Mall
OSO ENTERTAIN	Orlando Sentinel Online: Entertainment
OSO GOVERNMENT	Orlando Sentinel Online: Government
OSO HOMES	Orlando Sentinel Online: Homes
OSO JOBS	Orlando Sentinel Online: Jobs
OSO LIVING	Orlando Sentinel Online: Living
OSO MAGIC MAG	Orlando Sentinel Online: Magic
OSO MERCHANDISE	Orlando Sentinel Online: Merchandise
OSO MOVIES	Orlando Sentinel Online: Movies
OSO NET	Orlando Sentinel Online: OSOnet
OSO PHOTOS	Orlando Sentinel Online: Photos
OSO POLITICS	Orlando Sentinel Online: Government
OSO PREDATORS	Orlando Sentinel Online: Predators
OSO REAL ESTATE	Orlando Sentinel Online: Classified Real Estate
OSO RELIGION	Orlando Sentinel Online: Religion News
OSO SERVICES	Orlando Sentinel Online: Services
OSO SOUND OFF	Orlando Sentinel Online: Sound Off
OSO SPACE	Orlando Sentinel Online: Space
OSO SPORTS	Orlando Sentinel Online: Sports
OSO STORM	Orlando Sentinel Online: Hurricane Survival Guide
OSO THEME PARK	Orlando Sentinel Online: Theme Parks
OSO TO DO	Orlando Sentinel Online: Things To Do
OSO TOP	Orlando Sentinel Online: Top Stories
OSO TRANS	Orlando Sentinel Online: Transportation
OSO WANT ADS	Orlando Sentinel Online: Jobs
OSO WEATHER	Orlando Sentinel Online: Weather
OTHER NEWS	The Hub: The Other News
OTHER PEOPLES PROBLEMS	Other People's Problems
OTR	Over The Rainbow: Travel News for Gay Men & Lesbians
OUR WORLD	News Channel
OUT OF THE BLUE	Out Of The Blue TV Show
OUT ONQ	onQ: Coming Out
OUT WEST	Out West Online
OUTDOOR ADVENTURE	Outdoor Adventures Online
OUTDOOR FUN	The Exchange: Outdoor Fun
OUTEREDGE	OuterEdge
OUTPROUD	!OutProud!
OVER THE RAINBOW	Over The Rainbow: Travel News for Gay Men & Lesbians
OWENS CORNING	Owens Corning
P1	Stock Portfolio #1
P2	Stock Portfolio #2
P3	Stock Portfolio #3
P4	Stock Portfolio #4
P5	Stock Portfolio #5
P7	Stock Portfolio #7
P8	Stock Portfolio #8
P9	Stock Portfolio #9
PACERS	Pro Basketball
PADRES	Major League Baseball Team: San Diego Padres
PAGAN	Pagan Religions & Occult Sciences
PAGEBOOK	Pager Address Book
PAGER	Consumer Electronics
PAIN	Pain Relief Center
PALLADIUM	Book Central: Palladium Live Events
PALM COMPUTING	Palm Computing
PALMTOP	PDA/Palmtop Forum
PANGEA	Pangea Toy Net
PANTHERS	Carolina Panthers Football Coverage
PAP	Applications Forum
PAPER MAIL	Fax/Paper Mail (Discontinuation Notice)
PAPUA	Papua New Guinea
PARADOX	DC Comics Online
PARASCOPE	Parascope
PARENT	AOL Families
PARENT SOUP	Parent Soup
PARENT SOUP CHAT	Parent Soup: Chat
PARENT SOUP LOCAL INFO	Parent Soup: Local Information
PARENTAL CONTROLS	Parental Controls
PARENTS	AOL Families
PARGH	Andy Pargh/The Gadget Guru
PARKS	America's National Parks
PARLOR	Games Parlor
PARROT KEY	Parrot Key: Tropical Rock Forum

PARSONS	Parsons Technology
PARTY SUPPLIES	Your Business: Party Supply Community
PASSOVER	Jewish Holidays
PASSPORT NEWS	Passport Newsletter
PASSPORT TO LOVE	Passport to Love
PASSWORD	Change your password*
PATERNO	Paterno Imports
PATHFINDER	Time Warners's Pathfinder [WWW site]
PAWNBROKER	Your Business: Pawnbroker Community
PBM	Play-By-Mail Forum
PBM CLUBS	Play-By-Mail Clubs & Messaging
PC	People Connection
PC ANIMATION	PC Graphics Forum
PC APS	PC Applications Forum
PC AUD	AOL Live!
PC BEGINNERS	PC Help Desk
PC CHAT	PC Computing Forums: Chats and Conferences
PC DADS	PC Dads
PC DATA	PC Data
PC DESKMATE	DeskMate
PC DEV	Developers Forum [Platform dependent]
PC DM	DeskMate
PC FINANCIAL	PC Financial Network
PC FORUMS	Computing Channel [Platform dependent]
PC GAMES	PC Games Forum
PC GRAPHICS	PC Graphics Forum
PC HARDWARE	PC Hardware Forum
PC HELP	PC Help Desk
PC MUSIC FORUM	PC Music and Sound Forum
PC PLAZA	People Connection Plaza
PC SECURITY	Computing Channel [Platform dependent]
PC SOFTWARE	PC Software Center
PC STUDIO	PC Studio
PC TELECOM	PC Telecom/Networking Forum
PC TOOL	PC Virtual Toolbox
PC WORLD	PCWorld Online
PCD	Professional Cutlery Direct
PCF	Personal Finance Channel
PCFN	PC Financial Network
PCH	PC Help Desk
PCM	PC Telecom/Networking Forum
PCS	MobileMedia
PCW NETSCAPE	PC World: Netscape
PDA	PDA/Palmtop Forum
PDA DEV	PDA Development SIG
PDA FORUM	PDA/Palmtop Forum
PDA SHOP	PDA Forum: PDA Shop
PEAPOD	Peapod Online
PEN	Personal Empowerment Network
PEN PAL	Digital City Pen Pal or International Pen Pal
PENGUINS	NHL Hockey
PENNSYLVANIA	Digital Cities: Mid-Atlantic
PEOPLE	People Connection
PERFUME	The Fragrance Counter
PERISCOPE	Parascope
PERSONAL CHOICES	Personal Choices Area
PERSONAL EMPOWERMENT	Personal Empowerment Network
PERSONAL FINANCE	Personal Finance Channel
PERSONAL PUBLISHER 2	Personal Publisher
PERU	Peru
PEST CONTROL	Your Business: Pest Control Community
PET CARE	Pet Care Forum
PET STORE	Your Business: Pet Store Community
PETER NORTON	Symantec
PETS & ANIMALS	Hobby Central: Pets & Animals
PETS ONQ	onQ: Holidays
PF ANALYSIS	Personal Finance: Technical Analysis
PF BASICS	Personal Finance: Investing Basics
PF BONDS	Personal Finance: Bonds
PF FUNDS	Personal Finance: Funds
PF FUTURES	Personal Finance: Futures & Options
PF SAVINGS	Personal Finance: Financial Planning
PF SEARCH	Personal Finance: Search
PF SOFTWARE	Personal Finance Software Center
PF STOCKS	Personal Finance: Stocks & Investing
PFSS	Personal Finance Software Support
PHD	Pharmacy Help Desk
PHILADELPHIA	Digital Cities: Philadelphia
PHILADELPHIA EAGLES	Philadelphia Eagles Online
PHILIPPINES	Philippines
PHILLIES	Major League Baseball Team: Philadelphia Phillies
PHISH	Grateful Dead: The Phish Phorum
PHL	Digital City Philadelphia: WPHL Channel 17
PHONE BOOK	Phone Directories
PHONE HELP	Local access numbers*
PHONE NUMBER	Accessing America Online*
PHOTO	Photography Area
PHOTOSHOP	Photoshop SIG

PHS	Practical Homeschooling
PHW	PC Hardware Forum
PHYSICALLY DISABLED	DisABILITIES Forum
PIERIAN	Pierian Spring Software
PILOTS	Flying Magazine
PIPE	Food & Drink Network
PIRATES	Major League Baseball Team: Pittsburgh Pirates
PISCES	AOL UK: Astrology AOL UK
PISTONS	Pro Basketball
PITTSBURGH PIRATES	Major League Baseball Team: Pittsburgh Pirates
PIZZA	Your Business: Pizza Community
PLACES	P.L.A.C.E.S. Forum
PLACES RATED	Places Rated Almanac
PLANET EALING	Planet Ealing
PLANET REEBOK	Reach!
PLAY-BY-MAIL	Play-By-Mail Forum
PLAYBILL	Playbill Online
PLAYTEX	One Hanes Place
PLUG IN	Plug In
PLUS	Plus ATM Network
PLUS & TALLS	JCPenney: Plus & Talls
PMM	PC Multimedia Forum
PMU	PC Music and Sound Forum
PNC BANK	PNC Bank Online
POET	Writers Club: Poetry Place
POKER	Kesmai's Casino Poker
POLAND	Poland
POLARIS	Polaris Grants Center
POLICY REVIEW	Heritage Foundation Area
POLITICS	Politics Area
POLL ONQ	onQ: Poll
PONTIAC CARS	Pontiac Command Center
POP MUSIC	Popular Music Forum
POP PHOTO	Popular Photography Online
POPE	Catholic Community
PORK	Pork Online
PORTFOLIO	Portfolio Summary
PORTUGAL	Portugal
POSITIVE LIVING	onQ: Positive Living
POST OFFICE	Mail Center
POSTAL STAMPS	Comic Strip Centennial
POSTCARDS	Virtual Post Card Center
POV	3D Forum
POWER BOATS	Boating Online

POWERBOOK	PowerBook Resource Center
POWERMAC	PowerMac Resource Center
POWERTOOLS	American Woodworker: Tool Reviews
PP2	Personal Publisher
PPI	Practical Peripherals Inc.
PPL	Passport to Love
PR	Pain Relief Center
PR ACHES	Pain Relief Center: Minor Aches and Pains
PR AIDS	Pain Relief Center: AIDS/HIV
PR ARTHRITIS	Pain Relief Center: Arthritis
PR BACK	Pain Relief Center: Back Pain
PR CANCER	Pain Relief Center: Cancer
PR HEADACHES	Pain Relief Center: Headaches
PRAYER NET	The Prayer Network
PREFERRED MAIL	Preferred Mail*
PREMIERE	Premiere Online
PRESCHOOL	Preschool/Early Childhood SIG
PRESENTING	Presenting... on AOL
PRESIDENT	President's Day [May disappear without notice]
PRESS RELEASE	AOL Press Release Library
PREVIEW VACATIONS	Preview Vacations
PRICING	New Pricing*
PRIDE PRESS	onQ: Pride Press
PRIMASOFT	PrimaSoft PC Inc.
PRIME HOST	PrimeHost
PRIN	Principians Online
PRINCETON	The Princeton Review Online
PRINO	Principians Online
PRINT ARTIST	Print Artist Special Interest Group
PRINTER	Mac Printer Knowledge Base
PRINTSHOP	Your Business: Printshop Community
PRISM ELITE	Prism Elite Software
PRIVATE PARTS	Digital City Philadelphia: Howard Stern
PRO HOOPS	Pro Basketball
PRO INSIDER	SportsFan Radio: The Insider
PRODUCTIVITY	Applications/Business/Productivity Forum [Platform dependent]
PROFILE	Edit your member profile
PROGRAMMER U	Programmer University
PROGRAMMING	Development Forum [Platform dependent]
PROPERTY MANAGE	Your Business: Property Management Community
PSC	Public Safety Center
PSCP	Parascope
PSYCH ONLINE	Psych Online

Keyword	Destination
PSYCHOLOGY	Psychology Forum
PT	Parsons Technology
PTC	PC Telecom/Networking Forum
PUBLIC POLICY	Politics Area
PUBLIC RADIO	National Public Radio Outreach
PUBLIC SAFETY	Public Safety Center
PUBLICATIONS	The Newsstand
PUBLISHER	Your Business: Publishing Community
PUERTO RICO	Puerto Rico
PURDUE	Purdue University [WWW site]
PUZZLE	The Puzzle Zone
Q&A	Reference Q&A
Q101	Q101 (Chicago)
QATAR	Qatar
QB1	NTN's QB1
QMODEM	Mustang Software
QOTD	The Grandstand: Sport Trivia Question of the Day
QUANTUM GROUP	the.quantum.group: World Wide Web Specialists [WWW site]
QUARK	Quark Inc.
QUE	PC Studio
QUE'S DICTIONARY	Computer and Internet Dictionary
QUEST	Adventures by Mail
QUEST TEST	Quest Test
QUESTION	One Stop Infoshop*
QUESTIONS	Member Services*
QUICK	Marketplace Quick Gifts
QUICK FIND	Search Database of Files and atOnce Software Search [Platform dependent]
QUICK FIXES	net.help: QuickFixes
QUICK GIFTS	Marketplace Quick Gifts
QUICK PRINTERS	National Association of Quick Printers Area
QUILT	Quilting Forum
QUOTATION	New York Public Library's Book of 20th Century Quotations
QUOTE	StockLink: Quotes & Portfolios Area
QUOTES PLUS	Quotes Plus
R HUNTER	Grateful Dead: Robert Hunter's Archives
R&B	R&B Music Forum
R&R	ABC Online: Rock & Road
R&T	Road & Track Magazine
RABBITJACK'S CASINO	RabbitJack's Casino
RADIO	Entertainment's Radio Forum
RADIUS	Radius Inc.
RAGU	Mama's Cucina by Ragu
RAIDERS	Oakland Raiders
RAILROADING	The Exchange
RAM DOUBLER	Connectix Corporation
RANDOM	Random AOL Keyword
RANGERS	Major League Baseball Team: Texas Rangers
RAPTORS	Pro Basketball
RAW	World Wrestling Federation
RAY TRACE	3D Forum
RAZORBACKS	AOL College Football
RDI	Free-Form Gaming Forum
RE	Real Estate Center
RE/MAX	RE/MAX of Southern Pennsylvania
REACH	Reach!
REACH OUT	The Reach Out Zone
REACTOR	Reactor
READ USA	Online Bookstore
REAL DEAL	Real Deals on AOL
REAL ESTATE	Real Estate Center
REAL LIFE	MoneyWhiz
REALMS OF CHANCE	Realms of Chance
REBA	Reba McIntire [May disappear without notice]
REC CENTER	Sports Channel
REC ROOM	Family Computing: Rec Room
REC SKATING	Recreational Skating MiniForum
RECIPES	Woman's Day Online
RECORDS & TAPES	Your Business: Recording Community
RECOVERIES	Addictions and Recovery Forum
RED RAIDERS	AOL College Football
RED SOX	NESN: New England Baseball
RED STAR STATION	Red Star Station
RED WINGS	NHL Hockey
RED ZONE	NESN: New England Football
REDI	TRW REDI Property Data
REDIALER	AOL Autodialer
REDS	Major League Baseball Team: Cincinnati Reds
REDSKINS	Washington Redskins
REF 50	The Fifty States
REF ART	Art and Music Reference
REF GOVERNMENT	Government Reference
REF HOT	Hot Reference
REF MATH	Science and Math Reference
REF MUSIC	Art and Music Reference
REF NEWS	Reference Desk Newsletter
REF SCIENCE	Science and Math Reference

REF USA	The Fifty States
REFERENCE	Research & Learn Channel
REGIONAL	Your Business: Regional Resources
REGIONS	Regions Bank
REI	REI Recreation Equipment Inc.
@RELATIONSHIPS	Thrive@AOL: Sex
RELIGION NEWS	Religion News Update
RELIGIONS	Religion & Ethics Forum
REMAX	RE/MAX of Southern Pennsylvania
REMINDER	Gift Reminder
REMODELING	Furniture Selections: American Woodworker -or- Home Magazine Online
RENAISSANCE	onQ: Transgender Organizations
RENDER	3D Forum
RENT	Digital City Boston: Rent
REPAIRE	HouseNet
REPRISE	Warner/Reprise Records Online
REPUBLIC BANK	Republic Bank
REPUBLICAN	Republican National Committee
RESEARCH	Academic Assistance Center
RESEARCH ZONE	Research Zone
RESERVATION	Preview Travel
RESTAURANTEUR	Your Business: Restaurant Community
RETAIL TOYS	Your Business: Retail Toys Community
RETIREMENT	MoneyWhiz
REV WAR	Revolutionary War Forum
REWARD	Reward Town
RGRANT	Russell Grant's Stars
RHODE ISLAND	Digital Cities: Northeast
RICK STEVES	Europe Through The Back Door
RICKI LAKE	The Ricki Lake Show
RICOCHET	Metricom Inc.
RIDDLER	Riddler.Com (online games) [WWW site]
RIT	Rochester Institute of Technology [WWW site]
RNB	Republic Bank
ROAD TO COLLEGE	Road to College
ROAD & TRACK	Road & Track Magazine
ROADTRIP	AOL Roadtrips
ROC	Realms of Chance
ROCK	Rock Music Forum
ROCK AND ROLL	Rock and Roll Hall of Fame
ROCK & ROAD	ABC Online: Rock & Road
ROCKETS	Pro Basketball
ROCKIES	Major League Baseball Team: Colorado Rockies

ROCKNET	RockNet Information & Web Link
ROCKWELL AUTOMATION	Rockwell Automation/Allen-Bradley [WWW site]
RODEO	Rodeo MiniForum
ROGER WAGNER	Roger Wagner Publishing
ROLAND	Roland Corporation U.S.
ROLE PLAYING	Role-Playing Forum
ROLLER DERBY	Roller Derby MiniForum
ROLLER HOCKEY	Roller Hockey MiniForum
ROLLER SKATING	Inline/Aggressive/Roller Skating
ROLLERSKATING	The Grandstand: Other Sports
ROLLING STONE	Rolling Stone Online
ROMANCE GROUP	Writer's Club: Romance Writers & Readers
ROME	Time Out Rome
ROOFING	Owens Corning
ROOTS	Genealogy Forum
ROSES	1-800-FLOWERS
ROSH HASHANA	Rosh Hashanah
ROSIE	Rosie O'Donnell Online
@ROTUNDA	Rotunda Auditorium
ROYALS	Major League Baseball Team: Kansas City Royals
ROYALTY	Royalty Online
ROZ	The Reach Out Zone
RPGA NETWORK	Fellowship of Online Gamers/RPGA Network
RPM TRAVEL	RPM Worldwide Entertainment & Travel
RR	ABC Online: Rock & Road
RSFL	The Grandstand: Simulation Football
RSP	RSP Funding Focus
RSS	Red Star Station
RUN	AOL Sports: Running
RUNNER'S WORLD	Runner's World
RUSSELL GRANT	Russell Grant's Stars
RUSSIA	Russia
RW	Runner's World
RYOBI	Ryobi
S.F. GIANTS	Major League Baseball Team: San Francisco Giants
SA	Shopper's Advantage Online
SA MED	Scientific American Medical Publications
SABRES	NHL Hockey
SAC KINGS	Sacramento Kings
SAF	Scientific American Frontiers
SAFETY	Public Safety Center
SAGE	Sage Mutual Funds Area
SAGINAW DCITY	Digital Cities: Saginaw

SAILING	Boating Selections
SAINT	Religion & Beliefs: Christianity
SALES	Your Business: Sales & Marketing Community
SALES & MARKETING	Sales & Marketing Online
SALON	Internet Salon [WWW site]
SALTWATER FISHING	Fishing Broadcast Network
SAN DIEGO PADRES	Major League Baseball Team: San Diego Padres
SAN FRAN	Major League Baseball Team: San Francisco Giants
SAN FRANCISCO	Digital Cities: San Francisco CA
SAN JOSE	Mercury Center
SAN MARINO	San Marino
SANTA	Santa's Home Page
SANTA FE	Digital Cities: Albuquerque/Santa Fe NM
SANWA	Sanwa Bank California
SAYINGS	New York Public Library's Book of 20th Century Quotations
SBA	Small Business Administration
SBC	Your Business
SCA	The History Channel: Living History Forum
SCANNERS	Digital Imaging Resource Center
SCHOLARS' HALL	Scholars' Hall
SCHOLARSHIPS	RSP Funding Focus
SCHOLASTIC	Scholastic Network Preview Area
SCHOOL	Back to School [May disappear without notice]
SCHOOL MATCH	School Match
SCHOOLHOUSE	Electronic Schoolhouse
SCI AM	Scientific American
SCI FI	Fictional Realm
SCIENCE FAIR	Science Fair Projects
SCIENCE FICTION	Fictional Realm
SCIENTIFIC AMERICAN	Scientific American
SCIFI CHANNEL	The Sci-Fi Channel
SCIFI.COM	scifi.com [WWW site]
SCOREBOARD	Sports Scoreboard
SCORPIO	AOL UK: Astrology
SCOUNDREL	Military City Online: Villains of Fact & Fiction
SCOUTS	Scouting Forum
SCRAPBOOK	Member Scrapbook
SCREEN NAME	Add, change, or delete screen names
SCUBA	Scuba Club
SCUBA FORUM	SCUBA FORUM
SCUDDER	Scudder Funds Online
SD COMM	Digital City San Diego: Community
SD DIGITAL CITY	Digital Cities: San Diego CA
SD ENTERTAINMENT	Digital Cities: San Diego Entertainment
SD MAG	Digital City San Diego: San Diego Magazine
SD NEWS	Digital City San Diego: News & Weather
SD PEOPLE	Digital City San Diego: People
SD REAL ESTATE	Digital City San Diego: Real Estate
SD TOUR	Digital City San Diego: City Tour
SDK	Developer's Studio
SEARCH	Software Center [Platform dependent]
SEARCH AOL LIVE	Search AOL Live
SEARCH.COM	CINet Search.com [WWW site]
SEARCH NEWS	Search News articles
SEATTLE	Digital Cities: Seattle/Tacoma WA
SEATTLE MARINERS	Major League Baseball Team: Seattle Mariners
SECOND CHANCE	Your Second Chance
SECRET BARGAINS	Arthur Frommer's Secret Bargains
SECURITY	Consumer Electronics
SECURITY SERVICE	Your Business: Security Community
SELF HELP	Self Help Area
SEMINOLES	AOL College Football
SENATORS	NHL Hockey
SEND PAGE	Page Sender
SENEGAL	Senegal
SENIOR FRIENDS	Columbia's Health Today
SENSATION	Tandy Sensation Support Center
SERVENET	SERVEnet
SERVICE	Member Services*
SEVENTEEN	Seventeen Magazine Online
SEVENTH	Seventh Level Software
SEW	Needlecrafts/Sewing Center
SEW NEWS	Sew News Magazine
SEWING	Woman's Day Online
SEYCHELLES	Seychelles
SF	Fictional Realm or San Francisco
SF Chat	Digital City San Francisco: Chat Room
SF COMM	Digital City San Francisco: Community
SF NEWS	Digital City San Francisco: News & Weather
SF PEOPLE	Digital City San Francisco: People
SF TOUR	Digital City San Francisco: City Tour
SFRN	@SportsFan Radio
SHADOW TRAFFIC	Traffic Center
SHALOM	Jewish.COMMunity
@SHAPE EXPERTS	Thrive@AOL: Ask the Experts
@SHAPE LIVE	Thrive@AOL: Chat and Auditorium Events

SHAREWARE	Software Center [Platform dependent]
SHAREWARE SOLUTIONS	Shareware Solutions
SHARKS	NHL Hockey
SHARP	PDA/Palmtop Forum
SHARPER IMAGE	The Sharper Image
SHAWN GREEN	Shawn Green's Journal
SHIFT	Shift Magazine
SHIP CRITIC	Cruise Critic
SHOE	Your Business: Shoe Retail Community
SHOPOLOGIST	Shopologist
SHOPPERS ADVANTAGE	Shopper's Advantage Online
SHOPPING	Shopping Channel
SHOPPING EXPERT	Shopologist
SHORTHAND	Online Shorthands
SHORTHANDS	AOL Shorthands
SHOW TIMES	MovieLink
SHOWBIZ NEWS	Showbiz News & Info
SIERRA	Sierra On-Line
SIERRA.COM	Sierra On-Line [WWW site]
SIERRA LEONE	Sierra Leone
SIFS	Computing Channel [Platform dependent]
SIGHTINGS	Sightings Online
SIGNS	Your Business: Signage Community
SIGNUP	Online Campus
SILLY PUTTY	The Physics of Silly Putty
SIM	Simming Forum
SIM RACING	iRACE
SIMBA	Cowles/SIMBA Media Information Network
SIMI WINERY	Simi Winery
SIMMING	Simming Forum
SIMON & SCHUSTER	Simon & Schuster College Online
SIMULATION LEAGUES	The Grandstand: Fantasy & Simulation Leagues
SINGAPORE	Singapore
SINGLE	Love@AOL
SIXERS	Pro Basketball
SKI	AOL Skiing
SKI REPORTS	Ski Reports
SKI ZONE	The Ski Zone
SKIING	iSKI
SKIN	Skin Hair & Nails
SKINET	SkiNet
SKY DIVING	Aviation Forum
SKYLINE AIRWAYS	Virtual Airlines
SLATE.COM	Slate Magazine [WWW site]
SLINGO	Slingo Game
SLOVAKIA	Slovakia
SLOVENIA	Slovenia
SMALL BUSINESS	Your Business
SMART BOOKMARKS	Smart Bookmarks [WWW site]
SMART KIDS	Youth Tech
SMARTMOUTHS	Smart Mouths
SMITHSONIAN	Smithsonian Online
SMITHSONIAN MAGAZINE	Smithsonian Magazine
SN LIBRARIES	Scholastic Libraries
SN LIT GAME	Bookwoman's Literature Game
SN SPACE	Space and Astronomy
SNGUESTS	Scholastic Network: Special Guests
SNLITGAME	Bookwoman's Literature Game [K-6]
SNOWBOARD	Snowboarding Selections
SOAP DIGEST	Soap Opera Digest
SOAPLINE	ABC Daytime/Soapline
SOFT SHOP	AOL Software Shop
SOFTWARE	Software Center [Platform dependent]
SOFTWARE COMPANIES	Computing Company Connection
SOFTWARE HARDTALK	Software Hardtalk with John C. Dvorak
SOFTWARE UNBOXED	Software Unboxed
SOFTWORD	Softword Technical
SOHO	Home Office Computing Magazine
SOL	Snowboarding Online
SOLIII	Sol III Play-by-Email Game
SOLOMON ISLANDS	Solomon Islands
SOMALIA	Somalia
SONICS	Pro Basketball
SOONERS	AOL College Football
SOPH CIR	Sophisticated Circuits
SOS	Wall Street SOS Forum
SOUND ROOM	Sound Room*
SOURCERER	The Hub: Sorcerer
SOUTH AFRICA	South Africa
SOUTH CAROLINA	Digital Cities: South
SOUTH DAKOTA	Digital Cities: Midwest
SOUTHEAST	Digital Cities: South
SPACE	Space Exploration Online
SPACE COAST	Florida's Space Coast
SPAIN	Spain
SPAM UPDATE	Mail Spam Update
SPC	Software Publishing Corporation
SPECIAL DELIVERY	Special Delivery: International Penpals

SPECULAR	Specular International
SPEED SKATING	Speed Skating MiniForum
SPIDERMAN	Marvel Online
SPIN	Spin Online
SPINNING	Needlecrafts/Sewing Center
SPIRITUAL	Spiritual Mosaic
SPORTING NEWS	The Sporting News
SPORTS	Sports Channel
SPORTS ARCHIVE	AOL Sports Archive
SPORTS BOARDS	The Grandstand: Sports Boards
SPORTS CHAT	The Grandstand: Chat Rooms
SPORTS CIRUIT	New England Sports Network
SPORTS HOT	What's Hot in Sports
SPORTS LIBRARIES	The Grandstand: Libraries
SPORTS LIVE	AOL Sports Live
SPORTS MAGS	Sports Magazines and Clubs
SPORTS NEWS	Sport News
SPORTS ODDS	Sports Odds
SPORTSCHANNEL	SportsChannels
SPORTSFAN	@SportsFan Radio
SPORTSLINE.COM	Sportsline USA [WWW site]
SPORTSRADIO	The Fan AM 950 Denver
SPRING	Computing Spring Fling [May disappear without notice]
SPURS	Pro Basketball
SQUARES	MetaSquares
SSS	Craig Anderton's Sound Studio & Stage
SSS NEWS	Sound Studio
SSSI	SSSi
ST. LOUIS CARDINALS	Major League Baseball Team: St. Louis Cardinals
ST PAUL	Digital Cities: Minneapolis/St. Paul
ST PETERSBURG	Digital Cities: Tampa/St. Petersburg
STAGE	Playbill Online
STAMP PRO	Your Business: Stamp Professionals Community
STAMPS	The Exchange
STANFORD	AOL College Football
STANFORD UNIVERSITY	Stanford University [WWW site]
STAR TREK	Star Trek Club
STAR WARS	Star Wars Sim Forum
STARBUCKS	Caffe Starbucks
STARFISH	Starfish Software
STARS	Galileo Mission to Jupiter [May disappear without notice]
STARS AND SHOWS	ABC Online: Stars and Shows

STATS	Pro Sports Center by STATS Inc.
STATS BASKETBALL	Pro Basketball Center by STATS Inc.
STATS CFB	STATS College Football
STATS FB	STATS Pro Football
STD	Sexually Transmitted Diseases Forum
STEREO	Stereo Review Online
STERN	Digital City Philadelphia: Howard Stern
STEVE CASE	Community Updates from Steve Case*
STOCK	StockLink: Quotes & Portfolios Area
STOCK CHARTS	Decision Point Forum
STOCK PORTFOLIO	Portfolio Summary
STOCK QUOTES	StockLink: Quotes & Portfolios Area
STOCK REPORTS	Stock Reports
STORE ONQ	onQ: Store
STRAIGHT DOPE	Straight Dope
STRANGE	Parascope
STRATEGY	Strategy & Wargaming Forum
STRIKE-A-MATCH	Boxer*Jam Gameshows [WAOL only]
STUDENT HANGOUT	Campus Life's Student Hangout
STUDY BREAK	Compton's Study Break
STUDY SKILLS	Study Skills Service
SUCK	suck.com [Web site]
SUGGEST	Suggestion boxes*
SUMMER MOVIES	New Movie Releases
SUMMER SLAM	World Wrestling Federation
SUN DEVILS	AOL College Football
SUN SENTINEL	Digital City South Florida: Sun-Sentinel
SUN TRAVEL	Endless Sun
SUNAIR EXPRESS	Virtual Airlines
SUNS	Pro Basketball
SUPERCARD	SuperCard Scripting Center
SUPERDISK	Alysis Software
SUPERLIBRARY	MacMillan Information SuperLibrary
SUPERMAN	Superman Selections
SUPERSONICS	Pro Basketball
SUPERSTORE	Softdisk Online
SUPPORT	Member Services*
SURF	SurfLink
SURF SHACK	The Surf Shack
SURFBOARD	SurfLink
SURVIVAL	Survival
SURVIVAL WORLD	Survival World
SUSAN	The Hub: Susan
SWEDEN	Sweden

SWIMMING	The Grandstand: Other Sports
SWISS BANKS	Swiss Bank Mystery
SWITCHBOARD	Switchboard Interactive Directories [WWW site]
SWITZERLAND	Switzerland
SYMANTEC	Symantec
SYSOP	Member Services*
SYSTEM 7	Mac Operating Systems Forum
SYSTEM RESPONSE	System Response Report Area*
T ROWE PRICE	T. Rowe Price Mutual Funds
T TALK	Teachers' Forum
TA	Traveler's Advantage
TA FOOTRACE	Trans-America Footrace
TAC	Top Advisor's Corner
TACKY	The Ultimate Tacky Page
TACOMA	Digital Cities: Seattle/Tacoma WA
TAIWAN	Taiwan
TALENT	Talent Bank
TALK	People Connection
TALK SHOW	Future Labs Inc.
TAMPA	Digital Cities: Tampa/St. Petersburg
TAMPA COMM	Digital City Tampa: Community
TAMPA NEWS	Digital City Tampa: News & Weather
TAMPA PEOPLE	Digital City Tampa: People
TANNING SALON	Your Business: Tanning Salon Community
TAROT	The Crystal Ball Forum
TAURUS	AOL UK: Astrology
TAVERN	Taverns, Pubs & Bars
TAVERN	Your Business: Tavern Community
TAX	Tax Planning
TAX CHANNEL	NAEA Tax Channel
TAX FORUM	Tax Forum
TAXI CAB	Your Business: Taxi Community
TAXLOGIC	TaxLogic
TAYLOR UNIVERSITY	Taylor University
TBR	The Book Report
TCF	onQ: Transgender Community Forum
TCW	Today's Christian Woman
TEACHER PAGER	Teacher Pager
TEACHERS' LOUNGE	Teachers' Lounge
TEAM	Team Concepts
TEAM NFL	Team NFL
TECH LIVE	Member Services*
TECHNOLOGY	Computing Channel [Platform dependent]
TECHNOLOGY WORKS	Technology Works
TECHWEB	Techweb: The Technology Super Site [WWW site]
TEEN	Teen Selections
TEEN BEAT	Teen Style: Teen Beat
TEEN HANGOUT	Teen Scene
TEEN SCENE	Teen Selections
TEEN WRITER	Teen Writers
TEENS	Teen Selections
TEENWRITER	Writers Club: Teen Writers Area
TEL AVIV	Isr@el Interactive
TELECOM	Communications/Telecom/Networking Forum [Platform dependent]
TELECOMM	Your Business: Telecommunications Community
TELECOMMUNICATIONS	Communications/Telecom/Networking Forum [Platform dependent]
TELEPHONE NUMBERS	Phone Directories
TELEPHONE SERVICE	Your Business: Telephone Service Community
TELEPORT	Global Village Communication
TELESCAN	Telescan Users Group Forum
TELEVISION	TV Main Screen
TELL US	Tell Us Your Story
TELNET	Telnet
TEMPLE DCITY	Digital Cities: Waco/Temple/Bryan TX
TEMPO II	Affinity Microsystems
TEMPS	Your Business: Employment Community
TEN	The Educator's Network
TENNESSEE	Digital Cities: South
TENNIS	AOL Tennis
TERMS	Terms of Service*
TEST TUBE	ABC Online: Test Tube
TEXAS RANGERS	Major League Baseball Team: Texas Rangers
THANKSGIVING	Thanksgiving@AOL [May disappear without notice]
THE BIZ	The Biz!
THE BOOK REPORT	The Book Report
THE DAILY FIX	The Daily Fix
THE DEAD	Grateful Dead Forum
THE ENTREPRENEUR ZONE	Your Business
THE EXCHANGE	The Exchange
THE GRANDSTAND	The Grandstand
THE HOLE	Mighty Mites: The Hole
THE HUB	The Hub
THE HUB INDEX	The Hub: Index
THE INDUSTRY	The Industry: Entertainment News
THE KEYS	The Florida Keys

THE LAB	The Lab
THE LIMIT	The Limit Software
@THE.MOVIES	@the.movies
THE ODYSSEY PROJECT	The Odyssey Project
THE POST OFFICE	Mail Center
THE REALM	The Realm
THE ROYCE FUNDS	The Royce Fund
THE SPORTING NEWS	The Sporting News
THE TOY NET	Pangea Toy Net
THE WALL	Vietnam Veterans Memorial Wall
THE WB NETWORK	The WB Network
THE WEATHER CHANNEL	The Weather Channel [WWW site]
THE WHITE HOUSE	White House Forum
THE WORLD	The World
THE ZONE	Your Business
THEATER	Playbill Online
THEFAN	The Fan AM 950 Denver
@THENEWSROOM	The News Room Auditorium
THESAURUS	Merriam-Webster's Thesaurus
THIS WAY OUT	This Way Out
THREE SIXTY	Three-Sixty Software
THRIVE	Thrive@AOL
THRIVE@EATS	Thrive@AOL: Eats
THRIVE EXPERTS	Thrive@AOL: Experts Grouping
THRIVE@HEALTH	Thrive@AOL: Health
THRIVE MARKETPLACE	Thrive@AOL: Marketplace
THRIVE@OUTDOORS	Thrive@AOL: Outdoors
THRIVE@SEX	Thrive@AOL: Sex
THRIVE@SHAPE	Thrive@AOL: Shape
THRIVE TALK	Thrive@AOL: Thrive Message Boards & Chat
TI	Texas Instruments
TICKER	AOL NewsTicker
TICKET SALES	Your Business: Ticket Sales Community
TICKETMASTER	Ticketmaster
TIGER	TIGERDirect Inc.
TIGERS	Major League Baseball Team: Detroit Tigers
TIMBERWOLVES	Pro Basketball
TIME OUT	Digital City London: Time Out
TIME OUT ROME	Time Out Rome
TIMES ARTS	@times: Art & Entertainment Guide
TIMES DINING	@times: Dining Out & Nightlife
TIMES FILM	@times: Film
TIMES MUSIC	@times: Music & Dance
TIMES SPORTS	@times: Sports News

TIMES STORIES	@times: Page One—Top Stories
TIMES THEATER	@times: Theater
TIMEWORKS	GST Technology
TIP	Discover America Online (New Member Area)
TIPS	Top Tips for AOL
TITF	Today in Computers & Software [Platform dependent]
TLC ED	The Discovery Channel: Education
TMS	TV Quest -or- TMS Peripherals
TNC	The Nature Conservancy
TNEWS	Teachers' Newsstand
TNPC	The National Parenting Center
TO MARKET	Marketplace Gift Valet
TODAY PITCH	The Motley Fool: Finance & Folly
TODAY'S OTHER	The Hub: Today's Other News
TODAYS NEWS	News Channel
TODD ART	The Image Exchange: Ask Todd Art
TOE	The Outer Edge
TOLL FREE	AT&T 800 Directory (WWW site)
TONYS	Playbill Online: Tony Awards Central
TOOL	American Woodworker: Tool Reviews
TOON	InToon with the News
TOONS	Cartoon Network World
TOP ADVISOR	Top Advisor's Corner
TOP COMP SITES	Top Computing Internet Sites
TOP COMPANY SITES	Companies on the Internet
TOP MODEL	TopModel Online
TOP TIPS	Top Tips for AOL
TORONTO	Digital Cities: Toronto
TORONTO BLUE JAYS	Major League Baseball Team: Toronto Blue Jays
TORRE	The Book Report: Joe Torre Chasing the Dream
TOS	Terms of Service*
TOUR	AOL Highlights Tour
TOUR CHAMPIONSHIP	iGolf: Tour Championship
TOUR DE FRANCE	Bicycling Magazine: Tour de France Coverage
TOWER	Tower Records
TOY NET	Pangea Toy Net
TOY STORE	JCPenney's Toy Store [May disappear without notice]
TOYBUZZ	Pangea Toy Network: ToyBuzz
TPI	Trivial Pursuit Interactive
TPN	The Prayer Network
TRADE	Your Business: International Trade Community
TRAFFIC	Traffic Center

TRAILBLAZERS	Pro Basketball
TRANSCRIPT	AOL Live! Event Transcripts
TRANSGENDER	Transgender Community Forum
TRANSPORT	Your Business: Transport Community
TRANSSEXUAL	onQ: Transgender Community Forum
TRANSWORLD	Transworld SNOWboarding
TRAVEL	Travel Channel
TRAVEL ADVISORIES	US State Department Travel Advisories
TRAVEL ALABAMA	Travel Alabama
TRAVEL ALBUQUERQUE	Travel Albuquerque
TRAVEL AMERICA	Travel America...Online
TRAVEL ARIZONA	Travel Arizona
TRAVEL CALIFORNIA	Travel California
TRAVEL CHICAGO	Travel Chicago
TRAVEL CINCINNATI	Travel Cincinnati
TRAVEL COLORADO	Travel Colorado
TRAVEL CONNECTICUT	Travel Connecticut
TRAVEL DALLAS	Travel Dallas
TRAVEL DAYTONA	Travel Daytona
TRAVEL FLORIDA	Travel Florida
TRAVEL FORUM	Travel Forum
TRAVEL HAWAII	Travel Hawaii
TRAVEL HOUSTON	Travel Houston
TRAVEL INDUSTRY	Your Business: Travel Industry Community
TRAVEL KANSAS	Travel Kansas
TRAVEL KENTUCKY	Travel Kentucky
TRAVEL KEY WEST	Travel Key West
TRAVEL LAKE TAHOE	Travel Lake Tahoe
TRAVEL LAS VEGAS	Travel Las Vegas
TRAVEL & LEISURE	Travel & Leisure Magazine
TRAVEL LONG BEACH	Travel Long Beach
TRAVEL LOS ANGELES	Travel Los Angeles
TRAVEL LOUISVILLE	Travel Louisville
TRAVEL MAINE	Travel Maine
TRAVEL MASSACHUSETTS	Travel Massachusetts
TRAVEL MEMPHIS	Travel Memphis
TRAVEL MIAMI	Travel Miami
TRAVEL MINNEAPOLIS	Travel Minneapolis
TRAVEL MINNESOTA	Travel Minnesota
TRAVEL NEW HAMPSHIRE	Travel New Hampshire
TRAVEL NEW ORLEANS	Travel New Orleans
TRAVEL NEW YORK	Travel New York
TRAVEL NEW YORK CITY	Travel New York City
TRAVEL NORTH DAKOTA	Travel North Dakota
TRAVEL OAKLAND	Travel Oakland
TRAVEL OHIO	Travel Ohio
TRAVEL ORLANDO	Travel Orlando
TRAVEL PHOENIX	Travel Phoenix
TRAVEL PICKS	What's Hot in Travel
TRAVEL RHODE ISLAND	Travel Rhode Island
TRAVEL SACRAMENTO	Travel Sacramento
TRAVEL SALT LAKE CITY	Travel Salt Lake City
TRAVEL SAN DIEGO	Travel San Diego
TRAVEL SAN FRANCISCO	Travel San Francisco
TRAVEL TAMPA	Travel Tampa
TRAVEL TENNESSEE	Travel Tennessee
TRAVEL TEXAS	Travel Texas
TRAVEL UPDATE	Travel Update
TRAVEL UTAH	Travel Utah
TRAVEL VIRGINIA	Travel Virginia
TRAVEL VISA	Traveling with Visa
TRAVEL WASHINGTON DC	Travel Washington DC
TRAVELER	Travel Forum
TRAVELERS ADVANTAGE	Traveler's Advantage
TRAVELERS CORNER	Traveler's Corner
TREASURY	The U.S. Department of Treasury [WWW site]
TREK	Star Trek Club
TREKKER	800-TREKKER: 24 Hour Sci-Fi Collectibles Hotline
TRENDSETTER	Trendsetter Software
TRENDZINE	Teen Style: Trendzine
TRIB	Chicago Tribune
TRIB ADS	Chicago Tribune: Classifieds
TRIB COLUMNISTS	Chicago Tribune: Columnists
TRIB SPORTS	Chicago Tribune: Sports Area
TRIBE	Major League Baseball Team: Cleveland Indians
TRIBUNE.COM	Chicago Tribune [WWW site]
TRIPLE A	AAA Online
TRIPLE CROWN	VISA Triple Crown Challenge
TRIPOD	Tripod: Tools for Life [WWW site]
TRIVIA	Trivia Forum
TRIVIAL PURSUIT	Trivial Pursuit Interactive
TRIVIANA	Digital City San Francisco: Trivian Games
TROJANS	AOL College Football
TROPICAL STORM	Tropical Storm and Hurricane Info
TRUE TALES	True Tales of the Internet
TRW REDI	TRW REDI Property Data
TSN	The Sporting News
TSP	Tom Snyder Productions

TSQUARE	Apple Computer: Town Square Chat
TSR ONLINE	TSR Online
TU	Fly-Fishing Broadcast Network
TUNE UP	Tune Up Your PC
TURKEY	Turkey
TURKMENISTAN	Turkmenistan
TURTLE SYS	Turtle Beach Systems
TUTORING	Academic Assistance Center
TV	Main TV Screen
TV DEALER	Your Business: TV Dealer and Repair Community
TV GOSSIP	TV Shows Gossip
TV GUIDE	TV Quest
TV NETWORKS	TV Networks Area
TV PEOPLE	TV People
TV REPAIR	Your Business: TV Dealer and Repair Community
TV SHOWS	TV Shows
TV SPOOFS	TV Spoofs
TV VIEWERS	TV Viewers Forum
TWO MARKET	Marketplace Gift Valet
TWSNOW	Transworld SNOWboarding
U2	U2 Popmart
UA	Unlimited Adventures
UCAL	University of California Extension
UG LV	Unofficial Guide to Las Vegas
UG WDW	Unofficial Guide to Walt Disney World
UGF	User Group Forum
UHA	Homeowner's Forum
UIOWA	University of Iowa [WWW site]
UIUC	University of Illinois at Urbana-Champaign [WWW site]
UK	AOL UK Main Menu
UK WRITERS	UK Writers
UKRAINE	Ukraine
ULTIMATE	Ultimate Fighting Championships
ULTRALIGHTS	Aviation Forum
UMD	Universal Multimedia & Design Inc. [WWW site]
UMICH	University of Michigan [WWW site]
UNION	Union Bank of California
UNITARIAN	Humanism-Unitarianism Forum
UNITED KINGDOM	United Kingdom
UNITED MEDIA	United Media [WWW site]
UNIVERSAL	Universal Studios [WWW site]
UNIVERSITY	Electronic University Network
UNLIMITED ADVENTURES	Unlimited Adventures
UNOFFICIAL VEGAS	Unofficial Guide to Las Vegas
UNOFFICIAL WDW	Unofficial Guide to Walt Disney World
UNPROFOR	Balkan Operation Joint Endeavor
UPENN	University of Pennsylvania [WWW site]
UPGRADE	Upgrade to the latest version of AOL* [Platform dependent]
URBAN ACTION	Urban Action
URBAN LEAGUE	National Urban League
URBAN LEGENDS	Urban Legends
US MAIL	Fax/Paper Mail (Discontinuation Notice)
US NEWS	U.S. & World News Area
US ROBOTICS	U.S. Robotics Online
USA	USA Weekend
USA	The Fifty States
USA TODAY.COM	USA Today [WWW site]
USA WEEKEND	USA Weekend
USEFUL THINGS	The Hub: Useful Things
USELESS THINGS	The Hub: Useless Things
USENET	Internet Usenet Newsgroup Area
USER GROUP	User Group Forum
USER NAME	Add, change, or delete screen names
USERLAND	Userland
USFSA	United States Figure Skating Association
USPS	United States Postal Service
USR	U.S. Robotics Online
USSBA	Small Business Administration
UTAH	Utah Forum
UTAH JAZZ	Pro Basketball
UTEXAS	University of Texas at Austin [WWW site]
UTILITIES	Utilities Forum [Platform dependent]
UTILITY	Your Business: Utilities Community
UZBEKISTAN	Uzbekistan
V	Vices & Virtues
V PLACES	Virtual Places Beta
V103	Digital City Chicago: V103 Online
VA	Virginia Forum
VAA	Virtual Airlines
VACATION	Preview Vacations
VACATIONS.COM	Preview Travel: Vacations.com [WWW site]
VALET	Marketplace Gift Valet
VALUES	Ethics & Values
VAN KAMPEN	Van Kampen American Capital
VANGUARD	Vanguard Online
VANITY	Vanity Bag

VAULT	Mutual Fund Center: Vault
VB	Visual Basic Area
VCOMMS	Vanguard Online: Communications
VEGAN	Cooking Club: Vegetarians Online
VEGETARIAN	Cooking Club
VENDING	Your Business: Vending Machine Community
VERMONT	Digital Cities: Northeast
VERONICA	Internet Gopher
VERTIGO	DC Comics Online
VERTISOFT	Vertisoft
VETERINARIAN	Pet Care Forum
VETS	Military and Vets Club
VFR	Flying Magazine
VGAP	VGA Planets
VGS	Video Games Area
VH	Virtual Christian Humor
VH1	VH1 Online
VIC	Virus Information Center
VICES	Vices & Virtues
VIDEO GAMES	Video Games Forum
VIDEO MAG	Video Selections
VIDEO MAGAZINE	Video Magazine
VIDEO PRODUCTION	Your Business: Video Production Community
VIDEO SIG	Video SIG
VIDEO ZONE	PC Multimedia's Video
VIETNAM	Vietnam Veterans Memorial Wall
VIEWER	Viewer Resource Center
VILLAIN	Military City Online: Villains of Fact & Fiction
VIN	Veterinary Information Network
VIRGIN RECORDS	Virgin Records
VIRGINIA	Virginia Forum
VIRGO	AOL UK: Astrology
VIRTUAL AIRLINES	Virtual Airlines
VIRTUAL REALITY	Virtual Reality Resource Center
VIRTUAL VINEYARDS	Virtual Vineyards
VIRUS	Virus Information Center
VIS HELP	PC Help Forum: Visual Help
VISA	AOL Visa Card
VISALIA DIGC	Digital Cities: Fresno/Visalia CA
VISION VIDEO	Vision Video
VISUAL HELP	PC Help Forum: Visual Help
VITAMIN EXP	Health and Vitamin Express
VKAC	Van Kampen American Capital
VOLLEYBALL	AVP Pro Beach Volleyball
VOLUNTEERS	AOL Community Matters!
VP	Virtual Places
VR	Virtual Reality Resource Center
VSTATS	Vanguard Fund Information
VV	Vision Video
WACO	Digital Cities: Waco/Temple/Bryan TX
WAIS	Internet Gopher
WALES	Virtual Wales
WALL STREET WORDS	Wall Street Words
WALLPAPER	Windows Wallpaper & Paint Center
WAND TV	ABC Online: WAND-TV in Decatur IL
WARNER	Warner/Reprise Records Online
WARNER BROS.COM	Warner Bros. [WWW site]
WARNER BROS. STORE	Warner Bros. Studio Store
WARRIORS	Pro Basketball
WASH PERSONALS	Digital City Washington: Personals
WASHINGTON	Politics Forum
WASHINGTON POST	WashingtonPost.com [WWW site]
WASHINGTON UNIVERSITY	University Of Washington [WWW site]
WATE TV	ABC Online: WATE-TV in Knoxville TN
WAY TO GO	Prism Elite Software
WAYLON G JENNINGS	Country Music Forum
WB	The WB Network
WB17	Digital City Philadelphia: WPHL Channel 17
WB56	Digital City Boston: WLVI Channel 56
WBAY TV	ABC Online: WBAY-TV in Green Bay WI
WBNET	The WB Network
WBRC TV	ABC Online: WBRC-TV in Birmingham AL
WBRZ TV	ABC Online: WBRZ-TV in Baton Rouge LA
WC CHAT	Writer's Club: Chat Rooms
WCN	World Crisis Network
WCRG	Writer's Club: Romance Writers & Readers
WCVB TV	ABC Online: WCVB-TV in Boston MA
WD	Woman's Day Online
WD KITCHEN	Woman's Day Kitchen
WDC	Western Digital
WDHN TV	ABC Online: WDHN-TV in Dothan AL
WDIO TV	ABC Online: WDIO-TV in Duluth MN
WDTN TV	ABC Online: WDTN-TV in Dayton OH
WE	Web Essentials
WEAR TV	ABC Online: WEAR-TV in Pensacola FL
WEASEL	Cheeky Weasel
WEATHER	Weather
WEATHER MALL	WSC Weather Mall

WEATHER NEWS	Weather News
WEAVING	Needlecrafts/Sewing Center
WEB	www.aol.com [WWW site]
WEB ART	Web Page Clip Art Creation Center
WEB DEVELOPER	Web Developer [WWW site]
WEB ENT	WebEntertainment
WEB ESSENTIALS	Web Essentials
WEB HELP	The Web Diner
WEB HUMOR	Hecklers Online
WEB KEYWORDS	Web Keywords
WEB MAKEOVER	Web Makeover
WEB PUB	Web Publishing SIG
WEB RESEARCH	Reference: Web Research
WEB REVIEW	Web Review
WEB U	Web University
WEBCRAWLER	WebCrawler Web Search [WWW site]
WEBFIND	AOL NetFind
WEBSITE	The Web Diner
WEBSOURCE	Websource
WEBSTER	Merriam-Webster's Collegiate Dictionary
WEDDING	The Knot: Weddings
WEEKLY READER	Weekly Reader News
WEEKLY WORLD NEWS	Weekly World News
WEIGAND	Weigand Report
WEIGHTLIFTING	AOL Weightlifting & Bodybuilding
WEIRD SISTERS	The Hub: Weird Sisters
WEISSMANN	Traveler's Corner
WELLS FARGO	Wells Fargo Bank
WEST DIGC	Digital Cities: West
WEST VIRGINIA	Digital Cities: Mid-Atlantic
WESTERN DIGITAL	Western Digital
WESTWOOD	Westwood Studios [WWW site]
WF	Wells Fargo Bank
WFAA TV	ABC Online: WFAA-TV in Dallas/Ft. Worth TX
WFTV TV	ABC Online: WFTV-TV in Orlando FL
WGGB TV	ABC Online: WGGB-TV in Springfield MA
WGNX	Digital City Atlanta: WGNX Channel 46
WGTU TV	ABC Online: WGTU/WGTQ-TV in Traverse City MI
WHALERS	NHL Hockey
WHALEZ	Tartan Software
WHAT'S HOT	What's Hot on America Online
WHAT'S HOT IN HEALTH	What's Hot in Health
WHAT'S NEW	New Features & Services

WHEELS	Wheels
WHEELS EXCHANGE	Wheels Exchange
WHERE	Where Magazines
WHERE IS IT	Click & Go: Where Is It?
WHITE HOUSE	White House Forum
WHITE HOUSE.GOV	The White House [WWW site]
WHITE PAGES	Switchboard Interactive Directories [WWW site]
WHOI TV	ABC Online: WHOI-TV in Peoria/Bloomington IL
WHTM TV	ABC Online: WHTM-TV in Harrisburg PA
WICCA	Pagan Religions & Occult Sciences
WICS	Women in Community Service
WILHELMINA	Wilhelmina Studios
WIMBLEDON	Wimbledon [May disappear without notice]
WIN	Windows Forum
WIN MAG	Windows Magazine
WIN NEWS	Windows News Area
WIN NT	Windows NT Resource Center
WINDOWS	Windows Services
WINDOWS TIPS	Family Computing Forum: Tip of the Day
WINDSURFING	Sailing Forum
WINMAG.COM	Windows Magazine [WWW site]
WINNER	AOL Contest Area
WINNER'S CIRCLE	ABC Track
WINSOCK	Winsock Central [WAOL only]
WIRED	Wired Magazine
WIRELESS	Wireless Communication
WISC	University of Wisconsin-Madison [WWW site]
WISCONSIN	Digital Cities: Midwest
WIXT TV	ABC Online: WIXT-TV in Syracuse NY
WIZARD	Wizard World
WJBF TV	ABC Online: WJBF-TV in Augusta GA
WJCL TV	ABC Online: WJCL-TV in Savannah GA
WKBW TV	ABC Online: WKBW-TV in Buffalo NY
WKRC TV	ABC Online: WKRC-TV in Cincinnati OH
WKRN TV	ABC Online: WKRN-TV in Nashville TN
WLOS TV	ABC Online: WLOS-TV in Asheville NC
WLOX TV	ABC Online: WLOX-TV in Biloxi MS
WLS	WLS Chicago
WLVI	WLVI Boston MA
WMBB TV	ABC Online: WMBB-TV in Panama FL
WMDT TV	ABC Online: WMDT-TV in Salisbury MD
WMUR TV	ABC Online: WMUR-TV in Manchester NH
WNEP TV	ABC Online: WNEP-TV in Scranton/W-B PA
WOKR TV	ABC Online: WOKR-TV in Rochester NY

WOLFF BOOKS	Internet Connection Store
WOLO TV	ABC Online: WOLO-TV in Columbia SC
WOLVERINES	AOL College Football
WOMAN	Woman's Day Online
WOMAN BOARDS	Women's Network: Message Boards
WOMAN NEWS	Women's Network: News
WOMAN'S DAY	Woman's Day Online
WOMEN	Women's Network
WOMEN CLASS	Women's Network: Online Courses
WOMEN ONLY	Consumer Reports Complete Drug Reference Search
WOMEN ONQ	onQ: Women's Space
WOMEN'S HEALTH	Women's Health Forum
WOMEN'S HEALTH WEB	Women's Health Internet Sites
WOMENS SPORTS	Women's Sports World
WONDERLINK	Creative Wonders
WOODWORKER	American Woodworker
WORD HISTORIES	Word Histories
WORD PERFECT	Word Perfect Support Center
WORD PROCESSING	Mac Desktop Publishing/WP Forum
WORK	Workplace Channel
WORKSTYLE	About Work: WorkStyle
WORLD	The World
WORLD BELIEFS	World Beliefs
WORLD CAFE	World Cafe
WORLD CRISIS	World Crisis Network
WORLD NEWS	U.S. & World News Area
WORLD WIDE WEB	www.aol.com [WWW site]
WORLDVIEW	Fodor's Worldview
WORTH	Worth Magazine Online
WOTV TV	ABC Online: WOTV-TV in Battle Creek MI
WOW COM	Wow-Com
WP	Word Processing Resource Center
WPBF TV	ABC Online: WPBF-TV in West Palm Beach FL
WPDE TV	ABC Online: WPDE-TV in Myrtle Beach SC
WPHL	Digital City Philadelphia: WPHL Channel 17
WPLJ TV	ABC Online: WPLJ-TV in New York NY
WPTA TV	ABC Online: WPTA-TV in Fort Wayne IN
WQAD TV	ABC Online: WQAD-TV in Moline IL
WQOW TV	ABC Online: WQOW-TV in Eau Claire WI
WRD	Christianity Online: Word Publishing
WRESTLING	World Wrestling Federation
WRITE	Writer's Club Chat Rooms
WRITERS	Writer's Club
WRQX TV	ABC Online: WRQX-TV in Washington DC
WRTV TV	ABC Online: WRTV in Indianapolis IN
WSB TV	ABC Online: WSB-TV in Atlanta GA
WSJ	The Wall Street Journal [WWW site]
WSJV TV	ABC Online: WSJV-TV in South Bend IN
WSW	Wall Street Words
WSYX TV	ABC Online: WSYX-TV in Columbus OH
WTEN TV	ABC Online: WTEN-TV in Albany NY
WTG	Prism Elite Software
WTNH TV	ABC Online: WTNH-TV in Nashville TN
WTOK TV	ABC Online: WTOK-TV in Meridian MS
WTVC TV	ABC Online: WTVC-TV in Chattanooga TN
WTVQ TV	ABC Online: WTVQ-TV in Lexington KY
WUSTL	Washington University in St. Louis
WVA	AOL College Football
WVEC TV	ABC Online: WVEC-TV in Norfolk VA
WVII TV	ABC Online: WVII-TV in Bangor ME
WWE	Hot Education Internet Sites
WWF	World Wrestling Federation
WWIR	Washington Week in Review Magazine
WWN	Weekly World News
WWOS	ABC Online: Wide World of Sports
WWW	www.aol.com [WWW site]
WWW HELP	net.help: WWW Help
WWW KEYWORDS	Web Keywords
WX MALL	WSC Weather Mall
WXLV TV	ABC Online: WXLV-TV in Winston/Salem NC
WXOW TV	ABC Online: WXOW-TV in LaCrescent MN
WZZM TV	ABC Online: WZZM-TV in Grand Rapids MI
X FILES	X Files Forums
X FILES SIM	X Files Sim Forum
X2	U.S. Robotics x2 Modem Field Trial
XCMD	XCMD SIG
YACHTING	Sailing Forum
YACHTS	Boating Online
YANKEES	Major League Baseball Team: New York Yankees
YB	Your Business
YC	Your Church Magazine
YEAR	1996: The Year in News
YELLOW JACKETS	AOL College Football
YELLOW PAGES	Business Yellow Pages
YHA	Youth Hostel Association

YOUNG CHEFS	Young Chefs
YOUR BUSINESS LUNCH	Your Business Lunch
YOUR SPORTS	NESN Sports Circuit
YOUR TOONS	The Cartoons Forum
YOUTH HOSTEL	Youth Hostel Association
YOUTH TECH	Youth Tech
YOUTHNET	National Network for Youth
YOYO	Yoyodyne Entertainment
YOYO GAMES	Yoyodyne Entertainment: Games
YT	Youth Tech
YUGOSLAVIA	Balkan Operation Joint Endeavor
YUKON	Digital Wilderness
ZAGAT	Zagat Hotel/Resort/Spa Surveys
ZD	ZDNet
ZDNET.COM	ZD Net [WWW site]
ZEN	ChipNet Online: ZENtertainment
ZEO	Pangea ToyNet: Power Rangers Zeo!
ZEOS	Zeos International Ltd.
ZIP CODE	Zip Code Directory
ZIPPO	Original Zippo's News Services [WWW site]
ZODIAC	Astronet
ZODNAS	Sandoz Online
ZON	Zondervan Publishing House
ZOO	America's Favorite Zoos and Aquariums
ZOOM T	Zoom Telephonics Inc.

Glossary

This glossary was coauthored by George Louie (screen name: NumbersMan), to whom we express our heartfelt thanks for a job very well done. It's updated regularly and posted online. To find it, use the keyword: **Keywords** and open the Learn More About AOL folder, or use the keywords: **File Search** and search with the criterion "VirtuaLingo."

800 and 888 numbers America Online provides 800 and 888 numbers, at a modest hourly rate, to U.S. and Canadian members who are without local access numbers. To use these numbers, you must have Windows AOL 2.5 (or higher) or Mac AOL 2.5.1 (or higher). If you have a version below 4.0 of either software, you may need the AOLnet CCL file available at keyword: **Modem**. Additional information on these numbers can be found at keyword: **Access**. See also **access number** and **AOLnet**.

$im_off/$im_on The commands for ignoring Instant Messages (IMs). Sending an IM to the screen name $im_off will block incoming IMs. Conversely, sending an IM to $im_on will allow you to receive IMs again. When you use these commands to turn IMs off or on, type the letters exactly as shown. To initiate the command, either type some text in the message box and send the IM (by clicking on the Send button) or simply click on the Available? button. You will receive confirmation in the form of an America Online dialog box when you turn IMs either on or off. If members try to send you an IM or use the Available? button on the IM window, they will be told that "<your screen name> cannot currently receive Instant Messages." Note that IMs can be turned off for specific individuals using your Buddy List's Privacy Preferences. See also **Buddy List** and **IM**; contrast with **Ignore** and **parental chat controls**.

<< and >> These symbols are used to quote text, and they're often used in e-mail and posts. Members using Windows AOL 2.5 or higher, or Mac AOL 3.0 or higher, can get automatic quoting simply by selecting and copying a block of text in an e-mail and then clicking Reply. See also **e-mail** and **post**.

//roll The command for rolling dice. When entered in a chat or conference room, AOL's host computer will return a random result for two six-sided dice to the room. For example:

```
OnlineHost : NumbersMan rolled 2 6-sided dice:  2 4
```

The command can also be used to roll other types and quantities of dice. The full syntax of the command is //roll -diceXX -sidesYYY (where *XX* is 0-15 and *YYY* is 0-999). Be sure to include the spaces. It is considered rude to roll dice in Lobbies or other public chat areas (with the exception of the Red Dragon Inn, sims, and other special game rooms). This command is often used when role-playing or in lieu of "drawing straws." See also **chat rooms**, **OnlineHost**, and **sim**.

/ga This is common shorthand for "go ahead," often used during conferences with protocol. See **protocol**.

abbreviations Acronyms for common online phrases used in chat, IMs, and e-mail. Examples include LOL (laughing out loud) and BRB (be right back). See also **chat** and **shorthand**; contrast with **body language** and **emoticons**.

access number A phone number (usually local) your modem uses to access America Online. To find an access number online, go to keyword: **Access** or **AOLnet**. If you aren't signed on to AOL, there are a number of ways to get access numbers:

- Choose Add Number from the Setup menu (in Windows AOL 4.0), sign on with the New Local# (Windows AOL or Mac AOL 3.0) or Get Local# (Mac AOL 2.7 and lower) option in the Set Up & Sign On window.
- Delete all your numbers in Setup; America Online will automatically call the 800 number and let you choose from the list of access numbers.
- Phone the network: Call SprintNet at 1-800-877-5045, press 1, and then press 2; call SprintNet's automatic access number listings at 1-800-473-7983; or call Tymnet at 1-800-336-0149, ext. 2.
- Dial up SprintNet's Local Access Numbers Directory: Using a general telecommunications program, you can call in to a SprintNet node directly. Once connected, type **@D** and press the Enter key twice. At the @ prompt given, type **c mail** and press Enter. Then type p**hones** for the username and **phones** again for the password. You can look up any local SprintNet number available.

- Call America Online's Customer Service Hotline at 1-800-827-6364 (within the United States) or 1-703-893-6288 (from Canada or overseas); it's open 24 hours a day, 7 days a week.
- Call America Online's FAXLink service at 1-800-827-5551 and request that a list of access numbers be faxed to you. An automated voice menu will guide you through the choices.
- Dial up America Online's Customer Service BBS with a standard telecommunications program at 1-800-827-5808 (settings: 8 data bits, no parity, 1 stop bit, up to 14.4K).

If you don't have a local access number, read the information in the Access Number area (keyword: **Access**) on how to obtain one. See also **800 and 888 numbers**, **AOLnet**, **SprintNet**, **Tymnet**, and **node**.

address There are two types of addresses you'll hear about on America Online and the Internet. The first is an e-mail address, which you use to send an e-mail to anyone on AOL, the Internet, and just about any other online service. You can look up addresses for America Online members at keyword: **Members** and addresses for Internet denizens at various places on the WWW (World Wide Web). The second is a location address for information on America Online or the WWW, which is better known as a URL. An example of an address on AOL is aol://1722:keyword, which, when entered into the keyword window, takes you to the Ultimate Keyword List area. On the Web, the address http://members.aol.com/jennifer/ will take you to Jennifer's home page. See also **e-mail**, **e-mail address**, **Internet**, **URL**, and **WWW**.

Address Book An America Online software feature that allows you to store screen names for easy access. Your Address Book may be created, edited, or used through the Address Book icon available when composing mail. You can also create or edit them with the Edit Address Book or Address Book option under your Mail menu. To use, click the New Person or New Group icon to add a new entry—note that you can include a photo (or graphic) on the second page of any entry (click the tab at the top to get there). To use the names in your Address Book, be sure to choose Compose Mail from the Mail menu first and then click on the Address Book icon. See also **e-mail** and **screen names**.

Adobe Acrobat Commercial software that allows you to create Portable Digital Format (PDF) documents that retain their original appearance across computer platforms when read with the freely distributed Adobe Acrobat Reader.

AFK Common shorthand for "away from keyboard." It's most often used in chat and IMs when it's necessary to leave the keyboard for an extended length of time. Upon return, BAK is used, meaning "back at keyboard." See also **shorthands**, **abbreviations**, and **chat**; contrast with **body language** and **emoticons**.

Alt key A special function key on the PC keyboard. It's usually located near the space bar; you'll find Alt printed on it. Holding down the Alt key while another key is pressed will often activate a special function. For example, Alt+ H will bring up the Help section under Windows AOL and Geos AOL. (Note: Some Macintosh keyboards also have a key labeled Alt, but this is primarily for use when operating a PC emulator on the Mac and is otherwise defined as the Option key.) See also **Control key**, **Command key**, and **Option key**.

alphanumeric Data or information consisting of the letters of the alphabet *A* through *Z* (upper- and lowercase), the digits *0* through *9*, punctuation marks, and other keyboard symbols.

America Online, Incorporated (AOL) The nation's leading online service, headquartered in Virginia. Formerly known as Quantum Computer Services and founded in 1985, America Online has grown rapidly in both size and scope. AOL has over 10 million members and hundreds of alliances with major companies. America Online's stock exchange symbol is AOL. To contact AOL headquarters, call 1-703-448-8700 or use 1-800-827-6364 to speak to a representative. See also **AOL**.

analog Information composed of continuous and varying levels of intensity, such as sound and light. Much of the information in the natural world is analog, while man-made information, such as from computers, is digital. For example, the sound of your significant other asking you politely and sensitively to get off America Online for the 10th time is analog. Yet if you were to convert that information to a computer sound file, it would become digital. Contrast with **digital**.

AOL Abbreviation for America Online, Inc. Occasionally abbreviated as AO. See also **America Online, Incorporated**.

AOL Instant Messenger Software that allows people with Internet accounts to send and receive Instant Messages from America Online members. Once a person has downloaded, installed, and registered the AOL Instant Messenger software, America Online members will be able to add them to their Buddy Lists and send Instant Messages to them as if they were using the AOL service rather than another service or ISP. See also **IM**.

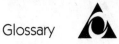

AOL NetFind America Online's exclusive Internet directory and search service available at http://www.aol.com or at keyword: **NetFind**. It was created through AOL's partnership with Excite, Inc.

AOL Radio A forthcoming feature on AOL that is similar to Progressive Network's RealAudio. AOL Radio will allow members to listen to real-time broadcasts of news, music, and advertisements.

AOL Slideshows An AOL-exclusive presentation consisting of a series of images, animation, and sound. AOL Slideshows take advantage of streaming technology to begin playback before the entire slideshow downloads. Slideshows are only available for version 3.0 or later clients.

AOL Talk A future feature on AOL that will allow members to talk to other members in real-time through AOL. AOL Talk will probably require AOL 4.0, a microphone and sound card, and a 28.8 Kbps or better connection to be useful.

aol.com America Online's home page on the Web, located at http://www.aol.com.

AOLiversary The date on which a person first became an active member of America Online. Celebrated yearly, it is considered to be an accurate yardstick by some to determine their state of addiction. See also **AOLoholic**.

AOLnet America Online's own data network, which provides members with local access numbers up to 56 Kbps. To use this network, you must have Windows AOL 2.5 (or higher) or Mac AOL 2.5.1 (or higher). If you have a version below 3.0 of either software, you may need the AOLnet CCL file available at keyword: **AOLnet**. AOLnet numbers are located across the country. For members who do not have a local access number, there is also an 800 number that is more affordable than most long-distance fees. An alternative is to sign on to AOL through an Internet or ISP (Internet Service Provider) connection. To find AOLnet local access numbers, go to keyword: **AOLnet**. See also **800 and 888 numbers**, **packet-switching network (PSN)**, and **access number**; contrast with **SprintNet** and **Tymnet**.

AOLoholic A member of AOL who begins to display any of the following behaviors: spending most of their free time online; thinking about AOL even when offline (evidenced by the addition of shorthands to non-AOL writings); attempting to bring all their friends and family online; and/or thinking AOL is the best invention since the wheel. A 12-step plan is in development. Many, but not all, AOLoholics go on to become community leaders. See also **community leader** and **member**.

ARC Short for archive, this is an older compression utility that was the PC standard prior to ZIP. This utility will compress one file or multiple files into a file called an archive, which will make for shorter transfer time while uploading or downloading. Some older files online are still packaged in the ARC format. See also **archive**, **file**, **file compression**, **PKZip**, and **StuffIt**.

archive 1. A file that has been compressed with file compression software. See also **file**, **file compression**, **ARC**, **PKZip**, and **StuffIt**. 2. A file that contains message board postings that may be of value but have been removed from a message board due to their age, inactivity of topic, or lack of message board space. These messages are usually bundled into one document and placed in a file library for retrieval later. See also **file** and **library**.

article A text document intended to be read online, but may be printed or saved for later examination offline. Usually articles are less than 25K, as anything larger would probably scroll off the top of your window. See also **document**; contrast with **file**.

asbestos Means flame-retardant. Used as a modifier to anything intended to protect one from flames. For example, "donning asbestos underwear." This is usually used just before saying something that is expected to produce flames. See also **flame**.

ASCII Acronym for American Standard for Computer Information Interchange (or American Standard Code for Information Interchange). ASCII is the numeric code used to represent computer characters on computers around the world. Because only seven bits are used in ASCII, there are no more than 128 (2^7) characters in the standard ASCII set. Variations of ASCII often extend the available characters by using an 8-bit means of identifying characters and thus may represent as many as 256 characters. The standard ASCII code set consists of 128 characters ranging from 0 to 127. America Online supports characters 28-127 in chat areas, IMs, and message boards. Pronounced "ask-key." See also **ASCII text**.

ASCII art Pictures created with no more than the 128 ASCII characters. ASCII art can be humorous, entertaining, or serious. It is popular in some chat rooms. Some members find it disruptive when large ASCII art is displayed in a chat room, so you are advised to ask before scrolling it. See also **ASCII** and **ASCII text**.

ASCII text Characters represented as ASCII. Sometimes called *plain text*; it is compatible with all platforms represented on AOL. See also **ASCII**; contrast with **rich text**.

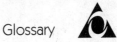

Ask the Staff button See **Comment to Staff button**.

asynchronous Data communication (via modem) of the start-stop variety where characters do not need to be transmitted constantly. Each character is transmitted as a discrete unit with its own start bit and one or more stop bits. AOL is asynchronous. See also **synchronous**.

attached file A file that hitches a ride with e-mail. Be the file text, sound, or pictures, it is said to be attached if it has been included with the e-mail for separate downloading by the recipient (whether addressed directly, carbon-copied, or blind-carbon-copied). E-mail that is forwarded will retain any attached files as well. Files are usually attached because the information that they contain is either too long to be sent in the body of a regular e-mail message or is impossible to send via e-mail, such as software programs. Multiple files may be attached by compressing the files into one archive and attaching the archive to the piece of e-mail with the Attach File icon. See also **archive, download, e-mail**, and **file**.

auditorium Auditoriums are specially equipped online "rooms" that allow large groups of AOL members to meet in a structured setting. Currently, there are several auditoriums: AOL Live, The Bowl, The Coliseum, Cyberplex, CyberRap, The Globe, International, News Room, and The Odeon (all for special and general events); Rotunda (for computing-related topics or computing company representatives); and Tech Live (for questions and help on AOL—this is in the free area). The auditoriums are divided into two parts: the stage, where the emcee and the guest speaker(s) are located, and the chat rows, where the audience is located. Upon entering an auditorium, a user is assigned to one of the chat rows, which consist of up to 15 other audience members. Audience members in the same row may talk to each other without being heard by those on stage or by those in other rows. Normally, nothing said in the audience can be heard by anyone on stage, although anything said on stage can be "broadcast" and heard by everyone in the audience. The OnlineHost will broadcast important information throughout the conference. The emcee moderates the conference and will broadcast more specific information. You can tell the difference between what is said on stage and what is said in your chat row because what is said in your chat row is preceded by a row number. More information on auditoriums can be found at keyword: **Live**. See also **emcee, OnlineHost**, and **Tech Live**; contrast with **chat rooms** and **conference room**.

Automatic AOL An automated feature that can send and receive your e-mail and files as well as receive message board and newsgroup postings. Formerly known as FlashSessions. Auto AOL can be set up to run at any time, including while you are online. It is accessible under your Mail Center icon. See also **e-mail**, **file**, **flashmail**, and **newsgroup**.

avatar A graphical representation or depiction of a person used in online games or chat rooms. Avatars are usually customizable, have limited animated actions or expressions, and interact with other avatars. See also **People Connection**, **chat rooms**, and **conference room**.

bandwidth A measure of the amount of information that can flow through a given point at any given time. Technically, bandwidth is the difference, in Hertz (Hz), between the highest and lowest frequencies of a transmission channel. However, as typically used, it more often refers the amount of data that can be sent through a given communications circuit. To use a popular analogy, a low bandwidth is a two-lane road while a high bandwidth is a six-lane superhighway.

bash A get-together or party of AOL members in a particular area. Members who attend are often referred to as bashees, and popular bashes are the Big Apple Bash (in NYC) and the Texas Bash. Information on bashes can usually be found in The Quantum Que, a community message board available at keyword: **Que**.

basher A particularly vile form of snert. A basher will usually target a certain group and harass them for the basher's pleasure. This usually takes place in a People Connection chat room dedicated to that group, but it may also occur in conference rooms. See also **snert**, **People Connection**, **chat rooms**, and **conference room**.

baud rate A unit for measuring the speed of data transmission. Technically, baud rates refer to the number of times the communications line changes states each second. Strictly speaking, baud and bits per second (bps) are not identical measurements, but most nontechnical people use the terms interchangeably. See also **bps**.

BBS (bulletin board system) A system offering information that can be accessed via computer, modem, and phone lines. While that definition technically includes AOL, BBSes are typically much smaller in size and scope. Most BBSes maintain message boards and file libraries and some feature Internet access, newsfeeds, and online games. For more information online, go to keyword: **BBS**. BBSes are sometimes abbreviated as simply "board," and should not be confused with message boards on AOL. Contrast with **message board**.

beta test A period in a new product's or service's development designed to discover problems (or "bugs") prior to its release to the general public. AOL often selects members to beta test its new software. If you are interested in beta testing AOL software, you may be able to apply at keyword: **BetaA Apply**. See also **bug**.

blind carbon copy (bcc) A feature of the AOL e-mail system that allows you to send e-mail to a member or members without anyone other than you being aware of it. To send a blind carbon copy, simply place parentheses around the screen name(s). For example, (JoeShmo) or (JoeShmo, HughHamstr). Mac AOL 3.0 users can use the small pop-up menu to change an address to BCC. When a blind carbon copy is made, it is said to be bcc'ed. See also **e-mail**; contrast with **carbon copy**.

board An abbreviated reference to a message board or bulletin board system (BBS). See also **message board** and **BBS**.

body language An online expression of physical movement and nonverbal emotions through text. Two popular methods have developed on AOL: colons (:::yawning:::) and brackets (<yawning and trying to stay awake for 10 straight hours in front of a monitor>). See also **chat**; contrast with **abbreviations**, **emoticons**, and **shorthand**.

Boolean search A search that uses logical operators from Boolean algebra to narrow the number of matches. For example, a search in the classifieds for "car" would yield many matches, but not exactly what you want. A search for "car AND brown AND (Firebird OR TransAm)" would help you find exactly what you were looking for.

bounce To return something, such as e-mail. For example, e-mail sent to recipients outside of AOL may bounce and never make it to its intended destination, especially if it was not addressed correctly. Sometimes users who are punted will refer to themselves as bounced. See also **e-mail** and **punt**.

bps (bits per second) A measurement of data transmission speed. Currently, 1200 through 57,600 bps are supported on AOL (see keyword: **AOLnet** for more information). See also **baud rate**.

BRB Common shorthand for "be right back." It is used by AOL members when participating in chat/conference rooms or talking in IMs (Instant Messages). See also **shorthands, abbreviations**, and **chat**; contrast with **body language** and **emoticons**.

browse To casually explore rather than examine in detail. Typically used in reference to message boards and file libraries. Browsing information online without a specific target is one prominent trait of an budding AOLoholic. Contrast with **search**.

browser A way of accessing the World Wide Web. On Mac AOL 3.0 and Windows AOL 2.5 and higher, the browser is an integrated component of the software. On Mac AOL 2.6 and 2.7, it is a separate piece of software. See also **favorite place**, **Internet**, **hot list**, **page**, **Personal Filing Cabinet**, **site**, and **WWW**.

BTW Common shorthand for "by the way." It is used in IMs, chat/conference rooms, e-mail, and message postings. See also **shorthands**, **abbreviations**, and **chat**; contrast with **body language** and **emoticons**.

buddy A friend or family member who has an AOL membership or is using AOL Instant Messenger, and has been added to your Buddy List. See also **AOL Instant Messenger** and **Buddy List**.

Buddy List A special list that stores your "buddies" (screen names of friends, family members, coworkers, etc.) and informs you when they sign on or off AOL. You add (or remove) buddies yourself, and you can define several groups of buddies as you like. The Buddy List is a feature of the Windows AOL and Mac AOL 3.0 software. The buddy list preferences (accessible via keywords: **Buddy List**) allow you to configure your buddy list as you like; don't neglect the Privacy Preferences either, where you can keep others from seeing or even IMing you. See also **buddy** and **invitation**.

bug A problem or glitch in a product, be it software or hardware. A bug may be referred to jokingly as a "feature." You can report a problem with AOL software or services by going to keyword: **Questions** and clicking on Error Messages. See also **GPF**.

bulletin board See **message board** and **BBS**.

cache A portion of a data storage device, RAM, or processor set aside to temporarily hold recently accessed or frequently accessed information. By saving the information locally, performance is improved because it is quicker to receive the information from the cache than from the original source. For example, AOL's client software saves the artwork and icons for those areas that you visit often so that they don't need to be downloaded every time.

carbon copy (cc) A feature of the AOL e-mail system that allows you to address e-mail to a member for whom the e-mail is either not directly intended or of secondary interest. The primary addressee(s) are aware that the copy was made; it is similar to the carbon copy convention used in business correspondence. As such, the members carbon-copied are not usually expected to reply. When a carbon copy is made, it is said to be cc'ed. Also known as a courtesy copy. See also **e-mail**; contrast with **blind carbon copy**.

CCL (Communication Control Language) A script that allows you to control your modem. CCL scripts are most useful when the connection process is more complicated than can be handled by a modem file. For example, if your modem needs certain commands every time a connection is established, you can use or write a CCL script to automate this process. America Online uses standard CCLs and modem files to control your modem; in other words, you shouldn't need to worry about CCLs when connecting to AOL. See also **modem files**.

Center Stage See **auditorium**.

channel This is the broadest category of information into which America Online divides its material. Also known as department. At this writing, these are the channels for the different areas online: AOL Today, News, Sports, Influence, Travel, International, Personal Finance, Workplace, Computing, Research & Learn, Entertainment, Games, Interests, Lifestyles, Shopping, Health, Families, Kids Only, and Local.

chat To engage in real-time communications with other members. AOL members who are online at the same time may chat with each other in a number of ways: Instant Messages (IMs), chat/conference rooms, and auditoriums. "Chatting" provides immediate feedback from others; detailed discussions are better suited toward message boards, and lengthy personal issues are best dealt with in e-mail if a member isn't currently online. See also **Instant Message**, **chat rooms**, **conference room**, and **auditorium**; contrast with **message board** and **e-mail**.

chat rooms Online areas where members may meet to communicate and interact with others. There are two kinds of chat areas—public and private. Public chat areas can be found in the People Connection area (keyword: **People**) or in the many forums around America Online (see keywords: **AOL Live** for schedules). Public rooms may either be officially sanctioned rooms or member-created rooms (which are listed separately). All public rooms are governed by AOL's Terms of Service (TOS) and are open to anyone interested. Private chat rooms are available from most chat areas and are open only to those who create them or know their names and meeting times. All chat rooms accommodate at least 23 members, while some of the chat areas in forums other than People Connection may hold up to 100 members. The chat rooms that can be created by members (both public and private) must have names with no more than 20 characters, begin with a letter, and contain no punctuation. See also **private room**, **chat**, **host**, **Guide**, **TOS**, and **People Connection**; contrast with **auditorium** and **conference room**.

chat sounds Sounds may be played and broadcast to others in chat areas by typing: **{S <sound>}** and sending it to the chat area. Be sure to type it exactly as shown and insert the exact name of the sound you wish to play where <sound> appears in the example. For example, {S Welcome} will play America Online's "Welcome" sound in a chat area. New sounds can be found online by searching the libraries. To install sounds into your AOL software for playing, you'll need a sound utility (also found in the libraries online). Keep in mind that other members will need to have the same sound installed in their AOL software to hear it when played. Please note also that Geos AOL users cannot hear chat sounds, nor can those without sound capabilities. See also **chat rooms** and **library**.

client A computer that requests information from another. On America Online, your computer is generally the client and the Stratus is the host. Contrast with **host (1)**.

close box The small box in the upper left corner of your window. Clicking on this box closes the window on the Mac and gives you the option to close the window on the PC. Not to be confused with a shoe box, a boom box, or even a clothes box. See also **window**; contrast with **zoom box**.

club See **forum**.

Command key A special function key on the Mac. Usually located near the space bar. You'll find printed on it either an open Apple symbol or a cloverleaf symbol (or both). Holding down the Command key while another key is pressed will often activate a special function. Also known as the Open-Apple key. See also **Control key**, **Option key**, and **Alt key**.

Comment to Staff button A button available in file libraries that takes you to the Download Info Center, which offers a great deal of information about libraries and allows you to send a note to the managers of the library. Note that it doesn't send a note to the uploader, only the library managers (often a forum leader or assistant). Also note that this is labeled Ask The Staff on

Windows AOL and Geos AOL. The Download Info Center is also available directly at keywords: **Info Center**. See also **download** and **library**.

community leader AOL members who help in the various forums and areas. They usually work from their homes, not AOL headquarters, hence they have been called "remote staff" in the past. Often they are Guides, Hosts, Forum leaders/assistants/consultants, and so on. When community leaders work with partners, they usually do not work at the partner's offline physical location; those who do are known as corporate staff rather than community leaders. See also **Guide**, **host**, **partner**, and **uniform**; contrast with **corporate staff** and **in-house**.

compression See **file compression**.

conference room A specific kind of chat area found in forums all around AOL where members can meet, hold conferences, and interact in real-time. Conference rooms can hold up to 48 or 100 members at any one time (depending on location) and are located outside of the People Connection. Currently, there are over 700 public conference rooms with more being added all the time. Often special events are held in these rooms, and a protocol system may be used to make them proceed smoothly. Hosts or moderators often facilitate the discussions and conferences here. See also **host**, **moderator**, and **protocol**; contrast with **chat rooms** and **auditorium**.

Control key A special function key, usually located on the bottom row of keys, you'll find either Ctrl or Control printed on it. Holding down the Control key while another key is pressed will often activate a special function. (Note: Some Macintosh keyboards also have a key labeled Control, but it is primarily for use when operating a PC emulator on the Mac.) See also **Command key**, **Option key**, **Alt key**, and **Open-Apple key**.

corporate staff Members who are usually company or partner (information provider) employees and work at the corporate offices of the company. In-house AOL, Inc. staff is often referred to in this manner as well. See also **in-house** and **partner**; contrast with **community leader**.

cracker One who violates security. Coined by hackers in the 1980s in defense against the growing assumption that all hackers are malevolent. A password scammer is a cracker. See also **password scammer**; contrast with **hacker**, **phisher**, and **snert**.

cross-post To make the same message in several folders, message boards, or newsgroups. Overuse is bad netiquette and may result in having your posts hidden (if on AOL) or your mailbox barraged with flaming e-mail (if on the Internet). See also **flame**, **newsgroup**, **post**, and **spam**.

CS Live See **Tech Live**.

Customer Relations America Online's Customer Relations Hotline is open from 7:00 A.M. to 2:45 A.M ET, seven days a week. You can reach them at 1-800-827-6364. See also **Tech Live**.

cyberpunk First used to designate a body of speculative fiction literature focusing on marginal people in technologically enhanced cultural "systems." Within the last few years, the mass media has used this term to categorize the denizens of cyberspace. Cyberpunks are known to cruise the information landscapes with alacrity, or lacking that, eagerness.

cyberspace An infinite world created by our computer networks. Cyberspace is no less real than the real world—people are born, grow, learn, fall in love, and die in cyberspace. These effects may or may not be carried over into the physical world. America Online is an example of cyberspace created through interaction between the energies of the members, community leaders, staff, and computers. See also **online community**.

daemon An automatic program that performs a maintenance function on America Online. For example, a board daemon may run at 3:00 A.M. in the morning and clean up old posts on a message board. Rumored to stand for "Disk And Execution MONitor."

database A collection of information stored and organized for easy searching. A database can refer to something as simple as a well-sorted filing cabinet, but today most databases reside on computers because they offer better access. Databases are located all over AOL, with prominent examples being the Find databases (keyword: **Find**) and the Member Directory database (keywords: **Member Directory**). See the AOL Research & Learn channel (keyword: **Research**) for a large collection of databases. See also **Boolean search**, **Member Directory**, and **searchable**.

Delete An AOL e-mail system feature that allows you to permanently remove a piece of mail from any and all of your mailboxes. To use it, simply select and highlight the piece of mail you wish to delete (from either your new mail, read mail, or sent mail) and click the Delete button at the bottom of the window. The mail will be permanently deleted and cannot be retrieved. Mail you have deleted without reading first will appear as "(deleted)" in the Status box of the sender. The Delete feature is useful for removing unneeded mail from your Old Mail box. Do not confuse this feature with the Unsend option, which will remove mail you've sent from the recipient's mailbox. See also **e-mail** and **Status**; contrast with **Ignore** and **Unsend**.

demoware Demonstration software. Often full-featured versions of commercial software, with the exception being that the Save or Print features are often disabled. Some demos are only functional for certain periods of time. Like shareware, demonstration software is a great way to try before you buy. Contrast with **freeware**, **public domain**, and **shareware**.

department See **channel**.

digital Information that is represented by discrete states. Most information in the real world is not digital but must be converted into this form to be used by computers. The converse is also true; digital information normally needs to be converted into analog information before people can use it. For example, AOL chat sounds, which are stored as digital information, must be converted into their analog equivalents before they are actually heard by us. Contrast with **analog**.

document An information file, usually relating specific details on a topic. On America Online, they can be in the form of articles (which are read-only) or modifiable documents, usually created with the New (Memo) menu command within AOL. See also **article** and **file**.

DOD Abbreviation for Download On Demand, a method of receiving artwork updates that was used prior to progressive artwork downloading; still used on Mac AOL 2.7 and Windows AOL 2.5 and lower. AOL was unique in that as it grew and new areas were added, the custom artwork associated with new services and areas was added on the fly. When you enter an area that includes new artwork, such as a logo or icon, it is automatically downloaded and stored on your computer. Once you have visited an area, you never have to wait for the artwork to download again. Similarly, if you never enter a new area with artwork updates, you do not need to wait for the DODs. The difference between DOD and Smart Art (progressive artwork downloading) is that, with DOD, your computer is tied up while the download is in progress and you do not see the artwork until the download has completed. Contrast with **Smart Art** and **UDO**.

domain In Internet addresses, usually everything to the right of the @ symbol is referred to as the domain. For example, the domain name for AOL member addresses is aol.com. See also **address**, **e-mail**, **e-mail address**, and **Internet**.

DOS Abbreviation for Disk Operating System, also called PC DOS or MS-DOS (Microsoft). DOS is the most widely used operating system for IBM PCs and compatibles. Pronounced "dahss." Contrast with **OS/2**, **system**, and **Windows**.

download The transfer of information stored on a remote computer to a storage device on your personal computer. This information can come from AOL via its file libraries or from other America Online members via attached files in e-mail. Usually, downloads are files intended for review once you're offline. You download graphics and sounds, for instance. *Download* is used both as a noun and a verb. For example, you might download a graphic file to your hard drive, where you store your latest downloads. See also **archive**, **attached file**, **download count**, **Download Manager**, **FileGrabber**, and **library**.

download count The download count refers to the number of times a certain file has been downloaded. It is often used as a gauge of the file's popularity. While this may not be too significant for a new upload, it is a good indication of the popularity of files that have been around for a while. Often, however, the number of downloads is more reflective of the appeal of a file's name or description rather than of its content. Note that a newly uploaded file on AOL will always have a download count of 1, even though it hasn't been downloaded yet. So to divine the true number of downloads, always subtract one from the total. Also, if the system is slow, the download count visible at the top level of the library may not update immediately. See also **file**, **library**, and **download**.

Download Manager An America Online software feature that allows you to keep a queue of files to download at a later time. You can even set up your software to automatically sign off when your download session is complete. You can schedule your software to sign on and grab files listed in the queue at times you specify. See also **download**, **file**, **Automatic AOL**, and **Personal Filing Cabinet**.

e-mail Short for electronic mail. One of the most popular features of online services, e-mail allows the exchange of private communications electronically from one person to another. No wasted paper, leaky pens, or terrible tasting envelope glue involved. E-mail is usually much faster and easier to send than ordinary mail; the shortcomings are that not everyone has an e-mail address to write to and your mail resides in electronic form on a computer system, although e-mail is considered as private and inviolable as regular mail. With AOL's e-mail system, mail can be sent directly to scores of people; carbon copies and blind carbon copies can be sent, messages can be forwarded, and they can even include attached files. E-mail can also be sent (and forwarded) to any other service that has an Internet address. On version 3.0, there is no limit to the size of mail that can be sent and received. On Windows AOL and Mac AOL below version 3.0, mail up to 32K in size can be sent and received.

Your screen name's mailbox is limited to 550 pieces of mail at any one time, including both read and unread mail. Unread mail will remain in your New Mail box for four weeks after the date it was sent and mail you have read remains in your Old Mail box for three days. If the amount of mail in your mail box exceeds 550 pieces, AOL will start to delete excess mail, starting with read mail—America Online will not delete any of your unread mail, however. These limits almost never present a problem for even frequent America Online users. See also **attached file, blind carbon copy, carbon copy, Delete, e-mail address, flashmail, gateway, Ignore, Keep as New, mailbomb, massmail, Personal Filing Cabinet, return receipt**, and **Status**; contrast with **snail mail, message**, and **IM**.

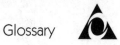

e-mail address A cyberspace mailbox. On America Online, your e-mail address is simply your screen name; for folks outside of AOL, your address is yourscreenname@aol.com. For example, if our friend Sharon wants to e-mail us from her Internet account, she can reach us as jennifer@aol.com or numbersman@aol.com. See also **address, e-mail**, and **screen name**.

Easter egg A hidden surprise in software; often left in at the whim of the programmers. Both Macintosh and Windows applications have Easter eggs. There are also some Easter eggs scattered around America Online, but be forewarned, they come and go as quickly as chocolate bunnies on Easter Sunday.

emcee A member who has been trained to moderate and host events held in auditoriums. See also **auditorium**; contrast with **host** and **moderator**.

emoticons Symbols consisting of characters found on any keyboard; they are used to give and gain insight on emotional states. For example, the symbol :) is a smile—just tilt your head to the left and you'll see the : (eyes) and the) (smile). The online community has invented countless variations to bring plain text to life, and you'll see emoticons used everywhere from chat rooms to e-mail. Emoticons, like emotions, are more popular in "face-to-face" chat, and some consider them unprofessional or overly cute. Regardless, they are one of the best methods of effective communication online. Emoticons may also be referred to as smileys and collectively with other chat devices as shorthands. A brief list is available at keyword: **Shorthands**. See also **shorthands** and **chat**; contrast with **abbreviations** and **body language**.

encryption The manipulation of data in order to prevent any but the intended recipient from reading it. There are many types of data encryption, and they are the basis of network security.

ET (EST or EDT) Abbreviation for Eastern Time. Most times are given in this format because America Online is headquartered in this time zone. Mac AOL users can change the default time zone through their Preferences settings under the Members menu.

FAQ Short for Frequently Asked Questions. FAQs may take the form of an informational file containing questions and answers to common concerns/issues. They are used to answer questions that are brought up often in message boards or discussions. These files may be stored online in an article or archived in a file library. See also **message board** and **library**.

favorite place 1. On Windows AOL 2.5 and Mac AOL 3.0 and higher, this refers to a feature that allows you to "mark" America Online and WWW places you'd like to return to later. Your favorite places are stored in your Personal Filing Cabinet. Any WWW site can be made a favorite place, as well as any America Online window with a little heart in the upper right hand corner. See also **Personal Filing Cabinet**. 2. On Mac AOL 2.7 and lower and Geos AOL, a favorite place is one of the user-definable locations at the bottom of the Go To menu. You can edit these favorite places with the Edit Favorite Places option.

fax (facsimile) A technique for sending graphic images (such as text or pictures) over phone lines. While faxes are usually sent and received with a stand-alone fax machine, they may also be sent to or from computers using fax software and a modem. Contrast with **e-mail** and **snail mail**.

file Any amount of information that is grouped together as one unit. On America Online, a file can be anything from text to sounds and can be transferred to and from your computer via America Online. Collections of files are available in libraries for downloading, and files may be attached to e-mail. See also **download**, **library**, and **software file**; contrast with **article**.

file compression A programming technique by which many files can be reduced in size. Files are usually compressed so they take up less storage space, can be transferred quicker, and/or can be bundled with others. Compressed files must be decompressed before they can be used, but the America Online software can be set to automatically decompress most files (check your Preferences). See also **file** and **download**.

file library See **library**.

File Transfer Protocol See **FTP**.

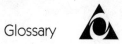

FileGrabber A piece of software built into Windows AOL and Mac AOL that will automatically decode encoded data (also known as *binaries*) such as that found in some newsgroups. Besides making sure that your newsgroup preferences are set to allow you to decode files, you don't need to do anything to use it—FileGrabber will automatically detect encoded data and ask you if you want to download the file. For more information, see the aol.newsgroups.help.binaries newsgroup. See also **download**, **file**, **Internet**, and **newsgroup**.

filename extensions Filename extensions are usually three-character codes found suffixing a file name and are primarily used for PC files. A comprehensive list would take several pages, but here are some common extensions:

Some common filename extensions	
Text/word processor formats:	
DOC	Microsoft Word document
HLP	Help file
HTM	HyperText Markup Language (WWW) format
HTX	Hypertext document
LF	Line Feeds added to text format
LET	Letter file, as to a friend (e.g., friend.let)
LOG	America Online log file, usually text
MW	MacWrite document
RTF	Rich text format
SAM	Ami Professional document
TXT	Unformatted ASCII text
WS	WordStar document
WP (or WPD)	WordPerfect document
Graphic formats:	
ART	Johnson Grace ART
BMP	OS/2 or Windows bitmap
EPS	Encapsulated PostScript
GIF	Graphics Interchange Format
JPG	Joint Photographic Experts Group (JPEG)
MAC	MacPaint (also PNT)
PIC	Macintosh PICT
PCX	Zsoft Paintbrush
TIF	Tagged-image file format (TIFF)
WPG	WordPerfect graphic

➡

Some common filename extensions *(continued)*	
Compressed formats:	
SIT	StuffIt
ZIP	PKZip
ARC	Abbreviation for ARChive; similar to PKZip
SEA	Self-extracting archive
Other formats:	
AVI	Audio-Video Interlaced animation
BAT	Batch file; executable file; DOS
BIN	Binary program file; often a subdirectory name
BMK	Windows Bookmark file; references Help segment
COM	Executable program file; DOS
DAT	Data file or subdirectory with data files
DBF	DBase file
DLL	Dynamic link library; program files recognized by Windows
EXE	PC executable file, can be a self-extracting archive
GRP	Windows Program Group
INI	Initialization file for Windows and other applications
MAC	Macro
MOV	QuickTime movie
MPG	MPEG animation
PDF	Adobe Acrobat Portable Document Format
PM4	PageMaker version 4.x file
SLK	SYLK file
SYS	Device driver or System file
WAV	Windows sound file
XLC	Excel chart
XLS	Excel worksheet

flame Made popular on the Internet, to flame means to chat, post messages, or send e-mail about something that is considered inflammatory by other members and may cause fires among those who read and respond to it. "Flaming" may spark a lively debate when selectively and appropriately used. More often, it will cause misunderstandings and divided parties. Harassment and vulgarity are not allowed on America Online, and if you see it occurring, you may report the occurrence at keyword: **TOS**. See also **asbestos**, **chat**, **message board**, **e-mail**, and **TOS**.

flashmail See **Automatic AOL**.

form A window for an area online—usually comprises a text field, a list box (scrollable), and one or more icons. Often special artwork will be placed in the form as well, as in a logo. Examples of forms include Star Trek Club (keyword: **Trek**), MTV Online (keyword: **MTV**), and the Mac Games Forum (keyword: **MGM**). See also **icon** and **window**.

format Generally, to organize information into a regular form. When on America Online, you format text using the various commands in the Text Format toolbar (which may be built in to your windows already). See also **rich text**.

forum A place online where members with similar interests may find valuable information, exchange ideas, share files, and get help on a particular area of interest. Forums (also known simply as areas or clubs) are found everywhere online, represent almost every interest under the sun, and usually offer message boards, articles, chat rooms, and libraries, all organized and accessible by a keyword. Forums are moderated by forum hosts or forum leaders. For example, in the Computing channel, each forum has a forum leader (denoted by PC at the beginning of their screen name), who is assisted by forum assistants (denoted by PCA), and often assisted even further by forum consultants (denoted by PCC). See also **form** and **keyword**.

freeware A file that is completely free and often made available for downloading in libraries of online services like America Online. Unlike public domain files, you are not able to modify freeware and the author retains the copyright. Since the author or programmer usually posts freeware and the user downloads it, distribution is direct and nearly without cost. Users are generally encouraged to make copies and give them to friends and even post them on other services. Check the file's documentation for limits on use and distribution. VirtuaLingo is freeware—you are encouraged to pass this along to anyone who may be interested, but please do not modify or incorporate it into another work without permission. See also **file**, **shareware**, and **public domain**.

FTP Abbreviation for File Transfer Protocol. A method of transferring files to and from a computer that is connected to the Internet. America Online offers FTP access via the keyword: **FTP**, as well as personal FTP sites at keywords: **My Place**. See also **Internet**, **WWW**, and **home page**; contrast with **library**.

Fwd: Short for "forward," as in forwarding e-mail to someone. See also **e-mail**.

gateway A link to another service, such as the Internet or a game (Gemstone III). Gateways allow members to access these independent services through America Online. Used as both a noun and a verb. It is also rumored that the celestial gateway to Heaven is hidden somewhere online. See also **Internet**.

Geos AOL The PC platform's DOS version of the older AOL client software, which is based on the GeoWorks graphical operating system. The current version is 1.5a, although a special 2.0 version exists for Geos users. America Online has no plans to continue upgrading this software, but members may continue to use the current versions for the time being. May also be referred to as PC/Geos, PCAO, or GAOL. Contrast with **Mac AOL** and **Windows AOL**.

GIF (Graphics Interchange Format) A type of graphic file that can be read by most platforms; the electronic version of photographs. GIFs can be viewed with your AOL software or with a GIF viewer utility, which you can locate at keyword: **Viewers**. Member GIFs are also located in the Portrait Gallery (keyword: **Gallery**). To view a Mac GIF on a PC, you may need to strip off the Macintosh header with an application called AOMAC2PC. This utility is located in the Viewer Resource Center. The *g* in *GIF* should not be pronounced like the *j* in the brand of peanut butter, but rather like the *g* in *gift*. (Yes, we know others claim otherwise, but if it were to be pronounced like "JIF," it would have been spelled that way.)

Gopher A feature of the Internet that allows you to browse huge amounts of information. The term implies that it will "go-fer" information to retrieve it for you. It also refers to the way in which you "tunnel" through the various menus, much like a gopher would. See also **WAIS** and **Internet**; contrast with **newsgroups** and **WWW**.

GPF Abbreviation for general protection fault. If you get a GPF error, it means that Windows (or a Windows application) has attempted to access memory that has not been allocated for use. GPFs are the scourge of Windows America Online members everywhere. If you experience an GPF while using Windows AOL, write down the exact error message and then go to keywords: **GPF Help** for assistance. Note: As you may have guessed, GPFs occur only on PCs with Microsoft Windows installed. See also **bug**.

GUI Graphical User Interface. Some examples of GUIs include the Mac Operating System, OS/2, and Windows. See also **operating system**, **system**, **OS/2**, and **Windows**.

Guide Experienced America Online members who have been specially chosen and trained to help other members enjoy their time online. All on-duty Guides wear their "uniforms"—the word *Guide* followed by a space and a 2- or 3-letter suffix in all caps. If you would like to apply to become a Guide, send a request to the screen name GuideApply or ask a Guide for a copy of the application. Applicants must be at least 18 years of age, have an account that has been active 6 months or more, and be a member in good standing (no TOS or billing problems). To offer a compliment or lodge a complaint against a Guide, send e-mail to Guide MGR. See also **Guide Pager**, **Lobby**, and **uniform**; contrast with **host** and **moderator**.

Guide Pager A feature of America Online that allows you to page a Guide when there is a problem in a chat or conference room or when someone is requesting your password (a big no-no). Simply go to keyword: **Guidepager** and you will be presented with a simple form to complete regarding the problem. Kids have a special Guide Pager of their own at keywords: **Kids Pager**. If a Guide is unavailable, you may report the offending text at keyword: **TOS** or through the button on your chat window. See also **Guide** and **TOS**.

hacker Hackers are (usually) self-taught computer gurus who take an unholy delight in discovering the well-hidden secrets of computer systems. Blighted by a bad reputation of late, hackers do not necessarily denote those who intend harm or damage. There are those, however, who feed upon the pain inflicted by viruses. See also **password scammers**, **phishers**, and **virus**.

handle An outdated term for your electronic *nom de plume*, or screen name. See also **e-mail address** and **screen name**.

header The information at the top (or bottom) of e-mail received from the Internet. Contains, among other things, the message originator, date, and time. Headers can also be found in newsgroup postings. See also **e-mail**, **Internet**, and **newsgroup**.

help room Online "rooms" where members can go to get live help with the AOL software/system as well as assistance in finding things online. There are two types of help rooms: Guide-staffed and Tech Live. The Guide-staffed rooms are located in the People Connection > Public Rooms area (keyword: **People**). On weekdays, there is a generic help room, AOL Help, open from 3:00 P.M. to 6:00 P.M. ET, with platform-specific rooms open from 6:00 P.M. to 3:00 A.M. ET. On weekends, the generic help room opens at noon, and the platform-specific rooms are open from 3:00 P.M. to 3:00 A.M. For more information on the Member Help Interactive rooms, go to keyword: **Help**. See also **Guide**, **Help**, and **MHM**.

home page 1. The first "page" in a World Wide Web site. 2. Your own page on the WWW. Every member on America Online can now create his or her own home page—see keywords: **My Home Page** for more information. 3. The page you go to when you first enter the WWW. See also **browser, favorite place, hot list, page, site, URL**, and **WWW**.

host 1. The America Online computer system, affectionately referred to as the Stratus (which is actually an outdated term, but it is particularly tenacious). See also **Stratus**. 2. An America Online member who facilitates discussion in chat rooms. They are usually chat-fluent, personable individuals with particular expertise in a topic. You can find hosts all over the system, and they will often be wearing "uniforms"—letters in front of their names (usually in all caps) to designate the forum they host for. See also **Guide, chat rooms, conference room**, and **uniform**.

hot chat A safe, euphemistic term that means to chat about (read "flirt") and engage in the popular online dance of human attraction and consummation. Virtually, of course. And usually in private rooms or IMs.

hot list On Mac AOL 2.6 and 2.7 with the WWW browser, this is a place for storing your favorite WWW site addresses. See also **browser, page, site, URL**, and **WWW**.

HTML Acronym for HyperText Markup Language. This is the language used to create most WWW pages; it's interpreted by your WWW browser to display those pages.

HTTP Acronym for HyperText Transfer Protocol. HTTP is the Internet standard that defines Universal Resource Locators and how they are used to retrieve resources on the Internet. Perhaps most importantly, HTTP enables Web authors to embed hyperlinks in Web documents. See also **URL**.

icon A graphic image of a recognizable thing or action that leads to somewhere or initiates a process. For example, the icons in the Write Mail window may lead you to the Address Book, allow you to attach a file, send the mail, or look up help. Icons are activated by clicking on them with a mouse; some may even be used with keyboard shortcuts. See also **keyboard shortcuts**.

Ignore 1. Chat blinders; a way of blocking a member's chat from your view in a chat/conference room window. Ignore is most useful when the chat of another member becomes disruptive in the chat room. Note that the Ignore button does not block or ignore IMs from a member—it only blocks the text from your own view in a chat or conference room. To ignore a member's chat, double-click on the member's screen name from the list of member names in the upper right hand corner of the Chat room window. You will be presented with a dialog box that offers an option to ignore the selected member's text. Ignore can be confirmed on all platforms by either checking for the word *Ignored* next to the screen name in question in the People in This Room window or by selecting their name and checking to see if the Ignore check box is enabled. Once ignored, a member's chat can be reinstated through the same process. See **$im_off/$im_on** for instructions on ignoring IMs. 2. An America Online e-mail system feature that allows you to ignore mail in your New Mail box, causing it to be moved to your Old Mail box without having to read it first. To use, simply select and highlight the piece of mail you wish to ignore in your New Mail box and then click on the Ignore button at the bottom of the window. Mail you have ignored without reading first will appear as "(ignored)" in the Status box. Note: This feature is not currently available on Windows AOL 4.0. See also **e-mail** and **Status**.

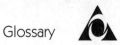

IM (Instant Message) America Online's equivalent of passing notes to another person during a meeting, as opposed to speaking up in the room (chat) or writing out a letter or memo (e-mail). Instant Messages (IMs) may be exchanged between two America Online members signed on at the same time; they are useful for conducting conversations when a chat room isn't appropriate, available, or practical. To initiate an IM conversation, choose Send Instant Message from the Member menu (or use the keyboard shortcuts listed below), enter the recipient's screen name and a message, and finally send the IM by clicking on Send (or using the keyboard shortcuts). If your intended victim is currently online, he or she will receive the IM within seconds. IMs may be exchanged at any time and from any part of the service, although IMs may not be sent when you are in the free area or when you are uploading a file. IMs may be ignored (see **$im_off/$im_on**). It is also possible to send an IM to yourself, and this is often used as a therapy exercise for recovering AOLoholics. IM is used as a noun ("I have too many IMs") or a verb ("I'm IMing with him now"). See also **AOL Instant Messenger** and **IMsect**.

Keyboard shortcuts for IMs:	
Mac AOL:	
Command+I	Brings up a new IM window.
Command+Return or Command+Enter	Sends the IM.
Windows AOL:	
Control+I	Brings up a new IM window.
Control+Enter	Sends the IM.
Geos AOL:	
Control+I	Brings up a new IM window.
Tab to Send button; then press Enter	Sends the IM.

IMsect An annoying Instant Message (IM). They are usually from someone who insists on IMing you when you're busy or when you've indicated you'd rather not talk in IMs. If this happens, you have the option of turning your IMs off completely (see **$im_off/$im_on** for directions). If someone persists in IMing you even though you've politely asked them to stop, it may be considered harassment and you should report it via keyword: **TOS**. See also **IM**.

in-house Used to describe those employees who actually work at America Online's Virginia-based headquarters or one of the satellite offices. May also be referred to as corporate staff. In-house employees are different than community leaders, many of whom are actually volunteers and work from their homes. See also **community leader** and **corporate staff**.

insertion point The blinking vertical line in a document marking the place where text is being edited. The insertion point may be navigated through a document with either the mouse or the arrow keys. Also called *cursor*.

Instant Messenger See **AOL Instant Messenger**.

interactive Having the ability to act on each other. America Online is interactive in the sense that you can send information and, based upon that, have information sent back (and vice versa). The chat rooms are an excellent example.

Internet The mother of all networks is not an online service itself but rather serves to interconnect computer systems and networks all over the world. America Online features the Internet Connection channel, which includes access to e-mail service to and from Internet addresses, Usenet newsgroups, Gopher & WAIS databases, FTP, and the World Wide Web. Telnet access is now available with version 3.0 of the AOL software. To receive mail through the Internet gateway, you need to give others your Internet mailing address, which consists of your America Online screen name (without any blank spaces) followed by the @ symbol and aol.com (e.g., jennifer@aol.com). To obtain more information about the Internet, use the keyword: **Internet** to go to the Internet Connection. For information about TCP/IP access to America Online, see **TCP/IP**. See also **address**, **browser**, **domain**, **FTP**, **gateway**, **Gopher**, **header**, **IRC**, **newsgroups**, **page**, **site**, **URL**, and **WAIS**.

Internet Explorer See **Microsoft Internet Explorer**.

invitation A request by another member to join a chat or visit an area on America Online; made possible by a special feature of the software available on Windows AOL and Mac AOL 3.0. To use this feature, add someone to your Buddy List, select his or her name, and click the Invite button. You will then be prompted to fill in the information regarding the Invite. Note that you may need the address (or URL) or an area in order to invite someone to it. See also **address**, **buddy**, **Buddy List**, and **URL**.

IP (Information Provider) See **partner**.

IRC (Internet Relay Chat) The Internet protocol for chat, allowing one to converse in real-time with others connected to the Internet. Although it's similar to America Online chat rooms, there are many differences—America Online's chat rooms are more intuitive and user-friendly, while IRC chats offer greater control over the environment. See also **Internet**; contrast with **chat rooms**.

ISDN Acronym for Integrated Services Digital Networks. ISDN is a relatively new type of access offered by local telephone companies. You can use an ISDN to connect to other networks at speeds as high as 64,000 bps (single-channel). See also **TCP/IP**; contrast with **packet-switching network**.

ISP Acronym for Internet Service Provider. An ISP generally provides a point to which you can connect and access various Internet-based services such as WWW sites, FTP, e-mail, Gopher, and newsgroups. Some ISPs also provide more advanced services that range from hosting Web sites and servers to wide area networking. See also **FTP**, **e-mail**, **Gopher**, **newsgroups**, and **WWW**.

Java A computer language developed by Sun Microsystems. Java is similar to C++ and is used to develop platform-independent applications commonly known as applets.

K56flex One of two competing implementations for 56 Kbps modem data delivery. K56flex was conceived by Lucent Technologies and Rockwell and competes with U.S. Robotics's X2 technology. Neither X2 nor K56flex is an international standard; look for a finalized 56 Kbps standard in 1998. America Online has begun field-testing this technology; appropriate access numbers can be located at keyword: **Access**. See also **X2**.

Keep as New An America Online e-mail system feature that allows you to keep mail in your New Mail box, even after you've read or ignored it. To use, simply select and highlight the piece of mail you wish to keep (in either your New Mail or Old Mail list (a.k.a. Mail You Have Read list) and then click on the Keep as New button at the bottom of the window. Returning read mail to your New Mail box with the Keep as New button will not change the time and date that appears in the Status box of the sender. See also **e-mail**.

keyboard shortcuts The AOL software provides us with keyboard command equivalents for menu selections. For example, rather than choosing Send Instant Message from the menu, you could type Control+I on the PC (Windows AOL or Geos AOL) or Command+I on the Mac. For a complete list of these keyboard shortcuts, see Appendix B of this book, or check keyword: **Keyword**.

keyword 1. A fast way to move around within America Online. For example, you can "beam" directly to the Star Trek Forum by using the keyword: **Trek**. To use a keyword, simply type it into the toolbar and click the Go button. You can also type either Command+K on the Mac or Control+K on the PC and then type the keyword followed by the Return or Enter key. Keywords are communicated to others in a standard format—Keyword: **Name**. The name of the keyword is shown in all caps to distinguish it from other words around it, but it does not need to be entered that way. Currently, there are over 10,000 public keywords. An updated list of all public keywords is available at keyword: **Keyword**. 2. A single word you feel is likely to be included in any database on a particular subject. A keyword is usually a word that comes as close as possible to describing the topic or piece of information you are looking for. Several of America Online's software libraries, mainly those in the Computers & Software channel, can be searched for with keywords.

lamer A colloquial term for someone who follows others blindly without really having a grasp on the situation. Used frequently within the hacker culture. See also **hacker**.

library An area online in which files may be uploaded to and downloaded from. The files may be of any type: text, graphics, software, sounds, and so on. These files can be downloaded from America Online's host computer to your personal computer's hard disk or a floppy disk. Some libraries are searchable, while others must be browsed. You may also upload a file that may interest others to a library. A library is the best way to share large files with other America Online members. To search libraries available for your platform, go to keyword: **Filesearch** and click Download Software. See also **file**, **download**, **upload**, **search**, and **browse**; contrast with **FTP**.

line noise Extraneous noise on telephone lines that is often heard as clicks or static. While line noise is usually only a nuisance to voice communications, it means trouble for data being transmitted through modems. If you are having problems remaining connected, it may be the result of line noise. This problem can sometimes be solved by signing off, redialing, and getting a new connection.

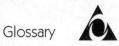

link A pointer that takes you to another place when you activate it (usually by clicking on it). America Online has literally millions of links that criss-cross the service, but they can't compare to the links on the WWW (often called hyperlinks). Links can cross continents without you knowing it. See also **address, browser, favorite place, hot list, page, site, URL**, and **WWW**.

listserv An automated mailing list distribution system that allows a group of e-mail addresses to receive (and often send) e-mail to one another as a group. You can subscribe to a listserv mailing list as a member of America Online. More information and a database of available mailing lists are available at keyword: **Listserv**. See also **e-mail** and **mailing list**.

Lobby Often seeming more like the Grand Central Station of America Online rather than a sedate hotel foyer, the Lobby is the default chat room of the People Connection. When you first enter the People Connection, you will most likely enter a Lobby where any other number of members are also gathered. Some prefer the bustling atmosphere of the Lobby, while others use it as a way station for other rooms in the People Connection. There will usually be a Guide present in the main Lobby at all times. If the main Lobby is full (with a maximum of 23 members at any one time), additional Lobbies will be created and suffixed with 1, 2, 3, and so on. To get to the Lobby, go to keyword: **Lobby**. Stop by on a chilly night for a warm mug of cocoa, but beware of pie fights and desk burnings. See also **chat, chat rooms**, and **Guide**.

LOL Shorthand for "laughing out loud"; often used in chat areas and Instant Messages. Another variation is ROFL, for "rolling on floor laughing." See also **shorthands, abbreviations**, and **chat**; contrast with **body language** and **emoticons**.

lurk To sit in a chat room or read a message board, yet not contribute anything. See also **chat** or **conference room**.

lurker One who lurks in a chat room or message board.

Mac AOL The Apple Macintosh version of the AOL client software. The current version is 3.0. May also be referred to as MAOL. Contrast with **Geos AOL** and **Windows AOL**.

macro A "recording" of keystrokes or mouse movements/clicks on a computer that allows you to automate a task. Macros are usually created with shareware and commercial software and can be initiated with a single keystroke. They may contain something as simple as your signature for an e-mail note or a complex sequence that opens an application, converts the data, saves it in a special format, and shuts your computer down. Online, macros are most useful for sending large amounts of text to a chat area or for automating tasks such as archiving a message board or saving e-mail.

mail controls A set of preferences that enable the master account holder to control who you receive mail from. It can be set for one or all screen names on the account. Changes can be made by the master account holder at any time. To access controls, go to keywords: **Mail Controls**. You can also block junk mail from your e-mailbox at keywords: **Preferred Mail**. See also **e-mail**.

mailbomb What you have when one person sends you an excessive amount of e-mail, which is usually done in retaliation for a perceived wrong. This is a serious offense, as it not only inconveniences you but occupies mail system resources. If you receive a mailbomb, you can report it at keyword: **TOS**. See also **e-mail**, **snert**, and **TOS**.

mailing list A group of e-mail addresses that receive e-mail on a regular basis about a topic in which the participants have a mutual interest. Mailing lists can be as simple as a few friend's addresses that you often e-mail or as complex as a daily digest of news delivered to the e-mailboxes of millions of addresses. See also **address**, **e-mail**, and **listserv**.

massmail The act of sending a piece of e-mail to a large number of members. Also used a noun. See also **e-mail**, **cc**, and **bcc**.

megabyte 1,048,576 bytes of data.

member An America Online subscriber. The term *member* is embraced because "AOLers" are members of the online community. There are currently over nine million members on America Online. See also **online community**.

Member Directory The database of America Online member screen names that have profiles. To be included in this database, a member need only create a Member Profile. Note that profiles for deleted or ex-members are purged periodically, and therefore it's possible to have a Member Profile for a deleted screen name. You can search for any string in a profile. Wildcard characters and Boolean expressions also may be utilized in search strings. The Member Directory is located at keyword: **Members**. See also **member**, **Member Profile**, **database**, and **searchable**.

Member Help Interactive Previously known as CS Live, this is a free area where you can ask questions of America Online staff and community leaders live. Member Help Interactive is open from 7:00 A.M. to 2:45 A.M. Eastern Time, 7 days a week. Here you can get live help from experienced Customer Relations staff working in-house at America Online headquarters or remotely. This service is available in the Unlimited Use (free) area through keyword: **Help**. See also **Customer Relations**.

Member Profile A voluntary online information document that describes oneself. Name, address information, birthday, sex, marital status, hobbies, computers used, occupation, and a personal quote may be provided. This is located a keyword: **Members** or keyword: **Profile**. See also **member** and **Member Directory**.

message A note posted on a message board for other members to read. Message titles are limited to 30 characters. There is no limit to the number of messages in a topic. A message may also be referred to as a *post*. See also **message board**.

message board An area where members can post messages to exchange information, ask a question, or reply to another message. All America Online members are welcome and encouraged to post messages in message boards (or boards). Because messages are a popular means of communication online, message boards are organized with "topics," wherein a number of messages on a specific subjects (threads) are contained in sequential order. Members cannot create new topics, so they should try to find an existing topic folder before requesting a new one. There are two kinds of message boards in use on America Online right now: regular and response-threaded. Message boards may be grouped together in a Message Center to provide organization and hierarchy. Message boards are occasionally called bulletin boards. See also **cross-post**, **folder**, **message**, **Message Center**, **spam**, and **thread**.

message board pointer An automatic place-marker for message boards. America Online keeps track of the areas you have visited by date, allowing you to pick up where you left off upon your return. Once you've visited a message board, clicking on the List Unread button will show you only the new messages that have been posted since your last visit. The pointers are updated each time you return.

Message Center A collection of message boards in one convenient area. See also **message board**.

MHM (Members Helping Members) A message board in the free area where America Online members can assist and get assistance from other members. Located at keyword: **MHM**.

Microsoft Internet Explorer The Web browser software integrated in all AOL 3.0 or later clients. See also **Netscape Navigator**.

modem An acronym for modulator/demodulator. This is the device that translates the signals coming from your computer into a form that can be transmitted over standard telephone lines. A modem also translates incoming signals into a form that your computer can understand. Two modems, one for each computer, are needed for any data communications over telephone lines. Your modem speaks to a modem at America Online through a network of telephone lines provided by AOLNet, SprintNet, or Tymnet, for example.

modem file An information file that stores your modem settings for connecting to America Online. As modems differ, you often need to use a modem file configured specifically for your modem. Luckily, America Online offers over 100 standard modem files you can select from in the Setup window. If you cannot find a modem file for your modem, you can call AOL Customer Service, try the Modem Help area (keywords: **Modem Help**), or edit your modem file. See also **CCL**.

moderator Typically a host who facilitates a discussion during a conference. The moderator usually manages protocol, if used. See also **host**, **conference room**, and **protocol**.

MorF Acronym for Male or Female. Used to ask other members their sex. This happens frequently in Lobbies and chat rooms in the People Connection, but it is considered ill-mannered by most seasoned onliners. BorG is another manifestation of this virus that seems to infect some members. See also **Lobby**, **chat rooms**, and **People Connection**.

MSIE See **Microsoft Internet Explorer**.

Net Abbreviation for the Internet. See **Internet**.

NetFind See **AOL NetFind**.

netiquette Net manners. Cyberspace is a subculture with norms and rules of conduct all its own—understanding them will often make your online life more enjoyable and allow you to move through it more smoothly. Online etiquette includes such things as proper capitalization (don't use all caps unless you mean to shout). Basically, the most important rule to keep in mind is one we learned offline and in kindergarten, of all places: Do unto others as you'd have them do unto you (a.k.a. The Golden Rule). See keyword: **Shorthands** for a primer in America Online etiquette.

Netscape Navigator An Internet browser produced by the Netscape Corporation. Today, Netscape Navigator and Microsoft Internet Explorer are struggling to achieve dominance in the WWW browser market. You can use Netscape Navigator in place of America Online's built-in browser with AOL 3.0 or later. See also **Microsoft Internet Explorer**, **TCP/IP**, and **Winsock**.

network A data communications system that interconnects computer systems at various sites. America Online could be considered a network.

Network News America Online maintenance broadcasts and feedback that are displayed in a small window when transmitted. Network News can be enabled or disabled with the AOL software (select Preferences under the Members menu).

newbie Affectionate term for a new member (under six months). Good places for the new member to visit are keywords: **Discover AOL**, **Top Tips**, **Keywords**, and **Tour**. Contrast with **wannabe**.

newsgroups The Internet's version of a public message board. Available on America Online at keyword: **Newsgroups**. See also **FileGrabber**, **header**, and **Internet**; contrast with **FTP**, **Gopher**, **WAIS**, and **WWW**.

node A single computer or device accessible via a phone number and used by one or more persons to connect to a telecommunications network such as America Online. Everyone signs on to America Online via a node, which is usually local to them and doesn't involve long-distance charges. Sometimes a bad connection is the result of a busy node and can be corrected by trying a new node. See also **packet-switching network**, **800 and 888 numbers**, **access number**, **AOLnet**, **SprintNet**, and **Tymnet**.

online The condition of a computer when it is connected to another machine via modem. Contrast with offline—the condition of a computer that is unconnected.

online community A group of people bound together by their shared interest or characteristic of interacting with other computer users through online services, BBSes, or networks. Because of the pioneer aspects of an online community, established onliners will welcome newcomers and educate them freely in most cases. On America Online, elaborate conventions, legends, and etiquette systems have developed within the community. See also **cyberspace**.

OnlineHost The screen name of America Online's host computer that is used to send information and is usually seen in chat rooms, conference rooms, and auditoriums. The OnlineHost screen name may signal when a member enters or leaves the room. On all platforms, the OnlineHost screen name will give you the result of dice rolled. See also **chat rooms, conference room, auditorium**, and **//roll**.

Open-Apple key See **Command key**.

Option key A special function key commonly found on Mac keyboards. Usually located on the bottom row of keys and labeled Option. Holding down the Option key while another key is pressed will often activate a special function.

OS (operating system) The software that is used to control the basic functions of a computer. Operating systems are generally responsible for allocation and control of a computer's resources. Some common operating systems are System 7, MS-DOS, UNIX, and OS/2. See also **DOS**, **system**, **UNIX**, and **Windows**.

OS/2 IBM's 32-bit operating system that offers a Macintosh-like interface for IBM PC and compatible machines. The current release of OS/2 is called OS/2 Warp and runs Windows 3.1, DOS, and OS/2-specific applications. See also **operating system**, **DOS**, and **Windows**.

packet-switching network (PSN) An electronic network that enables you to access a remote online service by dialing a local phone number. Information going to and from your computer is segmented into "packets" and given an address. The packets are then sent through the network to their destination much as a letter travels through the postal system, only much faster. America Online uses a variety of PSNs to supply local nodes (local telephone numbers) for members' access. Also see **access number**, **node**, **AOLnet**, **SprintNet**, and **Tymnet**; contrast with **ISDN**.

page A document on the World Wide Web; presented in the browser window. WWW pages can contain any combination of links, text, graphics, sounds, or videos. A set of pages is often referred to as a site. See also **browser**, **favorite place**, **home page**, **hot list**, **HTML**, **link**, **site**, **URL**, and **WWW**.

palmtop See **PDA**.

parental chat controls Parental Control enables the master account holder to restrict access to certain areas and features on America Online (such as blocking IMs and rooms). It can be set for one or all screen names on the account; once Parental Control is set for a particular screen name, it is active each time that screen name signs on. Changes can be made by the master account holder at any time. To access controls, go to keywords: **Parental Control**. Contrast with **$im_off/$im_on** and **ignore**.

parity A method of error correction used at the character level when information is sent via modems. Error correction occurs less frequently now—every 1,024 characters isn't rare—so parity is almost a thing of the past.

partner A person or party that supplies material for use on the AOL service and/or is responsible for the content of an area on the America Online service. Also known as an information provider or IP. See also **corporate staff** and **community leader**.

password Your secret four- to eight-character code word that you use to secure your account. Because password security is so important, we've included a number of password-creation tips and reminders. Please read them and pass them along to your friends (and enemies). See also **phish**.

- Your password should be as long as possible (use all eight characters, if you can).
- Your password should not include any word found in your profile, any of your names (or your spouse's/kid's names), or anything commonly found in a dictionary.
- Your password should be a combination of letters and numbers.
- Try using the first letter of each word in an eight-word sentence.
- Or, use a word that is easy to remember and insert numbers into it such as SU8M3ER. (Important: Do *not* use any passwords you have seen used as examples.)
- Change your password often (use keyword: **Password**).

password scammer See **phish**.

PC/Geos See **Geos AOL**.

PC-Link A discontinued service for PC users that utilized a Deskmate-style interface with special support areas provided by the Tandy Corporation. PC-Link was phased out in late 1994. Abbreviated PCL. See also **AOL** and **Q-Link**.

PDA Short for Personal Digital Assistant. A hand-held computer that performs a variety of tasks, including personal information management. PDAs are gaining in popularity and variety, although America Online is only officially supported on the Zoomer (Casio Z7000/Tandy Z-PDA/AST Gridpad 2390), the Sharp PT9000, the Sony Magic Link, and the Motorola Envoy. The Zoomer, Magic Link, and Envoy versions of America Online only allow you to access a limited number of features. PT9000 allows almost complete access, and it can be run on the Zoomer. For those with an HP100LX, HP200LX, or other DOS-based palmtop with CGA capability, a workaround with Geos AOL v1.6 is possible. On the Newton, a shareware program called Aloha allows you to access your America Online e-mail. For more information, check out the PDA Forum at keyword: **PDA**. PDAs may also be referred to as palmtops.

People Connection (PC) An America Online area dedicated to real-time chat. Many different rooms can be found here: Lobbies, officially sanctioned rooms, member-created rooms, private rooms, the AOL Live area, and PC Plaza. You can access this area with keyword: **People**. See also **channel** and **chat rooms**; contrast with **conference room**.

Personal Filing Cabinet On Mac AOL 3.0 or Windows AOL 2.5 and higher, this is a special feature of the AOL software that organizes your mail, files, newsgroups postings, and favorite places. Note that everything in your Personal Filing Cabinet is stored on your hard disk. You can set your Filing Cabinet preferences by opening Preferences from the Members menu and selecting Personal Filing Cabinet. This feature is not currently available for those on Mac AOL 2.7 and lower or Geos AOL. See also **e-mail**, **favorite place**, **file**, and **newsgroup**.

PKZip A compression utility for PCs to compress one file or multiple files into a smaller file (called an archive), which will make for quicker up-/downloading. The latest version is 2.04g. Windows AOL 2.5 and Mac AOL 2.6 (and higher) can automatically decompress 2.04 ZIP archives. See also **archive**, **download**, **file**, **file compression**, **ARC**, and **StuffIt**.

phish The act of tricking members into revealing their passwords, credit card numbers, or other personal information. Phishers will often disguise themselves as America Online staff, but remember that America Online staff will *never, ever* ask you for your password or credit card information while you are online. They may also ask you to send certain files to them or do something that seems odd to you. Phishers should always be reported to America Online so they don't continue to prey on other, less-knowledgeable members. If you get an IM from them, save the IM and then report them at keyword: **Guidepager** immediately. See also **hacker** and **password**.

phisher One who phishes. See also **cracker**, **hacker**, and **snert**.

polling The act of requesting information from everyone in a chat room. For example, a member may ask, "Everyone here who is cool press 1," and the chat room will scroll with 1s for several minutes. This is considered disruptive and shouldn't be done in a public room. See also **chat rooms**.

post 1. The act of putting something online, usually into a message board or newsgroup. 2. A message in a message board or newsgroup. See also **message board** and **message**; contrast with **upload**.

postmaster The person responsible for taking care of e-mail problems, answering queries about users, and taking care of other e-mail-related issues at a site. America Online's postmaster can be reached at, you guessed it, screen name Postmaster. You can also reach other postmasters by simply adding the @ symbol and the domain name you wish to reach, such as postmaster@gnn.com. See also **domain** and **e-mail**.

PPP An acronym for Point-to-Point Protocol. PPP is one method of specifying how computers connect to the Internet through a dial-up connection. See also **SLIP**.

private The state of being in a private room. It is considered taboo by some members to be "seen" in a private room because this is often the communication channel of choice for "hot chatters." In reality, however, private rooms are a convenient way to meet with someone when IMs would get in the way. If you are private and another member does a search for your screen name, they will be told that "<screen name> is online, but in a private room." See also **private room** and **hot chat**; contrast with **chat rooms** and **conference room**.

private room A chat room created by a member via an option in the People Connection; the name of a private room is not public knowledge. Private room names have the same restrictions as chat room names: they may only contain up to 20 characters, must begin with a letter, and cannot contain punctuation. Some commonly named private rooms are rumored to be open 24 hours a day; AOLoholics have been known to make a hobby out of finding these "hidden" rooms. If you happen to stumble into a private room already occupied by other members, proper etiquette calls for you to stay silent for a few minutes to catch any interesting tidbits, and then disappear as silently as you entered. (In fact, etiquette also calls for you to sign off immediately to avoid irate "hot chatters.") See also **chat rooms** and **hot chat**; contrast with **conference room** and **auditorium**.

profile America Online allows each screen name to have an informational file (a profile) attached to it. A profile tells a bit about who you are, where you live, what your interests are—anything you want others to know about you. A profile can be created or updated at keyword: **Profile**. You can only modify the profile of the screen name you are using in your current session, and each screen name has a unique profile. To read another member's profile, press Control+G (Command+G on the Mac), enter his or her screen name, and press Enter. Not all members have profiles. You may search profiles through the Member Directory. See also **member**, **Member Directory**, and **screen name**.

protocol A system used in conference rooms to keep order and facilitate a discussion. When you have a question, you type **?**, when you have a comment, you type **!**, and when you are finished, you type **/ga**. A queue of those waiting with questions and answers is displayed at regular points throughout the conference, and members will be invited to speak by the moderator or host. It is considered impolite and a breach of protocol to speak out of turn. See also **conference room**, **host**, and **moderator**.

public domain A file that's completely free, not copyrighted, and typically posted on services like America Online for distribution (via downloading) directly to the user. Since the producer (or programmer) usually posts the file and the user downloads it, distribution is direct and nearly without cost. Users are generally encouraged to make copies and give them to friends—even post them on other services. Often little, or no, documentation is available for it, though. Contrast with **freeware** and **shareware**.

push technology A technology that allows online services to deliver content to your computer automatically during times when your computer is otherwise inactive. America Online is developing push technology to deliver content to your desktop.

'puter An affectionate abbreviation for one's computer; often employed by enthusiasts and AOLoholics.

Q-Link A discontinued service for Commodore 64 and 128 users. See also **America Online** and **PC-Link**.

quoting To include parts of an original message in a reply. One or two greater than characters (>) is the standard method for setting off a quote from the rest of the message. They are usually placed to the left of the sentence, followed by a space, but they may also be placed on the right. For example:

```
> Wow! That's great! How did you come by it? (Internet-style)

>> Wow! That's great! How did you come by it?

>> Wow! That's great! How did you come by it? <<

<< Wow! That's great! How did you come by it? >>
```

Mac AOL 3.0 and Windows AOL 2.5 and higher members can quote text automatically in e-mail by first selecting it, then copying it (Ctrl+C on the PC or Command+C on the Mac), and then clicking on Reply. See also **<< and >>**.

Re: Short for "regarding" or "reply." See also **e-mail** and **message**.

real-time Information received and processed (or displayed) as it happens.

RealAudio A streaming audio data format that allows Internet users and America Online members to listen to music and events in real-time. The basic RealAudio player is available free for individual use from Progressive Networks at http://www.realaudio.com. See also **AOL Radio**.

release 1. Version. 2. To make something available to the general public, such as a file in a file library. See also **file** and **library**.

remote staff See **community leader**.

return receipt A feature available with the Mac AOL software that returns a piece of e-mail acknowledging that mail you sent to another AOL member (or members) has been received. To enable this function, you must check the Return Receipt check box on the e-mail window before it is sent. Once the e-mail has been read by the member(s) it was addressed to (including those carbon-copied and blind-carbon-copied), mail with the date and time it was read will be automatically generated and returned to the sender immediately. One note is sent for each member that reads the mail. If you check return receipt on a letter that is carbon-copied to 100 people, 100 notes will trickle in as each addressee reads the mail. In general, return receipts are unnecessary as the Status feature can be used to determine when any piece of mail was read. Return receipts are most useful when you need to be immediately informed that the mail was read, usually so you can contact that person as soon as possible. Return receipts should be used sparingly as they can clutter up your mailbox. See also **e-mail**, **carbon copy**, **blind carbon copy**, and **status**.

revolving door A chat or conference room has a "revolving door" when members are quickly moving in and out of the room. Lobbies and many popular chat rooms in the People Connection will often have revolving doors. See also **chat rooms**, **conference room**, and **Lobby**.

rich text Rich text takes advantage of HTML tags to control positioning, size, color, and other attributes of appearance. America Online members using version 3.0 or later can use rich text formatting in e-mail and on America Online's new-style message boards.

Road Trip An America Online feature that is available for Mac AOL 3.0 or Windows AOL 2.5 (or higher) members; it allows you to create "tours" of the WWW and America Online and then present them to others. For more information, see keywords: Road Trip. See also **WWW**.

savvy To be knowledgeable or perceptive at something. Often seen as "computer-savvy" or "online savvy." Contrast with **newbie** and **wannabe**.

screen name The names, pseudonyms more often than not, that identify America Online members online. Currently, screen names may contain no fewer than 3 and no more than 10 characters. They must be unique and cannot contain vulgarity or vulgar references. Also, some combinations of letters are reserved for community leaders (such as Guide or host). Screen names may not start with a number. Any one account may have up to 5 screen names to accommodate family members or alter-egos, and each screen name can have its own unique password. Either way, you cannot delete the original screen name you set up the account with, and the person who establishes the original screen name and account is responsible for all charges incurred by all 5 screen names. To add or delete your screen name, go to keyword: **Names**. Note that when you add a new screen name, it will be automatically blocked from entering Member Rooms in the People Connection. To disable this block, you will need to switch to the master screen name and use the Parental Control feature (keywords: **Parental Control**). See also **address**, **e-mail address**, **member**, and **uniform**.

scroll 1. Refers to the movement of incoming text and other information on your computer screen. See also **scroll bar**. 2. The act of repeatedly typing similar words on the screen or spacing out the letters of a word. For example, if a member typed the word *hello* seven times in a row, with returns between each word, this would be scrolling. So would pressing Return after each letter of a word. Polling also causes scrolling. Scrolling is prohibited in America Online's Terms of Service and you may be given a warning if observed by a Guide or host. Go to keyword: **TOS** for more information. See also **polling**.

scroll bar The bar on the right-hand side of a window; it allows you to move the contents up and down. Also the bar on the bottom of a window for moving things to the left or right. The area on the scroll bar between the up and down arrows is shaded if there is more information than fits in the window or white if the entire content of the window is already visible. See also **scroll (1)**.

search Typically used in association with libraries and other searchable databases, the term *search* refers to a specific exploration of files or entries themselves rather than a casual examination done line by line. See also **searchable**, **database**, **file**, and **library**; contrast with **browse**.

searchable A collection of logically related records or database files that serves as a single central reference; a searchable database accepts input and yields all matching entries containing that character string. The Members

Directory is an example of a searchable database. See also **search**, **database**, **Directory of Services**, and **Members Directory**.

self-extracting archive A compressed file that contains instructions to automatically decompress itself when opened; the software that originally compressed it is not needed. On the Mac, these files can be decompressed simply by double-clicking on the icon and are usually identifiable by the .sea extension. On the PC, they are often identified by an .exe extension. See also **file compression** and **StuffIt**.

server A provider of resources, such as a file server. America Online uses many different kinds of servers, as do several of their partners, such as Air Warrior.

shareware A fully functional file that is distributed with the promise of "try before you buy." Made available with the downloader's good conscience in mind, the authors of shareware ask that if you continue to use their product, you pay the fee requested in their documentation. Shareware is often made available in libraries of online services like America Online for downloading or is distributed via CD-ROM collections. There are shareware programs of exceptional quality and many are often comparable to commercially distributed software. There are a great number of variations of the shareware theme: demoware, which is often fully functional except for printing or saving functions or is only functional for a short period of time; postcardware, which requests that a postcard be sent to the author; contributionware; and so on. See also **file**; contrast with **demoware, freeware**, and **public domain**.

shorthands The collective term for the many emoticons and abbreviations used during chat. These devices were developed by members over time to give information on the writer's emotional state when only ASCII text is available. A brief list is available at keyword: **Shorthands**. See also **emoticons**, **abbreviations**, and **chat**; contrast with **body language**.

sig Short for signature. A block of text that some folks include at the end of their newsgroup postings and/or e-mail. You can designate a sig for your own newsgroup postings through your newsgroup preferences. See also **newsgroup** and **post**.

sign-on kit The free software, registration codes, and directions for creating a new America Online account. There are a number of ways to obtain sign-on kits. Online, go to keyword: **Friend** and follow the directions there to have the kit sent via snail mail. Offline, you can always find a "free offer" card in a magazine, particularly those magazines that have online forums, like MacUser Magazine. You may also find the sign-on kits themselves bundled with commercial software, modems, and computers. Sign-on kits can also be ordered via phone (1-800-827-6364, ext. 7776). If you simply need new AOL software but not an entirely new account, you can download the latest software for your platform at keyword: **Upgrade** or use the AOL Support BBS (see **access number** for information regarding the AOL Support BBS). If you need to download Mac AOL 2.7, use keyword: **Get 27**.

sim Short for simulation. A sim is a free-form game where participants role-play in various scenarios. Sims are generally held in a chat or conference room and may have rules associated with them. Check out the Simming Forum at keyword: **Sim**. See also **//roll**, **chat rooms**, and **conference room**.

simulchat A chat held simultaneously with a radio call-in broadcast. Online chat participants listen to the broadcast and discuss the same topics being discussed on the air. The radio broadcast takes questions and comments from the online chat as well as from callers. Simulchats are organized through the Digital City Chicago Online (keyword: **Chicago**) and Craig Crossman's Computer America (keyword: **Crossman**). See also **chat**.

site A specific place on the Internet, usually a set of pages on the World Wide Web. See also **address**, **link**, **page**, **URL**, and **WWW**.

slideshow See **AOL Slideshows**.

SLIP An acronym for Serial-Line Internet Protocol. The SLIP protocol specifies how computers connect to the Internet through a dial-up connection. SLIP is used by some ISPs to connect their members to the Internet. See also **PPP**.

Smart Art A capability of the AOL 4.0 software; it downloads system art to your computer progressively as you watch. You can stop the art download at any time by clicking a button or closing the window. Smart Art is a significant improvement over the old DOD style of art download, which forced you to wait for new artwork when you opened a window that required it. Contrast with **download**, **DOD**, and **UDO**.

smileys See **shorthands** and **emoticons**.

snail mail Mail that is sent via the U.S. Postal Service. Not meant as derogatory, but to point out the difference between nearly instantaneous e-mail versus the delivery of tangible packages. Despite its relative slowness, snail mail will be used until matter transfer becomes possible. See also **e-mail**.

snert Acronym for Sexually Nerdishly Expressive Recidivistic Trolls. A member who is disruptive or annoying. Contrast with **cracker**, **hacker**, **phisher**, and **troll**.

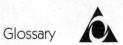

software file A file available in an America Online software library. Often, a software file online is actually multiple files (a program, its documentation, etc.) that are compressed together for shorter uploading or downloading. Every file posted online for download must meet America Online's Terms of Service standards and be checked for functionality and viruses. See also **archive**, **file**, **file compression**, **library**, **TOS**, **virus**, **ARC**, **PKZip**, and **StuffIt**.

sounds See **chat sounds**.

Spam To barrage a message board, newsgroup, or e-mail address with inappropriate, irrelevant, or simply numerous copies of the same post (as in cross-posting). Not only is this annoying, but it is exceedingly bad netiquette. Members who "spam" will often have their posts removed (if in an America Online message board) or find their mailbox full of e-mail from angry onliners (if in a newsgroup). See also **cross-posting**, **e-mail address**, **message board**, and **newsgroup**; contrast with **flame**.

SprintNet Formerly known as Telenet, SprintNet is a packet-switching network that provides members with 1200, 2400, 9600, 14,400, and 28,800 bps local access numbers to America Online. SprintNet networks are owned and operated by U.S. Sprint. To find SprintNet local access numbers, go to keyword: **Access** or call 1-800-877-5045, press 1, and then press 2. See also **packet-switching** and **access number**; contrast with **AOLnet** and **Tymnet**.

Status (of e-mail) An America Online feature that allows you to check whether e-mail has been read yet and, if read, when. The status for an e-mail message will be either not yet read, ignored, or deleted or will show the precise date and time when the mail was read. Status information includes recipients who were carbon-copied (and even those who were blind-carbon-copied, if you were the sender). To check the current status of e-mail on the Mac platform, select and highlight the piece of mail you are interested in (either in the New Mail, Mail You Have Read, or Mail You Have Sent window) and then click on the Status button at the bottom of the window. On the PC platform, first choose the Check Mail You've Sent option from the Mail menu, select and highlight the piece of mail, and then click on the Show Status button on the bottom of the window. See also **e-mail**, **carbon copy**, **blind carbon copy**, and **return receipt**.

Stratus America Online's host computer is known as the Stratus and is actually a collection of computers manufactured by outside companies, including the Stratus Corporation. These days America Online uses other types of computers for specific purposes, but Stratus continues to indicate the collective group of computing power. The Stratus features a fault-tolerant system. This is achieved through "redundant" multiple processors, disks, and memory banks. The Stratus runs 365 days a year, 24 hours a day, and it's backed up by a standby diesel generator in case the power fails.

streaming A method whereby information, usually in the form of audio or video, is delivered to your computer and becomes available for immediate playback. Information that is delivered through streaming technology differs from normal download because you don't have to wait for the entire file to download before it becomes usable. See also **AOL Radio**, **AOL Slideshows**, **download**, and **RealAudio**.

StuffIt A popular compression program for the Apple Macintosh that is currently published by Aladdin Software and written by Raymond Lau. StuffIt is the standard method of compressing Mac files for uploading to America Online's file libraries. With StuffIt, it's possible to combine several files into one archive, which is a convenient way to transfer several files at once. StuffIt files, also called archives, are often recognizable by the .sit extension to the filename. A file that has been compressed with StuffIt is said to be "stuffed." Files compressed with StuffIt can be automatically "unstuffed" when downloaded from Mac America Online or when opened using the Mac AOL software. StuffIt is currently distributed both as a shareware product, StuffIt Lite, and a commercial product, StuffIt Deluxe. Programs to extract stuffed files are free and exist both for the IBM and Mac. See also **archive**, **file compression**, **self-extracting archive**, **download**, and **shareware**; contrast with **ARC** and **PKZip**.

surf To cruise in search of information not readily evident in the hope of discovering something new. Usually paired with another word to describe the type of information being sought. Examples are room surfing and keyword surfing. See also **password scammer**.

synchronous Data communication technique in which bits are transmitted and received at a fixed rate. Used to transmit large blocks of data over special communications lines. Much more complex than asynchronous communication, this technique has little application for most personal computer users. See also **asynchronous**.

sysop Abbreviation for system operator. The individual who operates and maintains a computer service—usually including a message board, a library or collection of libraries, and a chat room. Forum leaders are sometimes referred to as sysops, although that term isn't favored by many on America Online. Pronounced "sis-op." See also **forum**, **host**, and **uniform**.

system Short for operating system, it refers to the software that controls the basic operations of a computer. System can also refer to the collection of components that have a functional existence when combined. Some examples are your computer system, the telephone system, or the America Online system. See also **operating system**, **OS/2**, and **Windows**.

TCP/IP Acronym for Transmission Control Protocol/Internet Protocol. The protocol language that Internet machines use to communicate. Windows AOL 2.5 and Mac AOL 2.6 and higher allow you to sign on via TCP/IP, and you can use other TCP/IP-capable applications through Mac AOL 3.0 at the same time. See also **Internet**.

Tech Help Live See **Member Help Interactive**.

Telnet An Internet protocol that lets you connect to another computer without hanging up your modem and dialing again; you can use the connection you've already established with your local provider. Bulletin boards, online stores, and multiuser games are just some of the things you can tap into using Telnet. Telnet is available on America Online at keyword: **Telnet**. See also **Internet**.

thread In general terms, a discussion that travels along the same subject line. More specifically, a thread refers a group of posts in a message board under the same subject and (hopefully) topic. See also **message board**.

thwapp To hit someone upside their screen name; a virtual slap. For example, you may be ::thwapped:: for requesting an age/sex check in a chat room.

timeout 1. What happens when you've got two computers connected online and one gets tired of waiting for the other; that is, when the hourglass (PC) or beachball (Mac) cursor comes up and the "host fails to respond." You can report problems with frequent timeouts at keywords: **System Response**.
2. The result of remaining idle for a certain amount of time while signed on to America Online. This timeout time is usually 30 minutes, but it may vary with different modems. In this case, America Online's computers are tired of waiting for you. It's also protection against staying signed on all night when an AOLoholic falls asleep at the keyboard.

title bar The portion of a window where the name of the window is displayed. On the Mac, the title bar also may include the close box and the zoom box. See also **close box**, **window**, and **zoom box**.

toast Something totally ruined or unusable. For example, "Well, that file is toast." Also used as a verb.

topic Groupings of messages by subject within message boards are termed topics on America Online. You cannot create topics. See also **message** and **message boards**.

TOS Short for America Online's Terms of Service—the terms of agreement everyone agrees to when registering for and becoming a member of America Online. These terms apply to all accounts on the service(s). You can read them at keyword: **TOS** (in the free area) or by going to keywords: **PC Studio** and clicking on Terms of Service. Also included are avenues for reporting TOS violations to America Online. See also **TOSAdvisor** and **TOS warning**.

TOS warning An onscreen warning given by a trained Guide or host for violating America Online's Terms of Service. These warnings are reported to America Online, who takes action (or not, depending on the severity of the breach). See also **TOS**.

TOSAdvisor In days of olde, this was the screen name to which all TOS violations observed by members were sent to. These days, if you feel something violates TOS, you should go to keyword: **TOS** to report it. The Terms of Service Staff area can also be reached at keywords: **PC Studio > Terms of Service/Parental Controls > Write to Terms of Service Staff**. See also **TOS**, **TOS warning**, and **OSW**.

TOSsable The state of being likely to receive a TOS warning. For example, a TOSsable word is one which a TOS warning could be given to if typed online. See also **TOS** and **TOS warning**.

Tour Guide This book.

trojan horse A destructive program that is disguised within a seemingly useful program. For example, one trojan horse was a file called aolgold, which claimed to be a new version of AOL but actually corrupted files if it was executed. A trojan horse is only activated by running the program. If you receive a file attached to e-mail from a sender you are not familiar with, you are advised not to download it. If you ever receive a file you believe could cause problems, forward it to screen name TOSEmail1 and explain your concerns. Contrast with **virus**.

troll An online wanderer who often leaves a wake of disgruntled members before crawling back under his or her rock. Contrast with **cracker**, **hacker**, **password scammer**, and **snert**.

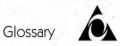

Tymnet A packet-switching network that provides members with surcharged local access numbers to America Online. Tymnet networks are owned and operated by MCI. To find Tymnet local access numbers, call 1-800-336-0149. See also **packet-switching** and **access number**; contrast with **AOLnet** and **SprintNet**.

typo 1. A typographical error. 2. A dialect that many onliners have mastered with the advent of keyboards and late nights.

UDO An older method of receiving updates to the AOL software. Upon signing on to America Online, the UDO sends all the necessary updates to your computer before you can do anything else. Rumor has it UDO stands for Unavoidable Delay Obstacle, but we haven't been able to verify it. Contrast with **DOD** and **Smart Art**.

uniform The screen name that's often "worn" by a staff member, either in-house or remote (community leader), when working online. The screen name usually consists of an identifiable prefix and a personal name or initials. Uniforms aren't usually worn when the member is off-duty. See also **Guide**, **host**, and **screen name**. Some current uniforms include:

AFL	Apple/Mac Forum leader
AFA	Apple/Mac Forum assistant
AFC	Apple/Mac Forum consultant
AOLive	AOL Live leader
FCA/FCC	Family Computing leader
Guide	General system guide
HOST	People Connection host
IC	Computing Company Connection
MHMS	Members Helping Members staff (Tech Live)
On Q	onQ Forum leader
PC	PC Forum leader
PCA	PC Forum assistant
PCC	PC Forum consultant
PCW	PC World Online
Rnger	People Connection Ranger
REF	Reference Desk host
QRJ	RabbitJack's Casino leader
AOLTech	Tech Live representative (in-house)

UNIX An easy-to-use operating system developed by Ken Thompson, Dennis Ritchie, and coworkers at Bell Laboratories. Since it also has superior capabilities as a program development system, UNIX should become even more widely used in the future. America Online does not currently have software for the UNIX platform. See also **operating system**; contrast with **DOS**, **Windows**, and **system**.

Unsend An America Online e-mail system feature that allows you to retrieve mail that has been sent but not yet read. To use, simply select and highlight the piece of mail you wish to unsend from the Check Mail You've Sent window and click on the Unsend button at the bottom of the window. The mail will be permanently deleted and cannot be retrieved. Note that only mail sent to other America Online members can be "unsent" or retrieved; Internet e-mail cannot be retrieved. See also **e-mail**.

upload 1. The transfer of information from a storage device on your computer to a remote computer, such as America Online's host computer. This information may be uploaded to one of America Online's file libraries or it may be uploaded with a piece of e-mail as an attached file. Generally, any file over 16K (with the exception of text files) should be compressed before uploading to make the transfer faster and save system resources. Approved compression formats are ZIP, ARC, SIT, and SEAs. Important note: When uploading to America Online file libraries, be sure that the library you wish to upload to is the last one you've opened after clicking on the Upload button; there is a bug that sends your file to the last opened library regardless of whether it was the one in which you initially clicked on the Upload button or not. See also **file**, **file compression**, and **library**; contrast with **download**.
2. The file or information that is sent or uploaded.

urban legend A story, which may have once started with a kernel of truth, that has become embroidered and retold until it has passed into the realm of myth. It is an interesting phenomenon that has spread to the Internet and America Online. You may come across several urban legends, such as the $250 Neiman-Marcus Cookie Recipe or the Get Well Cards for the Sick Kid. Use keywords: **Urban Legends** for more fun.

URL An address for an Internet resource, such as a World Wide Web page or an FTP site. URL stands for Uniform Resource Locator. You can use a URL address to go to a WWW site by entering it directly into the toolbar or the WWW browser, or by typing it into the America Online keyword box (on Windows AOL 2.5 and Mac AOL 2.6 or higher). There is no list of URL addresses as they are constantly changing and growing. America Online's home page URL is http://www.aol.com. See also **address**, **browser**, **favorite place**, **hot list**, **page**, **site**, and **WWW**.

Usenet See **newsgroup**.

Virtual Places An Internet-based chat room system that used avatars to represent the chat participants and allowed people to collectively tour the World Wide Web. Virtual Places was created by Ubique Ltd., which was later purchased by America Online. Virtual Places was beta-tested on America Online for several months before disappearing from the service. Do not be surprised to see the technology surface again, but this time as a surcharged service.

virus Computer software that has the ability to attach itself to other software or files, and does so without the permission or knowledge of the user. Virus prevention software and information may be found at keyword: **Virus**. Contrast with **trojan horse**.

WAIS Acronym for Wide Area Information Server. A database that allows you to search through huge amounts of information on the Internet, similar in some respects to a Gopher. WAIS databases are now widespread throughout the Internet. See also **Gopher** and **Internet**; contrast with **FTP**, **newsgroups**, and **WWW**.

wannabe Someone who aspires to something. Wannabes are often spotted by their obvious enthusiasm or their frustration at not being able to acquire a skill. Most wannabes are self-proclaimed and are considered a stage above newbies. For example, "He's a Guide wannabe." See keyword: **Wannabe**. Contrast with **newbie**.

Web See **WWW**.

weeding (Yes, that's "weeding," as in a garden of bliss.) An online wedding. Often held in the People Connection chat rooms like Romance Connection or in the LaPub. Nuptial announcements and well-wishes can often be found in The Que message board at keyword: **Que**.

window A portion of the computer screen in which related information is contained, usually with a graphical border to distinguish it from the rest of the screen. Especially important in graphical user interfaces, windows may generally be moved, resized, closed, brought to the foreground, or sent to the background. Some common America Online windows include the chat room window, e-mail windows, and IM windows.

Windows A graphical extension to the DOS operating system used on IBM PCs and compatibles. Developed by Microsoft, the Windows environment offers drop-down menus, multitasking, and mouse-oriented operation. See also **DOS**, **system**, and **UNIX**.

Windows AOL The PC platform's Windows version of the America Online client software. At the time the glossary was written, the current version was 3.0, but version 4.0 was right around the corner. (You can look up your revision number by choosing About America Online from the Help menu and then pressing Control+R). Contrast with **Mac AOL** and **Geos AOL**.

Winsock Short for Windows Socket. Winsock is a standard that specifies how applications should support TCP/IP. Using Winsock, America Online versions 3.0 (or later) for Windows allow other applications such as RealAudio to take advantage of your connection to America Online and the Internet. See also **RealAudio** and **TCP/IP**.

WWW Abbreviation for World Wide Web. One of the more popular aspects of the Internet, the Web is actually a general term for the many hypertext documents that are linked together via a special protocol called HyperText Transfer Protocol (or HTTP). WWW information is accessed through a WWW browser, and browsers are available with Windows AOL 2.5 or Mac AOL 2.6 (or higher). You use URL addresses to get to various WWW sites, or pages, much like you use keywords on America Online. See also **browser**, **favorite place**, **home page**, **hot list**, **Internet**, **page**, **site**, and **URL**.

X2 One of two competing implementations for 56 Kbps modem data delivery. X2 was conceived by U.S. Robotics and competes with Rockwell's and Lucent Technologies's K56flex technology. Neither X2 nor K56flex is an international standard; look for a finalized 56 Kbps standard in 1998. America Online is field-testing this technology; appropriate access numbers can be located at keyword: **Access**. See also **K56flex**.

ZIP See **PKZip**.

zoom box The zoom box is the small box in the upper right corner of the window. Clicking on the zoom box will cause a reduced window to zoom up to fill the entire screen; clicking on the zoom box of a maximized window will cause it to zoom down to its reduced size. Compare with **close box**.

Index

B

D

E

F

I

J

K

L

M

O

Q

R

S

T

U

V

W

X

Y

Z

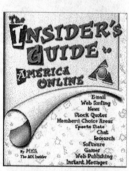

Order your Books and AOL Planner Collections Today

To order by phone: **1-800-884-3372**, ext. 1022
To order by fax: 1-800-827-4595

Item #	Title	Quantity	Unit Price	Total Price
5532	AOL Official Guide the Internet, 2nd Edition		$24.95	
5517	World Wide Web Yellow Pages AOL Edition		$34.99	
5469	AOL Insider's Guide to Finding Information Online		$24.95	
5053	America Online Tour Guide, Version 4.0		$24.95	
5468	The Official America Online Yellow Pages		$24.95	
5461	The Insider's Guide to America Online		$24.95	
5055	Upgrade & Repair Your PC on a Shoestring		$24.95	
6550	America Online's PowerSuite		$29.95	
6708	America Online's GraphicSuite		$29.95	
6748	AOL's Internet AcceleratorSuite		$39.95	
2817	The AOL Mouse Netbook		$29.95	
2807	Watermen Pen for AOL Members		$29.95	
2809	AOL Pocket Netbook		$15.95	

Prices subject to change without notice.

Shipping and Handling:
Under $20.00 = $4.00
$21.00 - $30.00 = $4.25
$31.00 - 40.00 = $4.75
Over $50.00 = $5.00

Subtotal $ ________
Shipping & Handling $ ________
Sales Tax may be applicable $ ________
Total $ ________

ORDERED BY:

Name ______________________________

Address ______________________________

City/State/Zip Code ______________________________

Daytime Phone Number (____) _____ - ________

SHIP TO: (if different from above)

Name ______________________________

Address ______________________________

City/State/Zip Code ______________________________

Daytime Phone Number (____) _____ - ________

METHOD OF PAYMENT

- ☐ VISA
- ☐ MasterCard
- ☐ Discover
- ☐ American Express

☐☐☐☐☐☐☐☐☐☐☐☐☐☐☐☐☐
Account Number

Expiration Date: ☐☐ - ☐☐

____
Signature
(Required for all credit card orders)

Send order form and payment to:
America Online, Inc.
Department 1022
P.O. Box 2530
Kearneysville, WV 25430-9935

BB22

Blue-Wings-Flying

Blue-Wings-Flying

by Elizabeth Willis De Huff

Illustrations by Dorothea Sierra

Addison-Wesley

To my Indian friends of many years
Fred and Alice Kabotie, Isabel Atencio,
Marie Martinez, George and Juanita Blue Spruce
and the memory of Steve Honani,
Regina Cata and Velino Shije-Herrera

Addison-Wesley Publishing Company, Inc.
Reading, Massachusetts 01867
Printed in the United States of America
ABCDEFGHIJ – WZ – 7987

Library of Congress Cataloging in Publication Data

De Huff, Elizabeth Willis, 1892 –
Blue-Wings-Flying.

SUMMARY: A young Indian boy longs for a sister in order to participate in traditional family ceremonies.
[1. Indians of North America — Fiction. 2. Brothers and sisters — Fiction] I. Sierra, Dorothea. II. Title.
PZ7.D3667Bl [Fic] 76-18102
ISBN 0-201-01539-0

Book Design by Designworks

Blue-Wings-Flying lay wrapped in his blanket like a cocoon. His thin mattress was spread on the hard-packed clay floor. It lay beneath the one small window in the adobe house. Dawn was already tinting to rose the thin cloth hanging over the window, and the smell of a match and burning piñon sap filled the room.

Through his sleep, Blue-Wings-Flying felt the pressure of a hand upon his shoulder. He awakened and looked up into the face of Yu-Yu, his mother. She smiled and nodded toward the window.

At once, the boy wriggled out of his blanket. He took his moccasins from beside the mattress and put them on. Then he rolled up the mattress and pushed it against the wall between Yu-Yu's and his father, Tah-Tah's. Yu-Yu covered it with his sleeping blanket. Now all three beds were ready to be used as seats during the day.

Tah-Tah had built a fire in the wood stove and was placing the two stove lids over the blaze. He went to the pole-for-hard-things suspended high on the wall near the door. From it hung bows and arrows, pots, tools and a small bowl in a nest of deerskin thongs. Tah-Tah took a pinch of sacred cornmeal from it. Next Yu-Yu took a pinch. Then Blue-Wings-Flying reached in for his pinch.

The three went out swiftly and walked through the quiet Hopi village. Their moccasins made soft scraping sounds on the hard earth. The air was cool and fresh to breathe. Mingled odors from the porous adobe house walls, the smell of piñon smoke, the faint smell of drying pelts, sheep wool and the corrals came to Blue-Wings-Flying, but he did not notice. He was so used to them.

When they reached the eastern edge of the Mesa, they stood still, awaiting their Helper, the Sun. Soon its golden rim rose above the far off, blue mountain peaks. They blew their pinches of sacred meal from the palms of their hands and gave silent thanks to the Bringer of the new day.

They stood silently watching across the painted land until the whole shining ball had risen into view, shining over the Petrified Forest and the Painted Desert. Then they turned to walk back through the village.

As they walked Blue-Wings-Flying remembered with a start that today was a special day, a day of ceremony for his family. Feathery-Snow-Flake, his mother's younger sister, would put on her black blanket dress and her mother's cotton, wedding blanket cloak and would go to the plaza to grind corn with two other girls. As they ground, a chorus of men and boys would sing to let everyone know that the girls were grown-up and ready for marriage. Blue-Wings-Flying wished he could sing in the chorus. He sighed as he remembered that only the grinder's brothers and her mother's brothers could sing for her. "Everybody needs a sister," he thought sadly.

For weeks Yu-Yu and her mother, his grandmother So-Oh, had been teaching Feathery-Snow-Flake to grind cornmeal. Now she could grind almost as well, if not quite so rhythmically and fast, as Yu-Yu and So-Oh.

Both Yu-Yu's house and So-Oh's house, next door, were burdened with baskets piled with cornmeal. But much would be needed to feed everyone who might come to wish Feathery-Snow-Flake happiness after the grinding that day.

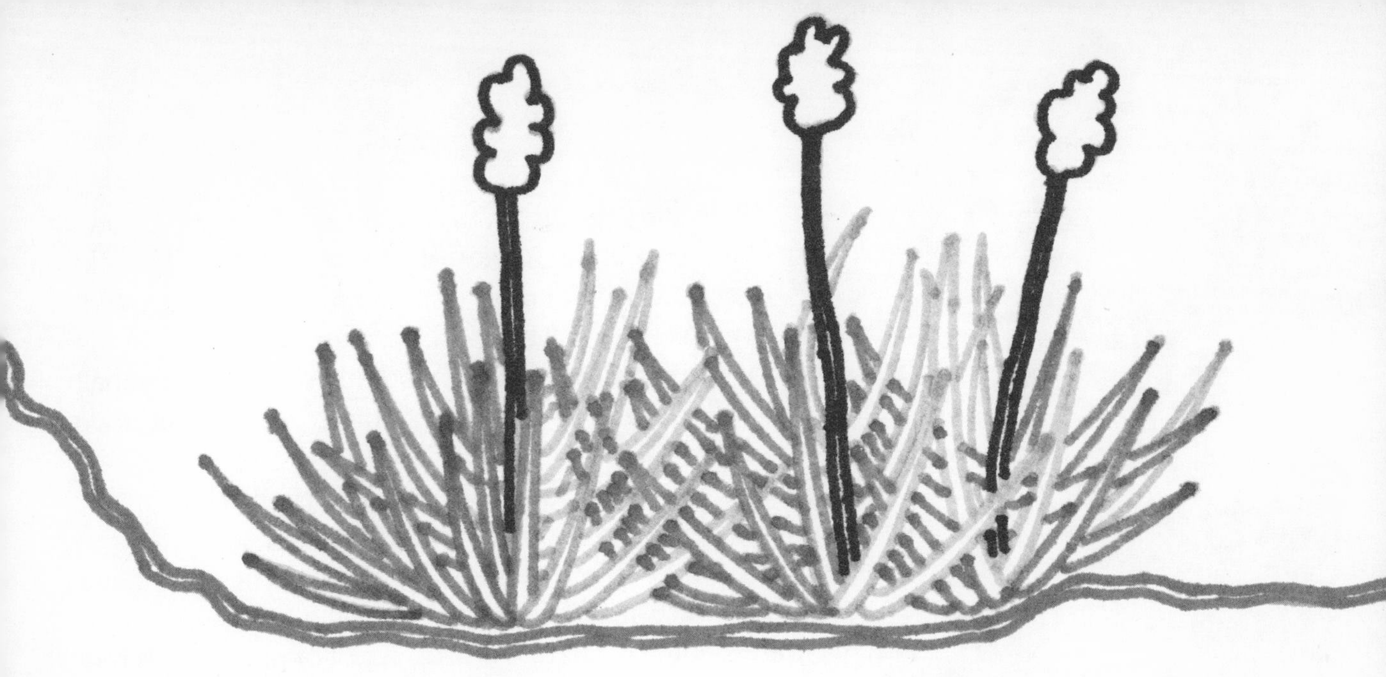

Two days before, Tah-Tah and Blue-Wings-Flying had gone far out from the Mesa to dig up roots of an amole, a yucca plant. Tah-Tah had beaten the roots with a stone against a big rock until they were frazzly strings of wood. Yu-Yu had put them in a big bowl with some water to soak over night.

Then yesterday, she had rolled up her sleeve and whipped and whipped the water with her hand until the bowl was filled with foamy suds. Feathery-Snow-Flake had stuck her head into the suds and begun to wash her long hair. The suds foamed and crackled and disappeared taking with them the dirt from the hair. Yu-Yu pulled strands of hair between her thumb and finger, and they squeaked. "It's clean now," she said as her sister sat up again.

After picking out all the tiny bits of woody string, Yu-Yu brushed and brushed the hair with short straws bound in a tight bunch with thongs. The black hair shone so much it looked dark blue. When Blue-Wings-Flying sniffed it, it smelled clean and fresh like the woods on the mountains.

When they reached Yu-Yu's house, Feathery-Snow-Flake brought a basket of meal to So-Oh. The old lady scooped handfuls of it into a bowl, dampened it with water, put in a little salt scraped from the rock of salt in the tiny storeroom, and rolled it into a ball. Then she patted the ball into a big round pancake and flapped it onto one of the hot stove lids.

Feathery-Snow-Flake put a spoonful of fresh coffee in the tin pot and placed it on the other stove lid to boil. She had put the fresh coffee right on top of the old grounds. When too many coffee grounds accumulated in the pot, they would be emptied and the coffee would be started afresh. A pot of pinto beans had been cooking all the day before. It was put beside the coffeepot to warm up.

Yu-Yu and Feathery-Snow-Flake ate first because they had the most to do. They scooped up the beans with pieces of their corn pancakes and drank coffee from tin cups bought at the trading post.

"The cups shine almost like silver bracelets," thought Blue-Wings-Flying.

While the others ate their breakfast, Yu-Yu brought the one chair, a straight one, into the middle of the floor for Feathery-Snow-Flake to sit upon. With a comb from the trader's she parted her young sister's long, glossy hair down the middle of her head, back and front. She tied each bunch of hair at either side of her head with leather strings.

Yu-Yu kept brushing and smoothing so that every hair would stay in place. Then beginning on one side, she brushed and twisted the hair into a fat rope which she bent around in a figure eight, upside down with the big loop at the top. She tied the place where the loops crossed with the strings already holding up the hair. She pulled the knot very tight with her teeth and hand, and made the big loop of hair stand out from Feathery-

Snow-Flake's head. As So-Oh lifted the lid of the stove to put in another piece of wood, the hair shone like satin from the light of the flames.

"She looks pretty," whispered Blue-Wings-Flying, and quickly put his hand to his mouth. He knew that Yu-Yu had forgotten he was there, or she would have reminded him of his chores. Sure enough, now she said, "There is no room in a beehive for a drone. Go and help Tah-Tah with the animals. You can see Feathery-Snow-Flake when she is grinding."

Blue-Wings-Flying did not want to go, but when So-Oh clicked her tongue and looked at him, he ran out to find Tah-Tah.

The ceremony was ready to begin when Tah-Tah and Blue-Wings-Flying reached the plaza. The three girls, dressed alike, were kneeling on blankets behind three metates, grinding stones, which were fastened into the same crib. On the ground before each stone was a flat basket.

Deep-toned drums beat the rhythm of the men's song. Blue-Wings-Flying liked the strong way Swift-Eagle, his uncle and the brother of Feathery-Snow-Flake, beat his drum and sang. Then he remembered he could never beat a drum for the grinding ceremony, because he had no sister.

The girls scattered corn grains upon the large, rough metate. Then together they pushed down the small handstone over the corn kernels. They rubbed it, bending up and down in rhythm with the drum beats. The song ceased and the drums just rumbled. Then the girls took short straw brooms and brushed the meal from the metates into the flat baskets. Once more the drums beat; the singing and the grinding went on until the meal had to be swept up again.

All stopped when the baskets were piled high and would hold no more. The girls picked up their baskets and each went to her home. Soon relatives would come to be fed and to taste flat cakes made from the freshly ground cornmeal.

During the celebration at Yu-Yu's house, Blue-Wings-Flying giggled when relatives teased Feathery-Snow-Flake and made her shake her head to see if the handsome hair-do would fall down.

The teasing made Blue-Wings-Flying wonder which man would come to leave gifts at the door of Feathery-Snow-Flake, which was So-Oh's door, too. The gifts would say, "Please be my wife." If Feathery-Snow-Flake took them into her home, that would say, "Thank you, I will." If she left them outside, her answer was, "No, I will not marry you." Then the man had to come and take the gifts away.

"I bet the man who comes to leave presents at your door will be a green frog-man," teased someone.

"And an old toad-man will be fighting him to push him away," said another.

Feathery-Snow-Flake laughed happily, as she patted and baked the pancakes.

Blue-Wings-Flying had seen Running-Deer and another young man each weaving a cream-colored cotton blanket with blue and red stripes at the ends. He knew they were wedding blankets. Running-Deer had also killed a deer. He had removed the hide, stretched it, tanned it and worked it between his fists many, many days to make it soft for moccasins. But Blue-Wings-Flying did not know which girls these young men liked.

Men did not like to be seen bringing gifts, so they usually came at twilight when people would not be watching. Neither did they like to bring gifts too soon, so they would wait a few days.

Blue-Wings-Flying grew impatient for something to happen. Tah-Tah kept him busy. Cornstalks had to be chopped up for the sheep and the goat. Cockscomb and chamisa flowers had to be gathered to make red and yellow dye. The dye was for straw, to be woven into baskets, and for yarn, to be woven into blankets, and for coloring thin piki bread. The sheep and the goat had to be taken out to pasture. Water had to be fetched from the well. There was much to do.

But in the late afternoons, Blue-Wings-Flying found excuses to go outside to look beside So-Oh's doorway. Tah-Tah noticed.

"Didn't the old men in the kiva last winter tell you about the Little People with the long red tongues?" asked Tah-Tah.

Blue-Wings-Flying nodded. He was afraid even to mention them. They played cruel tricks on children who talked about them or tried to see them. "I went to sleep, though. I was too tired to hear all the story."

"But you did hear that First Man turned them into little people, because they sneaked around spying and gossiping," said Tah-Tah. "Now they don't want people to do to them what they did to others. They cannot hurt grown people except through hurting their children, so they punish children if children try to spy on them. That should teach us not to peek into other people's affairs or to talk about others. If a boy is busy with what concerns him, his family and their needs, he will not have time to snoop around others." Tah-Tah turned and went inside. He knew that his son would follow him indoors.

That night after Blue-Wings-Flying had rolled himself up in his blanket and lain down on his mattress, he could not sleep. But he had to close his eyes and pretend he was asleep, or Yu-Yu would want to know what troubled him. He could not talk about the Little People with long red

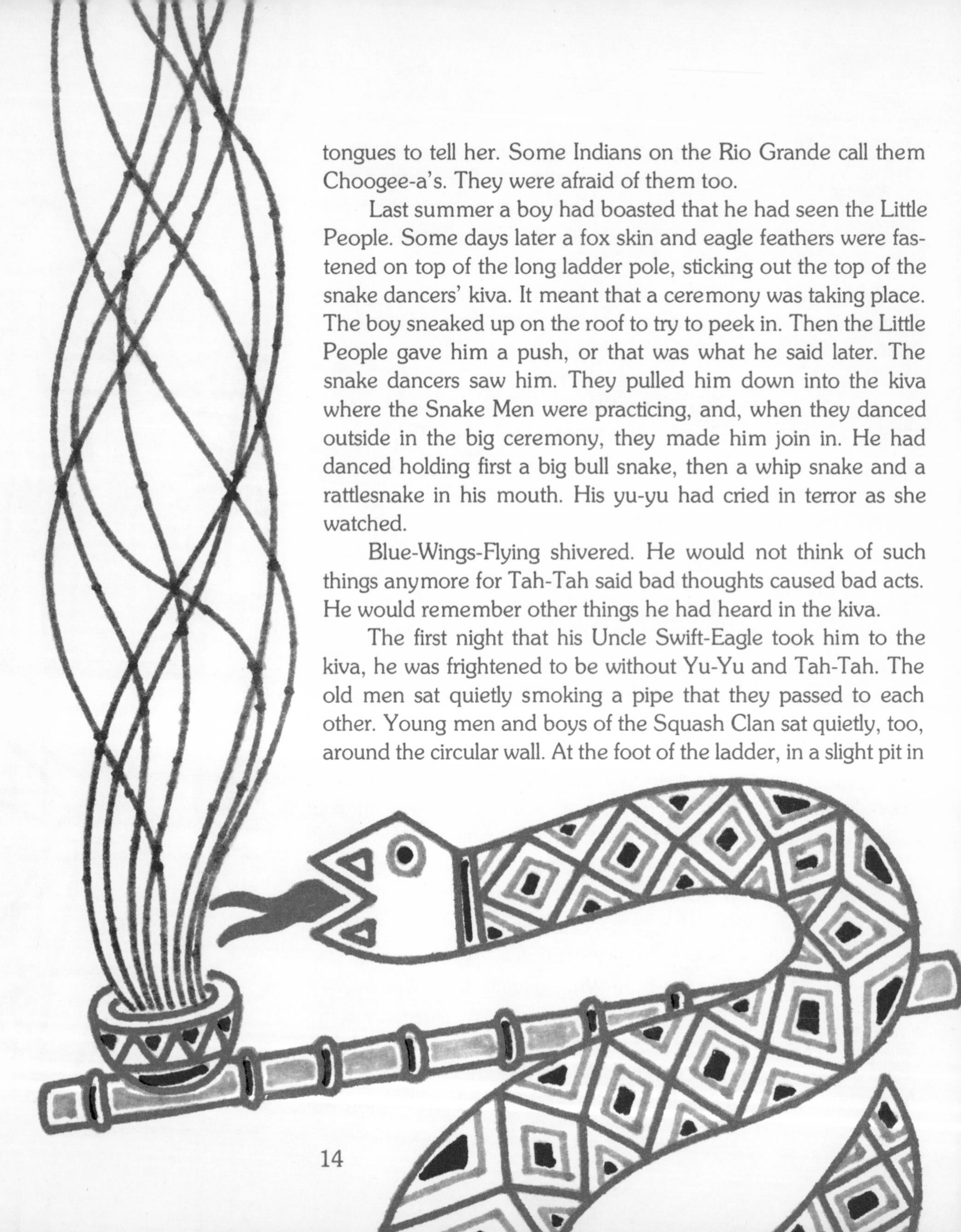

tongues to tell her. Some Indians on the Rio Grande call them Choogee-a's. They were afraid of them too.

Last summer a boy had boasted that he had seen the Little People. Some days later a fox skin and eagle feathers were fastened on top of the long ladder pole, sticking out the top of the snake dancers' kiva. It meant that a ceremony was taking place. The boy sneaked up on the roof to try to peek in. Then the Little People gave him a push, or that was what he said later. The snake dancers saw him. They pulled him down into the kiva where the Snake Men were practicing, and, when they danced outside in the big ceremony, they made him join in. He had danced holding first a big bull snake, then a whip snake and a rattlesnake in his mouth. His yu-yu had cried in terror as she watched.

Blue-Wings-Flying shivered. He would not think of such things anymore for Tah-Tah said bad thoughts caused bad acts. He would remember other things he had heard in the kiva.

The first night that his Uncle Swift-Eagle took him to the kiva, he was frightened to be without Yu-Yu and Tah-Tah. The old men sat quietly smoking a pipe that they passed to each other. Young men and boys of the Squash Clan sat quietly, too, around the circular wall. At the foot of the ladder, in a slight pit in

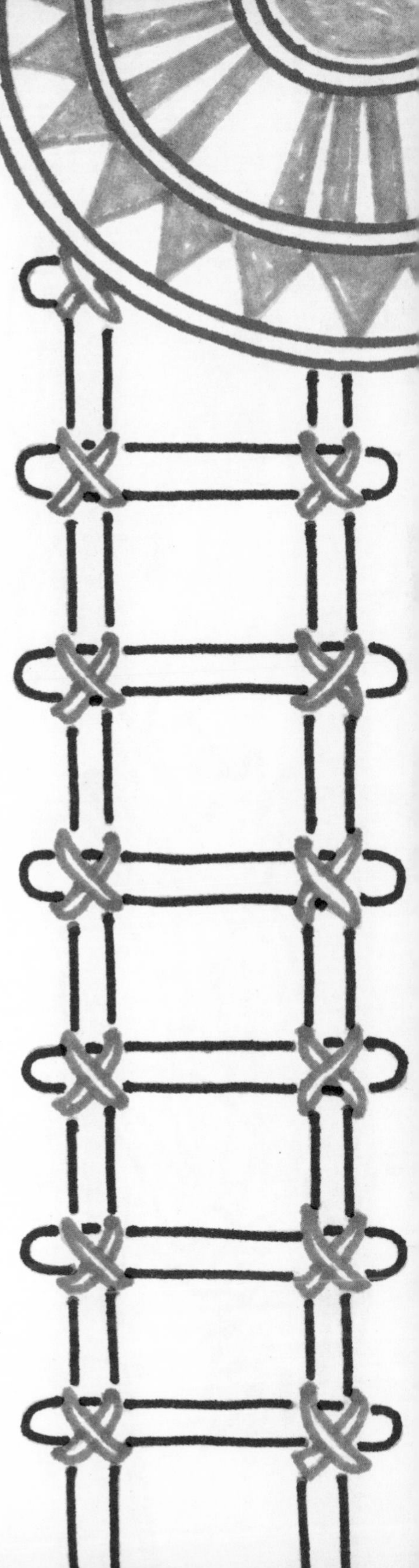

the clay floor, a wood fire burned. When someone came or went on the ladder or moved around in the room, the smoke swirled around the kiva. It stung Blue-Wings-Flying's eyes and almost choked him. Then, when no one was moving, the smoke went straight up from the pit to the opening above. There were cloud and rain symbols painted on the walls with colored dyes, and there were marks on the wall showing where sunlight touched it in daytime. The marks told the time of the day and the seasons of the year.

When the old men finished smoking and the story teller started talking, Blue-Wings-Flying was already very tired. So every time he went to the kiva, he heard only a little bit before he fell asleep.

He had heard this much — everybody and everything had come up from the Underworlds, and everybody would go back to Underworlds when they died. At first all the people — the animal people and the men-and-women people—were big like giants. As more and more people were born, the round Underworld had become too crowded, so the good, smart people had built a ladder and climbed into a new world.

When the people came into this world, he remembered, it was all dark. First Man, who was the leader, scraped up a pile of shining mica rocks and made a big round shining disc. He cut down giant trees and made a ladder to reach the Sky. Up there he placed the shining disc.

The Owl-people, the Fox-people and all the animal people who prowl and feed at night hooted and howled, "We want it dark! We want it dark!"

So First Man took down the shining disc. "Who will carry this disc across the sky for people who want light for half a day, and then take it into the Underworld for the other half day for those who want the world dark?"

A man called out, "I will. I know the Underworld-people. I'll carry the shining disc across from East to West. Then I'll go into the Underworld to visit and come back into the East to make a new day. But I will not do so if I can be seen and watched."

"Fine!" said First Man. "On a day of fair skies that are blue, you will ride a blue horse and wear a blue robe. On days of billowy, white clouds and cloudiness, your horse will be a pinto and will be spotted. On gray days you will wear gray and ride a gray horse. You will always be invisible to other men."

Again the night-people complained. "We need a little light to see our prey. It is now too dark."

So First Man made a smaller disc that was not so shiny. He fastened on it a long, invisible thong of hide. He told Sun-Carrier to tie the other end of the thong to his saddle and let the new disc drag far behind him. Sometimes it stays up straight and is round like the sun disc. Sometimes it topples and one sees only a part of the shining disc. So the night-people had a moon. Still they complained.

"Well," said First Man, "I will make many small shining discs and place them here and there in the sky to shine all the time. They will give some light to help when the moon is not dragging right."

First Man got his tall ladder and climbed up to the sky with a big bag of shiny mica. He was busy placing tiny discs — stars — over the dark sky. He had not noticed that Giant Coyote, the trickster, had climbed up behind him. Coyote grabbed the bag from First Man and blew the mica across the sky to make the Milky Way. He blew so hard that he tumbled from the ladder. His landing made a deep crack in the earth, a great canyon that is still there today. "We go near the rim of it to get our salt," ended the story teller.

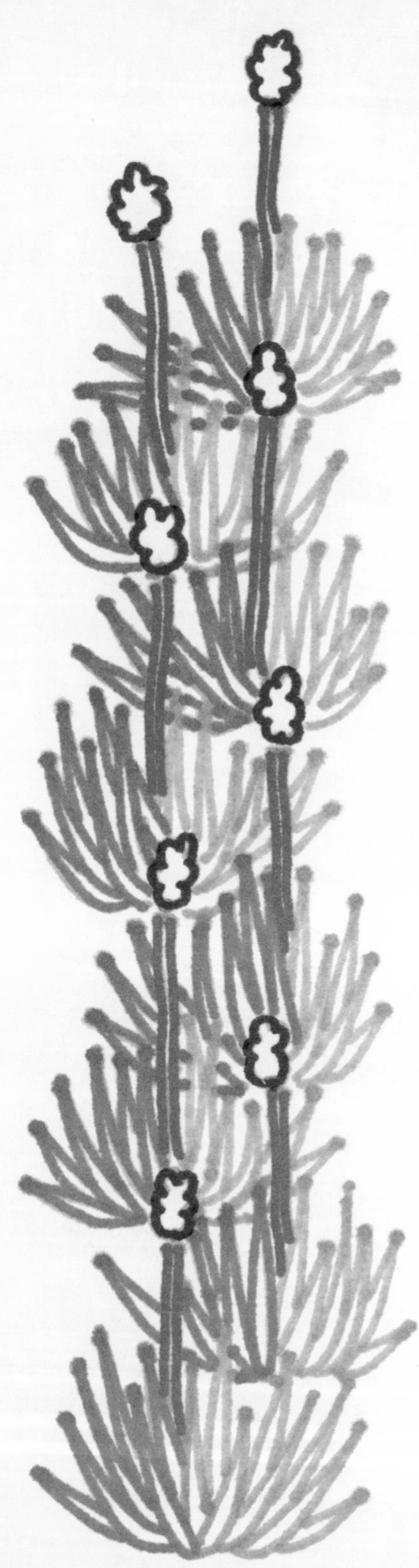

Blue-Wings-Flying liked that story; his thoughts had journeyed far from fear of the Little People. He heard the soft breathing of Yu-Yu. Tah-Tah gave a tiny snore and turned himself over. Quick steps outside with the soft scrape of moccasins, the opening and closing of a door gave him comfort. It told him that somebody else was also awake, some neighbor coming home late from his work.

A piece of charred wood fell in the stove, sharpening for the moment the scent of piñon smoke still lingering in the air. Blue-Wings-Flying yawned, took a deep breath of the smoke smell, closed his eyes and went to sleep.

The next morning, Blue-Wings-Flying went with Yu-Yu to cut long yucca leaves for basket weaving. The leaves were too tough for Yu-Yu to cut them alone. They didn't return until late afternoon. As soon as they had eaten baked beans, bread and coffee for their supper, Yu-Yu handed a bunch of the yucca leaves to Blue-Wings-Flying.

"Take this to So-Oh. She wants to begin splitting this to-night so she can start a new basket in the morning. Her teeth are old, and her fingernails break easily. She can only hold the leaf with her teeth and split it with her thumbnail for a short time. That makes her work slowly." Yu-Yu also handed him a bunch of long, dried grass, about which the yucca strips would be wound.

Blue-Wings-Flying took them and ran out. Suddenly he stopped. He saw Badger, a gray-haired man, placing a big pile of things beside So-Oh's door for Feathery-Snow-Flake. Badger owned the trading post on the Mesa. His son-in-law took charge of it now for Badger had so many things to look after. He owned more sheep than anyone else.

He was carrying piles of Navajo blankets, piles of silver bracelets set with turquoise stones and every other treasure that Blue-Wings-Flying could imagine — blankets, jewelry, boxed and canned foods and more things.

"How did Badger get it all here?" Blue-Wings-Flying wondered. Quickly he went back into his house. He looked with wonder at Tah-Tah, as he, too, came in.

"I wasn't snooping," he said to his father. "Yu-Yu sent me out. But I saw Badger going away from So-Oh's door, and he left a great, big pile of all kinds of things. But I don't want her to marry an old man like that. His wife is dead and his children are older than Feathery-Snow-Flake."

"It is for Feathery-Snow-Flake to decide. Not for us," said Tah-Tah.

"Swift-Eagle will talk to her about marriage to an old man," said Yu-Yu. "Put the yucca and grass with the others. You can take them to So-Oh tomorrow. Run like the blowing wind now and tell Swift-Eagle what you saw and come right back here."

In a few moments, Blue-Wings-Flying was back. Yu-Yu looked at him with a question in her eyes. He nodded and said, "Yes, Swift-Eagle has come to So-Oh's."

"Come," said Tah-Tah. "Let's start cutting a new thong from the cowhide. The old one fastening the sheep corral is badly worn."

Blue-Wings-Flying watched Tah-Tah get the hide from the tiny storage room. He sat on a sheepskin on the floor to hold it tight for his father. He knew that Tah-Tah wanted to keep him from thinking about old man Badger and Feathery-Snow-Flake. They cut until Tah-Tah saw Blue-Wings-Flying nod and knew he was sleepy.

"That's enough for tonight," he said, as he went and put the hide, the cut thongs and the knife away.

Soon all three, Blue-Wings-Flying, Yu-Yu and Tah-Tah were asleep.

Next morning, on their way to greet the Sun-Carrier, they saw the pile of gifts still beside So-Oh's doorway. They smiled and walked on quickly. Very soon afterward the young man, Running Deer, whom Blue-Wings-Flying had seen weaving the blanket wrap and softening deerskin for moccasins, brought them and left them beside Feathery-Snow-Flake's door. She did not wait for him to get out of sight before she opened the door, grabbed them up, hugged them and took them inside.

Badger took his gifts to a widow with two children and she accepted them. Feathery-Snow-Flake went with her sleeping blanket and mattress to the home of Running-Deer's mother to grind corn for his mother for one week. Running-Deer still slept with his young clansmen in their kiva. He measured his bride-to-be's feet on cowhide he had tanned for soles, and in the kiva he made her some moccasins out of the deerskin with tops laced up with narrow thongs. He made them blue with a wash of copper dust and trimmed them at the top with porcupine quills.

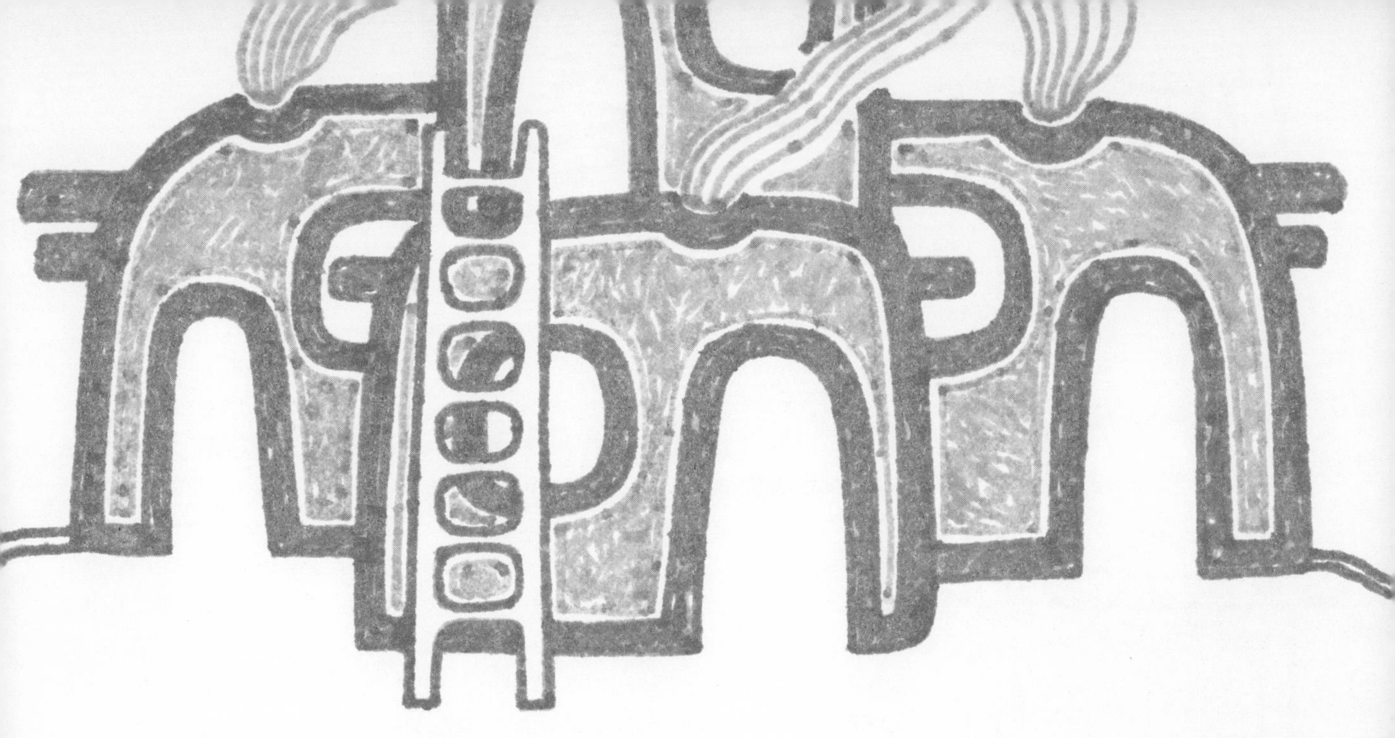

Blue-Wings-Flying had never seen such pretty ones before. Yu-Yu's wedding moccasins had been worn in so many ceremonies that the blue had worn off, and they were all scuffed. They were not pretty any more.

Then Feathery-Snow-Flake and Running-Deer stayed at So-Oh's house while they built a one-room house with a tiny storeroom on top of So-Oh's house. They left a little space in front of the house to stand on while they opened their door to enter. Running-Deer made a ladder to climb up to the little porch. Swift-Eagle and Tah-Tah helped with the building of the walls, and Yu-Yu and Running-Deer's sisters helped to plaster the walls with adobe mud.

"It is nice to have a new uncle and a new house to visit," thought Blue-Wings-Flying. He helped, too, to bring pails of adobe to the women. They would take it up in their hands and rub it with their palms against the rough stonewalls.

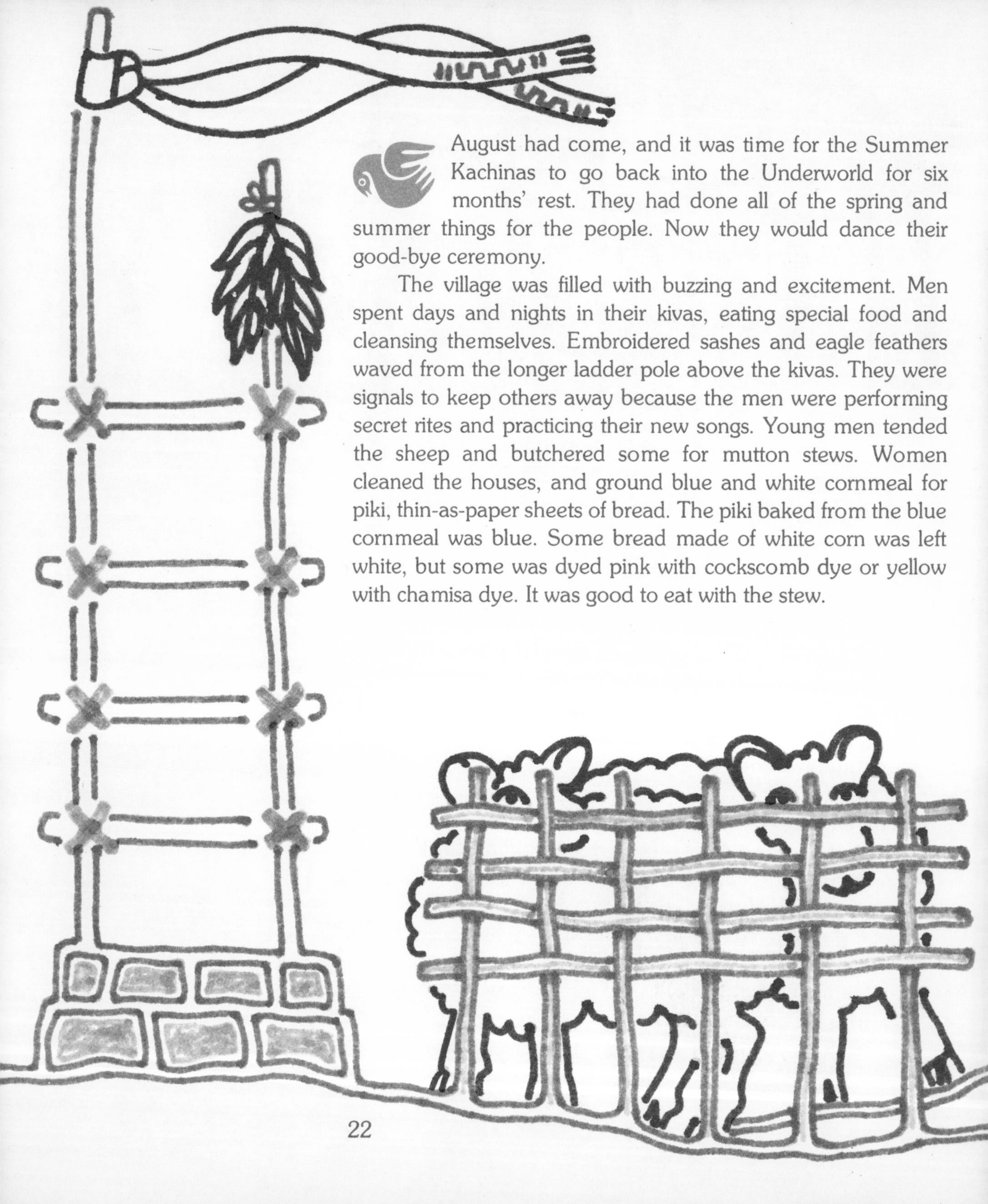

August had come, and it was time for the Summer Kachinas to go back into the Underworld for six months' rest. They had done all of the spring and summer things for the people. Now they would dance their good-bye ceremony.

The village was filled with buzzing and excitement. Men spent days and nights in their kivas, eating special food and cleansing themselves. Embroidered sashes and eagle feathers waved from the longer ladder pole above the kivas. They were signals to keep others away because the men were performing secret rites and practicing their new songs. Young men tended the sheep and butchered some for mutton stews. Women cleaned the houses, and ground blue and white cornmeal for piki, thin-as-paper sheets of bread. The piki baked from the blue cornmeal was blue. Some bread made of white corn was left white, but some was dyed pink with cockscomb dye or yellow with chamisa dye. It was good to eat with the stew.

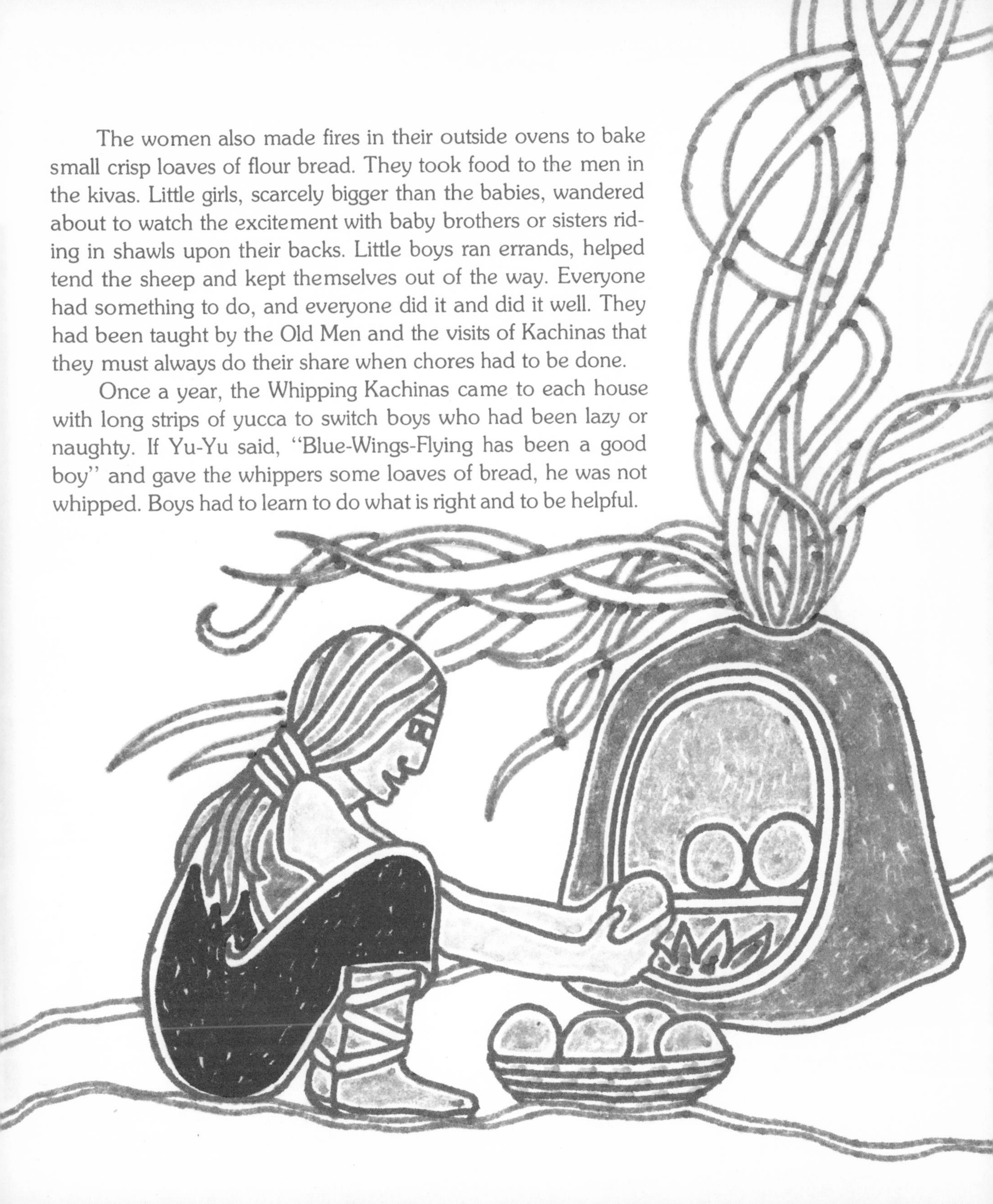

The women also made fires in their outside ovens to bake small crisp loaves of flour bread. They took food to the men in the kivas. Little girls, scarcely bigger than the babies, wandered about to watch the excitement with baby brothers or sisters riding in shawls upon their backs. Little boys ran errands, helped tend the sheep and kept themselves out of the way. Everyone had something to do, and everyone did it and did it well. They had been taught by the Old Men and the visits of Kachinas that they must always do their share when chores had to be done.

Once a year, the Whipping Kachinas came to each house with long strips of yucca to switch boys who had been lazy or naughty. If Yu-Yu said, "Blue-Wings-Flying has been a good boy" and gave the whippers some loaves of bread, he was not whipped. Boys had to learn to do what is right and to be helpful.

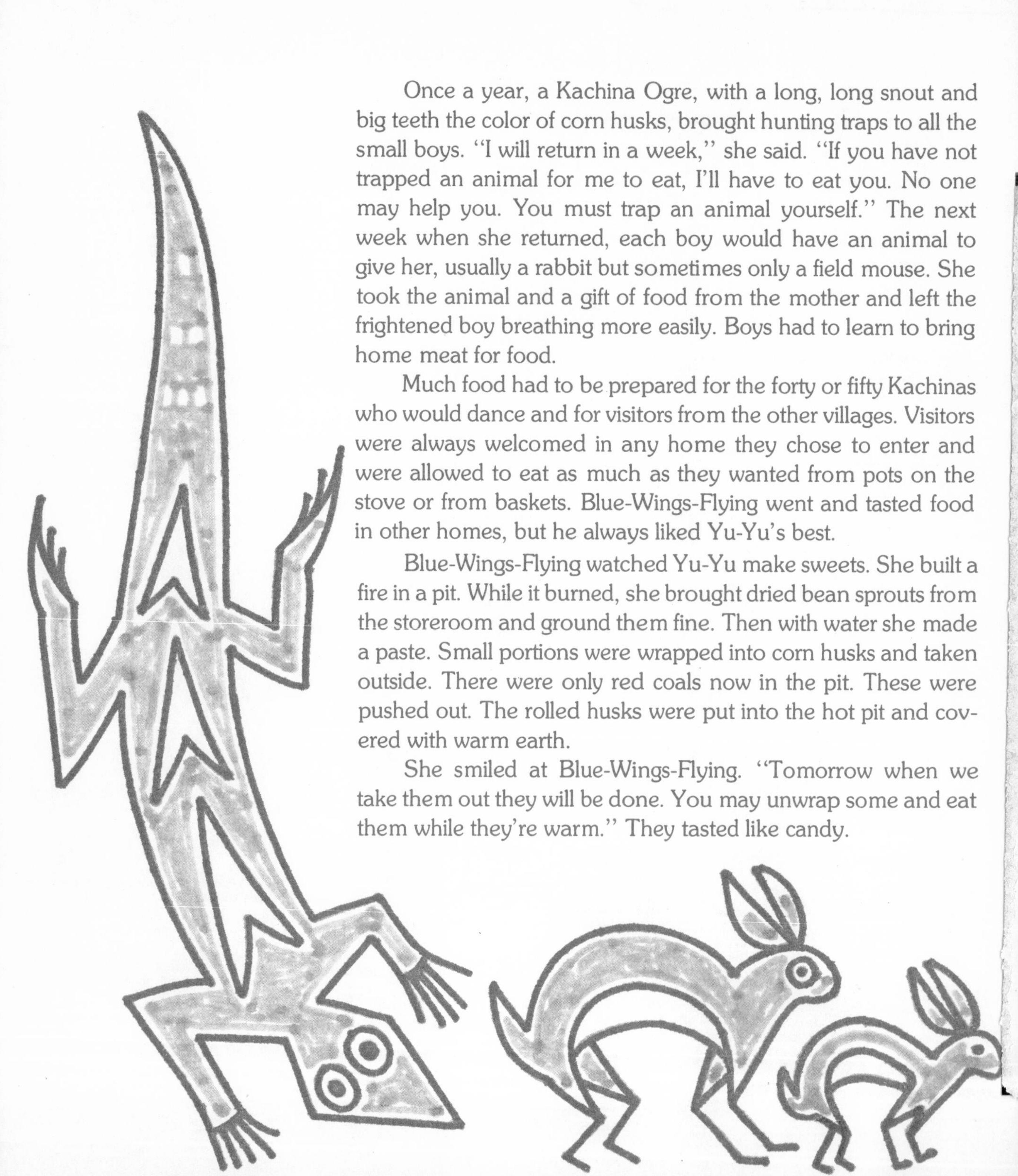

Once a year, a Kachina Ogre, with a long, long snout and big teeth the color of corn husks, brought hunting traps to all the small boys. "I will return in a week," she said. "If you have not trapped an animal for me to eat, I'll have to eat you. No one may help you. You must trap an animal yourself." The next week when she returned, each boy would have an animal to give her, usually a rabbit but sometimes only a field mouse. She took the animal and a gift of food from the mother and left the frightened boy breathing more easily. Boys had to learn to bring home meat for food.

Much food had to be prepared for the forty or fifty Kachinas who would dance and for visitors from the other villages. Visitors were always welcomed in any home they chose to enter and were allowed to eat as much as they wanted from pots on the stove or from baskets. Blue-Wings-Flying went and tasted food in other homes, but he always liked Yu-Yu's best.

Blue-Wings-Flying watched Yu-Yu make sweets. She built a fire in a pit. While it burned, she brought dried bean sprouts from the storeroom and ground them fine. Then with water she made a paste. Small portions were wrapped into corn husks and taken outside. There were only red coals now in the pit. These were pushed out. The rolled husks were put into the hot pit and covered with warm earth.

She smiled at Blue-Wings-Flying. "Tomorrow when we take them out they will be done. You may unwrap some and eat them while they're warm." They tasted like candy.

The Sun-Carrier was riding his blue horse. The warm, dry air was filled with a bouquet of smells — freshly ground corn, bubbling mutton stew, boiling coffee and, the most delightful, baking bread, all blended with the aroma of burning piñon and juniper sticks and the peculiar scent of old, absorbent walls.

In midmorning, a call, "Hoodle-Who!" came from far away. All the villagers hurried to the western edge of the Mesa. In the distance, they could see groups of Niman Kachinas, approaching the village from the entrance to the Underworld, among the San Francisco peaks. Wooden tablitas on the masks covering their heads shone with colored sun, clouds, rain and other symbols; white eagle feathers on top waved in the breeze from their rapid walking. Once in a while one called "Hoodle-Who!" Women rushed back to their homes. Many children followed. But some children stayed to watch until the eerie figures reached the foot of the path leading up on the Mésa. Then awed and frightened by the Kachinas, they ran home to their mothers.

Blue-Wings-Flying stood close beside Yu-Yu in the adobe house, waiting. Soon a Kachina entered, and with funny talk,

handed Yu-Yu a bunch of fresh bean sprouts. They were not only tender and good to eat but, having been ceremonially grown in the kiva, they would bring plenty of food to her home. Yu-Yu put them into the pot of boiling water that she had waiting on the stove. She salted it and let it cook a while, so that every member of her family could have a bit to eat. While the families were thus occupied, the Kachinas formed a long line in the plaza and began to stamp their feet and chant. The families stepped from their houses and stood about in groups watching.

The deep voices of the Kachinas echoed among the cracks and cliffs, doubling the sound of the chant. Their stamping feet paused at intervals, emphasizing the importance of certain words in the songs. It made Blue-Wings-Flying think again of the great Kachina deeds that the Old Men told about in the kiva. Everyone was silent and thoughtful. When this first part of the dance was over, the Kachinas went among the children handing out gifts. Each boy received a decorated bow and arrows. Some also received throwing sticks and some moccasins, newly reddened with red clay wash.

Most of the little girls were given Kachina dolls to hang on their walls. One was given an Owl Kachina. She quickly covered it with her skirt and ran to hide it in her house. The real Owl Kachina flies away with cry-babies, and the little girl knew she had been given the doll because she had been crying too much. The other little girls looked at theirs with smiles and showed them to each other. They did not dare to hug them for the colors would rub off. Around the neck of each doll was a string with a loop. Soon they would be hanging on the walls of the little girls' homes, where they would remain always as reminders of what the little figures had come to teach them. Many babies were given figures with Kachina heads but flat bodies; these were given only as toys for the babies to play with.

Blue-Wings-Flying felt a bit of envy when he looked at the Kachina dolls. They would look pretty hanging on a white wall. There were none in his house for he had no sister to receive a doll. The ones that were given long ago to Yu-Yu were still hanging on So-Oh's wall. Yu-Yu would never take them away for the dolls were not ever supposed to be moved. He wanted pretty dolls on the wall at Yu-Yu's house. He wanted a sister.

The Niman Kachinas danced again in the afternoon before they went into kivas to feast. They would not go back into the Underworld until after dark. The men of the village were helping the Kachinas, so they did not get home until even later. Yu-Yu had Tah-Tah's bed all ready for him. She was very tired, so she and Blue-Wings-Flying were asleep and did not hear Tah-Tah come home.

For many days, there was much work for Tah-Tah and his son. Water had to be brought from the spring. Fields had to be smoothed over for the winter. Wood had to be cut, hauled to the Mesa, chopped, brought up on the burro's wood saddle and stacked by the house wall. Sheep had to be dipped to disinfect their wool. Bark of certain trees, far away, had to be cut in a way not to hurt the trees. The bark was used to dye yucca strips a warm brown color for baskets. Tah-Tah began to teach Blue-Wings-Flying how to clean wool, to dye some of it and to make it into yarn with his distaff. Blue-Wings-Flying was awkward. He grew discouraged. Tah-Tah noticed, as he always did, how Blue-Wings-Flying was feeling and thinking.

"Learning," said Tah-Tah, "is like climbing up the Mesa path. One does not get here at once with the first step. But step by step one goes ahead until he reaches the top. It takes time, and it takes first one step, and then another step; on and on, taking many steps. In a year, if you try over and over, you should spin fine yarn, good enough to weave."

Blue-Wings-Flying noticed that Yu-Yu was getting a bigger stomach. She grew tired more quickly, and So-Oh helped her more with heavy things. He knew what was happening, but it was something that one pretended not to see. It was private to Yu-Yu, so no one mentioned it. But he thought much about it. He wanted, he needed a sister. As he went to sleep one night, he decided what he would do. He would do it the very next day.

The sun was setting. Growing bigger and bigger, it went down below the far-away blue mountains, slipping into the Underworld. Blue-Wings-Flying, holding his bow and arrows, stood watching it.

Blue-Wings-Flying wanted the Sun-Carrier to take a message for him to the Mother Kachina in the Underworld. It was not easy to talk with someone he could not see. He looked all around the sun. Its brightness hid its Carrier. It was no use to look. Blue-Wings-Flying knew he would never see the Sun-Carrier nor his horse. But he knew the Carrier was there, holding the sun. So he whispered:

"Great Sun-Carrier. I'm the only child in my home. Please ask Mother Kachina to bring Yu-Yu a baby sister for me. A baby brother would be more fun to play with. But we need a baby sister. Houses belong to mothers, so there must be a sister in every house to grow up and have children. Then we will always have a family."

Blue-Wings-Flying was wishing so hard that he forgot about the bow and arrows in his hand. Suddenly one arrow slipped out. *Pinck*, he heard, as it struck the ground and bounced over the cliff. Putting down the others quickly, he looked over the Mesa's edge. The arrow had not fallen far. He squatted down to get it, and a round stone shot out from under his moccasin like a stone from a slingshot. With a gasp of surprise and horror, he fell, rolling down against a ledge.

He landed on his stomach and grew dizzy as he looked at the sheer wall going down, down, down to the stony bottom of

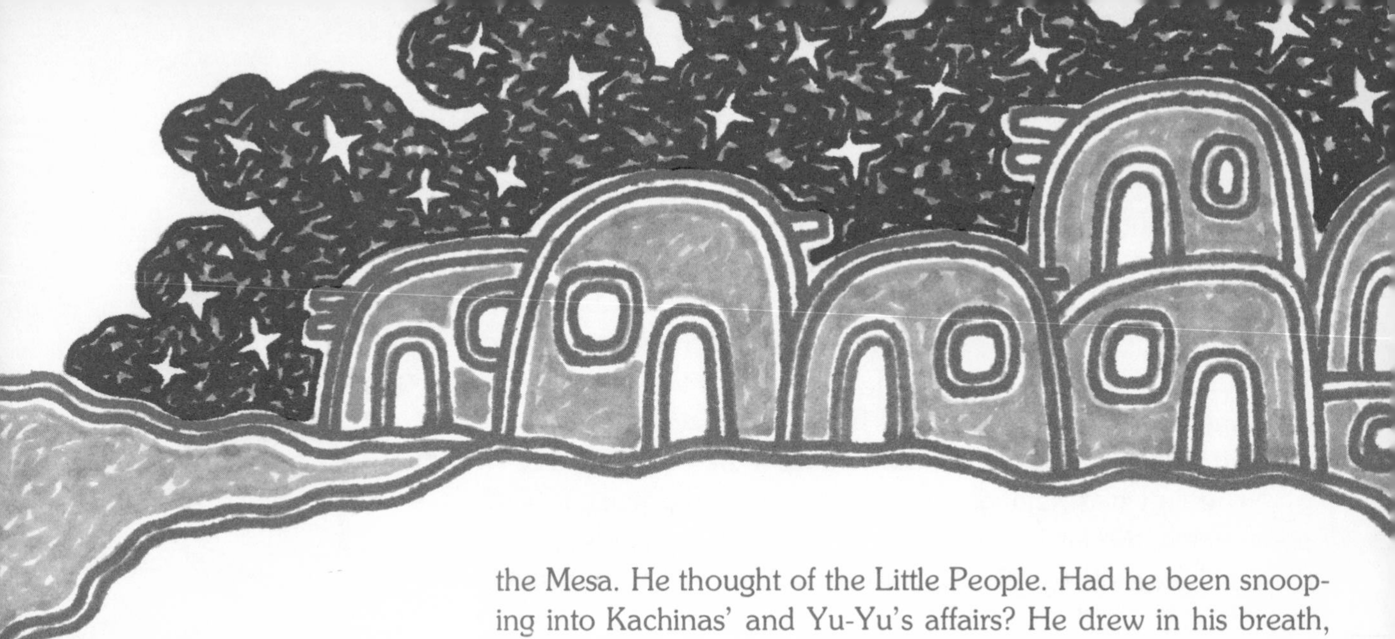

the Mesa. He thought of the Little People. Had he been snooping into Kachinas' and Yu-Yu's affairs? He drew in his breath, turned his face to the cliff and slowly, carefully got up on his knees. Then shivering and sweating he gingerly climbed to his feet, holding tight to ridges in the Mesa wall.

One by one, he yelled the names of his playmates. His voice echoed hollow and harsh between the canyon walls. No answer came. "They have gone into their houses," he thought, holding back tears.

Clinging tightly to the rough wall, he turned his head. He saw that the bright colors the Sun-Carrier dragged behind him were fading. Night was coming. The air was chill. Like cold claws, it slipped through his thin shirt and pants.

Blue-Wings-Flying heard doors shutting for the night. The patter of sheep's hooves drifted up from the corrals below as the animals huddled closer together. Could he slide all the way down and be with the sheep? No, there were too many ledges to stop him.

Far away a coyote gave his first howl of the night. Another answered, and Blue-Wings-Flying shuddered. Sometimes they came close to try to get a sheep. They could climb steep walls. He listened closely for some helpful sign. He heard none.

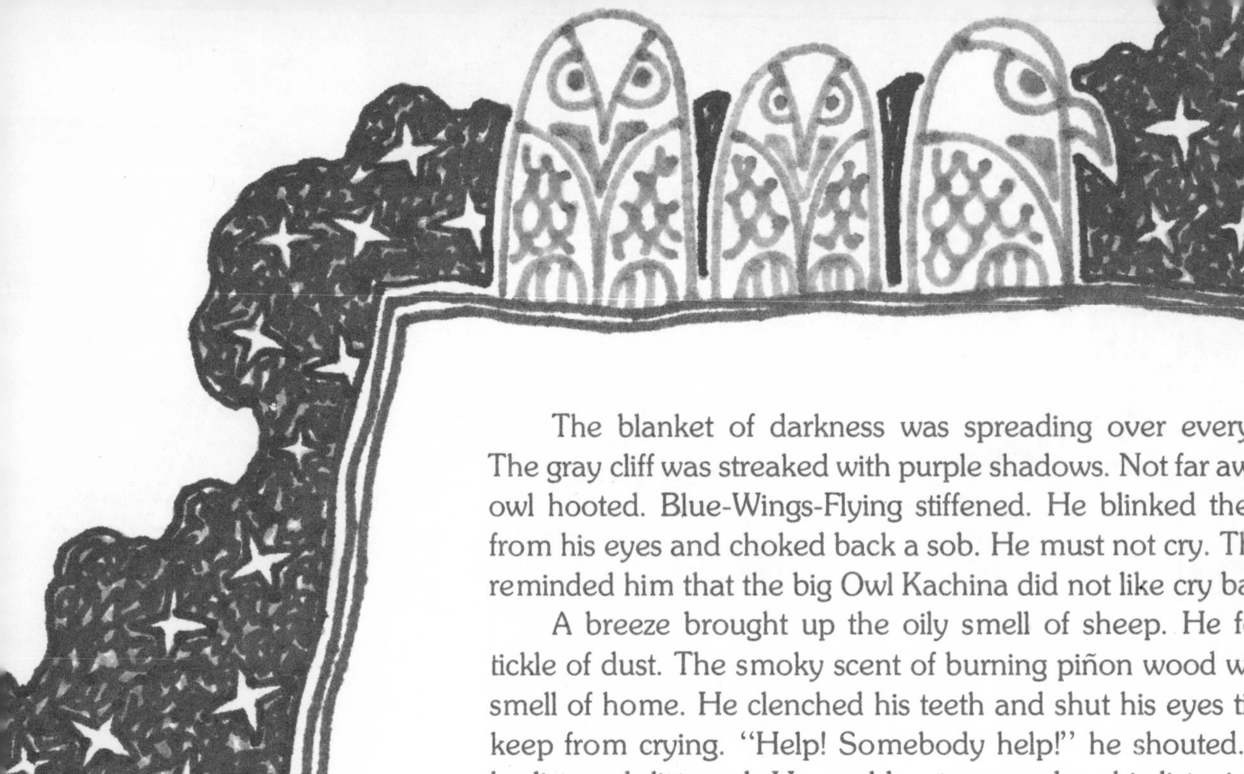

The blanket of darkness was spreading over everything. The gray cliff was streaked with purple shadows. Not far away an owl hooted. Blue-Wings-Flying stiffened. He blinked the tears from his eyes and choked back a sob. He must not cry. The owl reminded him that the big Owl Kachina did not like cry babies.

A breeze brought up the oily smell of sheep. He felt the tickle of dust. The smoky scent of burning piñon wood was the smell of home. He clenched his teeth and shut his eyes tight to keep from crying. "Help! Somebody help!" he shouted. Then he listened, listened. He could not see and so his listening was even more intense in the growing blackness. He waited and waited.

Then, at last, there was a sound — the scraping of moccasins on the hard earth. "Help. Please help me!" he called again. The footsteps hurried to a place above him. A head, blacker than the darkness, stuck out over the Mesa's edge.

"Is that you Blue-Wings-Flying? I have been looking for you." The voice of Swift-Eagle came down to him.

Blue-Wings-Flying could not answer. Dry sobs caught in his throat, making sounds like the dreaming noises of a sleeping pup. He swallowed and tried to call out, but his throat only grew tighter.

"It must be you down there. A boy's bow and arrows are here. I touched them with my foot. Hold tight," called Swift-Eagle. "Keep holding, I will come back with a rope."

His fingers grew numb with holding. "Hoot, Hoot," repeated the owl. Would Swift-Eagle never, never come? Then suddenly a dark form slipped down the wall and stood beside him.

"Hold tight, like a dirt dauber's nest to a wall, to the rope tied around my waist. Crawl up the cliff beside me as I climb," said Swift-Eagle. Then pulling on the stout rope, hand over hand, Swift-Eagle climbed with him to the top.

Blue-Wings-Flying crumpled to the ground, like a bundle of soft sheepskins. Swift-Eagle began looping the rope on his arms. "Feel around and pick up your bow and arrows," he said.

They walked back to untie the other end of the rope from the ladder pole of the kiva. Swift-Eagle spoke gravely to Blue-Wings-Flying. "You went too near the edge of the Mesa. You do not know what you should do and what you should not do. It is time for you to stay awake in the kiva each evening to listen to the Old Men. They must teach you all about the world. They must teach you what is right, what is wrong, what is good, what is bad, all the things that you do not know. I will begin taking you again next week."

"I want to go with Tah-Tah."

"You do not go with your father. You go with me," said Swift-Eagle. "Ask your mother."

Swift-Eagle held his arm, as they walked to Yu-Yu's house. When they reached the door, he gave the boy a gentle push and went to his own home.

A thankful sigh escaped from his lips as Blue-Wings-Flying entered his house. He shut the door tight against the owl, the coyote and the blackness. He tossed his bow and arrow into a corner.

"Tsch! Tsch!" his grandmother's tongue clicked in disapproval. He looked up in surprise. He had not expected So-Oh to be there. She was always in her own house after the sun went down. He couldn't tell about his fall while So-Oh was there. She would be frightened, and she scolded when she was scared.

But she was right about the bow and arrows. He picked them up from the corner where he had dropped them. Then he went to the wall and pulled down a strip of deerskin from the pole-for-soft-things. Squeezing the bow and arrows between his knees, he tied them together, leaving a loop in the knot. Then, going to the pole-for-hard-things, he slipped the loop over its end. So-Oh nodded her approval when he looked at her.

Yu-Yu was sitting on her rolled-up mattress with her back against the clay wall. He ran to sit by her and leaned against her shoulder.

"Why did I have to send Swift-Eagle for you? Why were you so late?" she asked.

He moved from her shoulder and looked into Yu-Yu's eyes to let her see him look at So-Oh. Then he whispered, "Tomorrow I can tell you." Yu-Yu understood that he did not want So-Oh to hear. She nodded.

So-Oh picked up a big pancake from a pile in a basket. She handed it to her grandson and motioned with pursed lips toward a pot on the cook-stove. The flickering lights from the stove deepened and multiplied the lines in her face.

Blue-Wings-Flying broke off a piece of pancake. He dipped it into the mutton stew in the pot and took a big bite. He was hungry. Without swallowing the first bite, he stuffed another piece in his mouth, and his cheeks bulged like a squirrel's.

"Tsch! Tsch!" So-Oh shook her head. "Coyotes gulp their food," she said, spanking another flat cake down on the hot stove top. He tried to grin, but his mouth was too full. He ate more slowly and looked around the long room.

Darkness had slipped in. Shadows filled three corners of the room. In the fourth corner, where a hole punctured the roof to let smoke out, there was brightness. A square hood had been built around the hole to draw the smoke up and keep it from filling the room. On the floor, under the hood, two very low, clay walls held the ends of a long, thin piece of slate. It was chiefly for cooking *piki,* and it had been used that evening. Three charred sticks of piñon wood that had burned under the slate now lay smoldering in the corner of the room. The piney odor was pleasant to sniff. Now and again, a spark popped out onto the clay floor. Then the embers darkened and the fire was out.

As his glance went on around the wall, Blue-Wings-Flying could tell that someone had been in the storeroom. The blanket that always hung over the low opening was fastened up. He could see the stacks of dried corn, the pots of dried beans, the extra sheepskins, a ball of deerskin and the cowhide thongs which were stored inside.

Next to the storeroom entrance were the double grinding stones. Two baskets beside them were filled with cornmeal. So-Oh or Yu-Yu had been grinding. Behind the stones, something big and fat leaned against the wall. It was tightly wrapped in the new blanket that Tah-Tah had brought from the kiva a few days ago. "What can it be?" wondered Blue-Wings-Flying. He would have to wait to see. Yu-Yu had told him that when things were wrapped up they were their owners' secrets. Others have to wait until things are unwrapped to know about them. He wished he did know!

Then he saw, lying close in front of the grinding stones, So-Oh's own blanket. The colors were old and faded. It was

wrapped around what Blue-Wings-Flying knew, from its shape, was So-Oh's rolled-up mattress. So-Oh was spending the night with them. That was strange.

He saw all of this in his glance around the room.

The door opened. A patch of light fell on the black ground outside. Tah-Tah came in with an armful of wood and placed it against the wall by the stove. So-Oh nodded thanks. Then he undid the blanket at the storeroom entrance and let it fall over the opening. Turning to Yu-Yu, he said, "I am going to the kiva. After the council meeting, I will stay there." Once more the opened door spilled light into the darkness. It closed, and Tah-Tah was gone.

Yu-Yu was still sitting on her rolled-up mattress with her back against the wall. Blue-Wings-Flying saw that her eyes looked tired. He saw pain in them, too. He went back to sit be-

side her and to lean against her arm. He wanted her well and happy again. Tomorrow So-Oh would go home and Yu-Yu would not be tired; then he would tell her about his fall. "Her eyes will show how glad she is that I'm not hurt." The pleasant thought made him happy.

Yu-Yu lifted a long lock of his black hair.

"The wind has given you the hair of an Old One," she said. "Bring the brush."

Blue-Wings-Flying took down the bunch of tied stiff straw from the pole-for-hard-things. Yu-Yu brushed and brushed his hair. Dust fell on his shoulders and in her lap. The scratching on his scalp felt good. He was sorry when it was time to put the brush away.

As she brushed the dust from his shoulders, Yu-Yu said softly, "Bluebirds put their heads under their wings at night. They sleep and rest to be strong for tomorrow's flights. Your blanket will be your feathers to warm and rest you in sleep. Tah-Tah made it just for you."

He lifted his blanket off his rolled-up mattress. When the mattress was spread upon the floor, he sat and pulled off his moccasins. Then he rolled himself tightly in the blanket.

As he lay awake in his cocoon, he watched So-Oh spread her mattress on sheepskins by the grinding stones. There, near the smoldering piñon sticks, the clay floor was warmer. She did not take off her moccasins. Did she forget? It didn't matter. She didn't walk much outside, so her moccasins were old and soft.

The warmth from the clay-plastered walls made him feel comfortable. He drew in a deep breath of the good, piney warmth. It was the smell of home, the smell of safety with Yu-Yu and Tah-Tah. But he had too many *Wonder Thoughts* to go to sleep. Too many things had happened today. Deep inside was his wish, the wish for a baby sister. Had the Sun-Carrier heard his message? Had the Little People pushed him off the cliff?

Yu-Yu came to him. "You are not sleeping, my Blue-Wings," she whispered. "What troubles you?"

"I have too many *Wonder Thoughts*." He sighed and looked up at her. "Why am I going to Swift-Eagle's kiva with him? I want to go to Tah-Tah's kiva with Tah-Tah. I want his Old Men to teach me all about the world and how things were made. I want to go to Tah-Tah's kiva to learn to weave blankets."

Yu-Yu came close. She didn't want to disturb the sleeping So-Oh. She put her hand on his head. Softly she said, "You can't go to Tah-Tah's kiva. You don't belong to his clan. His kiva is the secret house for the Shell Clan. Long ago, when the world was young, the Wise Men divided Indian men and women into groups called clans. Someone asked, 'What about the children? Have they a separate clan?'

" 'Children will always belong to their mother's clan,' said a Wise One. 'Then there will be no fuss over where they belong.' "

"So Swift-Eagle and I belong to So-Oh's clan, for she is our mother. You belong to my clan, for I am your mother. You and Swift-Eagle and I all belong to the same clan, to So-Oh's Squash Clan," explained Yu-Yu.

Blue-Wings-Flying lay silent for a moment, frowning. Then he asked, "What about Tah-Tah?"

"Tah-Tah belongs to his mother's clan, the Shell Clan. Children are taught the same truths in all the kivas. You will understand better when you are older."

He was silent again, thinking. In a moment, he said, "Then when I'm a man, my children will go to my wife's kiva."

Yu-Yu nodded.

"I will have no children to take to my kiva unless I have the children of a sister?" he asked anxiously. "I need a sister. I want a baby sister."

"It would be nice," said Yu-Yu. "Now go to sleep. Sometimes tomorrows bring good things." Yu-Yu went to fix her bed.

Suddenly the rhythm of muted drum beats sounded in the darkness, like the blanket of night flapping softly.

"Listen," whispered Yu-Yu. "The old chief is thinking. Drum beats are marching his thoughts down the trail of truth."

The beats went on and on. Blue-Wings-Flying felt his thoughts grow fainter and fainter. Soon he was asleep.

Most mornings the sunlight sent its shining fingers through the little window and awakened Blue-Wings-Flying. This morning the window was curtained. Something else awakened him. He heard something he had heard before. He listened. *"A-laa a-laa, a-laa,"* he heard. It was the cry of a tiny baby.

He wiggled out of his blanket and sat up. So-Oh was seated by the stove with a basket of soft gray ashes beside her. Gently she rubbed sifted ashes over the body of a newborn baby. Then she sprinkled the child with cornmeal. Tah-Tah was standing on the wooden chair, hanging the baby cradle to a ceiling beam. Blue-Wings-Flying knew at once that the cradle had been the bundle behind the grinding stones. The new blanket had been woven for the baby.

Yu-Yu was sitting on her rolled-up mattress. He ran to her unable to ask the question.

"Yes," said Yu-Yu, "you have a baby sister."

She put her arm around him. He held tightly to her softness, feeling that he might burst open with gladness, like a heated popcorn kernel.

His new sister was wrapped in cloths and a blanket grown soft with much use. So-Oh handed the baby to Yu-Yu, who held her a moment for Blue-Wings-Flying to see. He touched a cheek

with his finger, then Yu-Yu took the baby and placed its mouth to her breast.

Suddenly he felt afraid. He placed his hand on the baby and asked, "Will this baby sister stay with us?"

"Yes, she will stay if she keeps well and happy and has a pretty name." Yu-Yu smiled.

"The other little baby, the little brother, went to sleep and would not wake up." He reminded her.

"He wanted to go back into the Underworld from where all things and all Indians have come." Yu-Yu's voice was soft and comforting.

"Is that why you dressed up the baby and put on his moccasins?" he asked. "Tah-Tah wrapped the baby's new blanket around him and put him in the deep crack in the Mesa."

"He put him there to make it easier for him to return to the Underworld. He is happier there." Yu-Yu looked down at the nursing baby.

"The baby did not stay long in the crack. So-Oh took me there to see, because I wanted him back. He had gone." The memory made him sad for a moment. Then he smiled and touched the baby bundle.

"We will keep this little sister. I will play with her to make her happy, and I will find a pretty name for her. She will love me best if I name her."

"We will have to see," said Yu-Yu. "So-Oh, Tah-Tah, your uncles and aunts and cousins will all be watching for the prettiest thing they see or feel on this day of her birth. Then on her Naming Day the one who has the nicest idea will be the one to name her."

"That will be many names. How will we know the best one?" asked Blue-Wings-Flying.

"The one that we begin to call her, after we hear all of them, will be her name."

"I will go and look and look until I find a beautiful name," said Blue-Wings-Flying.

Yu-Yu gave him a pat on the shoulder. "Now you must eat your pancake and beans. Tah-Tah will be waiting. You must help him fill the water jars at the spring." He slowly shook his head. "I don't want to go, Yu-Yu. I want to look for a pretty name."

"You don't have to look faraway for a name," said Yu-Yu. "There are pretty things everywhere for an eye to see. Keep your eyes open. Thoughts and eyes work together. Have beautiful thoughts and you see beautiful things."

Tah-Tah came in and picked up the big water jar. "Come, my boy," he said, "the burro and I are waiting."

Blue-Wings-Flying dragged his moccasins on the clay floor as he went outside, eating the last of his pancake. Tah-Tah was fastening the jar in one end of the blanket across the burro's back. He had already tied So-Oh's jar on the other side.

"Ar-ray!" he called to the burro. The jars swung in rhythm as the burro trotted to the head of the steep path. His pace slowed as he began to go downhill, but he still moved very quickly. Blue-Wings-Flying followed at a half run. He frowned; there was no time to look for pretty things.

Tah-Tah noticed. "Nothing will look pretty if you frown, my boy."

The frown left the boy's face, but unhappiness did not leave his heart. He was worried. He knew his cousin Blue-Flower had gone out to get yucca strips for baskets. His cousin Quick-Hawk had gone out with the family sheep. They would see many things, different things for new names.

At one turn of the path, there was a crevice in the high wall. Blue-Wings-Flying had seen blossoms of Indian paint brush

there. He stopped to look inside. As he did, Tah-Tah spoke. "No need to look for flowers. They only bloom when it rains, and no rain has come for many months. The flowering plants are dried up." At the foot of the path, the burro went slower to nibble dried grass here and there. Near them a lizard lay on a rock, warming in the sunshine. "A lizard is not pretty enough for a name," said Blue-Wings-Flying to himself. "It is not smart either."

As he watched, a road-runner ran by. It picked up the little lizard by the neck. Holding its head high, the bird began to swallow the lizard, which wiggling its hind legs and lashing its tail slipped into the long throat. Then, as fast as it had come, the road-runner vanished behind a mesquite bush.

Blue-Wings-Flying felt trembles in his stomach, as if it were empty and a heavy rock had fallen in to shake it. He felt sorry for the little lizard.

"Road-runners are ugly, mean birds," thought Blue-Wings-Flying. "Only witch people or bad people could be named Road-Runner-Swallowing-a-Lizard."

Clouds could make pretty names, he thought. He looked up into the clear blue sky. There were no real clouds today, just small strands of white froth moving slowly here and there, far, far away.

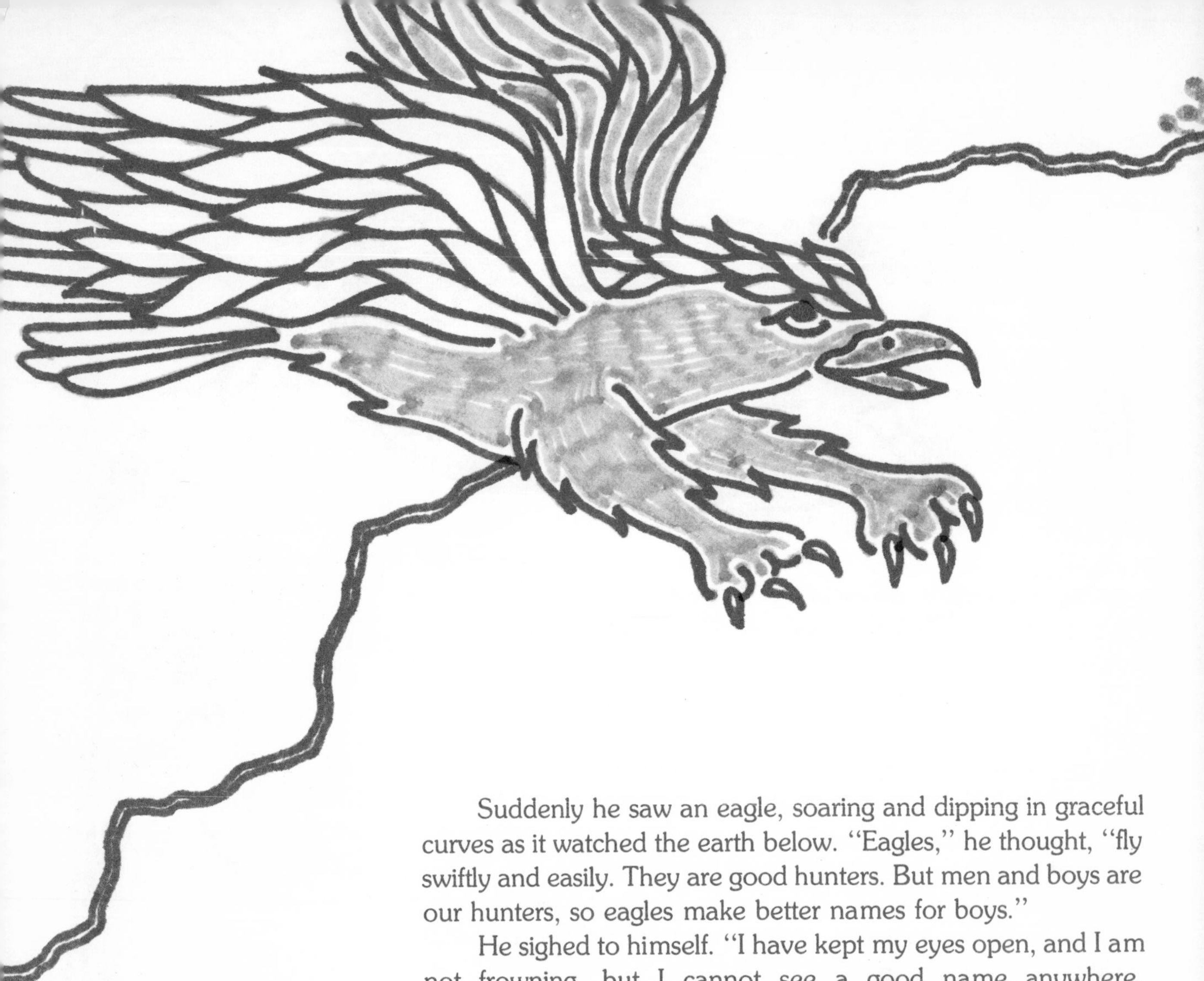

Suddenly he saw an eagle, soaring and dipping in graceful curves as it watched the earth below. "Eagles," he thought, "fly swiftly and easily. They are good hunters. But men and boys are our hunters, so eagles make better names for boys."

He sighed to himself. "I have kept my eyes open, and I am not frowning, but I cannot see a good name anywhere. Everyone will have a pretty name but me."

Suddenly the burro stiffened his legs and stopped. With eyes wild with terror, he wheeled around, snorted and dashed away as fast as the bumping jars would let him go.

Tah-Tah and Blue-Wings-Flying looked to see what had alarmed him. It was a rattlesnake, coiling itself into rings, one upon another. Its lifted tail was shaking angrily; the horny rings at the tip rattled to warn them off. Its forked tongue flickered from its wide-open mouth between the two sharp poisonous fangs.

Blue-Wings-Flying stood as one turned into a stone statue.

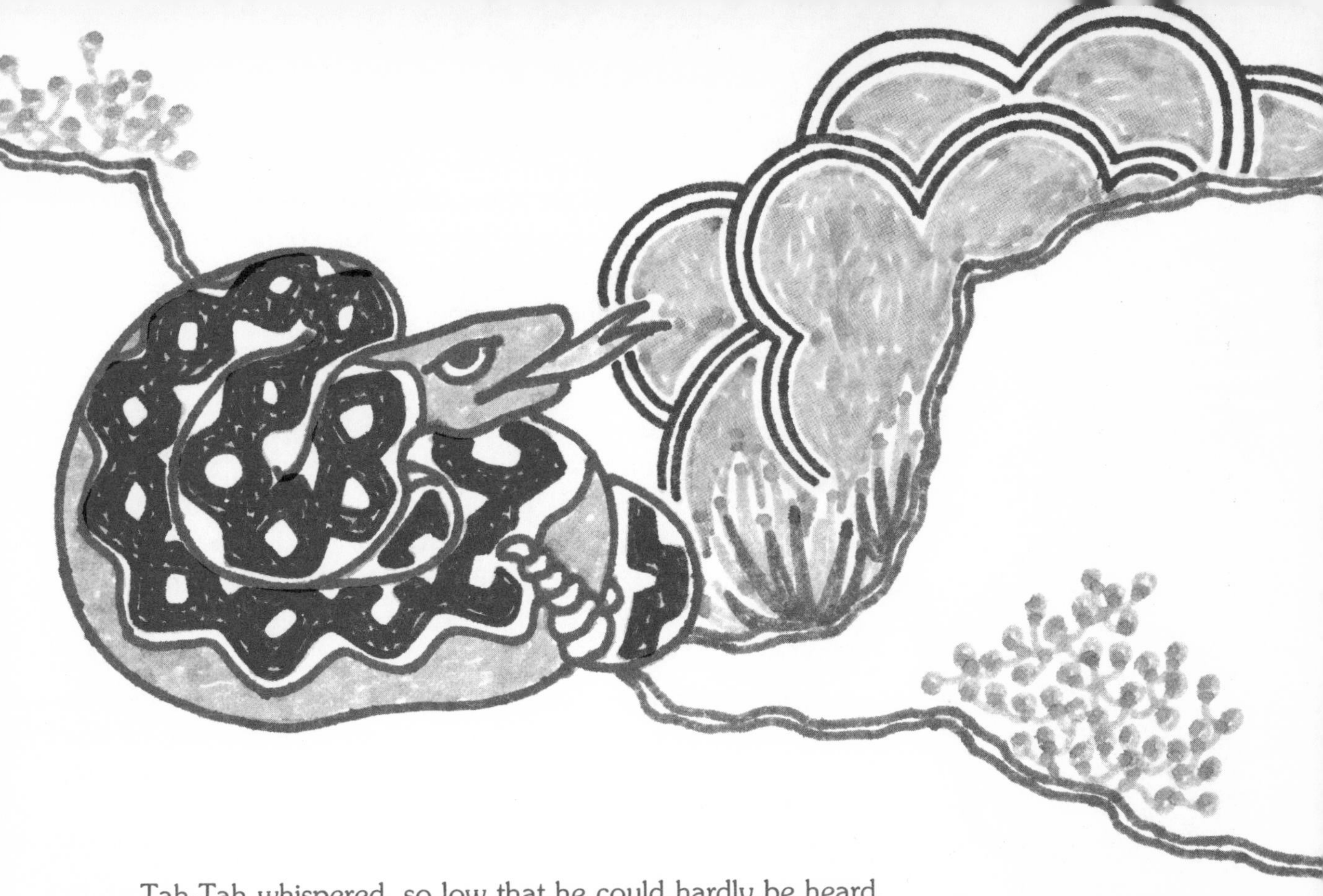

Tah-Tah whispered, so low that he could hardly be heard, "Don't move. Don't show fear. Let the snake know that we are his brothers."

Blue-Wings-Flying could not help feeling afraid, but he stood still. Not even his eyes moved from the coiled snake. Tah-Tah stood still and stiff beside him.

The snake drew in its forked tongue. It closed its mouth, lowered its blunt head, and straightened its shiny body, coil by coil, along the sand. Then it slithered among the shadows of the scattered plants and rocks and was gone.

After a few moments, Blue-Wings-Flying sighed with relief. Tah-Tah went to get the burro.

"There are pretty marks on the snake," thought Blue-Wings-Flying, as he waited. "But a snake name would frighten a child." So he stopped thinking about the snake and began to feel very sorry for himself instead.

Somehow Tah-Tah knew what he was thinking. "If you want to bring sorrow, then be sorry for yourself." He looked gravely at Blue-Wings-Flying. The boy looked back at him and slowly smiled with understanding.

When they reached the spring, they unfastened the jars from the burro, and Tah-Tah said, "So-Oh's jar is made of better clay. It is lighter. Take it and fill it in the spring while I let the burro drink below." Tah-Tah slapped the burro's rump to let him know that he was free to drink.

His arms barely reaching around the big jar, Blue-Wings-Flying walked unsteadily to the pool of water. He slowly lowered the jar into the water, but it was difficult to get a good grip on the cumbersome jar. And suddenly — clink — the top slipped from his hands, struck the stone wall and shattered; a fragment flew into the air and vanished in the spring.

For a moment, Blue-Wings-Flying could not move. His throat tightened and his eyes filled with tears. So-Oh loved the jar; it had belonged to her own grandmother. The museum man from Santa Fe had tried to buy it for his collection, but So-Oh had wanted it for herself. To break the pot was to break her heart.

Catching the good part of the jar's top, he tilted it to fill with water. A ray of sunlight made a rainbow in the mist, rising from the spring, but Blue-Wings-Flying looked at it without seeing. His thoughts were all on So-Oh's sadness.

To spare his son greater shame, Tah-Tah had turned away, but now he lifted the jar and carried it to the burro. He gave Blue-Wings-Flying the other jar to fill, to show his trust. Then he put his hand on the boy's head, "There will be other jars. Things that can break do not last forever." Together they reloaded the burro and began to climb the steep path.

So-Oh was cooking pancakes when they reached home. Blue-Wings-Flying watched her slowly shake her head as Tah-Tah brought in the water jars. He ran to her, the words tumbling out, "Your jar was heavy, So-Oh. It slipped and hit the spring wall." So-Oh could not speak; she stood very still, looking at the broken jar. Finally she turned and went back to cooking pancakes. Blue-Wings-Flying knew she was sad. He knew, too, that she would not scold; he would feel better if she would.

Yu-Yu stood by the cradle, swinging the baby. Blue-Wings-Flying went to her and buried his face in her dress. She whispered, "I will weave a big basket and trade it to someone in the village of First Mesa for a new jar for So-Oh."

"But it will not be an old jar," said Blue-Wings-Flying, blinking to keep back the tears.

"It will be old for your sister when she is old like So-Oh," Yu-Yu smiled. He felt a little better.

Suddenly he wondered what time it was. He lifted a corner of the cloth over the window and looked out. The shadow of a little boy running by was long. It was time for the Sun-Carrier to ride behind the distant mountain tops. He must hurry. Just in time, he reached the edge of the Mesa.

"Sun-Carrier," he whispered toward the West. "I like my baby sister, but I have no name for her. Thank the Mother Kachina for sending her to me!"

As always, the shining ball of sunlight slipped down into the Underworld, pulling behind it a great blanket of colors. Watching it, Blue-Wings-Flying felt that he had forgotten something, something important, something he should remember. He dragged his feet as he went home.

The blanket of night spread quickly over the village. Silence, too, lay as still and soft as the blankets covering Tah-Tah, Yu-Yu and Blue-Wings-Flying, at rest on their mattresses. The baby slept in Yu-Yu's arms, but the boy lay wide awake, wondering what the sunset had tried to tell him. Then a picture came into his mind. He saw again the spring and the broken jar filling with water. He saw it clearly, and all at once he had a name for his baby sister. He longed to say it aloud, once, just to hear how it sounded. But it was a secret to keep until his turn to name the baby. He closed his eyes, the picture still in his mind. Soon he was asleep.

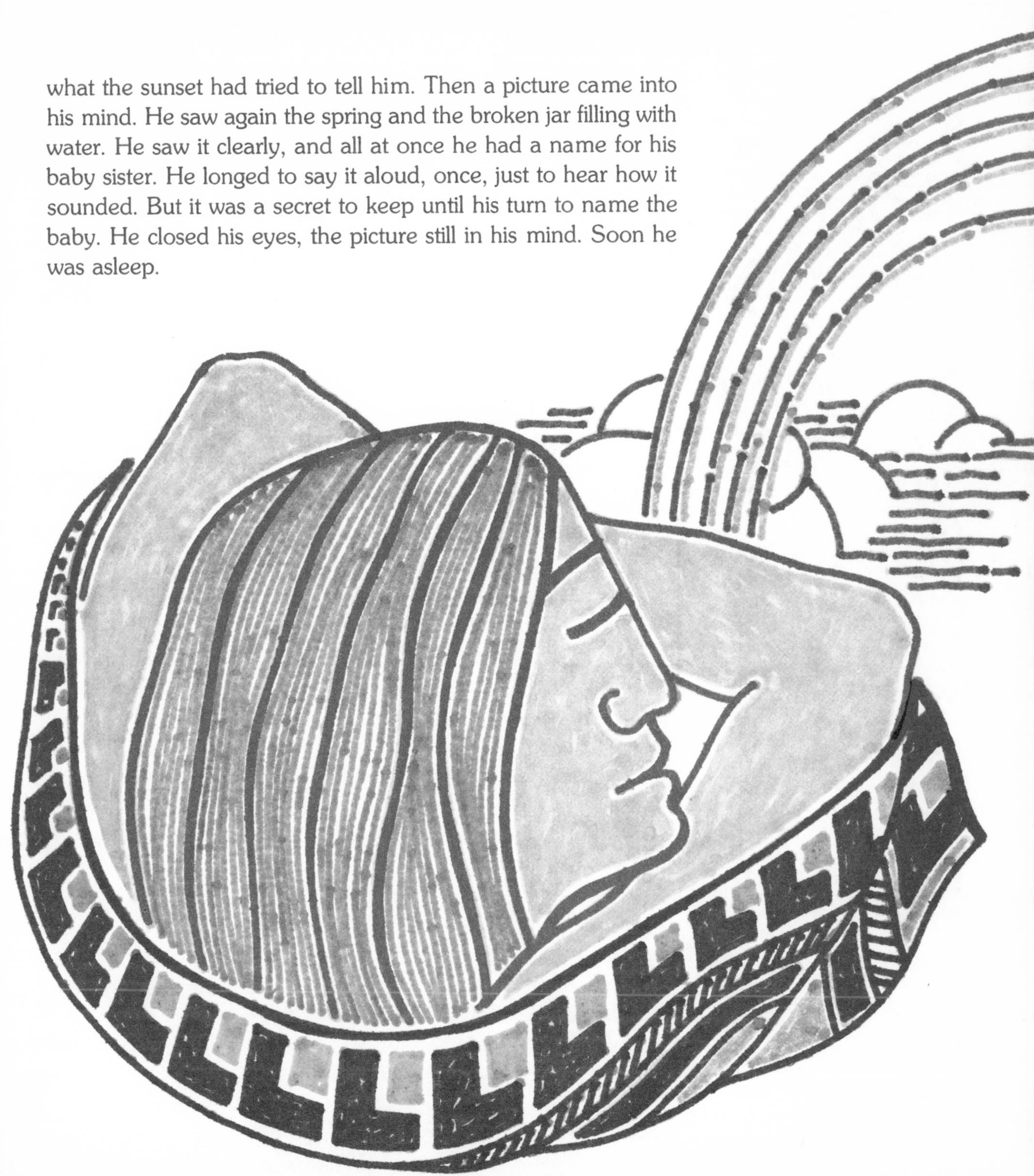

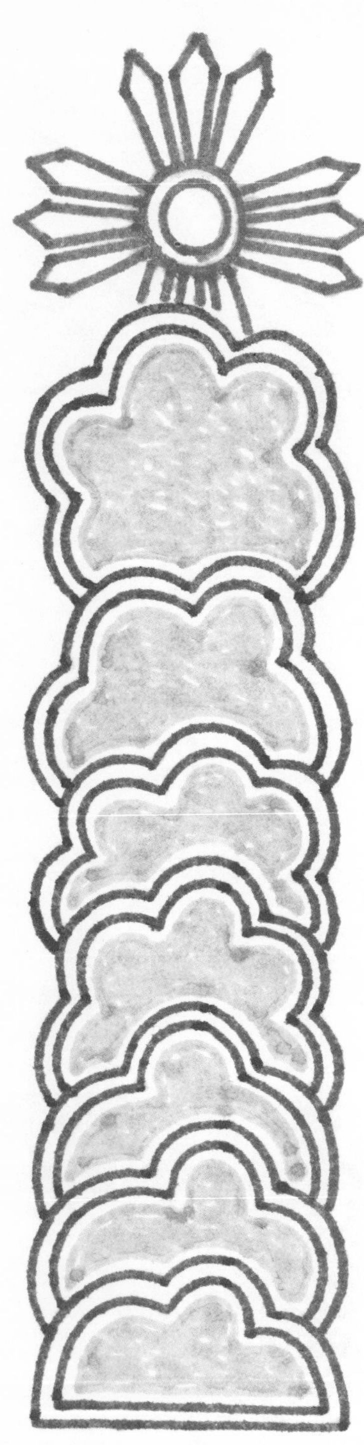

Blue-Wings-Flying slept late the next morning. By the time he did wake up, Tah-Tah had already gone to slaughter a sheep. He ran down to the corral to watch, but he was too late. Tah-Tah was cutting the animal into quarters and wrapping the pieces in cloth. He handed one hind quarter to Blue-Wings-Flying. "Is this too heavy for you to carry?"

"No," boasted Blue-Wings-Flying. But when he held it in his arms, he could hardly walk. So Tah-Tah tied the mutton to the boy's back, then he put the rest in a sling on his own back.

"Take your load home for the stew. I am going to the trading store," he said.

All his women relatives were there when Blue-Wings-Flying returned home with the cloth bundle. They had come to help prepare the Naming Feast. So-Oh was kneeling beside the hot slate stone and spreading thin blue corn batter over the surface. He liked to watch her neat, quick movements as she peeled off the thin-as-paper bread, and folded it into long flat sticks. Blue-Wings-Flying thought of the hornet's nest he had seen. Pieces of it were much like the pancakes, the same color and thinness.

One of his cousins lifted a cloth bag of oak ashes from a brown pot and laughed. He ran over to see what was funny. In the bottom of the pot, the eyes of the corn kernels were popping out. The corn was puffing up and breaking the hulls. They did look funny. She poured off the lye from the ashes and washed the puffy corn in clean water. It would taste good in the mutton stew. He watched as he waited for Tah-Tah to come from the store.

Tah-Tah came in with many heavy bundles. Blue-Wings-Flying helped him to unpack. There were wonderful bottles of orange and grape drinks and paper boxes of cookies.

"Careful," warned Tah-Tah, as Blue-Wings-Flying began pulling out the bottles. "Don't break the bags of sugar and coffee." When they had finished he turned to the boy, "This house is now an ant hill. You had better go out and play."

Blue-Wings-Flying went out to find his friends, but he did not go far away from his own house. When he saw relatives coming from all directions, he ran to go inside with them.

The baby had been fed so she would sleep on Yu-Yu's lap. As soon as the relatives were seated on rolled-up mattresses and sheepskins around the walls of the big room, So-Oh got up. She held an ear of white corn. Touching the baby's head with the corn, she said, "I name you Pink-Clouds-in-the-morning."

Blue-Wings-Flying looked around. He saw most of the relatives smile and nod their heads. "They like that name," he thought.

Tah-Tah took the ear of corn. He touched the baby's head with it. "I name you Singing-Corn-Leaves-in-the-wind," he said. Blue-Wings-Flying remembered the soft rustle of a corn stalk by the dry river bed. It was a nice sound. Some of the relatives nodded.

Yu-Yu's young cousin took the corn. "I name you Sparkling-Sunshine-on-a-bright-tin-can." A few visitors put hands to their mouths and grinned. Yu-Yu smiled down at the baby.

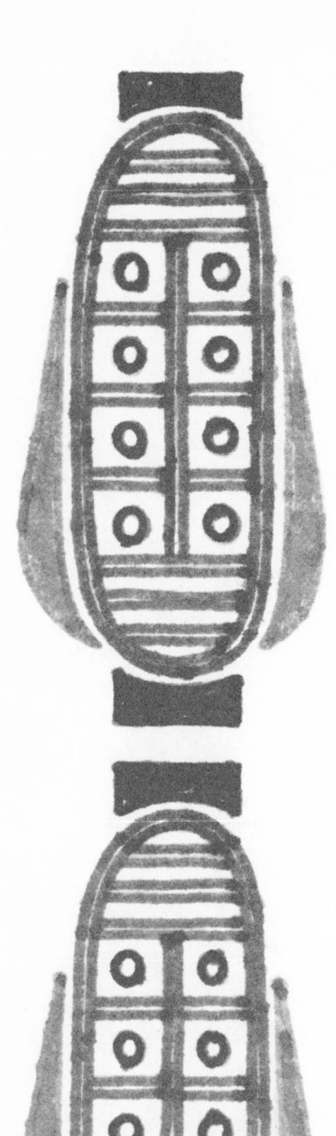

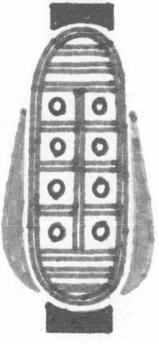

Another cousin took the corn and said, "I name you Whispering-Breezes-on-the-cliffs." Blue-Wings-Flying remembered his adventure on the cliffs and did not want that name.

Another said, "I name you Running-Chipmunk."

One by one, each of the relatives gave a name. Then it was the turn of Blue-Wings-Flying-in-sunlight. He was the last because he was the youngest.

Yu-Yu whispered, "Let the ear of corn touch like a butterfly." He nodded.

He touched the baby's head lightly and said, "I name you Rainbow-Mist-at-the-spring."

He looked shyly around the room. No one nodded. No one was smiling but Yu-Yu. So-Oh had the frown of thought on her forehead. Then they all stood up to eat. "Perhaps they did not even hear my name," he thought.

Blue-Wings-Flying ate little. When the other children had stuffed themselves, one of the girls said, "Come play." She pulled his arm and together they went outside, followed by the others. The girl picked up a short stick and, not too gently, struck Blue-Wings-Flying's head with it, calling out, "I name you the Bray-of-the-long-eared burro."

He grabbed the stick from her. She ran away, and he raced after until he was near enough to hit her head and say, "I name you Sticky-Stick-in-the-mud."

Someone else snatched the stick. He caught another girl. Tapping her head, he yelled, "I name you the Fat-Frog-croaking-at-the-water-hole."

He tried to keep the stick, but another boy grabbed it and struck a girl too hard. Turning, she made a face at him, as he called, "I name you Horse's-Tail-switching-flies."

She snatched the stick. Hitting him a good blow, she said, "I name you the Wobbly-Legs-of-a-skinny-colt." He staggered away on wobbly legs, and they all laughed.

Blue-Wings-Flying slipped away. He wanted to be inside to hear what name the baby was being called. He went into the house and saw that most of the relatives had gone away. So-Oh sat holding the baby in her lap. Yu-Yu came to take her, and as she lifted the tiny bundle, she said, "Come, little Rainbow-Mist, you must get back into your cradle."

So-Oh got up. "Good-night, little Rainbow-Mist," she said. "The day has been long. I must go home to rest." She gathered up a small bundle of food and went out. The other relatives went with her.

In his happiness Blue-Wings-Flying hugged himself and laughed out loud. He went to the cradle and touched his mother's arm. When she looked, he smiled and watched her smile back.

"Will the baby stay with us?" he whispered.

"Yes, surely she will stay," answered Yu-Yu. "The Government is building an automobile road up to our village on the Mesa. The Government nurse will come to see the baby. The trading store has canned milk and little jars of baby food to keep her well fed. You will play with her to make her happy. And she has a beautiful name that you found for her. She will stay."

Blue-Wings-Flying peeped into the cradle and said softly, "Good-night, little Rainbow-Mist."

Soon they would have her kachina dolls on their white wall. Someday she would have a grinding ceremony, and he would sing. And maybe she would have a son, a nephew to take to his kiva, the kiva of the Squash Clan. Blue-Wings-Flying closed his eyes. In a moment he was asleep.

Glossary Terms

KACHINAS — mythical people who gave the Hopi corn, rain, clouds and all other natural phenomena. NIMAN KACHINAS watch over the planting and harvest seasons.

KIVA — sacred underground meeting place for men.

MESA — plateau or tableland.

METATE — grinding stone.

PIÑON — desert pine tree.

SO-OH — Grandmother.

TAH-TAH — Father.

YUCCA — desert plant.

YU-YU — Mother.

The Hopi Indians call themselves *Hopituh Shi-mu-mu* which means "The Peaceful People." They live in northern Arizona on three fingers of the Black Mesa, the first, second and third mesas, overlooking the Petrified Forest and the Painted Desert. The San Francisco Mountains rise to the west. The villages on top of the mesas are practically invisible from below; the Indians chose this location because it provided natural fortification against mauraud-ing tribes who came to steal their harvests. It is a truly magnificent sight to look out across the country — seeing for miles and miles — from the top of the mesas.

The Hopi have no tribal government. Each village has its own organization, and each individual has his or her own responsibilities in this organization. The society is matriarchal. Women own the houses, food, seed for the next year's planting, the springs, the cisterns and the small gardens they work. Men do the herding, hunting and all farming outside of the village. They gather and haul wood for fuel. They do the sheep shearing and the blanket weaving and perform the sacred ceremonial dances organized by their clans.

Perhaps more than any other Indian tribe, the Hopi adhere to their clan system. Clan membership is passed from mother to child and accounts for the physical structure of Hopi villages. Adobe houses are built in blocks adjacent to the house of the matriarch or "mother" of the clan. A Hopi boy leaves his mother's house when he reaches adolescence; he then lives in the kiva of his clan until he is ready to marry. A Hopi girl remains at home with her mother until she receives and accepts a marriage proposal. Prior to marrying she spends one month in the home of her future mother-in-law; she grinds corn and helps with other daily tasks to prove her capabilities as a wife. After marriage, the couple builds a house adjacent to that of the wife's mother and raises their children as members of the wife's clan.

I have never known a simpler, more patient relationship between a parent and a child than among the Hopi. They are a gentle, kind people who have been less influenced by contact with white people than have their neighbors. They never accepted Christianity but continued to follow their old customs and beliefs, including the ritual name-choosing for a child. While Navaho children are known simply as "boy" or "girl" until the idiosyncrasies of later life suggest a name, "Many Sheep," for example, a Hopi child's name is of deep religious significance. A name binds a child to his environment by establishing a link between nature and good fortune. Thus, Blue-Wings-Flying's great joy in finding the name for his baby sister.

Elizabeth Willis De Huff

Elizabeth De Huff lived and taught in Hopiland for more than thirty years. She was one of the first white people invited to witness the sacred Snake Dance, and she gave noted Hopi and Pueblo painters, Fred Kabotie and Velino Herrera, their start with water colors, paper and encouragement in the livingroom of her house.

Dorothea Sierra has been coloring ever since she can remember. As a illustrator and graphic designer she is fascinated by Indian art because it translates the real world into a system of shapes and spaces—a very sophisticated and magical symbolism. Ms. Sierra lives in Cambridge, Massachusetts where she plays tennis, the flute, keeps a firm grip on her magic markers and sings her songs on paper.